7 ⁹⁵

The U.S. Government and the

Vietnam War

COMMITTEE ON FOREIGN RELATIONS

CHARLES H. PERCY, Illinois, *Chairman*

HOWARD H. BAKER, JR., Tennessee
JESSE HELMS, North Carolina
RICHARD G. LUGAR, Indiana
CHARLES McC. MATHIAS, JR., Maryland
NANCY L. KASSEBAUM, Kansas
RUDY BOSCHWITZ, Minnesota
LARRY PRESSLER, South Dakota
FRANK H. MURKOWSKI, Alaska
PAULA HAWKINS, Florida

CLAIBORNE PELL, Rhode Island
JOSEPH R. BIDEN, JR., Delaware
JOHN GLENN, Ohio
PAUL S. SARBANES, Maryland
EDWARD ZORINSKY, Nebraska
PAUL E. TSONGAS, Massachusetts
ALAN CRANSTON, California
CHRISTOPHER J. DODD, Connecticut

SCOTT COHEN, *Staff Director*
GERYLD B. CHRISTIANSON, *Minority Staff Director*

THE U.S. GOVERNMENT AND THE VIETNAM WAR

Executive and Legislative Roles
and Relationships

PART II: 1961-1964

William Conrad Gibbons

PRINCETON UNIVERSITY PRESS

PRINCETON, NEW JERSEY

Published by Princeton University Press, 41 William Street,
Princeton, New Jersey 08540
In the United Kingdom: Princeton University Press, Guildford, Surrey
Preface copyright © 1986 by Princeton University Press

Library of Congress Cataloging in Publication Data will be found
on the last printed page of this book

First Princeton Paperback printing, 1986
First Princeton hardcover printing, 1986

LCC 86-3270
ISBN 07715-0   ISBN 02255-0 (pbk.)

This book was prepared for the Committee on Foreign Relations of the United States
Senate by the Congressional Research Service of the Library of Congress. It was
originally published by the U.S. Government Printing Office in February 1985. The
"Letter of Submittal" and "Foreword" are deleted and some typographical corrections
have been made. Otherwise, contents and pagination are the same.

Clothbound editions of Princeton University Press books are printed on acid-free
paper, and binding materials are chosen for strength and durability. Paperbacks,
while satisfactory for personal collections, are not usually suitable for library
rebinding.

Printed in the United States of America by Princeton University Press,
Princeton, New Jersey

For my children
Robert, Frances, Stephen and Gayle
with love

PREFACE

This second part of the study of the U.S. Government and the Vietnam war covers the period 1961-64, from the inauguration of President John F. Kennedy through President Lyndon B. Johnson's first year in office. During these four years, the U.S. commitment was expanded and the number of American military personnel in Vietnam rose from 800 to almost 20,000.

Indochina and Cuba were the first two items on President Kennedy's foreign policy agenda when he took office on January 20, 1961. The day before, he had met with President Dwight D. Eisenhower, who reportedly warned him that the situation in Laos was becoming serious and that the U.S. would have to act, with force if necessary, to block the Communists. Ten days after becoming President, Kennedy approved a new counterinsurgency plan for South Vietnam. This was followed by a concerted effort to supply the South Vietnamese with U.S. advisers trained in counterinsurgency warfare, based on President Kennedy's decision that the U.S. should demonstrate its determination to defeat Communist "wars of national liberation," and that, "Come what may," the U.S. would win in South Vietnam. Meanwhile, after threatening to use U.S. forces if necessary, the President, with advice from Congress, decided that a political settlement in Laos was preferable to military action, and negotiations were begun which led to the Geneva (Laos) Accords of 1962.

During the summer of 1961, after the June meeting between President Kennedy and Premier Nikita Khrushchev in Vienna had strengthened Kennedy's resolve to stand fast in Vietnam, partly to demonstrate U.S. determination on Laos, as well as in anticipation that greater U.S. assistance might be necessary in Vietnam itself, White House and departmental officials developed contingency plans for direct military action against North Vietnam. This led to a trip to Vietnam in October 1961 by White House advisers Gen. Maxwell D. Taylor and Walt W. Rostow who reported that the Communists were much stronger, and that the U.S. needed to take "vigorous action" to help save South Vietnam. They recommended sending 6,000-8,000 U.S. troops and "inserting" Americans into operational positions in the Government of Vietnam to show the Vietnamese "how the job might be done." Kennedy did not act on the suggestion to send the troops, but he approved the recommendation to increase U.S. aid, including military advisers, provided the South Vietnamese would increase their commitment.

By 1963, the situation in South Vietnam had not improved, and the Kennedy administration decided that new political leadership was necessary. In early November, President Ngo Dinh Diem was deposed and assassinated in a coup encouraged and assisted by the United

States. The result, however, was even greater political instability and lack of progress.

When Lyndon B. Johnson became President after Kennedy's assassination a few weeks later, he vowed to continue the U.S. commitment to South Vietnam. In early 1964, the military situation in the South became more critical, and the Johnson administration stepped up its aid and prepared a plan for U.S. military action against North Vietnam. In June 1964, however, with the Presidential election pending in the fall, and apparently feeling that the situation in Vietnam did not require such a move at that time, the President decided to postpone further consideration of the plan.

In August 1964, North Vietnamese boats attacked a U.S. destroyer, and Congress approved the Gulf of Tonkin Resolution authorizing President Johnson to take "all necessary steps" to defend South Vietnam. His advisers recommended increased pressure on North Vietnam, but Johnson, then waging a political campaign in which the keeping of peace was a central issue, and apparently still unwilling to agree to a greater commitment, approved only minor changes in the U.S. program.

On the eve of the U.S. Presidential election in early November 1964, however, the Communists attacked a U.S. installation in South Vietnam, and his military advisers urged the President to retaliate. He declined to do so, but immediately after the election he directed an interdepartmental group to prepare a plan for further U.S. action based on the plan developed earlier in the year. On December 1, President Johnson approved the new plan, a two-stage program of "measured" military pressure against North Vietnam beginning with covert actions (OPLAN 34-A) and escalating, if necessary, to "sustained reprisal" by air, and, if that was not sufficient, to the use of U.S. ground forces. By early 1965, it was becoming clear that the United States was once again headed into war in Asia.

A number of persons have contributed to the preparation of this second part, including most of those who assisted with Part I, and the author wants to thank all of them for their help. Reviewers of the first part who also reviewed this part were Mr. William P. Bundy, Gen. Andrew J. Goodpaster, Ambassador U. Alexis Johnson, Dr. Francis O. Wilcox, Dr. Carl Marcy, Mr. Boyd Crawford, and Dr. Robert Klaus. There were two new reviewers for Part II who, with the others, deserve thanks. They were: W. W. Rostow (for the 1961 period), a former professor of Cambridge and Oxford universities and the Massachusetts Institute of Technology, and now a professor at the University of Texas, who was a Deputy Special Assistant for National Security Affairs to President Kennedy, and Counselor and Chairman of the Policy Planning Council in the Department of State, and then Special Assistant for National Security Affairs to President Johnson; and William H. Sullivan, former U.S. Ambassador to Laos and Iran, and now President of the American Assembly at Columbia University, who actively participated in Vietnam policymaking during his many years in the Foreign Service, including serving as Chairman of the Vietnam Coordinating Committee and as a member of the negotiating team for the Paris peace talks leading to the 1973 cease-fire.

In addition, the following members of the staffs of the John F. Kennedy Library and the Lyndon B. Johnson Library were very cooperative: from the Kennedy Library, Martin McGann, Archivist, Barbara Anderson, Archivist, Suzanne Forbes, Classification Review Archivist, and Ronald Whealan, Librarian, and, from the Johnson Library, Dr. David Humphrey, Senior Archivist, Tina Lawson, Supervisory Archivist, Linda Hansen, Archivist, and Nancy Smith, Archivist. Ted Gittinger, a historian in charge of Vietnam oral history interviews for the Johnson Library, was also helpful, as were Betty Austin, head of Special Collections, University of Arkansas Libraries, and Sheryl Vogt, head of the Richard B. Russell Library, University Libraries, University of Georgia.

CONTENTS

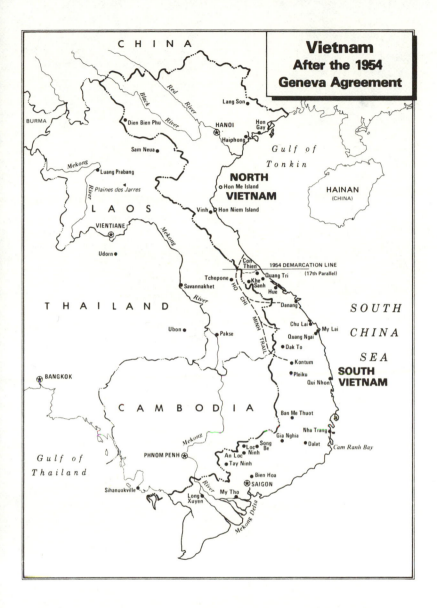

Vietnam
After the 1954
Geneva Agreement

CHINA

Lang Son

BURMA

Dien Bien Phu

HANOI

Hon Gay

Haiphong

Gulf of Tonkin

Sam Neua

Mekong

NORTH VIETNAM

Luang Prabang

Red River

Black River

HAINAN
(CHINA)

Hon Me Island

River

Plaines des Jarres

LAOS

VIENTIANE

Vinh • Hon Niem Island

Udorn •

Mekong

Con Thien

1954 DEMARCATION LINE
(17th Parallel)

Tchepone •

Quang Tri

THAILAND

Savannakhet •

River

Khe Sanh
Hue

Danang

HO CHI MINH TRAIL

SOUTH

Ubon •

Pakse •

Chu Lai
My Lai

CHINA

Quang Ngai
Dak To

Kontum

SEA

Pleiku

SOUTH VIETNAM

Qui Nhon

CAMBODIA

Ban Me Thuot

Nha Trang

Gia Nghia

BANGKOK

Mekong

Loc Ninh
An Loc
Tay Ninh

Song Be

Dalat

Cam Ranh Bay

PHNOM PENH

Bien Hoa

Gulf of Thailand

Sihanoukville

River

My Tho

SAIGON

Long Xuyen

Mekong Delta

SOUTH CHINA SEA

CHAPTER 1

THE 1961 DECISION TO STAND FIRM IN VIETNAM

By 1961, after years of U.S. support for existing governments in Vietnam and Laos, the Communists appeared to be making greater inroads in those countries, and it seemed clear to U.S. policymakers that further action needed to be taken to protect American interests in Southeast Asia.[1] In Vietnam, the government of Ngo Dinh Diem was becoming increasingly unpopular, while being faced with more intense military and political pressures from the Communists. In November 1960, the Communists, together with some of the non-Communists who opposed the Diem government, organized a new political action group, the National Liberation Front, as a part of the growing movement to bring about changes in the government. In November 1960, there was also an abortive military coup against Diem as dissatisfaction spread. In late 1960, U.S. officials proposed a new counterinsurgency plan for South Vietnam which called for more U.S. aid, as well as more Vietnamese self-help.

In Laos, the rightist government supported by the U.S. faced a serious threat from the Communists by the end of 1960, and appeared to be failing rapidly.

Events in other parts of the world also affected U.S. attitudes toward the situation in Southeast Asia, and had a direct bearing on America's involvement in Vietnam.

The relationship of the United States and the People's Republic of China continued to be hostile. In 1954-55, the Chinese had attacked the Pescadores islands off the China coast which were occupied, as was the island of Formosa, by National Chinese forces who had fled the mainland when it was overrun by the Communists in 1949. The United States responded by increasing its military aid to the Nationalists and by threatening to intervene directly in the conflict. In 1955, Congress passed the Formosa Resolution, the first of five such resolutions between 1955 and 1965, giving the President advance approval for the use of the armed forces in the area "as he deems necessary." (The other resolutions were the Middle East Resolution in 1957, the Cuba Resolution in 1962, the Berlin Resolution in 1962, and the Gulf of Tonkin Resolution in 1964.) Faced with the threat of U.S. action, especially the possibility of air attacks which might have involved atomic bombs, the Chinese pulled back and the situation became less critical. A similar series of events occurred in 1958, and once again the threat of direct U.S.

---

[1] For background information on years prior to 1961, see William Conrad Gibbons, *The U.S. Government and the Vietnam War: Executive and Legislative Roles and Relationships*, Part I, 1945-1960 (Princeton: Princeton University Press, 1986).

military action appeared to have successfully deterred the Chinese. Although there was no further repetition of these attacks, the relationship between the U.S. and the People's Republic of China did not improve noticeably after the 1958 incidents, and by 1961, China, together with the Soviet Union, the "Sino-Soviet Bloc" as it was called, was still viewed as the major threat to the security of Southeast Asia.

Competition and conflict between the U.S. and Russia, which had eased somewhat during the middle 1950s, increased in the late 1950s. In 1958-1959, after nine years of relative quiet, the Russians resumed their pressure on the U.S. in Berlin. Tension eased again later in 1959 after President Dwight D. Eisenhower sought to revive the spirit of *détente* which had existed earlier. He invited Russian Premier Nikita Khrushchev to come to the United States, and this, together with a meeting of the two leaders during that visit, led to renewed hope for greater cooperation. In the spring of 1960, they met again in Paris for a "summit conference" to discuss outstanding issues, but as the meeting was about to begin, an American intelligence aircraft was brought down in the Soviet Union, and Khrushchev denounced the U.S. and left the meeting.

The Eisenhower administration also suffered a setback in its efforts to prevent the Communists from gaining power in countries like Vietnam and Laos which were faced with political insurgencies. Having successfully used American power to prevent this from happening in those two countries, as well as in Iran and Guatemala, the administration was confronted with a new threat to American security when Fidel Castro came to power in Cuba in 1959 and the new government soon established close ties with the Soviet Union and other Communist countries. This resulted in the decision by Eisenhower in March of 1960 to approve a CIA plan for training Cuban refugees for a possible anti-Communist insurgency operation in Cuba.

Meanwhile, developments in the Russian missile program were posing what many American leaders regarded as a basic challenge to U.S. security. In August 1957, the Russians had successfully fired an intercontinental ballistic missile, and in October and November they launched the world's first earth satellites. The Eisenhower administration reacted by accelerating the U.S. missile and space programs, but there was widespread concern that the U.S. was falling behind technologically, and that the Russians were in a position to gain strategic military superiority over the United States by the early 1960s. Despite the successful launching of a U.S. space satellite in January 1958, and rapid development of the U.S. missile program during 1958, there was increased criticism of alleged weaknesses in the U.S. defense posture.

In November 1957, after the announcement of the first Russian satellite, a committee which had been appointed to advise the White House on defense needs, the Gaither committee, whose chairman was H. Rowan Gaither, chairman of the board of the Ford Foundation, recommended a large increase in defense spending to prevent the Russians from becoming strategically superior. One of its recommendations was that the U.S. should develop greater capability to fight limited wars, the logic being that such

limited conflicts were more apt to occur because of the destructive-
ness of a general nuclear war.

The major recommendations of the Gaither committee were rejected by President Eisenhower for what, in retrospect, would seem
to have been substantially valid reasons, but they were supported
by many prominent Americans, including a number of leading
Democrats, and the "missile gap" became one of the principal
themes in the 1960 Presidential campaign of Senator John F. Kennedy (D/Mass.).[2]

The need for improving limited warfare capability also became a
major theme in the late 1950s among some military leaders, academic theorists and politicians, including Senator Kennedy. Army
Generals Maxwell D. Taylor, Matthew B. Ridgway, and James M.
Gavin argued that rather than relying on strategic airpower and
the ultimate use of atomic bombs, the U.S. needed a "flexible response," in Taylor's words, to situations involving the possible use
of force, especially in a non-nuclear limited war.[3]

The Kennedy Administration and the Defense of Southeast Asia

In November 1960, John F. Kennedy defeated Vice President
Richard M. Nixon for the Presidency, thus ending eight years of
Republican control of the White House and setting the stage for
changes in response to these trends in the world situation and in
U.S. foreign and defense policy.

In his inaugural address on January 20, 1961, Kennedy set an ex-
pansive, militant tone for his administration:[4]

> Let every nation know, whether it wishes us well or ill, that
> we shall pay any price, bear any burden, meet any hardship,
> support any friend, oppose any foe to assure the survival and
> the success of liberty.

"In the long history of the world," Kennedy added, "only a few
generations have been granted the role of defending freedom in its
hour of maximum danger. I do not shrink from this responsibility;
I welcome it."

He also promised to continue assisting countries in the third
world, especially those, like Vietnam, threatened by the Communists: "To those new states whom we welcome to the ranks of the
free, we pledge our word that one form of colonial control shall not

---

[2]For an excellent analysis of the arguments involved, and of Eisenhower's position, see John
Lewis Gaddis, *Strategies of Containment: A Critical Appraisal of Postwar American National Se-
curity Policy* (New York: Oxford University Press, 1982), ch. 6. For an analysis by a prestigious
Rockefeller Foundation study group, headed by Henry A. Kissinger, which supported the
Gaither committee's findings, see the report "International Security. The Military Aspect," published in 1958 and reprinted in *Prospect for America: The Rockefeller Panel Reports* (New York:
Doubleday, 1961).
    As historian Anna Nelson has explained, the Eisenhower administration was not oblivious to
the problem of fighting limited wars while relying on a strategic nuclear deterrent. At an NSC
meeting on May 1, 1958, she reports, there was a candid discussion of the problem, and the
Council agreed to develop a supplementary strategy for "defensive wars which do not involve
the total defeat of the enemy." Anna Kasten Nelson, "The 'Top of Policy Hill': President Eisenhower and the National Security Council," *Diplomatic History,* 7 (Fall 1983), p. 311.
[3]Maxwell Taylor, *The Uncertain Trumpet* (New York: Harper and Bros., 1960). Major academic studies included Henry A. Kissinger *Nuclear Weapons and Foreign Policy* (New York: Harper
and Bros., 1957); Bernard Brodie, *Strategy in the Missile Age* (Princeton: Princeton University
Press, 1961); Robert E. Osgood, *Limited War: The Challenge to American Strategy* (Chicago: University of Chicago Press, 1957).
[4]U.S., President, *Public Papers of the Presidents of the United States* (Washington, D.C.: Office
of the Federal Register, National Archives and Records Service), John F. Kennedy, 1961, pp. 1-3.

have passed away merely to be replaced by a far more iron tyranny." U.S. assistance to those trying to "help themselves," he said, would continue "for whatever period is required, not because the Communists may be doing it, not because we seek their votes, but because it is right."

This statement of intent, together with Kennedy's own beliefs, and those of his top associates, about the importance of defending Southeast Asia, and of making American power credible throughout the world, had a direct and, as it turned out, critical bearing on the Kennedy administration's decision to reaffirm and to expand the U.S. commitment. (When Kennedy became President there were approximately 750 U.S. military advisers in Vietnam. At the time of his assassination in late 1963 there were almost 20,000, many of whom were actively engaged in combat despite their formal, legally-prescribed noncombatant status.) He believed, as had Dwight D. Eisenhower and Harry S Truman before him, in containment, and in the policy of providing assistance to countries threatened by the Communists.[5] He also believed in the efficacy of American action, and his activist political style, among other things, caused him to engage in an activist foreign policy involving increased intervention in situations in which the use of American power was considered desirable. Thus, as one historian aptly says, "Kennedy did not represent a sharp break with the past or a uniqueness in the fundamental tenets of American foreign policy. Yet the different methods he chose to use, the personal elements he applied to diplomacy, did matter in heating up the Cold War, threatening nuclear war, and implanting the United States in the Third World as never before."[6]

With respect to Southeast Asia, and Vietnam in particular, President Kennedy had long taken the position that the U.S. should help to defend that area against the Communists, both for the sake of the countries themselves, and in order to protect vital U.S. interests in the region.[7] As a Member of the U.S. House of Representatives, he visited Vietnam in 1951, denounced French colonialism, and declared, "There is no broad, general support of the native Vietnam Government among the people of that area. To check the southern drive of communism makes sense but not only through reliance on the force of arms. The task is rather to build strong native non-Communist sentiment within these areas and rely on them as a spearhead of defense. . . . To do this apart from and in defiance of innately nationalistic aims spells foredoomed failure."

In 1954-55, Kennedy strongly supported the U.S. choice of Ngo Dinh Diem for premier of South Vietnam after the country was divided at the Geneva Conference of 1954, and opposed the plan for

---

[5]See Gaddis, *Strategies of Containment,* ch. 7. In the words of James A. Nathan and James K. Oliver, *United States Foreign Policy and World Order,* 3d ed. (Boston: Little, Brown, 1985), p. 237, Kennedy's inaugural message "was an eloquent reaffirmation of the Truman Doctrine. It was containment with vigor."

[6]Thomas G. Paterson, "Bearing the Burden: A Critical Look at JFK's Foreign Policy," *Virginia Quarterly Review,* 54 (Spring 1978), p. 195.

[7]The following is taken from pt. I of the present study, cited above, which contains source notes and further discussion.

nation-wide elections in Vietnam in 1956 as stipulated by the Geneva Declaration.

In 1955, Kennedy joined the newly-organized American Friends of Vietnam, and was its keynote speaker at a symposium on Vietnam in June 1956. His statement on that occasion was the most definitive explanation given during his service in the Senate, as well as during his Presidency, of his position on "America's Stake in Vietnam," the title of the speech. These were his major points:

(1) *First,* Vietnam represents the cornerstone of the Free World in Southeast Asia, the keystone to the arch, the finger in the dike. Burma, Thailand, India, Japan, the Philippines and obviously Laos and Cambodia are among those whose security would be threatened if the red tide of Communism overflowed into Vietnam. . . .

(2) *Secondly,* Vietnam represents a proving ground of democracy in Asia. However we may choose to ignore it or deprecate it, the rising prestige and influence of Communist China in Asia are unchallengeable facts. Vietnam represents the alternative to Communist dictatorship. If this democratic experiment fails, if some one million refugees have fled the totalitarianism of the North only to find neither freedom nor security in the South, then weakness, not strength, will characterize the meaning of democracy in the minds of still more Asians. The United States is directly responsible for this experiment—it is playing an important role in the laboratory where it is being conducted. We cannot afford to permit that experiment to fail.

(3) *Third* and in somewhat similar fashion, Vietnam represents a test of American responsibility and determination in Asia. If we are not the parents of little Vietnam, then surely we are the godparents. We presided at its birth, we gave assistance to its life, we have helped to shape its future. As French influence in the political, economic and military spheres has declined in Vietnam, American influence has steadily grown. This is our offspring—we cannot abandon it, we cannot ignore its needs. And if it falls victim to any of the perils that threaten its existence—Communism, political anarchy, poverty and the rest—then the United States, with some justification, will be held responsible; and our prestige in Asia will sink to a new low.

(4) *Fourth,* and finally, America's stake in Vietnam, in her strength and in her security, is a very selfish one—for it can be measured, in the last analysis, in terms of American lives and American dollars. It is now well known that we were at one time on the brink of war in Indo-China—a war which could well have been more costly, more exhausting and less conclusive than any war we have ever known. The threat of such war is not now altogether removed from the horizon. Military weakness, political instability or economic failure in the new state of Vietnam could change almost overnight the apparent security which has increasingly characterized that area under the leadership of President Diem. And the key position of Vietnam in Southeast Asia, as already discussed, makes inevitable

the involvement of this nation's security in any new outbreak of trouble. . . .

. . . We should not attempt to buy the friendship of the Vietnamese. Nor can we win their hearts by making them dependent upon our handouts. What we must offer them is a revolution—a political, economic and social revolution far superior to anything the Communists can offer—far more peaceful, far more democratic and far more locally controlled. Such a revolution will require much from the United States and much from Vietnam. We must supply capital to replace that drained by the centuries of colonial exploitation; technicians to train those handicapped by deliberate policies of illiteracy; guidance to assist a nation taking those first feeble steps toward the complexities of a republican form of government. We must assist the inspiring growth of Vietnamese democracy and economy, including the complete integration of those refugees who gave up their homes and their belongings to seek freedom. We must provide military assistance to rebuild the new Vietnamese Army, which every day faces the growing peril of Vietminh armies across the border.

The position stated in Kennedy's inaugural address was uniquely applicable to Vietnam, which, at the time, was probably the foremost representative of a "new state" freed from colonialism and threatened by communism. Thus, when he took office, Kennedy, whose personal commitment to Diem and to the defense of Vietnam was consonant with the commitment to Vietnam made by previous Presidents, did not seriously question or feel the need to reexamine U.S. policy toward Vietnam. He readily approved a major expansion of the U.S. commitment only a few days after becoming President, possibly doubting whether the proposal he was approving was the most effective way to accomplish the desired objective, but without having any apparent misgivings or uncertainty as to the validity of the objective itself.

Kennedy's views of the responsibility of the U.S. toward Vietnam were shared by all but two of his new policymaking team. (One was Chester Bowles, Under Secretary of State until November 1961, when he became Ambassador at Large and later Ambassador to India. The other was George W. Ball, who replaced Bowles.) So, too, were the general lines of U.S. foreign and military policy which characterized at least the first few weeks of the new administration, until the trauma produced by the failure of the Cuban (Bay of Pigs) invasion in April 1961 resulted in a hardening of attitudes and a reassessment of existing patterns of policymaking, and, to some extent, of policy and operations.

Kennedy's choice as Secretary of State, Dean Rusk, who had been a key member of the State Department's Far East team during the Truman administration, fully shared Kennedy's view of the importance of defending Southeast Asia. As he stated later:[8]

. . . collective security was the key to the prevention of World War III. My generation of students had been led down the path to the catastrophe of World War II which could have

---

[8]Letters to CRS from Dean Rusk, Apr. 1, 1983 and Oct. 22, 1984.

been prevented. We came out of the war deeply attached to the idea of collective security; it was written very clearly and strongly into Article 1 of the United Nations Charter and was reinforced by certain security treaties in this hemisphere, across the Atlantic and across the Pacific. When the Kennedy administration took office, the SEATO Treaty was a part of the law of the land. How we responded under the SEATO Treaty was strongly linked in our minds with the judgments that would be made in other capitols as to how and whether we would react under other security treaties such as the Rio Pact and NATO.

"Indeed," Rusk added, "NATO had been severely tested in the Berlin crisis of 1961-62 and the Rio Pact had been severely tested in the Cuban missile crisis. President Kennedy was very much aware of the question as to what might have happened had Chairman Khrushchev not believed him during that Berlin crisis and the Cuban missile crisis. The reputation of the United States for fidelity to its security treaties was not an empty question of face or prestige but had a critical bearing upon the prospect for maintaining peace."

Kennedy's views toward containment and toward Vietnam were also highly compatible with those of most Members of Congress. Although some cracks had begun to appear in the consensus established at the end of World War II and during the beginning of the cold war, in 1961 there was still strong support in Congress for containment and for U.S. assistance to countries threatened by Communist expansion or subversion. Defense of Vietnam and of Southeast Asia as a whole was still a specific article of congressional faith, despite the growing doubts of some Members about Diem himself.[9]

What distinguished the Kennedy administration was not its policy assumptions or its worldview, but its approach to problem solving. It is here that a key can be found to understanding the administration's handling of Vietnam, as well as many of the other foreign policy problems of the time. "The style, personality, and mood of the Kennedy team," as Thomas G. Paterson has written, "joined the historical imperatives to compel a vigorous, even belligerent foreign policy. . . . Bustle, zeal, energy, and optimism became the bywords.

"The Kennedy people considered themselves 'can-do' types, who with rationality and careful calculation could revive an ailing nation and world. Theodore H. White has tagged them 'the Action Intellectuals.' They believed that they could *manage* affairs. . . .

"With adequate data, and they had an inordinate faith in data, they were certain they could succeed. It seemed everything could be quantified. When a White House assistant attempted to persuade Secretary of Defense Robert S. McNamara, the 'whiz kid' from Ford Motors, that the Vietnam venture was doomed, the efficient-minded McNamara shot back: 'Where is your data? Give me

---

[9] For more information on congressional support for U.S. policy toward Indochina in the 1950s, see pt. I of this study, cited above.

something I can put in the computer. Don't give me your poetry.'"[10]

At another point, Frederick E. ("Fritz") Nolting, Jr., who replaced Elbridge Durbrow as U.S. Ambassador to Vietnam in March 1961, objected to some of the proposed reforms which Washington policymakers were considering for Vietnam, saying that it would be difficult if not impossible to put a Ford engine into a Vietnamese ox-cart. McNamara is reported to have replied that although it might be difficult, "We can do it."[11]

Beginnings

Prior to taking office, Kennedy had met twice with Eisenhower to discuss problems facing the U.S., as well as other questions pertaining to foreign and domestic policy and the operation of the government. In preparation for their first meeting on December 6, 1960, Kennedy, who had already been briefed a number of times by CIA Director Allen Dulles, suggested an agenda on which the first three items (in order) were Berlin, the Far East, and Cuba. The White House notified Kennedy that the President intended to discuss seven subjects, including Laos. Vietnam was not specifically mentioned on either list.[12] In preparing Kennedy for the meeting, his foreign policy team, headed by John H. Sharon and George W. Ball, drafted memoranda on each subject. In their memorandum on Laos they concluded by suggesting, in the form of questions, that neutralization of Laos might be the most desirable course to pursue, provided the Communists could be excluded from participating in a neutralist government. They asked, "If a neutralist government can be established without Communist participation, may not this now be the best the West can hope for?" and, "Taking into account the strong evidence of neutralist sentiment, and the danger inherent in attempting to get Laos to take sides in any future conflict involving the Communist states and SEATO, may not Laos make its best contribution to the peace of Southeast Asia, as well to its own security, by carrying on as a neutral buffer state?"[13]

The only available account of the December 6 meeting is Eisenhower's notes, in which he states that he and Kennedy discussed several foreign policy subjects, but that most of the meeting concerned organization and staffing in the area of national security affairs.[14]

The second Kennedy-Eisenhower meeting was held on January 19, 1961, the day before the inauguration. Meanwhile, the situation in Laos had taken a decided turn for the worse in the eyes of the Eisenhower administration. The Prime Minister of Laos, Prince

---

[10]Patterson, "Bearing the Burden: A Critical Look at JFK's Foreign Policy," pp. 201, 203.
[11]Michael Charlton and Anthony Moncrieff, *Many Reasons Why* (New York: Hill and Wang, 1976), p. 82.
[12]Vietnam or Laos (or Indochina) was not even on a list of seven topics which the chief of staff of the Foreign Relations Committee, Carl Marcy, proposed to Chairman Fulbright as the most important foreign policy problems for the committee to consider during 1961. University of Arkansas, Fulbright Papers, Marcy to Fulbright Memorandum, Dec. 27, 1960, series 48, box 1.
[13]Kennedy Library, POF Spec. Corres. File, Memorandum to Senator John F. Kennedy from John H. Sharon and George W. Ball, Dec. 5, 1960.
[14]For the text of Eisenhower's notes see *Waging Peace, 1956-1961* (Garden City, N.Y.: Doubleday, 1965), pp. 712-716.

Souvanna Phouma, who was considered by the administration to be too closely associated with the Laotian Communists (the Pathet Lao), had been toppled on December 8 by a rightist coup led by Gen. Phoumi Nosavan and supported by the U.S. In turn, the Russians and the North Vietnamese increased their assistance to the Pathet Lao. By the end of December 1960, as Pathet Lao forces advanced, U.S. policymakers in Southeast Asia and in Washington became very concerned about the possibility that the Communists would gain control of Laos. Eisenhower viewed this with alarm, and began to consider military action. As he said in his memoirs:[15]

This was disturbing news. Possibly we had another Lebanon on our hands. While we needed more information—such as indisputable proof of North Vietnamese or Red Chinese intervention—before taking overt action, [he had already approved covert action],[16] I was resolved that we could not simply stand by. I thought we might be approaching the time when we should make active use of the Seventh Fleet, including landing parties.

In an NSC meeting on December 31, 1960, Eisenhower declared, "We cannot let Laos fall to the Communists, even if we have to fight, with our allies or without them."[17]

By the time Eisenhower and Kennedy met on January 19, the situation had eased only slightly, and Kennedy himself put Laos at the top of the agenda for that meeting. Vietnam was not included.[18] At this second meeting, Eisenhower reportedly said to Kennedy, "with considerable emotion," that the U.S. could not afford to let the Communists take Laos. If Laos, the "key to the whole area," were to fall, "it would be just a matter of time until South Vietnam, Cambodia, Thailand and Burma would collapse." The U.S. had a responsibility under the SEATO Treaty to defend Laos, Eisenhower added, but Britain and France were opposed to SEATO intervention. If efforts to achieve a political settlement failed, the U.S. "must intervene in concert with our allies. If we were unable to persuade our allies, then we must go it alone."[19]

Thus, Kennedy, who earlier had told one of his assistants that he hoped "whatever's going to happen in Laos, an American invasion, a Communist victory or whatever," would happen "before we take over and get blamed for it,"[20] was faced upon taking office with his

---

[15]*Ibid.*, p. 610.

[16]See *ibid.*, p. 609.

[17]*Ibid.*

[18]Kennedy Library, POF Spec. Corres. File, Memorandum of Subjects for Discussion at Meeting of President Eisenhower and Senator Kennedy on Thursday, January 19, 1961, n.d. (The other items on the list under "State" were, in order after Laos, "Cuba, Dominican Republic and Caribbean area; The Congo, and the African situation generally; Berlin; Nuclear Test Talks and Disarmament; Algeria, and other current problems with France." The list also included one item for Defense and one item for Treasury.)

[19]These excerpts are from a memorandum on the meeting prepared in 1969 for President Lyndon B. Johnson by Clark Clifford, who, along with the newly appointed top Cabinet officials, Secretary of State Dean Rusk, Secretary of Defense Robert S. McNamara, and Secretary of the Treasury Douglas Dillon, accompanied Kennedy to the meeting. The memorandum is reprinted in *Pentagon Papers*, Gravel ed. (Boston: Beacon Press, 1971), vol. II, pp. 635-637 (hereafter cited as *PP*). There is an earlier, shorter but similar memorandum on the meeting to Kennedy from Clifford, Kennedy Library, POF Spec. Corres. File, Jan. 24, 1961. Eisenhower does not discuss the details of the meeting in his memoirs.

[20]Theodore C. Sorensen, *Kennedy* (New York: Bantam Books ed., 1966), p. 722.

first potential "crisis," and with applying the principles of his inaugural speech to a very knotty problem.[21]

Because of the seriousness with which the Laotian "crisis" was perceived at the time, there was concern in Congress, and key Members were being kept abreast of the situation. Some Senate Democrats close to Kennedy and interested in the Far East, particularly Mike Mansfield (D/Mont.), were also communicating with him privately.

On January 21 and 23, 1961, Mansfield, who had just been elected Senate majority leader, sent memos to Kennedy urging that Laos be neutralized—an idea that the State Department was already considering, and that had been recommended by Winthrop G. Brown, U.S. Ambassador to Laos, in a cable to Washington on January 18, 1961. Mansfield said he had received a personal communication, via the State Department, from Souvanna Phouma, then in Cambodia, in which Souvanna criticized the U.S. for exaggerating the Communist threat in Laos—there were "at the most," he said, 100 Laotian Communists—and for blocking Laotian neutrality, which he told Mansfield was the only practicable course for Laos because of its cultural characteristics and geographical location. In his memo, Mansfield added that, from his standpoint, another major shortcoming of U.S. policy was "The corrupting and disrupting effect of our high level of aid on an unsophisticated nation such as Laos."

In discussing the need for Laotian neutrality, Mansfield said, among other things, "It is difficult to see how the U.S. commitment can be limited or a SEATO military involvement avoided except by an active attempt by this country to neutralize Laos in the pattern of Burma or Cambodia." "There are risks in such a policy," he added, "but the risks in our present policies seem even greater for they create the illusion of an indigenous Laotian barrier to a communist advance when, in fact, there is none."

In order to achieve a neutral Laos, Mansfield said, the U.S. should seek to establish a commission for Laos similar to the International Control Commission (ICC) established for Indochina under the 1964 Geneva Accords, but it should consist entirely of Asians (the ICC was composed of India, Canada and Poland). He recommended India, Pakistan and Afghanistan as members. Second, U.S. involvement should be reduced, "primarily by cutting down our military aid commitments while working for the restoration of the French military training mission to replace our own."

The significance of the plan proposed in these two memos, Mansfield said, "is that it may permit us to extricate ourselves from an untenable over-commitment in a fashion which at least holds some promise of preserving an independent Laos without war."[22]

On January 6 and February 2, 1961, the Foreign Relations Committee met in executive session for hearings, the first on the world

---

[21]For details of this and other aspects of the Laotian aspect of the Indochina War see the standard works, Arthur L. Dommen, *Conflict in Laos: The Politics of Neutralization*, rev. ed. (New York: Praeger, 1971), and Charles A. Stevenson, *The End of Nowhere: American Policy Toward Laos Since 1954* (Boston: Beacon Press, 1972). For 1960-1961 specifically see Bernard B. Fall, *Anatomy of a Crisis: The Laotian Crisis of 1960-61* (New York: Doubleday, 1969).

[22]The two memos are in the Kennedy Library, POF Country File, Laos, where there is also a translation of Souvanna Phouma's letter of Jan. 7, 1961, to Mansfield.

situation, with Secretary of State Christian A. Herter (John Foster Dulles had died in 1959) and Assistant Secretary of State for Far Eastern Affairs, J. Graham Parsons, and the second with Winthrop Brown, U.S. Ambassador to Laos, to discuss the Laotian situation. (There was another executive session hearing on January 11, 1961, with CIA Director Dulles, but only eight pages were transcribed. It appears to have dealt primarily with Cuba.) In the first hearing there were questions on Laos (none on Vietnam), but fewer than on the Congo, which was considered another "crisis" area. In the second hearing, members of the committee were interested in why the U.S., unlike the British and the French, had not supported Souvanna Phouma. There were also questions about U.S. covert involvement in Laos.[23] The committee did not, however, indicate any strong disagreement with the administration's Laotian policy.

On February 28, 1961, the Foreign Relations Committee met in executive session for a general review of the world situation by Secretary of State Rusk. There was no discussion of Vietnam, but Laos was discussed to some extent. Rusk reported to the committee that the administration was interested in getting Laos "into a stable and independent position" and removing it as a "major battle ground in the cold war." Laos, he said, was "something of a quagmire."

Rusk said that the U.S. did not want Laos to be set up as a "strongly pro-western ally." The United States was not looking for an ally, he said, but wanted to prevent Laos from becoming an ally of the Communists, a Communist "puppet." He told the committee that the Russians had proposed an international conference, but, "We feel that an international conference for the purpose of settling Laos would not be particularly productive at this time and could, indeed, simply further inflame the situation . . . at the present time we do not see how a conference can bring about a solution which we would find tolerable."[24]

The urgency of the Laotian situation was so compelling that Kennedy is said to have spent more time on Laos during February and March 1961 than on anything else.[25] Vietnam, however, was also of great concern to the President, partly as a result of a report on the subject from Gen. Edward G. Lansdale (the famed CIA agent who had played a central part in the U.S. role in Vietnam 1954-56). On January 27, in preparation for a meeting on January 28 to discuss Cuba and Vietnam, McGeorge Bundy (Kennedy's new national security adviser), sent a memorandum to Rusk, Secretary of Defense Robert S. McNamara, and Allen Dulles in which he said, "The President's interest in Cuba needs little explanation. His concern for Vietnam is a result of his keen interest in General Lansdale's recent report and his awareness of the high importance of this country."[26]

---

[23]U.S. Congress, Senate, Committee on Foreign Relations, *Executive Sessions of the Senate Foreign Relations Committee* (Historical Series), vol. XIII, pt. 1, 87th Cong., 1st sess. (Washington, D.C.: U.S. Govt. Print. Off., 1984), pp. 1-38, 49-90 (hereafter this series will be cited as *SFRC His. Ser.*).

[24]*Ibid.*, pp. 188-190.

[25]Arthur M. Schlesinger, Jr., *A Thousand Days* (Boston: Houghton Mifflin, 1954), p. 329, and Sorensen, *Kennedy*, p. 722.

[26]Kennedy Library, NSF Country File, Vietnam.

According to Walt W. Rostow, the new deputy to McGeorge Bundy, Kennedy's comment after the meeting was, "This is the worst one we've got, isn't it? You know, Eisenhower never mentioned it. He talked at length about Laos, but never uttered the word Vietnam."[27]

Lansdale's report, dated January 17, 1961, was made after a trip to Vietnam January 2-14, during which he talked to Diem and a number of other Vietnamese leaders, as well as to members of the U.S. mission.[28] In the report he warned that "The free Vietnamese, and their government, probably will be able to do no more than postpone eventual defeat—unless they find a Vietnamese way of mobilizing their total resources and then utilizing them with spirit." He proposed that the U.S. treat Vietnam as a "combat area of the cold war, as an area requiring emergency treatment," and that under such conditions we should send to Vietnam "our best people," people who are "experienced in dealing with this type of emergency . . . who know and really like Asia and the Asians, dedicated people who are willing to risk their lives for the ideals of freedom. . . ." In addition to a new Ambassador with these skills and attitudes he suggested that a similar person be sent to Vietnam for "political operations, whose primary job would be to work with the "oppositionists," with the goal of establishing a responsible opposition party by which to "promote a two-party system which can afford to be surfaced, end much of the present clandestine political structures, and give sound encouragement to the development of new political leaders." "There are plenty of Aaron Burr's, a few Alexander Hamilton's and practically no George Washington's, Tom Jefferson's or Tom Paine's in Saigon today," he added, "largely as a result of our U.S. political influence. This certainly was not the U.S. policy we had hoped to implement."

Lansdale said that Diem was "still the only Vietnamese with executive ability and the required determination to be an effective President," and that "We must support Ngo Dinh Diem until another strong executive can replace him legally. President Diem feels that Americans have attacked him almost as viciously as the Communists, and he has withdrawn into a shell for self-protection." The U.S. needed, Lansdale said, to understand Diem, and to treat him as a friend. "If the next American official to talk to President Diem," he said, "would have the good sense to see him as a human being who has been through a lot of hell for years—and not as an opponent to be beaten to his knees—we would start regaining our influence with him in a healthy way." "If we don't like the heavy influence of Brother [Ngo Dinh] Nhu," he added, "then let's move someone of ours in close."

Lansdale also recommended that American military advisers be allowed to work in combat areas, and that the effects of the U.S. aid program on the Vietnamese—which "has filled their bellies but has neglected their spirit"—should be reassessed. "The people have more possessions but are starting to lose the will to protect their

[27] W. W. Rostow, *The Diffusion of Power* (New York: Macmillan, 1972), p. 265.
[28] The text of the report is in *PP*, DOD (Department of Defense) ed., (Washington, D.C.: U.S. Govt. Print. Off., 1971), book 2, IV. A. 5., pp. 66-77, as well as in book 11, pp. 1-13.

liberty. There is a big lesson here to be learned about the U.S. aid program."

Shortly after returning from his trip, Lansdale met with Secretary of Defense McNamara, who had requested that Lansdale brief him on Vietnam. (At that point Lansdale was an assistant to McNamara.) Lansdale has recounted their meeting:[29]

> I had a lot of Viet Cong weapons, punji stakes, and so on, that I'd collected in Vietnam to get the Special Forces to start a Fort Bragg museum of guerrilla weapons. They still had Vietnamese mud on them, rusty and dirty. They were picked up from the battle field. So, I tucked all of these under my arm and went to his office. He had told me on the phone that I had five minutes to give him a briefing on Vietnam. I went in and he was sitting at his desk, and I put all of these dirty weapons down—crude looking, and including those big spikes that they had as punji stakes with dried blood and mud on them—I put them on this beautiful mahogany desk—I just dumped them on that. I said, "The enemy in Vietnam used these weapons—and they were just using them just a little bit ago before I got them. The enemy are barefoot or wear sandals. They wear black pajamas, usually, with tatters or holes in them. I don't think you'd recognize any of them as soldiers, but they think of themselves that way. The people that are fighting them, on our side, are being supplied with weapons and uniforms and good shoes and all of the best that we have; and we're training them. Yet, the enemy's licking our side," I said. "Always keep in mind about Vietnam, that the struggle goes far beyond the material things of life. It doesn't take weapons and uniforms and lots of food to win. It takes something else, ideas and ideals, and these guys are using that something else. Let's at least learn that lesson." Somehow I found him very hard to talk to. Watching his face as I talked, I got the feeling that he didn't understand me.

Counterinsurgency Plan Approved for Vietnam

In submitting to Washington in January 1961 the counterinsurgency plan for Vietnam which had been developed during the fall of 1960, Ambassador Durbrow stated that he had reservations about one of the proposals, which would increase the Vietnamese Army by 20,000 men (from 150,000 to 170,000), primarily for action against the Communist insurgents. He preferred, he said, that "more calculated risks . . . should be taken by using more of the forces in being to meet the immediate and serious guerrilla threat." Some of the proposals for reforms, Durbrow added, would probably be unpalatable to the Government of Vietnam. "Consideration should, therefore, be given to what actions we are prepared to take to encourage, or if necessary to force, acceptance of all essential elements of the plan."[30]

---

[29]CRS Interview with Edward G. Lansdale, Nov. 19, 1982.
[30]From the text of Durbrow's cable, in *PP*, DOD ed., book 10, p. 1359. See also Durbrow's cable of Dec. 4, 1960, excerpted in *ibid.*, book 2, IV. A. 5., pp. 63-65, in which he described the situation in Vietnam after the attempted coup in November, and explained why the U.S. needed to continue to insist on reforms and liberalization. The text of the counterinsurgency plan and its annexes is still classified, but a portion of the plan is in *ibid.*, pp. 87-93.

The proposed plan provided for a substantial increase in U.S. military assistance to Vietnam. In addition to an increase of 20,000 men in the army, it called for increasing the Civil Guard by 32,000 (to 68,000). The total cost of these increases would be about $42 million, added to approximately $225 million a year already being paid by the U.S. for maintaining Vietnamese forces.

The plan also called for Diem to institute certain political reforms, including having opposition leaders in the Cabinet, giving the National Assembly power to investigate charges of mismanagement and corruption in the executive, improving "civic action" and other means of winning more popular support. The position of Durbrow and of the Department of State was that Diem's cooperation in achieving these reforms should be required before the U.S. agreed to provide the additional aid, and this was the position that was accepted, however tacitly, by the President when he approved the plan.

It is also of interest to note that the memorandum setting forth the proposed counterinsurgency plan is said to have stated that if the provisions of the plan were carried out, "the war could be won in eighteen months."[31]

Indicative of the prevailing attitude about the importance of providing such additional assistance was a memorandum on February 1 from Robert W. Komer (a former CIA employee then serving as Rostow's deputy) and an unnamed State Department official in the Far East bureau, "Forestalling a Crisis in South Vietnam," in which they said, among other things, that such aid ". . . will probably require circumvention of the Geneva Accords. We should not let this stop us."[32]

At the White House meeting on January 28 at which the new counterinsurgency plan was discussed, Kennedy asked whether increases in Vietnam's Armed Forces "would really permit a shift from the defense to the offense," which the plan purportedly would do, or "whether the situation was not basically one of politics and morale."[33] This led to a discussion of the situation in Vietnam in which Lansdale argued that the Communists considered 1961 "as their big year," but that a "maximum American effort" in 1961 could thwart their plans, and enable South Vietnam, with U.S. help, to "move over into the offensive in 1962." In his comments, as in his written report, Lansdale stressed the need to support Diem. "The essentials were three," he said: "First, the Americans in Viet-Nam must themselves be infused with high morale and a will to win, and they must get close to the Vietnamese; secondly, the Vietnamese must, in this setting, be moved to act with vigor and confidence; third, Diem must be persuaded to let the opposition coalesce in some legitimate form rather than concentrate on the task of killing him." ("It was Diem's view," Lansdale said, "that there are Americans in the Foreign Service who are very close to those who tried to kill him on November 11, [1960] . . . Diem felt confidence

---

[31]Schlesinger, *A Thousand Days,* p. 541. In writing this book, Schlesinger had access to classified materials, many of which, such as the counterinsurgency memorandum, are still classified.

[32]Kennedy Library, NSF Country File, Vietnam.

[33]This account of the meeting is from a memorandum at the Kennedy Library, NSF Country File, Vietnam, W. W. Rostow to McGeorge Bundy, Jan. 30, 1961.

in the Americans in the CIA and the MAAG [Military Assistance Advisory Group].")

Secretary of State Rusk commented that U.S. diplomats in Vietnam faced an ". . . extremely frustrating task. They were caught between pressing Diem to do things he did not wish to do and the need to convey to him American support. It was a difficult balance to strike; and Diem was extremely sensitive to criticism."

Kennedy said he would like to see guerrillas operating in North Vietnam, and asked about this possibility. CIA Director Dulles replied that four teams of eight men each had been organized for harassment, but had been used only in the south, despite CIA interest in more offensive operations. Dulles urged a build-up of counterguerrilla forces before the addition of the 20,000 men to the regular army, and also advocated increased U.S. training of such forces.

Lansdale mentioned the importance of Laos to the defense of Vietnam. ". . . if Laos goes to the Communists," he said, "we might not have time to organize the turn-around required in American and Viet-Nam morale and action."

As the meeting ended, Kennedy concluded by asking ". . . how do we change morale; how do we get operations in the north; how do we get moving?" And, referring to the four "crisis areas: Viet-Nam; Congo; Laos; and Cuba," he said ". . . we must change our course in these areas and we must be better off in three months than we are now."

Kennedy's approval of the counterinsurgency plan two days later (January 30), as the *Pentagon Papers* observes, "was seen as quite a routine action."[34] Kennedy's major concern seems to have been to make the U.S. role more effective, to "get moving." He wanted to do more rather than less, including expanding operations by undertaking, among other things, espionage and sabotage by guerrilla infiltration into North Vietnam. According to former Ambassador Durbrow, who had received a photostat from the State Department, Kennedy made a notation in the corner of the cover page of his copy of the counterinsurgency plan, to the effect, "Why so little? JFK. January 28."[35]

Thus, the expansion of the U.S. role in Vietnam provided for by the counterinsurgency plan was approved by the President quickly, firmly and without change. Presidential aide Theodore C. Sorensen later commented, ". . . an abandonment of Vietnam, an abandonment of our commitment would have had a very serious adverse effect on the position of the United States in all of Southeast Asia. Therefore, we had to do whatever was necessary in order to prevent it, which meant increasing our military commitment."[36]

On February 3 (National Security Action Memorandum—NSAM—2), Secretary McNamara was directed to make a report on conducting guerrilla operations in North Vietnam.[37] On March 9

---

[34]*PP*, Gravel ed., vol. II, p. 27.
[35]CRS Interview with Elbridge Durbrow, Oct. 25, 1978.
[36]Kennedy Library, Oral History Interview with Theodore C. Sorensen, Mar. 26, 1964, p. 97.
[37]The subject of the first NSAM was "Separate Budgeting of Spending Abroad." A list of all Kennedy NSAMs by number and subject was provided CRS by the Kennedy Library. A similar listing of NSAMs during Johnson's administration, made available by the Johnson Library, does

Continued

(NSAM 28), McNamara was again directed to make the report on guerrilla operations "in view of the President's instructions that we make every possible effort" to undertake such activities "at the earliest possible time."[38] Kennedy also suggested (NSAM 9, February 6, 1961), that Lansdale's ". . . story of the counterguerrilla case study would be an excellent magazine article for magazine like the *Saturday Evening Post.* Obviously it could not go under Lansdale's signature, but he might, if the Department of Defense and the State Department think it is worthwhile, turn this memorandum over to them and they could perhaps get a good writer for it. He could then check the final story."[39]

Khrushchev's Speech and the Special Group (Counterinsurgency)

While approving the new plan for Vietnam, and taking prompt action to prevent further Communist gains in Laos, the Kennedy administration launched a new counterinsurgency program to combat Communist "wars of national liberation." As described by Russian Premier Nikita Khrushchev in a speech on January 6, 1961, such "wars of liberation or popular uprisings," which began as "uprisings of colonial peoples against their oppressors" and developed into "guerrilla wars," were supported "without reservation" by the Communists.

Khrushchev's speech, the meaning and significance of which may have been exaggerated or even misinterpreted by Kennedy and his associates, made a "conspicuous impression" on the President, and besides sending copies of it to his newly appointed top aides and associates, he ". . . read the Khrushchev speech time and again—in his office, at cabinet meetings, at dinners with friends, alone. At times he read it aloud and urged his colleagues to comment."[40]

Spurred by what he and his associates considered to be a direct challenge to the U.S., as well as by the need they felt to respond more vigorously to Communist subversion in Indochina and elsewhere in the third world, Kennedy began, as a "personal project," the development of a U.S. counterguerrilla or counterinsurgency program. He personally looked over the Army's field equipment for counterguerrilla warfare, studied the training manuals, and read studies on the subject, including Communist doctrine.[41] He then ordered the Army to expand its counterguerrilla training, and to augment its Special Forces, or "Green Berets." Counterinsurgency training courses were eventually required for all personnel, civilian as well as military, serving in countries facing Communist subversion. "The hybrid word [counterinsurgency] became a passkey to the inner councils of government, to the trust of the President. If a high official expressed skepticism about the significance or newness ascribed to this style of warfare, it was said, he risked shortening

---

not provide, for alleged security reasons, and at the direction of the NSC staff, the subjects of most NSAMs issued during Johnson's administration. The texts of all NSAMs cited herein were provided by the two libraries unless otherwise noted.

[38]NSAMs 2 and 28 are also in the *Pentagon Papers,* DOD ed., book 11, pp. 17-18.

[39]This was done and the piece in question appeared in the *Saturday Evening Post,* May 20, 1961, under the title, "The Report the President Wanted Published," By an American Officer ("whose name, for professional reasons, cannot be used").

[40]Schlesinger, *A Thousand Days,* p. 302, and Marvin Kalb and Elie Abel, *Roots of Involvement, The U.S. in Asia, 1784-1971* (New York: W. W. Norton, 1971), p. 110.

[41]Schlesinger, *A Thousand Days,* p. 341.

his tenure in office. McNamara, [Maxwell] Taylor, and Rostow became early converts, and their White House standing soared. Rusk never converted."[42]

In March 1961, Kennedy established a counterinsurgency task force, headed by Richard Bissell, a Deputy Director of the CIA, which in January 1962 became the Special Group (CI) chaired by Presidential adviser Maxwell D. Taylor, with the Deputy Under Secretary of State, the Deputy Secretary of Defense, the Chairman of the JCS, the Director of the CIA, the Special Assistant to the President for National Security Affairs, the Administrator of the Agency for International Development, and the Director of the U.S. Information Agency, as members.[43]

Maxwell Taylor, a distinguished General and Army Chief of Staff in the latter part of the 1950s, who took early retirement from the Army in 1959 because of his disagreement with current strategy, and W. W. Rostow, who had been a professor at the Massachusetts Institute of Technology before becoming McGeorge Bundy's deputy, were foremost leaders in the development of U.S. counterinsurgency doctrine and programs, along with Roger Hilsman, the new head of the State Department's Bureau of Intelligence and Research, who had a strong academic and research background as well as having been a West Point graduate and a member of the U.S. commando unit in Southeast Asia in World War II, "Merrill's Marauders."

One of the earliest proponents of a shift in strategy was Henry A. Kissinger, who propounded in 1955 an argument for defense of the "grey areas" around the periphery of the Soviet Union by a military policy based on fighting "little" or "local" wars, rather than on the threat of "massive retaliation" by strategic forces.[44] Rostow and other Kennedy theorists carried Kissinger's argument to its ultimate conclusion. In order to fight "little" or "local" wars in which the Communists were seeking to "liberate" countries through internal, indirect aggression, assisted from outside but not involving open, external aggression, the U.S. needed, to paraphrase Hilsman, to use the tactics of the guerrilla against the guerrilla. Whereas Kissinger advocated building up the indigenous capacity for self-defense, the counterinsurgency argument of the Kennedy era was open-ended, as experience later demonstrated. When the U.S. was unable to develop adequate indigenous strength, it began to substitute American strength.

One of the experts recruited for counterinsurgency planning in the Kennedy administration later described the early Kennedy period as "one of change, of ferment, of self confidence—of 'knowing' what had to be done and of unquestioning 'can do.'" Kennedy, he said, "Taking seriously the threat to American power and influence implicit in Khrushchev's words, . . . set about building our

---

[42]Kalb and Abel, p. 124.
[43]See Douglas S. Blaufarb, *The Counterinsurgency Era* (New York: Free Press, 1977). The Special Group (CI) was established by NSAM 124, Jan. 18, 1962, which is reprinted in *PP*, DOD ed., book 12, pp. 442-444. Other relevant documents are NSAM 131, Mar. 13, 1962, "Training Objectives for Counter-Insurgency" in *ibid.*, pp. 457-459, and NSAM 162, June 19, 1962, "Development of U.S. and Indigenous Police, Paramilitary and Military Resources," in *ibid.*, pp. 481-486.
[44]Henry A. Kissinger, "Military Policy and Defense of the 'Grey Areas,'" *Foreign Affairs*, 33 (April 1955), pp. 416-428. For a more complete discussion of Kissinger's argument, see pt. I of this study.

military and government instruments to meet an obvious and serious challenge. That challenge may appear shadowy and full of braggadocio from the vantage point of the bitter experience of all parties in the late sixties. But who can deny that it was uttered seriously, and was meant to succeed, if it could, ten years earlier?"[45]

Many policymakers in the Kennedy administration, like those under Eisenhower, did not have the specialized knowledge required to deal with Southeast Asia, however, and this factor greatly complicated the attempt to intervene in situations in which such knowledge could be decisive. One of Kennedy's closest advisers has singled this out as a key lesson to be learned from studying the development of U.S. policy toward Vietnam after 1961:[46]

> . . . our system has many strengths and the drawing of talent from outside the government and bringing it into government brings many advantages. But it also brings many costs, and one of the costs is bringing people into high policy-making positions who *aren't* prepared to deal with many of the questions they face. . . . So I think in a very real sense we assumed responsibilities unprepared; we didn't see clearly the full extent of those responsibilities; there were very few resources in the country to draw upon. And I mention all of this because I think it colored the behavior thereafter. And I don't think to this day it is understood. What, in a sense, evolved as a feeling of public officials misleading the public was, in a major respect, much worse than that; much different—let me put it this way. It was public officials not seeing the problem clearly, and, at least in hindsight, not acting in the public interest.

What To Do About Laos?

In early February 1961, Kennedy established a task force on Laos consisting of the Assistant Secretary of State for the Far East, J. Graham Parsons, and his Deputy, John Steeves, both of whom had been appointed to those posts during the Eisenhower administration, as well as Kennedy's new Assistant Secretary of Defense for International Security Affairs, Paul H. Nitze, (who had worked on Indochina under Truman and his Secretary of State, Dean G. Acheson), W. W. Rostow from the NSC staff, and others from State, the military and the CIA.

A day or so later, Secretary Rusk sent a memorandum to Kennedy in which he said that the task force had completed a draft report. He enclosed a proposed cable to set in motion a new plan for Laos.[47] This plan called for the King of Laos to declare the neutralization of the country, followed by establishment of a Neutral Nations Commission by Cambodia and Burma, among others. At

[45]Seymour J. Deitchman, *The Best-Laid Schemes* (Cambridge, Mass.: MIT Press, 1976), pp. 4-5. In Schlesinger's description, "The future everywhere . . . seemed bright with hope. . . . The capital city, somnolent in the Eisenhower years, had come suddenly alive. The air had been stale and oppressive; now fresh winds were blowing. There was the excitement which comes from an injection of new men and new ideas, the release of energy which occurs when men with ideas have a chance to put them into practice." *A Thousand Days,* p. 206.

[46]Confidential CRS Interview, Feb. 1, 1979. (emphasis in original)

[47]Undated memo from Rusk to Kennedy in the Kennedy Library, POF Country File, Laos.

the same time, General Phoumi was to conduct an offensive against the Pathet Lao for the purpose of strengthening the position of the government. These actions would be supported by SEATO moves, including the deployment of a U.S. military unit to Thailand.

On February 7, in preparation for a White House meeting to discuss the Laos plan, McGeorge Bundy and W. W. Rostow sent the President a memorandum commenting on the plan and suggesting possible questions to raise.[48] They called the plan a "carefully worked out and intelligent attack on a very tough problem." As for questions, they suggested the President might ask whether deploying the U.S. military unit to Thailand was "the best way of signalling support to Sarit [Sarit Thanarat, the leader of the military junta then ruling the country] and general concern for the area?"

They also suggested linking Laos to the broader question of U.S. relations with the Soviet Union:

> Does this whole approach fully recognize that the decisive dialogue here is with Khrushchev? Are we not coming to a time when something should be said directly to him? In this area where all the local advantages are against us, one clear asset is that Khrushchev wants serious talks with you, there must be a real cooling-off in Laos. Should we not move in ways which make it as easy as possible for him to face down the CHICOMS [Chinese Communists] on this point, while emphasizing quietly the depth of our commitment?

Kennedy approved most of the proposed plan, with the exception of sending the U.S. military unit to Thailand, and on February 19 the King of Laos issued a neutrality declaration and asked Cambodia, Malaya and Burma to form a neutral commission. Only Malaya agreed to do so, however. Meanwhile, Phoumi's offensive failed, and U.S. policymakers were back at square one.

On March 1, Rusk sent Kennedy a memo reporting on the status of U.S. plans for Laos in which he said that the "key obstacle" to acceptance of the U.S. position by countries like Cambodia and Burma was the "narrow composition" of the Laotian Government, i.e., that it did not include Souvanna Phouma.[49]

A few days later, the Laos Task Force sent Kennedy another proposed plan. By this point, according to a memo to the President from Rostow on March 9, in which he recounted events during February, "our initial dispositions with respect to Laos, both diplomatically and militarily, have not succeeded, and we enter a new phase."[50]

The task force recommended that in this "new phase" there should be increased military assistance to Laos, as well as U.S. military moves to demonstrate U.S. determination to resist Communist control of Laos. A "seventeen-step escalation ladder" was proposed. The members of the group, according to one knowledg-

---

[48]Same location.
[49]Same location.
[50]Same location.

able source, "were much more willing to favor the use of American force than the President and his senior advisers."[51]

This plan was discussed and generally approved by the President and his advisers on March 9, 1961. Possible intervention by U.S. forces was not ruled out, but there was considerable reluctance to take such a step, and the President decided to continue efforts to find a diplomatic solution. These efforts, specifically the attempt to get the Russians to terminate their airlift into Laos, were unsuccessful, however, and within a few days there was a plan in the works to undertake limited U.S. military action. According to a memorandum from Rostow to the President on March 17,[52]

> State is preparing for the Secretary's consideration a plan for the movement of an international SEATO force into Laos. If SEATO did not accept, the idea is that the U.S., Asian members of SEATO, and possibly Australia and New Zealand, would work on a modified plan. Diplomatically it would be based on the Lebanon case; that is, it would be triggered by an appeal from the King of Laos for us to hold the line and permit peace to be negotiated, looking to an independent, neutral country. The troops would go in merely to hold certain key centers for diplomatic bargaining purposes, not to conquer the country. They would only shoot if shot at. There would be talks with the Russians explaining our position and a report to the UN. The total force envisaged is about 26,000, which seems a bit high. At least half would be Asian troops. There would be U.S., Australian and, hopefully, New Zealand contributions.

On March 20-21 this plan was discussed by the President and his advisers. Details of these meetings are still classified, but apparently Rostow, on behalf of the task force, argued the case for deploying U.S. forces to Thailand. The Joint Chiefs, however, argued that this could result in North Vietnamese moves into Laos, and possible war with China, and that if U.S. troops were to be used there would have to be an adequate force to insure a favorable outcome. They estimated that a U.S. move into Laos would require 60,000 men, as well as air cover, and the use, if necessary, of atomic bombs against targets in North Vietnam and China.

Kennedy, it is said, recognized the difficulties involved in committing a large force to Laos. He had learned, for one thing, that if 10,000 men were sent to Southeast Asia there would be almost no strategic reserve force for other emergencies.[53]

He is also said to have recognized that a neutralization of Laos was the "only feasible alternative." Remembering what had happened in Vietnam in 1954, however, he did not want to negotiate prior to a cease-fire.[54] He thought that Laotian anti-Communist forces, with U.S. help, had to hold Vientiane, the capital city of Laos, in order to establish a stronger basis for negotiations, and in order to prevent a defeat that would have repercussions on the credibility of the United States in other areas. "We cannot," he

[51]Stevenson, *The End of Nowhere*, p. 142. One senior adviser, Under Secretary of State Chester Bowles, was strongly opposed to a U.S. military commitment in Laos. See Bowles' *Promises to Keep* (New York: Harper and Row, 1971), pp. 335-407.
[52]Kennedy Library, POF Staff Memos File.
[53]Cited in Stevenson, *The End of Nowhere*, p. 135.
[54]Sorensen, *Kennedy*, p. 724.

was quoted as saying, "and will not accept any visible humiliation over Laos."[55]

In addition, Kennedy recognized and apparently alluded in the meetings to what he considered to be the "contradictions" in American public opinion, ". . . between the desire to 'get tough' with the communists and the disinclination to get involved in another Asian War. . . ." But he apparently also felt, and confirmed in consultations with Members of Congress, that the public would support U.S. intervention in Laos if that became necessary.[56]

The meetings of March 20-21 resulted in a decision to undertake a limited show of force by the U.S., to be followed by possible SEATO action. Kennedy authorized (there was no NSAM on the subject) immediate military moves similar to the ones made by Eisenhower in December 1960:[57]

Three aircraft carriers moved toward Laos with 1,400 marines. Long-range troop and cargo transport planes flew from the continental United States to the Philippines. About 150 marines were dispatched to Udorn, Thailand, to service fourteen additional helicopters being given to the Royal Lao Army. On Okinawa Task Force 116 was alerted and its staffs brought up to operational size. . . . Two thousand marines in Japan were pulled away from a movie which they were assisting in filming. . . . In all, about 4,000 troops were ready for battle in Laos—not enough to carry out the intervention plans, but, hopefully, enough to force a change in the diplomatic stalemate.

At the same time, Kennedy authorized various covert actions, including increased reconnaissance flights over Laos. These had previously been conducted primarily by the Thais, but when the Thai Government decided in February 1961 not to continue such flights the JCS recommended that they be made by the U.S. Air Force. Instead, Kennedy told the U.S. military to borrow planes from the Philippine Air Force (RT-33s), paint them with Laotian markings, and use U.S. Air Force pilots in civilian clothes to fly reconnaissance over Laos. "On April 24, 1961, the first American-piloted RT-33 sortie flew from Udorn under the code name 'Field Goal.' "[58]

On March 23, 1961, Kennedy took his case to the public. Speaking on nationwide television, he said that the U.S. supported a neutral and independent Laos. Without mentioning the military moves which he had already authorized, he said that attacks by "externally supported Communists" would have to cease, and if they did not that the U.S. would "honor its obligations." "No one should doubt our resolutions [sic] on this point," he added "The security of all Southeast Asia will be endangered if Laos loses its neutral independence."[59]

[55]Schlesinger, *A Thousand Days*, p. 332.
[56]*Ibid.*, p. 333. There are few available details on the consultations that apparently were held with Congress during the latter part of March, including an executive session of the Senate Foreign Relations Committee on Mar. 22 which was not transcribed.
[57]Stevenson, *The End of Nowhere*, p. 146.
[58]Earl H. Tilford, Jr., *Search and Rescue in Southeast Asia, 1961-1975* (Washington, D.C.: Office of Air Force History, United States Air Force, 1980), pp. 34-35. On Mar. 24, 1961, the first U.S. Air Force plane piloted by an officer in uniform had been shot down in Indochina while flying an electronic surveillance mission over Laos. See *ibid.*, p. 33.
[59]*Public Papers of the Presidents*, John F. Kennedy, 1961, p. 214.

Congress reacted favorably to Kennedy's speech, with both Democrats and Republicans declaring their support for negotiations while also supporting Kennedy's firmness and determination to honor U.S. commitments. Except for the concern of some Republicans and a few Democrats about having Communists included in the government of a neutral Laos, there was no dissent in Congress to the administration's proposals for handling the Laotian situation.[60]

In a letter to Kennedy on March 24, the day after the speech, Senate Foreign Relations Committee Chairman J. William Fulbright (D/Ark.) said, "Your explanation of the Laotian situation was extremely effective." He enclosed a study on Vietnam for Kennedy's use, saying that he thought it would be of interest: "The thought occurred to me," Fulbright added, "that the extent to which you might be willing to go in defending Laos could possibly be influenced by the stability in Viet-Nam. It would be embarrassing, to say the least, to have Viet-Nam collapse just as we are extended in Laos."[61]

Meanwhile, after the White House meetings of March 20-21, the U.S. had informed the British of the military moves which it was making, and had urged them to join in getting SEATO to implement "Plan 5/60" (usually referred to as SEATO Plan 5, this was a contingency plan for the deployment of a major SEATO force to Laos and Vietnam which would seek to defend Southeast Asia from a position on the Mekong River) under which U.S. Marines would be augmented by the Mobile Commonwealth Brigade consisting of troops from Britain, New Zealand and Australia. The British, however, urged continued efforts to achieve a cease-fire, and stated their reservations about military intervention. Kennedy then asked British Prime Minister Harold Macmillan to discuss the matter. The two leaders met on March 26, 1961, and according to Macmillan, Kennedy ". . . was not at all anxious to undertake a military operation in Laos. If it had to be done (as a sort of political gesture) he definitely wanted it to be a SEATO exercise. He did *not* want to 'go it alone.'" Kennedy, he said, commented that a number of people in the U.S. would consider British support to be the "determining factor," and that unless the British decided to join the U.S. in such an effort "he was not sure he could get his people to accept unilateral action by the United States."

Kennedy told Macmillan that he was considering a very limited force of four or five battalions to hold Vientiane and other key posts, apparently referring to a modified version of the Vietnam Task Force proposal. Macmillan said he understood Kennedy's need to convince the Russians, "at the beginning of his presidency," that the U.S. would not be "pushed out" of Laos, and that he would agree to participate, with cabinet approval, in "the *appearance* of resistance and in the necessary military planning." But

---

[60]See *Congressional Record*, vol. 107 (Washington, D.C.: U.S. Govt. Print. Off.), pp. 4706-4708, 5114-5115, 5292-5293, (hereafter cited as *CR*).

[61]Kennedy Library, POF Country File, Laos. The 16-page study enclosed with the letter was "The Struggle in South Vietnam," prepared in Mar. 1961 by Oliver E. Clubb, Jr., Legislative Reference Service, Library of Congress. In 1962, Clubb, then at the Brookings Institution, prepared the study, *The United States and the Sino-Soviet Bloc in Southeast Asia* (Washington, D.C.: Brookings Institution, 1962).

while undertaking such planning, the U.S. and Britain should make every effort to get the Russians to agree to a cease-fire and a conference.[62]

On April 1, Khrushchev responded favorably to the idea of an international conference on the subject, and tension eased momentarily.

At this point, a very serious event occurred, an event which critically affected the foreign policy of the Kennedy administration. Carrying out a plan developed in the Eisenhower administration, Kennedy agreed to let Cuban refugees, trained, armed and supported by the CIA, invade Cuba (Operation Zapata). After the resulting fiasco, commonly referred to as the "Bay of Pigs," the Kennedy administration, seeking to prove to the world, and especially to the Russians, that the U.S. was not the "paper tiger" it appeared to be, assumed an even more militant (although perhaps less bold) foreign policy stance which, in turn, may well have affected U.S. policy toward Vietnam.[63]

Some have suggested that the failure of the Bay of Pigs, together with the subsequent "bullying" to which Khrushchev is said to have subjected Kennedy at their "summit meeting" in June 1961, heavily influenced the Kennedy administration's decision to stand and fight the Communists in Vietnam, on the grounds that the U.S. had to demonstrate its determination to confront them, by force if necessary, and that Vietnam was the most auspicious place for such a confrontation. There is considerable validity to this argument. Most U.S. policymakers apparently did assume that the U.S.

---

[62]Harold Macmillan, *Pointing the Way, 1959-1961* (New York: Harper and Row, 1972), pp. 333-338. Quotations from the book are from Macmillan's diary.

[63]Immediately after the Bay of Pigs failure, President Kennedy asked Maxwell Taylor, Robert Kennedy, Adm. Arleigh Burke (Chief of Naval Operations) and Allen Dulles to review the operation, as well as "governmental practices and programs in the areas of military and paramilitary, guerrilla and anti-guerrilla activity." With respect to the Bay of Pigs (Operation Zapata), the Cuban Study Group concluded after a month of secret hearings, ". . . we are of the opinion that the preparations and execution of paramilitary operations such as Zapata is a form of cold war action in which the country must be prepared to engage. If it does so, it must engage in it with a maximum chance of success." With respect to the broader question of U.S. cold war operations, the group concluded that there was need for " . . . a changed attitude on the part of the government and of the people toward the emergency which confronts us. The first requirement of such a change is to recognize that we are in a life and death struggle which we may be losing, and will lose unless we change our ways and marshall our resources with an intensity associated in the past only with times of war. To effect this change, we must give immediate consideration to taking such measures as the announcement of a limited national emergency, the review of any treaties or international agreements which restrain the full use of our resources in the cold war, and the determination to seek the respect of our neighbors, without the criteria being international popularity, and a policy of taking into account the proportioning of foreign aid to the attitude shown us by our neighbors. In the light of the strained situation in Laos and the potential crisis building up over Berlin, we should consider at once affirmative programs to cope with the threat in both areas. There should be a re-examination of emergency powers of the President as to their adequacy to meet the developing situation." For one comment on the Kennedy administration's response to these recommendations see Arthur M. Schlesinger, Jr., *Robert Kennedy and His Times* (Boston: Houghton Mifflin, 1978), pp. 459-460. See below for actions taken by Kennedy.

The Cuban Study Group also recommended a division of responsibility between the CIA and the military that was later implemented in Vietnam: ". . . the Department of Defense will normally receive responsibility for overt paramilitary operations. Where such an operation is to be wholly covert or disavowable, it may be assigned to CIA, provided that it is within the normal capabilities of the agency. Any large paramilitary operation wholly or partly covert which requires significant numbers of militarily trained personnel, amounts of military stocks and/or military experience of a kind and level peculiar to the armed forces is properly the primary responsibility of the Department of Defense with the CIA in a supporting role."

These quotations from the Cuban Study Group report are from *Operation Zapata: The "Ultrasensitive" Report and Testimony of the Board of Inquiry on the Bay of Pigs* (Frederick, Md.: University Publications of America, 1981), pp. 43, 51-52, and 48-49.

could not back down in Vietnam, and that it was Vietnam, rather than Laos, where, if necessary, a confrontation should occur. "What happened," commented James C. Thomson, Jr. (an Asian specialist, who was then assistant to Under Secretary Bowles, and subsequently a member of the NSC staff dealing with Vietnam), "as my colleagues put it at the time, was that we discovered that the Laotians were not Turks. That was the phrase of the moment. What did that mean? That meant that they would not stand up and fight. And, once we discovered that the Laotians were not Turks, it seemed advisable to pull back from confrontation in Laos. . . . But once Laotians were discovered not to be Turks, the place to stand one's ground, it was thought, was Vietnam because the Vietnamese were Turks. . . . That's my recollection of the climate—let's call it 'the search for Turks.'"[64]

Former Ambassador William H. Sullivan, who was very closely associated with Indochina affairs for many of his years in the State Department, gave this description of the prevailing attitude:[65]

The attitude was that Laos was a secondary problem; Laos was a poor place to get bogged down in because it was inland, had no access to the sea and no proper logistics lines . . . that it was rather inchoate as a nation; that the Laos were not fighters, et cetera. While on the other hand if you were going to have a confrontation, the place to have it was in Vietnam because it did have logistical access to the sea and therefore, we had military advantages. It was an articulated, functioning nation. Its troops were tigers and real fighters. And, therefore, the advantages would be all on our side to have the confrontation and showdown in Vietnam and not get sucked into this Laos operation.[66]

Sullivan made a very important additional point: ". . . I think, in saying that the White House recognized and that all of us did recognize that Vietnam was the main show, it wasn't at all the same to say that people were afraid of Vietnam as a quagmire; people were looking at Vietnam as something that could be a more solid instrument for settling this thing."[67] In other words, Vietnam

[64]CRS Interview with James C. Thomson, Jr., Oct. 17, 1978. In his very perceptive article, "How Could Vietnam Happen?" *Atlantic Monthly* (April 1968), p. 48, Thomson stated: ". . . the legacy of the fifties was apparently compounded by an uneasy sense of a worldwide Communist challenge to the new Administration after the Bay of Pigs fiasco. A first manifestation was the President's traumatic Vienna meeting with Khrushchev in June, 1961; then came the Berlin crisis of the summer. All this created an atmosphere in which President Kennedy undoubtedly felt under special pressure to show his nation's mettle in Vietnam—if the Vietnamese, unlike the people of Laos, were willing to fight."

[65]Kennedy Library, Oral History Interview with William H. Sullivan (second of two), Aug. 5, 1970, p. 33.

[66]Of interest is a portion of a "Dear Joe" letter of Mar. 18, 1967, from Sullivan, then serving as U.S. Ambassador to Laos, to Joseph W. Alsop, the noted U.S. journalist, regarding a series of articles Alsop had just written on Laos (Library of Congress, Joseph Alsop Papers): ". . . you may wish some documentary support for your contention that President Kennedy deliberately put Laos on the back burner so that he could pursue the confrontation more advantageously in Vietnam. There will be those who will accuse you of hindsight in this regard. To silence them, I would refer you to an article which appeared in the *New York Times* Sunday magazine some time in the late summer of 1962 over the signature of Averell Harriman. This article made precisely the point which you are contending; namely, that the President did not intend to handle the situation in the same manner as in Laos. I recall this article well because I wrote it and it had the President's personal clearance before it was printed."

[67]Kennedy Library, Second Oral History Interview with William H. Sullivan, p. 33.

was more than just an auspicious place to confront the Communists and to demonstrate the American commitment to containment—it was a "solid instrument" for proving U.S. mettle; for "settling" the question of defending "free" countries against wars of national liberation. Thus, as Sullivan said, Vietnam was not feared as a quagmire; it was perceived as an opportunity.

W. W. Rostow made this same point in a memorandum to Kennedy on June 17, 1961, after Kennedy's meeting with Khrushchev, entitled "The Shape of the Battle."[68] Rostow said that the administration was heading into "our crucial months of crisis," and that to "turn the tide" it was necessary to win two "defensive battles"—Berlin, and Vietnam. If these battles could be won, he said, the U.S. could then "provide a golden bridge of retreat from their present aggressive positions for both Moscow and Peking." Berlin would have to be held against the Russians, he added, and the Communists would have to be turned back in Vietnam, in order to demonstrate that wars of national liberation could and would be defeated, which, in turn, would deter guerrilla activities in other unstable situations.

This argument doubtless would have been made if there had not been a Bay of Pigs invasion or a summit meeting, but those incidents seem to have caused the Kennedy administration to take a firmer stand in Vietnam, both to convince the Communists that the Bay of Pigs was an aberration, and to demonstrate that the U.S. could use its power effectively—and in unconventional ways if necessary—in combatting wars of national liberation, despite the failure of the unconventional means used in the attempt to overthrow the Communists in Cuba.

Ironically, it was also the Bay of Pigs that may have prevented active U.S. military involvement in Laos, and strengthened the President's resolve to find a diplomatic solution for Laos by which the U.S. could avoid having to fight in an area of lesser importance, and one where it would be at such a disadvantage militarily. After the failure of the Cuban invasion, Kennedy became much more cautious about the advice he was getting. As Presidential assistant Sorensen said,[69]

> . . . the Bay of Pigs fiasco had its influence. That operation had been recommended principally by the same set of advisers who favored intervention in Laos. But now the President was far more skeptical of the experts, their reputations, their recommendations, their promises, premises and facts. He relied more on his White House staff and his own common sense; and he asked the Attorney General and me to attend all NSC meetings. He began asking questions he had not asked before about military operations in Laos. He requested each member of the Chiefs of Staff to give him in writing his detailed views on where our intervention would lead, who would join us, how we would react to a massive Red Chinese response and where it would all end. Their answers, considered in an NSC meeting on May 1, looked very different from the operations originally envisioned; and the closer he looked, the less justifiable and de-

---

[68]Kennedy Library, POF Staff Memos File.
[69]*Kennedy*, p. 726.

finable those answers became. "Thank God the Bay of Pigs happened when it did," he would say to me in September. . . . , "otherwise we'd be in Laos by now—and that would be a hundred times worse."[70]

Cease-Fire in Laos

Before turning to the developments occurring during February-May 1961 with respect to Vietnam, this discussion of events in Laos, culminating in May with the agreement between the U.S. and the U.S.S.R. to negotiate a settlement for Laos, should be concluded. Prior to the Laos negotiations, which began in Geneva on May 16, 1961, the U.S., facing a renewed offensive by the Pathet Lao, and fearing that the Russians were stalling, again considered using American forces. On April 27, Kennedy met with his advisers. Rostow, speaking for the Laos Task Force, again recommended limited troop deployment to Thailand.[71] W. Averell Harriman, who had been appointed Ambassador at Large, and was to head the U.S. team in Geneva, agreed with this proposal. He thought the presence of U.S. forces in Thailand would strengthen the negotiating position of the U.S. The JCS again argued that if there was to be a show of force, there should be an adequate force available to undertake a military offensive, should one be required. This time, possibly in part because of the Bay of Pigs experience, the JCS proposed a force of 120,000-140,000 men, with authority to use nuclear weapons if necessary. There were so many differences of opinion expressed by military representatives attending the meeting, however, that Vice President Lyndon B. Johnson finally suggested to Kennedy that each one be asked to state his views in writing. Kennedy agreed, and they were asked to do so. As a result, Kennedy received separate statements from all four members of the JCS, from all three service secretaries, and from McNamara. Although the Army apparently predicted problems of supplying U.S. troops in Laos, as well as difficulties in effectively fighting guerrillas holed up in the mountains, "The majority," according to Sorensen,[72] "appeared to favor the landing of American troops in Thailand, South Vietnam and the government-held portions of the Laotian panhandle. If that did not produce a cease-fire, they recommended an air attack on Pathet Lao positions and tactical nuclear weapons on the ground. If North Vietnamese or Chinese then moved in, their homelands would be bombed. If massive Red troops

---

[70]As Schlesinger, *A Thousand Days*, p. 339, recounts the story, Kennedy told him on May 3, "'If it hadn't been for Cuba, we might be about to intervene in Laos.' Waving a sheaf of cables from Lemnitzer [Gen. Lyman L. Lemnitzer, Chairman of the JCS], he added, 'I might have taken this advice seriously.'" In a memorandum on June 1, 1961, Robert Kennedy took a similar position. See Schlesinger, *Robert Kennedy and His Times*, p. 702.

[71]On Apr. 28, the day following this meeting, Rostow sent the President a memorandum, (still classified), stating his views on what should be done about Laos. The President asked him to give him another memorandum on the "action consequences" of his memo of Apr. 28, and on May 6 he did so. Kennedy Library, NSF Regional Security File, Southeast Asia. Included was this comment:

". . . our total effort must be more expensive than it now is and the American public must gear itself to the self-discipline required to sweat out this protracted battle, notably by devising a method of voluntary wage restraints to be combined with price cuts geared to productivity increases. In addition, our society must understand that it is in a protracted struggle which will require from time to time that we face with unity, poise, and determination very dangerous tests of will."

[72]*Kennedy*, p. 727. The memoranda are still classified.

were then mobilized, nuclear bombings would be threatened and, if necessary, carried out. If the Soviets then intervened, we should 'be prepared to accept the possibility of general war.' "

In an interview some years later, David E. Bell, then Director of the Bureau of the Budget, recalled: "To us outsiders, that is to say to those of us who weren't part of the Pentagon-State Department complex, this was a shocking meeting, because at least two of the Joint Chiefs . . . were extremely belligerent, as we saw it, and were ready to go in and bomb the daylights out of them or land troops or whatever." ". . . there was a predisposition," he added, "in some members of the military leadership to go shooting off into the Southeast Asian jungles on what at that time was plainly no substantial provocation. It seemed to most of us to have been simply a militaristic adventure, not at all justified in terms of American foreign policy interests."[73]

According to Arthur M. Schlesinger, Jr.,[74] "The President was appalled at the sketchy nature of American military planning for Laos—the lack of detail and the unanswered questions," and in a meeting on April 29 after the memoranda were submitted he questioned military representatives on a number of points, and was said to have been quite dissatisfied with the answers he received.

Despite their differences of opinion, the military had already begun to order contingency plans for military action. On April 26, the JCS alerted the U.S. Pacific Command (CINCPAC) to be prepared to undertake airstrikes against North Vietnam and possibly southern China, and after the meeting on April 29 CINCPAC was told to prepare to move 5,000 U.S. combat troops into Thailand and another 5,000 into Vietnam, together with supporting units, including air. The cable ordering this move said that Washington hoped to give a "SEATO cover" to these actions.[75]

In addition, on April 20 Kennedy had ordered U.S. military advisers in Laos to put on their uniforms, to organize openly and officially as a MAAG, and to start advising on combat operations. (Approximately 400 U.S. advisers had been sent to Laos by Eisenhower in 1960, ostensibly to advise the French military mission—the only military mission permitted in Laos by the 1954 Geneva Accords—on technical matters, but they had worn civilian clothes to avoid the charge of violating the Accords.)

On April 29, there was an important meeting of top policymakers, including Rusk, McNamara, McGeorge Bundy, and the four service Chiefs, as well as Attorney General Robert F. Kennedy (who was sitting in, as a result of the Bay of Pigs experience, to represent his brother and to protect the President's interests), to discuss Laos.[76] In response to a question by Robert Kennedy, who asked where would be the "best place to stand and fight in Southeast Asia, where to draw the line," McNamara replied that he thought the U.S. would take a stand in Thailand and Vietnam. Kennedy asked again, saying that what he wanted to know was not only whether any of Laos could be saved by U.S. forces, but wheth-

---

[73] CRS Interview with David E. Bell, Oct. 27, 1978
[74] *A Thousand Days*, p. 338.
[75] *PP*, Gravel ed., vol. II, p. 41.
[76] See *ibid.*, DOD ed., book 11, pp. 62-66.

er the U.S. would stand up and fight. McNamara said that "we would have to attack the DRV" [Democratic Republic of Vietnam, in North Vietnam] if Laos were to be given up. Army Chief of Staff Gen. George H. Decker said that there was "no good place to fight in Southeast Asia but we must hold as much as we can of Viet-Nam, Cambodia and Laos." Adm. Arleigh Burke, Chief of Naval Operations, urged that U.S. forces be sent into Laos. Burke said that "each time you give ground it is harder to stand next time. If we give up Laos we would have to put US forces into Viet-Nam and Thailand. We would have to throw enough in to win—perhaps the 'works.' It would be easier to hold now than later. The thing to do was to land now and hold as much as we can and make clear that we were not going to be pushed out of Southeast Asia."

John Steeves, Deputy Assistant Secretary of State for the Far East, said that if the U.S. decided that defense of Laos was not tenable, "we were writing the first chapter in the defeat of Southeast Asia."

Rusk also took the position that U.S. forces should be sent to Laos. "The Secretary suggested that Thai and US troops might be placed together in Vientiane and, if they could not hold, be removed by helicopter. Even if they were defeated they could be defeated together and this would be better than sitting back and doing nothing."

General Decker added, ". . . we cannot win a conventional war in Southeast Asia; if we go in, we should go in to win, and that means bombing Hanoi, China, and maybe even using nuclear weapons. He suggested that U.S. troops be moved into Thailand and Vietnam in an effort to induce agreement on a cease-fire. Robert Kennedy, playing his role as provocateur, ". . . said we would look sillier than we do now if we got troops in there and then backed down." Again he asked "whether we are ready to go the distance." Responses were mixed and unclear. Rusk said that if a cease-fire was not achieved quickly it would be necessary to resort to SEATO Plan 5 under U.N. auspices.

During the meeting, Under Secretary of State Chester Bowles, who later became known for his opposition to U.S. military involvement in Vietnam, "said he thought the main question to be faced was the fact that we were going to have to fight the Chinese anyway in 2, 3, 5 or 10 years and that it was just a question of where, when and how. He thought that a major war would be difficult to avoid."

The meeting adjourned without agreement on a specific course of action.

On Sunday, April 30, Rusk sent Kennedy a memorandum discussing two alternative solutions for Laos.[77] "Track No. 1" discussed the procedures to be followed if the Communists agreed by Tuesday, May 2, to a cease-fire. "Track No. 2" discussed what would need to be done if there was no cease-fire. In this event, Rusk said, Laos, supported by the U.S. and Britain, should take its case to the U.N. At the same time, there should be action by SEATO, either SEATO Plan 5, or deployment of a SEATO force

---

[77]Kennedy Library, POF Country File, Laos.

into Thailand which could move into Laos if necessary. (If Plan 5 were implemented, SEATO forces would not undertake offensive action against the Communists, or be deployed near the sensitive northern frontier.)

Rusk's conclusions were as follows:

> If either Track 1 or Track 2 succeed in getting a cease-fire we will then face the real issue: what kind of a Laos to envisage emerging from the Conference. Our actions and the realities of Laos will all anticipate a "mixed up Laos." The more we can fracture it the better.
>
> It will be best for the time being for Laos to become a loose federation of somewhat autonomous strong men. Given the military capability of the Pathet Lao, a centralized government under a coalition government would tend to become a Communist satellite. Even partition would be a better outcome than unity under leadership responsive to the Communists.

Rusk went on to suggest that the U.N. act as a "third party" in Laos between the two contending forces in order to preserve the peace and promote development.

Meanwhile, congressional committees had been kept informed of Laotian developments. On April 11, for example, there was a long executive session briefing of the Foreign Relations Committee by Secretary of State Rusk.[78] On April 27, President Kennedy and Vice President Johnson met with congressional leaders and found that with the exception of Senator Styles Bridges (R/N.H.), they were opposed to the use of U.S. forces in Laos.[79] According to Admiral Burke, who briefed the congressional group at the April 27 meeting, after he told the leaders that the U.S. should stand firm in Laos, even at the risk of war, the President asked others for their advice, and only the Vice President supported Burke's position.[80] Other reactions were reported by U. Alexis Johnson, a veteran Foreign Service officer who had been a ranking member of the U.S. delegation to the Geneva Conference in 1954 and U.S. Ambassador to Thailand, 1958-61, and who became Deputy Under Secretary of State in April 1961. "'I think the whole thing would be rather fruitless,' said Mansfield. 'When we got through we would have nothing to show for it,' said Senate Republican leader Everett McKinley Dirksen (Ill.). 'We should get our people out and write the country off,' said Senator Richard B. Russell (D/Ga.). But if not Laos, then where would we draw the line? Some of the senators favored putting American troops in Vietnam and Thailand but letting Laos alone."[81]

[78]See *SFRC His. Ser.*, vol. XIII, pt. 1, pp. 281-307.

[79]Rostow, *The Diffusion of Power*, p. 268. The notes on that meeting are still classified. Attending the meeting were, from the Senate, Democrats Richard B. Russell (Ga.), Fulbright, and Hubert H. Humphrey (Minn.) and Republicans Everett McKinley Dirksen (Ill.), Bridges, Leverett Saltonstall (Mass.), Alexander Wiley (Wis.) and Bourke B. Hickenlooper (Iowa); from the House, Speaker Sam Rayburn (D/Tex.) and Democrats Carl Albert (Okla.), Carl Vinson (Ga.) and Thomas E. Morgan (Pa.), and Republicans Charles A. Halleck (Ind.), Leslie C. Arends (Ill.) and Robert B. Chiperfield (Ill.).

[80]Stevenson, *The End of Nowhere*, p. 152, based on Stevenson's interview with Admiral Burke.

[81]U. Alexis Johnson with Jef Olivarius McAllister, *The Right Hand of Power* (Englewood Cliffs, N.J.: Prentice-Hall, Inc., 1984), p. 324.

Appearing on the television program "Meet the Press" on April 30, 1961, Senator Fulbright, Chairman of the Foreign Relations Committee, said he did not think the U.S. should send troops to Laos. Conditions there, including the terrain and the peaceful nature of the people, were factors against such a move, he said. But he added, interestingly enough, that he thought it would be entirely proper to send U.S. troops to Thailand and South Vietnam if those countries were willing to cooperate with us, and requested such assistance. In both of these countries, he said, the terrain and other conditions, including the public's interest in self-defense, were much more conducive to the success of such an operation than were the conditions in Laos.[82]

After a private meeting with Kennedy on May 4, Fulbright, who had asked for the meeting, reiterated this position, declaring that he would support U.S. troop commitments to Thailand and Vietnam if such forces were considered necessary and if those countries wanted them. He said that the Thais and the South Vietnamese, unlike the Laotians, appeared willing to defend themselves. But he emphasized that he was not willing to make the United States the primary defensive factor in Southeast Asia over a long period of time. He said it was up to Japan and India to play a role.[83]

On May 6, the *New York Times* in an editorial noted Fulbright's views, but discounted the possibility of getting India or Japan to play such a role, and concluded: "An important defensive role for the United States in Southeast Asia must therefore be envisaged for an indefinite time if this area is to be protected from Communist aggression. . . ."

Other congressional leaders indicated their support for the President and for his leadership in handling the Laotian "crisis." It should be remembered that the traditional "honeymoon" between Congress and the President, during which there is customarily a higher degree of tolerance and deference between the branches, was still in effect at the time, and that this support reflected that fact. It also obviously reflected the continuing tendency of Congress to defer to the President in the making of decisions and the use of the armed forces.

In an appearance on May 7, 1961, on ABC-TV's "Issues and Answers," for example, Senate Majority Leader Mansfield and Senator George Aiken (R/Vt.), both members of the Foreign Relations Committee, took the position that although the President should and would confer with Congress before using the armed forces in Southeast Asia, he had the power under the Constitution, as reinforced by the SEATO Treaty, to deploy troops as necessary. Mansfield was asked "Do you think the Congress would approve of sending troops to any of these [SEATO] countries?" He replied:

Oh, I am quite certain that the President would confer with the necessary individuals in the Congress before any action was undertaken, but we must remember that under the Constitution, the President is charged with the conduct of our foreign

---

[82]*New York Times,* May 1, 1961. For a staff background briefing paper for Fulbright's use in preparing for the program, see the memorandum from John Newhouse to Carl Marcy, Apr. 26, 1961, University of Arkansas, Fulbright Papers, series 48, box 2.
[83]*New York Times,* May 5, 1961.

policy, and he is the Commander in Chief of our armed services, and furthermore, we do have this treaty [SEATO] which
we are obligated to adhere to.

Mansfield and Aiken were then asked, "Do you think it is worth
risking a global war to keep the Communists from getting, say,
Vietnam, Thailand, and Cambodia?" Mansfield's reply was that
this was a question no one could answer at that time, adding, "I
would again have to refer you to the responsibility of the President
of the United States as far as this country is concerned." Aiken
agreed with Mansfield, saying, "The final determination is up to
the President of the United States. He would supposedly act upon
the best advice which he could get and the best opinions which he
could secure and I am sure that the Congress of the United States
would support him in whatever his decision might be."[84]

During this time Mansfield continued to communicate privately
with the President, and on May 1, 1961, he sent another memo to
Kennedy on the Laotian situation in which he took the position
that, beginning with Laos, the U.S. needed to bring commitments
in Southeast Asia into line with American interests in that
region.[85] The U.S. needed, he said, referring specifically to Laos,
"to get out of the center of this thing and into a position more commensurate with our limited interests, our practical capabilities,
and our political realities at home." Laos, he said, was not like Lebanon, to which the U.S. had sent troops in 1958. Among other
things, in Laos the Russians could "call all the shots" without intervening, meanwhile condemning the U.S. for the bloodshed.

Referring to the administration's plan to use ground forces from
Thailand, Pakistan and the Philippines (at a SEATO meeting on
March 27, the U.S. had been given preliminary indications that
this would be possible), and to limit U.S. participation to air and
sea power, Mansfield said that the U.S. might end up having to use
its own ground forces as well. Moreover, pressures could be put on
the United States elsewhere, including South Vietnam. Intervention could also prove costly at home:

> If we intervene, we can possibly anticipate an initial reaction
> of public approval for your "standing firm." If the intervention
> succeeds in the Lebanese pattern, there will be some sustained
> approval but it is not likely to drown out the complaints about
> the increased costs of aid which will follow. If the intervention
> involves U.S. forces, the initial approval, such as it is, will
> start to disappear as soon as the first significant casualty lists
> are published. And it will not be long before the approval of
> "standfirm" gives way to the disapproval of "Kennedy's War"
> and "what are we doing in Laos?"

On the contrary, he said, although the U.S. would take some
risks by not intervening, they would be small compared to the costs
of intervention. If the U.S. did not intervene militarily, Souvanna
Phouma would emerge after negotiations as the principal leader,
and while he might cooperate with the Communists, there would
be greater advantages in such a situation than in U.S. intervention. Mansfield described these, and said that even if there were to

---

[84]From the text of the program, reprinted in *CR*, vol. 107, pp. 7587 ff.
[85]Kennedy Library, POF Country File, Laos.

be a government which cooperated with the Communists, "we will at least be in a position to cut our losses with some measure of dignity and we will be relieved of an enormous over-commitment." Adverse reaction in the U.S., he added, would be "mild" compared to the reaction if the U.S., "with American blood and treasure," tried to keep the existing government in power.

Mansfield concluded by recommending that the U.S. concentrate on assisting Vietnam, which he thought had the "greatest potential in leadership, human capacities and resources" in the area, and on cultivating neutral, friendly relations also with Cambodia, Burma, Malaya, Indonesia and Thailand, rather than continuing to search for "cold-war 'allies.'" By the same token, he, like Fulbright, advocated that the U.S. seek to encourage India to play a more active role in Southeast Asia, beginning with possible Indian efforts to prevent the situation in Laos from worsening prior to the forthcoming Geneva Conference.

Mansfield suggested that if the U.S. reduced its military program in Laos those funds could be redirected to Vietnam, but that in doing so the U.S. should avoid raising the level of aid "so high that it atrophies the will of the Viet Namese government to do what it must do to strengthen its ties among the Viet Namese people."

Facing a difficult choice, and feeling the effects of the Bay of Pigs, Kennedy struggled with the possibility of "losing" Laos to the Communists, apparently feeling that the domestic political consequences of such an outcome would be more serious than Mansfield estimated. He is said to have told Rostow that whereas Eisenhower was able to withstand the political fall-out from the loss of Dien Bien Phu because it was the French, rather than the Americans, who were defeated, "I can't take a 1954 defeat today."[86]

On May 1, Kennedy met again with his advisers. The situation in Laos was more ominous, and the group decided that the U.S. had no choice but to threaten to take military action unless a cease-fire was arranged. Unlike the meeting on April 29, at which they were divided, the military were all agreed on the need to act. During the meeting, McGeorge Bundy sent Kennedy the following note:[87]

Mr. President:

On Saturday [April 29] the Joint Chiefs of Staff divided 1-1 (Navy-Air vs. Army-Marine) on going into Laos; it's not at all clear why they now are unanimous. . . .

The diplomatic result of the meeting is probably best described by British Prime Minister Macmillan, based on messages he was receiving that day from Washington:[88]

6 p.m. [London] Meeting on Laos. . . . The Americans, supported by Australia and New Zealand, now want to take the preliminary troop movements for a military intervention. . . . They want to declare the alert at the SEATO meeting tomorrow. Their reason is that the two sides have not yet managed to meet to discuss the cease-fire; that the Pathet Lao are obviously stalling till the whole country has fallen; that they are

[86]Schlesinger, *A Thousand Days*, p. 339.
[87]Undated handwritten note in Kennedy Library, POF Country File, Laos.
[88]*Pointing the Way*, p. 346.

advancing all the time; that the Thais are getting restless; that only the United Kingdom and France are out of step, etc., etc.

Later that day, however, cease-fire talks were agreed upon, and the alert was postponed and then cancelled when it became clear that the Geneva Conference would be held.

It should be noted, however, that on May 5 Rusk met with the members of the newly-created Vietnam Task Force to discuss whether the U.S. should send combat forces to South Vietnam prior to the Geneva Conference on Laos as another means of demonstrating U.S. determination to take a stand in Southeast Asia. It was decided not to do so at that point, but to keep the possibility under review.[89] (It should also be noted that the day before the Geneva Conference was to begin, Kennedy, in connection with increased U.S. assistance to Vietnam, authorized covert military operations against the North Vietnamese in both North Vietnam and Laos. Among other things, he approved intelligence and harassment missions by South Vietnamese units into southeastern Laos, and the use of U.S. advisers, "if necessary," in attacks on the North Vietnamese supply center in Tchepone, Laos, on the Ho Chi Minh Trail.)[90]

Later that day (May 5), Kennedy met with his advisers to discuss the Laos situation as well as Vietnam. "Most agreed the chance for salvaging anything out of the cease-fire and coalition government was slim indeed." The group discussed ways in which to reassure Vietnam and Thailand, one of which was a visit to Vietnam by Vice President Johnson, which was agreed upon and announced after the meeting.[91]

Vietnam Moves Up on the Agenda

During February and March 1961, Ambassador Durbrow attempted to extract from Diem the agreement on reforms which the U.S. was insisting be reached before the new counterinsurgency plan for Vietnam was implemented. As these negotiations dragged on, U.S. military leaders became restive, and began to urge that the plan be implemented even though Diem had not met the prior conditions established by Washington.

The President was also restive. On March 14, McGeorge Bundy sent a memorandum to Lucius D. Battle, Executive Secretary for the State Department, expressing Kennedy's concern that Nolting would not be arriving in Saigon until June. "This is simply one sample," Bundy said, "of repeated questioning which we get here on Vietnam from the President. He is really very eager indeed that it should have the highest priority for rapid and energetic action, and I know that anything the Secretary [Rusk] can do to encourage him on that point will be much appreciated."[92]

By the end of March, Rostow, who had been given primary NSC staff responsibility for Vietnam, was urging Kennedy to organize for an "effective counter-offensive" in Vietnam.[93] Among other

---

[89]*PP*, DOD ed., book 11, pp. 67-68.

[90]Schlesinger, *A Thousand Days*, p. 336, and Stevenson, *The End of Nowhere*, p. 153.

[91]*PP*, Gravel ed., vol. II, p. 9.

[92]Kennedy Library, NSF Country File, Vietnam. (Nolting's arrival in Vietnam subsequently was moved up to late March.)

[93]Memorandum from Rostow to the President, Mar. 29, 1961, same location.

things, he advocated having Diem visit Washington, or sending Vice President Johnson on a visit to Vietnam. "In any case," he added, "we must help [Ambassador] Nolting persuade him that our support for him is unambiguous, but that he must face up to the political and morale elements of the job, as well as its military component."

Rostow also said, "We must somehow bring to bear our unexploited counter-guerrilla assets on the Viet-Nam problem: armed helicopters; other Research and Development possibilities; our Special Forces units. It is somehow wrong to be developing these capabilities but not applying them in a crucial active theater. In Knute Rockne's old phrase, we are not saving them for the Junior Prom."

On March 28, in a special message on the defense budget, the President asked Congress for authority to increase limited warfare forces, including counterinsurgency, in addition to a larger force of intercontinental ballistic missiles.[94]

Senator Richard B. Russell, chairman of the Armed Services Committee, agreed. In a memorandum on April 20, 1961, addressed to both Kennedy and Johnson, Russell said, among other things, "The President's suggested program for specialized training in ranger or counterguerrilla operations for certain units of the Army and Marine Corps should be prosecuted with relentless vigor."[95]

The JCS was also recommending accelerated action in Vietnam. After receiving a report on March 28, 1961, from Lt. General T. J. H. Trapnell (former head of the MAAG in Indochina in the early 1950s), who had just returned from a review of the situation in Vietnam and Laos, the JCS agreed with most of Trapnell's suggestions, and asked the Secretary of Defense to approve those actions requiring his concurrence. These included letting the MAAG operate independently of the Embassy, and increasing U.S. support for the Civil Guard.[96]

In conjunction with moves concurrently underway with respect to Laos, orders also were given on March 26, 1961, for U.S. planes to destroy "hostile aircraft" over South Vietnam, but to avoid publicity. According to the JCS cable to Saigon:[97]

> . . . it is mandatory that . . . you work out ways and means to ensure maximum discretion and minimum publicity. This effort must be kept in lowest possible key. In the event of loss of US aircraft, a plausible cover story or covering action must be ready.

On March 29, Lt. Gen. Lionel C. McGarr, Chief of the U.S. Military Assistance Advisory Group (MAAG) in Saigon, with Nolting's concurrence (his arrival had been moved up), replied that such a plan had been devised, and that, among other things, "In event an enemy aircraft is destroyed by US air action we will remain silent. *No* results US missions will be passed via air-ground radio. . . . In the event a US aircraft is lost on an operations mission from any

---

[94]*Public Papers of the President*, John F. Kennedy, 1961, pp. 230 ff. On May 25, this was followed by a "Special Message to the Congress on Urgent National Needs," same source, pp. 396-397, in which Kennedy asked also for approval of a large civil defense program to support the credibility of U.S. strategic forces.
[95]Johnson Library, Vice Presidential Security File.
[96]*PP*, DOD ed., book 11, pp. 19-21. These proposals were not approved by McNamara.
[97]Kennedy Library, NSF Country File, Vietnam.

cause whatsoever, the explanation in reply to press query is that accident occurred while aircraft engaged in routine operational flight. . . ."[98]

On April 12, Rostow recommended to Kennedy, among other things, that he appoint a top-level Washington coordinator for Vietnam, (Rostow was thinking of Lansdale), raise the MAAG ceiling, and, besides sending Vice President Johnson to see Diem he suggested that Kennedy consider writing a letter to Diem like that of Eisenhower's in 1954, reaffirming U.S. support, stating what new assistance the U.S. was prepared to give, and urging him to make more progress toward creating a "more effective political and morale setting for his military operation. . . ."[99]

On April 19, Lansdale recommended that "The President should at once determine the conditions in Vietnam are critical and establish a Washington Task Force for the country."[100] Among other things he proposed that he himself should accompany the new U.S. Ambassador to Vietnam "to facilitate good working relationships with the Vietnamese Government" as well as to implement the actions of the task force. After getting Diem's consent, one of his first goals would be ". . . to call non-Communist political opposition leaders together and encourage them to rely on legal means of opposition, to help in the fight against the Communist Viet Cong, and to ease scheming *coup d'etats*." To help him with this and other tasks Lansdale asked that all those who had worked with him in 1954-55 be sent to Vietnam, along with Generals John W. O'Daniel and Samuel T. Williams, former chiefs of the Saigon MAAG, and other personnel as needed.

Among other steps to achieve U.S. goals in Vietnam, Lansdale recommended that the U.S., as a way of weakening the position of the North, "Encourage again the movement of refugees into the South by stimulating the desire to do so among the people in the North, by establishing better means of ingress to the South, and by re-establishing the highly successful refugee settlement program. . . . The goal should be a million refugees."

On April 20, the day after the Bay of Pigs invasion ended in failure, Kennedy established a Vietnam Task Force. (Prior to that time Vietnam had been handled also by the Laos Task Force, which, at least by the end of March, was being called the Laos-Viet-Nam Task Force.) This new group was to be headed by Deputy Secretary of Defense Roswell Gilpatric, with Lansdale as operations officer. Other members included, Rostow, Paul Nitze, (Assistant Secretary of Defense for International Security Affairs), Gen. Charles H. Bonesteel III from the JCS, U. Alexis Johnson (Deputy Under Secretary of State), and Desmond FitzGerald, (then Chief of the Far East Division of the covert side of the CIA). The group was told to recommend by April 27 measures to "prevent Communist domination" of Vietnam.

In an interview some years later, Gilpatric reflected on a basic problem that faced the task force:[101]

[98]Same location.
[99]*PP*, Gravel ed., vol. II, pp. 34-35.
[100]*Ibid.*, DOD ed., book 11, pp. 32-34.
[101]CRS Interview with Roswell Gilpatric, Jan. 9, 1979.

The first thing that we ran into was what I felt then and still feel was a basic lack of understanding of what motivated the people in the whole Indochina area, their culture, their history, their politics. And we really went on the basis of recommendations from people in prior administrations. In other words, none of us of the new group that came in with the President, who were charged with responsibility for this area, had any preparation for this problem. What we didn't comprehend was the inability of the Vietnamese to absorb our doctrine, to think and to organize the way we did. We just assumed they would react the way our Western European allies had. We really were dealing with a mentality and a psychology that we didn't understand.

Gilpatric added that it would have been difficult for any of the policymakers involved to have gained such an understanding, and that "You certainly couldn't do it under the kinds of conditions that we were faced with in 1961 and 1962 when we were making these decisions—exchange of cables and hurried meetings and this development and that development. All of us did a great deal of reading. We were briefed. But we really didn't understand what kinds of people we were dealing with and how they would respond to this assistance, direction, support that we were trying to give them, initially, to make them more effective."

Gilpatric was asked to speculate as to what the task force would have done differently in preparing its report if it were to do it again, and he replied:

I think it would be a much more tentative, exploratory longer-phased program than we came up with. I think we wouldn't have been as brash and bold in just assuming that we could, within certain time frames, train certain units and bring about certain results. I think we would have been far less confident of our judgments than we were then. We took all of these masses of suggestions that came in from all of these people, Lansdale and others, who had been out there and we talked them over and threw them around at various sessions we had at State and Defense, and came up with this whole package of different measures. I think we bought that whole line and then put it forward as our own with much more assurance than I would ever do again. I think we were kidding ourselves into thinking that we were making well-informed decisions.

"Come what may, the U.S. intends to win this battle"

On April 26, the Vietnam Task Force submitted the first draft of its report.[102] Noting that South Vietnam "is nearing the decisive phase in its struggle for survival," the report recommended that primary emphasis should be placed on internal security, and that additional U.S. assistance should be given to strengthen the programs approved earlier in January in the CIP. Included were proposals for financing the increase of 20,000 in the armed forces as well as for the entire Civil Guard and Self-Defense Corps; 100 more

---

[102]For the text see *PP*, DOD ed., book 11, pp. 43-56.

men for the MAAG; installation of a radar surveillance system for monitoring overflights; and support for a Vietnamese junk force to prevent Communist supply and infiltration by water.

The report also strongly reflected Lansdale's concerns about political and psychological warfare, especially his emphasis on attacking the problem in the rural areas rather than insisting on reforms that were of interest primarily to urban elites. It also assumed that Lansdale would return to Vietnam to take charge of implementing the report and subsequent follow-up action, with Gilpatric and the other members of the task force serving as the key coordinating group in Washington.

The report, which contained an annex dealing with the situation in Laos, was predicated on the assumption that the level of Communist activity in South Vietnam would remain substantially the same. If it increased, either directly or as a result of a "collapse" of Laos, the draft stated, additional assistance would be needed, and preparations should be made for that eventuality.

The reaction of top White House staff members, partly as a result of the Bay of Pigs experience, was that the task force report was inadequate, and that the President needed "a more *realistic* look." (emphasis in original) In a memorandum to Kennedy, on April 28, 1961, his Counsel, Theodore Sorensen, speaking also for McGeorge Bundy and David Bell, Director of the Bureau of the Budget, urged that at the NSC meeting on April 29 at which the report was to be discussed, the President should approve "only the basic concept of an all-out internal security effort to save Vietnam."[103] The memo proposed that the report be reshaped and taken by Vice President Johnson to Vietnam for discussion with Diem. It might become necessary, it said, if Johnson and Diem reached agreement, for the report then to be recast as a joint plan to be implemented by both countries.

Besides raising various specific questions about the report, the Sorensen-Bundy-Bell memo challenged two broad aspects of the task force report:

> To the extent that this plan depends on the communists being tied down in Laos and lacking further forces, on our blocking land corridors through which communist support flows, or on our obtaining effective anti-infiltration action from

---

[103]Kennedy Library, NSF Country File, Vietnam. Also in that location there are memos to Rostow on Apr. 28, 1961, from two other NSC staff members, Robert W. Komer and Robert H. Johnson, assistants to Rostow, commenting on the task force report. Both urged that greater pressure be put on Diem. As Komer said, "If we are bailing Diem out, why aren't we entitled to *insist* . . . that he overhaul tax system, halt waste of foreign exchange and devalue currency to a realistic rate? To my mind one of the flaws of our Korean operation has been that we always gave and never demanded. This is war for Diem too; he's got to understand that continued procrastination on his part will be fatal." (emphasis in original) Komer also urged that the U.S. demonstrate its determination: "At a minimum, why not give Diem now a public commitment that if things get to the stage of overt fighting, we will come to his support. We should consider ways and means of putting token US forces in South Vietnam as further evidence (if this is possible under Geneva Accords)." By May 4, Komer was arguing that a way needed to be found to "'seal' off South Vietnam in such a way as to deter another Laos." He said he was not convinced that the U.S. should send troops to Vietnam, but he questioned whether the decision should be postponed until after the Laos conference had begun, and the situation in Vietnam had deteriorated even further. He also questioned whether a large force was needed. "The purpose of sending forces is *not* to fight guerrillas. It would be to establish a US 'presence'; this could be accomplished by no more than a battalion supported by naval power." Memorandum from Komer to Bundy and Rostow, May 4, 1961, same location. (emphasis in original)

Laos, Cambodia and the Laotian negotiations, the outcome is highly doubtful.

To the extent that it depends on wider popular support among the Vietnamese, tax and foreign exchange reforms by Diem, and his agreement to the military and governmental reorganizations required, the outcome is speculative at best.

In other words, Sorensen, Bundy, and Bell questioned whether the U.S. could count on reforms by Diem, and also doubted whether it was realistic to think that Communist infiltration into Vietnam could be blocked, even by U.S. military action.

These three advisers went on to say that the U.S. could not prevent the "loss" of South Vietnam, but that U.S. insistence on reforms was justified in order to help the South Vietnamese save themselves:

There is no clearer example of a country that cannot be saved unless it saves itself—through increased popular support; governmental, economic and military reforms and reorganizations; and the encouragement of new political leaders. We do not want Vietnam to fall—we do not want to add to Diem's burdens—and the chief purpose of insisting upon such conditions should not be the saving of American dollars but the saving of Vietnam.

Kennedy appears to have been influenced by or to have agreed with the advice of Sorensen, Bundy, and Bell, and at the NSC meeting on April 29 at which the report of the Vietnam Task Force was considered, he approved only a few of the recommendations of the task force, including its proposal that the MAAG be increased by approximately 100 in order to assist in training the Self Defense Corps, that there should be additional 20,000 men for the armed forces, and the suggestion that U.S. military assistance funds be used to support the entire Civil Guard force.

On May 1, 1961, a revised draft of the task force report was distributed. At this point, the primary responsibility was transferred from Defense to State, doubtless at the insistence of the White House, and the report was redrafted on May 3 to reflect State's views.

The task force was also downgraded in importance, with a Foreign Service officer, Sterling J. Cottrell, appointed as Director, and another FSO, Chalmers B. Wood, as Executive Officer, thus making it an interagency working group rather than a sub-Cabinet level task force. Lansdale was not even made a member of the group.

In arguing for State's direction of the group it was said that Rusk ". . . was able to turn the trick with a phrase. 'If you want Vietnam,' he said to McNamara, 'give me the Marines.'"[104]

On May 6 the task force report was again redrafted for an NSC meeting on May 11. In this, its final form, the report, which stated that "come what may, the U.S. intends to win this battle" (this language had been in the first draft of the report), recommended that in addition to the actions approved by the President on April 29, he approve other military moves, including dispatching 400 U.S. Special Forces to help train Vietnamese Special Forces; consideration

---

[104]Roger Hilsman, *To Move A Nation* (Garden City, N.Y.: Doubleday, 1967), p. 41.

of increasing the Vietnamese Armed Forces from the newly-ap-
proved 170,000 to 200,000; and consideration also of sending U.S.
forces to Vietnam should this be agreed upon in the meetings of
Vice President Johnson and Diem. The paper stated that the Defense Department had begun a study of the use of U.S. forces, and
that one action being considered was the deployment of two U.S.
battle groups (with supporting units) and an engineer battalion.

In one of the annexes to the report these military moves were
discussed at greater length.[105] With respect to the use of U.S.
forces, it was stated in the annex that such a U.S. military group
would be "specifically designed for carrying out a counterguerrilla—civic action—limited war mission in South Vietnam," in
which "In the absence of intelligence indications of an overt attack
on the G.V.N., it is contemplated that this composite force would
be deployed throughout the country in small 'task force' units on
specific mission assignments of a counter-guerrilla or civic action
nature."

The report itself also proposed that these troops be stationed in
Vietnam under a U.S.-Vietnam defensive alliance. Advantages and
disadvantages of having U.S. forces in Vietnam were discussed.
One of the advantages would be that "It would place the Sino-
Soviet Bloc in the position of risking direct intervention in a situation where U.S. forces were already in place, accepting the consequences of such action. This is in direct contrast to the current situation in Laos."

Among the disadvantages was the following: "The danger that a
troop contribution would provoke a DRV-CHICOM, [Democratic Republic of Vietnam—Chinese Communist] reaction with the risk of
involving a significant commitment of U.S. force in the Pacific to
the Asian mainland."

The report also discussed political, economic and psychological
aspects, as well as covert action and unconventional warfare.

Also in preparation for the May 11 NSC meeting, McNamara
asked the JCS to review the question of deploying U.S. forces in
Vietnam. JCS Chairman Gen. Lyman L. Lemnitzer stopped by
Vietnam on his return from another trip, and on May 9 the JCS
recommended to McNamara that Diem should "be encouraged" to
request that the U.S. fulfill its SEATO obligation, by sending "appropriate" forces to Vietnam:[106]

Assuming that the political decision is to hold Southeast
Asia outside the Communist sphere, the JCS are of the opinion
that U.S. forces should be deployed immediately to South Vietnam; such action should be taken primarily to prevent the Vietnamese from being subjected to the same situation as presently exists in Laos, which would then require deployment of
US forces into an already existing combat situation. . . . Sufficient forces should be deployed to accomplish the following
purposes:

A. Provide a visible deterrent to potential North Vietnam and/or Chinese Communist action.

---

[105] Annex 2, the text of which is in *PP*, DOD ed., book 11, pp. 93-100. For the final May 6 task
force report and all of the annexes see pp. 70-130.
[106] A copy of this JCS paper is in the Johnson Library, Vice Presidential Security File.

B. Release Vietnamese forces from advanced and static defense positions to permit their fuller commitment to counterinsurgency actions.

C. Assist in training the Vietnamese forces to the maximum extent consistent with their mission.

D. Provide a nucleus for the support of any additional major US or SEATO military operation in Southeast Asia.

E. Indicate the firmness of our interest to all Asia nations.

On May 10, Rostow sent Kennedy a memorandum commenting on the task force report that was to be discussed the next day, and it is of interest to note his position on a possible coup against Diem:[107]

Although we have no alternative except to support Diem now, he may be overthrown, as the accompanying cables suggest. If so, we should be prepared to move fast with the younger army types who may then emerge. Such a crisis is not to be sought, among other reasons because its outcome could not be predicted; but should it happen, we may be able to get more nearly the kind of military organization and perhaps, even, the domestic political program we want in Viet-Nam but have been unable to get from Diem.

On May 11, Kennedy approved additional steps recommended by the task force, including the proposals for covert action, and deployment of a 400-man Special Forces team, which was the first open violation by the U.S. of the Geneva Accords. (Both sides had been violating the Accords for many years.) The military were told to assess the value of increasing the Vietnamese Armed Forces from 170,000 to 200,000. With respect to the possible use of U.S. forces, he ordered a complete study of this question, including the "diplomatic setting" for such a move. He also authorized Ambassador Nolting to begin to negotiate a bilateral U.S.-Vietnam defense pact, but to make no commitment until receiving further approval from the White House.

Kennedy's decision, which became known as the "Presidential Program for Vietnam," was promulgated by NSAM 52, May 11, 1961, the opening statement of which reaffirmed the long-standing U.S. commitment to the defense of Vietnam:[108]

The U.S. objectives and concept of operations stated in report are approved: to prevent Communist domination of South Vietnam; to create in that country a viable and increasingly democratic society, and to initiate, on an accelerated basis, a series of mutually supporting actions of a military, po-

---

[107]Kennedy Library, NSF Country File, Vietnam.

[108]The text of NSAM 52 is in *PP*, Gravel ed., vol. II, pp. 642-643. After the NSAM was issued, there were progress reports about every two weeks on the status of the 33 actions (later 44) which were proposed. The first of these reports was issued on May 23, 1961, and the last on July 1, 1962. (After the Nov. 15, 1961, decision to increase U.S. aid to Vietnam—see below—the reports were broadened to cover also the new "limited partnership" program.) Copies of some of these reports are now available at the Kennedy Library, NSF Country File, Vietnam, and others are at the Johnson Library, Vice Presidential Security File. Generally the reports are very uninformative except for details on the implementation of specific forms of assistance.

On Mar. 20, 1972, the Senate Foreign Relations Committee issued a brief staff study on this subject, *Vietnam Commitments, 1961,* based on the *Pentagon Papers.*

litical, economic psychological and covert character designed to achieve this objective.

This is William P. Bundy's comment on the significance of Kennedy's decision:[109]

The decision to compromise in Laos made it essential to convey by word and deed that the US would stand firm in South Vietnam and in the rest of Southeast Asia. And the situation was deemed too critical to permit a more leisurely approach, or an effort to enlist systematic allied support in the SEATO framework. . . . What was going on in Vietnam seemed the clearest possible case of what Khrushchev in January had called a "war of national liberation." The Administration was impregnated with the belief that Communism worldwide . . . was on the offensive, that this offensive had been allowed to gain dangerous momentum in the last two years of the Eisenhower Administration, and that it must now be met solidly. . . . Although some have suggested that Kennedy was reluctant in this early decision this was certainly not the mood of his advisors nor the mood that he conveyed to them. Rather, the tone was: "Sure, Diem is difficult, but this one has got to be tackled."

Johnson's Trip and the Increased U.S. Commitment

In order to affirm and promote the U.S. commitment, as well as to extract more of a commitment from Vietnam, Kennedy decided, as was indicated earlier, that Vice President Johnson should confer with Diem. There were several reasons for sending Johnson, in addition to emphasizing the importance of the mission. He was an experienced politician who was known for his ability to persuade, and thus might be able to influence Diem. He also had considerable power and influence in Congress, and the President anticipated that Johnson would, as he did, become more committed himself, and work to get congressional support for increased aid to Vietnam.

Another important reason for sending Johnson to Vietnam was that it could be (and was) made to appear that Johnson's conclusions and recommendations were his own, and represented his point of view rather than Kennedy's. Thus, while controlling every important aspect of the trip, the White House could give the impression that the President was not directly involved in the taking of another important step toward a major expansion of U.S. assistance to Vietnam. At the same time, the fact that these recommendations were coming from Johnson would not only help Kennedy gain approval for the program in Congress, but would help insulate him from criticisms by some of the conservatives, who, by the same token, would hesitate to criticize Johnson.

Johnson's mission to Vietnam, May 9-15, 1961, was a very important step in the evolution of U.S. policy toward Vietnam. It has often been ridiculed and belittled by those who have reacted nega-

---

[109]For this and subsequent observations which will be cited as Bundy MS., CRS is indebted to William P. Bundy for permission to quote from his unpublished manuscript, written in 1970-72, dealing with key decisions concerning Southeast Asia in the period from early 1961 to early 1966. The quotation here is from ch. 3, pp. 36, 41-42.

tively to Johnson's reference to Diem as the "Winston Churchill of Southeast Asia," unaware, perhaps, of the fact that Johnson had been directed to laud Diem and his accomplishments.[110]

When he arrived in Vietnam, Johnson gave Diem a letter from Kennedy in which the President told Diem of the additional assistance he had approved, and said that ". . . we are ready to join with you in an intensified endeavor to win the struggle against Communism and to further the social and economic advancement of Viet-Nam."[111] It was to be, Kennedy said, a "joint campaign."

Acting on explicit instructions from the White House, Johnson raised with Diem the key questions being considered in Washington, namely, whether there should be a U.S.-Vietnam mutual defense pact, and whether U.S. combat troops should be sent to Vietnam to establish a visible American military presence. Diem was not in favor of either proposal, but he said he would welcome U.S. troops for training. (Based on this, General McGarr requested that 16,000 U.S. troops be sent to Vietnam, ostensibly for training purposes, or 10,000 if Diem rejected the larger number.)[112]

Johnson also discussed with Diem the reforms that the U.S. wanted him to make, and although Diem again appeared to be agreeable, it is questionable whether Johnson accomplished any more than others had or would.

On May 13, Johnson and Diem issued a joint communiqué, drafted by State Department officials in Saigon and Washington, which had been completely cleared in Washington, summarizing the talks.[113] It was evident from this document that the Kennedy administration was expanding the U.S. commitment to Vietnam in an effort to prevent the country from being overrun by the Communists. Eight points of agreement on new programs were announced, including the various measures approved earlier by Kennedy through which the joint effort would be intensified. These measures, the communiqué said, ". . . represent an increase and acceleration of United States assistance to the Republic of Viet-Nam. These may be followed by more far-reaching measures if the situation, in the opinion of both governments, warrants."

---

[110]It had been agreed in the administration that one of the principal purposes of the Johnson mission was to create in Diem a higher sense of his own importance in the eyes of the United States and the world, and Johnson's statements, written for him by State Department representatives on the trip, deliberately sought to convey this impression. This same point was made in the instructions Johnson received from the State Department prior to the trip, which were conveyed in a letter from Under Secretary Bowles, Kennedy Library, NSF Trips and Conferences File, May 8, 1961.

According to one member of the Johnson group, Francis Valeo, (Mansfield's assistant, who had been asked by Johnson to go with him as a "foil" against the advice he would be getting from the State Department), Johnson's comparison of Diem to Churchill may have been suggested by one of the State Department representatives on the mission.

Valeo also concluded that as a result of this trip Johnson became committed to Vietnam, and that this affected his handling of the matter after he became President. CRS Interview with Francis Valeo, Oct. 29, 1978.

After the trip, Valeo himself concluded that the mission had been useful. In a cable to Mansfield on May 21 as the group was returning to Washington he said, "Over-all effect of mission highly useful in Southeast Asian area. Opens up possibility of great improvement in our performance here if it is followed by adjustments in policy at home and follow-through with tight and unmuddled administration in Southeast Asia." Kennedy Library, NSF Trips File.

[111]PP, DOD ed., book 11, p. 132. For Diem's reply, see pp. 155-156. For whatever reason, Kennedy's letter to Diem was not included in the Public Papers of the Presidents.

[112]PP, Gravel ed., vol. II, p. 11.

[113]The text is in the Department of State Bulletin, June 19, 1961.

The communiqué stated that the United States recognized "its responsibility and duty, in its own self-interest as well as the interest of other free peoples, to assist a brave country in the defense of its liberties against unprovoked subversion and Communist terror," and also recognized that Diem "is in the vanguard of those leaders who stand for freedom on the periphery of the Communist empire in Asia."

Ambassador Nolting cabled Washington on May 15 that Johnson had "avoided any commitments beyond those in President Kennedy's letter to Diem. . . ." He said Johnson had "repeatedly stressed necessity of having adequate evidence to convince Congress it should vote additional aid funds especially in economic field. We believe general expectation left with Diem is that additional aid will be forthcoming."[114]

This expanded commitment by the President of the United States, with the acquiescence of Congress, raised the level and enlarged the scope of existing U.S. commitments to Vietnam. Previously the U.S. had taken the position that it was assisting Vietnam in its efforts to defend itself. Although in practice the United States was deeply involved in activities in Vietnam, it had never taken the position that this was a joint effort by the two countries—a concept with many implications for the role of the United States and the role of Vietnam, as well as for the relationship between the U.S. and Vietnam.

This shift from providing assistance to assuming responsibility for part of a joint effort was based on a recognition of two salient facts. First, the previous commitment was not adequate and existing programs were not working. The situation in Vietnam was deteriorating, and a stronger commitment as well as new programs were required in order to prevent this from happening and to achieve U.S. objectives. Second, by 1961 the failure of the South Vietnamese to act effectively to prevent substantial Communist gains in the country had convinced the new Kennedy administration that the U.S. had to intervene more fully, and play a stronger, more direct role in Vietnam in order to prevent the Communists from winning.

It is important in this connection to understand that the Kennedy administration did not consider negotiating a settlement of Vietnam, even though there was a move among several State Department officials to do so in conjunction with the Geneva Conference on Laos. In a subsequent interview, Kennedy's assistant Theodore Sorensen explained the administration's conception of the differences between Laos and Vietnam, and the reasons for not seeking a negotiated settlement for Vietnam:[115]

> In Laos it was clear that a negotiated settlement was the best we could reach. It was not accessible to American forces. It was up against the border of the Red Chinese. A policy of trying to establish an American protege there was contrary to the wishes of our allies. And therefore, inasmuch as a negotiated settlement was possible, since negotiations with the Soviet Union were possible, that was the most desirable alternative.

---

[114]Kennedy Library, NSF Trips File.
[115]Kennedy Library, Oral History Interview with Theodore Sorensen, Mar. 26, 1964, p. 96.

In Vietnam, on the other hand, exactly the opposite was true. It was militarily more accessible, and there was no obvious route to negotiations inasmuch as we were not and could not be in a position of dealing directly with the Red Chinese and the North Vietnamese. And therefore, the President felt that we would have to maintain our military presence there until conditions permitted a settlement which would not be a disaster for the United States.

Carl Kaysen, who was interviewing Sorensen on this occasion, and who himself had been on Kennedy's NSC staff, noted that the U.S. had negotiated with the Chinese over Korea, and then asked Sorensen, "Were the possibilities or prospects for a settlement by negotiation ever considered, to your knowledge, examined—any sounding made?"

Sorensen. No, not to my knowledge.

Kaysen. So the President assumed from the first that we had to deal with this problem by military means?

Sorensen. That's right.

Sorensen added that Kennedy did not consider it to be just a military problem. "He felt that getting the enthusiastic support of the country, its population, and its army was at least one-half of the problem and, therefore, would require economic and political and social reforms as well as military action on our part."

Kaysen. Yes, but from the first, there was this judgment that we have to support military action with whatever also was required to do that. And throughout the whole of the President's Administration, we found ourselves increasing our commitment to Vietnam, although at no time did the prospects improve. Did this reflect a judgment that a favorable decision in Vietnam was really vital to U.S. interests?

Sorensen. It reflected rather the converse of that—that an unfavorable decision, or a retreat, an abandonment of Vietnam, an abandonment of our commitment would have had a very seriously adverse effect on the position of the United States in all of Southeast Asia. Therefore, we had to do whatever was necessary to prevent it, which meant increasing our military commitment.

Sorensen added: ". . . I think the President did feel strongly that for better or worse, enthusiastic or unenthusiastic we had to stay there until we left on terms other than a retreat or abandonment of our commitment."

Johnson Reports, and Fulbright Becomes Concerned

On May 24, 1961, Johnson returned to Washington and gave Kennedy an oral and a written report on his trip.[116] For the oral report Kennedy invited selected congressional leaders to the White House to hear Johnson in a closed 1 hour session attended also by Rusk.[117] In his written report, which State Department officers on the trip and in Washington had also prepared, and which had been cleared and approved by the White House itself, Johnson began by

---

[116]The text of the written report is in *PP*, DOD ed., book 11, pp. 159-166.

[117]Kennedy's appointments calendar does not list the participants in that meeting, nor did published reports in the press.

emphasizing that the mission had helped to offset the adverse affects in Asia (he visited India, Pakistan, Taiwan and the Philippines as well as Thailand and Vietnam) created by the Lao situation. Laos, he said, ". . . has created doubt and concern about the
intentions of the United States throughout Southeast Asia. No
amount of success at Geneva can, of itself, erase this. The independent Asians do not wish to have their own status resolved in
like manner in Geneva." He said, however, that the mission had
". . . arrested the decline of confidence in the United States. It did
not—in my judgment—restore any confidence already lost. The
leaders were as explicit, as courteous and courtly as men could be
in making it clear that deeds must follow words—soon.

"We didn't buy time—we were given it.

"If these men I saw at your request were bankers, I would
know—without bothering to ask—that there would be no further
extensions on my note."

The principal conclusion of the report was as follows:

> The basic decision in Southeast Asia is here. We must decide
> whether to help these countries to the best of our ability or
> throw in the towel in the area and pull back our defenses to
> San Francisco and a "Fortress America" concept. More impor-
> tant, we would say to the world in this case that we don't live
> up to treaties and don't stand by our friends. This is not my
> concept. I recommend that we move forward promptly with a
> major effort to help these countries defend themselves.

Johnson said that combat troops were neither required nor desirable:

> Asian leaders—at this time—do not want American troops
> involved in Southeast Asia other than on training missions.
> American combat troop involvement is not only not required,
> it is not desirable. Possibly Americans fail to appreciate fully
> the subtlety that recently-colonial peoples would not look with
> favor upon governments which invited or accepted the return
> this soon of Western troops.

He added this interesting and important point:

> To the extent that fear of ground troop involvement domi-
> nates our political responses to Asia in Congress or elsewhere,
> it seems most desirable to me to allay those paralyzing fears in
> confidence, on the strength of the individual statements made
> by leaders consulted on this trip. This does not minimize or dis-
> regard the possibility that open attack would bring calls for
> U.S. combat troops. But the present probability of open attack
> seems scant, and we might gain much needed flexibility in our
> policies if the spectre of combat troop commitment could be
> lessened domestically.

Johnson concluded the report by reiterating the need for deciding whether to make a "major effort" in Southeast Asia: "The fundamental decision required of the United States—and time is of the
greatest importance—is whether we are to attempt to meet the
challenges of Communist expansion now in Southeast Asia by a
major effort in support of the forces of freedom in the area or
throw in the towel." He underlined the implications: "This decision
must be made in a full realization of the very heavy and continuing costs involved in terms of money, of effort and of United States

prestige. It must be made with the knowledge that at some point we may be faced with the further decision of whether we commit major United States forces to the area or cut our losses and withdraw should our other efforts fail." And then there was this haunting sentence: "We must remain master in this decision."

The next day, May 25, 1961, Johnson went to Capitol Hill to report to the Senate on his trip. The meeting was hosted by the Foreign Relations Committee, and 57 Senators were present. (Prior to going to Asia, Johnson had talked to Fulbright, Mansfield and others.)[118] Johnson repeated for the group the conclusions he had stated in his report to the President, including the need to understand that a decision to make a major effort in Southeast Asia could later entail, on the one hand, a decision to withdraw, or, on the other, to commit major forces.

Tailoring his language for his political audience, Johnson, saying that he favored such a major effort, added, "If a bully can come in and run you out of the yard today, tomorrow he will come back and run you off the porch."

During the question period Johnson was asked whether Laos was a "lost cause." "No," he said, "I did not get that feeling out there, but I have been very depressed about Laos. I don't see what we can do there. I don't think anything is going to come out of the conference.

"I think that the Russians are going to bust it up, and I think that the Communists will practically have it." He added that he was glad he did not have to discuss this subject with Asian leaders, "because there was not any hope I could give them or any promises I could make."

Congressional reaction to Johnson's trip was generally favorable. Senator Thomas J. Dodd (D/Conn.), the newest member of the Foreign Relations Committee, and a committed anti-Communist who was also a strong supporter of Johnson, praised the Vice President, but argued that the U.S. should increase its role in Asia. Based on a trip he had just completed, he said, ". . . the drama which may toll the death knell for the United States and for Western civilization is now being played out in southeast Asia." Laos is the center of that crisis, he said, but throughout the area there is a "crisis of confidence" in U.S. leadership. He proposed a plan of action in which the U.S. would insist at Geneva that Laos be "truly free," without Communists in a coalition government, and that if this could not be achieved the U.S. should then "make an inviolable commitment of our prestige and our resources to achieve an independent Laos by force of arms." Moreover, the U.S. should increase its aid to freedom-loving countries, and carry the battle to the enemy. Guerrillas should be sent into North Vietnam ". . . to equip and supply those patriots already in the field; to make every Communist official fear the just retribution of an outraged humanity; to make every Communist arsenal, government building, communications center, and transportation facility a target for sabotage; to provide a rallying point for the great masses of oppressed

---

[118]Lyndon B. Johnson, *The Vantage Point* (New York: Holt, Rinehart and Winston, 1971), p. 53. For Johnson's meeting with the Senators, see *SFRC His Ser.*, vol. XIII, pt. 1, pp. 629-651. Quotations here are from p. 640.

people who hate Communism because they have known it." Also, if sending SEATO forces to Laos resulted in an increased Communist offensive, the U.S. should "carry the offensive to North Vietnam, and wherever else it may be necessary."[119]

There was another reaction of interest, given his later opposition, beginning in 1967, to the war. This was the position taken by Representive Paul Findley (R/Ill.), then in his first year in Congress, who criticized Johnson's announcement that he would not recommend the deployment of U.S. combat forces to Vietnam. Findley said, "U.S. combat forces are the most effective deterrent to aggression, and we should publicly offer such forces to South Vietnam without delay." "If we commit our forces in advance of Communist action," he argued, "the attack will probably never come. If we get into the fight in midstream, we may trigger a big war." He said that no country in which U.S. forces had been stationed had ever been attacked, and that for the Vice President to state that we would not send forces to Vietnam was "an invitation to trouble." Another Laos "was in the making," he added. "Supplies and training are not enough. Sooner or later, we will be forced to send combat forces to a war already in progress, or once more be identified with failure."[120]

This same argument was made within the executive branch only a few months later by a number of civilian and military advisers, including the Vietnam Task Force itself.

Fulbright also reacted. Although he had indicated in early May that he would support using U.S. combat troops in Vietnam or Thailand if necessary, by the beginning of June, partly as a result of his reaction to Johnson's trip and to what he correctly perceived to be the beginning of a major expansion of U.S. military aid to Vietnam and of the U.S. role in Southeast Asia, he began to have second thoughts. This led him to send a private memorandum to Kennedy as the President was preparing for his "summit meeting" with Khrushchev, in which he urged Kennedy to "reconsider the nature of American policies in Southeast Asia, specifically U.S. programs in Korea, Taiwan, South Vietnam, Laos and Thailand."[121]

On June 29, Fulbright continued this line of argument in an important foreign policy speech in the Senate in which he said that it was "dangerous doctrine" to argue that because the U.S. was strong it would commit its strength to the "active defense of its policies anywhere outside the Communist empire . . . nothing would please Communist leaders more than to draw the United States into costly commitments of its resources to peripheral struggles in which the principal Communist powers are not themselves directly involved." The attempt by the U.S. to make Laos into an "armed anti-Communist bastion," he said, ". . . was a mistake, because it [U.S. policy] was not related to the needs of the country or to the nature of its people and their interests." South Vietnam, however, deserved U.S. support. Its people were anti-Communist,

[119]*CR*, vol. 107, pp. 9176.
[120]*Ibid.*, p. 8587.
[121]Haynes Johnson and Bernard M. Gwertzman, *Fulbright, The Dissenter* (Garden City, N.Y.: Doubleday, 1968), p. 178. The Kennedy Library staff reports that they have not located this document in their files.

and its regime, although "perhaps unnecessarily severe," had been strong. But he warned that U.S. programs in Vietnam had been "too heavily weighted on the military side," and more attention was needed in the "struggle for dignity and economic independence." Referring to the success of Magsaysay in the Philippines, he said that the proper role for the U.S. in countries such as Vietnam was to enable "well-intentioned governments" to bring about social and economic reforms that, with the necessary security, would cause the populace to reject Communist domination.[122]

Fulbright's words fell on deaf ears. No effort had been or was thereafter made by the administration to review or reevaluate U.S. policy in Southeast Asia, except for the decision to seek a negotiated settlement of Laos.

The Staley Mission

After meeting early in June 1961 with Khrushchev, who seemed agreeable with respect to the neutralization of Laos but was truculent on almost every other subject, Kennedy and his associates became even more intent on getting an agreement on Laos, on the one hand, and stepping up U.S. assistance to Vietnam on the other. In an interview some years later, Dean Rusk commented:[123]

> When Kennedy met with Khrushchev in Vienna in June 1961, they seemed to reach some kind of understanding about Laos. That was the only positive thing to come out of that meeting. At the same time, Khrushchev tried to intimidate and bully this young President of the United States with an ultimatum. He told Kennedy, "We Russians are going to go ahead now and make this peace treaty with East Germany; if the West tries to interfere, there will be war." Kennedy said, "Mr. Chairman, there will be war. It is going to be a very cold winter." It was a tough situation. Kennedy was very much aware of this as he looked at the problem of Vietnam. I think he felt up to the point of his death that he was being tested by Khrushchev. Of course, that feeling was underscored by the Cuban missile crisis.

Just after his meeting with Khrushchev, Kennedy told James Reston of the *New York Times,* "Now we have a problem in making our power credible, and Vietnam looks like the place."[124]

---

[122]*CR*, vol. 107, pp. 11702-11705. At several points in the 1961 public hearings on the foreign aid bill, as well as in executive session hearings on June 13 and 14, Fulbright asked administration witnesses whether the executive branch had reviewed the program in order to "affirmatively decide" which aid commitments were in the U.S. national interest, and whether it was "within our capacity to continue to try to support every area in the world that is not now within the Communist orbit." (The witnesses said that no such review had been made.) He said, referring specifically to South Vietnam, but including also Laos, Cambodia, Thailand, Burma, and South Korea, "I am really questioning the validity of the concept which we are trying to fulfill, if it is not a false one, basically false, that it is impossible, and I am inclined at the moment to think that it probably is, due to reasons beyond our control; these are things we cannot change." For these and other comments by Fulbright in the public hearings see U.S. Congress, Senate, Committee on Foreign Relations, *International Development and Security,* Hearings on S. 1983, pts. 1 and 2, 87th Cong., 1st sess. (Washington, D.C.: U.S. Govt. Print. Off., 1961), pp. 86-87, 586-587, 606-608, 644-645, 866-869.

[123]CRS Interview with Dean Rusk, Nov. 17, 1978.

[124]David Halberstam, *The Best and the Brightest* (New York: Random House, 1972), p. 76. Of interest also are Reston's comments in his column in the *New York Times* for June 10, 1979 (for his original report on this subject see the *Times* for Jan. 18, 1966):

Continued

But if Vietnam rather than Laos was "the place," then it was all the more important that a negotiated settlement be reached on Laos. Accordingly, after returning from Europe, Kennedy called Harriman to stress the need for an agreement. According to Harriman, the President said, " 'You understand Averell' or Governor, he always used to call me, 'that I want a settlement. I don't want to send troops.' "[125]

There was still something of a disjunction, however, between the White House and the working level in the departments. Despite Kennedy's emphasis on Laos negotiations, the Vietnam Task Force continued to take the position, which the Laos Task Force had taken earlier in the year, that the U.S. should undertake military action in Laos. Such action was recommended to the task force at a meeting on June 19, 1961, by the Director, Sterling Cottrell, in a draft report which argued that this action was necessary in order to defend South Vietnam. On June 20, Robert H. Johnson, a member of the NSC staff, sent Rostow a memorandum on this new report, saying that he had "expressed some surprise" in the meeting at Cottrell's statement "that, unless we undertake military action in Laos, it would be virtually impossible to deal effectively with the situation in Viet-Nam."[126]

Johnson's comment itself is somewhat surprising, in view of the fact that there had long been very strong support in State and Defense for the proposition that the defense of Southeast Asia, including Vietnam, necessarily was based on a defense line along the Mekong River—SEATO Plan 5. Even after the agreement on Laos in 1962, many planners continued to argue that such a line of defense was the key to protecting all of Southeast Asia, and that unless the infiltration of men and supplies into Vietnam through Laos could be controlled, the insurgency in Vietnam could last indefinitely. (This argument—that U.S. (SEATO) forces should be sent to Laos in order to protect Vietnam—was made, especially by the JCS, during the weeks of planning for action in Southeast Asia preceding the Taylor mission in October 1961.)

The President and his associates lost no time in implementing the Johnson-Diem communiqué. On June 14, 1961, Kennedy met with Diem's key Cabinet officer, Nguyen Dinh Thuan, to discuss

---

"I had an hour alone with President Kennedy immediately after his last meeting with Khrushchev in Vienna at that time. Khrushchev had assumed, Kennedy said, that any American President who invaded Cuba without adequate preparation was inexperienced, and any President who then didn't use force to see the invasions through was weak. Kennedy admitted Khrushchev's logic on both points.

"But now, Kennedy added, we have a problem. We have to demonstrate to the Russians that we have the will and the power to defend our national interests. Shortly thereafter, he increased the defense budget, sent another division to Europe and increased our small contingent of observers and advisors in Vietnam to over 16,000.

"I have always believed, on the basis of that private conversation, that this particular summit was an event of historic significance, leading to Khrushchev's decision to send nuclear weapons to Cuba and to Kennedy's decision to confront Khrushchev by increasing our commitment in Vietnam.

"Kennedy dealt with Khrushchev's misjudgment by forcing him to turn back his nuclear weapons for Cuba or risk the possibility of war. Khrushchev turned them back, but the American commitment to Vietnam went on. The Kennedy people have always denied that there was any connection between Khrushchev's threats in Vienna and Kennedy's decision to confront the Communist threat to South Vietnam. But I know what I heard from Kennedy in Vienna 17 years ago, and have reflected on the accidents of summit meetings ever since."
[125]CRS Interview with Averell Harriman, Sept. 26, 1978.
[126]Kennedy Library, NSF Country File, Vietnam.

Diem's suggestions for implementing that agreement. These were contained in a letter of June 9 from Diem to Kennedy, which Thuan presented, in which Diem recommended, among other things, an increase in the Vietnamese Armed Forces from the 170,000 men just approved in May to 270,000 men, with the increase occurring over 3½ years.[127] (It is interesting to note, by the way, that this increase would be in regular army units, rather than in local militia or the Civil Guard. By this time, however, a large percentage of the regular army was engaged in fighting the guerrillas.) This plan, which had been worked out in conjunction with General McGarr, would necessitate, Diem said, a "considerable expansion" of the U.S. military assistance group, but, "Such an expansion, in the form of selected elements of the American Armed Forces to establish training centers for the Vietnamese Armed Forces, would serve the dual purpose of providing an expression of the United States' determination to halt the tide of communist aggression and of preparing our forces in the minimum of time." In other words, Diem apparently had been persuaded to agree to the American formula of having U.S. forces deployed in Vietnam for training purposes as well as serving as an armed presence, or "trip wire," that might deter the Communists.

In this meeting, Kennedy asked, among other things, about the problems of infiltrating guerrillas into North Vietnam. According to the memorandum of the conversation, "Mr. Thuan replied that a few highly trained troops were available but that if Viet-Nam were to risk these men in an attempt to stir up unrest in North Viet-Nam, the United States should be prepared to make a major effort to give them the full support needed to carry out such an action to a successful conclusion."[128]

The President seemed to agree completely with Diem's proposals. He instructed the State Department to expedite financing for the 20,000 increase already approved for the Vietnamese Army, and told McNamara to give a copy of Diem's letter to the Senate Armed Services Committee, where the Secretary was testifying that day, ". . . in order that the Senators could better understand and appreciate the magnitude of the task involved in helping Viet-Nam to maintain its independence." He also asked which Members of Congress Thuan would be seeing, and suggested he see some Republican Senators, especially Everett McKinley Dirksen (Ill.) and Bourke B. Hickenlooper (Iowa). The State Department said it would arrange these meetings. It had already arranged for Thuan to see Fulbright, Mansfield, and Frank J. Lausche (D/Ohio), the

---

[127]For the text of the letter see *PP*, DOD ed., book 11, pp. 168-173.
[128]Kennedy Library, NSF Country File, Vietnam, Memorandum of Conversation, June 14, 1961.

Consistent with President Kennedy's interest in increasing covert activity, especially against North Vietnam, the CIA authorized William E. Colby, then the Station Chief in Saigon, to accelerate operations against the North. ". . . we pressed ahead," Colby said. "Flights left Danang in the dusk headed north with Vietnamese trained and equipped to land in isolated areas, make cautious contact with their former home villages and begin building networks there. Boats went up the coast to land others on the beaches, and we started leaflet drops and radio programs designed to raise questions in North Vietnamese homes about their sons being sent to South Vietnam to fight and about the vices of Communist rule." William Colby, *Honorable Men* (New York: Simon and Schuster, 1978), p. 173.

chairman of the Far East Subcommittee of the Foreign Relations Committee.[129]

On the sensitive subject of U.S. forces, Kennedy carefully avoiding making a commitment, even though he agreed that the MAAG should be increased in order to speed up the training of Vietnamese forces, adding that ". . . this increase should be done quietly without publicly indicating that we did not intend to abide by the Geneva Accords."

In mid-June 1961, in accordance with the Johnson-Diem agreement, the U.S. sent a team of specialists to Vietnam to work with a Vietnamese team on a financial plan. The U.S. group (U.S. Special Financial Group) was headed by a private economist, Dr. Eugene Staley, president of SRI (Stanford Research Institute), but most of its members were from the government.

After spending a month in Vietnam the group made its report.[130] Although it was responsible for developing a financial plan, it had necessarily become involved in discussions of military force levels on which such a plan would rest. Two projections were made. Alternative A called for a level of 200,000, an increase of 30,000 over the level already approved. Alternative B called for increasing forces to the level of 278,000, which was 8,000 more than had been recommended by Diem. The first alternative assumed a continuation of the existing level of the insurgency, whereas the second assumed a significant increase in Communist activity in Vietnam, and a deterioration in Laos ending in *de facto* control by the Communists. The report then analyzed the costs involved in each alternative, and how these funds could be provided jointly. Other economic and political programs were discussed, including the Vietnamese plan to build 100 agrovilles ("strategic hamlets" or fortified villages) during the next 18 months. Calling these "one of the more promising counter-guerrilla methods tried up to this time," the report recommended that agrovilles be given top priority.

The report stated that although the military situation was the most critical, an "emergency" plan of economic and social action was also needed, especially in the rural areas. The long-run success of military operations, it said, would hinge on the success of economic and social action.

The concept of this "Joint Action Program," the report stated, was, by applying adequate resources in a prompt and effective manner, to achieve an early victory or "breakthrough." "Our joint efforts must surpass the critical threshold of the enemy's resistance, thereby putting an end to his destructive attacks, and at the same time we must make a decisive impact on the economic, social, and ideological front."

On August 4, 1961, President Kennedy approved the Staley group's recommendations, including alternative A (a 200,000 man army).[131] (Because the level of 200,000 could not be achieved for

---

[129]Kennedy Library, NSF Country File, Vietnam, cables to Saigon from Washington, June 15, 1961.
[130]The text is in *PP*, DOD ed., book 11, pp. 182-226.
[131]The Joint Chiefs had recommended alternative A. See *ibid.*, p. 239.

over a year, he thereby left himself the option of moving later to a higher number.) He also agreed that the U.S. would pay most of the increased costs involved in these new actions, but he urged that Vietnam increase its own financial efforts, including tax reform and an increase in the exchange rate for U.S. commodities under the commodity import program, and that Diem provide more of an opportunity for non-Communist opposition political groups to participate in public life.[132]

On its face, the Staley report appeared innocuous enough. Consistent with the announced mission of the group to develop a financial plan, the report discussed at length the financial and economic aspects of the situation in Vietnam at that time. What was not apparent was the extent to which the Staley plan was a military-security plan. Furthermore, approval of the plan, which seems to have been almost automatic, set in motion another series of incremental actions by which the United States strengthened its military-security commitment to Vietnam.

In its actions during the summer of 1961 on the authorization and appropriation bills for the foreign aid program, Congress approved the administration's increased assistance to Vietnam resulting from the Johnson and Staley missions. Although there were more policy questions than in previous years, especially on the part of Fulbright, as was indicated earlier, support for U.S. assistance to Vietnam continued to be strong, and the requested funds were generally approved without significant change. Once again, however, it is appropriate to note that although some of its leaders may have been informed about the decisions on Vietnam being made in the executive branch, Congress was largely acting on this legislation without knowledge of those decisions and of the growing U.S. commitment in Vietnam. Although Kennedy consulted leaders of Congress about sending U.S. forces to Laos, and included them in the meeting with Johnson upon his return from Vietnam, there is no record of similar consultations with Congress about the decisions made during the early months of 1961, as well as during the summer and fall, to increase the commitment and role of the U.S. in Vietnam. In part this lack or absence of consultation resulted from the customary reluctance of executive branch personnel to divulge information to Congress. It also reflected the reluctance of Congress to press the administration for information on sensitive foreign policy subjects, or to attempt to ferret out information in investigations or trips to the field. The President also was still enjoying to some extent his "honeymoon" with Congress, and, being a

---

[132]The decision on the Staley plan was promulgated as NSAM 65, Aug. 11, 1961, and appears in *ibid.*, pp. 241–244. At the same time Kennedy appears to have approved a letter to Diem, as suggested by the State Department, confirming and explaining the U.S. decision. No copy of this has been found. The memoranda to the President from the State Department, signed by George Ball (n.d.), and from Rostow (Aug. 4, 1961) in which the proposed plan was explained and Presidential action requested, are in the Kennedy Library, POF Staff Memos File. Rostow noted in his memo that the draft of the letter to Diem was a compromise between the two basic views within the U.S. Government on the best methods for getting the Vietnamese to act. State and Defense, he said, believed that this could best be achieved "not by specific conditions on our aid, but by creating a general atmosphere of cooperation and confidence," whereas "staff levels" in the Bureau of the Budget and the foreign aid program "believe that such action is much more likely to be forthcoming if our aid is specifically conditioned upon Vietnamese performance. . . ."

Democrat, he tended to have the presumption of support from a Democratic Congress.

There was also a tendency to exclude Congress from the decision-making process when the White House itself was taking the lead in debating alternatives, making plans, and recommending action. Thus, during July-October 1961, when Rostow and Maxwell Taylor, both on the President's staff, took personal charge of planning the next moves in Vietnam, Congress appears to have been almost totally excluded from the process.[133]

While there may have been some consultation or at least communication with a few Members and committees, especially on military matters, the general exclusion of key Members and committees of Congress from Vietnam decisionmaking during the last half of 1961 also had the effect of dulling Congress and the public's interest in the subject. In two executive sessions of the Foreign Relations Committee to discuss the world situation with Rusk, one on September 20 and the other on December 20, there was not even any mention of Southeast Asia or of Vietnam or Laos, either by Rusk or by members of the committee.[134] With the exception of the foreign aid bill, and of one hearing on Laos on August 16 by the Far East Subcommittee (which kept no transcript or minutes of the meeting), no hearings on Southeast Asia were held by the Foreign Relations Committee during the balance of the year after Johnson's report on his visit in late May. As was previously indicated, this did not imply a lack of interest in the area by the chairman and other key Members.

During the late summer and fall of 1961, however, the overriding foreign policy concern of the President and Congress was the growing tension with the Russians over Berlin, culminating in late August with the construction of the Berlin Wall. As had been the case earlier in the year, this more important foreign policy problem tended to eclipse the situation in Southeast Asia.

Contingency Planning for Action in Southeast Asia

Although Berlin was the primary focus, Southeast Asia continued to be of great concern. By late June 1961, the small group of White House staff members, supported by a few agency personnel, chiefly from the State Department, had begun to develop contingency plans for that area. They were particularly worried about the course of U.S. policy in the event that the Laos negotiations failed to produce a settlement, and/or the Communists increased their military activities in South Vietnam.

The principal persons working on Southeast Asia in the White House at the time were Gen. Maxwell Taylor, who had become a special assistant to Kennedy in June, and W. W. Rostow. Others directly involved were NSC staff members Robert Komer and Robert Johnson. From outside the White House the key participant was Deputy Under Secretary of State U. Alexis Johnson.[135]

---

[133] As Henry Fairlie has observed, however, "There was always sufficient knowledge within the public realm on which to form a political judgment. . . ." "We Knew What We Were Doing When We Went Into Vietnam," *Washington Monthly*, 5 (May 1973), pp. 7-26.

[134] *SFRC His. Ser.*, vol. XIII, pt. 2, pp. 605 ff. and 629 ff.

[135] John Steeves of the Far East Bureau, who was made the director of the Southeast Asia Task Force in July 1961, as well as Cottrell, the director of the Vietnam Task Force, were active in assisting U. Alexis Johnson.

On June 20, 1961, Rostow sent President Kennedy a memorandum on "The Present Situation in Southeast Asia," which he also sent to U. Alexis Johnson on July 6 with a note saying that he was attempting through the memorandum to do two things:[136]

(1) To get the town [Washington] to examine the question of whether there might not be a better and more persuasive military contingency plan than putting many thousands of troops in the Mekong Valley [SEATO Plan 5].

(2) To get the town to consider more explictly the military and political links between the Laos and the Viet-Nam problems.

On July 10, Rostow thanked Johnson for responding and said, "The crucial issue that remains, it seems to me, is whether we take the initiative fairly soon to raise the question of aggression against Viet-Nam in some international forum."[137] ". . . the crucial role of the Viet-Nam—as a diplomatic issue," he added "—is to provide a political base for more persuasive military posture; for I assume we agree that without the other side becoming persuaded that we mean business in Southeast Asia, there is unlikely to be a Laos settlement acceptable to us."

Rostow continued:

It goes without saying, of course, that we should not raise the Viet-Nam issue on the international level unless we are prepared to see it through, if international action is unnecessary. Here, as you know, I favor designing and looking hard at an air-sea (iron-bomb)[138] counter-guerrilla war, with as many SEATO friends as will play, along with continued vigorous efforts within Diem's boundaries. But if that more ambitious course should be rejected, we would have still strengthened our position before the world, should it be necessary for us sharply to increase our assistance to Diem inside South Viet-Nam. And, at the minimum, this seems likely.

On July 12, Rostow made these same points in a conversation with Rusk. For his part, Rusk emphasized that if the U.S. raised the Vietnam issue in the U.N. as a case of aggression under the U.N. Charter, it would have to be "ready to go" in following up on that charge.[139] In a memo to Rusk on July 13, Rostow said he agreed:[140] "We must know quite precisely what kind of international action we want—action which might radically reduce the external component in Diem's guerrilla war." But if the U.S. was not able to get effective international action, Rostow said, this would "free our hands and our consciences for whatever we have to do." He said that he believed—and he thought U. Alexis Johnson agreed—that in order to achieve a satisfactory settlement in Laos the U.S. had to persuade the Communists that it would "fight." He did not think that the existing SEATO Plan 5, which was based primarily on defending the area from the Mekong Valley to the south, would be an adequate deterrent. He favored the develop-

---

[136]Kennedy Library, NSF Country File, Vietnam. The memorandum itself is still classified.
[137]Same location. Johnson's response is still classified.
[138]I.e., non-nuclear bomb.
[139]Kennedy Library, NSF Country File, Vietnam, Memorandum from Rostow to Rusk, July 13, 1961.
[140]*Ibid.*

ment of a plan under which the U.S. would take direct action against North Vietnam.

Rostow told Rusk that if the U.S. was not able to get adequate help from the U.N., it would need to be prepared for these three levels of action:

—A sharp increase in the number of Americans in South Viet-Nam for training and support purposes;

—A counter-guerrilla operation in the north, possibly using American Air and Naval strength to impose about the same level of damage and incovenience that the Viet Cong are imposing in the south;

—If the Vietminh cross their border substantially, a limited military operation in the north; e.g., capture and holding of the port of Haiphong.

On July 14, 1961, Rostow sent Kennedy a memorandum in response to a question the President had apparently asked concerning the implications of the Southeast Asia situation for the handling of the Berlin crisis. Rostow, who noted that Taylor had approved the memo, said that rather than focusing just on Berlin, the President should, for a variety of reasons (which he stated), deal with the broader question of the increasing seriousness of the world situation, including Southeast Asia, and the need for the U.S. to prepare to meet the growing threat to its security. He also suggested the desirability of doing so under the President's emergency powers by a "modification" of the state of emergency arrangements which were still in effect as a result of World War II and the Korean war. This, he said, could help provide a legal basis for such preparations, as well as strengthening the administration's case for foreign aid, the space program, and education.[141]

On July 18, Rostow and Taylor met with U. Alexis Johnson to discuss the "inter-connection between various elements of policy in Southeast Asia. . . ."[142] Among the topics considered were the urgent need for creating and funding a program for Northeast Thailand; the need for "clearing out the Pathet Lao pocket at Tchepone," on the Ho Chi Minh Trail, and "the difficulties of doing it while the ceasefire still operated in Laos"; the need for developing a "common feeling among the Vietnamese, the Cambodians, and the Thais . . . in relation to the possibility of mounting a local effort to protect that area from guerrilla warfare and subversion." (The memorandum of conversation on the meeting added: "It was agreed that, while the job might not be impossible, important political and psychological obstacles would have to be overcome. The crucial long-term need for such an association of effort was emphasized.")

At this meeting, held three years before the U.S. retaliated against North Vietnam after the Gulf of Tonkin incident, "The possibility of using evidence of North Viet-Nam aggression as a foundation for more aggressive limited military action against North Viet-Nam" was also discussed. U. Alexis Johnson agreed, on behalf of State, to "collect and examine the persuasiveness of the evidence of North Viet-Nam aggression against South Viet-Nam," as well as

---

[141]Kennedy Library, NSF Regional Security File, Southeast Asia General, 1961.
[142]Kennedy Library, Thomson Papers, Memorandum of Conversation, July 18, 1961.

to examine "the best diplomatic forum or series of forums in which the issue might be raised."[143]

A part of the planning process included contingency planning for information programs on Vietnam, both internationally and in the United States itself, to be used in conjunction with military action, and one of the more interesting documents of the period is a plan for a "Contingency Information Program" in the United States, prepared by a member of the Public Affairs staff of the State Department for the Vietnam Task Force, describing the means by which the public and Congress could be persuaded to support military action.[144] "Before we could use force or publicly announce our decision to use force," the paper said, "American public opinion would have to be conditioned to support such action. The Congress would also have to be fully informed and convinced of the necessity for such action." This, according to the paper, would be accomplished by the following means:

a. *Perspectives.* The Task Force should float perspective articles through selected newspaper columns such as those of Messrs. Alsop, Drummond, Childs, Reston, etc. While these would reach one audience, a broader exposition for a different audience should be made through Sunday newspaper supplements such as the American Weekly, Parade, the *New York Times* Magazine and, if time permits, through the *Saturday Evening Post* and movie newsreels which have a claimed audience of 40 million weekly.

It might be profitable for later exploitation to place some profile articles on Gen. Maxwell Taylor as an expert on limited warfare.

b. *Consultations.* The Senate, or some of its key members, should be taken into the confidence of the Executive early in the process and they should be told why alternative courses of action are unacceptable. We should induce some senators to make public speeches on the seriousness of the situation, etc.

c. *Backgrounders.* Following publication of the perspectives, the Task Force should analyze public reaction to them and assess any weak points in the argumentation which may have been revealed by public reaction. From this analysis and assessment, material might be prepared for backgrounders to be given by top level officials, among whom might be Messrs. Bowles, Johnson, McConaughy, Bohlen, Nitze and General Taylor.

d. *Press conferences, etc.* If by this time public opinion has not begun to call for positive action, we should begin to withdraw to a fall-back position; we should prepare now the terrain to which we might be obliged to withdraw.

---

[143]This resulted in the State Department's "White Paper" on Vietnam prepared by William J. Jorden, which was issued in Dec. 1961. (See p. 103 below.) The Vietnam Task Force was already preparing a number of papers for the White House on other aspects of the possible use of U.S. military forces in Southeast Asia in accordance with a task force directive issued earlier in the summer, which was supplemented on June 24, 1961, by a memorandum entitled "Regional Action to Protect Vietnam" setting forth the steps to be taken under a SEATO Plan 5 operation.

[144]Kennedy Library, NSF Country File. This document is not dated, but it appears to have been prepared during July 1961, and is filed accordingly.

If, on the other hand, public opinion has become more receptive, high level officials should move into the open with public statements on the choices facing us. From this point onward in the information program, the sequence of events should, ideally, move very rapidly.

The Secretary, Senators Fulbright, Mansfield, Humphrey or Javits might take a public supporting position and Gen. Taylor could state his views. The means would be television interview programs, press conferences and—again if time permits—newsreels.

e. *Spot News.* At this point, our Asian allies might request token deployment of American combat troops to help them in the defense of Southeast Asia against external aggression.

f. *Fireside telecast.* Very quickly after the Asians request combat help, President Kennedy should, in a telecast to the nation, announce that action has been taken. He should also explain the reasoning behind his decision and the unacceptable nature of the alternatives, and the fact that [it] is defensive, not aggressive action. He should stress that we shall cross no borders uninvited.

As for the messages to be sent to the public by these means, the paper recommended that the public and Congress be told about the history of Communist aggression and subversion in Vietnam, as well as the consequences of Communist control of Laos, and that "The 'domino theory' should be fully explained."

In general; the aim should be to (i) give our Asian allies full credit for the efforts, social and economic as well as military, that they have made; (ii) show the peril to our own defenses; and (iii) indicate that subversion in Southeast Asia is a Communist export, not an indigenous product. Finally, we should develop the theme that the Communist propaganda campaigns have often struck Berlin like a gong to distract our attention from the actual exercise of force in Asia, but that we do not intend to be diverted.

As the planning process continued, Robert Komer sent Rostow a memorandum on July 20 entitled "Are We Pushing Hard Enough in South Vietnam?"[145] He proposed, as was being recommended by the Staley group, a "crash" program for Vietnam:

. . . While it may simply be too early to tell, we do not yet have things turned around in Vietnam. In part this reflects one of the real problems for any government—how to get adequate follow-through. We whack up a big exercise on a crash problem, take some strong initiatives, and then the agencies tend to slip back toward business as usual with only the White House providing much of a prod.

But more important, there are some strong political reasons for stepping up the momentum in South Vietnam. I believe it very important that this government have a major anti-Communist victory to its credit in the six months before the Berlin crisis is likely to get really hot. Few things would be better calculated to show Moscow and Peiping that we mean business

---

[145]Kennedy Library, NSF Country File, Vietnam. (misspellings and emphasis in original)

than an obvious (if not yet definitive) turnaround in Vietnam. Moreover, here the odds are still in our favor, which makes Vietnam a better place than Laos to achieve the desired result.

Such a victory is also indispensable to the process of reassuring our Far East allies, most of whom have been led by Laos to wonder whether we have the moxie to protect them any longer.

What should we do? How about the President directing that all wraps are off in the counter-guerilla operations, etc. in South Vietnam? We will fund and pay for any crash measures, however wasteful, which will produce quick results. We will do anything needed in sending arms and ammunition, providing MAAG advisers, and in associated social and economic operations designed to win back the countryside. The objective—to achieve before the end of the year a major defeat of the Viet Cong.

The important thing would be a change in operational philosophy. Instead of haggling with Diem over who should finance what proportion of the effort, *we would regard this as a wartime situation in which the sky's the limit.* The only caveat would be that outlays must be related to the counter-guerrilla campaign. Hence, we would not give Diem a blank check on economic development or on building up the regular army for defense of the 17th parallel as McGarr would have us do.

Komer added that while such a program would cost more, the cost of not acting could be higher in the long-run. He emphasized, moreover, that "Simultaneously, we must put the blocks to Diem on finally doing the necessary to regain popular support," and suggested that the U.S. might be able to use the proposed program as a "lever" for that purpose.

Komer's conclusion was as follows:

What do we lose if such an initiative fails? Are we any worse off than before? Our prestige may have become a little more heavily engaged but what else? And the risk involved if we fail to prevent the Viet Cong threat from developing into a full-fledged civil war is clearly overriding. After Laos, and with Berlin on the horizon, we cannot afford to go less than all-out in cleaning up South Vietnam.

Kennedy is Skeptical of Proposed Military Action

President Kennedy doubtless shared the feeling of Komer and other advisers that there was an important linkage between the posture of the U.S. in Southeast Asia and relations with the Russians, especially with respect to Berlin. He probably also agreed with Rostow's contention that the administration could use the Communist threat in Southeast Asia, among other things, to increase U.S. public and congressional support for a military build-up, as well as for promoting foreign aid and other legislation which the White House considered important. But Kennedy was reluctant to move as fast or as far as some of his advisers recommended. At a meeting on July 28, 1961 with all of the key participants in the planning process (including Rusk, U. Alexis Johnson, Ball, Taylor, Rostow), Kennedy made it clear that he was skeptical about military plans for Laos, and that he wanted more information before approving a counterinsurgency plan for using U.S. forces in Southeast Asia.

In advance of the meeting, the State Department's newly-established Southeast Asia Task Force, under the direction of John Steeves, had prepared a brief report for Kennedy on a proposed course of action in Southeast Asia.[146] According to the report, the "consensus" of the task force was that "It is essential to our policy interests in Asia, and indeed globally, to ensure the security of Southeast Asia against further communist advancement. . . . The loss of Southeast Asia to the free world would be highly inimical to our future strategy and interest." The group had also concluded that "We should make the basic decision now to resist this encroachment by appropriate military means, if necessary, with or without unanimous SEATO support."

The task force took the position that North Vietnam was "the immediate focal point of the threat to the peninsula and whatever action is taken should bear on this objective if both Laos and Viet-Nam are to be secured and the approaches to the rest of the peninsula blocked."

Among its recommendations, the task force proposed that the U.S. insist on having an effective International Control Commission for Laos as the "minimum price" for U.S. military withdrawal. In addition, the U.S. should "keep a steady rein" on the royalist government of Laos to keep it from agreeing to a coalition government that could be controlled by the Communists.

With respect to Vietnam, the task force recommended that the Staley plan be approved. In addition, "In carrying out our programs based in Viet-Nam covert action be conducted to interdict North Vietnamese pressure on South Viet-Nam and if these contacts do not prove successful, eventually give covert indication that the continuation of DRV [Democratic Republic of Vietnam] aggressive policy towards Laos and Viet-Nam may result in direct retaliatory action against her."

Finally, the report recommended that because SEATO Plan 5 did not envisage action against North Vietnam, the U.S. should develop a military plan based on the possibility of such action, with or without other SEATO countries.

On July 27, Taylor and Rostow sent Kennedy a memo in which they listed the issues which would be presented at the meeting the following day.[147] The choices for the U.S., they said, were "to disengage from the area as gracefully as possible; to find as soon as possible a convenient political pretext and attack with American military force the regional source of aggression in Hanoi; or to build as much indigenous military, political and economic strength as we can in the area, in order to contain the thrust from Hanoi while preparing to intervene with U.S. military force if the Chinese Communists come in or the situation otherwise gets out of hand." They said they assumed that the latter course was what Kennedy preferred, but that it would be helpful for him to indicate his posi-

---

[146]The report, which is not dated, is in the Kennedy Library, NSF Regional Security File, Southeast Asia General, July 1961.
[147]Same location.

tion and to have a discussion of the situation and the options available.

At the meeting which then took place with the President on July 28, U. Alexis Johnson began the discussion of the Southeast Asia Task Force report by stating that the Communists did not appear to want a neutral Laos; that "they are very confident about the current military situation and see no reason for concessions." The U.S., therefore, needed to "introduce a new element which will change their estimate of the situation." This new element would be a plan to "take and hold" the southern part of Laos with troops from Laos, Thailand, Vietnam and the U.S., if the minimum U.S. condition for a negotiated settlement (a strong ICC) was not accepted in Geneva. Furthermore, Johnson said, continuing his discussion of the task force report, if the Viet Minh then intervened substantially in Laos and/or Vietnam, the U.S. should consider using air and naval forces in direct attacks on North Vietnam. As he explained some years later, Johnson thought that the U.S. needed to inhibit the North Vietnamese from using the Ho Chi Minh Trail in Laos to supply Communists forces in South Vietnam. He argued that if there was to be a negotiated settlement, its inspection provisions must have "teeth." "Laos was really the key to Vietnam" Johnson said, and our failure in 1962 to dislodge the Pathet Lao from Tchepone [the strategic town on the southern end of the Ho Chi Minh trail] eventually acted to seal the fate of Vietnam."[148] At the same time, Johnson recognized that his hope for a settlement with stronger inspections provisions was probably "futile." As to whether the direct use of U.S. forces in Laos would have been effective in preventing the North Vietnamese from using the Ho Chi Minh Trail, he concludes: "We probably lacked the means to do this; certainly we lacked the will."[149]

As the meeting on July 18, 1961 continued, President Kennedy asked several questions about details of the plan, and from the responses it was clear that such details had not been developed. Moreover, "It was not clear how great an effect action against Haiphong or Hanoi would have on Northern Viet-Nam, nor whether it would be easy to hold what had been taken in a single attack. Similarly, no careful plan has yet been developed for an operation to take and hold Southern Laos."[150]

Kennedy expressed "the need for realism and accuracy" in plans for military action in Laos. "He had observed in earlier military plans with respect to Laos that optimistic estimates were invariably proven false in the event. He was not persuaded that the airfields and the existing situation in Southern Laos would permit any real operation to save that part of the country, and he emphasized the reluctance of the American people and of many distinguished military leaders to see any direct involvement of U.S. troops in that part of the world." He said he was very reluctant to make a decision to use U.S. forces in Laos, and in order to find out more about the situation he would like for General Taylor to go to

---

[148]Letter to CRS from U. Alexis Johnson, July 31, 1984.

[149]U. Alexis Johnson with Jef Olivarius McAllister, *The Right Hand of Power*, p. 326.

[150]From the July 31, 1961, "Memorandum of Discussion on Southeast Asia," July 28, 1961, prepared by McGeorge Bundy, Kennedy Library, NSF Regional Security File, Southeast Asia General, 1961.

Vietnam on a study mission. Meanwhile, he wanted to pursue the
Laos negotiations. He also agreed to accept the Staley recommendations, but did not want to be committed in advance to specific
levels of funding.

After the meeting, Rostow, with Taylor's concurrence, sent a
memorandum to Kennedy on August 4 in which he attempted to
state his and Taylor's understanding of Kennedy's position:[151]

> As we understand your position: You would wish to see
> every avenue of diplomacy exhausted before we accept the ne-
> cessity for either positioning U.S. forces on the Southeast
> Asian mainland or fighting there; you would wish to see the
> possibilities of economic assistance fully exploited to strength-
> en the Southeast Asian position; you would wish to see indige-
> nous forces used to the maximum if fighting should occur; and
> that, should we have to fight, we should use air and sea power
> to the maximum and engage minimum U.S. forces on the
> Southeast Asian mainland.

The memo went on to reiterate the proposals of the task force for
developing a contingency plan for controlling southern Laos, and, if
necessary, ". . . attacks from the air—also, possibly, from the
sea—in the Haiphong-Hanoi area." "This graduated pressure," the
memo added, "could take the form of air strikes against the land
lines of communications and supply centers, and sea interdiction of
logistical traffic along the east coast of Viet-Nam. It could also include a naval blockade in the Gulf of Tonkin to isolate the Port of
Haiphong."

Moreover, the memo stated, the contingency plan should include
possible U.S. action against China if the Chinese Communists intervened in Indochina.

Meanwhile, Taylor had sent his own proposal to U. Alexis Johnson on July 31, in which he suggested a meeting of the leaders of
Vietnam, Thailand and Laos "to consider ways of making common
cause against the infiltration into Laos," and sending reconnaissance groups from SEATO Plan 5 forces to military installations in
Thailand and Laos to check on military needs prior to implementing any contingency plans. "Word of these happenings," he added,
"would get around."

As planning for possible military action in Southeast Asia continued, the President asked Rostow and Taylor on August 7 to advise
him on the means for bringing to the attention of "world public
opinion" the actions of North Vietnam, both in Laos and in South
Vietnam. He added, "I agree with you that ground work has to be

---

[151]Same location. In a memorandum to Rostow, on Aug. 14, 1961, "Strategy for Southeast
Asia," Robert Johnson questioned the military and political feasibility of Rostow's proposal for
action against North Vietnam, but concluded, ". . . to use the current cliché, I think that this is
the point where we are going to have to bite the bullet. If we are going to save Southern Laos
and a strip along the Mekong, it seems to me that we have to face the possibility that a substantial U.S. manpower contribution may be required." He said he thought the U.S. should seek a
"de facto partition of Laos by a sub-limited war approach" involving increased covert activity,
but that in so doing "we must take such initial action with a full awareness of, and commitment
to, the possibility that we may have to move from sub- limited war to limited war and that a
substantial commitment of U.S. forces in Southern Laos may be necessary." Kennedy Library,
Thomson Papers.

laid or otherwise any military action we might take against Northern Vietnam will seem like aggression on our part."[152]

On August 10, the JCS presented to Kennedy their plan for Southeast Asia. There are no records available as to what the plan contained or as to the discussion of it with the President, but there is the record of a meeting on August 12 which included Taylor and Rostow from the White House, Johnson and Steeves from the State Department, and Lemnitzer and others from the JCS (but no Department of Defense civilians, which is an indication of the fact that the discussions had not attained the level of a full-scale policy process), to continue the August 10 discussion of the JCS proposal. There was apparently no civilians in attendance from the Defense Department, which is an indication that the discussions on Southeast Asia which had been initiated by the White House staff had not attained the level of a full-scale policy process. At this meeting it was agreed that a "comprehensive area plan" was needed to provide for military action in the event of a possible partition of Laos. Participants in the meeting further agreed that in the case of the first contingency, "a visible, stepped-up invasion from the North," SEATO Plan 5 should be invoked. "Hanoi would have been warned in advance that invasion would bring SEATO forces and air attacks on targets in North Vietnam." In the second contingency, that of increased infiltration and pressure on areas controlled by the pro-western forces, SEATO forces should be given greater support, including as many as 2,000 more military advisers for Laotian forces, mostly from the U.S.[153]

On August 14, Taylor drafted a memorandum for Kennedy to send to Rusk commenting on both the August 10 JCS briefing and the August 12 meeting of State and the JCS.[154] The memo indicated approval of the proposed area plan to defend the "flanks"—Vietnam and Thailand—from Communist infiltration and attack through cooperative military efforts of Vietnam, Thailand and Laos, but took the position that U.S. military participation was the "minimum" required to get these three countries to cooperate. It noted, moreover, that even if such a cooperative plan were feasible, "it will require very considerable effort to develop the political framework to support it."

Rostow left for vacation while the "comprehensive area plan" was being developed, but before leaving he sent Kennedy a memorandum on August 17 in which he explained what the area plan would probably include, and offered his own suggestions as to how to proceed.[155] "I suspect your planners," he said, "will tell you this: to hold the present line and to mop up behind it nothing will suffice very much short of the introduction of forces (or the firm commitment to introduce forces) into Southeast Asia from outside the mainland on the scale of the SEATO Plan 5 if to overcome the

[152]Kennedy Library, POF Staff Memos File. For Rostow's reply see his memorandum to the President on Aug. 11, 1961, "Southeast Asia," NSF Regional Security File, Southeast Asia General, 1961.
[153]Kennedy Library, NSF Regional Security File, Southeast Asia General, 1961, Memorandum for Record, Aug. 12, 1961.
[154]Same location. The files do not indicate whether or not the memo was sent to Rusk by Kennedy.
[155]Same location.

three fundamental weaknesses we face: Diem's preoccupations; Sarit's uncertainties; and Phoumi's incompetence." (Sarit Thanarat was then in power in Thailand, and Phoumi Nosavan was in command of the non-Communist government in Laos.) Because of these weaknesses, and the difficulty of intervening from outside, Rostow felt that a negotiated settlement of the Laotian conflict was essential. But he again argued that in order to get the Communists to agree to a reasonable settlement the U.S. and the other SEATO powers had to convince them that they would make a "substantial" military commitment if the Communists refused to agree. He proposed to the President a plan to demonstrate American determination in the event the Communists decided to stall and to try to take more territory in South Laos, which would also avoid, at least initially, the deployment of U.S. forces to Laos. To do this he suggested that the U.S. establish a SEATO military headquarters in Thailand, staffed by an American commander and supporting personnel, to develop contingency plans with Sarit and Diem for the deployment of a SEATO combat force. Then, with or without the participation of the British and French, the U.S. should develop contingency plans for such an action with other SEATO powers.

Rostow said, "This kind of revival of SEATO appears, then, the only way I can perceive of salvaging Averell [Harriman] in Geneva [negotiating on Laos] and laying the basis for holding the area for the long pull without excessive U.S. commitment on the mainland. But it takes a bold U.S. commitment in principle—very soon indeed."

"This is a hard decision," he said, "for our troubles with the British and French in SEATO have permitted us a bit of the luxury of the drunk at the bar who cries "Let me at 'em," while making sure he is firmly held by his pals.

"On the other hand, to go this route is, in fact, to recognize commitments we already have upon us—but to act on them positively. Surely we are hooked in Viet-Nam; surely we shall honor our bilateral assurances to Sarit, as well as our SEATO commitment; and—I suspect—despite everything it implies, we shall fight for Laos if the other side pushes too far its advantages on the ground."

Rostow added, "Your decision here is not easy. It involves making an uncertain commitment in cold blood. It is not unlike Truman's commitment on Greece and Turkey in March 1947; for, in truth, Southeast Asia is in as uncertain shape as Southeast Europe at that time. But—like Truman's commitment—it has the potentiality of rallying the forces in the area, mobilizing the will and strength sufficient to fend off the Communist threat, and minimizing the chance that U.S. troops will have to fight in a situation which has further deteriorated."

The next day (August 18), Rostow sent a memo to Robert Kennedy in which he said, "I deeply believe that the way to save Southeast Asia and to minimize the chance of deep U.S. military involvement there is for the President to make a bold decision very soon."[156] (By this he meant before the end of the rainy season in Laos, which would occur by early October.)

---

[156] Same location.

On August 22, 1961, Taylor sent a memorandum to U. Alexis Johnson recommending that certain interim steps be taken while final U.S. plans for Southeast Asia were being completed, and that these be assigned to appropriate U.S. agencies for implementation. These steps would include political discussions with Thailand, Laos and Vietnam to determine their willingness to establish a common front against the Communists, as well as "the price which the United States might be obliged to pay for effective collaboration"; establishing, as Rostow had suggested, a SEATO headquarters and staff in Thailand; and increasing the numbers of foreign advisers with Laotian troops. The major question, Taylor said, was the amount of U.S. and other SEATO force commitments. "It presently appears that we must be willing to make some commitment at the outset in order to assure Sarit's support."[157]

On August 24, a top-level meeting of those working on Southeast Asia plans was held in Rusk's office. A draft of a proposed plan prepared by the Southeast Asia Task Force (drafted primarily in State) was the subject of the discussion. According to a report of the meeting, the proposal, which generally reflected Rostow's ideas, was vigorously attacked by McNamara and Harriman, joined by Rusk, who saw it as inconsistent with, if not antagonistic to, the President's plan for a negotiated settlement in Laos. Despite efforts by Taylor and Steeves to defend the plan, it was thoroughly repudiated, leaving the subordinates on the task force without any support for their positions from their agency heads.[158]

After this debacle, the State Department drafted a modified proposal for Kennedy which stressed the negotiation of a settlement for Laos, and suggested courses of action in the event these negotiations were successful or not, with proposals for military and other action in the latter case.[159]

On August 29, 1961, Kennedy met with his advisers to consider the revised proposal. The memorandum from Rusk asked that he decide on these points:

1. Authorization immediately to undertake talks with our SEATO allies both bilaterally and with the SEATO Council representatives in Bangkok, and also with South Vietnam, as appropriate, in which we would explore their receptivity to:

(a) enlarging the concept of SEATO Plan 5 so that if the Communists renew their offensive and the decision is made to implement Plan 5 the objective would be the expulsion of Communist forces from all of Southern Laos and the Mekong River line, including the Luang Prabang area. The establishment of such an objective would be conditional upon the willingness of Thailand and South Vietnam, and to a lesser extent possibly some other SEATO countries such as the Philippines, Pakistan, Australia and New Zealand, to commit additional forces to Plan 5.

(b) in the event neither a peaceful settlement is achieved nor has there been a sufficient renewal of the offensive by

---

[157]Same location.
[158]Memorandum for McGeorge Bundy from Robert H. Johnson, Aug. 25, 1961, same location.
[159]Memorandum for the President, Aug. 29, 1961, same location, with attached "Plan for Southeast Asia," "sanitized"—the government term used to refer to material deleted for security reasons when a document is declassified—and made public in 1978.

the Communists to justify consideration of implementing SEATO Plan 5, the carrying out of a SEATO exercise in Thailand about October 10 employing ground combat troops, supported by tactical air units and, on completion of the exercise, leaving behind in Thailand a SEATO command and communications "shell" prepared on a contingency basis to expedite the implementation of SEATO Plan 5.

(c) undertaking additional rotational training of SEATO combat units in Thailand.

(d) introducing into Thailand a SEATO River Patrol along the line of the Mekong, and

(e) declaring at an appropriate time a SEATO charter yellow or charter blue condition [stages of military alerts].

2. Immediately increasing our mobile training teams in Laos and seeking Thai agreement to supplying an equal number of Thais for the same purpose.

3. Immediately increasing by 2,000 the number of Meos being supported so as to bring the total up to the level of 11,000.

4. Authorizing photo reconnaissance———[160] over all of Laos. (This has for the most part been suspended during the cease-fire.)

5. As soon as the details are worked out with ICA and Congressional action has been taken on the aid bill, a letter from you to Sarit offering a $150,000,000 line of credit.

Kennedy approved most of the proposed actions, including SEATO discussions (but not the actual steps suggested in States' memo, 1. [b] through 1. [e]), as well as the increase in mobile training (bringing U.S. advisers in Laos to a total of 500), the increase in CIA assistance to Meos tribesmen, and photo reconnaissance of Laos "by Thai or other sanitized aircraft."[161]

Several days later the State Department gave the White House a new memorandum on steps to take in Laos if the Communists resumed military activity and if the U.S. did not intervene militarily. As summarized by Robert Johnson for Rostow, "The objective of the proposed actions . . . is not to clean out, sanitize or seal off the Mekong and South Laos areas, but rather, through harrassment, to prevent the Communists from obtaining a secure base area from which to launch attacks on Thailand and Vietnam." "It seems to me," Johnson added, "that we should be preparing for the kinds of actions suggested on an urgent basis."[162]

As outlined by State (either in the same paper described by Johnson or a later and similar one), the U.S. would, among other things, continue its various forms of covert assistance to Laotian forces;

---

[160] When this document was sanitized by the Department of State the missing portion of this sentence in item 4 was stricken.

[161] NSAM 80, Aug. 29, 1961, *PP*, DOD ed., book 11, pp. 247-248. As will be noted, all or most of the sanitized words in the State Department proposal of the same date appear to have been included in this printing of NSAM 80.

The President apparently did not approve State's proposal that Sarit, as an inducement for and in recognition of his cooperation, be given an open line of credit of $150 million. For a memorandum from the Bureau of the Budget on Aug. 30, 1961, criticizing this proposal see Kennedy Library, NSF Regional Security File, Southeast Asia General, 1961.

[162] Johnson memo to Rostow, Sept. 12, 1961, same location.

consider sending a combat battalion to Vietnam and another to Thailand for training purposes, as well as to establish the presence of U.S. troops, and deploy an engineering battalion to Vietnam and another to Thailand. All of these moves would be made unilaterally by the U.S. without the involvement of other SEATO countries.[163]

A JCS survey team under direction of Brig. Gen. William H. Craig, which had just returned from a trip to Laos and Vietnam, recommended on September 15, 1961, that SEATO Plan 5 should be activated immediately in order to forestall action by the Communists when the rainy season ended in early October. The team also recommended that the U.S. "get tough with Phoumi" to improve the Laotian military performance, and that the U.S. be prepared to support Phoumi's forces with tactical air operations if hostilities resumed. "The future of the US in Southeast Asia is at stake. It may be too late unless we act now one way or another."[164]

In a memo to Kennedy on September 26, 1961, however, Taylor confirmed the President's earlier concern about the potential logistical problems involved in military action by ground forces in Laos. Taylor reported that "The more we study the Southeast Asia problem the more we are convinced of the critical importance of logistic factors. A study of the logistic problem from the point of view of the Communists and ourselves indicated that it sets an upper limit to the possibility of escalation of military action. . . . Without much work on the logistical facilities, we should not introduce and support many more troops in Laos and Thailand than those contemplated in SEATO 5."[165]

A meeting with the President on October 5, 1961 to discuss Southeast Asia, for which Rostow, Taylor and U. Alexis Johnson had been organizing papers from the several departments concerned, was postponed. Instead, the President met with Harriman, who was returning to Geneva, to discuss the next moves the U.S. would make in the Laos negotiations, especially the possibility of getting the Russians to agree that continued infiltration by the North Vietnamese into South Vietnam would be a breach of the broad U.S.-U.S.S.R. understanding being developed at Geneva, and what the responsibility of the Russians might be toward enforcing such an understanding on infiltration. Harriman apparently was also authorized at this point to explore with the Russians "ways and means whereby relations between North and South Viet-Nam could be stabilized."[166]

The Taylor-Rostow Trip is Scheduled

On October 11, the President held the meeting with his advisers to discuss Southeast Asia which had been postponed from October 5. By this time the situation in Laos was fairly stable, and negotiations were continuing in Geneva. In Vietnam, however, the situation was becoming more serious, and it was apparent that further

[163]Same location. The paper "Limited Holding Actions (Southeast Asia)," was dated sometime between Sept. 20 and 30, 1961, but the exact day cannot be discerned from the copy in the file. The final version of this paper, "Southeast Asia," Oct. 3, 1961, is in the same file.
[164]Same location.
[165]Same location.
[166]"Draft Instructions for Ambassador Harriman," Oct. 1961, same location.

action might be needed. As Rostow stated in a memo to Kennedy on October 5:[167]

> The contingency plan for an overt resumption of the offensive in Laos is in tolerably good shape; but it is now agreed that it is more likely that the other side will concentrate on doing Diem in than on capturing the Mekong Valley during this fighting season.
>
> As for Viet-Nam, it is agreed that we must move quite radically to avoid perhaps slow but total defeat. The sense of this town is that, with Southern Laos open, Diem simply cannot cope.

Rostow's own proposal was that the U.S. should tell the Russians "the destruction of Diem via infiltration could not and would not be accepted," and that Harriman should emphasize this point in the Geneva talks. Secondly, the U.S. should seek U.N. agreement on a United Nations inspection mission in Southern Laos. This would have the advantage, he said, of causing the Communists to reduce their activity in the area of the Ho Chi Minh Trail, as well as bringing the U.N. into the Southeast Asia situation, a move which Rostow said he thought was "essential in the long run." Thirdly, he proposed deploying a 25,000-man SEATO border patrol force in Vietnam. Among other things, this would have the advantage of bolstering Diem and giving the U.S. more leverage on military matters, restraining a North Vietnamese invasion of South Vietnam, and strengthening U.S. bargaining power with the Russians by making the withdrawal of such a U.S. force a "bargaining counter in a Vietnamese settlement." Above all, "The presence of a SEATO force in South Viet-Nam would make it clear . . . that the attempt to destroy the South Vietnamese government by force could not be carried forward to a conclusion without risking an escalation of the fight. This would not merely threaten Hanoi with air and naval action, but would threaten Soviet or Chinese Communist involvement. And this I doubt Moscow wants."

In conclusion, Rostow repeated his recommendation that Taylor and Lansdale be sent to Vietnam for a review of the situation, and said, "For us the gut issue as I see it is this: We are deeply committed in Viet-Nam; if the situation deteriorates, we will have to go in; the situation is, in fact, actively deteriorating; if we go in now, the costs—human and otherwise—are likely to be less than if we wait."

As policymakers in the executive branch, without any apparent knowledge of or participation in such proceedings on the part of Congress, continued to discuss what action should be taken in view of the increasing threat to Vietnam, the JCS was asked for its reaction to Rostow's proposal for a SEATO border patrol force. It replied on October 9 that this proposal was not feasible. Instead, the JCS again recommended the implementation of SEATO Plan 5 in a "concentrated effort" in Laos which would also have the effect of protecting the Vietnamese border as well as giving "concrete evidence of US determination to stand firm against further communist advances world-wide."[168] ". . . lacking an acceptable political

---

[167]Same location.
[168]For JCS objections to Rostow's proposal, see *PP*, DOD ed., book 11, pp. 297-298.

settlement prior to the resumption of overt hostitlities," the JCS said, "there is no feasible military alternative of lesser magnitude which will prevent the loss of Laos, South Vietnam and ultimately Southeast Asia."

If SEATO Plan 5 deployments caused escalation, the JCS added, there would have to be additional mobilization in the U.S. in order to maintain U.S. strategic reserves, adding, ". . . we cannot afford to be preoccupied with Berlin to the extent that we close our eyes to the situation in Southeast Asia, which is more critical from a military viewpoint." "It is not a question of the desirability of having two limited war situations going at the same time. The fact of the matter is that we may be faced with such a contingency."[169]

According to the plan suggested by the JCS on October 9, the SEATO force would be stationed in South Vietnam near the Laotian border in the vicinity of Pleiku for the purpose of controlling the central highlands, the key area for defending Laos and South Vietnam. There would be 22,800 men, of whom approximately 9,600 would be ground combat troops, including 5,000 from the U.S. (Of the total force, 13,200 would be from the U.S.) A U.S. brigade would also be stationed in Thailand. "Our military posture," the JCS stated, "is such that the employment of the SEATO forces would not adversely affect our capability to conduct planned operations in Europe relating to Berlin."

The JCS plan called for offensive action by the SEATO force against Communist threats to the border of South Vietnam or to the force itself, and retaliation against North Vietnam for any overt military intervention in South Vietnam or Laos.

If North Vietnam were to "overtly intervene," the SEATO force would need to be increased to more than 200,000, including an increase in U.S. forces to 129,000 from the original 13,200. If the Chinese intervened, 278,000 SEATO troops would be needed, and consideration would have to be given "whether to attack selected targets in North China with conventional weapons and whether to initiate use of nuclear weapons against targets in direct support of Chinese operations in Laos."[170]

As preparations for a meeting with the President on October 11 continued, William P. Bundy, then Acting Assistant Secretary of Defense for International Security Affairs, sent a memorandum on October 10 to McNamara in which he, too, advocated an "early and hard-hitting" military operation in Vietnam by a SEATO force:[171]

> For what one man's feel is worth, mine—based on very close touch with Indochina in the 1954 war and civil war afterwards till Diem took hold—is that it *is* really now or never if we are to arrest the gains being made by the Viet Cong. . . . An early and hard-hitting operation has a good chance (70% would be my guess) of *arresting* things and giving Diem a chance to do better and clean up. Even if we follow up hard, on the lines the JCS are working out after yesterday's meeting, however, the chances are not much better that we will in fact be able to *clean up* the situation. It *all* depends on Diem's effectiveness,

[169]*Ibid.*, pp. 297-298.
[170]For the JCS plan, see *ibid.*, pp. 300-311.
[171]*Ibid.*, p. 312. (emphases in original)

which is very problematical. The 30% chance is that we would wind up like the French in 1954; white men can't win this kind of fight.

On a 70-30 basis, I would myself favor going in. But if we let, say, a month go by before we move, the odds will slide (both short-term shock effect and long-term chance) down to 60-40, 50-50, and so on. Laos under a Souvanna Phouma deal is more likely than not to go sour, and will more and more make things difficult in South Viet-Nam, which again underscores the element of time.

Bundy commented later on this memo, with its "breathless character." "I do not recall," he said, "that my prognosis was argued specifically, or necessarily shared. The memorandum was not circulated beyond McNamara and a few others; all it does in history is to express a mood that was widely shared, that we had to act fast and hard if we were to act at all. Also that it was not an open-and-shut decision."[172]

For the October 11 meeting with the President the principal document was a paper of October 10, 1961, drafted by U. Alexis Johnson, which combined the ideas of Taylor, Rostow and the Southeast Asia Task Force with the military proposals of the JCS.

This paper, "Concept for Intervention in Viet-Nam," proposed the use of SEATO (primarily U.S.) forces "to arrest and hopefully to reverse the deteriorating situation" in Vietnam, while at the same time having a favorable effect on the Laos negotiations."[173] Deployment of SEATO forces, however, "cannot be taken without accepting as our real and ultimate objective the defeat of the Viet Cong, and making Viet-Nam secure in the hands of an anti-Communist government."

Initially these forces, which would be stationed at Pleiku, would consist of 11,000 ground combat forces, which would be supported by 11,800 air, naval, and other forces, bringing the total to 22,800. To "clean up the Viet Cong threat" in South Vietnam, however, as many as 40,000 might be needed. This number would increase if the North Vietnamese intervened in force in South Vietnam, and would increase further if the Chinese intervened. There might ultimately be a requirement for as many as four divisions, plus supporting forces, from the U.S.-based reserve forces, and this might necessitate "a step-up in the present mobilization, possibly of major proportions."

The paper pointed out that the ultimate force requirements would depend "above all on whether the effort leads to much more and better fighting by Diem's forces. They alone can win in the end."

The "rules of engagement" for these forces would allow them to do battle with any Communist forces "encountered in any reasonable proximity to the border or threatening the SEATO forces." In addition, they could engage in "hot pursuit" into Laos and possibly into Cambodia if necessary.

[172]Bundy MS., ch. 4, pp. 12A, 13.
[173]Johnson's paper, including two "supplemental notes," was declassified, with some sanitation, in 1982, and is in the Kennedy Library, NSF Country File, Vietnam.

The paper advocated prompt action in deploying these SEATO forces before a Laos settlement could be reached, because of the fact that with a settlement "it would be much more difficult to find a political base upon which to execute this plan."

The "pros" and "cons" of the proposed action were presented. Among the "cons" was: "The plan itself would not itself solve the underlying problem of ridding SVN of communist guerrillas." Also, "It breaks the Geneva Accords and puts responsibility on the U.S. for rationalizing the action before the U.N. and the world." Furthermore, there would be the "risk of being regarded as interlopers a la the French. . . ." In addition, the Communists might react by a "change of tactics back to small-scale operations [which] might leave this force in a stagnant position."

Among the "pros" was that such a move could strengthen the Vietnamese as well as U.S. influence with the Vietnamese and the U.S. bargaining position with the Russians. Moreover, "If we go into South Viet-Nam now with SEATO, the costs would be much less than if we wait and go in later, or lose SVN."

In connection with this paper, Ambassador Nolting had reported on October 1 that Diem had asked for a bilateral defense treaty with the U.S. Diem was said to be concerned that the situation in Laos would become more serious, and that the effectiveness of the proposed deployment of SEATO forces would be reduced by British and French resistance to getting involved. According to Nolting, "changing U.S. policy in Laos, especially SEATO decision to use force if necessary to protect SVN and Thailand, would relieve pressure for bilateral treaty."[174] (On October 13, Nolting reported that Minister Nguyen Dinh Thuan had requested, on behalf of Diem, U.S. combat forces in lieu of a defense treaty.)[175]

At the meeting on October 11, President Kennedy decided to send General Taylor, accompanied by Rostow, Lansdale, William J. Jorden (Department of State) and Cottrell, to Vietnam to review the political and military feasibility of deploying U.S. forces, either a larger group as proposed by the Johnson memo, or a smaller group with "a more limited objective than dealing with the Viet Cong; in other words, such a small force would probably go in at Tourane and possibly another southern port principally for the purpose of establishing a U.S. 'presence' in Vietnam." The group was also asked to review other alternatives to the use of U.S. forces, such as more economic and military aid.

In addition, Kennedy approved certain specific actions recommended in the Johnson paper, including sending the Air Force's "Jungle Jim" Squadron (12 planes especially equipped for counterinsurgency warfare); initiating attacks against Communist installations at Tchepone, using U.S. advisers if necessary; preparing publication of the white paper on Vietnam, and developing plans for presenting the Vietnam case to the U.N.. Other unspecified actions were approved.[176]

---

[174]*PP,* Gravel ed., vol. II, p. 649.
[175]*Ibid.,* pp. 651-652.
[176]NSAM 104, Oct. 13, 1961, in *ibid.,* DOD ed., book 11, p. 328. (There is no available summary of the meeting.) The NSAM did not reveal the instruction to the Taylor group concerning the review of the use of U.S. forces. This was provided by a memorandum from Roswell Gilpatric summarizing the meeting, which is reprinted on pp. 322-323.

With respect to the decision to use the "Jungle Jim" Squadron, there is this additional information in the Air Force history of the Vietnam war:[177]

On October 11, 1961, President Kennedy authorized the sending of a U.S. Air Force unit to South Vietnam. The following day, a detachment of the 4400th Combat Crew Training Squadron, code-named "Farm Gate," flew to South Vietnam. Stationed at Bien Hoa Air Base just north of Saigon, the 4400th CCTS flew combat modified T-28 fighter-bomber trainers, SC-47s, and B-26s, redesignated "Reconnaissance Bombers" (RB-26s) in deference to the 1954 Geneva Conventions prohibition against the introduction of bombers into Indochina. On December 16, Secretary of Defense Robert S. McNamara authorized participation in combat operations, provided a Vietnamese crewmember was aboard the strike aircraft.

In order to conceal the purpose of the Taylor trip, in part to prevent premature speculation about the question of using U.S. forces, Kennedy said in the NSC meeting that he was going to announce it as an "economic survey." He apparently decided not to do so, but on October 14 the *New York Times* ran a story to that effect, stating, among other things, that military leaders, as well as General Taylor, were reluctant to use U.S. forces, and that local forces assisted by the U.S. would be used instead. As the *Pentagon Papers* says, "this was simply untrue." Kennedy was not pleased about Diem's request for troops, as well as about news stories that troops would be sent, and had decided to plant the version contained in the *New York Times*. That story, as the *Pentagon Papers* adds, ". . . had the desired effect. Speculation about combat troops almost disappeared from news stories, and Diem never again raised the question of combat troops: the initiative from now on came from Taylor and Nolting, and their recommendations were very closely held."[178]

---

[177] Tilford, *Search and Rescue in Southeast Asia*, p. 36.
[178] *PP*, Gravel ed., vol. II, p. 82.

CHAPTER 2

THE NEW U.S. COMMITMENT: "LIMITED PARTNERS"

General Taylor and his party left for Vietnam on October 17, 1961, stopping at Honolulu to confer with Adm. Harry D. Felt, the U.S. Commander in Chief, Pacific (CINCPAC). Felt recommended against deploying U.S. forces in Vietnam "until we have exhausted other means for helping Diem." He was concerned that the use of U.S. forces would raise the colonialist issue, spur the Communists into greater action, and eventually involve U.S. troops in extended combat. He agreed, however, that the U.S. had to play a stronger role in Vietnam, and thought that SEATO forces might eventually be required in Laos to prevent infiltration of South Vietnam along the Ho Chi Minh Trail.[1]

After arriving in Vietnam on October 18, the group spent about 10 days reviewing the situation and conferring with Diem and his associates, and then stopped briefly in Thailand before returning to Washington on November 2.[2]

Taylor said later that he and his party were in Vietnam, ". . . at a time when the situation was the darkest since the early days of 1954."[3] He added:

> Vietcong strength had increased from an estimated 10,000 in January 1961 to 17,000 in October; they were clearly on the move in the delta, in the highlands, and along the plain on the north central coast. The South Vietnamese were watching with dismay the situation in Laos and the negotiations in Geneva, which convinced them that there would soon be a Communist-dominated government in Vientiane. The worst flood in dec-

---

[1] Kennedy Library, NSF Country File, Vietnam, CINCPAC to Washington, Oct. 20, 1961. Subsequently, however, Admiral Felt agreed with the proposal made by Taylor to send U.S. military units to Vietnam under the guise of helping with flood relief. CINCPAC to Washington, Oct. 24, 1961, same location.

[2] In connection with the Taylor group's visit to Thailand, the U.S. Ambassador, Kenneth T. Young, a respected Foreign Service officer who had worked on Southeast Asia for many years both in Defense and in State, gave Taylor a memorandum outlining his views on the situation. Kennedy Library, NSF Regional Security File, Southeast Asia General, 1961. "Defensibility of Southeast Asia and United States Commitments," Oct. 27, 1961, "I believe denial of Southeast Asia to Viet Cong, Chinese or Russian control," he said, "is indispensible for United States interests and purposes in the whole world. . . . Southeast Asia is the critical bottleneck stopping Sino-Soviet territorial and ideological expansion—territorial in Asia, ideological in the whole world. Southeast Asia is something like the hub of a wheel; lose the hub and the wheel collapses. And Laos, plus South Vietnam, is the cotter-pin holding the hub. If we let Laos-South Vietnam go, the Viet Cong and Chinese Communists will soon dominate all of Southeast Asia, including Indonesia. The United States will be forced off the mainland of Asia, Australia will be surrounded and actually flanked, while India and Japan will be permanently separated. All of this is what the Communists are trying to do in Asia. Their success there will intensify their impact in Africa and South America."

Young outlined a strategy to defend Southeast Asia against "Communist small-scale, rural aggression," which he said was the heart of the problem. A central feature of this proposal was establishment of an "American Southeast Asian Unified Command" (under CINCPAC) in Thailand, with small U.S. combat teams in southeast Thailand, Vietnam and Laos to "reverse the trend of doubt, discouragement and despair in Southeast Asia."

[3] Maxwell Taylor, *Swords and Plowshares* (New York: W. W. Norton, 1972), p. 228.

ades was ravaging the Mekong delta, destroying crops and live-stock and rendering hundreds of thousands homeless. . . . In the wake of this series of profoundly depressing events, it was no exaggeration to say that the entire country was suffering from a collapse of national morale—an obvious fact which made a strong impression on the members of our mission. In subsequent weeks as we meditated on what the United States could or should do in South Vietnam, the thought was always with us that we needed something visible which could be done quickly to offset the oppressive feeling of hopelessness which seemed to permeate all ranks of Vietnamese society.

Whether or not this assessment of the state of affairs was accu-rate—and one might wonder how well-equipped Taylor and his as-sociates were to make such sweeping psychological and social judg-ments about a culture with which (with the possible exception of Lansdale) they were almost totally unfamiliar—they apparently be-lieved that it was accurate, and acted accordingly. They proposed in their report to President Kennedy that the U.S. take "vigorous action" to assist South Vietnam:[4]

From all quarters in Southeast Asia the message on Viet-nam is the same; vigorous American action is needed to buy time for Vietnam to mobilize and organize its real assets; but the time for such a turn around has nearly run out. And if Vietnam goes, it will be exceedingly difficult if not impossible to hold Southeast Asia. What will be lost is not merely a cru-cial piece of real estate, but the faith that the U.S. has the will and the capacity to deal with the Communist offensive in that area.

Two things were needed, the report said: first, a military commit-ment to demonstrate U.S. resolve, and, second, an "insertion" of Americans into military and government operations in Vietnam in order to "show them how the job might be done. . . ." By this "shift in the American relation to the Vietnamese effort from advice to limited partnership," the report stated, ". . . Vietnamese performance in every domain can be substantially improved if Americans are prepared to work side by side with the Vietnamese on the key problems."

The proposal for "inserting" Americans as governmental advis-ers came from Lansdale, who called it "U.S. political-psychological-military-economic encadrement in Vietnam. . . ," in which highly selected Americans, acting as "collaborators," would provide "oper-ational guidance" at key decision points in the top of the Vietnam-

---

[4]The Taylor report (including its tabular material), often referred to as the Taylor-Rostow report, has been largely declassified and is in the Kennedy Library, NSF Country File, Vietnam. The report itself is 25 pages long. Attached are eight appendices of reports from each of the functional areas to which Taylor made assignments. These were as follows:
1. Political-Social, Sterling Cottrell and William Jorden
2. Military, General William H. Craig
3. Political Warfare, W. W. Rostow
4. Unconventional Warfare, General Edward Lansdale
5. Covert Activities, Joseph Smith of the CIA;
6. MAAG and Military Aid, Rear Adm. Luther C. Heinz
7. Economic Aid, James W. Howe
8. Research and Development, Dr. George W. Rathjens and Mr. William H. Godel
For ease of reference, the *Pentagon Papers*, which contains excerpts from the report, is cited herein as the source for most of the quoted material.

ese government.[5] "It will take Americans who are willing to stake all on the outcome, who know their tasks, and who can act with great understanding in collaboration with the Vietnamese." "I believe that one year of devoted duty by such Americans," Lansdale said, "would spark a complete psychological change in Vietnam's situation, give the Vietnamese the hope of winning and take the initiative away from the Communists. . . ." Without this "spark," Lansdale added, the Vietnamese were going to "lose their country." With such direct American help he thought that "much of the present Vietnamese bickering and hesitancy would disappear as a new sense of direction is given them."

Lansdale's position was that "Vietnam is dangerously far down the road to a Communist takeover, against the will of its people. . . . Mistrust, jealousy, and the shock of Communist savagery have contributed to making a none-too-certain government bureaucracy even more unsure of itself. Pride and self-protection still cover this unsureness, but the cover is wearing thin."

"It is time that we in the free world got angry about what is happening in Vietnam and about what is happening elsewhere in Southeast Asia. With our anger, there should come a deep commitment to stop the Communists in their tracks and hit back hard."

If the U.S. encadrement plan could be used effectively, he added, ". . . we will have found the means of meeting similar Communist threats elsewhere . . . this fuller U.S. role in helping free nations remain free will give a new spark to freedom throughout the world."

In order to provide the necessary sense of national purpose and administrative flexibility under which to conduct such a program, Lansdale said, "The U.S. needs to declare a 'sub-limited' war on the Communists in Vietnam and then to wage it successfully. Since such an action is not envisioned by our Constitution, a way of so doing must be found which is consistent with our heritage. The most natural declaration would be a proclamation by the President, which would state U.S. objectives and clearly outline the principles of human liberty involved. The U.S. Congress would vote support of these objectives and principles. Implementing action would then be carried out by Executive Order."

Although Lansdale felt that the encadrement of U.S. advisers had become necessary, he was not critical of Diem. This was not the case with William Jorden, however. In his report to Taylor on the political situation, Jorden took the position that "Pressures for political and administrative change in South Viet Nam have reached the explosion point. Without some badly needed reforms, it is unlikely that any program of assistance to that country can be fully effective."[6] "The arguments in favor of change, almost any change," he added, "are impressive." Indeed, "If change does not come in an orderly way, it will almost certainly come through forceful means carried out by an alliance of political and military elements."

---

[5]These quotations from Lansdale are from a memorandum he sent to Taylor during the trip, entitled "Unconventional Warfare," and a subsequent and longer memorandum to Taylor entitled, "Vietnam," which was included as part of the unconventional warfare appendix of Taylor's report. Both, undated, are located with the Taylor report in the Kennedy Library.
[6]"The Political Situation in South Viet Nam," Oct. 30, 1961, included in the Taylor report.

In this situation, Jorden said, U.S. options ranged from doing nothing to engineering a coup. He rejected both extremes, saying that a coup ". . . is not something we do well. It has little to recommend itself." His recommendation was that the U.S. should avoid identification with Diem, and should support changes which would lead to necessary reforms:

The situation provides an opportunity for the United States to stand once again for change in this part of the world, to press for measures that are both efficient and more democratic. We must identify ourselves with the people of Viet Nam and with their aspirations, not with a man or an administration. We must do what we can to help release the tremendous energy, ability and idealism that exist in Viet Nam. We must suggest, not demand; we must advise not dictate; but we must not hesitate to stand for the things that we and the Vietnamese know to be worthwhile and just in the conduct of political affairs.

If the new U.S. program resulting from the Taylor mission's recommendations did not produce the necessary improvement in the Vietnamese government, however, Jorden said that the U.S. would then have to consider "backing changes that would reduce sharply the role of the President [Diem] and would alter his status to that of figurehead and symbol."

In his report for Taylor, Sterling Cottrell was less sanguine about the possibility of achieving changes in Diem's government.[7] "Diem," he said, "like Sukarno, Rhee, and Chiang is cast in the mold of an oriental despot, and cannot be 'brought around' by threats, or insistence on adoption of purely Western concepts. . . . Diem, having been subject to military coups, cannot be expected to delegate concentrated authority to the military. . . . Diem is not a planner, in the Western sense. . . . Diem is not a good administrator, in the Western sense." Cottrell's conclusion was that "Given the virtual impossibility of changing perceptibly the basic weaknesses of Ngo Dinh Diem, and in view of our past unsuccessful efforts to reform the GVN from the top down, we should now direct our major efforts from the bottom up, and supply all effective kinds of military and economic aid." But Cottrell was opposed to a U.S. commitment to Vietnam in the form of a mutual security pact: "Since it is an open question whether the GVN can succeed even with U.S. assistance, it would be a mistake for the U.S. to commit itself irrevocably to the defeat of the Communists in SVN."

In his report to Kennedy, Taylor said that he and his associates had considered but rejected "the removal" of Diem because "it would be dangerous for us to engineer a coup under present tense circumstances," and because they believed that Diem's administrative weaknesses could be overcome ". . . by bringing about a series of *de facto* administrative changes via persuasion at high levels; collaboration with Diem's aides who want improved administration; and by a U.S. operating presence at many working levels,

---

[7]"Viet-Nam," Oct. 27, 1961, included in the Taylor report.

using the U.S. presence . . . for forcing the Vietnamese to get their house in order in one area after another."[8]

A few weeks earlier, a suggestion for handling Diem had been made by Frank C. Child, formerly a member of the Michigan State University group in Vietnam. In a memorandum of October 5, 1961, which was sent to Carl Kaysen of the NSC staff, who in turn gave it to staff member Robert Johnson, Child said that Diem "can only postpone defeat . . . he cannot win." "Projecting the present trend," he added, "South Viet Nam will surely fall to the Viet Cong in 12-18 months. . . ." There was an alternative, he said, after referring to the abortive but poorly led coup of 1960: "There are intelligent and able men in Viet Nam who could provide effective leadership and even capture the imagination of the population. A military *coup*—or an assassin's bullet—are the only means by which this leadership will ever be exercised."[9]

On October 31 Johnson replied to Kaysen:

> . . . the analysis is generally sound. The prescription is one which the Government is unlikely to adopt. We are going to make at least one more effort to do the job with Diem. It has been the policy of this Administration to let up somewhat on continuous haggling with him over reforms. I believe—or perhaps it would be better to say hope—that we will now condition our military intervention (if it occurs) on real performance on a whole series of reforms designed primarily to make the governmental operations—including military operations—more efficient.

With respect to the military aspect of the Taylor group's proposal for having Americans work side by side with the Vietnamese, the report stated, "To execute this program of limited partnership requires a change in the charter, the spirit, and the organization of the MAAG in South Vietnam. It must be shifted from an advisory group to something nearer—but not quite—an operational headquarters in a theater of war. . . . The U.S. should become a limited partner in the war, avoiding formalized advice on the one hand, trying to run the war, on the other."[10]

In proposing that the U.S. make a military commitment (6,000-8,000 troops, some logistical and some combat, to be sent initially under the guise of assisting with recovery from the flood), Taylor and his group took the position that the U.S. effort to defend Vietnam could not succeed without such a move. They said they accepted the fact that if this first contingent was not adequate, it would be difficult to resist the argument that additional troops would be needed, and with each increase the prestige of the U.S. would become more involved and Communist retaliatory moves more likely. Moreover, if U.S. forces were used to protect (close) the frontier and "clean-up" the insurgency in South Vietnam, ". . . there is no limit to our possible commitment (unless we attack the source in Hanoi.)" Despite these risks, the Taylor group, based on unani-

[8]For specific suggestions for the assignment of U.S. advisers, see the excerpts from the report in *PP*, Gravel ed., vol. II, pp. 652-654.

[9]Kennedy Library, NSF Country File, Vietnam. On Child's typescript someone crossed through the words "—or an assassin's bullet—are" and added the word "is" after the word "coup." See also Child's article "Vietnam—The Eleventh Hour," *New Republic* (December 1961).

[10]*PP*, Gravel ed., vol. II, p. 653.

mous agreement among U.S. personnel in Vietnam, as well as among Vietnamese officials, concluded that such a military commitment was necessary.[11]

In this connection, a section of the report proposed and written by W. W. Rostow posed the question of how the U.S. could effectively combat the insurgency in South Vietnam, and elsewhere, and raised the possibility of ultimately striking at North Vietnam:[12]

> It is my judgment and that of my colleagues that the United States must decide how it will cope with Khrushchev's "wars of liberation" which are really para-wars of guerrilla aggression. This is a new and dangerous Communist technique which bypasses our traditional political and military responses. While the final answer lies beyond the scope of this report, it is clear to me that the time may come in our relations to Southeast Asia when we must declare our intention to attack the source of guerrilla aggression in North Vietnam and impose on the Hanoi Government a price for participating in the current war which is commensurate with the damage being inflicted on its neighbors to the south.

Sterling Cottrell was even more specific. "If the combined U.S.-GVN efforts are insufficient to reverse the trend," he said, "we should then move to the 'Rostow Plan' of applying graduated punitive measures on the DRV with weapons of our choosing."[13]

With respect to covert action, Smith of the CIA, who had been responsible for studying this aspect of the situation, recommended to Taylor that the U.S. should apply in Vietnam the doctrine learned from experience in the Philippines and in Greece:[14]

> This doctrine generally concerns itself with three kinds of measures that are needed to extinguish classical Maoist guerrilla tactics such as those employed in Vietnam. These three basic measures are:
>
> 1. The establishment of a tough, mobile striking force in sufficient numbers to meet the guerrillas on their own terms and defeat them in the jungles or mountains where they thrive. This force, wherever possible, should take advantage of the technological advantages we possess and thus be equipped with the capacity for vertical envelopment by parachute, helicopter, or fixed wing aircraft. The

---

[11] *Ibid.*, pp. 90-91. In his report to Taylor, General Craig, the U.S. military representative on the mission, took the position that the proposed introduction of U.S. forces into South Vietnam (which he referred to as SEATO Plan 7), while helping the South Vietnamese, "would not contribute substantially to the over-all problem of SE Asia. . . ." (Tab D of the Taylor report.) From the military standpoint, he said, ". . . any concept for the defense of SE Asia which does not include Laos or substantial parts of it is militarily unsound." The preferred way of defending Southeast Asia, he said, was to implement SEATO Plan 5 in Laos. This would also have the advantage of cutting off infiltration into Vietnam via the Ho Chi Minh Trail, and was therefore "the method of saving SVN by intervention offering the greatest chance of success. . . ."

[12] *PP*, Gravel ed., vol. II, p. 98.

[13] *Ibid.*, p. 96. (This was called by some, "Rostow Plan 6.") Taylor and his group proposed the 8,000-10,000 man force as a token unit to provide an American presence, to provide security in the area they were stationed, and to act as an advance party if additional forces were sent subsequently. Some years later Taylor was asked about the decision to recommend such a limited commitment. He replied, "Had I known what the future held the better course would have been to introduce a strong American combat force right then, and see whether that wouldn't deter the enemy when they saw that indeed the United States was ready to fight for this place if necessary." Charlton and Moncrieff, *Many Reasons Why*, pp. 74-75.

[14] "Covert Annex," included in the Taylor report.

primary mission of this force should be to harrass the enemy, his lines of communication and his bases of supply, and to prevent the enemy from fighting "set piece" engagements.

2. The sympathy of the populace among which the communist guerrillas exist must be denied to the communists and won to the side of free forces. This involves a whole variety of programs in the political, psychological, economic realm, basic to which is the friendliest possible relationship between the free forces and the civilian populace.

3. To the maximum extent feasible and possible, the fight must be taken to the enemy. The enemy must be given cause for concern for his own home area and thus restricted in his capability to provide for the needs of his guerrilla movement in another area.

Most of the specific covert action proposals in the appendices of the Taylor report are still classified, but one suggested by Lansdale, which was never implemented, was to use Chinese Nationalist soldiers to provide "human defoliation" in Zone D north of Saigon which was generally controlled by the Communists:

The timber in this jungle contains valuable hardwoods. If the timber concession was let to Chinese Nationalists, say a commercial firm which was composed of veterans who volunteered for the task, the "fire-break" plan of sectioning Zone D might be carried out at minimal cost, with a politically-acceptable introduction of Chinese Nationalists, and with definite benefit to both the welfare and morale of Chinese veterans in Taiwan. A small Vietnamese unit could be attached to such an outfit, as "protection" to give proper commercial coloration to the venture. However, the Chinats should be sufficiently armed for self-protection, which would include patrolling in the vicinity of the lumber operation. The Vietnamese unit could forward intelligence reports from this operation, as well as furnish coordination when larger Viet Cong units were used and the Vietnamese Armed Forces were needed for the strike at the enemy.

Lansdale also mentioned (this, too, was not implemented) that consideration was being given to having ". . . a group of about 2,000 [Nationalist Chinese] veterans, ages 35-40, to come into Vietnam as Vietnamese, being 'sheep-dipped' in Cholon [the Chinese suburb of Saigon] and given Vietnamese names. They will train village Self Defense Corps in handling weapons, patrol action, and intelligence reporting."[15]

Washington Debates the Taylor Report

Upon returning to Washington on November 2, 1961, Taylor submitted the group's report to the President. On November 4, Taylor met with the members of the NSC, and on November 5 with the President, to discuss the report.

---

[15]These proposals are included in Lansdale's memorandum for Taylor, "Vietnam," cited above.

This is William Bundy's account of the November 4 meeting chaired by Ball:[16]

> The Saturday [November 4, 1961] discussion was long and pointed. Almost at once there was dissatisfaction with the half-in, half-out, nature of the "flood relief task force," and a consensus of disbelief that once thus engaged the US could easily decide to pull the force out. McNamara in particular argued that the gut issue was whether to make a "Berlin-type" US commitment. By this phrase he and others meant a categorical pledge to use every US resource to prevent a result [communist victory]. . . .
>
> Without such a categorical commitment, the argument ran, sending any significant forces was a confused action, while with a commitment the question of forces becomes a relatively simple question of what was needed for practical missions. To use military force for what were conceded to be primarily psychological purposes made not only the JCS but the civilian leaders in the Pentagon uneasy.

In these and subsequent discussions leading up to final decisions on November 15, the major issue continued to be that of U.S. military involvement. This was intertwined with the problem of Diem's leadership, however, and whether, if the U.S. got involved, there would be a Vietnamese government worth fighting for. In this connection, in preparation for another White House meeting on November 7, Washington cabled Ambassador Nolting on November 4, requesting his views on the possibility of getting Diem to accept, as a *quid pro quo* for U.S. agreement to a "joint effort," a plan for delegating authority in order to make the Vietnamese Government more efficient.[17] The cable stated, "Feeling is strong that major changes will be required if joint effort is to be successful in that US cannot be asked further to engage its prestige and forces while machinery of Diem government remains inadequate and thus full capabilities South Vietnamese forces and population not be realized."

The cable proposed several changes, the principal one being that a National Emergency Council should be established (based on Diem's declaration of a national emergency in October, just prior to Taylor's arrival), headed by a key figure ("if possible Vice President Nguyen Ngoc Tho"), with Nguyen Dinh Thuan as Secretary, through which all business to and from Diem and the departments of the government would be transacted, with Diem's brother Nhu as the go-between.

Moreover, "a mature hard-headed" American would participate in all decisions of the Council, and coordinate with the U.S. Government.

Nolting replied on November 7 that Diem would probably agree to the establishment of such a council, but probably only if it were chaired by Nhu. Concerning the proposal for an American to participate in council decisions, Nolting said he did not think Diem would agree. "This step would, I think, be interpreted by him and by most Vietnamese as handing over Govt of SVN to US."[18]

[16]Bundy MS., ch. 4, pp. 22-23. Notes of the meeting are still classified.
[17]Kennedy Library, NSF Country File, Vietnam, Washington to Saigon 545, Nov. 4, 1961.
[18]Saigon to Washington 608, Nov. 7, 1961, same location.

During debate on the Taylor report various approaches were proposed by the various participants. Defense supported Taylor's recommendations, but preferred a larger force, while most policymakers in State (Washington, not Saigon or Bangkok) preferred new and stronger programs to exact a better performance from Diem, and deployment of U.S. forces only if these failed.

In both Defense and State there was concern about the consequences of Taylor's proposal to send only a small force to Vietnam in connection with flood relief. As NSC staff member Robert Johnson told McGeorge Bundy on October 31, "many in Washington are convinced that the longer the forces remained in Viet-Nam, the more they would come under attack and the more they would become involved in combat." This, he said, led to the conclusion that "If we do not intend to be forced out of SEA [Southeast Asia] altogether, there is real doubt as to whether, once we committed forces, we could withdraw them until reasonable security had been restored in Viet Nam." Thus, Johnson said, ". . . in making a decision on the Taylor proposal we need to face and to decide in principle the question of whether we are prepared, if necessary, to step up very considerably our military commitment in Viet Nam. If we commit 6-8,000 troops and then pull them out when the going got rough we will be finished in Viet Nam and probably in all of Southeast Asia."

Johnson reported that the Vietnam Task Force had developed an alternative to Taylor's plan, under which only 1500 U.S. troops, part combat and part logistical, would be sent to the flood zone. They would be assigned to work only on flood relief, and although prepared to defend themselves, they would withdraw if attacked. Meanwhile, the U.S. would make the commitment of additional troops contingent on Vietnam's performance, as well as making a decision, should such troops be sent, to move to a full-scale SEATO operation.[19]

Robert Johnson's own position on the Taylor group's proposals was one of general concurrence. While he thought there should be agreement in principle to commit combat forces if necessary, he did not believe they should be sent at that time. Concerning the proposal for attacking Hanoi, he told Rostow that he shared "some of Bill Bundy's doubts as to whether we will, in fact, be able to convince the neutrals of the justice and our allies of the wisdom of such a course. . . ."[20]

By November 14 (six days later), however, Johnson had apparently agreed to the proposed deployment of some U.S. troops to Vietnam. In a memorandum to Rostow he said:[21]

> I fear that we are losing a strategic moment for the introduction of U.S. troops units. The world has been made aware of the crisis in Viet Nam as a result of the Taylor mission. Both the [Communist] Bloc and the Free World are going to look upon the *actions* we take now as the key to our future actions no matter what we may *say*. A plate glass window on the 17th

---

[19]Same location.
[20]Johnson memo to W. W. Rostow, Nov. 8, 1961, same location. Three months earlier Johnson had taken the position that U.S. forces might have to be sent to Laos. See fn. 151, p. 61.
[21]Kennedy Library, NSF Country File.

parallel or a flood relief task force could make a great political difference not only in Viet Nam, but in the whole area. Such intervention later might have much less political effect and may have to be on a much larger scale to have military effect. In any event, in the interim uncertainty as to our intentions will grow.

Johnson was also concerned about "the relationship between our actions and the diplomatic noise we make." He thought it would be a mistake to tell other nations, especially the Soviet Union, that the U.S. intended to defend Vietnam before deciding to do so. "I myself think," he said, "that we ought to *decide* now the key question of whether we are prepared to introduce combat troops if necessary even if we are not going to introduce them now. That is obviously the ultimate test of whether we are prepared to prevent the fall of Viet Nam."

If troops were not sent, Johnson added, the U.S. should make clear its intention to defend South Vietnam, either by agreeing to the request of the South Vietnamese for a bilateral defense agreement, or by an announcement that the U.S. considered its SEATO obligations binding regardless of the position of other SEATO countries.[22]

NSC staff member Robert Komer again urged military intervention, and on October 31 he sent a memo to McGeorge Bundy making the argument "why over-reacting, if anything, is best at this point":[23]

> Though no admirer of domino theory, I doubt if our position in SEA could survive "loss" of S. Vietnam on top of that of Laos. Moreover, could Administration afford yet another defeat, domestically?
>
> Perhaps there are alternatives to sending US troops which would have fair chance of doing the job. But I doubt it. And if the alternatives fail, we still face the question of sending troops—at a later and less satisfactory time.
>
> The case for acting now is that in the long run it is likely to be the most economical. True, we may end up with something approaching another Korea, but I think the best way of avoiding this is to move fast now before the war spreads to the extent that a Korean type commitment is required.
>
> Sending troops now would also lead to much recrimination and some risks of escalation, *but both risks and recriminations would be much greater, say, a year from now* when the whole situation is a lot more heated up.
>
> Admittedly, intervention alone does not solve our problem—but at least it buys us time to do so. . . .
>
> . . . I'm no happier than anyone about getting involved in another squalid, secondary theatre in Asia. But we'll end up doing so sooner or later anyway because we won't be willing to accept another defeat. If so, the real question is not whether but how soon and how much!

---

[22]This interpretation which was subsequently stated in the so-called Rusk-Thanat agreement of March 1962, had been first raised in March 1961. See fn. 102, p. 114.
[23]Kennedy Library, NSF Regional Security File, Southeast Asia General, 1961, "The Risks in Southeast Asia." (emphasis in original)

Komer added, however, "If we move in, we must exact in turn from Diem a whole series of iron-clad commitments."

Harriman, Bowles, as well as John Kenneth Galbraith (a Harvard economist, then U.S. Ambassador to India) and Abram J. Chayes (a member of the Harvard law school faculty, and at the time serving as the Legal Adviser of the State Department), proposed variations of an alternative plan. To avoid military intervention, as well as a long-term U.S. commitment to Vietnam, they recommended the neutralization of Vietnam along the lines of the agreement being negotiated for Laos. In memoranda for the President, Harriman, as well as Galbraith and Chayes, also argued that the U.S. should seek to impress upon Diem, in the strongest possible terms, that, as Harriman said, "we mean business about internal reform."[24] This, they said, would require a very strong Ambassador, who could make these demands stick. Galbraith and Chayes suggested Harriman, David E. Lilienthal or George C. McGhee.

In an earlier personal letter on October 17 to Arthur Schlesinger, Jr., one of Kennedy's assistants, Harriman had expressed the hope that the Taylor group would pay particular attention to the political situation in Vietnam. "I am afraid that some feel that military action will cure political difficulties. Our experience with Chiang Kai-Shek may not be quite applicable, although it has some similarity. Against the value of the introduction of American troops to strengthen morale, there is certain adverse political reaction, particularly when a country has just emerged from colonial rule."

In another communication on October 13, Harriman said he recognized, however, that "we may be sitting on a powder keg which may blow up." And he added a sentence of considerable interest in retrospect, given the key part he played in the U.S. role in the coup against Diem two years later: "This might not necessarily be disastrous if set off by constructive forces."[25]

Although the relevant documents on this subject are not yet available, there is some evidence that the President took seriously the proposal of Harriman, Galbraith and Chayes. He discussed it with Harriman and Galbraith, and then on November 7 with Galbraith, Rusk, and Indian Prime Minister Jawaharlal Nehru, who was in Washington on an official visit. However, while he may have been attracted to the idea of avoiding a long-term commitment, as well as military intervention, the President ended up rejecting neutralization as an alternative.

In a later interview, Chayes commented on the lack of support for the proposal in the State Department.[26]

   . . . it didn't fly partly because we didn't have enough people for it. Bowles was at that time on his way out. He was not a powerful figure. I think Harlan Cleveland [Assistant Secretary of State for International Organization Affairs] was identified with it, also. We had all of the non-power in the Department, and so it just never flew. We talked to the Secretary

---

[24]Harriman's memorandum of Nov. 11, 1961, is in the Kennedy Library, NSF Country File, Vietnam, and the Galbraith-Chayes memorandum of Nov. 3 is in POF Country File, Vietnam General. For Bowles' position see *Promises to Keep*, pp. 408-409.
[25]The communications of Oct. 13 and 17 are in the Kennedy Library, POF Country File, Vietnam General Security, 1961.
[26]CRS Interview with Abram Chayes, Oct. 13, 1978.

about it, but it was simply regarded as not within the realm of possibility.

In some ways the most interesting paper during this period, in terms of the range of possibilities being considered and their likely outcomes, was a memorandum prepared only in draft by William Bundy, entitled "Reflections on the Possible Outcomes of US Intervention in South Vietnam."[27] This, said Bundy, was "the range of possible outcomes":

"Good" Scenarios

Scenario A: Diem takes heart and also takes the measures needed to improve efficiency, with only the 8000 man force and US specialist help. Hanoi heeds our warning and lays low, so that control is reasserted in South Vietnam. (Laos is a big question mark here and in other Scenarios.)

Scenario B: The struggle continues to go against Diem, and his own efforts at improvement are feeble. Thus, the US moves into the driver's seat and *eventually brings the situation* under control, using forces on the *scale of 25,000-75,000. Hanoi* and Peiping do not intervene directly, and we do not attack Hanoi.

Scenario C: As the struggle becomes prolonged, the US strikes at Hanoi (or Hanoi and Peiping intervene overtly). The U.S. wins the resulting conflict, i.e. obtains at least a restoration of the status quo, after inflicting such punishment on Hanoi and/or Peiping that further aggressive moves are forestalled for a long time to come.

"Bad" Scenarios

Scenario X: The US decides not to put in the 8000 men, or later forces, and Diem is gradually overcome.

Scenario Y: The US puts in the 8000 men, but when Diem fails to improve his performance pulls out and lets him be overcome.

Scenario Z: Moscow comes to the aid of Hanoi and Peiping, supplying all necessary equipment (including a limited supply of air-deliverable nuclear weapons to retaliate in kind against US use) so that the outcome is a stalemate in which great destruction is wreaked on the whole area.

    *   *   *   *   *   *   *

Of these, only A is truly a good outcome from all long-term standpoints—it stiffens us generally vis-à-vis the Bloc, holds the area (save perhaps Laos), does not discomfit us unduly in the neutral world, excellent for domestic US will and drive. Only trouble is—it's unlikely! *However,* it is still so much better than any other that it is worth accepting some added degree of difficulty in achieving B and C to give A every chance to happen.

The choice between B and C is a hard one. Despite all our warnings and Jorden Reports, our case of aggression against Hanoi will not convince neutrals of its accuracy and justice, or major allies of its wisdom and practicality.

---

[27]Kennedy Library, NSF Country File, Vietnam, Second Draft, Nov. 7, 1961. (asterisks and emphases in original)

On the other hand, B is a road that has almost no end in sight. The US is poorly cast as a permanent protecting power, but the local capabilities would be so low at the end of such a struggle that we would almost have to assume that role. There is a very considerable chance that under continuing US protection, South Vietnam and the area as a whole would become a wasting asset and an eyesore that would greatly hamper all our relations worldwide. On the whole, the short-term onus attached to C may be preferable. However, as we play the hand toward C (especially if we use Moscow as the channel to Hanoi) we may well raise the chances of Moscow acting to bring on Z.

On the "bad" side, X and Z are clearly nightmares. Though X means loss of the area for a long time to come, it is probably better in the long run than Z. The chances of the Soviets acting to bring about Z do not appear great in the short run, but we must certainly try to keep those chances low (e.g., by making our dealings with Moscow private).

Y is also a nightmare. It loses the area. Moreover, vis-à-vis the Bloc it would be worse than X, since they would take it as an almost final proof that we would not stand up. It might have some compensating gains in the neutral world, at least in the short run. But on the whole it seems the worst possible outcome.

The basic strategic issues are:

a. How long to give A a chance?

b. Whether B is preferable to the weighted odds of C vs. Z?

On November 2, 1961, President Kennedy also received a memorandum from Senator Mansfield urging him not to send combat forces to Vietnam:[28]

The sending of American armed forces to Viet Nam may be the wrong way and probably would be, in present circumstances. In the first place, we would be engaged without the support of significant allies. Our troops would be engaged by third-string communist forces (North Vietnamese). Then, they could very well become engaged against the second-string—the Chinese Communists, who might be drawn into the fray and could outmatch us and our Asian allies many times in manpower. If American combat units land in Viet Nam, it is conceivable that the Chinese Communists would do the same. With shorter lines of communication and transportation, with much more manpower available, South Viet Nam, on that basis, could become a quicksand for us. Where does an involvement of this kind end even if we can bring it to a successful conclusion? In the environs of Saigon? At the 17th parallel? At Hanoi? At Canton? At Peking? Any involvement on the mainland of Asia would seem to me to weaken our military capability in Berlin and Germany and, again, leave the Russians uncommitted.

---

[28]Kennedy Library, NSF Country File, Vietnam, "The Vietnamese and Southeast Asia Situation."

It appears to me that the presence of American combat troops in South Viet Nam could be misinterpreted in the minds of millions of Southeast Asians and could well be considered as a revival of colonial force. Moreover, we must be extremely wary of any seemingly simple solution that would have Asian SEATO nations do the intervening at our behest to avoid this appearance. If we give them the go-ahead, then there is every likelihood that we shall have to follow militarily or if we do not, we will suffer disastrous repercussions throughout all of Asia and we will indeed become the laughing stock of the world.

While Viet Nam is very important, we cannot hope to substitute armed power for the kind of political and economic social changes that offer the best resistance to communism. If the necessary reforms have not been forthcoming over the past seven years to stop communist subversion and rebellion, then I do not see how American combat troops can do it today. I would wholeheartedly favor, if necessary and feasible, a substantial increase of American military and economic aid to Viet Nam, but leave the responsibility of carrying the physical burden of meeting communist infiltration, subversion, and attack on the shoulders of the South Vietnamese, whose country it is and whose future is their chief responsibility.

Mansfield added that if U.S. combat forces were sent to Vietnam, this ". . . might provide that bare minimum of effectiveness which would permit a solution of the guerrilla problem in South Viet Nam or prevent further encroachment southward—assuming of course that the Chinese Communists, let alone the Russians, do not become involved. Even then, we will have achieved a 'victory' whose fruits, if we could conserve them, will cost us billions of dollars in military and aid expenditures over the years into the future."

As an alternative, and in order to minimize U.S. involvement, Mansfield recommended larger and more effective economic and political programs by which to increase popular support for the Diem government and democratic participation in politics at all levels. Among these recommendations, which he said he had first made in a memorandum to Kennedy on September 20, 1961, Mansfield advocated "a dramatic and sincere effort to enlist Vietnamese intellectuals in all aspects of the government's activities, primarily by the lifting of the shroud of fear which hangs over political life in Saigon and by acceptance of a genuine opposition in the National Assembly."[29] He also proposed "A campaign by Diem and his officials to develop close personal ties with the people by a continuous [Lyndon] Johnson-like shirt-sleeve campaign from one end of the country to the other."

Here, once again, is an example of the tendency to apply American values and practices to Vietnam. Although Mansfield had more training and experience in Asian cultural and political traditions than most Members of Congress and many U.S. officials dealing with Vietnam, his basic frame of reference was his own cultural

---

[29]The Kennedy Library staff reports that it cannot find the Sept. 20 memorandum from Mansfield.

and political training and experience. Thus, he apparently assumed that an American-style political campaign technique would produce similar results in Vietnam.

On November 8, as the debate on the Taylor report continued, the Defense Department circulated its draft of a memorandum to the President signed by McNamara, Gilpatric and the JCS. They endorsed Taylor's recommendations, but advocated a much clearer and stronger U.S. commitment to the defense of Vietnam. Such a commitment, they also argued, should be supported by whatever military action might be necessary, and the announcement of the commitment should be accompanied by a warning through diplomatic channels to the North Vietnamese to desist or risk punitive actions. This is the text of that important memorandum:[30]

MEMORANDUM FOR THE PRESIDENT

The basic issue framed by the Taylor Report is whether the U.S. shall:

a. Commit itself to the clear objective of preventing the fall of South Vietnam to Communism, and

b. Support this commitment by necessary immediate military actions and preparations for possible later actions.

The Joint Chiefs, Mr. Gilpatric, and I have reached the following conclusions:

1. The fall of South Vietnam to Communism would lead to the fairly rapid extension of Communist control, or complete accommodation to Communism, in the rest of mainland Southeast Asia and in Indonesia. The strategic implications worldwide, particularly in the Orient, would be extremely serious.

2. The chances are against, probably sharply against, preventing that fall by any measures short of the introduction of U.S. forces on a substantial scale. We accept General Taylor's judgment that the various measures proposed by him short of this are useful but will not in themselves do the job of restoring confidence and setting Diem on the way to winning his fight.

3. The introduction of a U.S. force of the magnitude of an initial 8,000 men in a flood relief context will be of great help to Diem. However, it will not convince the other side (whether the shots are called from Moscow, Peiping, or Hanoi) that we mean business. Moreover, it probably will not tip the scales decisively. We would be almost certain to get increasingly mired down in an inconclusive struggle.

4. The other side can be convinced we mean business only if we accompany the initial force introduction by a clear commitment to the full objective stated above, accompanied by a warning through some channel to Hanoi that continued support of the Viet Cong

[30]*PP*, Gravel ed., vol. II, pp. 108-109.

will lead to punitive retaliation against North Vietnam.

5. If we act in this way, the ultimate possible extent of our military commitment must be faced. The struggle may be prolonged and Hanoi and Peiping may intervene overtly. In view of the logistic difficulties faced by the other side, I believe we can assume that the maximum U.S. forces required on the ground in Southeast Asia will not exceed 6 divisions, or about 205,000 men (CINCPAC Plan 32-59, Phase IV). Our military posture is, or with the addition of more National Guard or regular Army divisions, can be made, adequate to furnish these forces without serious interference with our present Berlin plans.

6. To accept the stated objective is of course a most serious decision. Military force is not the only element of what must be a most carefully co-ordinated set of actions. Success will depend on factors many of which are not within our control—notably the conduct of Diem himself and other leaders in the area. Laos will remain a major problem. The domestic political implications of accepting the objective are also grave, although it is our feeling that the country will respond better to a firm initial position than to courses of action that lead us in only gradually, and that in the meantime are sure to involve casualties. The over-all effect on Moscow and Peiping will need careful weighing and may well be mixed; however, permitting South Vietnam to fall can only strengthen and encourage them greatly.

7. In sum:

a. We do not believe major units of U.S. forces should be introduced in South Vietnam unless we are willing to make an affirmative decision on the issue stated at the start of this memorandum.

b. We are inclined to recommend that we do commit the U.S. to the clear objective of preventing the fall of South Vietnam to Communism and that we support this commitment by the necessary military actions.

c. If such a commitment is agreed upon, we support the recommendations of General Taylor as the first steps toward its fulfillment.

The McNamara-Gilpatric-JCS memorandum had been drafted by William Bundy, who says that his first draft of November 5 "took the Taylor recommendations to their logical conclusion." Before the memo was sent to the President on November 8, however, Bundy says that the words "inclined to recommend" (in 7. b.) were added because of the ". . . steady growth of doubt all that week." ". . . the sense of how much any commitment depended on South Vietnamese performance was sinking in," he adds. "It was one thing to commit the US to the defense of Berliners who had shown themselves staunch in the hardest adversity. It was quite another to make a categorical commitment in a South Vietnam whose political divisions and weaknesses had now been highlighted more than ever by the Taylor Report and its Annexes."[31]

Although the Defense Department and the JCS had reached common agreement on a position, the State Department was more divided. State's representatives on the trip, Cottrell and Jorden, concurred with the recommendations of the Taylor group, but Secretary of State Rusk had some serious reservations, and he cabled from Tokyo on November 1 that ". . . special attention should be given to critical question whether Diem is prepared take necessary measures to give us something worth supporting. If Diem unwilling trust military commanders to get job done and take steps to consolidate non-communist elements into serious national effort, difficult to see how handful American troops can have decisive influence. While attaching greatest possible importance to security in SEA, I would be reluctant to see U.S. make major additional commitment American prestige to a losing horse."[32]

George Ball, Under Secretary of State for Economic Affairs, who was to replace Chester Bowles as the Under Secretary of State a few weeks later, had even more serious reservations about the proposed use of U.S. troops. Ball, a New York international lawyer, who had been associated with the French on legal matters during the last years of French military operations in Indochina, thought that the U.S. would suffer a fate similar to that of France if it became militarily involved in Vietnam: ". . . I knew something about Indochina," he said in a later interview,[33] "and the people around me, really, had very little background. This is one of the observations that I would make out of our whole Vietnam experience, the tragedy of the fact that people who were making decisions really had so little historical acquaintance with earlier situations that could have cast considerable light on this. I used to sit in meetings with the President, and McNamara would be holding forth and I would say, 'Well, Bob, look, I've heard all of that before; the kill ratios, the cost effectiveness aspects of various operations, the body counts. The French had exactly the same statistics and they lost.'"

Ball discussed the Taylor recommendations with McNamara and McGeorge Bundy, who argued that the commitment should be made even if it should ultimately require, as Ball predicted, a large U.S. troop commitment. Ball also made his case with the President:[34]

> I told Kennedy at that time that if we went down that road, we would have 300,000 men in the jungles and paddies in five years' time and that it was an impossible terrain, both politically and militarily, and that the last thing in the world we ought to do is get involved in this. But he said, "Well, George, I always thought you were one of the brighter guys in town, but I think you're crazier than hell. It isn't going to happen."[35]

---

[31]Bundy MS., ch. 4, pp. 25–26.
[32]*PP*, Gravel ed., vol. II, p. 105. See also George Ball's comment in his memoirs, *The Past Has Another Pattern* (New York: W. W. Norton, 1982), p. 368.
[33]CRS Interview with George Ball, Sept. 30, 1980.
[34]*Ibid.* See also George Ball, *The Past Has Another Pattern*, p. 366.
[35]In another interview Ball stated that Kennedy probably meant that he would not let it happen, but, Ball added, "I will only remind you that at the time he was killed we had 16,500

Continued

At about this same time Kennedy met with John J. McCloy, a senior U.S. business leader with extensive U.S. Government experience, who told the President that he should consider very carefully making a commitment to Vietnam of the kind recommended by Taylor because once the U.S. became involved it would be very difficult to withdraw. According to a report of that meeting, "Kennedy stated that he had very few, if any options. . . . McCloy thought President Kennedy felt he could do this [increase U.S. involvement] without making an irretrievable commitment." [36]

There were also warnings in a Special National Intelligence Estimate prepared on November 5, 1961.[37] According to the *Pentagon Papers* summary of this prophetic SNIE, which reviewed the probable responses of the Communists to increasing levels of U.S. military action, "The gist of the SNIE was that North Vietnamese would respond to an increased U.S. commitment with an offsetting increase in infiltrated support for the Viet Cong. . . . On the prospects for bombing the North, the SNIE implies that threats to bomb would not cause Hanoi to stop its support for the Viet Cong, and that actual attacks on the North would bring a strong response from Moscow and Peiping, who would regard the defense of North Vietnam against such an attack as imperative."[38]

Action on the Taylor Report

On November 8, the day McNamara sent the DOD-JCS memorandum to Kennedy, there was another top-level meeting without the President, at which the State Department took the position that the decision to send forces should be postponed, but that all of the other Taylor recommendations should be accepted. According to William Bundy's account of the meeting, "On the issue of committing the US to prevent the fall of South Vietnam, the discussion that day was inconclusive. On the one hand, it was thought that a posture of total firmness, communicated privately to Hanoi and with the implicit threat of bombing of the North, might cause a drop in Communist external support for the VC. On the other hand, it was strongly argued by George Ball that to make a commitment and yet stop short of immediate major units was the worst of both worlds."[39]

On November 11, 1961, in order to give the President an interdepartmental policy paper which he could accept and on which he could act, Rusk and McNamara sent a joint memorandum to Kennedy (drafted by William Bundy and U. Alexis Johnson) incorporating the findings and recommendations of the Taylor mission and the McNamara-Gilpatric-JCS memorandum, including the recommendation for a greatly increased MAAG. Based on the discussions

---

men in Vietnam and there were two or three thousand more ready to go over. So that certainly the escalation was proceeding fairly rapidly at that point." Charlton and Moncrieff, *Many Reasons Why*, p. 78.

[36] Cited by Leslie H. Gelb with Richard K. Betts, *The Irony of Vietnam* (Washington, D.C.: Brookings Institution, 1979), p. 77, fn. 35.

[37] For excerpts of this SNIE, which is still classified, see *PP*, Gravel ed., vol. II, p. 107. The text of an SNIE on the same subject prepared on Oct. 10, 1961, is in *ibid.*, DOD ed., book 11, pp. 313-321.

[38] *Ibid.*, Gravel ed., vol. II, pp. 107-108.

[39] Bundy MS., ch. 4, p. 28.

of previous days, they did not recommend, however, that U.S. combat forces be sent in the initial phase of the proposed plan.[40]

"The loss of South Viet-Nam to Communism," they said, in describing U.S. interests in defending Vietnam, "would not only destroy SEATO but would undermine the credibility of American commitments elsewhere. Further, loss of South Viet-Nam would stimulate bitter domestic controversies in the United States and would be seized upon by extreme elements to divide the country and harass the Administration." They described the U.S. objective as follows:

The United States should commit itself to the clear objective of preventing the fall of South Viet-Nam to Communism. The basic means for accomplishing this objective must be to put the Government of South Viet-Nam into a position to win its own war against the guerrillas. We must insist that that Government itself take the measures necessary for that purpose in exchange for large-scale United States assistance in the military, economic and political fields. At the same time we must recognize that it will probably not be possible for the GVN to win this war as long as the flow of men and supplies from North Viet-Nam continues unchecked and the guerrillas enjoy a safe sanctuary in the neighboring territory.

We should be prepared to introduce United States combat forces if that should become necessary for success. Dependent upon the circumstances, it may also be necessary for United States forces to strike at the source of the aggression in North Viet-Nam.

With respect to putting the Government of South Vietnam "into a position to win its own war against the guerrillas," Rusk and McNamara endorsed the recommendations of Taylor's group for a series of actions to help strengthen Vietnamese military and governmental activities. Most of these would involve the participation of U.S. military or civilian personnel in the administration of those programs, including a recommendation to "Provide individual administrators and advisers for insertion into the Governmental machinery of South Viet-Nam in types and numbers to be agreed upon by the two Governments."

With respect to U.S. forces, the memorandum differentiated between "(A) Units of modest size required for the direct support of South Viet-Namese military effort, such as communications, helicopter and other forms of airlift, reconnaissance aircraft, naval patrols, intelligence units, etc.," which should be sent "as speedily as possible," and "(B) larger organized units with actual or potential direct military missions . . . [which] pose a more serious problem in that they are much more significant from the point of view of domestic and international political factors and greatly increase the probabilities of Communist bloc escalation." Moreover, the use of forces in category (B) ". . . involves a certain dilemma: if there is a strong South-Vietnamese effort, they may not be needed; if there is not such an effort, United States forces could not accomplish their mission in the midst of an apathetic or hostile popula-

---

[40]The text of the memorandum is in *PP*, Gravel ed., vol. II, pp. 110-116.

tion." ("This point," William Bundy says, "hammered out in oral arguments I well recall, bore heavily on the recommendation to defer decision, and planted itself deeply in the minds of all those who had participated in the policy process during the week.")[41]

Rusk and McNamara recommended that to prepare for possible deployment of U.S. forces the Department of Defense should make plans for the use of troops for one or more of these purposes:

(a) Use of a significant number of United States forces to signify United States determination to defend South Viet-Nam and to boost South Viet-Nam morale.

(b) Use of substantial United States forces to assist in suppressing Viet Cong insurgency short of engaging in detailed counter-guerrilla operations but including relevant operations in North Viet-Nam.

(c) Use of United States forces to deal with the situation if there is organized Communist military intervention.

In their discussion of the question of using larger units of U.S. forces in Vietnam, Rusk and McNamara made one very important point which reflected Kennedy's own position, as well as Harriman's: "It must be understood that the introduction of American combat forces into Viet-Nam prior to a Laotian settlement would run a considerable risk of stimulating a Communist break of the cease fire and a resumption of hostilities in Laos." They added this highly significant comment, which in itself might have been considered adequate justification for delaying the decision to send larger units of U.S. forces: "After a Laotian settlement, the introduction of United States forces into Viet-Nam could serve to stabilize the position both in Viet-Nam and in Laos by registering our determination to see to it that the Laotian settlement was as far as the United States would be willing to see Communist influence in Southeast Asia develop."

This paper was then discussed by the President with Rusk, McNamara, Taylor, and General Lemnitzer, at a meeting that same day (November 11, 1961). The President went into the meeting armed with a set of eight questions prepared for him by the White House staff which raised such issues as whether the program proposed by Rusk and McNamara would be effective without the 8,000-10,000 military force recommended by Taylor, how the U.S. would explain to Diem its reasons for not sending these troops, under what circumstances the U.S. would consider sending such troops, whether the offer of assistance was to be contingent on reforms, and whether the commitment should be "a public act or an internal policy decision of the U.S. Government."[42]

According to William Bundy's account of the meeting (the only one available), Kennedy agreed with the recommendation of Rusk and McNamara not to send U.S. forces at that time: ". . . the thrust of the President's thinking was clear—sending organized forces was a step so grave that it should be avoided if this was hu-

---

[41]Bundy MS., ch. 4, p. 30.
[42]Kennedy Library, POF Country File, Vietnam General Security, 1961. Attached to this is the Rusk-McNamara memorandum which had been transmitted that morning by U. Alexis Johnson to McGeorge Bundy "for discussion with the President at the noon meeting today." The text of that memorandum and of the memorandum as printed in the *Pentagon Papers* is identical.

manly possible." Bundy adds that although the Rusk-McNamara memorandum had recommended a ". . . categorical commitment to prevent the loss of South Vietnam, JFK decided at this meeting not to do this. . . . As I recall the sense of the discussion, there was a distinct switch to support George Ball's argument that a flat commitment without combat forces was the worst of both worlds."[43]

Following the meeting of November 11, the President met again with Rusk and McNamara on November 14.[44] Prior to the meeting he received a memorandum from Rostow urging that he approve a program of action in Vietnam which would demonstrate U.S. decisiveness and resolve and thereby strengthen the hand of the United States in any subsequent negotiations.[45] Rostow said, "It is universally agreed that the objective of the proposed exercise in Viet-Nam is to induce the Communists to cease infiltration, return to the Geneva Accord, while assisting South Viet-Nam in reducing the force of some 16,000 guerrillas now operating in the country. This track unquestionably will require extensive talks with the Bloc countries and, at some stage, probably formal negotiations." He argued, however, that the U.S. should put deeds before words; if it did not, the Communists would use the negotiations as a pretext behind which to continue to "dismantle" South Viet-Nam, and there would also be a ". . . major crisis of nerve in Viet-Nam and throughout Southeast Asia. The image of U.S. unwillingness to confront Communism—induced by the Laos performance—will be regarded as definitively confirmed. There will be real panic and disarray."

"In Viet-Nam," Rostow said, "the gut issue is not whether Diem is or is not a good ruler. . . . The gut issue is whether we shall continue to accept the systematic infiltration of men from outside and

---

[43]Bundy MS., ch. 4, p. 31. In several memoirs and other sources on the period it has been argued that because the NSAM directing the implementation of the President's decision of Nov. 15 did not include the statement of the U.S. objective contained in the Rusk-McNamara memorandum, the President was thereby refraining from endorsing that objective. Although the NSAM did not contain any rhetorical commitment to the defense of South Vietnam, General Taylor explained that Kennedy probably saw no need for such a statement in the NSAM since the commitment had been made in the NSAM of May 11. According to Taylor, "President Kennedy never indicated any opposition of which I was aware to the thesis that we must be prepared to go all the way if we took this first step—one of the prime lessons of the Bay of Pigs." *Swords and Plowshares*, p. 248. This interpretation is further confirmed by the State Department's Nov. 15 cable to Ambassador Nolting explaining the President's decision, which makes it clear that although the decision on troops was being postponed, partly to avoid interfering with the Laos negotiations, and partly in order to try other methods first, combat forces would be sent if necessary. The text of the cable is in *PP*, DOD ed., book 11, pp. 400-405.

Rostow himself wrote that "As Kennedy rose from the cabinet table, having indicated the elements in the Taylor report he finally approved, he remarked: 'If this doesn't work perhaps we'll have to try Walt's Plan Six'; that is, direct attack on North Vietnam. He acted, in short, in precisely the spirit of Taylor's and my paraphrase of his view as of August 4: he took the minimum steps he judged necessary to stabilize the situation, leaving its resolution for the longer future, but quite conscious that harder decisions might lie ahead." *The Diffusion of Power*, p. 278.

John Lewis Gaddis, *Strategies of Containment*, p. 246, adds this explanation: "The full Taylor-Rostow recommendations, he [Kennedy] thought, would have constituted too abrupt an escalation of pressure; he preferred, instead, a more gradual approach, involving an increase of American economic and military aid to Saigon, together with the introduction of U.S. 'advisers.' Nothing in this procedure precluded the dispatch of ground troops at a later date if that should become necessary. . . . Kennedy's actions reflected doubts only about the appropriate level of response necessary to demonstrate American resolve, not about the importance of making that demonstration in the first place."

[44]At this writing, there are no available notes on this meeting.

[45]Kennedy Library, NSF Country File, Vietnam.

the operations from outside of a guerrilla war against him which has built up from 2,000 to 16,000 effectives in two years. The whole world is asking a simple question: what will the U.S. do about it?"

Rostow said he was aware of the possibilities of escalation and of war, but experience had demonstrated that war could be best avoided by strong, decisive action. "The Korean War," he added, "arose from the withdrawal of U.S. forces from South Korea and the opening it appeared to offer the Communists. In other cases where we have acted strongly on our side of the line we have come home free: Northern Iran; Greece; the Berlin blockade; Lebanon-Jordan; Quemoy-Matsu. In Laos, the alerting and loading of the Seventh Fleet induced a cease-fire."

"If we act indecisively now," Rostow said, "I fear we shall produce excessive fears on our side and excessive hopes on the other side; and then we shall have to over-react to correct a disintegrating situation worse than the present. In those circumstances there would, indeed, be a danger of war. As in Korea we would have first tempted the enemy by an apparent weakness and then double-crossed him. It is that circumstance I would wish to see us avoid."

> Therefore, I suggest that we make the moves we believe required to stabilize the situation and to buy time in South Viet-Nam; and then by imaginative communication and diplomacy—addressed to all elements in the Bloc as well as the Free World—we bring maximum pressure on Hanoi to call off the invasion of South Viet-Nam now under way. Such communication should begin the day we publish the Jordan [sic] Report—or the day before.[46]

Meanwhile, President Kennedy appears to have dictated, on November 14, the following memorandum to Rusk and McNamara:[47]

> I think we should get our ducks in a row for tomorrow morning's meeting. I believe we should make more precise our requests for action. In the papers which I have seen our requests have been of a general nature.
>
> 1. I would like to have you consider the proposals made by Governor Harriman. I am wondering if he should return, perhaps on Friday to discuss the matter further with [Georgi] Pushkin [Deputy Foreign Minister of the U.S.S.R.].
>
> 2. In the meantime what action should be taken toward South Viet Nam pending the arrival of Harriman.

---

[46]On November 13, Galbraith sent the President a memorandum on "Neglected Parts of General Taylor's Report on South Vietnam," in which he said he had just finished reading the entire report. ("I am advised," he added, "that few others have done so.") He thought the President should pay particular attention to certain comments about problems with Diem's government and the performance of Vietnamese Armed Forces, arising, in part, because of problems in the government. That same day Rostow sent a memo to the President replying to Galbraith. He agreed that there were problems, but said that Galbraith had ignored other aspects, and he added: "There is simply no doubt whatsoever that the problem in South Vietnam is tough. South Vietnam could be lost. On the other hand, the situation is better than it was when we accepted the responsibility of Greece in 1947; better than the Philippines and Malaya at their worst; better than South Vietnam itself in 1954-55. If Ken [Galbraith] is advocating that we disengage promptly from Vietnam and let Southeast Asia go, I think he should say so. In my view South Vietnam is not yet lost and one of the crucial variables is that we go forward with a clear-eyed view of our assets as well as an equally tough-minded view of our liabilities and problems.'" Both memos are in the Kennedy Library, NSF Country file, Vietnam.

[47] Same location.

3. I would like a letter to be written to the Co-Chairmen of the Geneva Conference to call a meeting of the conference to consider immediately South Viet Nam as a breach of the accord. As we will be breaching the Geneva accords ourselves it is important that we lay the groundwork. The Jordan [sic] report will do some of this. Has anyone examined the political implications in their efforts.

4. Should I address a statement today to Krushchev [sic] concerning South Viet Nam stating how dangerous we thought the situation was.

5. If we are going to send a military man as a Commanding Officer at the four star level for South Viet Nam, perhaps we could name a younger general and give him a star or do you know someone who already has the stars who can handle the situation.

6. I gather you felt that we should have a general military command set up. We want to make sure that someone like George McGee, [sic] heads it, in fact, it might be well to send McGee.

7. I would like to have someone look into what we did in Greece. How much money and men were involved. How much money was used for guerrilla warfare? Should we have not done it at the company level rather than at the battalion level? It is proposed by the military that we should operate from the battalion level or even below this.

Are we prepared to send in hundreds and hundreds of men and dozens and dozens of ships? If we would just show up with 4 or 5 ships this will not do much good. Or am I misinformed?

I think there should be a group specially trained for guerrilla warfare. I understand that the guns that have been used have been too heavy. Would carbines be better? Wonder if someone could make sure we are moving ahead to improve this.

Perhaps we should issue some sort of a statement on what we propose to do. Our actions should be positive rather than negative. As I said on Saturday concerning Laos—we took actions which made no difference at all. Our actions should be substantial otherwise we will give the wrong impression.

8. We should watch Laos very carefully for any fighting that might break out again even though we decide not to intervene.

This memorandum may not have been sent, but the file copy contains a notation from McGeorge Bundy that it was used by the President, together with one page of Rostow's memo of November 14 in which he emphasized the need to stand firm, as the President's talking paper in the November 14 meeting with Rusk and McNamara.

Kennedy Makes a New Commitment to Defend Vietnam

The NSC met again on November 15, 1961, to consider the draft of a National Security Action Memorandum based on the Rusk-

McNamara memorandum of November 11.[48] The draft was almost identical to the Rusk-McNamara draft recommendations except for omission of the language about a U.S. commitment to Vietnam. Included was language from the memorandum concerning the use of U.S. troops for achieving one or more of three stated purposes.

On the day of the meeting, Kennedy received a memorandum from McGeorge Bundy in which Bundy, in response to the President's specific request, stated his own views on what the U.S. should do about Vietnam:[49]

A. *We should now agree to send about one division **when needed** for military action inside South Vietnam.*

1. I believe we should commit *limited* U.S. combat units, if necessary for *military* purposes (not for morale), to help save South Vietnam. A victory here would produce great effects all over the world. A defeat would hurt, but not much more than a loss of South Vietnam with the levels of U.S. help now committed or planned.

2. I believe our willingness to make this commitment, *if necessary,* should be clearly understood, by us and by Diem, before we begin the actions now planned. I think without that decision the whole program will be half-hearted. *With* this decision I believe the odds are almost even that the commitment will not have to be carried out. This conclusion is, I believe, the inner conviction of your Vice President, your Secretaries of State and Defense, and the two heads of your special mission, and that is why I am troubled by your most natural desire to act on other items now, without taking the troop decision. Whatever the reason, this has now become a sort of touchstone of our will.

3. I believe the actions now planned, *plus* the basic decision to put in limited combat troops if necessary, are all that is currently wanted. I would not put in a division for morale purposes. I'd put it in later, to fight if need be. After all, Admiral Felt himself recommended, on balance, against combat troops less than a month ago. It will be time enough to put them in when our new Commander says what he would do with them.

4. The use of force up to a total of 20-25,000, *inside* Vietnam, is not on the same footing as the large forces that might become necessary if the Vietminh move to direct invasion. I would *not* make the larger decision on a war against North Vietnam today.

B. *We can manage the political consequences of this line of action.*

5. I believe South Vietnam stands, internally and externally, on a footing wholly different from Laos. Laos was

---

[48] For the text of the draft NSAM see Kennedy Library, NSF Country File, Vietnam.

[49] Same location. In the memorandum, McGeorge Bundy said he agreed with Rusk and McNamara that a new U.S. military man should be put in charge of U.S. efforts in Vietnam in place of General McGarr, and that Ambassador Nolting "should be judged as his complement, not as your head man in South Vietnam." Bundy, however, preferred to have George McGhee replace Nolting, as he stated in another memorandum to the President on Nov. 15, "Notes for Talk with Secretary Rusk—Nov. 15," same location.

never really ours after 1954. South Vietnam is and wants to be. Laotians have fought very little. South Vietnam troops are not U.S. Marines, but they are usable. This makes the opinion problem different at home and abroad.

6. I believe the Jorden Report, the exchange of letters, and Stevenson and Rusk, can coolly justify this basic line of action, not to all the world, but to an effective fraction. I do not expect that these actions will lead to rapid escalation of the conflict, since they remain essentially on our side of the line, and since the Communists do not want that kind of test.

7. I think this solution will put a serious strain on our position in Laos, but that has always been a bad bargain. My advice would be to give the game promptly to Souvanna and hope for the best, meanwhile holding hard to our new course in South Vietnam. Souvanna may make noises against the action, but I don't think he'll fight or be overthrown by the PL [Pathet Lao] for a while.

According to notes of the November 15 NSC meeting which are now available, the President again expressed concern about becoming more involved in Vietnam, both from the standpoint of the nature of the war, and from the standpoint of domestic and international opinion:[50]

Mr. Rusk explained the Draft of Memorandum on South Viet Nam. He added the hope that, in spite of the magnitude of the proposal, any U.S. actions would not be hampered by lack of funds nor failure to pursue the program vigorously. The President expressed the fear of becoming involved simultaneously on two fronts on opposite sides of the world. He questioned the wisdom of involvement in Viet Nam since the basis thereof is not completely clear. By comparison he noted that Korea was a case of clear aggression which was opposed by the United States and other members of the U.N The conflict in Vietnam is more obscure and less flagrant. The President then expressed his strong feeling that in such a situation the United States needs even more the support of allies in such an endeavor as Viet Nam in order to avoid sharp domestic partisan criticism as well as strong objections from other nations of the world. The President said that he could even make a rather strong case against intervening in an area 10,000 miles away against 16,000 guerrillas with a native army of 200,000, where millions have been spent for years with no success. The President repeated his apprehension concerning support, adding that none could be expected from the French, and Mr. Rusk interrupted to say that the British were tending more and more to take the French point of view. The President compared the obscurity of the issues in Viet Nam to the clarity of the positions in Berlin, the contrast of which could even make leading Democrats wary of proposed activities in the Far East.

---

[50]Johnson Library, Vice Presidential Security File, "Notes on National Security Council Meeting 15 November 1961," sanitized in 1982 and again in 1984. These notes, which are unattributed, are not in the Kennedy Library.

Mr. Rusk suggested that firmness in Viet Nam in the manner and form of that in Berlin might achieve desired results in Viet Nam without resort to combat. The President disagreed with the suggestion on the basis that the issue was clearly defined in Berlin and opposing forces identified whereas in Viet Nam the issue is vague and action is by guerrillas, sometimes in a phantom-like fashion. Mr. McNamara expressed an opinion that action would become clear if U.S. forces were involved since this power would be applied against sources of Viet Cong power including those in North Viet Nam. The President observed that it was not clear to him just where these U.S. forces would base their operations other than from aircraft carriers which seemed to him to be quite vulnerable. General Lemnitzer confirmed that carriers would be involved to a considerable degree and stated that Taiwan and the Philippines would also become principal bases of action.

With regard to sources of power in North Viet Nam, Mr. Rusk cited Hanoi as the most important center in North Viet Nam and it would be hit. However, he considered it more a political target than a military one and under these circumstances such an attack would "raise serious question." He expressed the hope that any plan of action in North Viet Nam would strike first of all any Viet Cong airlift into South Viet Nam in order to avoid the establishment of a procedure of supply similar to that which the Soviets have conducted for so long with impunity in Laos.

Mr. [McGeorge] Bundy raised the question as to whether or not U.S. action in Viet Nam would not render the Laotian settlement more difficult. Mr. Rusk said that it would to a certain degree but qualified his statement with the caveat that the difficulties could be controlled somewhat by the manner in which actions in Viet Nam are initiated.

The President returned the discussion to the point of what will be done next in Viet Nam rather than whether or not the U.S. would become involved. [the following one-half page of notes has been deleted]

General Taylor said that although the tone of some of the papers and of the discussion at the meeting was somewhat pessimistic, he was optimistic about what could be done. He said he envisioned two phases: "(1) the revival of Viet Nam morale, and (2) initiation of the guerrilla suppression program."

McNamara "cautioned that the program was in fact complex and that in all probability U.S. troops, planes and resources would have to be supplied in additional quantities at a later date." The President asked McNamara if he would recommend taking action even if SEATO did not exist, and McNamara replied that he would. The President asked for the justification for U.S. military action in Vietnam, and General Lemnitzer replied that otherwise ". . . the world would be divided in the area of Southeast Asia on the sea, in the air and in communications. . . . Communist conquest would deal a severe blow to freedom and extend Communism to a great portion of the world." The President asked how he could justify the proposed course of action in Vietnam while not acting against

Cuba. Lemnitzer replied that the JCS still believed that the U.S. "should go into Cuba."

As the meeting ended, Kennedy repeated his concern about having the support of other countries, as well as that of Congress and the American public. He said he did not think that even the Democrats in Congress were fully convinced that the U.S. should become further involved in Vietnam.

The President's decision to approve the revised Taylor-Rostow plan, and to make a new U.S. commitment to Vietnam, was based to an important extent on perceptions of the world situation, especially the need for the U.S. to stand up to the Communists. This is William Bundy's analysis:[51]

> When JFK later told James Reston that he would never have made the Vietnam decisions of the fall of 1961 unless he had been moved by their relevance to Berlin, he was expressing a connection never stated in the formal papers but present in the train of thought of every participant. It was not that everyone believed that Communist actions in Vietnam emanated from a monolith; rather, it was that the US itself seemed the single crucial sustaining power against multiple Communist threats. If the US seemed weak and faltering in Asia, it would be thought likely to falter in Europe. . . . Thus, Berlin and what it represented was surely the major unseen force that was thought to compel a generally firm decision. But the strategic arguments derived from the Asian context alone, had, I am sure, great weight and acceptance as well. They were not subjected to detailed criticism or reassessment, but they were believed. Altogether, the US had to act, in the universal judgment and feeling of all.

Bundy adds that if the November 15 decision "had a single thread, I would call it 'pragmatic resolve.'"[52]

Bundy's explanation of the U.S. domestic political considerations involved in the decision is also helpful in understanding that dimension of the policymaking process: ". . . a collapse in South Vietnam would set off sharp domestic controversy," he said. "This argued forcefully against doing nothing and was a clear part of the assessment of stakes." "[Moreover] . . . a hard and firm approach might be more politically acceptable than a gradual and long-drawn out one that ended up 'mired down.' Here surely was an indication that the domestic politics of 'gradualism' were distinctly negative."

According to Bundy, the twin specters of China and Korea were also "never out of the minds of JFK and his senior advisors . . . both political visions could be conjured up and were, I am sure, as much in the background of the policy circle's thinking as Berlin was at the surface." He adds, "In essence, the underlying arguments of domestic politics cancelled out. The Administration could be damned if it failed in Vietnam without trying; equally, it could be damned if it tried and got bogged down."[53]

---

[51]Bundy MS., ch. 4, pp. 34-35.
[52]*Ibid.*, p. 37.
[53]*Ibid.*, pp. 36-37.

After the NSC meeting on the morning of November 15, the President met that afternoon with Rusk. Final agreement was reached on a cable which was sent that evening to Ambassador Nolting informing him of the decision on the Taylor-Rostow report, and directing him to discuss the subject with Diem.

On November 22, 1961, NSAM 111 was issued. It consisted of the direction given Nolting about the components of the new U.S. plan, and the steps the U.S. expected the South Vietnamese to take, but it contained no reference to U.S. forces.[54]

The November 15 cable to Nolting, most of which was taken verbatim from the Rusk-McNamara memorandum of November 11 and the draft NSAM, stated that "President Kennedy, after conferring with General Taylor and carefully considering his report, has decided that the Government of the United States is prepared to join the Government of Viet-Nam in a sharply increased joint effort to avoid a further deterioration in the situation in South Viet-Nam and eventually to contain and eliminate the threat to its independence."[55] For its part in this joint effort, the cable said, the U.S. would immediately increase its military, economic, and other forms of assistance to South Vietnam, including additional military personnel (category "A"—military forces as proposed by the Rusk-McNamara memorandum of November 11), as well as providing personnel for assisting the South Vietnamese in administering their government.[56] For their part, the South Vietnamese would be expected to mobilize their "entire resources" in support of the war. "(This would include," the cable added, "a decentralization and broadening of the Government so as to realize the full potential of all non-Communist elements in the country willing to contribute to the common struggle.)" The South Vietnamese would also be expected to improve the organization and offensive capability of their army.

With respect to U.S. forces, the cable stated that Nolting should point out to Diem that the increased number of Americans who would be assigned for "operational duties" under the new plan would increase greatly the ability of the South Vietnamese to win the war. "You can also tell him," the cable added, "that the missions being undertaken by our forces, under present circumstances, are more suitable for white foreign troops than garrison duty or missions involving the seeking out of Viet Cong personnel submerged in the Viet-Nam population."

Nolting was also directed to tell Diem that the new joint plan would involve "a much closer relationship than the present one of acting in an advisory capacity only. We would expect to share in

---

[54]The text of NSAM 111 is in *PP*, DOD ed., book 11, pp. 419-421. On Nov. 30, 1961, in NSAM 115, Kennedy also authorized the use of U.S. planes and personnel for the first defoliant operation in Vietnam, code named "Operation Ranch Hand." (Originally, it was to have been called "Operation Hades.") See *ibid.*, p. 425. For a detailed study see William A. Buckingham, Jr., *Operation Ranch Hand: The Air Force and Herbicides in Southeast Asia, 1961-1971* (Washington, D.C.: Office of Air Force History, United States Air Force, 1982).

[55]For the text of the cable, Washington to Saigon 619, Nov. 15, 1961, see *PP*, DOD ed., vol. 11, pp. 400-405.

[56]During the several weeks after Taylor's mission, there was another proposal for which there was strong support, namely, that Lansdale be named to head the *encadrement* of American advisers and to become the chief U.S. participant in the affairs of the Vietnamese Government. This was abandoned after opposition, primarily from the State Department, similar to that which had developed in the spring of 1961 to an earlier version of the same proposal.

the decision-making process in the political, economic and military fields as they affected the security situation." Moreover, the U.S. contribution to the new plan would depend heavily on the cooperation of the South Vietnamese, and expressly on Diem's willingness to make genuine reforms, and to broaden the base of his government in such a way as to convince American and world opinion that the U.S. was not supporting an "unpopular or ineffective regime."

With the cable, Nolting was given the draft of a letter which Diem could use in writing to President Kennedy to accept the U.S. offer. The cable expressed the hope, however, that Diem's letter would not be a verbatim copy of the draft.

Thus, by the President's decision of November 15 the groundwork was laid for far greater U.S. involvement and for further "Americanization" of the war. The wheels may also have been set in motion for the 1963 coup against Diem. Various participants in the policymaking process, as well as knowledgeable observers from outside the government, were speculating even as early as the fall of 1961 that if the "performance" of Diem continued to be unsatisfactory, and the situation in Vietnam did not improve, the U.S. would have to play an active role in installing new leadership. One of these was Harriman. Another was Galbraith, who was asked by Kennedy to stop by Vietnam on his way back to India and to advise him on the situation. Galbraith did so, and reiterated his feeling that U.S. forces were not needed, and that ". . . it is those of us who have worked in the political vineyard and who have committed our hearts most strongly to the political fortunes of the New Frontier who worry most about its bright promise being sunk under the rice fields."[57] The problem, he said, was Diem, and if the U.S. was not able to get greater satisfaction—"performance" rather than continued "promises"—"the only solution must be to drop Diem." This would be neither difficult nor dangerous, he added:

> . . . a nod from the United States would be influential. At the earliest moment that it becomes evident that Diem will not and cannot implement in any real way the reforms Washington has requested we should make it quietly clear that we are withdrawing our support from him as an individual. His day would then I believe be over. While no one can promise a safe transition we are now married to failure.

Although these November 1961 Presidential decisions committed the United States to a new role in Vietnam, and to an open-ended utilization of U.S. military and civilian personnel, and despite the fact that in making such decisions the President was involving the United States in a situation in which, as his advisers had said, more drastic action by the United States might subsequently be required to meet its objectives, there appears to have been little if any consultation with Congress. Congress was not in session at the time the decision was being made, but most of the elected leaders as well as committee chairmen and ranking members could have been reached if it had been deemed necessary or desirable to seek their advice. But it was apparently not considered necessary to do

---

[57]For his cable, see *PP*, DOD ed., book 11, pp. 410-418.

so. Under the new Act for International Development of 1961,[58] the general authority for using U.S. assistance and personnel in aiding other countries, which had been first approved by Congress in 1949, was reenacted, thereby giving the President *carte blanche* authority to send more men and equipment to Vietnam and to expand the role of U.S. personnel. (The law still restricted them to a noncombatant role, however.) There was also sufficient money for this purpose in the new 1961 foreign aid appropriations bill (especially considering the broad transfer authority, which also had been reenacted), and in the Defense appropriations bill from which funds were used for the cost of the military advisory group. In addition, the 1960 Mutual Defense Assistance Agreement with Vietnam, which had been approved by Congress, gave authority to the U.S. to furnish matériel and services, and the right to station military personnel in Vietnam.

As to whether consultation with Congress about this new and potentially vast U.S. commitment was desirable, there seems to have been little thought given by the administration to taking such action, and it is even doubtful how many Members of Congress were personally informed (much less consulted) by the administration that such a decision was being or had been made. William Bundy says only, ". . . the record is sparse, but it appears that the general outlines of the program were conveyed to Congressional leaders orally in the latter part of November; this was done in low key and with little apparent comment one way or the other."[59]

Congress had certainly been alerted to the situation through public sources, however, and could have obtained information about the November 15 decisions if it had seen the need for such information and chosen to make the necessary inquiries.[60]

In addition to Mansfield's memos to Kennedy, however, there had been some informal communications during this period between some key Members of Congress and persons in the executive branch involved in Vietnam policymaking. One such contact resulted from a trip to Vietnam during the time of the Taylor group's visit by Senator Stuart Symington (D/Mo.), the newly-appointed chairman of the Subcommittee on the Middle East and South Asia of the Foreign Relations Committee (and formerly Secretary of the Air Force under Truman). Symington, who was also on the Armed Services Committee, sent Kennedy a personal, handwritten note from Saigon on October 21, 1961, in which he said he had talked to Taylor and Rostow as well as U.S. and Vietnamese officials in Saigon, and, "It seems to me we ought to try to hold this place. Otherwise this part of the world is sure to go down the drain." He added, "If you so decide, it will be my privilege to support your position to the best of my ability."[61]

---

[58]Public Law 87-195.
[59]Bundy MS., ch. 4, p. 42.
[60]See Fairlie, "We Knew What We Were Doing When We Went Into Vietnam." As Fairlie says, there had been numerous stories in the press about Taylor's trip and recommendations, as well as an article in the *New York Times* on Nov. 17, 1961, reporting on the White House meeting on Nov. 15 and on what the President had decided.
[61]Kennedy Library, POF Country File, Vietnam General. On Nov. 10, after returning from his trip, Symington sent Kennedy a memorandum outlining his views, in which he expressed concern about the declining prestige of the U.S., and, among other things, the need to stand

Continued

While he was in Vietnam, Symington paid a call on Diem, where he, like other Senators in earlier years, helped the State Department make its case on an important policy question. This concerned the Vietnamese request for a mutual defense treaty with the U.S., which the White House was resisting. Nolting said in his cable reporting on the Diem-Symington meeting:[62]

> Senator Symington (at my prior request) took line aimed at discretely discouraging Diem from pursuing idea of bilateral treaty at this time, principally by emphasizing delays and complications involved in Senate action on matter of this kind. . . . Reporting officer's distinct impression that Senator Symington's handling of this question cooled considerably the previous interest of Diem and Nhu in a bilateral treaty.

Symington and Diem also discussed the question of U.S. combat forces, and Symington took the same position that Mansfield and Aiken had taken earlier in the year, namely, that a decision to send U.S. forces was within the discretion of the President. (According to the cable, Symington added: "without referring it to Congress.") He also told Diem that once such a force was committed, "no responsible member of Congress would rise to ask that we back down."

Symington, who later became a strong opponent of the war, made another interesting observation. He said that Congress did not like to be asked to "reaffirm" the President's power to use the armed forces before the President makes a decision to do so. Presumably he was basing this statement on the reluctance of Members of Congress to go on record in favor of the use of U.S. forces, preferring to let the President suffer whatever political consequences might attend such a decision.

The New "Limited Partnership"

When Diem was told what the U.S. expected from him, and was informed that the U.S. would participate in the making of decisions of the Vietnamese Government, he reacted very adversely. According to Nolting, Diem said that "Viet Nam did not want to be a protectorate."[63] In Washington, Diem's renewed intransigence, as this reaction was generally perceived to be, produced a hardening of attitudes, especially in the State Department, where discussion of finding a successor for Diem was revived briefly, and consideration was also given to recalling Nolting for consultation in order to indicate U.S. disapproval.[64] It was apparent, however, that there was no satisfactory replacement, and by December 4 Nolting had succeeded in getting Diem to consent to most of the conditions requested by the U.S. Washington also softened its terms. Rather than re-

---

firm in Berlin and Vietnam. "Whether it be Saigon, or Berlin, or some other place," he said, "I do not believe this nation can afford to bend further. . . ." With respect to Vietnam, which he said "we are losing," and which would then result in the loss of Laos and Cambodia—"both already far gone"—as well as Thailand and Burma, he advocated the prompt establishment of a policy based on "whatever is necessary" to hold Vietnam.

Similar support for U.S. policy was voiced by a group from the House Foreign Affairs Committee that visited Vietnam in the Fall of 1961. See *Report of the Special Study Mission to the Far East, South Asia, and the Middle East,* Committee Print, 87th Cong., 2d sess. (Washington, D.C.: U.S. Govt. Print. Off., 1962).

[62]Kennedy Library, NSF Country File, Vietnam, Saigon to Washington A-145, Nov. 2, 1961.
[63]Kennedy Library, NSF Country File, Vietnam, Saigon to Washington 678, Nov. 18, 1961.
[64]Taylor, *Swords and Plowshares,* p. 248.

quiring participation in decisionmaking, U.S. policymakers were content, as a cable to Nolting on November 27, (following a meeting that day with the President), had stated, to have a partnership "so close that one party will not take decisions or actions affecting the other without full and frank prior consultation."[65]

In late 1961 and early 1962, the U.S. completed preparations for its new role in Vietnam by issuing (December 8, 1961), a State Department "White Paper" on North Vietnamese aggression against the south by which to justify U.S. abrogation of the Geneva Accords, and, based on this, the White House then responded favorably to a letter from Diem requesting assistance.

The two-part white paper, *A Threat to Peace: North Vietnam's Efforts to Conquer South Vietnam,*[66] drafted by William Jorden of State's Policy Planning Staff, which had been in preparation for several months, argued that, contrary to the Geneva Accords, North Vietnam was directing and supporting the insurgency in the south, and that North Vietnam's goal was to exercise Communist control over all of Vietnam. For this reason, under the doctrine of "collective self-defense," South Vietnam had the right to ask for outside assistance. Accordingly, on December 14, 1961, in response to Diem's letter asking for such assistance, Kennedy replied that because of Communist violations of the Geneva Acccords the U.S. was prepared to help South Vietnam.[67]

Having completed the formalities, the U.S. immediately began implementing the new partnership. McNamara held conferences in Honolulu in December 1961 and again in January 1962 at which basic decisions were made about the military aspects of the program. (At the meeting in January, General McGarr told McNamara that two divisions of the South Vietnamese Army would be able to "clean out" the guerrillas in War Zone D, an area northeast of Saigon that was heavily infiltrated by the Communists. One of McNamara's aides is said to have passed him a note reading, "This man is insane.")[68] One of these decisions, pursuant to Taylor's recommendations, was to strengthen the U.S. military command structure in Vietnam by replacing the MAAG with a Military Assistance Command Vietnam (MACV), a move that was made in February 1962 as Gen. Paul D. Harkins took over from McGarr.

As a result of these decisions, U.S. personnel and equipment began pouring into Vietnam. "Within weeks," George Ball said in his memoirs, "we had sent almost seventeen hundred men to Vietnam and more were to follow. That meant that the balloon was going up, and although it was not climbing as rapidly as some of my more belligerent colleagues would have liked, I had no doubt it was headed for the stratosphere."[69]

Perhaps more important at that point, however, were the steps being taken to activate programs through which the insurgency

[65]Kennedy Library, NSF Country File, Vietnam, Washington to Saigon 693, Nov. 27, 1961.
[66]Department of State, Publication No. 7308, Far Eastern Series 110 (Washington, D.C.: U.S. Govt. Print. Off., 1961).
[67]Diem's and Kennedy's letters were printed in the *Department of State Bulletin,* Jan. 1, 1962, pp. 13-14. For a State Department cable on the draft letter for Diem to send to Kennedy, see Kennedy Library, NSF Country File, Vietnam, Washington to Saigon 635, Nov. 17, 1961. The draft presented to Diem is not yet available.
[68]Henry L. Trewhitt, *McNamara* (New York: Harper and Row, 1971), p. 193.
[69]Ball, *The Past Has Another Pattern,* p. 369.

could be controlled and the country stabilized without having to resort to large-scale U.S. military involvement. Having decided against sending at that time any large body of U.S. combat forces, Kennedy and many of his associates wanted to find ways by which to defeat the "war of national liberation" without having to rely primarily on conventional military action.

Within the doctrinal framework of counterinsurgency, which the administration had already accepted as its response to wars of national liberation, what methods might be applicable to the situation in Vietnam? The answer had already been suggested by the CIA, which had been experimenting for about a year with a program to help villages defend themselves (with training provided by U.S. Special Forces) while at the same time improving their living conditions. William E. Colby, then the CIA Station Chief in Saigon, who originated the program, called it the "'Citizens' [or 'Civilian'] Irregular Defense Groups," a term he used "to clarify to the U.S. Special Forces units that implemented it, under CIA's over-all control, that it was a citizen's and not a military operation, that its objective was defense rather than offense, and that it should be kept irregular to meet the different needs of the different communities in which it was being carried out."[70]

Colby had also sold Diem and Nhu on the idea, and in the fall of 1961, with encouragement from the CIA, Diem invited a British group, the "British Advisory Mission," six men with experience in the successful campaign against the Communists in Malaya, to recommend a counterinsurgency plan for Vietnam. This group, led by Robert K. G. Thompson, recommended to Diem a plan for helping villages defend themselves (with protection also from regular military forces) and thus gain confidence in their security, while also helping them to improve their living conditions.[71] The result, Thompson's group said, would be better security, greater confidence, better intelligence about the Communists, leading to "more kills." Thus, they added, "Protection, confidence, intelligence and kills would be a constantly expanding circuit."

"The overall aim of any counter insurgency plan," the group stated, "must be to win the people. The killing of communist terrorists will follow automatically from that. If the main emphasis is placed mainly on killing terrorists there is a grave risk that more communists will be created than are killed. Winning the people must, therefore, be kept in the forefront of the minds of every single person, whether military or civilian, who is engaged in anti-terrorist operations."

The "Strategic Hamlet Plan," as this was called, was to function as follows:[72]

> The underlying concept of the [strategic hamlet] program was an abrupt break with the actual strategy of the GVN as

---

[70] *Honorable Men*, p. 169. The 400-man U.S. Special Forces group sent to Vietnam by Kennedy in May of 1961 was assigned to this project. Approximately 65,000 Montagnard soldiers were being supported in the strategic Highland Plateau adjacent to Laos. Although Colby emphasized their self-defense role, they were also active offensively in that area.

[71] The text of the plan presented to Diem by the Thompson group is in *PP*, DOD ed., book 11, pp. 347-358. See also Dennis J. Duncanson, *Government and Revolution in Vietnam* (New York: Oxford University Press, 1968). Duncanson was a member of the Thompson team.

[72] Blaufarb, *The Counterinsurgency Era*, p. 104.

well as with the proposals of the MAAG. Instead of emphasizing elimination of the armed bands of the VC by military means, the program attempted to go directly to the heart of the insurgency's strength, its ability to gain the willing or unwilling support of the rural population, which it was then able to organize to provide intelligence, food, money, and recruits for armed units. As was repeated endlessly in public explanations of the plan, the purpose was to dry up the sea of friendly peasantry in which swam the VC "fish."

Diem and Nhu generally approved Thompson's proposals, which were also supported by the CIA, and began implementing the strategic hamlet plan. Ambassador Nolting, pleased that the Vietnamese were taking the initiative to combat the Communists in rural areas, was also very supportive, and with his leadership the other components of the U.S. mission followed suit. The U.S. foreign aid mission (USOM) created an Office of Rural Development, the key figure in which was Rufus Phillips, a former member of Lansdale's 1954 team, who returned to Vietnam in 1962. The MAAG also set up a special office for that purpose, despite the continuing opposition of U.S. military leaders to schemes for shifting from conventional military operations to counterguerrilla warfare. The MAAG had opposed the efforts of the Michigan State University team in the 1950s to organize local police forces as a way of controlling the insurgency, and viewed the Thompson proposals in much the same light. As JCS Chief Lemnitzer wrote to Taylor on October 18, 1961, in urging Taylor to prevent Thompson's ideas from becoming officially approved, ". . . in recent months the insurgency in South Vietnam has developed far beyond the capacity of police controls."[73]

One seasoned observer, formerly a participant in CIA counterinsurgency programs in Vietnam and Laos, made this cogent comment about the effects of the dichotomy produced by these differences in perspective:[74]

. . . The military, despite concessions—no doubt sincere—to the importance of winning the population, was quite unshakably wedded to the idea that priority must go to destroying the enemy's armed force, and doing it by the familiar means of concentrating manpower and firepower at the right time and place.

Translating these doctrinal differences into the realities of the day, they meant that instead of one program to defeat the insurgency there were in fact two: strategic hamlets and all that went with them on the one hand, and the military effort to corner and destroy the VC main forces on the other. Except in such set-piece operations as Sunrise [the first major Strategic Hamlet project], which were preceded by military sweeps, seldom was there any real coordination and common planning between the two efforts. Nevertheless, the military persisted,

---

[73] *PP*, DOD ed., book 11, p. 325.
[74] Blaufarb, p. 119. The military became more cooperative in implementing the strategic hamlet plan, after responsibility for arming and training local self-defense forces was transferred from the CIA to the military beginning in late 1961 and ending in late 1963, ("Operation Switchback"), pursuant to the recommendations of the Bay of Pigs (Cuban Study Group) report that larger military operations should be run by the military rather than the CIA.

devising and obtaining GVN approval in November 1962 to a National Campaign Plan which called for the intensification of aggressive military operations in all corps areas.

Among the effects of this dichotomy was the gradual expansion of firepower in ways hardly suited to the nature of the war being fought. Available air power was increasing rapidly. Theoretically under careful control, it actually began to be used against any suspicious target and sometimes against none. Bombing and artillery barrages were a standard preliminary to large-scale operations and inevitably alerted the enemy, who was usually able to slip away in ample time. Pressures on the president to allow the use of napalm and of defoliants became so strong that he yielded and they became a common feature of the war. Inevitably, the bombing and the increased use of artillery involved destruction of property and death and injury of the very civilian population whose loyalty was being sought as the key to victory.

Although there was opposition to the strategic hamlet plan among military leaders, the plan received strong support among civilian officials in Washington who were actively engaged in promoting counterinsurgency programs. One of these was Roger Hilsman, Director of Intelligence for the State Department who, along with W. W. Rostow, had been a leader in the development during 1961 of the concepts of counterinsurgency and counterguerrilla warfare. In January 1962, Hilsman was told by Taylor (who had been in communication with Robert Thompson) that the President wanted him to go to McNamara's Honolulu Conference, and then to Saigon. He was to promote counterinsurgency ideas and report back on the state of affairs in Vietnam.

During his visit to Vietnam, in addition to numerous discussion of the strategic hamlet plan, Hilsman observed a large-scale conventional Vietnamese Army attack on Binh Hoa, a Communist stronghold, in which only civilians were killed while the Communists disappeared into the jungle.

When he returned to Washington, Hilsman reported to Taylor and then to the President. He told Kennedy about Binh Hoa, and the fact that ". . . it was not only fruitless but that it helped to recruit more Viet Cong than it could possibly have killed."

The President shook his head and said, "'I've been President over a year, how can things like this go on happening?'"

According to Hilsman, Kennedy was impressed with Thompson's ideas about how to develop a strategic concept for Vietnam, and told Hilsman to prepare a report with that title—"A Strategic Concept for Vietnam"—on which U.S. policy might be based. Hilsman did so.[75] In his report, which was, according to the *Pentagon Papers*, an "unabashed restatement of most of Thompson's major points,"[76] Hilsman said, "The struggle for South Vietnam . . . is essentially a battle for control of the villages." He stressed the need, therefore, for providing help "at the local level." He added,

---

[75] Hilsman, *To Move a Nation*, pp. 427-439.
[76] *PP*, Gravel ed., vol. II, p. 142. See also Hilsman's own description, pp. 435-436 of *To Move a Nation*. The report is now declassified, and is in the Kennedy Library, NSF Country File, Vietnam.

"As recommended in the Taylor Report, in sum, we need more 'working level friends and advisers'—Americans with technical competence, imagination, and human sympathy, and with the willingness and ability to live and work in the villages."

Hilsman's report presented a "strategic concept" for such action, the "first principle" of which was, *"The problem presented by the Viet Cong is a political and not a military problem—or, more accurately, it is a problem in civic action."* The second principle was to provide security to villagers, and for this purpose he proposed a plan involving strategic villages of the kind suggested by Thompson. (Hilsman said that in the areas most exposed to the Communists, there should be "defended villages," with more military protection.)

Lansdale relates a conversation with McNamara which illustrates also the difficulty some officials were having in applying managerial concepts and techniques to the less-measurable "human element" in the war:[77]

> . . . I remember when he was trying to computerize the war and he called me in one day. He had a long list of entries for a computer, including the body count type of stuff, enemy casualties. He had written them out in a hard-lead pencil, I remember, on graph paper. And I said, "Your list is incomplete. You've left out the most important factor of all." He said, "What is it?" I said, "Well, it's the human factor. You can put it down as the X factor." So, he wrote down in pencil, "X factor." He said, "What does it consist of?" I said, "What the people out on the battlefield really feel; which side they want to see win and which side they're for at the moment. That's the only way you're going to ever have this war decided." And he said, "Tell me how to put it in?" I said, "I don't think any Americans out there at the moment can report this to you." He said, "Oh, well," and he got out an eraser to erase it. I said, "No, leave it there." Then I took about a week trying to figure how you get answers on that, which I did finally. They later used the ideas for the hamlet evaluation system. Mine was a way to get our troops to report when they went in villages, whether the people, the kids, were smiling or present—a whole bunch of facts—a very complicated type of evaluation. But at the time I was pleading with McNamara not to codify a war and then believe what the figures were telling him. I said, "You're going to fool yourself if you get all of these figures added up because they won't tell you how we're doing in this war."

When asked what McNamara's response was, Lansdale said, "He asked me to please not bother him anymore. He used to say, 'Thank you, I've got something else to do now.' No, I could never talk to him. . . ."

Are U.S. Advisers Engaged in Combat?

In order to maintain a "low profile" for the new U.S. program in Vietnam, both for domestic and international reasons, the Kennedy

---

[77]CRS Interview with Edward G. Lansdale, Nov. 19, 1982.

administration tightened controls on the access of U.S. and other news media to potentially controversial aspects of the new program, especially the U.S. military role. On November 28, 1961, the U.S. mission in Saigon was told by Washington: "Do not give other than routine cooperation to correspondents on coverage current military activities in Vietnam. No comment at all on classified activities."[78]

Unlike the earlier situation in the middle 1950s, when the few U.S. journalists in Vietnam were generally supportive of the official U.S. position, in 1961-62 there were several journalists, notably Neil Sheehan of United Press International, Homer Bigart and later David Halberstam of the *New York Times* (who replaced Bigart in August 1962), Malcolm W. Browne of the Associated Press, François Sully of *Newsweek,* and Charles Mohr of *Time* Magazine, whose independent, aggressive reporting soon became a thorn in the flesh of the U.S. and Vietnamese Governments. (The Vietnamese, tried to expel Bigart and Sully in March of 1962, but withdrew the order. Sully, a French citizen, was expelled in September of that year despite strong protests from the other journalists and U.S. media representatives. Shortly afterwards, James Robinson, NBC's Southeast Asia correspondent, was also expelled.)[79]

Shortly after the new U.S. program got underway, questions began to be raised about the role of U.S. military advisers, based on press reports that these advisers were engaging in combat, a fact well-known to some key Members of Congress, especially on the Armed Services Committees. In an executive session of the Foreign Relations Committee on January 12, 1962, Ambassador Nolting was asked whether the U.S. was at war in Vietnam, and whether Americans were killing and being killed. Nolting said that one U.S. adviser had been killed, but that "as of now" U.S. advisers were not engaged in combat.[80]

President Kennedy was asked a similar question on January 15: "Mr. President, are American troops in combat in Viet-Nam?" He answered in one word: "No."[81]

Both Nolting and the President were attempting to conceal the fact that U.S. advisers were engaging in combat. Indeed, on January 13, 1962, two days before the President made his statement, the first U.S. air combat support mission in the FARM GATE series was flown to support a Vietnamese unit under attack, and by the end of January, FARM GATE crews had flown 229 combat sorties.[82]

---

[78]Kennedy Library, NSF Country File, Vietnam, Washington to Saigon 698, Nov. 28, 1961.

[79]See John Mecklin, *Mission in Torment* (Garden City, N.Y.: Doubleday, 1965), pp. 129-140. Sheehan and Halberstam subsequently were given a Pulitzer Prize for their reporting. They and Browne received the first Louis J. Lyons award from the Nieman Fellows of Harvard University for reporting "the truth as they saw it in the Vietnam conflict . . . without yielding to unrelenting pressure."

[80]U.S. Congress, Senate Committee on Foreign Relations, unpublished executive session transcript, Jan. 12, 1962. The transcripts of executive sessions of the Senate Foreign Relations Committee have been printed, as of this writing, through 1961. All future references in this study to executive sessions of the committee are to unpublished transcripts, most of which are still classified. All references used herein contain the date and names of major witnesesses, and quotations are used by authority of the committee.

[81]*Public Papers of the Presidents,* John F. Kennedy, 1962, p. 17.

[82]Tilford, *Search and Rescue in Southeast Asia,* 1961-1975, p. 37.

One of the reasons for wanting to conceal the combat role of U.S. military personnel was to avoid acknowledging that the U.S. was violating the Geneva Accords, in part because the U.S. was charging the Communists with violations, but also because new accords for Laos were then being negotiated.

During February, "Kennedy refused to admit that American troops were in combat, but his answers and statements became increasingly hard to believe. . . ."[83] On February 14, the *New York Times* stated in an editorial that the U.S. Government should not attempt to conceal the facts about American military involvement in Vietnam, and the possibility of an eventual major conflict. On that same day the paper carried a column by James Reston, who said, ". . . the United States is now involved in an undeclared war in South Vietnam."

Later that day, Kennedy was asked at his news conference whether he was being candid about Vietnam with Congress and the public. He replied by referring to the numerous meetings which he and other officials of the administration had held with Members of Congress."[84]

The next day, February 15, Majority Leader Mansfield gave a speech in the Senate replying to criticism that Congress and the public had not been kept informed about Vietnam. Citing the statistics about the number of meetings on Vietnam in which Members of Congress had been involved, he declared, ". . . it borders on the irresponsible to suggest that Congress had not been well informed on this situation for many years." He added, however, that it was important to respect the "line of demarcation" between the responsibilities of the President and the Congress. "It is the President's responsibility to act," he said. "It is ours to advise as we are able in our individual and collective wisdom, and, to the extent that it is constitutionally required, to consent."[85]

The two items from the February 14 *New York Times* caused considerable consternation in the administration, and pressure was exerted on the paper to modify its position. For one thing, Averell Harriman called Reston the next day (February 15) to suggest to him that he had not included facts that Harriman said he had given to the Senate Foreign Relations Committee on February 13.[86] According to Harriman's notes of the conversation, which he sent to the White House, Reston said he thought Harriman's criticism was "right." Harriman suggested that Reston pass the information on to the editorial staff.

Harriman also said that he had talked to Reston the night before at a private dinner party, ". . . pointing out that there were conflicting publicity pressures which had to be balanced—not only American opinion, but international opinion, including ICC [the International Control Commission for Indochina, established by the

---

[83]Fairlie, "We Knew What We Were Doing When We Went Into Vietnam," p. 20.
[84]*Public Papers of the Presidents,* John F. Kennedy, 1962, p. 136. He was also asked whether the U.S. had sent combat troops to Vietnam, and he replied, ". . . we have not sent combat troops in the generally understood sense of the word."
[85]*CR,* vol. 107, p. 2326.
[86]The unpublished transcript of this public hearing on Harriman's nomination as Assistant Secretary of State for the Far East is in the papers of the Committee on Foreign Relations in the National Archives, Record Group 46 (hereafter cited as RG).

Geneva Accords] and Co-Chairmen [the USSR and Britain, co-chairmen in Geneva and on a continuing basis thereafter], SVN and communist bloc—balancing them was not easy, particularly as the American correspondents' despatches plus photographs of recent helicopter flights had made the situation look like a US war, rather than a Vietnamese conflict which we were assisting."[87]

On February 20, 1962, Harriman testified in an executive session of the Senate Foreign Relations Committee on Laos and Vietnam, and was questioned by Senator Wayne Morse (D/Ore.) who said he had ". . . grave doubts as to the constitutionality of the President's course of action in South Vietnam."[88] Harriman replied that it was the North Vietnamese who had breached the Geneva Accords, and that he agreed with Kennedy that U.S. security was very much at stake in Vietnam, as well as with the decision not to send U.S. ground combat forces.[89]

Morse also said, as he had said in the January 12 meeting with Nolting, that a major war in Vietnam, in which "ships start coming back to the West Coast with flag-draped coffins of American boys," would seriously divide the American people. Senator Albert A. Gore (D/Tenn.) expressed concern about a statement made by Attorney General Robert Kennedy in Saigon on February 18, when Kennedy said, "We are going to win in Viet-Nam. We will remain here until we do win."[90] Gore said he was "uneasy about the public commitments which seem to be with us with respect to the presence of and the purposes for U.S. military personnel in Vietnam."

In the same hearing, Fulbright twice asked whether there was any alternative to Diem. Harriman's reply is interesting, particularly considering the central role he was to play in 1963 in the U.S. decision to sanction the coup against Diem. He told Fulbright, "He is the head of the government, and I would not have thought that it was a proper function of the U.S. to attempt to make or break governments."

---

[87]Kennedy Library, NSF Country File, Vietnam, "Memorandum of Telephone Conversation." In the same file, there is a letter from Arthur Sylvester, Assistant Secretary of Defense for Public Affairs, to McGeorge Bundy, Apr. 7, 1962, saying that, in response to Kennedy's concern, he had contacted the person in charge of the news at NBC/TV to ask NBC to withhold further use of a 2 minute segment of film used on NBC's nightly nationwide news program in which South Vietnamese soldiers were shown administering "rough treatment" to Communist prisoners. NBC agreed to keep the film "on the shelf."

[88]U.S. Congress, Senate, Committee on Foreign Relations, unpublished executive session transcript, Feb. 20, 1962.

[89]After the hearing Morse asked the State Department for answers to sixteen questions on Vietnam. In its reply on Mar. 16, 1962, which is still classified in part, State gave both classified and unclassified answers, depending on the question. One of the unclassified answers concerned the President's authority for activities of U.S. military advisers, in response to Morse's question about the provisions of the Constitution or treaty or statute under which Kennedy derived the right to order U.S. military personnel to engage in activities supporting military operations of the South Vietnamese. State cited the Foreign Assistance Act and the Mutual Defense Assistance Agreement, but gave as the primary authority the President's powers as Commander in Chief, as well as his foreign relations power as interpreted by the Curtiss-Wright decision. *United States* v. *Curtiss Wright Export Corp.*, 299 U.S. 304(1936).

Morse also asked whether it would be appropriate under the Constitution for the President to submit to Congress a resolution on Vietnam comparable to the Formosa Resolution and the Middle East Resolution. State replied that the President had the power under the Constitution to do what he was doing in Vietnam, but that it was desirable for Congress to understand and support these actions. Traditionally, the reply stated, this had been done by consultation, which had been extensive in the case of Vietnam.

[90]*New York Times*, Feb. 19,1962.

As a result of the questions being raised about the role of U.S. advisers, as well as other aspects of the new U.S. program, Kennedy ordered tighter restrictions on U.S. mission cooperation with reporters. In a cable (1006) on February 21, 1962,[91] that became rather notorious when a congressional committee conducted a hearing in May 1963 on the question of restrictions on press coverage in Vietnam,[92] the State Department told Nolting, "in absence of rigid censorship, US interests best be protected through policy of maximum feasible cooperation, guidance and appeal to good faith of correspondents," but he was also told that in order to avoid "harmful press repercussions on both domestic and international scene" he should seek to guide the press in ways that would minimize harmful reporting. Among the suggestions made by Washington were that "Correspondents should not be taken on missions whose nature such that undesirable dispatches would be highly probable," and that, "It [is] not repeat not in our interest . . . to have stories indicating that Americans are leading and directing combat missions against the Viet Cong." Moreover, "Sensational press stories about children or civilians who become unfortunate victims of military operations are clearly inimicable to national interest."

The cable also stressed that cooperation between the U.S. and the South Vietnamese Government was essential, and that "frivolous, thoughtless criticism of GVN makes cooperation difficult achieve." "We cannot avoid all criticism of Diem," it said. "No effort should be made to 'forbid' such articles. Believe, however, that if newsmen feel we are cooperating they will be more receptive to explanation that we are in a vicious struggle where support of South Vietnamese is crucial and that articles that tear down Diem only make our task more difficult."

The cable concluded with the following "for consideration and private use at Ambassador's discretion":

It should be possible for Ambassador and/or military to exact from responsible correspondents voluntary undertakings to avoid emphasis in dispatches of sensitive matters, to check doubtful facts with US Government authorities on scene. Seriousness of need for this may be duly impressed on responsible correspondents to extent that, in interests of national security and their own professionl needs, they can be persuaded to adopt self-policing machinery. Can be reminded that in World War II American press voluntarily accepted broad and effective censorship. In type struggle now going on in Viet-Nam such self-restraint by press no less important. Important to impress on newsmen that at best this is long term struggle in which most important developments may be least sensational

---

[91]Cable 1006 was declassified in 1983 after a mandatory review request from CRS, and is available in the Kennedy Library, NSF Country File, Vietnam, General.

[92]In its report on Oct. 1, 1963, (H. Rept. 88-797), the House Government Operations Committee (Foreign Operations and Government Information Subcommittee) concluded: "The restrictive U.S. press policy in Vietnam . . . unquestionably contributed to the lack of information about conditions in Vietnam which created an international crisis. Instead of hiding the facts from the American public, the State Department should have done everything possible to expose the true situation to full view."

and in which "decisive battles" are most unlikely, therefore stories imply sensational "combat" each day are misleading.

The President's Press Secretary, Pierre Salinger, said that the cable was intended to improve relations with the press, but he added that the Kennedy administration "was not anxious to admit the existence of a real war in Southeast Asia," partly because "their government was now going to be engaged in activities which were in clear violation of the Geneva Conference of 1954." He said that the President was "particularly sensitive" about press stories on the combat role of U.S. advisers. "It was my view at the time that we should be prepared to take the good stories with the bad in Vietnam, but the President pushed hard for us to tighten the rules there under which correspondents would observe field operations in person."[93]

According to John Mecklin, Public Affairs Officer for the U.S. mission to Vietnam from 1962-64 (formerly with *Time* Magazine, and a reporter in Vietnam 1953-55), Cable 1006, while recognizing the right of reporters to cover the war, ". . . was otherwise little more than codification of the errors the Mission was already committing." "The Mission persisted," he added, "in the practice of excessive classification, under the secret fraternity doctrine of the State Department cable No. 1006, to a degree that denied newsmen access to whole segments of U.S. operations in Vietnam."[94]

The "root of the problem," Mecklin said, "was the fact that much of what the newsmen took to be lies was exactly what the Mission genuinely believed, and was reporting to Washington. Events were going to prove that the Mission itself was unaware of how badly the war was going, operating in a world of illusion. Our feud with the newsmen was an angry symptom of bureaucratic sickness." "We were stuck hopelessly," he said, "with what amounted to an all-or-nothing policy, which might not work. Yet it *had* to work, like a Catholic marriage or a parachute. The state of mind in both Washington and Saigon tended to close out reason. The policy of support for Diem became an article of faith, and dissent became reprehensible."[95]

Laos Again Becomes a Problem

While increasing its assistance to Vietnam, the U.S. continued its efforts to neutralize Laos. A neutrality agreement had been reached in Geneva during the fall of 1961, but it was to become effective only after a coalition government had been formed by the Laotians and after that new government had declared the country's neutrality. General Phoumi, supported by various persons and groups in the U.S. State Department, the CIA, and the American military who were opposed to the position being developed by Harriman for the President, resisted the establishment of such a government. Finally, at the end of January 1962, the U.S. temporarily

[93]Pierre Salinger, *With Kennedy* (New York: Avon Books, 1967), pp. 394, 398. In Oct. 1963, when Arthur Sulzberger, publisher of the *New York Times,* visited Kennedy at the White House, the President suggested that David Halberstam be transferred to another post. The suggestion was rebuffed by Sulzberger. See David Halberstam, *The Making of a Quagmire* (New York: Random House, 1965), p. 268.
[94]Mecklin, *Mission in Torment,* pp. 111, 115.
[95]*Ibid.,* pp. 100, 105.

suspended monthly cash assistance payments to Phoumi's government as a way of forcing him to cooperate. He still refused.

In late February, the situation became more critical as Phoumi's forces in Nam Tha, a town near the Chinese border, which had been reinforced in response to a buildup of Pathet Lao forces in the area, came under attack by the Communists. Policymakers in Washington were concerned that the Pathet Lao might be planning another Dien Bien Phu, and that if Phoumi's forces were defeated at Nam Tha, the tentative agreement reached in Geneva might collapse, and the Communists might be in a position to take all of Laos.

The available record is very sketchy as to what alternatives were considered at this stage, but apparently the administration again began discussing the possibility of U.S. military intervention. As one step in this consideration, the President met on February 21, 1962, with Vice President Johnson and congressional leaders to discuss the situation.[96] One participant in that meeting, Senator Mansfield, took the position that if the administration was going to use U.S. forces, ". . . that they had better tell the whole truth to the American people, realize that this would be worse than Korea, would cost a great deal more and very likely bring us into conflict with the Communist Chinese. I said that I thought it was the worst possible move we could make." Mansfield added, "I think that the congressional leadership were in full accord with my views, and I have an idea that the President was too although he didn't say anything."[97]

At that meeting Senator Russell apparently took a similar position, arguing that the Laotians were not willing to fight, and that the U.S. should, if necessary, seek to block Communist expansion southward from Laos by stationing forces in Thailand. He was supported by Senator Hubert H. Humphrey (D/Minn.), (the newly-elected Democratic whip of the Senate).[98]

The situation in Laos was also discussed during testimony by Harriman before an executive session of the Foreign Relations Committee on February 20, 1962.[99] Harriman described for the committee the agreement for the neutralization of Laos, but said, interestingly enough, that he had no confidence that North Vietnam would comply with those arrangements, including the provision that Laos would not be used for access to any other country (which was intended to apply specifically to the Ho Chi Minh Trail). A good deal of the discussion that followed dealt with Vietnam, but Senator Lausche repeated his contention that Souvanna

---

[96]These Members of Congress were present at the Feb. 21 meeting: from the Senate, Democrats Mike Mansfield, Richard Russell, J. William Fulbright, Hubert Humphrey, George A. Smathers (Fla.) and Republicans Everett Dirksen, Leverett Saltonstall, Thomas H. Kuchel (Calif.), Bourke Hickenlooper, Alexander Wiley; from the House, Speaker John W. McCormack (Mass.) and Democrats Carl Albert, Hale Boggs (La.), Carl Vinson, Thomas Morgan, and Francis E. Walter (Pa.) and Republicans Charles Halleck, Leslie Arends, Robert B. Chiperfield (Ill.), Charles B. Hoeven (Iowa), and John W. Byrnes (Wis.)

[97]Kennedy Library, Oral History Interview with Mike Mansfield, June 23, 1964, p. 25.

[98]These comments are based on notes in the Russell Papers at the University of Georgia, Intra-office Communication Series, Memoranda File. In these papers there is also this note by Russell: "I advised Pres. Secty State-Defense and his advisors in Jan. or Feb. '61 to get out of Laos entirely while we could still save face."

[99]U.S. Congress, Senate, Committee on Foreign Relations, unpublished executive session transcript, Feb. 20, 1962.

Phouma was too closely connected to the Communists to be acceptable as the Prime Minister, and that a coalition government would lead to Communist control.[100] Harriman responded by saying that in Laos the U.S. had only three choices: to let the country be overrun by the Communists; to support the Phoumi government, which might require U.S. troops; or to work out a peaceful settlement. Vietnam, he said, was different. There the U.S. could help people who were willing to fight for themselves.

The situation in Laos during February also caused concern in Thailand, and toward the end of the month the U.S. responded by inviting the Thai Foreign Minister, Thanat Khoman, to Washington for discussions. One outcome of this was the so-called Rusk-Thanat Agreement, by which Rusk announced that the U.S. considered Thailand's independence and integrity "vital" to the national interests of the United States, and would honor its pledge to defend Thailand under the SEATO Treaty even if no other SEATO nations were willing to act.[101] This interpretation of SEATO, which was the first public assertion by the United States that the U.S. could act unilaterally under the treaty, even if other members were not willing to act, was subsequently given by the executive branch as a legal justification for U.S. unilateral action in Vietnam.[102]

Rusk said later: "Before we joined in the Rusk-Thanat communiqué, we talked to a number of senators who agreed that that was what the Treaty itself said."[103]

According to Kenneth T. Young, then the U.S. Ambassador to Thailand, "Bangkok and Washington were able in March 1962 to negotiate a significant interpretation of the SEATO Treaty which finessed Thailand's vigorous drive to modify the treaty in ways which the United States could not have accepted without creating serious constitutional difficulties." This interpretation of the right of unilateral action, he said, "amounts to a *de facto* bilateral defense alliance within the constitutional framework of the United States."[104]

On February 27, 1962, Harriman and Abram Chayes, the State Department's Legal Adviser, met in executive session with the Foreign Relations Committee to explain the concerns of Thailand, and the interpretation of SEATO which was to be announced in the communiqué on the Rusk-Thanat agreement. According to Harriman, the Thais wanted to be assured that if they were attacked by

---

[100]Similar comments were made by several members of the House Foreign Affairs Committee, especially Walter H. Judd (R/Minn.) and Clement J. Zablocki (D/Wis.), during hearings on the foreign aid bill in March. Judd called it a "retreat, retreat, retreat" policy. See U.S., Congress, House, Committee on Foreign Affairs, *Foreign Assistance Act of 1962*, Hearings, 87th Cong., 2d sess. (Washington, D.C.: U.S. Govt. Print. Off., 1962), pp. 654-655, 699.

[101]For the text see *Department of State Bulletin*, Mar. 26, 1962.

[102]According to William Bundy, the Thais were informed orally in March of 1961 that the U.S. was prepared to take such unilateral action under this interpretation of SEATO and of U.S. responsibilities under SEATO. "The substance of the Rusk-Thanat Communiqué a year later was thus conveyed privately at this time, and so far as the record shows with no particular thought that it was novel or a new departure." Bundy MS., ch. 3, p. 23. Bundy contends (ch. 5, p. 18), that such an interpretation was not and is not a novel interpretation of U.S. responsibilities under a multilateral treaty. "In no such case, surely, would the US, then or at any other time, accept the dissent or 'veto' of any single member as meaning that the American obligation ceased." See also U. Alexis Johnson with Jeff Olivarius McAllister, *The Right Hand of Power*, p. 305.

[103]Letter to CRS from Dean Rusk, Oct. 22, 1984.

[104]Quoted by Russell Fifield, *Americans in Southeast Asia: The Roots of Commitment* (New York: Crowell, 1973), p. 266, from an unpublished manuscript of Young's.

the Communists there would not have to be unanimous action on the part of SEATO in order for the U.S. to come to their defense.

Senator Gore asked Harriman why the proposed communiqué, if it constituted a commitment, was not being sent to the Senate for approval as a treaty. Harriman replied, ". . . the legal opinion is that there is no need to consult with this Committee. . . ." The communiqué, he said, would merely be stating publicly the interpretation of the treaty as presented to the committee by Dulles, and as explained previously to the Thais.[105]

In early May 1962, (a coalition government still had not been established), attacks on Nam Tha increased, and there were rumors that a nearby town had been overrun. This sent Phoumi's forces into headlong retreat southward until they crossed the Mekong River into sanctuary in Thailand. The leader of the U.S. Special Forces team advising the Laotians at Nam Tha is said to have told his headquarters: "The morale of my battalion is substantially better than in our last engagement. The last time, they dropped their weapons and ran. This time, they took their weapons with them."[106]

Although the seriousness of the Nam Tha defeat was probably overestimated by the Kennedy administration, there was an immediate reaction in Washington. Hilsman and Harriman argued that the U.S. had to respond with military moves that would convince the Communists that the United States would go to war, if necessary, to defend Laos, as well as reassuring the Thais of the U.S. commitment. At the same time, they said, the U.S. did not want to give Phoumi the impression that it was pulling away from our support for a coalition government. The JCS were again opposed to intervening unless adequate force was authorized to accomplish the objectives. They proposed that support for Phoumi be increased, and that there be a naval show of force.

In a meeting with his advisers on May 10, Kennedy agreed to send a naval task force from the Seventh Fleet toward the Gulf of Siam, the South China Sea, as proposed by the JCS. Hilsman's reaction to this at the time was that "the military [had] started going soft on us again, you know every time they beat their chests until it comes time to do some fighting and then they start backing down just like they did in Laos last spring. . . ." "'. . . the President is boxed' [in]. Because of the military softness he has 'only decided half of what is necessary to be effective in really deterring the Communists. And that is he hasn't decided enough to deter the Communists but he had decided more than enought [sic] to get into all sorts of political trouble.'"[107]

By the time another meeting was held on the following day (May 11, 1962), Kennedy had received Eisenhower's support for taking

[105]U.S. Congress, Senate, Committee on Foreign Relations, unpublished executive session transcript, Feb. 27, 1962.

[106]Stevenson, *The End of Nowhere*, p. 174.

[107]These and following quotations are from "'When Do I Have Time to Think?' John F. Kennedy, Roger Hilsman, and the Laotian Crisis of 1962," by Stephen E. Pelz, *Diplomatic History*, 3 (Spring 1979), pp. 215-230, based on notes dictated by Hilsman on May 11, 1962, and made public in 1979 by Hilsman and the Kennedy Library. For Hilsman's discussion of the contents of the memo which he and Harriman prepared, as well as his published description of the debate over Laos, see *To Move A Nation*, pp. 143 ff. In the Summer 1979 issue of *Diplomatic History*, pp. 345-348, he also commented on Pelz' article, followed by a reply from Pelz.

military action in Laos and, feeling less threatened politically, he approved stronger measures which came much closer to meeting the position taken by Harriman and Hilsman. In addition to sending a unit from the Seventh Fleet, he agreed to send approximately 5,000 U.S. troops to Thailand for deployment on the Mekong River border with Laos. According to Hilsman, Kennedy, in contrast to his attitude in May 1961, "was thinking much more about intervening this time. . . ." He had even asked Hilsman to prepare a memorandum on the Formosa and Middle East Resolutions, apparently with the thought of possibly sending a resolution to Congress to approve intervention in Laos.

It was also clear that Rusk and McNamara were more inclined than previously to consider more forceful measures. Rusk, according to Hilsman, proposed putting U.S. forces into North Vietnam (although Hilsman added that Rusk did not take a "strong stand.") McNamara recommended that the U.S. establish a command for all of Southeast Asia under General Harkins.

On May 12, after "barely going through the formality of asking the Thais to 'request' U.S. assistance under the SEATO Treaty,"[108] Kennedy ordered the military steps which he had decided to take. On May 15, only hours before the announcement was made to the press, Congress was brought into the picture when the President met with the Vice President and congressional leaders, some of whom had been informed over the weekend by telephone after the decision was made on Saturday. Secretary of State Rusk met separately with the Foreign Relations Committee.

According to a press report, Kennedy's meeting with the leadership was "more in the way of a briefing them than in asking their approval of his Administration's action."[109]

In his meeting with the Foreign Relations Committee, Rusk said that the action had been taken to reassure Thailand, and to have U.S. forces in position to implement, if necessary, the SEATO Treaty.[110] (It was not, he said, an action taken under the treaty.)

Senator Morse said he was concerned about sending U.S. forces into Laos to help the Laotians when they seemed so unwilling to fight for their country. Rusk replied that this was not an issue, but that if the Geneva talks collapsed it might become an issue. Morse said he intended to support "my government," but that the public would oppose U.S. military intervention if it was predominately a unilateral American effort. He reported that Senator A. Willis Robertson of Virginia, a conservative Democrat, had called him the day before to tell him of his concern about sending U.S. forces into Laos.

Rusk agreed that the prospects of sending U.S. troops into Laos, given the limiting factors of geography and cultural characteristics, was a "most unpromising prospect," and that rather than doing this the U.S. probably would "meet the situation on the coast in

---

[108]Sorensen, *Kennedy*, p. 730. This decision was not promulgated by a NSAM.

[109]*Washington Post*, May 16, 1962. Members of Congress attending the White House meeting were, from the Senate, Democrats Mansfield, Russell, and Humphrey, and Republicans Dirksen, Saltonstall, Kuchel and Wiley; and from the House, Speaker McCormack and Democrats Albert, Boggs, and Vinson and Republicans Halleck, Arends, and Chiperfield.

[110]U.S. Congress, Senate, Committee on Foreign Relations, unpublished executive session transcript, May 15, 1962.

some way, and specifically in North Vietnam," using air and sea power.

Senator Aiken then asked if Hanoi was the base of the "Russian supply operation" and Rusk answered "yes." Senator Aiken further asked whether, "if we become involved," our involvement would be limited to "strictly conventional weapons." Rusk replied that there could be no guarantee that this would be the case.

Senators Russell B. Long (D/La.), Symington and John J. Sparkman (D/Ala.) told Rusk that if the U.S. was going to get militarily involved on any substantial scale there should be action by Congress, possibly in the form of a resolution. They all agreed that it had been a mistake for the U.S. to become involved in the Korean war without such action. ". . . this silence-gives-consent business does not work too good," Long said, "when the thing starts going poorly."

After the May 12 decision and the dispatch of military forces, the debate over Laos continued in the administration. It was reported to be serious, and at times heated, as deep cleavages developed between the "all or nothing" view of the JCS, supported by others, including W. W. Rostow, and the Harriman-Hilsman preference for limited military action. Finally, according to Hilsman, those who favored more limited action were able to get agreement on action by the President on May 29, 1962 directing the development of contingency plans for military action in Laos, under which Thai forces, with U.S. assistance, would seek to take and hold a province on the Mekong River in the western part of Laos, while Thai, Vietnamese or U.S. forces would recapture and hold the "panhandle" in the Southern part of Laos.[111]

As a result of several factors, including the effects of U.S. military movements (although there is no indication that the Communists intended to wage a major offensive after Phoumi's troops fled Nam Tha), agreement was reached early in June 1962 on a coalition government, and on July 23 the Geneva Agreement (or Accords) on Laos ("Declaration on the Neutrality of Laos") was signed.

On July 13, Rusk, accompanied by Chayes, met with the Foreign Relations Committee in an executive session to discuss the Laos neutrality agreement.[112] He said that it would be signed by the President as an executive agreement, and that it required no action by Congress except to help pay for the costs of the control commission. Senator Morse asked why it had not been sent to the Senate as a treaty, and Rusk replied that it was not being sent because it was primarily a declaration of policy. Morse asked whether there were any new commitments to use force, and Chayes replied that it was not a "formal guarantee agreement" by which the U.S. would be obligated to act.

In a later interview Chayes was asked about the relation of Congress to the 1962 Geneva agreement. He replied:[113]

---

[111]NSAM 157, in *PP*, Gravel ed., vol. II, pp. 672-673.
[112]U.S. Congress, Senate, Committee on Foreign Relations, unpublished executive session transcript, July 13, 1962.
[113]CRS Interview with Abram Chayes, Oct. 13, 1978.

. . . we didn't choose to treat it as a treaty. Our view then was somewhat different than the views that are now advanced, especially by Congress, about the treaty power. Our views then were that the President as Commander in Chief is entitled to make agreements of this country without submitting them to Congress because they, in effect, were agreements about how the President would exercise his powers as Commander in Chief. But we've come a long way since 1962 and I think the development is such that you wouldn't regard it as that kind of an agreement.

I am confident that Harriman briefed congressional people from time to time on the Laotian settlement. But Congress was a very different animal, too. I mean, congressmen didn't want to get into these things. In fact, in a way, they'd just as soon not be briefed. They didn't want to have responsibility for these things, and if you briefed them they weren't probing or questioning. They wanted to keep their freedom of action, freedom to criticize when it was all over if they wanted to, but it was a very different atmosphere at that time. They were prepared to cede, in effect, presidential jurisdiction.

A similar observation about Congress' role with respect to the Geneva agreement, as well as the May 12, 1962 decision to dispatch U.S. forces, was made by William Bundy in an interview:[114]

I was recurrently appearing before interested congressional committees at this time, and I recall no serious questioning of the move [sending troops] as a matter of policy or of the President's authority to make such a move. What consultation there may have been, I do not know. But it's indicative of a period so different from today, that this kind of thing could take place. They weren't sent into combat; they were sent clearly for a sort of demonstrative purpose. It was the kind of deployment that would almost certainly be questioned sharply in today's atmosphere, but at the time I'd be quite confident, based on my more or less recurrent contacts with the Hill, it was not questioned at all. I think that the same goes for the Laos peace agreement. I don't recall that it had to be submitted for approval by the Senate.

Michael Forrestal, who replaced Rostow as McGeorge Bundy's deputy for the Far East in January 1962 (at that point Robert Johnson also moved with Rostow to the State Department's Policy Planning Staff) and was the primary White House staff liaison with Harriman on the final stages of the Geneva negotiations on Laos, also said in an interview that "no consideration" was given to submitting the Geneva agreement to the Senate for approval, and that there was "no demand" from the Senate that this be done:[115]

I think at that time the view was, assuming that the President had the right . . . to send economic and minor military assistance to a country that asks for it, that since he had that right he also had the right to pull out and that he didn't have to negotiate a treaty to do that. . . . So the issue of the Con-

[114]CRS Interview with William Bundy, Aug. 3, 1978.
[115]CRS Interview with Michael Forrestal, Oct. 16, 1978.

gress really didn't come up. And I can't remember a single person suggesting that [Senate approval].

Forrestal said that during the spring of 1962 he met with key Members of Congress, including Fulbright, Mansfield, Russell and John Stennis (D/Miss.), and Thomas E. Morgan (D/Pa.) and Clement J. Zablocki (D/Wis.) in the House, to keep them informed about the progress of the Geneva negotiations, but that with the exception of Mansfield none of them showed much interest in the matter. (Stennis, he said, was concerned about the effects of a Laos settlement on the rest of Southeast Asia, and on U.S. international prestige.) "My sense," Forrestal said, "is that they didn't want to hear much about it. . . . I think they felt that it was a messy subject. It wasn't going to be useful to them politically. They'd just rather have the administration handle it and not get involved." Forrestal added that in the case of the committee chairmen themselves (Fulbright, Russell, Morgan), they did not seem to want to have their committees involved, and did not suggest that the subject be brought before the committees. ". . . not until the very end were there even any hearings of any sort on the subject, and certainly no public ones." This was his explanation:

I think it's because at that time there seemed to be in Congress, among the leadership at any rate, a real disinclination to get into Executive foreign affairs, the foreign affairs conducted by the Executive, partly because so much information was classified; people's lives were involved overseas, and they didn't want to be burdened with the responsibility of knowledge. And even if they did have the knowledge, they probably felt, although none of them ever told me this, "What am I going to do about it? I know something, maybe, but I can't make a speech about it because it's all terribly secret. My constituents aren't really interested in this any way. . . . They hardly know where Laos is." We didn't have enough men over there to pose a political problem, with casualties and that sort of thing, so at that time it just didn't seem to be something they wanted to get involved in.

Congress accepted the 1962 Laos settlement with little open dissent, partly because of deference to the Executive, but primarily because few Members wanted to see the U.S. become more actively involved, especially militarily, in Laos. At the same time, many if not most Members were privately if not publicly skeptical that the settlement had "settled" anything, and there was considerable concern, especially among those who favored a strong stand by the U.S. in Southeast Asia, that it would work in the Communists' favor.[116]

Should Vietnam Also Become Neutral?

During the first several months of 1962, while efforts continued to bring about the neutralization of Laos, a few of Kennedy's associates and advisers again raised the possibility of making Vietnam neutral as well. They were not convinced that the new "limited

---

[116]For an example of these views see the private letters to Rusk and Harriman from Representative Melvin R. Laird (R./Wis.) on July 24 and Aug. 23, 1962, and their replies, printed subsequently in *CR*, vol. 110, pp. 12257-12258.

partnership" was workable, or that the U.S. could find a solution to the Vietnam problem, and they wanted, above all, to avoid the large-scale use of force as the ultimate answer. One of these was Ambassador Galbraith, who broached the possibility of a neutral Vietnam with Kennedy in early April 1962, during a trip to Washington. Kennedy, according to Galbraith, "was immediately interested," and asked him to talk to Harriman and McNamara and to give him something in writing. Both Harriman and McNamara, especially Harriman, were "warmly sympathetic," and on April 4 Galbraith gave Kennedy a memorandum on the subject which he said also reflected Harriman's ideas.[117] In it he warned the President of the perils of U.S. involvement in Vietnam, asserting that our "growing military commitment . . . could expand step by step into a major, long-drawn out and decisive military involvement." This, together with support of an ineffectual government and political leader, he said, posed the danger that the U.S. would ". . . replace the French as the colonial force in the area and bleed as the French did."

Galbraith reiterated his opposition to the use of U.S. troops or advisers in combat: "We should resist all steps which commit American troops to combat action and impress upon all concerned the importance of keeping American forces out of actual combat commitment." He also urged that the U.S. remain in the background in the case of the strategic hamlet program and the defoliation program, where the presence of an outside power might be resented, and where the U.S. might suffer from identification with unpopular activities. ("Americans in their various roles," he said, "should be as invisible as the situation permits.")[118]

Galbraith urged Kennedy to seek a political solution to the Vietnam problem, to reduce commitments to the Diem government, and to seek diplomatic support both for the establishment of a more viable non-Communist government and for efforts to bring an end to the insurgency, accompanied by U.S. withdrawal.

The Joint Chiefs of Staff, replying to a request for comment on the Galbraith memo, said that his suggestions would have the effect of putting the U.S. "in a position of initiating negotiations with the communists to seek disengagement from what is by now a well-known commitment to take a forthright stand against Communism in Southeast Asia." "Any reversal of U.S. policy," they added, "could have disastrous effects, not only upon our relationship with South Vietnam, but with the rest of our Asian and other allies as well."[119]

No action appears to have been taken on Galbraith's suggestion, but a short while later, toward the end of the Geneva Conference on Laos (the dates are not clear), Harriman was authorized by Kennedy himself to meet privately with North Vietnamese delegates to the Conference for the purpose of exploring possibilities of negotiations on Vietnam, including the possibility of a conference on neutralization of Vietnam similar to the one on Laos. Harriman, accompanied by his deputy, William Sullivan, went to the hotel suite

---

[117]John Kenneth Galbraith, *A Life in Our Times* (Boston: Houghton Mifflin, 1981), p. 477.
[118]From the text in *PP*, Gravel ed., vol. II, pp. 670-671.
[119]*Ibid.*, pp. 671-672.

of the Burmese delegation to the Conference, where they met with the North Vietnamese Foreign Minister, Ung Van Khiem, and one of his aides. The meeting was fruitless, Sullivan said later. "We got absolutely nowhere. We hit a stone wall."[120]

Harriman's position, which Sullivan said the President shared, was that ". . . once you get the Laotian settlement that you might be able to expand it into a larger area of understanding, and, particularly if you got the Soviets to recognize that it united their interests as well as ours to try to neutralize the whole Indochina area, that otherwise it might fall prey to the Chinese, and that we might be able to build therefore on the Laos settlement as something which would move toward a larger settlement in the whole Indochina area. . . . At least he [Kennedy] was constantly looking for opportunities to see if we could expand from the Laos agreement, but at the same time feeling more confident about his military posture in Vietnam once Laos had been tidied up [i.e., that Vietnam was a more suitable place to take a stand]."[121]

The failure of this attempt to probe the possible interests of the North Vietnamese in negotiations strengthened the resolve of Kennedy and his associates to prosecute the campaign against the Communists in Vietnam.[122] Some of them, including Rusk and U. Alexis Johnson, who had not favored the idea in the first place, were confirmed in their opinion that it was a mistake to seek such a solution, or to consider, at that stage, U.S. withdrawal from Vietnam. This position was supported by the reports coming in from Vietnam about improvements in the situation resulting from increased U.S. assistance. Many policymakers seemed to believe, and were telling Congress and the public, that they were optimistic.

John Newhouse, who was dealing with Vietnam for the Foreign Relations Committee, reported to Fulbright on February 23, 1962 on a long conversation he had held with the State Department desk officer for Vietnam, Chalmers Wood, who was also on the Vietnam Task Force in which Wood said that developments in Vietnam were encouraging. Newhouse concluded that if this evaluation was correct, ". . . it would seem very unlikely that the question of American combat forces need arise. What will be required of us is patience, because the process of eliminating the influence and presence of these hard core Viet Cong cadres will probably take years, five years some say. It will be difficult, but the actual fighting can presumably be left to the GVN forces, whose competence is expected to increase steadily."[123]

On March 16, 1962, McNamara testified before the House Appropriations Committee on the foreign aid appropriations bill, and said he was "optimistic" about the prospects in Vietnam. He main-

[120]Kennedy Library, Second Oral History Interview with William Sullivan, Aug. 5, 1970, p. 32; CRS Interview with William Sullivan, July 31, 1980.
[121]Second Oral History Interview with William Sullivan, p. 34.
[122]Following another trip to Southeast Asia in May 1962, Chester Bowles again urged Kennedy to seek a negotiated settlement of the Vietnam conflict. Kennedy and Rusk both expressed interest, but FE, Bowles said (he was referring to Harriman), was opposed, and a trip which he was to make to explore the idea was finally called off. See *Promises to Keep*, pp. 410-414. In the spring of 1963, Bowles made one last effort to persuade Kennedy to seek a negotiated settlement and to avoid a major U.S. military commitment to Vietnam. There was no response to his memorandum to the President.
[123]University of Arkansas, Fulbright Papers, series 48.

tained that the U.S. would attain its objectives, and suggested that the end was in sight: "I would say definitely we are approaching it from the point of view of trying to clean it up and terminating subversion, covert aggression, and combat operations. . . ." (He also took the position that U.S. forces might be detrimental: ". . . to introduce white forces—U.S. forces—in large numbers there today, while it might have an initial favorable military impact would almost certainly lead to adverse political and in the long run adverse military operations.")[124]

The administration was also waging at least a limited campaign to persuade the public that the new U.S. program in Vietnam was both necessary and effective, and that a negotiated settlement in Laos was the wisest course of action under the circumstances.

Harriman himself, while working behind the scenes to explore possible negotiations, publicly defended the new Vietnam program, and on May 27, 1962, the *New York Times* Magazine published an article by him on "What We Are Doing in Southeast Aisa," in which he explained U.S. policy toward both Laos and Vietnam.

George Ball, another skeptic behind closed doors, gave a rousing defense and justification for the U.S. role in Vietnam in a speech on April 30, 1962, before the Detroit Economic Club. He said, in part:

If the Vietnamese people were to lose the struggle to maintain a free and independent nation, it would be a loss of tragic significance to the security of Free World interests in the whole of Asia and the South Pacific.

And more than that, if the United States were to neglect its solemn commitments to the Vietnamese people, the consequences would not be limited even to those areas—they would be world-wide. For the Free World's security cannot be given away piecemeal; it is not divisible. When the going gets rough we cannot observe those commitments that are easy or near at hand and disregard the others.

What we do or fail to do in Viet-Nam will be felt both by our antagonists and our friends. Any United States retreat in one area of struggle inevitably encourages Communist adventures in another. How we act in Viet-Nam will have its impact on Communist actions in Europe, in Africa and in Latin America. Far from easing tensions, our unwillingness to meet our commitments in one tension area will simply encourage the Communists to bestir trouble in another.

Asserting that the struggle against the Communists in Vietnam would "definitely" be won, Ball said, "This is a task that we must stay with until it is concluded. But we should have no illusions. It will not be concluded quickly. It took eight years in Malaya.

"What we can expect in Vietnam is the long, slow arduous execution of a process. Results will not be apparent over night. For the

[124]U.S., Congress, House, Committee on Appropriations, *Foreign Operations Appropriations for 1963*, 87th Cong., 2d sess. (Washington, D.C.: U.S. Govt. Print. Off., 1962), p. 370. The quotation on U.S. forces was deleted from the printed text of the hearing by the Defense Department, but appears in a reprint of that part of the testimony in *PP*, Gravel ed., vol. II, p. 173. After a visit to Vietnam in May 1963, McNamara said privately that it would take 6 years to defeat the Communists, according to Maxwell Taylor, then Chairman of the JCS. *Swords and Plowshares*, p. 251.

operation is, of necessity, the patient winning back of a land to freedom, village by village."

According to Ball, "The United States has *no* combat units in Viet-Nam. We are not fighting the war, as some reports have suggested. We are *not* running the war, as the Communists have tried assiduously to argue."

The morning after Ball's speech, the *New York Herald Tribune* carried an article by its renowned reporter, Marguerite Higgins, in which she wrote that "American retreat or withdrawal from South Viet-Nam is unthinkable, according to Mr. Ball. The American commitment, moreover, is irrevocable." Ball immediately sent a memo to McGeorge Bundy asserting that the Higgins interpretation was not correct, and that his speech was intended to emphasize the limited nature of the U.S. involvement. He quoted passages from the speech, including those above, to buttress his point.

McGeorge Bundy sent Ball's memo and a copy of the speech to the President with a cover note saying, "I think George defends himself fairly against Maggie Higgins, but I also think that the speech has a tone and content that we would not have cleared, simply from the point of view of maintaining a chance of political settlement. From the way George has been telephoning to explain this speech, I doubt there will be another one without clearance over here."[125]

Messages contrary to the official optimism of Washington were being received, however, not only from U.S. and other media correspondents in the field, but from other informed persons who were concerned about the situation, and who were becoming increasingly alarmed about the trends they saw developing. One of these was Wesley R. Fishel, (former adviser to Diem and head of the Michigan State University group in Vietnam in the 1950s), who had just come back from a month's visit to Vietnam. He was very depressed over what he had found. (It will be recalled that the Michigan State University contract in Vietnam had just been finally terminated by Diem, allegedly because of articles in the U.S. press and periodicals by former members of the MSU team which were considered to be critical of the Diem government.) Fishel reported his findings to John A. Hannah, president of Michigan State, who sent them to President Kennedy with a covering letter in which he explained that although Michigan State regretted the termination of the contract, the purpose of his letter was to call Kennedy's attention to Fishel's views.[126]

In his report to Hannah, Fishel said, among other things:

For the first time in seven and one-half years I have become a pessimist about the fate of South Vietnam. In the two and

[125]Kennedy Library, POF Country File, Vietnam General, 1962. The speech was not published in the *Department of State Bulletin*, probably because of the reaction it received, and Ball does not mention it in his memoirs. The quotes above are from the *New York Times*, May 1, 1962.
[126]Fishel's letter of Feb. 17, 1962, Hannah's of Feb. 26, and an acknowledgement from McGeorge Bundy on Mar. 26, are in the Kennedy Library, NSF Country File, Vietnam. In his letter to Kennedy, Hannah, who had served as an Assistant Secretary of Defense under Eisenhower, made this interesting observation about the MSU contract: "We recognized at the beginning that we were involving ourselves in some activities that were hardly appropriate for a university to be concerned with, but because it seemed to be in the United States' national interest, and because our cooperation was requested by Mr. [Harold E.] Stassen and others near the center of the Eisenhower Administration, we agreed to do what we were asked to do."

one-half years since my last visit to that country there has been a most profound and distressing deterioration there, politically, socially, and psychologically. Economically, though some progress is still being made the gains of the past few years are in many cases being reversed. . . . Militarily, the recent influx of thousands of American officers and men, and dozens of helicopters, etc., is starting to make a distinct change in the situation already, turning what was a minus into a plus. I would hesitate to predict, however, that the plus will remain that for long, for I find it hard to believe that the Chinese and Viet Cong will allow this challenge to go unmet. Indeed, my travels to the high plateau, the center, and the Mekong delta last month have left me with the impression that a Viet Cong offensive is very likely in the next few weeks. By that I don't mean a major invasion out of the north, but rather a heavily intensified terrorization program that may spread even to the cities, with the intent of panicking the population and weakening the Diem government's hold still more.

Politically and psychologically things are at a low ebb. The commendable programs which were begun a few years ago have been allowed in many instances to lose their momentum by reason largely of a failure on the part of the Central Government to follow through on initial decisions and acts. The hopes and aspirations of 1954 and 1955 have been allowed to die, and a miasma of apathy pervades the atmosphere. I talked more than casually with 118 people during my four weeks in Vietnam. Almost all are people I have known for many years. None of them is politically part of the "opposition." At least two thirds of them were still Diem's strong adherents in 1959. Yet today, only three or four of these men and women supports the government with discernible enthusiasm. Then too, there is much popular fear: fear that "the Viet Cong are coming," and that the government is not going to be able to move to meet the Communist threat swiftly enough to save many people from being hurt or killed.

"Unless Vietnam experiences a major and favorable psychological shock within the next few months, I doubt seriously whether it will survive," Fishel added, "notwithstanding our efforts and our money and our men. The bright spots which were so clearly visible two and even one year ago are now fading into insignificance because the regime still has failed to mobilize the hearts and loyalties of the people."

Optimism Leads to a Plan for Reduction of the U.S. Role

Despite reports to the contrary, policymakers in Saigon and Washington continued to believe that the situation in Vietnam was improving. In a report on June 18, 1962 to Assistant Secretary of State Harriman, the Bureau of Intelligence and Research (Hilsman) discussed specific actions being taken along with a brief critique of each, and ended with a "Summary Assessment."[127] With

---

[127]The text is in *PP,* DOD ed., book 12, pp. 469-480.

respect to developments in the "military-security sector," the paper stated:

It is too early to say that the Viet Cong guerrilla-terrorist onslaught is being checked, but it can be said that it is now meeting more effective resistance and having to cope with increased aggressiveness by the Vietnamese military and security forces. Nonetheless, the Viet Cong continue to increase their armed strength and capability and, on balance, to erode government authority in the countryside.

There had not been as much improvement, Hilsman's report said, in other areas, and ". . . while there are encouraging signs of popular support for the government, there has been no major break-through in identifying the people with the struggle against the Viet Cong."

We conclude that:

1. there is no evidence to support certain allegations of substantial deterioration in the political and military situations in Vietnam;

2. on the contrary, there is evidence of heartening progress in bolstering the fighting effectiveness of the military and security forces;

3. however, there is still much to be done in strengthening the overall capacity of the Vietnamese Government to pursue its total counterinsurgency effort, not only in the military-security sector but particularly in the political-administrative sector;

4. a judgment on ultimate success in the campaign against the Communist "war of national liberation" in Vietnam is premature; but

5. We do think that the chances are good, provided there is continuing progress by the Vietnamese Government along the lines of its present strategy.

Operating on the assumption that U.S. efforts to assist the Vietnamese would continue to succeed, and, therefore, that the U.S. could and should begin to consider a plan for reducing its commitments and role in future years, McNamara, after consultation with the President, directed the military to begin such planning. At a meeting in Honolulu on July 23, 1962, the day the Laos agreement was concluded, he said that by fiscal year 1968 (beginning July 1, 1967), U.S. personnel should be reduced from the expected peak of 12,000 in 1963-64 to 1,500 (consisting only of MAAG headquarters staff), and U.S. military assistance funds from $180 million to $40.8 million.[128]

The optimism that generally prevailed at the time was further strengthened by reports at the Honolulu meeting that there had been "tremendous progress in South Vietnam." McNamara asked General Harkins how long it would take "before the VC could be expected to be eliminated as a significant force," and Harkins replied that it would take about a year from the time Vietnamese

---

[128]*Ibid.,* Gravel ed., vol. II, p. 160. The *Pentagon Papers* analyst notes (p. 161) that one of the reasons for the plan was to counteract bureaucratic pressures for increased involvement in Vietnam. "What Secretary McNamara did was to force all theater justifications for force build-up into tension with long-term phase-down plans."

forces were "fully operational and began to press the VC in all areas."[129] McNamara responded that it would be more prudent to assume that three years would be required. He then noted, as the *Pentagon Papers* states, that ". . . it might be difficult to retain public support for U.S. operations in Vietnam indefinitely. Political pressures would build up as losses continued. Therefore, he concluded, planning must be undertaken now and a program devised to phase out U.S. military involvement."[130]

Congress Accepts the New U.S. Program

Although McNamara correctly perceived the potential problem of maintaining public support for the U.S. program in Vietnam, as later events so clearly demonstrated, there were very few signs of public or congressional disagreement or discontent with the expanding U.S. role. During the hearings and debates in Congress in the spring and early summer of 1962 on the foreign aid authorization and appropriations bills, through which funds were provided for the new program (except for military advisers, who were paid from Defense Department funds), there were only scattered questions or comments about Vietnam and about the new program, and in the end Congress voted overwhelmingly for providing the authorization and the money requested by the Executive.

If anything, Congress was impatient to get on with the job. In public hearings of the House Foreign Affairs Committee some of the members were skeptical about the claims of the executive branch that U.S. advisers were not engaged in combat, and it was obvious from their comments that there was considerable support for having advisers serve as combatants. As Representative J. L. Pilcher (D/Ga.), a member of the Far East Subcommittee, said, "I am in favor of it. That is a hot war. . . . It is not a cold war. When you send those boys over there, they are going to shoot back."

Representative Zablocki, chairman of the Far East Subcommittee, referring to the training mission of U.S. advisers, said, "If we want to win against the enemy we will have to use them pretty soon." He added that he thought the American public was "prepared to assent" to this.[131]

The new U.S. program in Vietnam was, in fact, endorsed by some Members of Congress who had previously been uncertain about the role of the United States. Notable were the comments of Senators Humphrey and Morse on October 10, 1962, praising the administration's efforts to develop counterinsurgency programs, and to improve the capability of the U.S. to engage effectively in counterguerrilla warfare against the Communists.[132] Humphrey said that in Vietnam ". . . in recent months, the tide may well have turned for the forces of freedom against the Communist guerrillas of the north. . . . A number of striking successes have been achieved." He called for more effective programs and better weapons and supplies to "put out these brush fires" in Vietnam and in other less developed countries facing Communist guerrilla warfare.

[129]*Ibid.*, p. 164.
[130]*Ibid.*, p. 175.
[131]*Foreign Assistance Act of 1962*, pp. 252, 123.
[132]*CR*, vol. 108, pp. 22957-22961.

Morse, while critical of the unilateral burden being carried by the U.S. in Southeast Asia, agreed strongly with Humphrey, saying, "Unfortunately, a good many of the soldiers of freedom have not been in a position where they could successfully combat guerrilla warfare. Therefore, we must place ourselves in a strengthened position, so that the Communist world will know that we can meet them on every front—Cuba, Berlin, southeast Asia, Africa. We must let them know that wherever they wish to attack freedom, we will stand firm and protect freedom."

William Bundy, a principal executive branch witness on the military assistance portion of the 1962 foreign aid legislation, says of the phenomenon of congressional acceptance of the new Kennedy program:[133]

> . . . it is very striking to me in retrospect that I recall no significant expression of disagreement with that [the new U.S. program]. "How were we doing?" . . . they would want to get your latest evaluation . . . all of that. But there was no tendency to say, "Isn't this a very risky enterprise? Should we be in this deep?"

Why, besides its general agreement with U.S. policy in Vietnam, was Congress so accepting? In 1962, as in earlier years, it is clear that Congress was still playing its role as the "silent partner" of the Executive in foreign policy, based on the post World War II consensual pattern of executive-legislative relationships that still prevailed. For example, in a major speech on Vietnam on June 3, 1962, Senator Mansfield reiterated his belief that the determination of foreign policy is in the hands of the President. Referring to the recent U.S. troop deployment to Thailand, as well as the new U.S. military advisory role in Vietnam, he said, "Both steps represent a deepening of an already very deep involvement on the Southeast Asia mainland. In this, as in all cases of foreign policy and military command, the responsibility for the direction of the Nation's course rests with the President."[134] Although he suggested the need to reevaluate U.S. policy toward Southeast Asia, he seemed to assume that Congress' role was primarily that of a forum for public discussion of the issue.

At the time, Senator Fulbright held even stronger views about the role of the President. In an article in 1961 on "American Foreign Policy in the 20th Century under an 18th Century Constitution,"[135] which his critics later quoted with delight, Fulbright took the position that ". . . for the existing requirements of American foreign policy we have hobbled the President by too niggardly a grant of power." "The overriding problem of inadequate Presidential authority in foreign affairs," Fulbright added, "derives . . . from the 'checks and balances' of Congressional authority in foreign relations." Fulbright questioned ". . . whether in the face of the harsh necessities of the 1960's we can afford the luxury of 18th century procedures of measured deliberation. It is highly unlikely that we can successfully execute a long-range program for the

[133]CRS Interview with William Bundy, Aug. 3, 1978.
[134]From the text of Mansfield's speech at Michigan State University on June 3, 1962, reprinted in *CR*, vol. 108, pp. 10048-10050.
[135]*Cornell Law Quarterly*, 47 (Fall 1961), pp. 1-13.

taming, or containing, of today's aggressive and revolutionary forces by continuing to leave vast and vital decision-making powers in the hands of a decentralized, independent-minded and largely parochial-minded body of legislators. . . . I submit that the price of democratic survival in a world of aggressive totalitarianism is to give up some of the democratic luxuries of the past. We should do so with no illusions as to the reasons for its necessity. It is distasteful and dangerous to vest the executive with powers unchecked and unbalanced. My question is whether we have any choice but to do so."[136]

Mansfield and Fulbright's views were not atypical. They reflected the general attitude of most Members of Congress at that point in U.S. history. It is not surprising, therefore, that Congress should have asked so few questions during 1962 about the new U.S. role and program in Vietnam.

An additional and very important reason for Congress' acceptance of the new U.S. program in Vietnam was the somewhat hidden nature of that program. This factor, as was mentioned earlier, tended to maximize the role of the Executive and to minimize the role of Congress. As Carl Marcy, who was chief of staff of the Foreign Relations Committee during that period, said about the role of Congress, and specifically that of the Committee, in relation to Vietnam in 1962:[137] "I think it is fair to say that the committee did not pay much attention. The war was being waged by the executive branch. Committee members didn't feel that they were in a good position to criticize the professional, whether it be a professional in the military or whether it be a professional in clandestine activities of various kinds."

Moreover, during at least the first 6-9 months of 1962 the new U.S. program in Vietnam appeared, on the surface, at least, to be succeeding, and most Members of Congress were content, especially in an election year, to give it a chance to succeed. This was particularly true of the Democrats, who then controlled both the House and the Senate, and were not inclined to raise unnecessary questions about Kennedy's foreign policy. The Republicans were in a better position to do so, but they, too, were generally assentive.

There was also support in Congress for the new U.S. program in Vietnam among those Members—Humphrey being an example—who generally supported the kind of internationalist, interventionist foreign policy being conducted by the administration, and who were influenced by the prevailing intellectual and political fashion represented by the Special Group (CI).

Once again it is also important to note that at that stage Vietnam was a comparatively minor foreign policy problem, and therefore less salient for Congress than other foreign and domestic problems. For the first six months of 1962 Laos was a more compelling

[136]Years later, Fulbright commented, "The imperial presidency, in the wake of Vietnam and Watergate, seems to have fallen as fast as it rose. . . . I am not inclined, however, to revive my formulation of 1961, calling for a more generous grant of presidential power over foreign relations. A new, more generally serviceable formulation seems required, one that will take account of the essential congressional role in the authorization of military and major political commitments, and in advising broad policy directions, while leaving to the executive the necessary flexibility to conduct policy within the broad parameters approved by the legislature." J. William Fulbright, "The Legislator as Educator," *Foreign Affairs*, 57 (Spring 1979), p. 726.
[137]CRS Interview with Carl Marcy, Feb. 13, 1979.

issue, and for at least the last three months the Cuban "missile crisis," together with continuing problems in Berlin, eclipsed every other issue.

The Cuba and Berlin Resolutions: Immediate Precedents for the Gulf of Tonkin Resolution

Concern over both Cuba and Berlin prompted Congress to pass resolutions in the fall of 1962 supporting military action, if necessary, by the President at his own discretion, both of which, especially the Cuba Resolution, served as precedents and justification for the Gulf of Tonkin Resolution in 1964. In both cases, moreover, Congress seemed to be as insistent as the Executive that such action should be taken to demonstrate the "unified national will" to resist Communist aggression.

The Cuba Resolution,[138] which was enacted by Congress on September 26, 1962, stated the determination of the United States: "to prevent by whatever means may be necessary, including the use of arms, the Marxist-Leninist regime in Cuba from extending, by force or the threat of force, its aggressive or subversive activities to any part of this hemisphere," and "to prevent in Cuba the creation or use of an externally supported military capability endangering the security of the United States. . . ."[139]

By passing this resolution, which had no time limit, and which accepted and affirmed—but did not authorize—the use of the armed forces, if necessary, Congress gave its advance, open-ended approval to any decision by the President to use any or all of the armed forces of the United States to meet the perceived threat. By so doing, it implicitly accepted the President's own assertion of his constitutional right to undertake military action against Communism in Cuba without needing any action by or approval from Congress. In a speech on September 13, Kennedy had stated that "As President and Commander in Chief, I have full authority now to take such action."

Unlike previous resolutions (Formosa, Middle East), there was almost no debate in committee or on the floor with respect to the legal and constitutional aspects of the Cuba Resolution. The House Foreign Affairs Committee report made no reference to this subject, and the joint report of the Senate Foreign Relations and Armed Services Committees[140] brushed aside any possible questions by asserting that ". . . constitutional arguments over the relative powers of the President and the Congress respecting the use of American Armed Forces . . . have their place in American public life; but it is important in the current instance that they not obscure what the joint committee is convinced is the essential unity of purpose, not only of the Congress, but of the President and the American people as well." The joint committee voted unanimously to report the bill favorably to the Senate, where it was passed in one day with no significant debate. The vote was 86-1, with Senator Winston L. Prouty (R/Vt.) the only dissenter. He said

---

[138]Public Law 87-733.
[139]For a good synopsis of the background and congressional consideration of the Cuba Resolution see the *Congressional Quarterly Almanac* for 1962, pp. 331-340 (hereafter cited as *CQ*).
[140]S. Rept. 87-2111.

it was not strong enough. (Likewise, only a handful of Republicans, who felt as Prouty did, opposed the measure in a 384-7 House vote.) Silent were all those who had spoken up in 1955 and in 1957, when similar resolutions were being enacted, about their concerns for protecting Congress' war power. Conspicuously silent was Senator Wayne Morse, who, coincidentally or not, was running for reelection. He voted for the resolution, saying that he was doing so because it did not delegate the constitutional war-making power of Congress to the President.

The Berlin Resolution,[141] passed by Congress on October 10, 1962, declared the determination of the U.S. "to prevent by whatever means may be necessary, including the force of arms," any violation by the Communists of Allied rights in Berlin, and the commitment of the U.S. to help the people of Berlin maintain their freedom. It, too, was open-ended and time-unlimited, and took the position that the President could use at his discretion, and without further action by Congress (unless required by the need for increasing U.S. military forces), any or all of the armed forces of the United States to meet the stated objectives of our policy. Unlike the Cuba Resolution, however, it was a "sense of Congress" resolution, which did not require the President's signature and did not have the force of law. It did not, therefore, have the legal and constitutional significance of the Cuba Resolution, nor, for that reason, was it as important and direct a precedent for the Gulf of Tonkin Resolution.

In the case of the Cuba Resolution, as in the case of the Gulf of Tonkin Resolution, the domestic political situation was a key factor in Congress's action. The Cuban situation was a salient issue in the congressional campaign in 1962, and in 1964 the question of Presidential restraint in war making became a salient issue in the Presidential and, to some extent, congressional campaigns.[142]

Warnings

By the end of 1962, the "Comprehensive Plan for South Vietnam" (CPSVN), as the plan ordered by McNamara at the July Honolulu Conference was called, had been developed, and was being cleared at the various levels of command. There was much less optimism about the situation in Vietnam, however, than there had been in July.

On December 3, 1962, Hilsman sent Rusk and Kennedy a long memo[143] on the prospects in Vietnam. Its general conclusion was that very little progress was being made, and that "Elimination, even significant reduction, of the Communist insurgency will almost certainly require several years." The Communists, the paper reported, were stronger than ever, and "The sharp increase of the U.S. military presence in South Vietnam and the events of recent months in Laos apparently have not weakened Communist resolve to take over South Vietnam." Asserting that although the role of the U.S. may have caused the Communists to modify their

---

[141]H. Con. Res. 87-570.
[142]See the *CQ Almanac*, as well as the relevant literature on the Cuban "missile crisis," for information on how the Cuban issue was being handled politically in the 1962 election by both the Democrats and the Republicans.
[143]*PP*, Gravel ed., vol. II, pp. 690 ff.

tactics and their timetable, the paper added that the Viet Cong had not been weakened, and that they ". . . probably continue to look primarily to the long run in South Vietnam and to remain confident of eventual victory."

On the strategic hamlet program, the paper was optimistic, while stating that it was too early to evaluate the program. It was critical, however, of tactical bombing and crop destruction from defoliation, saying that these ". . . may well contribute to the development of militant opposition among the peasants and positive identification with the Viet Cong."

The Hilsman report also noted that, with increasing dissatisfaction among the populace, there was the possibility of a coup against Diem. If one occurred, the paper said, the role of the U.S. should be to avert a serious power struggle that could adversely affect the war effort, and to assist coup leaders in advance of the coup in avoiding precipitous action, and after the coup in establishing a new government.

Kennedy also received a disturbing first-hand report from Mansfield, who had visited Vietnam during late November and early December 1962. Others on the trip were Senators Claiborne Pell (D/R.I.), J. Caleb Boggs (D/Del.), and Benjamin A. Smith (D/Mass.).

David Halberstam, then in Vietnam with the *New York Times,* recounted his experience with Mansfield:[144]

Mike came through Saigon in the fall of 1962 and he wanted to have lunch with a group of us reporters, myself, Neil Sheehan, [UPI], Peter Arnett [AP], and possibly Mel Browne [Malcolm Browne, also AP]. If you wanted to get a non-official, non-embassy briefing in Saigon in those days, there was only one place—American reporters. . . . Mike already had his doubts, and, of course, by then we were all very, very discouraged and pessimistic and we had become the enemies of the mission and of the regime. . . . What we were saying was hardly that critical. We were quite pessimistic, but in terms of what was to come later, we were reasonably mild. So Mike had lunch with us and it lasted for five hours. I remember going on and on and on. . . . What was clear was that Mike Mansfield was really listening. He wanted to know.

Halberstam also recounted an incident at the airport the following day when Mansfield refused to make a parting statement written by the U.S. mission, (the mission acted "with incredible arrogance and stupidity" according to Halberstam),[145] and instead made his own, less optimistic statement.

Ambassador Nolting later said that he thought Mansfield was influenced by U.S. journalists, and that it was "a great mistake on the part of anyone who is as influential as Mansfield to come out there and sort of knock the legs from under U.S. policy, which ought to have been supported by the leader of the Senate." Nolting said that he went to see Diem after Mansfield left, and told Diem:

"Mr. President, I'm awfully sorry. Something must have gone wrong here. I don't know what it was but those were rather discouraging remarks." And Diem said, "I have been a

[144]CRS Interview with David Halberstam, Jan. 9, 1979.
[145]*Ibid.*

friend of Senator Mansfield and he has been so good to me for so many years that I'm not going to let that stand in the way of our friendship," or something to that effect. But he was shocked. He couldn't believe it. What impelled Mansfield to do this I've never understood.

According to Nolting, press accounts of Mansfield's report on his trip, and specifically his comments about Diem's leadership, were "the first nails in Diem's coffin."[146]

When the Mansfield party returned to Washington in mid-December 1962, Mansfield sent a private, confidential report on the trip to the President on December 18. In it, Mansfield, who noted that it was his first visit to Vietnam in seven years, summed up his conclusions by saying, ". . . it would be well to face the fact that we are once again at the beginning of the beginning." The "political structure in Saigon," he said, "is, today, far more dependent on us for its existence than it was five years ago. If Vietnam is the cork in the Southeast Asia bottle then American aid is more than ever the cork in the Vietnamese bottle."

Mansfield said he was told by both Vietnamese and U.S. officials in Saigon that the new program would solve the problem in a year or two. "Having heard optimistic predictions of this kind, with the introduction of other 'new concepts,' beginning with French General [Henry Eugène] Navarre in Hanoi in 1953, certain reservations seem to me to be in order." Among these he included estimates of Viet Minh casualties, and the success of the strategic hamlet program.

Concerning the strategic hamlets, Mansfield said that an ". . . immense job of social engineering, dependent on great outlays of aid on our part for many years and a most responsive, alert and enlightened leadership in the government of Vietnam" would be required before the plan could succeed in winning over the rural populace.

Mansfield expressed his continued confidence in Diem, but warned of the growing power of Nhu and "the great danger of unbridled power," which might prevent realization of the goal of the program to bring a new spirit of leadership and self-sacrifice to Vietnam.

Mansfield also expressed continued confidence in Kennedy's Vietnam program, which he said could be successful if the factors in the situation did not change drastically, and if there was adequate Vietnamese and American effort to make the program succeed.

The alternative, Mansfield said, was large-scale U.S. military intervention, which he vigorously opposed:

> . . . it is difficult to conceive of alternatives, with the possible exception of a truly massive commitment of American military personnel and other resources—in short going to war fully ourselves against the guerrillas—and the establishment of some form of new colonial rule in south Vietnam. That is an alternative which I most emphatically do not recommend. On the contrary, it seems to me most essential that we make crys-

---

[146]CRS Interview with Frederick Nolting, Dec. 7, 1978.

tal clear to the Vietnamese government and to our own people that while we will go to great lengths to help, the primary responsibility rests with the Vietnamese. Our role is and must remain secondary in present circumstances. It is their country, their future which is most at stake, not ours.

To ignore that reality will not only be immensely costly in terms of American lives and resources but it may also draw us inexorably into some variation of the unenviable position in Vietnam which was formerly occupied by the French. We are not, of course, at that point at this time. But the great increase in American military commitment this year has tended to point us in that general direction and we may well begin to slide rapidly toward it if any of the present remedies begin to falter in practice.

In conclusion, Mansfield returned to the theme of the speech he had made the previous June, in which he had questioned the value of the years of U.S. effort·and expenditure of funds in Southeast Asia, and suggested a possible new approach based on greater reliance on diplomacy and on collective action. If it was essential for the U.S. to maintain a "quasi-permanent position of power on the Asian mainland," he told Kennedy, then there was no choice but to take the steps required. "But if on the other hand it is, at best, only desirable rather than essential that a position of power be maintained on the mainland, then other courses are indicated. We would, then, properly view such improvement as may be obtained by the new approach in Vietnam primarily in terms of what it might contribute to strengthening our diplomatic hand in the Southeast Asia region. And we would use that hand as vigorously as possible and in every way possible not to deepen our costly involvement but to lighten it."[147]

After sending the report to Kennedy, Mansfield went to Palm Beach, Florida, on December 26, 1962, where he spent two hours going over the report with the President while sailing on Lake Worth. Kennedy, he said, had read the report ". . . in great detail and . . . questioned me minutely. He had a tremendous grasp of the situation."[148]

According to Halberstam,[149] "Kennedy had summoned Mansfield to his yacht, the *Honey Fitz,* where there was a party going on, and when the President read the report his face grew redder and redder as his anger mounted. Finally he turned to Mansfield, just about the closest friend he had in the Senate, and snapped, 'Do you expect me to take this at face value?' Mansfield answered, 'You asked me to go there.' Kennedy looked at him again, icily now, and said, 'Well, I'll read it again!' "

Kennedy told Kenneth P. O'Donnell, one of his closest aides, "I got angry with Mike for disagreeing with our policy so completely,

---

[147]Mansfield's private report to President Kennedy, Dec. 18, 1962, together with another such report which he made to President Johnson on Dec. 17, 1965, was eventually made public in Apr. 1973 in Senate Document 93-11. The public version of the report of the Mansfield group, *Viet Nam and Southeast Asia,* which is generally similar to his private report, was issued by the Foreign Relations Committee as a committee print in early 1963.
[148]Kennedy Library, Oral History Interview with Senator Mansfield, June 3, 1964, p. 24.
[149]*The Best and the Brightest,* p. 208.

and I got angry with myself because I found myself agreeing with him."[150]

In addition to the Mansfield group, three other Senators visited Vietnam late in 1962, Frank Church (D/Idaho), a member of the Foreign Relations Committee, Gale W. McGee (D/Wyo.), and Frank E. Moss (D/Utah). They reported that although the strategic hamlet program was working, the "vital ingredient"—"allegiance of the population to the present Government and their universal desire to win this struggle"—was lacking. The group concluded that despite the lack of progress, ". . . the alternatives to holding to our position there, both in the economic and military realms, are few indeed. The outlook must preclude either quick or decisive gains in the year ahead. A protracted struggle, at best, can be the only realistic forecast."[151]

The Hilsman-Forrestal Report

As the year (1962) ended, Kennedy sent Hilsman and Forrestal to Vietnam for a review of the situation. Both men were committed to the U.S. program, and their conviction that it could succeed apparently was strengthened as a result of the trip.[152]

In their report to the President, they said, among other things:[153] "The war in South Vietnam is clearly going better than it was a year ago. . . . The Viet Cong . . . are being hurt. . . . We are probably winning, but certainly more slowly than we had hoped. At the rate it is now going the war will last longer than we would like, cost more in terms of both lives and money than we anticipated, and prolong the period in which a sudden and dramatic event could upset the gains already made." The Communists, they reported, "continue to be aggressive and are extremely effective." Moreover, the strength of their regular forces had increased despite the fact that there was almost no infiltration from outside. ". . . it is ominous," the report stated, "that in the face of greatly increased government pressure and U.S. support the Viet Cong can still field 23,000 regular forces and 100,000 militia, supported by unknown thousands of sympathizers . . . the conclusion seems inescapable that the Viet Cong could continue the war effort at the present level, or perhaps increase it, even if the infiltration routes were completely closed."

The continuing success of the Communists in the countryside, said Hilsman and Forrestal, raised the "basic question of the whole war"—what is the attitude of the villagers?

No one really knows, for example, how many of the 20,000 "Viet Cong" killed last year were only innocent, or at least persuadable villagers, whether the Strategic Hamlet program is providing enough government services to counteract the sac-

---

[150]Kenneth P. O'Donnell, and David F. Powers, *"Johnny, We Hardly Knew Ye"* (New York: Pocket Book ed., 1973), p. 15.

[151]Senate Document 88-12, Mar. 15, 1963.

[152]In a memorandum to Kennedy on Sept. 18, 1962, Forrestal said, "While we cannot yet sit back in the confidence that the job is well in hand, nevertheless it does appear that we have finally developed a series of techniques which, if properly applied, do seem to produce results." Kennedy Library, NSF Country File, Vietnam. But he and Hilsman were also concerned about the slow progress being made in implementing the program, especially on the part of Diem.

[153]*PP*, Gravel ed., vol. II, pp. 717-725. For Hilsman's account see *To Move a Nation*, pp. 453-476.

rifices it requires, or how the mute mass of the villagers react to the charges against Diem of dictatorship and nepotism. At the very least, the figures on Viet Cong strength imply a continuing flow of recruits and supplies from these same villages and indicate that a substantial proportion of the population is still cooperating with the enemy, although it is impossible to tell how much of this cooperation stems from fear and how much from conviction. Thus on the vital question of villagers' attitudes, the net impression is one of some encouragement at the progress in building strategic hamlets and the number that resist when attacked, but encouragement overlaid by a shadow of uneasiness.

The report added, however, that the "basic strategic concept" on which the strategic hamlet program was founded—"not simply to kill Viet Cong, but to win the people"—was still sound, but needed to be better implemented. The U.S., they said, should press the Diem government to do more, and they cited specific weaknesses that needed remedying.

Forrestal and Hilsman concluded their report with several comments about the press, a subject that Kennedy had asked them to give particular attention. Concerning coverage of Diem, they said, "The American press representatives are bitter and will seize on anything that goes wrong and blow it up as much as possible." They advocated a "systematic campaign to get more of the facts into the press and T.V." to counteract the "pessimistic (and factually inaccurate) picture conveyed in the press."

In an "Eyes Only" (for the President only) secret annex to the report, they made two additional points.[154] First, they suggested the need for a person to replace Nolting and to coordinate the entire U.S. effort. Second, they recommended that the U.S. should use "the leverage we have to persuade Diem to adopt policies which we espouse." "In domestic politics," they added, "we have virtually no contact with meaningful opposition elements and we have made no attempt to maintain a U.S. position independent of Diem." "We should push harder," they said, "for a gradual liberalization of the authoritarian political structure and for the other programs discussed in the body of our report."

According to Hilsman, he and Forrestal had decided on the way to Vietnam that the "central judgment" of their report would be the question as to whether "the potential existed in South Vietnam to carry out the kind of tightly disciplined, precisely co-ordinated political, social, and military program that would be needed to defeat the guerrillas"; in other words, whether Diem could succeed or should be replaced. Their conclusion was a forecast of what lay ahead: "No matter how one twisted and turned the problem. . . ," Hilsman said, "it always came back to Ngo Dinh Diem."[155]

These conclusions were strengthened by the poor performance of Vietnamese forces at the battle of Ap Bac, which occurred during their trip. At Ap Bac, Vietnamese Army units, Hilsman said, suffered a "stunning defeat," which, he added, seemed to confirm the judgments of some U.S. advisers and journalists about the "ineffi-

---

[154]Kennedy Library, NSF Country File, Vietnam, declassified in 1982.
[155]*To Move a Nation*, pp. 459, 460.

ciency, bad leadership, and lack of aggressiveness of the Government forces. . . ." (Once again, the official Vietnamese and U.S. position was that it had been a victory.)[156]

"And thus," wrote Bernard Fall, in a fitting comment on the situation as 1962 came to an end, "the Second Indochina War goes on—from action to counteraction; from new devices which fail (such as 'defoliation' of forests and fields with chemicals) to older devices which work (small river craft and sea-going junk forces); from Vietnamese and French casualties in 1946-54 to Vietnamese and American casualties as of 1962. In South Viet-Nam, the West is still battling an ideology with technology, and the successful end of that Revolutionary War is neither near nor is its outcome certain."[157]

[156]For Hilsman's comments, see *ibid.*, pp. 447-449. See also Halberstam, *The Making of a Quagmire*, pp. 147 ff.

[157]Bernard Fall, *Street Without Joy*, 2d rev. ed., (Harrisburg, Pa.: Stackpole, 1962), p. 350.

CHAPTER 3

SOWING THE WIND: THE FALL OF NGO DINH DIEM

By the end of 1962, there were about 11,500 U.S. military personnel in Vietnam compared to about 3,000 at the beginning of that year, and their role, as well as the numbers and role of other U.S. personnel, had expanded sharply. Yet, as the CIA had correctly predicted in November 1961 during debate on the Taylor-Rostow report, there also seems to have been an equal or greater increase in Communist forces and activity.

President Kennedy, who had received very little solace from Mansfield or from Forrestal and Hilsman, had reason to wonder whether the new U.S.-Vietnamese partnership was succeeding or could succeed, or whether he had committed the United States to a course of ever-ascending increases in men and money leading only to higher levels of stalemate. Yet the alternatives, reducing the commitment or withdrawing from Vietnam, were considered unacceptable. Kennedy said in a news conference on March 6, 1963:[1]

> I don't see how we are going to be able, unless we are going to pull out of Southeast Asia and turn it over to the Communists . . . to reduce very much our economic programs and military programs in South Viet-Nam, in Cambodia, in Thailand.

> I think that unless you want to withdraw from the field and decide that it is in the national interest to permit that area to collapse, I would think that it would be impossible to substantially change it particularly, as we are in a very intensive struggle in those areas.

> So I think we ought to judge the economic burden it places upon us as opposed to having the Communists control all of Southeast Asia with the inevitable effect that this would have on the security of India and, therefore, really begin to run perhaps all the way toward the Middle East. So I think that while we would all like to lighten the burden, I don't see any real prospect of the burden being lightened for the U.S. in South-

---

[1] *Public Papers of the Presidents,* John F. Kennedy, 1963, pp. 243-244.

According to both Senator Mansfield and the President's assistant, Kenneth O'Donnell, some time in the spring of 1963, after a congressional leadership meeting at the White House at which Mansfield again criticized U.S. military involvement in Vietnam, Kennedy told Mansfield that he had changed his mind, and wanted to start withdrawing troops at the end of 1963. Charlton and Moncrieff, *Many Reasons Why,* p. 81. "But he said he couldn't withdraw all U.S. forces until after he was reelected. Otherwise there would be a 'wild conservative outcry' in the election campaign." According to O'Donnell, the President told him after Mansfield had left: "In 1965, I'll become one of the most unpopular Presidents in history. I'll be damned everywhere as a Communist appeaser. But I don't care. If I tried to pull out completely now from Vietnam we would have another Joe McCarthy red scare on our hands, but I can do it after I'm reelected. So we had better make damned sure that I *am* reelected." *"Johnny, We Hardly Knew Ye,"* p. 16.

Secretary of State Dean Rusk, among others, has questioned this story, and says that, in his judgment, Kennedy "did not reach any such conclusion in 1962 or 1963." *Many Reasons Why,* p. 82.

east Asia in the next year if we are going to do the job and meet what I think are very clear national needs.

Faced with this dilemma, the President, according to Forrestal, "More or less beginning then . . . began to take an interest in Vietnam. He began to get worried about it. It was a reaction of extreme nervousness—this thing is getting out of hand, and what am I going to do about it?"[2]

Forrestal was asked what Kennedy did after receiving the Forrestal-Hilsman report in January 1963:[3]

The thing that bothered him most about the report was that we were fighting a war, or helping Diem fight a war, with massive military means in a situation which was essentially a civil war—an elephant trying to kill a fly sort of thing. We were killing lots of other people at the same time we were trying to kill Viet Cong. So, the first thing he did was to try to get control of the kind of military operations that we were assisting the Vietnamese in undertaking, search-and-destroy, and great waves of battalions and regiments running all over the countryside pillaging and burning, doing all the things that soldiers do, which we thought had tended to make the political situation in Vietnam very much worse than it was, or should be. So his first reaction was to try—and he more or less succeeded—to cut back on the heavy military activity of the ARVN [Army of the Republic of Vietnam]—the use of napalm, the use of herbicides, the use of too many mines. And that was very difficult to do because our Army supported all those activities, and thought they were necessary and militarily justified.

In late January, Kennedy also received a report from the Army Chief of Staff, Gen. Earle C. Wheeler, on a trip he and others on a JCS team had just completed to Vietnam. Wheeler and his group were favorably impressed with the progress being made, but they, too, noted the increased strength of the Communists. The report concluded that unless there was increased pressure from the Communists, the present program could succeed in controlling the insurgency. ". . . we are winning slowly on the present thrust," the report said, and there is "no compelling reason to change."[4] "At the same time," the report added, "it is not realistic to ignore the fact that we have not given Ho Chi Minh any evidence that we are prepared to call him to account for helping to keep the insurgency in South Vietnam alive, and that we should do something to make the North Vietnamese bleed." Rather than direct U.S. attacks on North Vietnam, or the "minor intelligence and sabotage forays which lie within the competence of the Central Intelligency Agency," the group recommended that South Vietnamese military units, trained by U.S. military advisers, should engage in a "powerful military endeavor" of "sabotage, destruction, propaganda, and subversive missions against North Vietnam."

The report was also critical of the coverage of the war by the American press, and recommended a series of "sponsored visits to

[2] CRS Interview with Michael Forrestal, Oct. 16, 1978.
[3] *Ibid.*
[4] The report ("Report of Visit by Joint Chiefs of Staff Team to South Vietnam, January 1963") was declassified in 1984, and is in the Kennedy Library, NSF Country File, Vietnam.

Vietnam by mature and responsible news correspondents and executives."

On February 1, President Kennedy met with Wheeler, McNamara, Taylor, and CIA Director John A. McCone to discuss the report. According to a memorandum from Forrestal to the President on February 4, "The meeting with General Wheeler on Friday was a complete waste of your time, for which I apologize. It was intended to provide you an opportunity to initiate action on some of the problems in South Vietnam described in the Eyes Only Annex to Hilman's and my report. The rosy euphoria generated by General Wheeler's report made this device unworkable."[5]

Forrestal suggested that Harriman and he begin a "quiet campaign" to get action on this series of steps:

1. to get General Harkins a direct line of comunication to the JCS, or, alternatively and less desirably, to persuade CINC-PAC to delegate more responsibility to Saigon;

2. to look for a replacement for Fritz Nolting when his 2-year term is up in April;

3. to encourage our civilian and military people in Saigon to put across more forcefully to the GVN U.S. views on fighting the war and on foreign policy;

4. to develop gradually a more independent posture for the U.S. in South Vietnam and very carefully to dissociate ourselves from those policies and practices of the GVN of which we disapprove with good reason;

5. to stimulate Defense to examine more carefully whether our Special Forces camps and the strategic hamlets are getting effective close air support when they are attacked;

6. to make a rapid and vigorous effort to improve press relations in Saigon, even at some cost to our relationships with the Diem Government;

7. [sanitized]

8. to get the field to consider whether we are supporting too many paramilitary organizations and overlooking some of the specific needs, such as a police force for movement control.

It should also be noted in passing that General Wheeler's optimism in early 1963 was apparently shared by most Members of Congress. In two executive sessions of the Senate Foreign Relations Committee in January 1963 in which Secretary of State Rusk testified on the general state of the world, Vietnam and Southeast Asia were scarcely mentioned.

Growing Doubts about Diem

Even though Kennedy may have begun to worry more about the conduct of the war, the problem, as Hilsman and Forrestal had reported, was not the kind of war being waged; the problem was Diem. This feeling was widely shared among top White House and State Department officials, especially Forrestal, Hilsman, Harriman and Under Secretary Ball (in March 1963 Hilsman became Assistant Secretary of State for the Far East and Harriman became Under Secretary of State for Political Affairs) as well as by some

---

[5]Same location.

elements of the CIA, including many in the CIA Station in Saigon. On the other side were McNamara and the military, including Maxwell Taylor (then Chairman of the JCS) and General Harkins, Chief of the MAAG in Vietnam, General Lansdale, Ambassador Nolting, John McCone and the CIA Station chief in Saigon, John H. Richardson, as well as William Colby, (who had preceded Richardson as station chief, and was then chief of the CIA's Far East Division in the Directorate of Plans (which conducts the CIA's covert operations). They tended to believe that the U.S. could and should work with Diem, and that the principal emphasis should be on prosecuting the war against the Communists.

A similar view was held by Robert K. G. Thompson, the British adviser to Diem, whose counterinsurgency expertise, as was mentioned earlier, was widely respected by the Americans. In March 1963, Thompson visited CINCPAC while on a brief trip to the United States, and gave the officers of the Pacific Command a very glowing report on Diem and on the progress being made in Vietnam. According to the CINCPAC report to Washington, Thompson said, "One year ago we were neither winning nor losing in RVN. Now we definitely are winning."[6] He said the strategic hamlet program was going "much better in the last six months than he had ever expected." Moreover, the Government of South Vietnam was "stronger and more widely supported." A "coup attempt is remote," he added, but he was concerned about maintaining momentum and continuity, and said that "government throughout RVN would come to complete stop if Diem was eliminated."

The "greatest danger in RVN now," Thompson said, "is trying to do too much too rapidly. . . ."

Thompson suggested that at the end of the year, "if things go right," the U.S. should withdraw 1,000 U.S. military personnel from Vietnam. He recommended that the U.S. ". . . make big production out of this and publicize widely. This would show (1) RVN is winning; (2) take steam out of anti-Diemists; and (3) dramatically illustrate honesty of U.S. intentions." Whether or not this idea originated with Thompson, it was the plan subsequently carried out, at least on paper, by the Kennedy administration.

During April–June 1963, a series of events occurred in Vietnam that strengthened the Harriman-Hilsman-Forrestal position that Diem was "the problem," and led directly to the coup against Diem the following November.

Before examining these events it is important to note the broader framework within which U.S. policy was being made. From the beginning of Diem's rule in 1954, many U.S. policymakers had assumed that, under certain circumstances, the United States had not only the right but the responsibility to bring about a change of government in Vietnam. This assumption also prevailed with respect to relations with the government of some other countries in the world where U.S. interests were found to require such action, and in keeping with this philosophy the United States arranged and supported coups in 1954 in both Iran and Guatemala in which the putative leaders of those governments were replaced by leaders

---

[6]CINCPAC to Washington, Mar. 26, 1963, same location.

of U.S. choosing. (There were other similar but less successful efforts, including one in Cambodia and another in Indonesia.) One such plan, code-named Operation MONGOOSE, in which, after creating unrest in Cuba, the U.S. would seek to have the Cuban leader, Fidel Castro, removed from power directly or indirectly by one method or another, was underway, in fact, during the coup against Diem.[7]

Moreover, such action on the part of the U.S. Government had gained favor outside the government, primarily among those who supported U.S. intervention in the political affairs of other countries. These included persons of various political persuasions, but on the whole the support for such intervention appears to have come principally from individuals who tended to prefer political rather than military means, and who were strongly reformist in their political thinking. One of these was John Kenneth Galbraith, a professor at Harvard University then serving as U.S. Ambassador to India, who had advised Kennedy that if the Vietnamese failed to perform adequately under the new limited partnership, "the only solution would be to drop Diem." Another was Hans Morgenthau, a noted University of Chicago political scientist with access and influence in Washington, (who, it will be recalled, had been among those in the middle 1950s who had praised Diem's accomplishments in a speech at a meeting of the American Friends of Vietnam, while warning Diem himself that he should liberalize his attitude toward political opposition), who had decided that Diem was a liability. Morgenthau took the position that the U.S. was becoming overly involved in supporting regimes in countries like Vietnam "whose political weakness compels us in the end to commit ourselves militarily beyond what our national interest would require."[8] If the U.S. persisted in supporting Diem, he said, ". . . we are likely to be drawn ever more deeply into a Korean-type war, fought under political and military conditions much more unfavorable than those that prevailed in Korea and in the world a decade ago. Such a war cannot be won quickly, if it can be won at all, and may well last, like its Greek and Malayan counterparts, 5 or 10 years, perhaps only to end again in a stalemate, as did the Korean war." Such a war, Morgenthau warned, ". . . would certainly have a profound impact upon the political health of the Nation. McCarthyism and the change in the political complexion of the Nation which the elections of 1952 brought about resulted directly from the frustrations of the Korean War. The

---

[7]In the case of Vietnam, according to one account, "As early as 1957 some American government officials were talking about getting rid of Ngo Dinh Diem in South Vietnam." Thomas Powers, *The Man Who Kept the Secrets: Richard Helms and the CIA* (New York: Alfred A. Knopf, 1979), p. 126.

Powers also states (p. 127): "Later in the 1960s, a member of the President's Foreign Intelligence Advisory Board, Robert Murphy [a retired senior Foreign Service officer], asked why the CIA didn't kill Ho Chi Minh, since he was giving us so much trouble. . . . CIA officers responded with . . . what good would it do? Ho's successor might be even worse. How were you going to kill Ho Chi Minh secretly? You might be able to fool the *New York Times*, Robert Murphy was told, but how were you going to deceive the Vietnamese? They'd know what happened, they'd know who did it, and they'd probably be in a position and mood to retaliate. There is a tacit truce between nations on such matters: once you start killing them, they start killing you. The CIA simply does not have the assets to kill secretly a well-guarded figure like Ho Chi Minh in a security-conscious state like North Vietnam."

[8]Hans J. Morgenthau, "Vietnam – Another Korea?" *Commentary*, 33 (May 1962), pp. 369-374.

American people are bound to be at least as deeply affected by the frustrations of a Vietnamese War."

The alternative, Morgenthau said, was "the subordination of our military commitments to, and thus their limitation by, our political objectives in South Vietnam. These objectives must be defined as the restoration of a viable political order, which constitutes the only effective defense against Communist subversion." According to Morgenthau,

> It is obvious that such a political order can be established only through American intervention. It would be infantile to argue against such a policy on the ground that it is intervention; for if we had not intervened consistently since 1954 in the affairs of South Vietnam, Mr. Diem would not be its President today and South Vietnam itself would not exist. The choices before us are not between intervention and nonintervention, but between an intervention which serves our political interests and thereby limits our military commitments, and an intervention which supports to the bitter end the powers that be, even if their policies, by being counterproductive, jeopardize the interests of the United States.

The U.S., Morgenthau said, should "find a general" to replace Diem, and to establish a viable political order. "The idea that there is no alternative to Diem," he said, "is in the nature of a self-fulfilling prophecy. There appears to be no alternative to Diem only because we have placed all our bets on him."

Shortly after Morgenthau's views were published, a prominent American journalist, Theodore White, who had just returned from a trip to Asia, sent a personal letter to Kennedy in which he made a similar recommendation. Praising the negotiated settlement for Laos, White said:[9]

> But this South Vietnam thing is a real bastard to solve—either we have to let the younger military officers knock off Diem in a coup and take our chances on a military regime (as in Pakistan or South Korea); or else we have to give it up. To commit troops there is unwise—for the problem is political and doctrinal (in the long-range intellectual sense); until a government in South Viet-Nam comes about that inspires its people to die against Communism, as Communism inspires men to die against others, our troops can do no good.

Many of Diem's former supporters had also become disillusioned, and were actively promoting a change of leadership in South Vietnam. These included a large part of the membership of the American Friends of Vietnam, as well as most of those formerly associated with the Michigan State University project.

Joseph Buttinger, one of the organizers and principal leaders of the American Friends of Vietnam, had become disillusioned with Diem, and, beginning in 1960, worked for his removal. By 1962, he was, in his own words, a "determined opponent" of Diem.[10] In co-

---

[9] Kennedy Library, POF Country File, Vietnam General, 1962.

[10] Joseph Buttinger, *Vietnam: The Unforgettable Tragedy* (New York: Horizon Press, 1977), p. 50. Buttinger adds: "Two facts, however, prevented me from experiencing great satisfaction over the fall of Diem. I did not believe that his replacement by a military government offered much chance for the adoption of the policy of radical reforms I knew was called for; and I was deeply disturbed by the politically unnecessary and despicable murder of Diem and his brother Nhu."

operation with an exiled former official of Diem's government, he wrote a proclamation for clandestine distribution in South Vietnam which called on the people to help overthrow Diem. In June 1963, Buttinger convened a conference of American and Vietnamese social scientists to discuss the situation, and afterwards, at their behest, he prepared a memorandum, distributed in Washington, on the reasons why, in order for the war to be won, Diem had to be replaced. After the Vietnamese Ambassador to the United States resigned in protest in August 1963, Buttinger worked with him to convince the American public of the case against Diem.

One of the Michigan State group, Frank Child, as was noted earlier, said that the situation in Vietnam was critical; that new leadership was required; and that "A military *coup*—or an assassin's bullet—are the only means by which this leadership will ever be exercised." [11]

Wesley Fishel, who had been one of his close friends and advisers in the 1950s, was deeply discouraged about Diem's failure to "mobilize the hearts and loyalties of the people."

In Congress itself, where support for Diem had been a very important element in the U.S. commitment to Diem, Mansfield was very disillusioned by 1963. Morse put the Morgenthau article (quoted above) in the *Congressional Record*. Church, who was to play a supporting role in September 1963 in the power play mounted against Diem by the Kennedy administration, had returned from his trip to Vietnam feeling that the war was being lost because of the lack of Vietnamese public support for the government.

Fulbright, although silent on the subject, had indicated on several occasions in executive sessions of the Foreign Relations Committee that he was not opposed to U.S. efforts to bring about a change of leadership in Vietnam. Prior to the coup against Diem he had also received, probably in the spring of 1963, a memorandum from John Newhouse of the Foreign Relations Committee staff quoting from a letter from Stanley Karnow, a veteran Far East reporter, in which Karnow stated that the U.S. had its hands tied behind its back as long as Diem was in power. Karnow said, however, that the U.S. should not take the lead in overthrowing Diem; that the Vietnamese themselves would do so. [12]

Thus, by the spring of 1963, Diem's political support in Washington and among influentials in the U.S. had declined drastically, especially among Kennedy's own supporters. This, together with the lack of progress being made on the military front in Vietnam, provided the ingredients for the decision to "drop Diem," which was made during the period between May and August 1963, following numerous discussions of the matter during the spring and early summer in meetings of the Special Group (CI). [13]

Beginning in May 1963, and continuing during the summer, the case for withdrawing support from Diem was further strengthened as a result of the "Buddhist crisis," in which, following Buddhist demonstrations against the Diem government, including self-immo-

---

[11]See p. 76.
[12]University of Arkansas, Fulbright Papers, series 48, undated memorandum from Newhouse to Fulbright.
[13]Powers, *The Man Who Kept the Secrets*, p. 163.

lation by several monks, the government responded with what may have been or appeared to be excessive force.[14] These events, which were widely televised in the United States, created a sense of public revulsion, and policymakers in Washington became concerned that this reaction would have the effect of reducing American public support for the role of the U.S. in Vietnam.

The U.S. Decides to Act

On June 11, the first self-immolation of a Buddhist monk *(bonze)* occurred, and the U.S. warned Diem that unless the situation improved, the U.S. would have to dissociate itself from his treatment of the Buddhists.

There was also a sharp reaction from the American public to the burning of the Buddhist monk. Influential newspapers and leaders criticized the Diem government,[15] and a group of prominent New York clergymen, calling themselves the Ministers Vietnam Committee, organized a protest against U.S. policy, citing the following points:

1. Our country's military aid to those who denied him [the Buddhist monk] religious freedom.

2. The immoral spraying of parts of South Vietnam with crop- destroying chemicals and the herding of many of its people into concentration camps called "strategic hamlets."

3. The loss of American lives and billions of dollars to bolster a regime universally regarded as unjust, undemocratic, and unstable.

4. The fiction that this is "fighting for freedom."

The group, led by Dr. Donald Szantho Harrington, pastor of the Community Church of New York, a large unitarian universalist congregation, as well as vice chairman (later chairman) of the Liberal Party in the State of New York, placed an ad in the *New York Times* urging public support for the protest, and on August 15, 1963, sent President Kennedy a letter and a petition signed by 15,000 clergymen from around the country endorsing the four-point protest statement.[16]

This was one of the earliest protests against U.S. policy in Vietnam, and it attracted considerable support. According to Dr. Harrington, there were about 18,000 replies to the advertisement, and enough money was raised to cover the cost of both the first advertisement and another in the *New York Times* on September 15 in which the protest statement was repeated.[17]

Soon after the issuance of the protest, Dr. Harrington, Socialist Party leader Norman Thomas, and Robert Jones, the executive sec-

---

[14]The Buddhist uprisings are discussed in a a number of the books dealing with Vietnam. See especially Stanley Karnow, *Vietnam: A History* (New York: Viking, 1983); Mecklin, *Mission in Torment;* Halberstam, *The Making of a Quagmire;* Hilsman, *To Move A Nation;* Robert Shaplen, *The Lost Revolution* (New York: Harper and Row, 1965).

[15]See, for example, the *New York Times,* June 17, 1963, which said that if Diem " . . . cannot genuinely represent a majority then he is not the man to be President."

[16]Twelve of the country's foremost clergymen signed the protest, including Henry Emerson Fosdick, Reinhold Niebuhr, James A. Pike, and Ralph W. Sockman.

[17]Letter to CRS, Aug. 21, 1984. The money for the first advertisement had been advanced by a New York businessman, Daniel J. Bernstein, who, before his death in 1970, was one of the principal financial supporters of antiwar activities, primarily those of religious and business groups. Other antiwar activities of an informational or educational nature were supported by the Daniel J. Bernstein Foundation, known as the DJB Foundation.

retary of the Unitarian Universalist Washington office, organized the first picketing of the White House on the Vietnam question. In addition, Harrington's Liberal Party became the first political group to oppose the war.

Prior to the burning of the monk, the U.S. mission in Saigon had prepared a contingency plan for dealing with Diem in the event that the situation became more critical, and on May 23, 1963, Nolting submitted the plan to Washington for approval. On June 14, the State Department replied in a cable from Hilsman drafted by Chalmers Wood of the Vietnam Task Force, and cleared by Harriman, suggesting that in implementing this plan the U.S. mission consider Diem's Vice President, Nguyen Ngoc Tho as a replacement for Diem; that ". . . while there is no change in US policy of supporting Diem, we want Tho to know that in event situation arises due to internal political circumstances (in which US would play . . . no part) where Diem definitively unable act as President and only in this situation we would want to back Tho as constitutional successor. . . ." The cable added, "we would assume he would need military support," but it did not explain what was meant by "military support."[18]

"In view precarious situation," the cable continued, "it would seem worthwhile to run risk delivering such message now assuming Tho would not likely consider it in his interest to inform anyone else. We would have to tell Tho that if word leaked we would flatly deny." If the mission thought it advisable, the cable said, it might be preferable to tell Diem himself about the plan for succession.

As will be seen, it was indeed Nguyen Ngoc Tho, under the general authority of the military junta, who succeeded Diem as the civilian leader of Vietnam after the coup.

The cable also contained a second suggested action, which was deleted when the document was declassified in 1982. Judging by a reply from Saigon on June 16, this deleted recommendation had to do with the importance of maintaining contact with opposition leaders in the Diem government, especially those who might be involved in a coup.[19] In its comment on this suggestion the U.S. mission said: ". . . There are no bars whatsoever on contacts and we are receiving just now a surfeit of coup talk and antiregime comment. It is to be expected in such circumstances that one is never in contact with the people (if any) who really mean business, but we have all the lines out that we know how to put out and have had for some days. However, everyone is as usual under strict instructions . . . not to encourage coup talk and to meet any that arises with firm statement of US support for GVN."

As for Washington's suggestion about telling Tho or Diem about the plan for supporting Tho in the event Diem were no longer able to continue as President, the mission replied that the situation was more stable as a result of an agreement just concluded between the government and the Buddhists, and that it would not be wise to take such action at that time. "Our best move at this juncture . . .

---

[18] Kennedy Library, NSF Country file, Vietnam, Washington to Saigon 1219, June 14, 1963, same location.
[19] Saigon to Washington 1195, June 16, 1963, same location.

is to press Diem directly and indirectly to accept Buddhist crisis as blessing in disguise and to use agreement reached as a stepping stone to concessions to other groups (before they demand them). The whole operation would be keyed to building up popular support for regime prior to August parliamentary elections and importantly also to making sure that paper undertakings to Buddhists are carried out in full measure."

The U.S. mission was dubious about the chances for such a plan, however, as the cable admitted. "This scheme will doubtless be regarded as naive by anyone who knows this country (and it is certainly the longest of shots)." But the mission thought it should be given a "fair try." If Diem was "in a mood to freeze up, rather than move forward," the cable added, then "his days are numbered," and at that point the suggested approach should be made to Vice President Tho.

By July 1, 1963, the situation had not improved, and policymakers in Washington were once again concerned about a potential "crisis." At a meeting that morning, Ball, Harriman, Hilsman and Forrestal decided that they should notify McGeorge Bundy, who was with the President on a trip to Rome, of their appraisal of the situation. "We all believe," the ensuing White House cable stated, "one more burning Bonze will cause domestic U.S. reaction which will require strong public statement despite danger that this might precipitate coup in Saigon. Demarche to Diem insisting on removal of Nhu and wife to post outside SVN before such statement becomes necessary under consideration."[20]

Upon returning to Washington, Kennedy met with these advisers on the fourth of July.[21] They reported that the U.S. had put "extremely heavy pressure" on Diem, who had agreed to make a speech saying he would meet with Buddhist leaders. He was told that if he did not make the speech, and if the demonstrations resumed, the U.S. would be forced to take a public stand against his policy toward the Buddhists.

Hilsman told Kennedy, "Our estimate was that no matter what Diem did there will be coup attempts over the next four months." He said that there was general agreement, however, that "the chances of chaos in the wake of a coup are considerably less than they were a year ago." Hilsman added that Nolting thought a civil war would ensue if Diem were killed in a coup, but he said he disagreed with Nolting, feeling that in such an event a civil war was possible but not likely.

Forrestal reported Gen. Victor H. Krulak's (JCS Special Assistant for Counterinsurgency) view that even if there were chaos in Saigon, the Vietnamese Armed Forces would continue military actions against the Communists.

The group discussed the possibility of "getting rid of the Nhus," but the "combined judgment" was that this was not possible.

On that same day, Lucien Conein, the veteran CIA agent in Saigon, was contacted by General Tran Van Don, Acting Chief of Staff of Vietnamese Armed Forces, about the possibility of a military coup against Diem. Conein reported, and Washington was so

[20]Same location.
[21]*PP*, Gravel ed., vol. II, pp. 727-728.

informed, that General Don, his brother-in-law, General Le Van Kim, General Tran Thieh Khiem (Army Chief of Staff), and General Duong Van "Big" Minh, who had been a strong ally of Diem in 1954-55, had agreed on the necessity for a coup.[22] A week later, a CIA cable from Saigon said that if a coup occurred, the new government "might be initially less effective against the Viet Cong but, given continued support from the U.S., could provide reasonably effective leadership for the government and the war effort."[23]

The next day (July 5) Ball met with Ambassador Nolting, who was in Washington for a few days, and during the conversation he asked Nolting what would happen if there were a "change of government" in Vietnam. Nolting said, ". . . if a revolution occurred in Vietnam which grew out of the Buddhist situation, the country would be split between feuding factions and the Americans would have to withdraw, and the country might be lost to the Communists." As to the question of how much pressure the United States could bring to bear, Nolting said that Diem's government would fall if the U.S. were to repudiate it on the Buddhist question.[24]

On July 9, Nolting testified on Vietnam in an executive session of the Senate Foreign Relations Committee.[25] He said that the war was going well despite the Buddhist disturbances, and he defended the Diem government against charges of ruthlessness. Committee members seemed concerned about the situation, but only Senator Symington took a position on what should be done. He repeated earlier statements he had made publicly that the U.S. should either use greater military force to bring the conflict to an end (he preferred action directly against the north), or American forces should be withdrawn.[26]

On July 10, a Special National Intelligence Estimate on "The Situation in South Vietnam"[27] concluded that Diem and Nhu would resist further U.S. pressure, and that their inaction on the Buddhist "crisis" could then lead to a "better than even" chance of a coup or assassination.

On August 5, another *bonze* was burned, followed by another on August 16, as tension increased in Saigon.

On August 12, however, just before leaving Vietnam, Nolting talked to Diem, and reported to Washington that Diem had assured him that he would be conciliatory toward the Buddhists in order to satisfy world public opinion, even though he considered them sub-

---

[22]Conein's "After-Action Report," Nov. 1, 1963, cited by *Alleged Assassination Plots Involving Foreign Leaders, An Interim Report* of the Select Committee to Study Governmental Operations with Respect to Intelligence Activities, November 20, 1975, (S. Rept. 94-465), 94th Cong., 1st sess. (Washington, D.C.: U.S. Govt. Print Off., 1975), p. 218 (hereafter cited as Senate Report on Assassination Plots).

Don was the principal contact with the CIA. Minh was the leader of the group, and became the head of the military government which replaced Diem. Gen. Ton That Dinh, the III Corps commander in Saigon, joined the group in October and participated in the coup. Gen. Nguyen Khanh, II Corps commander in Pleiku was also involved, and later overthrew the Minh government in January 1965.

[23]Quoted by *U.S. News and World Report,* Oct. 10, 1983, "Untold Story of the Road to War in Vietnam," p. VN5. This special report was prepared by the magazine after three years of extensive research and interviewing.

[24]*PP,* Gravel ed., vol. II, pp. 728-729.

[25]U.S. Congress, Senate, Committee on Foreign Relations, unpublished executive session transcript, July 9, 1963.

[26]For Symington's position see his remarks during an appearance on "Meet the Press" on Apr. 28, 1963, reprinted in *CR,* vol. 109, pp. 17149 ff.

[27]*PP,* Gravel ed., vol. II, pp. 729-733.

versive. He also told Nolting that he would remove his brother's controversial wife, Madame Nhu (who, among other things, had been very outspoken in her defense of government actions against the Buddhists), from the country.

On August 21, while Nolting, Hilsman, and Henry Cabot Lodge, the new U.S. Ambassador to Vietnam, were meeting in Honolulu prior to Lodge's arrival in Saigon the following day, word came that Buddhist pagodas had been attacked in several cities. Originally it was thought that the attacks were carried out by Vietnamese Army units, but it soon became clear that they were conducted by police and Special Forces loyal to Nhu.

At this point, the U.S. Government began to put into effect the plan it had been developing for several months. First, Harriman and Forrestal drafted a statement denouncing and dissociating the U.S. from Diem's policies toward the Buddhists. Second, the U.S. began discussing with dissident Vietnamese army officers and others the possibility of a coup. On August 23, Conein, who had been contacted in July by General Tran Van Don, as was noted above, met again with Don, who discussed alternatives to Diem but refused to reveal the generals' plans.[28]

Also on August 23, Rufus Phillips, a CIA agent who had been one of Lansdale's associates in the middle 1950s, and had returned to Vietnam in 1962 as Assistant Director of Rural Development, was contacted by Nguyen Dinh Thuan, one of Diem's most intimate associates. In the cable to Washington reporting their conversation, Phillips said that Thuan recommended that the U.S. try to split the Nhus off from Diem. "Under no circumstances, Thuan said, should the U.S. acquiesce in what the Nhus had done. This would be disastrous." The U.S., Thuan added, "must not be afraid of leaving the door open to the Communists, by withdrawing support from the government as long as it contained the Nhus." The U.S. had to be "firm." If it was, Thuan said, "the army would respond."[29]

The August 24 Cable

Washington reacted in a cable from Hilsman to Lodge on August 24, 1963, the key part of which was as follows:[30]

US Government cannot tolerate situation in which power lies in Nhu's hands. Diem must be given chance to rid himself of Nhu and his coterie and replace them with best military and political personalities available.

If, in spite of all of your efforts, Diem remains obdurate and refuses, then we must face the possibility that Diem himself cannot be preserved.

We now believe immediate action must be taken to prevent Nhu from consolidating his position further. Therefore, unless you in consultation with Harkins perceive overriding objections you are authorized to proceed along following lines:

---

[28]Johnson Library, Declassified and Sanitized Documents from Unprocessed Files, The memorandum, sanitized with source deleted, dated 23 Oct. 1963, is entitled: "[first word or two deleted] Contacts with Vietnamese Generals, 23 August through 23 October 1963."

[29]Kennedy Library, NSF Country File, Vietnam, Saigon to Washington 324, Aug. 24, 1963.

[30]For the cable, Washington to Saigon 243, Aug. 24, 1963, see Johnson Library, Declassified and Sanitized Documents from Unprocessed Files.

(1) First, we must press on appropriate levels of GVN following lines:

(a) USG cannot accept actions against Buddhists taken by Nhu and his collaborators under cover martial law.

(b) Prompt dramatic actions redress situation must be taken. . . .

(2) We must at same time also tell key military leaders that US would find it impossible to continue support GVN militarily and economically unless above steps are taken immediately which we recognize requires removal of Nhus from the scene. We wish give Diem reasonable opportunity to remove Nhus, but if he remains obdurate, then we are prepared to accept the obvious implication that we can no longer support Diem. You may also tell appropriate military commanders we will give them direct support in any interim period of breakdown central government mechanism.

The cable added that the mission should "urgently examine all possible alternative leadership and make detailed plans as to how we might bring about Diem's replacement if this should become necessary."

This cable, which marked the beginning of active U.S. support for the coup against Diem, was drafted by Hilsman, with direct roles played also by Forrestal, Harriman and Ball. (It has usually been referred to as the "green light" cable, but there is said by one key official to have been a second "green light" cable on October 27 giving final approval for the coup.) It was cleared in Washington by various deputies—Ball for the State Department, Gilpatric for the Defense Department, Krulak for the JCS, and Richard Helms for the CIA, in the absence from Washington on that Saturday of all of the principals involved, as well as the President himself. A copy of the cable was teletyped to Kennedy in Hyannis Port, Massachusetts, and he cleared it after a phone conversation with Ball in which he told Ball that if Rusk (who was contacted by phone) and Gilpatric, as well as Ball himself, approved it, then it was all right with him.[31] According to Hilsman, the President "went over the cable word by word."[32]

The President had known that a proposal for such action was imminent. On August 24, prior to the drafting of the cable itself later that day, Forrestal sent Kennedy a memo for his "Week-end Reading File," as follows:[33]

I attach the latest cables on the situation in Saigon. It is now quite certain that Brother Nhu is the mastermind behind the whole operation against the Buddhists and is calling the shots. This is now agreed by virtually everyone here.

Agreement is also developing that the United States cannot tolerate a result of the present difficulties in Saigon which leaves Brother Nhu in a dominating position. There is disagreement on whether Diem has any political viability left,

---

[31] Charlton and Moncrieff, *Many Reasons Why*, p. 91.
[32] CRS Interview with Roger Hilsman, Sept. 23, 1980.
[33] Kennedy Library, NSF Country File, Vietnam.

and on whether he could even be brought to acquiesce in the removal of his brother.

Averell and Roger now agree that we must move before the situation in Saigon freezes. I am pressing them to get John McCone's endorsement of one of several courses of action which can be presented to you at the earliest opportunity.

Rusk was in New York on August 24, but according to Hilsman[34] he, too, was teletyped a draft, and both he and Kennedy, Hilsman says, "participated in the revisions" through "several telephone conversations." Hilsman also takes the position that Rusk added an important sentence (the final sentence in part [2] of the cable) promising direct assistance to the leaders of the coup, the "implication being," says Hilsman, "that if the generals revolted, and it wasn't immediately successful, we would attempt to supply the generals through Hue."[35] Rusk, for his part, denies that he added the sentence, and says that the cable was cleared by him by telephone, "but in the most guarded terms . . . I didn't have a text in front of me. It was cleared with me on the phone in rather general terms because we were on an open telephone line."[36] Ball agrees with Rusk's version, saying that after he talked to Kennedy he called Rusk and "paraphrased it to him, because I thought we had an open line." He said that Rusk replied that if the President approved, if Ball agreed, and if Defense agreed, then he would concur.[37] Hilsman contends that the telephone call occurred after Rusk had seen and revised the cable.[38]

Gilpatric, acting for McNamara, was telephoned at his farm near Washington by Forrestal, who told him of the contents of the cable, but stated that because it had already been approved by the President it did not need his concurrence. Gilpatric acquiesced, but then called Taylor, and the two agreed that both in substance and procedure the cable was unsatisfactory.[39] Meanwhile, according to Hilsman,[40] Taylor's concurrence had been given to Forrestal by General Krulak, then on the staff of the Joint Chiefs (of which Taylor was Chairman), after Krulak talked to Taylor by telephone at a restaurant. (Hilsman adds, however, that Krulak gave Taylor's clearance an hour and a half before actually receiving it from Taylor.) Taylor, on the other hand, says that he first heard of the cable when called at his residence by Gilpatric, and that he then called the Pentagon for a copy which was delivered later by Krulak.[41]

McCone was also out of town, but his deputy, Richard Helms, agreed emphatically, saying that it was time to take the proposed action.[42]

[34]*To Move A Nation*, p. 488.
[35]*Many Reasons Why*, pp. 90-91, 93.
[36]*Ibid.*, pp. 92-93.
[37]*Ibid.*, p. 91.
[38]David Wise, *The Politics of Lying* (New York: Random House, 1973), p. 1, fn. 20.
[39]Taylor, *Swords and Plowshares*, p. 292.
[40]*To Move A Nation*, p. 488.
[41]*Swords and Plowshares*, p. 292.
[42]*To Move A Nation*, p. 488. As Colby notes, however, Helms' action was not a clearance as such, in view of the fact that the cable concerned a policy matter rather than intelligence *per se*. See *Honorable Men*, p. 210.

Apparently, no Member of Congress was contacted or informed about the decision to support a coup against Diem, as represented by the cable.

By Monday, August 26, severe doubts about the cable were being expressed by McNamara, McCone and Taylor. The President himself, Schlesinger said, ". . . felt rather angrily that he had been pressed too hard and fast. He discussed the situation with Robert Kennedy, who talked in turn with McNamara and Maxwell Taylor. The Attorney General reported back with great concern that nobody knew what was going to happen in Vietnam and that our policy had not been fully discussed, as every other major decision since the Bay of Pigs had been discussed."[43]

According to Schlesinger, President Kennedy ". . . thought the August 24 cable impulsive and precipitate. 'He always said it was a major mistake on his part,' Robert Kennedy recalled the next year. '. . . The result is we started down a road that we never really recovered from.' " Schlesinger added that the President became, according to Robert Kennedy, " 'very unhappy' with Harriman—so much so that Robert noting that Harriman 'put on about ten years during that period . . . because he was so discouraged,' asked his brother 'if he couldn't rehabilitate him by just being nice to him . . . because he's a very valuable figure.' "[44]

Lodge replied the next day (Sunday, August 25) to Hilsman's August 24 cable. He generally agreed with the position taken in the cable, but questioned whether the U.S. should approach Diem directly with an ultimatum. This, he said, might strengthen Diem's defiance. Moreover, Diem was the one who should make amends. After receiving Lodge's cable, the State Department, after checking with others, agreed to postpone the question of talking directly to Diem.[45]

On Monday, August 26, Kennedy met with his top NSC advisers. According to Hilsman (the only available account of the meeting at this writing), he wanted to know ". . . how everyone stood. It was not too late to back off." The group discussed the "growing disaffection in Vietnam among the non-Communist elements of society whose support was essential if the war against the Viet Cong was to be pursued successfully." "What Rusk, Ball, Harriman, Forrestal, and I feared," Hilsman said, "was not only that there would be worldwide political repercussions if the situation continued as it was but that the heart would go out of the war effort. . . . McNamara, Taylor, and Krulak . . . wanted to try to find a way to get Diem to return to his old position and his old policies. . . . But they also agreed that in the circumstances we had to tell the generals that, although we would prefer to see Diem remain—without Nhu—if the Vietnamese decided otherwise, an interim, anti-Communist military government could expect that American support would continue."

"The consensus of the group," Hilsman said, "was that even though the present course of action was dangerous, doing nothing was even more dangerous, and the President went around the table

[43] A Thousand Days, p. 991.
[44] Robert Kennedy and His Times, p. 713.
[45] To Move A Nation, p. 488.

one by one to make sure. The Secretary of State summed it up by saying that if we acquiesced in what had happened and the present situation in Vietnam continued, we would be on an inevitable road to disaster. The decision would then be whether to get out and let the country go to the Communists or move United States combat forces into Vietnam and take over." The question of whether to approach Diem directly remained unanswered.[46]

Later that day (August 26), CIA Headquarters in Washington told the U.S. Mission to instruct Conein, and Alphonso G. Spera, also of the CIA, to discuss the coup with the generals, based on the August 24 cable, using the following points:[47]

(1) Solidification of further elaboration of action aspects of present thinking and planning. What should be done?

(2) We in agreement Nhus must go.

(3) Question of retaining Diem or not up to them [generals].

(4) Bonzes and other arrestees must be released immediately and five-point agreement of 16 June be fully carried out.

(5) We will provide direct support during any interim period of breakdown of central government mechanism.

(6) We cannot be of any help during initial action of assuming power of the state. Entirely their own action, win or lose. Don't expect to be bailed out.

(7) If Nhus do not go, and if Buddhists' situation is not redressed as indicated, we would find it impossible continue military and economic support.

(8) It is hoped bloodshed can be avoided or reduced to absolute minimum.

(9) It is hoped that during process and after, developments conducted in such manner as to retain and increase the necessary relations between Vietnamese and Americans which will allow for progress of country and successful prosecution of the war.

That same day (August 26), Conein and Spera discussed these points with Generals Tran Thien Khiem, Army Chief of Staff, and Nguyen Khanh, II Corps commander in Pleiku, two of the members of the group considering a coup. Khiem said that the generals agreed with the nine points. Khanh said he was not yet ready to move, and that he was waiting for indications that Nhu was preparing an accommodation with North Vietnam.[48]

On August 27, Khiem was again contacted, and told Conein that a committee of generals, headed by General Duong Van "Big" Minh, had discussed the question of a coup, and had agreed that one would occur within a week's time.[49]

The NSC advisers, along with Nolting, met again with the President the next day (August 27).[50] (In advance of the meeting, Ken-

[46] *Ibid.*, pp. 490-491.

[47] Director of Central Intelligence to Lodge, Aug. 26, 1963, cited in Senate Report on Assassination Plots, p. 239.

[48] "[first word or two deleted] Contacts with Vietnamese Generals, 23 August through 23 October 1963," cited above.

[49] *Ibid.*

[50] Kennedy Library, NSF Presidential Meetings File. Present besides the President were: the Attorney General, Rusk, McNamara, McCone, Ball, Gilpatric, Taylor, Hilsman, Nolting, Krulak, Helms, Colby, Edward R. Murrow (USIA Director), McGeorge Bundy, Forrestal, and General Marshall S. Carter, Deputy Director of the CIA.

nedy was told by Forrestal that a committee of South Vietnamese generals had been formed "for the purpose of bringing about a military coup within a week.")[51] Colby reported that the situation in Saigon was quiet, and the "unrest was not apparent in the countryside." He said that two generals had been interviewed by the CIA. "One general said the situation for a coup was favorable and forecast that one would take place within a week. The second general gave what was described as a jumpy answer."

The President then asked a series of questions. Among other things, he wanted to know about the effect of the civil disturbances on the war itself. Krulak replied that the effect was "slight."

In response to the President's question about why the peasants were not more disturbed about the attacks on the Buddhists, Nolting said the Buddhists were not an organized religious force, and that what happened in Saigon was of little concern to the rural population.

The President asked why Diem had not kept his promises. Nolting replied that Diem had kept his promises. "He said that there was no promise made to us which he [Diem] had not tried to keep. . . . Diem should be given an 'E' for effort. Diem is not a liar and is a man of integrity."

The President said that Hilsman had told him that Diem was not "forthright." Hilsman said he had gotten this impression from Nolting.

The President asked Nolting whether the situation between August 12, when Diem had promised conciliation, and August 21, when the pagodas were attacked, had caused Diem to change his mind, or whether Diem had lied to Nolting. Nolting replied that he thought Diem and Nhu had decided to "end the unrest once and for all and together they had moved from conciliation to the use of force."

Kennedy asked Nolting about the prospect for a coup. Nolting replied that there was not sufficient military support for a coup to be successful, but there might be if the U.S. told the Vietnamese that they had to get rid of Diem and Nhu. According to the official summary of the meeting, "Ambassador Nolting recalled that the circle had nearly been completed in a three-year period. Ambassador Durbrow had told Diem three years ago that Nhu must go. Diem refused to accept the suggestion and Durbrow was removed from Vietnam. (The President recognized the irony of this situation by smiling.)" Nolting added, ". . . we should not fight the internal political situation in Vietnam too hard. He urged that we keep our eye on fighting the Viet Cong." He said, however, "Diem must be forced to limit the authority of Nhu and get Madame Nhu out of the country. Diem would not respond if he were pushed, but he could be convinced by Ambassador Lodge that the situation must improve if we were to continue assisting Vietnam."

As the meeting ended, Rusk said that it was important to make clear to the U.S. mission that Washington was not changing the "existing directive," i.e., the August 24 cable authorizing U.S. support for a coup.

---

[51]Kennedy Library, NSF Country File, Vietnam, "Memorandum for the President," Aug. 27, 1963.

After the meeting, a cable was sent to Lodge and Harkins asking for their views on what the next move of the U.S. should be. They replied in a cable from Lodge on August 29, concurred in, with one exception, by Harkins, saying, "We are launched on a course from which there is no respectable turning back; the overthrow of the Diem government."[52] The cable continued:

We must press on for many reasons. Some of these are:

(a) Explosiveness of the present situation which may well lead to riots and violence if issue of discontent of regime is not met. Out of this could come a pro-Communist or at best a neutralist set of politicians.

(b) The fact that war cannot be won with the present regime.

(c) Our own reputation for steadfastness and our unwillingness to stultify ourselves.

(d) If proposed action is suspended, I believe a body blow will be dealt to respect for us by Vietnamese Generals. Also, all those who expect U.S. to straighten out this situation will feel let down. Our help to the regime in past years inescapably gives a responsibility which we cannot avoid.

Lodge added, "I realize that this course involves a very substantial risk of losing Vietnam. It also involves some additional risk to American lives. I would never propose it if I felt there was a reasonable chance of holding Vietnam with Diem."

Harkins, Lodge said, thought that Lodge should ask Diem to "get rid of the Nhus before starting the Generals' action." Lodge disagreed: ". . . I believe that such a step has no chance of getting the desired result and would have the very serious effect of being regarded by the Generals as a sign of American indecision and delay. I believe this is a risk which we should not run. The Generals distrust us too much already. Another point is that Diem would certainly ask for time to consider such a far-reaching request. This would give the ball to Nhu."

A cable on August 28 from CIA Station Chief Richardson to McCone, supported Lodge's position:[53] "Situation here has reached point of no return. . . . If the Ngo family wins now, they and Vietnam will stagger on to final defeat at the hands of their own people and the VC. Should a generals' revolt occur and be put down, GVN will sharply reduce American presence in SVN. Even if they did not do so, it seems clear that American public opinion and Congress, as well as world opinion, would force withdrawal or reduction of American support for VN under the Ngo administration. . . . It is obviously preferable that the generals conduct this effort without apparent American assistance. . . . Nevertheless, we all understand that the effort must succeed and that whatever needs to be done on our part must be done."

On that same day (August 28), Conein met with Generals Minh and Khiem. Minh asked for a "token" of U.S. determination to sup-

[52]The sanitized text of the cable, Saigon to Washington 375, Aug. 29, 1963, is in *PP*, Gravel ed., vol. II, pp. 738-739, and a copy of the cable is in the Johnson Library, Declassified and Sanitized Documents from Unprocessed Files.
[53]*PP*, Gravel ed., vol. II, p. 736.

port a coup in the form of a cutoff of economic aid "in order to force Nhu's hand." Conein said he did not reply specifically to this request.[54] In the weeks ahead, however, as will be seen, the U.S. decided to cut off aid to Nhu's Special Forces, thus giving the generals the token they wanted as the sign of American support for the coup.

The next day (August 29), the State Department received a cable from a Foreign Service officer, Paul Kattenburg, who had served in Vietnam during the 1950s, and at that time was director of the Vietnam Task Force under Hilsman. Kattenburg had been sent to Vietnam for a report on the situation, especially Diem's psychological state, and he cabled from Saigon that after talking with Diem, "while there is no doubt he is in full possession of his faculties, impression of growing neurosis cannot be escaped."[55]

Also on that same day, incidentally, the Public Affairs Bureau (Public Opinion Studies staff) of the State Department circulated within the government its latest "American Opinion Summary," based on the accounts of the news media and statements by Members of Congress, which concluded that there was general concern in Congress and the media about the effect of continuing to support Diem. "The Diem government's 'image,' insofar as a large number of those who commented are concerned," the Summary stated, "is 'beyond repair.'" Senator Morse was quoted as saying that "the sooner the U.S. ceases its support of the Diem government the better off we shall be."[56]

The White House also received a memorandum of a private conversation on the evening of August 27 between Lansdale and the former South Vietnamese ambassador to the U.S., Tran Van Chuong (who had resigned on August 22 in protest against the Diem government), and his wife, who were the parents of Madame Nhu. Both of them told Lansdale that, as he stated in his memo:[57]

The U.S. must act firmly and quickly to replace both Diem and Nhu with a new government. The Vietnamese people are aroused far more than ever before, and it is too late even to save Diem as a figure-head. The people, seeing VN special forces and police with U.S. weapons and equipment, knowing that Diem can only stay in power with U.S. support, will turn against the U.S. unless there is a change in the whole top of government.

Madame Chuong, Lansdale reported, said: "You must go to Saigon fast and tell Diem and the Nhu's to leave the country now. The people hate them and they shouldn't stay for the people to kill them. They will surely be killed if they stay, and nobody at the Palace now is telling them how the people really feel. They are cut off from reality. Why do they need power after nine years of it, if the family is killed. The US told Syngman Rhee to leave. Why not Diem and Nhu?"

On the morning of August 28, there was a rather contentious NSC meeting. Ball said that the battle with the Communists would

[54]"[first word or two deleted] Contacts with Vietnamese Generals, 23 August through 23 October 1963.'
[55]Kennedy Library, NSF Country File, Vietnam, Saigon to Washington 371, Aug. 29, 1963.
[56]Same location.
[57]Same location.

be lost if the U.S. continued to support Diem. Nolting responded that failure to support Diem would be contrary to our commitments. Ball replied that it was Diem who had broken commitments. At this point Harriman expressed very strong disagreement with Nolting, which, as Gilpatric recalls, was worse than any tongue-lashing he had ever witnessed in the presence of the President, and that, "I don't think it would have been tolerated by the President from anybody else." According to Robert Kennedy, the division among the President's advisers was so deep that "The government split in two. . . . It was the only time really, in three years, the government was broken in two in a very disturbing war [*sic*—probably should be "way"]."[58] Although the summary of this meeting is still classified, Schlesinger, who had access to a copy of the summary in the Robert Kennedy papers, says that Harriman, Ball, Hilsman, and Forrestal (quoting from the summary) " 'said that the U.S. must decide now to go through to a successful overthrow.' Taylor, McNamara, McCone, Lyndon Johnson strongly opposed a coup."[59]

That afternoon, in an effort to close ranks, Kennedy met with Rusk, McNamara and Taylor before meeting again with the larger group. (At the latter meeting, two of the contenders, Ball and Hilsman were not included. Rusk who had not been at the morning meeting, represented the Department of State.) Prior to the first of the two afternoon meetings, McGeorge Bundy sent Kennedy a memo suggesting who should attend. At the top of his list were Rusk, McNamara and Taylor. He then listed the Vice President, the Attorney General, (McGeorge) Bundy, Douglas Dillon and Harriman, with a question mark beside each one of this second group. Beside Harriman's name he wrote by hand, "Mike [Forrestal] thinks not." Beside the Attorney General there was the typed notation "(He and I have had a talk and he knows what is at stake and is at your disposal if you want him, and will go cruising if you do not.)"[60]

At this smaller meeting, agreement apparently was reached on putting aside personal differences and reaching a common position. There is no information available as to what was discussed at the meeting that followed, but when the larger group met again the next day (August 29), Kennedy polled those present and it was agreed by all that the decision announced in the August 24 cable should stand. Accordingly, a cable was sent to Saigon stating that "Highest level meeting today . . . reaffirmed basic course." The cable authorized Harkins to inform the generals of this decision. "He should stress that the USG supports the movement to eliminate the Nhus from the government, but that before arriving at specific understandings with the Generals, General Harkins must know who are involved, resources available to them and overall plan for coup. The USG will support a coup which has good chance of succeeding but plans no direct involvement of U.S. armed forces. Harkins should state that he is prepared to establish liaison with

---

[58]Both quotes are from Schlesinger, *Robert Kennedy and His Times*, p. 714.
[59]*Ibid.*, p. 713.
[60]Kennedy Library, POF Country File, Vietnam Security 1963.

the coup planners and to review plans, but will not engage directly in joint coup planning."

The cable also authorized Lodge to suspend U.S. aid to the Diem government if and when he decided this was necessary.

With respect to what the cable called the "last approach to Diem," Lodge was told that Rusk was sending him a separate cable on that subject.[61]

In his separate cable to Lodge, Rusk suggested further discussion of the possibility of separating Diem and the Nhus. Rusk said that, based in part on Paul Kattenburg's cable, he doubted whether Diem could be persuaded to take such an action. "Unless such a talk included a real sanction such as threatened withdrawal of our support, it is unlikely that it would be taken completely seriously by a man who may feel that we are inescapably committed to an anti-Communist Vietnam. But if a sanction were used in such a conversation, there would be a high risk that this would be taken by Diem as a sign that action against him and the Nhus was imminent and he might as a minimum move against the Generals or even take some quite fantastic action such as calling on North Vietnam for assistance in expelling the Americans."

To prevent this from happening, Rusk suggested that this sanction ". . . might properly await the time when others were ready to move immediately to constitute a new government," thus leaving it to the generals to make one last effort to separate Diem and the Nhus. "In any event, were the Generals to take this action it would tend to protect succeeding Vietnam administrations from the charge of being wholly American puppets subjected to whatever anti-American sentiment is inherent in so complex a situation."[62]

Lodge replied the next day (August 30) that he did not think the U.S. could remove the Nhus by working through Diem.[63] "In fact Diem will oppose it. He wishes he had more Nhus, not less. The best chance of doing it is by the Generals taking over the government lock, stock and barrel. After this has been done, it can then be decided whether to put Diem back in again or go on without him. I am rather inclined to put him back, but I would not favor putting heavy pressure on the Generals if they don't want him."

Lodge added:

> It is possible, as you suggested [several words deleted] for the Generals when, as and if their operation gets rolling to demand the removal of the Nhus before bringing their operation to fruition. But I am afraid they will get talked out of their operation which will then disintegrate, still leaving the Nhus in office.
>
> If the Generals' operation does get rolling, I would not want to stop it until they were in full control. They could then get rid of the Nhus and decide whether they wanted to keep Diem.

---

[61]A copy of the cable, Washington to Saigon 272, Aug. 29, 1963, is in the Johnson Library, Declassified and Sanitized Documents from Unprocessed Files.

[62]*PP*, Gravel ed., vol. II, pp. 737-738. A copy of the cable, Washington to Saigon 279, Aug. 29, 1963, is in the Johnson Library, Declassified and Sanitized Documents from Unprocessed Files.

[63]*PP*, Gravel ed., vol. II, pp. 739-740. A copy of the cable, Saigon to Washington 383, Aug. 30, 1963, is in the Johnson Library, Declassified and Sanitized Documents from Unprocessed Files.

It is better for them and for us for them to throw out the Nhus than for us to get involved in it.

I am sure that the best way to handle this matter is by a truly Vietnamese movement even if it puts me rather in the position of pushing a piece of spaghetti.

Lodge's cable had been preceded by discussions with Vietnamese leaders about the situation, and on the same day (August 30), he sent reports to Washington on two of these. One was with the Interim Secretary of State for Foreign Affairs, Truong Cong Cuu, and the other was with a prominent person whose name has been deleted from the cable reporting the conversation.[64] Cuu tried to reassure Lodge that measures were being taken by the Diem government to improve relations with the U.S., but he told Lodge "Please cease the efforts of your CIA to make us a nation of 'boys' "; and he asked him to stop the recruitment of spies "that we may be allowed to develop in our own way in dignity," adding ". . . the French tried to manipulate the Vietnamese people in this way and that is the reason why he had never been able to work with them."

Lodge reported that his other contact, a person who supported the U.S. program in Vietnam, advised against trying to remove the Nhus. The situation was improving, the informant said, and Diem, an excellent leader, needed Nhu. The war, he added, could be won by the Diem administration. As the conversation ended, he advised Lodge "First, try to calm American opinion and, second, no coups."

In addition to cabling Lodge and Harkins on August 29 to report agreement that the coup should be carried out as first ordered on August 24, President Kennedy personally sent Lodge that day the following top secret, "Eyes Only" cable marked "No Other Distribution Whatever":[65]

I have approved all the messages you are receiving from others today, and I emphasize that everything in these messages has my full support.

We will do all that we can to help you conclude this operation successfully. Nevertheless, there is one point on my own constitutional responsibilities as President and Commander in Chief which I wish to state to you in this entirely private message, which is not being circulated here beyond the Secretary of State.

Until the very moment of the go signal for the opposition by the Generals, I must reserve a contingent right to change course and reverse previous instructions. While fully aware of your assessment of the consequences of such a reversal, I know from experience that failure is more destructive than an appearance of indecision. I would, of course, accept full responsibility for any such change as I must bear also the full responsibility for this operation and its consequences. It is for this reason that I count on you for a continuing assessment of the prospects of success and most particularly desire your candid warning if the current course begins to go sour. When we go,

---

[64]Both cables, Saigon to Washington 380 and 384, Aug. 30, 1963 are in the Kennedy Library, NSF Country File, Vietnam.

[65] Kennedy Library, NSF Presidential Meetings File, CAP 63465. This cable was declassified in 1980.

we must go to win, but it will be better to change our minds than fail. And if our national interest should require a change of mind, we must not be afraid of it.

On August 30, Lodge replied to Kennedy in a cable marked "President only, pass White House directly, no other distribution whatever":[66]

1. I fully understand that you have the right and responsibility to change course at any time. Of course I will always respect that right.

2. To be successful, this operation must be essentially a Vietnamese affair with a momentum of its own. Should this happen you may not be able to control it, i.e., the "go signal" may be given by the Generals.

The Generals Hesitate, and the U.S. Regroups

Kennedy's personal cable to Lodge coincided with an apparent reluctance by the Vietnamese generals to proceed with the coup, and U.S. officials in both Washington and Saigon decided that the time was not yet ripe.

After a meeting of the NSC at the State Department on August 30, at which Secretary of State Rusk presided in the absence of the President, Rusk sent the following cable to Lodge:[67]

Generals so far appear have no plan and little momentum. Further, bits and pieces of information here suggest that Diem and Nhu are moving to normalize situation and head off possibilities of being upset. Prospects of changing government by strong and concerted Vietnamese elements seem very thin on basis of any hard information we have. This raises possibility that Nhu will try to ease internal and international pressures and perhaps bring about quiet liquidation of potential opposition. Possibility therefore increasingly is that if there is to be a change, it can only be brought about by American rather than Vietnamese effort. Obviously, an abortive effort inspired by or attributed to the United States will be disastrous. Central question therefore comes to be how much reality there is in attitude expressed by generals with whom contacts have been made and their capabilities and determinations with respect to what has been said thus far. The distinction between what is desirable and what is possible is one which we may have to face in the next few days. This telegram changes none of your instructions but expresses our uneasiness at the absence of bone and muscle as seen from here.

On August 31, the U.S. mission cabled Washington that planning for the coup had stopped because of doubts among the generals that they had enough forces under their control to undertake a successful coup, as well as about the commitment of the U.S. to support the coup. At that point, as the *Pentagon Papers* states,

[66]Kennedy Library, NSF Country File, Vietnam. This cable was declassified in 1983 as a request of a mandatory review request by CRS. A number of other cables between Washington and Saigon during the period Aug. 28-30, 1963, remain classified.
[67]Washington to Saigon 284, Aug. 30, 1963, same location.

". . . the U.S. found itself . . . without a policy and with most of its bridges burned."[68]

That same day, Lodge replied to Rusk's cable of August 30.[69] He noted that by then Washington had received Harkins' cable reporting that planning for the coup had stopped. "At some undeterminate date in the future," Lodge said, if "some other group with the necessary strength and lust for office comes forward, we can contemplate another effort."

Lodge said he thought Washington was "right" to instruct him to support a coup, ". . . not only because of the state of opinion in America and Free World but because the government of Viet-Nam have acted both as liars and criminals. But now the only attempt to change the government which would succeed would be one which the U.S. could mount itself and, of course, that is out of the question."

He suggested that the U.S. try to arrange for a go-between other than himself (he thought the coup planning and other factors had lessened his effectiveness to play such a role) to negotiate with Diem the departure from the country of Madame Nhu, as well as stripping Nhu of all functions except administration of the strategic hamlets. Archbishop Ngo Dinh Thuc, another of Diem's brothers, should also leave the country. The position of Prime Minister would be created to be filled by Thuan. Conciliatory steps would be taken toward the Buddhists and the students.

Lodge also asked whether, to strengthen his hand, it would be possible for the U.S. House of Representatives or the House Foreign Affairs Committee to "cut out appropriations for foreign aid for Viet-Nam? Giving me chance to get GVN to agree to our points on the ground that this would facilitate restoration of the item."

On August 31, there was another meeting of the NSC group at the State Department with Rusk presiding.[70] It was, or could have been, a significant meeting, because it was the first important high-level meeting of this kind during the Kennedy administration at which doubts were expressed about continued U.S. involvement in Vietnam. The meeting began with comments from Rusk as to why a coup had been considered by the U.S. in the first place. He listed three factors, the first two of which were the internal and external effects of Ngo Dinh Nhu and his wife on the situation in Vietnam, and the third was the pressure of U.S. public (and congressional) opinion. He said the time had come to take steps to improve the situation in Vietnam as well as to strengthen U.S. public support of Vietnam policy, but that it was unrealistic to begin by assuming that Nhu would have to be removed. McNamara said he agreed with Rusk, and urged that normal communications between the U.S. mission and Diem be resumed immediately. Hilsman then reviewed the reasons for supporting a coup.

At that point there occurred an exchange of some historical significance involving, on the one hand, Paul Kattenburg, and, on the other, Rusk, McNamara, Taylor, Nolting and Vice President John-

[68]*PP*, Gravel ed., vol. II, p. 240. The cable was based on a meeting on Aug. 31 between Harkins and Khiem.

[69]Kennedy Library, NSF Country File, Vietnam, Saigon to Washington 391, Aug. 31, 1963. Parts of this cable have been sanitized.

[70]*PP*, Gravel ed., vol. II, pp. 741-743.

son. It was, among other things, a sobering experience for anyone who might have had any thoughts about questioning the U.S. commitment. Kattenburg, who had just returned from Vietnam, commented that Lodge thought the United States would be thrown out of Vietnam in 6 months if the U.S. tried to continue working with the Diem regime. Kattenburg said he had known Diem for 10 years, and did not think that Diem would ever take the steps necessary to correct the situation. This, he said, would mean a steady deterioration in the situation, and he suggested that it would be better for the U.S. to withdraw honorably. Taylor questioned Kattenburg about what he meant by being forced out in 6 months, and Nolting disagreed with Kattenburg, but it was the response of Rusk, McNamara and Johnson that ended the argument. Rusk said that Kattenburg's comments were "largely speculative; that it would be far better for us to start on the firm basis of two things— that we will not pull out of Vietnam until the war is won, and that we will not run a coup." McNamara agreed. Rusk added that he thought there was "good proof that we have been winning the war." Vice President Johnson agreed also, adding that he had "great reservations with respect to a coup, particularly so because he had never seen a genuine alternative to Diem." He said that "from both a practical and political viewpoint, it would be a disaster to pull out; that we should stop playing cops and robbers and get back to talking straight to the GVN, and that we should once again go about winning the war."

Kattenburg later commented on this experience:[71]

> . . . I listened for about an hour or an hour and a half to this conversation before I was asked to say anything at the meeting and they looked to me absolutely hopeless, the whole group of them. There was not a single person there that knew what he was talking about. It simply looked, to me, that way. They were all great men. It was appalling to watch. I didn't have the feeling that any of them—Bobby Kennedy, Taylor, even down to my good old friend and buddy, Roger Hilsman— really knew. . . . They didn't know Vietnam. They didn't know the past. They had forgotten the history. They simply didn't understand the identification of nationalism and Communism, and the more this meeting went on, the more I sat there and I thought, "God, we're walking into a major disaster," and that's when I made what essentially was a very imprudent and also presumptuous remark, in a way. And the reaction to it was sort of what I had invited. They all just disregarded it or said it was not backed by anything.

After the meeting, the State Department sent Lodge two cables, one from Hilsman and the other from Rusk, both of which were read and approved by Kennedy.[72] In the cable from Hilsman, Lodge was told that policymakers in Washington agreed with his proposal for a "direct effort" in Vietnam. "U.S. cannot abandon Viet-Nam and while it will support Vietnamese effort to change government that has good prospects success U.S. should not and

[71] CRS Interview with Paul Kattenburg, Feb. 16, 1979.
[72] Kennedy Library, NSF Country File, Vietnam, Washington to Saigon 294 (Hilsman) and 295 (Rusk), Aug. 31, 1962.

would not mount and operate one. . . . In the meantime, our primary objective remains winning war and we concur your suggestion that we should now reopen communications with Diem." The cable continued:

As to general posture, it seems desirable to maintain both publicly and in our private talks with GVN the leverage of U.S. discontent with repression which has eroded war effort within Viet-Nam as well as support of Congress, U.S. public, and world. Impression should be, both privately and publicly, that U.S. engaged in candid and critical discussion to improve government not overthrow it. Decision on changing government is Vietnamese affair.

In your talk with Diem, our thought is you should first stress common interest in defeating Viet Cong. Then in frank but tough line point out that daily juxtaposition of continuing American casualties and massive U.S. aid with repressive measures contrary deepest American convictions will make it difficult for Executive and Congress to continue support. Common problem for U.S. and GVN in general and you and Diem in particular is to work out set of GVN policies and actions that will make possible continued U.S. support. But time is rather short. President Kennedy may well be obliged at next press conference to express U.S. disapproval of repressive measures. Should we find it impossible to reach an agreement with GVN on a program to undo the damage caused by recent GVN actions, then suspension of aid might soon be forced upon us.

Hilsman's cable concluded by stating that the President was going to comment on the situation in Vietnam in a televised interview on September 2. "While in this interview he will be as restrained as possible, if asked it will be impossible to avoid some expression of concern. This expression, however, will be mild in comparison to what may have to be said soon unless there is major improvement."

Rusk's August 31 cable to Lodge was as follows:

It seems to me that we must keep our eye fixed on the main purpose of our presence in South Viet-Nam and everyone on the U.S. side needs to review the bidding on this elementary purpose: why we are there, why are we asking our fellows to be killed and what is getting in the way of accomplishing our purpose. The actions of the GVN and the Nhus have eroded this purpose—inside Viet-Nam and internationally and they have also eroded our capacity to provide political leadership in the U.S. necessary to support the effort in Viet-Nam. To raise these questions is not merely an emotional reaction to two individuals. They involve the fundamental requirement of political leadership in Viet-Nam which is necessary to coalesce the Vietnamese people in a war effort which we can support. Diem must realize that his obligation of political leadership runs to the solidarity of his people which may require conciliatory actions which are distasteful to him personally. He must make a systematic effort to improve his international position, and a demonstration to the American people that we are not asking

Americans to be killed to support Madame Nhu's desire to bar-
becue bonzes.

On September 2, 1963, President Kennedy was interviewed on
CBS television by Walter Cronkite. When asked a prearranged
question about Vietnam by Cronkite, Kennedy gave this preplanned response:[73]

I don't think that unless a greater effort is made by the Government to win popular support that the war can be won out
there. In the final analysis, it is their war. They are the ones
who have to win it or lose it.

Kennedy was asked by Cronkite whether "this government has
time to regain the support of the people," and he replied that it
did; that "with changes in policy and perhaps with personnel I
think it can." He added that he did not agree with those who advocated U.S. withdrawal from Vietnam. "That would be a great mistake," he said. "We . . . have to participate—we may not like it—
in the defense of Asia."

Copies of Kennedy's comments during the Cronkite interview
were then cabled by the State Department to Saigon and to all
other relevant U.S. diplomatic missions with the notation, "They
represent the U.S. Government's attitude toward the situation and
should be followed as the official U.S. public position."[74]

On September 6, the *New York Times* said in an editorial on
Kennedy's interview: "The lessons of the present crisis are plain.
One is that the anti-Communist war in South Vietnam . . . is not
only, as President Kennedy declared, 'their war' but our war—a
war from which we cannot retreat and which we dare not lose."

A week later, in an interview with Chet Huntley on NBC television, Kennedy repeated that the U.S. should not withdraw from
Vietnam. He was also asked by Huntley whether he believed in the
"domino theory." He replied: "I believe it. I believe it. I think that
the struggle is close enough. China is so large, looms so high just
beyond the frontier, that if South Vietnam went, it would not only
give them an improved geographic position for a guerrilla assault
on Malaya, but would also give the impression that the wave of the
future in Southeast Asia was China and the Communists. So I believe it."[75]

According to William Bundy, Kennedy's opposition to withdrawal ". . . reflected exactly what the internal record shows was being
said by his senior advisers in council. Short of the most dire extremes, the U.S. simply should not think of withdrawing."[76]

In early September 1963, as the U.S. Government began regroup-
ing prior to new efforts to force Diem's hand, Lodge, who was deliberately avoiding a meeting with Diem, met for the second time
with Nhu (the first meeting had been on August 27). Accompanying Lodge were the Italian Ambassador and the Papal Delegate to
Vietnam. At this meeting, Nhu said that he was planning to resign
and to retire to the Vietnamese countryside (Dalat), and that
Madame Nhu would leave Vietnam for an extended trip. The

[73] *Public Papers of the Presidents,* John F. Kennedy, 1963, p. 652.
[74] Kennedy Library, NSF Country File, Vietnam, Washington to Saigon 306, Sept. 2, 1963.
[75] *Public Papers of the Presidents,* John F. Kennedy, 1963, p. 659.
[76] Bundy MS., ch. 10, p. 9.

Papal Delegate agreed to arrange for Archbishop Thuc to leave the country. Nhu also said that conciliatory steps would be taken toward the Buddhists, and that, as the U.S. had advocated, a Prime Minister would be appointed.[77] During the remainder of that week, the Italian Ambassador and the Papal Delegate urged Nhu to carry out these promises. One of the reasons they cited was the need to avoid a suspension of U.S. aid for Vietnam which was then being considered in the U.S. Senate. (On September 6, Nhu said again that he would resign, but that he would not leave the country. On September 7, the Papal Delegate "got Thuc out of the country," and on September 9, Madame Nhu left for Europe.[78] Nhu still had not resigned, however.)

On September 3, Kennedy met with his NSC advisers to consider new instructions for Lodge when he met again with Diem. The group discussed Lodge's meeting with Nhu on September 2 and agreed that it would be helpful if Nhu were to resign and leave Saigon, if only for Dalat. The President said he did not want to discourage Madame Nhu's trip, but that he did not want her to come to the United States, and particularly did not want her to make a speech in Washington. CIA Director McCone replied that "He believed we could handle the press in such a way that the trip would not increase Madame Nhu's prestige."[79]

Several hours after the meeting, a cable was sent to Lodge stating that Nhu's promises were hopeful, but that Lodge should meet with Diem as soon as possible.[80] "Bargain with Nhu," the cable said, "would only confirm his ascendency." Even if Nhu were in Dalat, "he could still be power behind throne."

Washington's "guidance" for Lodge in the September 3 cable was about the same as in the August 31 cables from Hilsman and Rusk:

> We will continue to assert publicly and privately U.S. discontent with repression which has eroded effort toward common goal of winning war until there are concrete results in GVN policies and posture. U.S. not trying to overthrow government, but engaged in candid and critical talks to improve it. Purpose of general posture is to give you leverage with GVN; avoid false public impression U.S. tried something and now backing off; and avoid seeming to acquiesce in repression, which would put U.S. on wrong side fence with majority of people inside Viet-Nam and the world.

In a memorandum reporting on a luncheon meeting he had that day (September 3) with journalists Peter Lisagor (*Chicago Daily News*), Hugh Sidey (*Time*), and Marguerite Higgins (*New York Herald Tribune*), Hilsman said in part:[81]

> I have been saying for several months that the U.S. would not attempt to "play God"; and the U.S. could not scurry about plotting and pulling strings on puppets in a country like Viet-Nam. The U.S. could not play God for three reasons: (1) it would undermine our efforts to build viable political systems

---

[77]*PP*, Gravel ed., vol. II, p. 242.
[78]*Ibid.*
[79]Kennedy Library, NSF Presidential Meetings File, "Memorandum of Conversation with the President," Sept. 3, 1963, portions sanitized.
[80]Washington to Saigon 317, Sept. 3, 1963, same location.
[81]Kennedy Library, NSF Country File, Vietnam.

throughout Asia; (2) it would open a new Vietnamese Government to a charge of being a U.S. puppet and set back the war effort; and (3) the CIA did not have the skill, the eptness or the perceptiveness into Asian societies to bring it off.

All this I have been saying for months. It remains true. What has happened here is that Nhu beat up the Pagodas without the Army knowing about it. It was an attempt to tar the Army with this brush and the U.S. The purpose was to lead the U.S. around by the nose to demonstrate to all of Viet-Nam that we were controllable. Faced with this action and these motives, the U.S. had to show Diem-Nhu and the Vietnamese people that the U.S. could not be made a puppet. It is true that we don't have the leverage that some think we do in calling the tune in a country we are helping, but we are not and cannot be their complete puppets. The motive behind the statement that the Army was not to blame was not an "invitation to rebellion" in exactly that sense. It did and was intended to put all concerned on notice that it was winning the war that we were concerned with and that, if the Vietnamese chose to change their government, we were not committed to Diem, the personality. It seemed to me that this was not "an invitation to rebellion."

(At the end of the last sentence, after "rebellion," Hilsman had added "if this is treason make the most of it," but he or someone else penciled out these additional words.)

At about this time, General Lansdale, even though involved in other assignments, met with Harriman to discuss the situation in Vietnam. This is his description of that conversation:[82]

. . . In the late summer of '63 I had breakfast one day with Harriman. He was asking me some questions about brother Nhu and Diem, and he told me he was very surprised at my viewpoints on things, I guess they sounded unusual to him. I urged him to create a place for Nhu up at Harvard. I remember he had John Kenneth Galbraith, a Harvard economist and Ambassador to India at the time, having breakfast with us at Harriman's house. I was saying that Galbraith and Harriman should get together and put up a group at Harvard and invite Nhu over from Vietnam to be a member there. I said, "Kick him upstairs. Tell him he's an intellectual. Listen to him and give him a job there. He'd come, and Diem would let him go. And once he's away, then Diem will be a very different person and be on his own and you won't have to worry so much about him." Galbraith sort of snorted negatively. And I said, "No, Nhu is a real smart guy. He's obnoxious like most of you intellectuals—he sort of gets on my nerves a little bit." Galbraith was so negative about it that I couldn't help teasing him. But it would have been one way out for Diem and Nhu.

Harriman liked the idea. He said, "I like the way you think and I like ideas like this." I said, "Well, Diem gave his father a sort of a death-bed promise that he would take care of his youngest brother, Nhu. And we Americans have come in and

---

[82]CRS Interview with Edward G. Lansdale, Nov. 19, 1982.

bluntly told him to get rid of Nhu. Well, his father's wishes mean more to him. He's a family man. Instead of that, if we had gone in and said, 'We have a real good job for Nhu and want you to help us convince him to go,' he'd do it. You know, he'd think it was good for his brother which it would be." And I said, "And Nhu is a real intellectual. He really is. He's a deep political student. I don't agree with him on a lot of things but that doesn't say that he doesn't have a lot on the ball, because he does." But we didn't do it. . . .

Lansdale said that he could "feel that something was happening," and he went to see Roger Hilsman in the State Department. "Roger kept talking about his forthcoming trip to Australia, and I said, 'No, Harriman wants me to talk about Vietnam to you. You must be about to do something. Tell me what it is, so I'll know, and maybe I can help you, come up with some ideas for you.' And he'd keep going back to Australia. He wouldn't talk about Vietnam at all." Lansdale also saw McNamara:

I went in and saw McNamara and he must have hinted at forthcoming changes in Saigon. I remember saying, "Don't forget there's a constitution there. Keep it alive. . . . don't go monkeying around trying to overcome the will of the people to make some new idea work. . . . And don't forget there's a constitutional vice president there," and so on.

Using Congress to Reinforce the Threat

In his cable of August 30, as was noted earlier, Lodge (a former Member of the U.S. Senate until he was defeated by John F. Kennedy) had suggested the possibility of having the House or the House Foreign Affairs Committee pass an amendment to reduce or suspend U.S. aid to Vietnam unless and until Diem agreed to the changes being suggested by the United States. On September 6, he suggested it again: "I am obviously looking for leverage for my talk with Diem," he said in a cable to Harriman.[83] "The following is clear to me: even though Vietnamese public mind would not differentiate, a congressional cut would, in GVN mind, clearly avoid much of the odium which would attach a suspension of U.S. aid by the executive branch. If our congressional system does, in fact, give us an advantage in handling the extremely explosive issue of aid suspension, we should certainly not overlook it."

Just before he sent this cable, Lodge received Hilsman's cable of September 5, in which Hilsman reported on an executive session of the Far East Subcommittee of the Senate Foreign Relations Committee where he had testified on the situation in Vietnam.[84] Hilsman told Lodge that the meeting ". . . revealed far-reaching doubts regarding not only Diem-Nhu leadership but also advisability of continued U.S. participation in Viet-Nam war."

Following the subcommittee meeting, the chairman of the subcommittee, Senator Frank Lausche, made a brief speech in the Senate, apparently drafted by or with the advice of the State Department, in which he said that he concurred with Kennedy's

---

[83]Kennedy Library, POF Country File, Vietnam Security, 1963, Saigon to Washington 423, Sept. 6, 1963.
[84]Washington to Saigon 335, Sept. 5, 1963, same location.

statement on September 2 about the need for a change of policy and possibly of personnel by the South Vietnamese, as well as Kennedy's opposition to the attacks on the Buddhists, which he called "a grave mistake of policy" on Diem's part.[85]

Later that day, Senator Frank Church, also a member of the Foreign Relations Committee, said that he was considering offering a resolution to suspend U.S. aid to Vietnam unless the Diem government instituted reforms. Senator Frank Carlson (R/Kans.), another member of the Foreign Relations Committee, said he would support such a move. This information was immediately cabled to Lodge by the State Department, and after a meeting of the NSC a cable was sent to Lodge directing him in talking to Diem, (which the cable urged him to do as a part of U.S. strategy), to "elaborate difficulties with U.S. public opinion and Congress using Hilsman meeting with Far East Subcommittee and statements of Lausche and Church. . . ."[86]

Lodge met with Diem on September 9, and afterwards he reported that "the greatest impact was probably made by the discussion of the grave reaction which Diem is courting in the U.S. Congress."[87]

When Church told Hilsman that he was thinking of introducing the resolution, Hilsman urged him not to offer specific language "without first checking with the Executive Branch on both wording and timing. . . ." Church agreed. The administration, which may have been responsible for initiating the resolution, pursuant to Lodge's suggestion, began encouraging Church, and working closely with him to maximize the impact of the proposal on the situation in Vietnam. McGeorge Bundy is said to have called Church on behalf of the President to tell him to 'Keep it up'; that they thought that was kind of helpful pressure."[88]

At a meeting of the NSC on September 10, the President raised the subject of a congressional resolution condemning Diem's actions.[89] Hilsman replied that "the problem was not to start Congress but to stop it." He discussed Church's interest in offering such a resolution, and said he thought Church would be amenable to suggestions from the administration on timing and wording. The President said ". . . we should decide whether we thought a revolution was advantageous. If we decided it was, we should then get the full support of Senators Mansfield and Dirksen. The worst possible situation would be to have a resolution put up and then defeated."

Following the NSC meeting, Hilsman went directly to Capitol Hill to talk to Church. He cautioned Church that it would not do to have a weak or contrary vote on the resolution. It had to be "near

[85]*CR*, vol. 109, p. 16397.
[86]Kennedy Library, NSF Country File, Washington to Saigon 341, Sept. 6, 1963, Vietnam; NSF Presidential Meetings File, Washington to Saigon 348, Sept. 6, 1963.
[87]Kennedy Library, POF Country File, Vietnam Security, 1963, Unsigned report by General Krulak on "Vietnam, 6-10 September 1963."
[88]CRS Interview with Church's former assistant, Bryce Nelson, Dec. 12, 1978. Bundy says he does not remember this phone call, but that it may have occurred. CRS Interview with McGeorge Bundy, Jan. 8, 1979.
[89]Kennedy Library, NSF Presidential Meetings File, "Memorandum of a Conference with the President," Sept. 10, 1963.

unanimous." Church replied that the proposed resolution had a "good prospect of getting real support."

Hilsman said he would work with Church on the language of the proposal. (At that time, Church's resolution provided for discontinuing aid to the government of South Vietnam because of its religious persecution which "offends the conscience of the American people. . . .")

In a meeting on September 11, the NSC agreed to support the Church resolution as one of a series of moves to bring new pressures to bear on Diem. The President said he thought it would be helpful, "but only if we could control the ensuing situation." There were these further comments:

> Mr. [McGeorge] Bundy said we could support the introduction of the resolution and then suggest that it not be acted upon in a hurry. Secretary Rusk and Senator Mansfield shared the view that the resolution should be introduced, but that hearings on it be delayed.

> The President expressed his concern that an effort would be made to attach the resolution to the aid bill. He wanted us to work with the Congressional Committees so that we would not end up with a resolution requiring that we reduce aid. The objective was a resolution merely condemning current actions of the Diem government. We must not get into a situation in which the resolution could be defeated. We should try to avoid having it tied to the aid program.

Following the NSC meeting, Church was given the go-ahead by Hilsman, and the next day, September 12, 1963, he introduced the resolution, as follows:[90]

> *Resolved,* That it is the sense of the Senate that unless the Government of South Vietnam abandons policies of repression against its own people and makes a determined and effective effort to regain their support, military and economic assistance to that Government should not be continued.

Cosponsoring the resolution were its principal cosponsor, Republican Senator Carlson, and 21 additional Senators (others joined subsequently), all but two of whom were Democrats, mostly liberals. Included among the cosponsors were some of the stalwarts among those who, in addition to Church, subsequently opposed the war: Morse, Ernest Gruening (D/Alaska), Gaylord Nelson (D/Wis.), Pell, Joseph S. Clark (D/Pa.), George S. McGovern (D/S. Dak.) and Stephen M. Young (D/Ohio).

Church's resolution had been drafted by the State Department, and, as stated in a note from a member of Hilsman's staff informing him that it been offered, "Church offered his resolution using exactly the same language as we had. No change."[91]

Following the introduction of the Church resolution, the State Department again cited congressional pressure as one of the arguments to be made to Diem. In the September 16 draft of instructions for Lodge, which was part of an overall action plan, he was to

---

[90]S. Res. 88-196. For Church's statement see *CR*, vol. 109, see p. 16824.

[91]Kennedy Library, Thomson Papers, Note to RH from Ginny, Sept. 12, 1963, reporting phone call from State's congressional liaison office. In the same file there are several other State Department drafts of the resolution.

tell Diem that "The Executive Branch considers any effort to contest moves in Congress to restrict or terminate U.S. aid programs in Vietnam bound to be ineffective under present circumstances."[92]

In the general plan of action prepared by State and sent to the President, Rusk, McNamara and McCone on September 16, Hilsman included this statement of "Congressional Action":[93]

A resolution expressing the "sense of the Senate" that aid to South Vietnam be terminated unless that regime reverses its policies of repression might be useful ammunition for Ambassador Lodge, if it were passed by a substantial margin. With tacit Administration approval, the Church-Carlson resolution has good prospects for passage. In terms of general strategy on the foreign aid bill, such a resolution should be delayed until Senate passage of the aid bill. Although a case can be made for earlier approval of this resolution, what is contemplated here is not a crash program of sudden aid termination but rather a carefully phased plan which might well benefit from Senate action at a later date.

The Debate Continues

Meanwhile, policymakers in the executive branch continued debating the next phase in the ongoing effort to bring about the desired changes in Vietnam. The NSC met again on September 6.[94] During the first part of the meeting, before the arrival of the President, there was a very pointed discussion among his advisers. Rusk said, "if the situation continues to deteriorate in Vietnam, if our relations with Diem continue to deteriorate, and if U.S. domestic opinion becomes strongly anti-Diem, we will be faced with no alternative short of a massive U.S. military effort." He said that Lodge should be directed to tell Diem that the United Nations was on the verge of passing a resolution condemning the repression of the Buddhists, and that the U.S. would not be able to prevent passage of that resolution. Moreover, unless Diem acted promptly there would be a "drastic effect in the U.S. involving both reduction in economic and military assistance and strong pressure to withdraw U.S. political support of Vietnam."

Robert Kennedy asked whether the war could be won if Diem and Nhu remained in power. Rusk replied that it could not be won unless changes were made. RFK wondered whether Diem would change, and said that the U.S. should get "tough." "Ambassador Lodge has to do more than say our President is unhappy. We will have to tell Diem that he must do the things we demand or we will have to cut down our effort as forced by the U.S. public." Rusk responded that pressure should be applied in ". . . two or three bites. It is very serious to threaten to pull out of Vietnam. If the Viet Cong takes over in Vietnam we are in real trouble." He recommended that the first step should be a discussion between Lodge and Diem, following which the U.S. would then be in a better posi-

---

[92]Kennedy Library, NSF Country File, Vietnam, Hilsman to Rusk and McNamara, "A Plan to Achieve U.S. Objectives in South Vietnam," Sept. 16, 1963.
[93]*Ibid.*, pt. C, phase I, p. 11.
[94]"Memorandum of Conference with the President," Sept. 6, 1963, cited above.

tion to know what to do, and could, if desirable, issue an "ultimatum."

McGeorge Bundy commented, ". . . this was not the moment of decision. When we say we can't win with Diem we are talking of a longer time period." He, too, thought they needed more information, particularly from Thuan.

Taylor observed that only three weeks earlier the U.S. believed that the war could be won with Diem, and he wondered whether recent events had changed that judgment. There apparently was no direct response to his query.

RFK asked again what the U.S. should do if it were concluded that the war could not be won with Diem. McNamara replied that this question could not be answered in Washington because of the lack of first-hand information on the state of affairs in Vietnam. Rusk agreed, and said that a reassessment was required. Taylor suggested that General Krulak should go to Vietnam to assess the "grass roots military view," and McNamara and Rusk agreed.

There was further discussion of the instructions to Lodge. Nolting argued that it would be a mistake to put too much pressure on Diem. "He asked that we not talk to Diem about sanctions, but describe to him flatly the situation as we saw it."

Rusk concluded this part of the meeting by calling the situation "stage one." He added, "There may be no stage two if we decide to pull out. If we pull out, we might tell Diem that we wish him well. Diem may be able to win the war without us, but this is unlikely."[95]

At this point the President joined the group and the meeting continued. McGeorge Bundy asked about the "essential minimum of our demands." Rusk replied, "if the Nhus stay on their present course we will continue to lose ground." The President remarked, "we should ask Diem to prohibit Madame Nhu from talking."[96] Nolting said that, on balance, he thought Ngo Dinh Nhu himself would "have to go." This, he added, "would mean a loss in Vietnam but a gain with U.S. public opinion." McGeorge Bundy said that if Madame Nhu would leave, "we could live with Nhu remaining in Saigon," but he again suggested getting Thuan's opinion. (Thuan had said two weeks earlier that the war could be won only if Nhu left.)

It was agreed that a team representing the two dominant points of view, Krulak from the DOD/JCS and Joseph A. Mendenhall, Director of the Far East Planning Office under Hilsman, should make a quick trip to Vietnam to survey the situation. McNamara ordered Krulak to leave in 90 minutes. Hilsman reported later that he personally had to have the departure of the plane delayed until Mendenhall could reach the airport.[97]

After the September 6 NSC meeting, a cable was sent to Lodge reporting on the meeting:[98]

It is clear that as a minimum we face a major problem with world, with U.S. Congress and with American public which

---

[95]Following this, Rusk's next sentence has been deleted.
[96]An additional comment by the President at this point has been deleted.
[97]*To Move A Nation*, p. 501.
[98]Washington to Saigon 348, Sept. 6, 1963, cited above.

will require GVN to take actions to restore its image so that
we may continue to support it. These actions included [here
there are one or two words sanitized] and removal from country of Madam Nhu, releasing of bonzes, students, etc., along
lines we have discussed.

What is not clear is whether these measures will suffice to
restore sufficient confidence in the Diem Government within
Viet-Nam to permit them to win the war.

Sense of meeting was that if the answer to this second question is that additional measures, such as departure of Nhu, are
essential, and if we cannot obtain these additional measures
after negotiating with Diem, then U.S. faced with question
whether to apply sanctions with all their risks rather than let
situation get steadily worse.

Lodge was urged to meet with Diem as soon as possible in order
to explain the U.S. position, and to get his reaction to that position.

Krulak and Mendenhall were gone for four days, September 6-10.
"It was a remarkable assignment" wrote John Mecklin,[99] the chief
U.S. public affairs officer in Saigon, who accompanied Krulak and
Mendenhall on the return trip, "to travel twenty-four thousand
miles and assess a situation as complex as Vietnam and return in
just four days. It was a symptom of the state the U.S. Government
was in." "The *non sequitur* tone of the whole trip," he added, "was
capped by the fact that the general and the FSO not only appeared
to dislike each other, but also disagreed on what should be done
about Vietnam. On the whole flight they spoke to each other only
when it was unavoidable."

On September 10, Krulak and Mendenhall presented their findings to the President and his advisers.[100] This was the meeting
made famous by the President's quip after hearing the reports
from the two men: "Were you two gentlemen in the same country?"[101]

Mendenhall ". . . emphasized the breakdown of civilian government in Saigon, accompanied by civilian fear and hate of the
Nhus. . . . He foresaw the possibility of a religious war or a large-
scale movement to the Viet Cong."[102]

Krulak, on the other hand, said that Mendenhall's report reflected the "metropolitan view," and that out in the countryside the situation was entirely different. Saigon's political problems, he said,
had not interfered with military operations against the Communists. "He believed strongly that we can stagger through to win the
war with Nhu remaining in control."[103]

The President asked why the judgments of the two men should
be so different. Hilsman responded that "it was the difference between a military and a political view."

---

[99]*Mission in Torment*, pp. 206-207.
[100]Kennedy Library, NSF Presidential Meetings File, Memorandum of Conference with the
President, Sept. 10, 1963.
[101]*Mission in Torment*, p. 208.
[102]The only written report made by Mendenhall was a cable, which is in the Kennedy Library, NSF Presidential Meetings File," Saigon to Washington 453, Sept. 9, 1963.
[103]For Krulak's complete report see "Visit to Vietnam," cited above. His general conclusions
are also in *PP*, Gravel ed., vol. II, pp. 243-244.

Nolting, however, who presumably also represented the political view, disagreed with Mendenhall's conclusions, and said that he thought "the present government will bear the weight of our program."

Rufus Phillips, who also came back with Krulak and Mendenhall, however, said that there was a "crisis confidence in Vietnam." (His comments immediately following this statement have been deleted.)[104] Phillips added that the U.S. had an obligation to adopt measures that would bring about a change of government in Vietnam. He recommended that Lansdale be sent to Vietnam. Lodge, he said, agreed.

Kennedy asked Phillips what the U.S. should do. Phillips replied that the U.S. should use the aid program to apply gradual and graduated pressure on Diem and Nhu. As one aspect of this, the U.S. should suspend aid to the special forces under the command of Colonel Le Quang Tung, who was under the control of Nhu. He believed that through this and other actions the U.S. could split Nhu from Diem, adding, "If we acquiesced in the actions which Nhu had taken against us, the result would be further loss of support from others in Vietnam."

Phillips also gave a pessimistic report on the military situation, with which Krulak disagreed, arguing that this was not the view of General Harkins. At this point the "Crocodile" (Washington's nickname for Harriman), according to Halberstam's detailed account of the meeting, ". . . went after Krulak: Harriman said he was not surprised that Krulak was taking Harkins' side—indeed he would be upset if he did not. Harriman said that he had known Krulak for several years and had always known him to be wrong, and was sorry to say it, but he considered Krulak a damn fool."[105]

The President then called on John Mecklin to state his views. Mecklin said that he agreed with Phillips and Mendenhall that the situation was critical and that strong action was required. He said that the policy of graduated pressure proposed by Phillips was not adequate, however. The Diem government was finished, and "The time had come for the U.S. to apply direct pressure to bring about a change of government, however distasteful." Mecklin said that this could be done without the U.S. appearing to play a direct role. Actions such as the withholding of certain types of aid would have the result of bestirring the generals to act on their own. This might create such chaos, however, that U.S. forces would have to be used to protect American lives.[106]

Mecklin also warned that the coup could provide an opening for the Communists, and therefore that the U.S. should resolve to use U.S. forces if necessary in order to prevent that from happening.

---

[104]From the official summary of the meeting, paraphrased in Hilsman, *To Move A Nation*, p. 504. Hilsman obviously had the benefit of the unexpurgated classified version of the summary when he wrote his book.

[105]Halberstam, *The Best and the Brightest*, p. 279.

Halberstam adds that the Army major who had written a report on Long An province that Phillips had used to illustrate his position "was reprimanded, given a bad efficiency report and immediately transferred out of Long An to the least attractive post available, which happened to be a National Guard slot. The stakes were getting higher and the game was getting tougher." *Ibid.*, pp. 279-280.

[106]These comments by Mecklin are from his book, *Mission in Torment*, p. 210. They have been deleted from the sanitized summary of the Sept. 10 meeting.

In a memorandum on September 10 to Edward R. Murrow, the noted radio and TV commentator who was then the director of the United States Information Agency, Mecklin (an employee of USIA) recommended using U.S. combat forces, if necessary, "both to promote unseating of the regime and against the VC, as well as a willingness to accept an engagement comparable to Korea if the Comunists choose to escalate."[107] Expanding on these points, he said:

In the writer's judgment, conditions in Viet-Nam have deteriorated so badly that the U.S. would be drawing to a three-card straight to gamble its interests there on anything short of an ultimate willingness to use U.S. combat troops. . . .

If we are not willing to resort to U.S. forces, it is wholly possible that efforts to unseat the Ngo Dinhs would produce results that would be worse, from the U.S. viewpoint, than a negotiated "neutral" settlement. . . .

On the other hand, a decision now to use U.S. forces if necessary would give the whole U.S. effort psychological lift, producing confidence that we need not be frustrated indefinitely, giving us a sure hand that has been lacking in the past. . . . Such a new sureness in our actions, with the clear implication that the U.S. "means business," would quickly get through to the Vietnamese and to third countries and thus conceivably itself remove the need to resort to force.

Perhaps it should also be noted that the present situation in Viet-Nam is confronting the U.S. with what was certainly an inevitable showdown on the thesis that Western industrial power somehow must always be frustrated by Communist guerrilla tactics applied against a weak, underdeveloped government that refused foreign advice and reforms of the very ills that the Communist live on. There are incipient insurrections of this sort all over the underdeveloped world and the outcome in Viet-Nam will have critical bearing on U.S. capability to prevent and/or suppress them.

In the writer's opinion, furthermore, there is a very real possibility that if and as Viet-Nam is conclusively being lost to the Communists, the U.S. will be forced to use force in any case as a last resort . . . just as we did so unexpectedly in Korea. It would be vastly wise—and more effective—to make this unpalatable decision now.

In this memorandum, and in his comments at the meeting with the President, Mecklin concluded that if diplomatic pressure failed to dislodge Diem and Nhu from power, and if selective suspension of aid also failed, that the U.S. should then begin covertly planning a coup. At that point, all aid should be suspended. If this, too, failed to produce the necessary changes, the coup should be carried out. "If this also failed, or only partly succeeded, there should be plentiful excuses to bring in U.S. forces, e.g. to restore order, protect American citizens, etc. Such forces should be prepared for attack by local GVN troops, but it is more likely that they would simply act as power in being, making it possible for the U.S. to have its way by seriously presenting the Ngo Dinhs with an ulti-

---

[107]Kennedy Library, NSF Country File, Vietnam, "A Policy for Vietnam."

matum. . . . And once U.S. forces had been introduced into Viet-Nam, it would be relatively simple—on the invitation of the new regime—to keep them on hand to help, if needed, in final destruction of the Viet Cong."

Subsequently, Phillips, in a memorandum that Forrestal sent along to McGeorge Bundy with the comment, ". . . Phillips' judgments of Vietnamese reactions are as good as any we have," took issue with Mecklin's suggestion for using U.S. troops. "Certainly," Phillips said, "no one should rule out the possibility of the ultimate use of U.S. troops and they should be ready to protect dependents if the going gets rough before Nhu topples but the entire policy should not be hinged on this contingency. The use of U.S. troops to fight the war against the VC would, in any case, be a mistake. The Vietnamese are willing to fight and can fight. If we help give them a government worth fighting for, this single action will be worth more than any number of U.S. troops."[108]

As the September 10 NSC meeting continued, Rusk observed that in May and June the U.S. had estimated that the war could be won with Diem. He suggested that events in July and August should be analyzed "to decide whether the situation can be returned to that which existed last May." Harriman's rejoinder was that as far back as May there had been warning signs that Diem was through. McCone said that intelligence reports as recently as the middle of July did not bear out Harriman's point, adding, "The current view of the intelligence community is not as ominous as that expressed by the civilian reporters today. The Vietnamese military officers will work with Nhu. Any aid cutoff would seriously affect the war effort."

At this point the President adjourned the meeting, asking that by the next meeting the following day (September 11) a paper be prepared on ways of cutting U.S. funds.

At 5:45 p.m. that same day (September 10), the NSC principals met at the State Department without the President to continue the morning's discussion.[109] McCone questioned whether there was an alternative to a government headed by Diem. Hilsman then described a ". . . two-prong pressure program on Diem with the aim of forcing him to change his present policies." According to the official summary of the meeting, "He acknowledged that if we started down this path we would have to be prepared to contemplate the use of U.S. forces on the ground in Vietnam." General Taylor commented that he was in favor of continuing to work with Diem, and the summary states that Taylor "revealed a reluctance to contemplate the use of U.S. troops in combat in Vietnam. . . ."

As the meeting concluded, McGeorge Bundy asked Hilsman to prepare two papers for the President, one on U.S. objectives, and the other on "a program of pressures against Diem with the aim of forcing him to meet our demands."

The NSC group met again the next day (September 11) at 6 p.m. without the President[110] and at 7 p.m. with the President. Earlier

---

[108]Kennedy Library, NSF Country File, Vietnam, "Comments on the Necessity for an Advance Decision to Introduce U.S. Forces in Viet-Nam," with transmittal memo of Sept. 17, 1963.
[109]Kennedy Library, "Meeting at the State Department," Sept. 10, 1963, NSF Presidential Meetings File. Some comments have been deleted.
[110]Records of this meeting are still classified.

that day a long cable had been received from Lodge, "Eyes Only for the Secretary of State," summarizing the situation in Vietnam.[111] It was a strong message, obviously intended to support the Harriman-Hilsman position, and to counteract the arguments of Krulak, McNamara and Taylor. Lodge said, ". . . the ship of state here is slowly sinking. . . . if there are effective sanctions which we can apply, we should apply them in order to force a drastic change in government. The only sanction which I can see is the suspension of aid and therefore I recommend that the best brains in the government study precise details of suspending aid so as to do ourselves the most good and the least harm."

Lodge directly questioned the reliability of Krulak's report, saying among other things:

I do not doubt the military judgment that the war in the countryside is going well now. But, as one who has had long connection with the military, I do doubt the value of the answers which are given by young officers to direct questions by generals—or, for that matter, by ambassadors. The urge to give an optimistic and favorable answer is quite unsurmountable—and understandable. I, therefore, doubt the statement often made that the military are not affected by developments in Saigon and the cities generally.

In addition to recommending that a study be made of ways to apply effective sanctions to the Diem government, Lodge said that the U.S. should be making "renewed efforts . . . to activate by whatever positive inducements we can offer the man who would take over the government—Big Minh [General Duong Van Minh, the leader of the coup group] or whoever we might suggest. We do not want to substitute a Castro for a Batista."

At the 7:00 p.m. meeting with the President on September 11, Hilsman summarized the proposed pressure plan. McGeorge Bundy observed that the difference between Hilsman's proposal and Lodge's was that Lodge wanted to suspend all aid. According to the official notes of the meeting, McGeorge Bundy added, "It turns out that it is not easy to cut U.S. aid without stopping the war effort."[112] Gilpatric agreed. Rusk said that Hilsman's proposal ". . . did not involve really important actions, but would have an important psychological effect. He recommended that Ambassador Lodge be told to tell Diem to start acting like the President of Vietnam and get on with the war." Rusk, McNamara, McCone, and Secretary of the Treasury Douglas Dillon all agreed that the U.S. should proceed cautiously, and should continue trying to work with Diem.

President Kennedy asked "whether deterioration has set in and whether the situation is serious." McCone replied that it was not serious, but might become serious within three months. McNamara agreed that it was not serious, and said that "we could not estimate whether the situation would become serious in three months."

[111]Kennedy Library, NSF Presidential Meetings File, Saigon to Washington 478, Sept. 11, 1963.

[112]"Memorandum of Conference with the President," Sept. 11, 1963, same location.

Kennedy also read to the group from a news report of Madame Nhu's latest statement, in which she again criticized the United States. He thought there should be a reply, and added, "How could we continue to have her making anti-American comments at the same time she is one of the leaders of a government we are supporting?"

As the meeting ended, Kennedy asked Hilsman for a detailed plan of action on the proposed sanctions. He also wanted a draft of new instructions for Lodge, "including in that instruction a request that he attempt to hush up the [U.S.] press in Saigon." Meanwhile, the President said, all further decisions on aid to Vietnam should be held up temporarily.

The following day (September 12), the NSC group met again (without the President) apparently for the primary purpose of agreeing on new instructions for Lodge.[113] Based on the documentation available, it would appear that the group agreed with Rusk, McNamara, Taylor, McCone and Nolting to make one last attempt to work with Diem, and approved the draft instruction to Lodge which had been personally drafted by Rusk for consideration at the meeting.[114] In that draft Rusk tried to put the situation in perspective, and to suggest that, given the alternatives, it was important to make another effort to get Diem to act on the problems facing his administration.

The draft cable began by recognizing Lodge's difficult assignment, but added that this was not the first time the U.S. had faced such a situation "in a country whose leadership stubbornly resists measures which we consider necessary to achieve desired results."

Rusk went on to reiterate that "Our central objective remains a secure and independent South Viet-Nam even though, at some future date, it may be possible to consider a free, independent and non-communist unified country. This central objective was what brought us into South Viet-Nam and its achievement is the condition for our leaving. No one would be happier than we to leave under that circumstance." The "outer limits" of our policy, he added, "within which we must therefore operate unless the situation forces us to break through those limits," are ". . . that we do not get out and turn South Viet-Nam over to the Viet-Cong. . . . [and] that we do not use large-scale force to occupy the country and run it ourselves."

Rusk said that the "key question" was what had happened to change the favorable developments of the first six months of 1963. The problem, he added, appeared to be the loss of political confidence, which he attributed primarily to "the two Nhus."

The next step should be "to concentrate on Diem himself to make him see that everything he has been working for for the past ten years is threatened with collapse and failure and that bold and far-sighted action on his part is required. . . ." What "pressures"

---

[113]It is impossible at this time to be certain of this, however, because the records of that meeting are still classified, and in the file at the Kennedy Library there is this notation concerning a one-page summary of the meeting: "Withdrawn because of high sensitivity and high national security classification and placed in special NLK (National Library Kennedy) security safe." This suggests that the discussion may have gone beyond the question of new instructions into the realm of more drastic U.S. action against Nhu, and against Diem if he did not cooperate.

[114]Kennedy Library, NSF Presidential Meetings File.

should be applied in getting Diem to act, the draft cable stated, would have to be determined by Lodge. "I am inclined," Rusk added, "to think that in the next immediate stage we should not threaten what we will not or cannot deliver and that we are not yet ready to cut off assistance which affects the war effort or which would inflict serious damage to the people as contrasted with the regime."

The draft cable concluded with this statement: "It may be that it will be impossible to succeed along this line but the alternatives are so far-reaching that the present effort seems to me to be worth the tedious and frustrating hours which will undoubtedly be required to get through to him and to get him to carry out his own full responsibility."

Development of a General Plan of Action to Enforce U.S. Demands

As the debate over U.S. policy continued, McCone dispatched a special CIA officer to make an independent evaluation of the situation, who reported in mid-September that "we had hastily expended our capability to overthrow the regime, that an aid suspension would not guarantee a constructive result, and that to prevent further political fragmentation we should adopt a "business as usual policy to buy time."[115]

Diem was also making some moves toward easing the tension in Saigon. On September 14, the government announced that martial law, imposed in August, would end, and that elections for the General Assembly, which had been originally scheduled for August but were postponed, would be rescheduled in September.

Meanwhile at the State Department, Hilsman and his associates were preparing the plan requested by the President at the September 11 meeting. On September 16 this was sent to the President and members of the NSC, and on September 17 the NSC met to consider it.[116]

This State Department plan, which became the basic action document for U.S. policy prior to the coup on November 1, had two parts or "tracks"—the "Reconciliation Track," and the "Pressures and Persuasion Track." They were not mutually exclusive. According to the cover memo from Hilsman to Rusk and McNamara, the latter track (Pressures and Persuasion Track) was "a phased program designed to persuade the GVN to take certain actions to ensure popular support necessary to win the war, including the removal of Nhu from his position of influence," whereas the former (Reconciliation Track) "proceeds from the assumption that the removal of Nhu is not feasible and attempts to develop a plan aimed at rehabilitating the GVN, even though Nhu continues in power."

Following the cover memo, there was this introductory statement to the two plans:

> The overall objective in South Vietnam is to win the war against the Viet Cong. It is our judgment that the recent repressive actions of the GVN have created disaffection which will inevitably affect the war effort, unless that government

[115]*PP*, Gravel ed., vol. II, p. 246.
[116]There are copies of the State Department plan, which was opened in a sanitized form in 1981, in the Kennedy Library, NSF Country File, Vietnam.

undertakes changes in both its policies and personnel that are effective and credible.

Withdrawal by the U.S. would be immediately disastrous to the war effort. On the other hand, acquiescence by the U.S. to recent GVN actions would be equally disastrous, although less immediately so. Our policy is therefore to discriminate; in the words of the President, "what helps to win the war we support. What interferes with the war effort we oppose."

Our problem is to implement this policy of persuasion coupled with pressure in such a way as to avoid triggering either civil violence or a radical move by the government of South Vietnam to make a deal with the DRV and remove the U.S. presence.

Following this introductory statement there was a 14-page statement on the Reconciliation Track, and a three-page "Checklist of Actions for GVN to Ensure Popular Support," which contained specific steps to be taken in conjunction with the Reconciliation Track. These steps included most of the reforms that the Kennedy administration had been urging Diem to adopt since the spring of 1961. The paper also suggested that U.S. efforts at reconciliation with Diem should be led by someone like Lansdale.

It was the second track, "Pressures and Persuasion," however, that was most fully articulated, because Hilsman and his associates considered that track to be more effective. Included was a paper on each of four phases of this track, together with six separate annexes.[117] The first of these papers was on the concept of the second track "pressure plan":

The general concept is to use phased, multiple pressures to persuade Diem and Nhu (1) that the GVN should reverse its recent policies of repression effectively and credibly; (2) that the GVN should be broadened; and (3) that the Nhu's influence in the GVN should be sharply and visibly reduced.

Phase 1 concentrates on suasion by a continuation of Lodge's conversations with Diem on the problem of U.S.-GVN relations in all its ramifications.

Phase 2, 3, and 4 add increasingly pressures to the continued conversations.

We recognize the possibility that this campaign may also result in resumed coup plotting. We propose at phases 1 and 2 to give no encouragement to such activities, although we remain ready to listen to serious approaches.

Although past experience does not lead us to be hopeful that suasion alone, as in phase 1, will accomplish the desired results, it seems essential to make the attempt if only to establish a record and lay the groundwork for phase 2.

We believe that the combination of phases 1 and 2 has a good chance of achieving our objective if skillfully and forcefully implemented.

---

[117]The annexes were as follows:
(1) Evacuation as a Pressure Device, (2) Evacuation Plan, (3) DOD Checklist on Military Aid, (4) AID checklist on Economic Aid, (5) CIA Checklist on Covert Aid, (6) Consequences for the United States if Nhu Remains in Power. In the Kennedy Library file, annexes (5) and (6) are not included, presumably because they are still classified.

Phase 3 and 4 increase the pressures considerably, and they begin to enter into a stage at which it will become increasingly difficult to reverse ourselves. At this time, we would recommend approval of phases 1 and 2, leaving our decision on 3 and 4 until a later date. At that point, it would seem advisable to bring Ambassador Lodge back to Washington for consultation.

Phase 1 of the Pressures and Persuasion Track was quite similar to the Reconciliation Track. It was to consist primarily of new efforts by Lodge to persuade Diem to make the reforms that the U.S. considered essential.[118] To help Lodge do so, there would be a new letter from Kennedy to Diem restating the U.S. position. (A copy of the suggested letter was included in the plan package.) ·

In phase 2 of this track the U.S. would selectively suspend aid to Vietnam, particularly to those projects and activities most closely controlled by Nhu, as well as general support funds in the commodity import program. The U.S. would also announce the evacuation of all American dependents from Vietnam. "These actions," the paper said, "have been so calculated as to bear minimal effect on the war effort and the conduct of counterinsurgency operations in VN. We are trying now and we will continue to try to avoid harming the little people in the villages and all those elements in VN which are continuing the fight against the VC."

In addition to these actions, of which Diem would be notified, certain additional actions would be taken without disclosure to Diem. "However, the fact that we are taking them will become apparent." These were "(A) Acquisition of substantial cash resources in piastres; (B) A series of covert actions;[119] (C) At Lodge's discretion, the [CIA] Chief of Station might talk directly with Ngo Dinh Nhu to persuade him to depart."

The explanation of phases 3 and 4 of the Pressures and Persuasion Track is still so sensitive that the entire introductory, explanatory statement for each phase was deleted when documents on the plan were opened in 1981. From the general description given earlier, however, and from the pages of that section of the report which have been opened, it is possible to ascertain that phase 3 was to be the first of the two-stage direct involvement of the United States in precipitating a coup against Diem, and that the principal public actions contemplated in phase 3 were the complete suspension of financial support under the commodity import program and the agricultural commodities[120] program, from which the Government of Vietnam derived half of its revenue.

If phase 3 failed to produce the necessary reforms or "change of personnel," to use Kennedy's earlier phrase, phase 4 would begin with a private or public announcement that the U.S. was dissociating itself from the Diem regime. "Such an announcement would reassert U.S. desires to continue support of the Vietnamese people in their fight for freedom, and to indicate U.S. willingness to support an alternative regime—either in Saigon or elsewhere in Viet-Nam. Actions accompanying this announcement include: immedi-

---

[118]For a listing of these reforms see below.
[119]Here the document refers to annex 5, "CIA checklist on Covert Aid," which is not included in the file and is still classified.
[120]The "P.L. [Public Law] 480 Program."

ate, preplanned evacuation of all nonessential U.S. personnel, turn-around of all shipping, and preparations to supply up-country military forces and strategic hamlets by direct pipeline. These actions now require the overthrow of the Diem regime by coup, or the establishment of a competing government outside of Saigon (and the attendant civil war chaos)."

This was the conclusion of the paper on phase 4:

If the U.S. correctly has estimated civil and military readiness to overthrow Diem, an alternate government should emerge with sufficient popular support to carry on the fight against the Viet Cong while coping with Diem, if he remains in the Saigon area. If the U.S. has not correctly assessed the readiness of the military to desert Diem and he, in fact, retains control of most major forces, the U.S. would face the final decision of U.S. military intervention or complete withdrawal from Viet-Nam. In this situation, U.S. military intervention to fight a former ally could serve no useful purpose, since there would not exist a sufficient popular base of support for U.S. objectives. Inherent in all Phase 4 activities is the element of extreme danger to U.S. essential personnel remaining in Viet-Nam. Casualties should be expected, particularly in the event that there is no popular abandonment of Diem.

On September 16, Hilsman sent Rusk the two draft cables to Lodge, one on each of the proposed two tracks, saying:[121]

. . . My own judgment is that the "Reconciliation Track" will not work. I think Nhu has already decided on an adventure. I think he feels that the progress already made in the war and the U.S. materiel on hand gives him freedom to launch on a course that has a minimum and a maximum goal. The minimum goal would be sharply to reduce the American presence in those key positions which have political significance in the provinces and the strategic hamlet program and to avoid any meaningful concessions that would go against his Mandarin, "personalist" vision of the future of Viet-Nam. The maximum goal, I would think, would be a deal with North Vietnam for a truce in the war, a complete removal of the U.S. presence, and a "neutralist" or "Titoist" but still separate South Viet-Nam.

On September 17, the President met with his NSC advisers to discuss the State Department's plan. The mood was one of determination. In addition to Kennedy's own public pronouncements on the need to defend Vietnam, Senator Fulbright had stated on September 15 on the CBS program "Face the Nation" that "A withdrawal of our forces at this time would . . . be unacceptable."[122]

It was also obvious, however, that the situation in Vietnam had improved very little, and that the U.S. was faced with having to take additional steps to enforce its demands. But while there was general agreement that the pressure plan was a good working concept, the division within the NSC was as deep as ever, and the appeal for more information on the situation struck a responsive chord with most members of the Council. Thus, after tentatively

[121]Kennedy Library, NSF Country File, Vietnam.
[122]New York Times, Sept. 16, 1963.

accepting the pressure plan at the September 17 meeting, the President approved another fact-finding mission by McNamara and Taylor, and postponed final action on the plan pending their report.

After the meeting, the White House cabled Lodge that the pressure plan had been tentatively approved, and requested his comments.[123] "We see no good opportunity for action to remove present government in immediate future; therefore, as your most recent messages suggest, we must for the present apply such pressures as are available to secure whatever modest improvements on the scene may be possible. We think it likely that such improvements can make a difference, at least in the short run. Such a course, moreover, is consistent with more drastic effort as and when means become available, and we will be in touch on other channels on this problem."

The cable authorized Lodge to suspend U.S. aid on a selective basis when desirable. He was also urged to resume discussions with Diem: "We ourselves can see much virtue in effort to reason even with an unreasonable man when he is on a collision course."

The cable also listed the conditions which Lodge should continue to insist upon:

A. Clear the air—Diem should get everyone back to work and get them to focus on winning the war. He should be broad-minded and compassionate in his attitude toward those who have, for understandable reasons, found it difficult under recent circumstances fully to support him. A real spirit of reconciliation could work wonders on the people he leads; a punitive, harsh or autocratic attitude could only lead to further resistance.

B. Buddhists and students—Let them out and leave them unmolested. This more than anything else would demonstrate the return of a better day and the refocusing on the main job at hand, the war.

C. Press—The press should be allowed full latitude of expression. Diem will be criticized, but leniency and cooperation with the domestic and foreign press at this time would bring praise for his leadership in due course. While tendentious reporting is irritating, suppression of news leads to much more serious trouble.

D. Secret and combat police—Confine its role to operations against the VC and abandon operations against non-Communist opposition groups thereby indicating clearly that a period of reconciliation and political stability has returned.

E. Cabinet changes to inject new untainted blood, remove targets of popular discontent.

F. Elections—These should be held, should be free, and should be widely observed.

G. Assembly—Assembly should be convoked soon after the elections. The government should submit its policies to it and should receive its confidence. An assembly resolution would be most useful for external image purposes.

---

[123]White House to Lodge, Sept. 17, 1963, in *PP*, Gravel ed., vol. II, pp. 743-745.

H. Party—Can Lao party [led by Nhu] should not be covert or semi-covert but a broad association of supporters engaged in a common, winning cause. This could perhaps be best accomplished by [words missing] starting afresh. . . .

J. Rehabilitation by ARVN [Vietnamese Army] of pagodas.

K. Establishment of Ministry of Religious Affairs.

L. Liberation of passport issuances and currency restrictions enabling all to leave who wish to.

M. Acceptance of Buddhist Inquiry Mission from World Federation to report true facts of situation to world.

"Specific 'reforms,'" the cable added, "are apt to have little impact without dramatic, symbolic move which convinces Vietnamese that reforms are real. As practical matter we share your view that this can best be achieved by some visible reduction in influence of Nhus, who are symbol to disaffected of all that they dislike in GVN. This we think would require Nhus departure from Saigon and preferably Vietnam at least for extended vacation. We recognize the strong possibility that these and other pressures may not produce this result, but we are convinced that it is necessary to try."

Lodge replied on September 19 that he agreed there was "no good opportunity for action to remove present government in immediate future . . . and that we should, therefore, do whatever we can as an interim measure pending such an eventuality."[124] He said that the list of reforms in Washington's cable had already been discussed with Diem and Nhu. "They think that most of them would either involve destroying the political structure on which they rest or loss of face or both. We, therefore, could *not* realistically hope for more than lip service. Frankly, I see no opportunity at all for substantive changes." Lodge also said that he doubted whether this kind of a "public relations package" would be effective, given the situation. He said he had talked the day before with General Minh, who said that the Communists were gaining ground and the Diem government was more corrupt and repressive than ever. He had also talked to Thuan, who said he wanted to leave the country.

With respect to using selective suspension of U.S. aid as a sanction, but without causing an economic collapse or impeding the war, Lodge said that this also was being studied by the U.S. mission, but without success. "If a way to do this were to be found," he added, "it would be one of the greatest discoveries since the enactment of the Marshall Plan in 1947 because, so far as I know, the U.S. had never yet been able to control any of the very unsatisfactory governments through which we have had to work in our many very successful attempts to make these countries strong enough to stand alone. . . . to threaten them with suppression of aid might well defeat our purposes and might make a bad situation very much worse."

Lodge said that whatever sanctions were used, they should be "directly tied to a promising coup d'etat and should *not* be applied without such a coup being in prospect."

---

[124]Saigon to Washington, Sept. 19, 1963, in *ibid.*, pp. 746-748.

With respect to the "dramatic symbolic moves" suggested by Washington, Lodge said he had talked to Nhu the night before about the matter, and that Diem and Nhu ". . . have scant comprehension of what it is to appeal to public opinion as they have really no interest in any other opinions than their own. I have repeatedly brought up the question of Nhu's departure and have stressed that if he would just stay away until after Christmas, it might help get the [foreign aid] Appropriation Bill through. This seems like a small thing to us but to them it seems tremendous as they are quite sure that the Army would take over if he even stepped out of the country."

In conclusion, Lodge told Washington that he had no objection to seeing Diem, but that he would "rather let him sweat for a while. . . . I would much prefer to wait until I find some part of the AID program to hold up in which he is interested and then have him ask me to come and see him."

The McNamara-Taylor Mission

On September 23, Kennedy met with McNamara and Taylor just before they left.[125] Among other things, he urged then to impress upon Diem the need for reform "as a pragmatic necessity and not as a moral judgment." He said he did not think the threats to cut off aid would be effective, and that, "Since in fact only small changes were likely to be made in the immediate future, it would be better to let such adjustments speak for themselves." Because Diem undoubtedly knew of U.S. involvement with the "opposition," he said it would be best for McNamara and Taylor to stress positive accomplishments, especially since 1961, and the strength of U.S. support for Vietnam.

Taylor suggested that it would be useful to work out ". . . a time schedule within which we expect to get this job done and to say plainly to Diem that we were not going to be able to stay beyond such and such a time with such and such forces, and that the war must be won in this time period." (The notes of the meeting do not indicate whether the President responded to this suggestion.)

When McNamara and Taylor (others on the trip were William Bundy, William Sullivan from the State Department, and William Colby from the CIA) arrived in Saigon on September 24, Lodge, who was fully aware of the politics of the situation, began lobbying hard for his position. According to Halberstam, who witnessed the incident, Lodge, who had invited McNamara to stay with him, met McNamara at the airport, where two of the Embassy's staffers had been assigned to block General Harkins so that Lodge would be the first to greet McNamara, ". . . leaving an angry Harkins pushing at the human barrier, shouting, 'Please, gentlemen, please let me through to the Secretary.' "[126]

After spending about a week surveying the situation in Vietnam, McNamara and Taylor met privately with Diem. McNamara told him that he thought the war was going well, and that the Communist threat could be satisfactorily met by the end of 1965 if the po-

---

[125]Kennedy Library, NSF Country File, Vietnam, "Memorandum for the Record, Meeting on McNamara/Taylor Mission to South Vietnam," Sept. 23, 1963.
[126]The Best and the Brightest, p. 283.

litical situation were stabilized and reforms were carried out by the Diem government. Taylor said he agreed.[127] McNamara added that such improvements were also required for continued support from Congress and the American public. According to the official summary of the meeting, Diem spoke at length, especially about the strategic hamlets, but did not seem at all responsive to the points made by McNamara and Taylor. "His manner was one of at least outward serenity and of a man who had patiently explained a great deal and who hoped he had thus corrected a number of misapprehensions."[128]

Upon their return to Washington on October 2, McNamara and Taylor immediately submitted their written report to the President, as well as reporting orally to the President that morning and to the President and the NSC that afternoon.[129] Their first conclusion was that "The military campaign has made great progress and continues to progress." They said that the timetable for final victory, ("If, by victory, we mean the reduction of the insurgency to something little more than sporadic banditry in outlying districts"), provided there was adequate political stability, was to win by the end of 1964 in all but the IV Corps (the delta), and sometime in 1965 in the IV Corps. But they also concluded that the political situation continued to be "deeply serious," and could affect the conduct of the war. U.S. pressure on Diem was required to produce change, but might make him even more uncooperative. A coup was not likely at that time, "although assassination of Diem or Nhu is always a possibility."

"The prospects that a replacement regime would be an improvement appear to be about 50-50," the report stated, adding that a new regime would probably be headed by a military officer, who would need to maintain order, and that "Such an authoritarian military regime, perhaps after an initial period of euphoria at the departure of Diem/Nhu, would be apt to entail a resumption of the repression at least of Diem, the corruption of the Vietnamese Establishment before Diem, and an emphasis on conventional military rather than social, economic and political considerations, with at least an equivalent degree of xenophobic nationalism."

Of the three alternatives—reconciliation, selective pressure, or active promotion of a coup, McNamara and Taylor said that the first would be ineffective and the third unwise. They favored the second, and recommended that the U.S. should continue to apply such selective pressures, primarily through withholding of aid funds, but that nothing should be done which would impede the war effort. "We should work with the Diem government but not support it." Although the U.S. should continue to develop relations with "an alternate leadership if and when it appears," it should not actively promote a coup at that time. ". . . whether or not it proves to be wise to promote a coup at a later time, we must be ready for the possibility of a spontaneous coup, and this too requires clandestine contacts on an intensive basis."

---

[127]See *Swords and Plowshares*, pp. 298-299.
[128]*PP*, Gravel ed., vol. II, p. 751.
[129]The McNamara-Taylor report to the President is in *ibid.*, pp. 751-766. For comments on the report see *Swords and Plowshares*, pp. 298-299, and *The Best and the Brightest*, pp. 284-285.

On the military side, they recommended an increase in combat operations, but with emphasis on "clear and hold" rather than "terrain sweeps which have little permanent value." Strategic hamlets should be strengthened, and more hamlet militia armed. More Vietnamese should be trained to replace U.S. forces by the end of 1965.

They also recommended announcement of the plan to withdraw 1,000 U.S. troops by the end of 1963: "This action should be explained in low key as an initial step in a long-term program to replace U.S. personnel with trained Vietnamese without impairment of the war effort."

At the conclusion of the second meeting on October 2, Kennedy, as recommended by McNamara and Taylor in their report, issued the following press statement:[130]

1. The security of South Viet-Nam is a major interest of the United States as of other free nations. We will adhere to our policy of working with the people and Government of South Viet-Nam to deny this country to communism and to suppress the externally stimulated and supported insurgency of the Viet Cong as promptly as possible. Effective performance in this undertaking is the central objective of our policy in South Viet-Nam.

2. The military program in South Vietnam has made progress and is sound in principle, though improvements are being energetically sought.

3. Major U.S. assistance in support of this military effort is needed only until the insurgency has been suppressed or until the national security forces of the Government of South Viet-Nam are capable of suppressing it.

Secretary McNamara and General Taylor reported their judgement that the major part of the U.S. military task can be completed by the end of 1965, although there may be a continuing requirement for a limited number of U.S. training personnel. They reported that by the end of this year, the U.S. program for training Vietnamese should have progressed to the point where 1,000 U.S. military personnel assigned to South Viet-Nam can be withdrawn.

4. The political situation in South Viet-Nam remains deeply serious. The United States has made clear its continuing opposition to any repressive actions in South Viet-Nam. While such actions have not yet significantly affected the military effort, they could do so in the future.

5. It remains the policy of the United States, in South Viet-Nam as in other parts of the world, to support the efforts of the people of that country to defeat aggression and to build a peaceful and free society.

---

[130]*Public Papers of the Presidents,* John F. Kennedy, 1963, pp. 759-760. Several changes were made in the wording suggested by McNamara and Taylor. They recommended that the statement read: "The security of South Vietnam remains vital to the United States security." As can be noted, the word "vital" was changed to "major interest." At Taylor's suggestion, (see *Swords and Plowshares,* pp. 296-297), the report also recommended that the press statement contain this sentence: "We believe the U.S. part of the task can be completed by the end of 1965, the terminal date which we are taking as the time objective of our counterinsurgency programs." This, too, was revised, as can be seen.

The wisdom of announcing the withdrawal of 1,000 U.S. troops, (which, it will be recalled, had been the objective of U.S. military planning since July of 1962) had been strenuously debated within the McNamara-Taylor mission, as well as among other top Presidential advisers. William Sullivan argued that it would be a mistake to include the statement:[131]

> . . . we were each drafting a separate chapter of this report and then exchanging the chapters around. When I got Max's [Maxwell Taylor] chapter—we all had offices in the old MACV [U.S. Military Assistance Command, Vietnam] out there—I went to Bob McNamara and I said, "I just can't buy this. This is totally unrealistic. We're not going to get troops out in '65. We mustn't submit anything phony as this to the president." And Bob agreed and he went in and talked to Max, and Max agreed to scrub it. Then on the plane on the way we talked about it a bit. Max said, "Well, goddammit, we've got to make these people put their noses to the wheel—or the grindstone or whatever. If we don't give them some indication that we're going to get out sometime, they're just going to be leaning on us forever. So that's why I had it in there." I said, "Well, I can understand that. But if this becomes a matter of public record, it would be considered a phony and a fraud and an effort to mollify the American public and just not be considered honest."

The decision to announce the withdrawal of 1,000 troops was made by Kennedy in a meeting with Rusk, McNamara and Taylor. Both Bundys questioned whether the announcement should be made, but when pressed by Chester L. Cooper, a member of the NSC staff, and others after the meeting, they said they were "under orders."[132] Sullivan called McNamara to ask ". . . why in hell is it back in public print again," and McNamara's reply, Sullivan said later, was "not all that convincing at the time."[133]

William Bundy has since commented that in retrospect there was a "clear internal inconsistency" in the report, namely, the finding on the one hand that political reforms were unlikely to occur, and the conclusion on the other that withdrawal could begin. He attributes this to the pressures of time and the effects of exhaustion, but says, "The words of the release on the military situation were extraordinarily unwise and extraordinarily haunting for the future."[134]

With respect to the results of the McNamara-Taylor trip, Bundy makes this informative observation:[135]

> In essence, McNamara, with the strong support of civilian members of his team, came to accept the judgment that had already been reached by Lodge, [William] Trueheart [Deputy Chief of Mission], and most (but not all) of the Embassy staff. This was that an unchanged Diem regime stood only a small chance of holding South Vietnam together and carrying the conflict with the Viet Cong and Hanoi to a successful conclu-

[131]Kennedy Library, Second Oral History Interview with William Sullivan.
[132]Chester L. Cooper, *The Lost Crusade* (New York: Dodd, Mead, 1970), p. 216.
[133]Kennedy Library, Second Oral History Interview with William Sullivan.
[134]Bundy MS., ch. 9, p. 26.
[135]*Ibid.*, ch. 9, pp. 19-20.

sion. What Diem and Nhu were doing was not merely repugnant, but seemed calculated to end in chaos.

Hence the McNamara group arrived at a series of concrete recommendations designed to dissociate the U.S. from Diem and to put substantial pressure on him.

After the meetings on October 2, Kennedy's top NSC advisers met without the President on October 3 and 4 to discuss the implementation of the McNamara-Taylor report. In the meeting on October 3, McNamara stated that ". . . we cannot stay in the middle much longer," and that the program proposed in the report "will push us toward a reconciliation with Diem or toward a coup to overthrow Diem."[136] Ball said, ". . . if we go down this road it will become known that we are using our aid as pressure on Diem. What position will we be in if we cut off aid, Diem does not do what we want him to do, and then we face a decision to resume aid because, if we do not, the effort against the Viet Cong will cease?" McNamara replied that he thought Diem would respond "by moving part way toward a position which will improve the political situation in Vietnam and therefore improve the military effort."

The group agreed that David Bell, administrator of the foreign aid program (AID), should tell Congress, which was then considering the 1963 aid bill, "that we are not suspending aid but were putting Diem on a shorter lease, which would mean that we have greater flexibility to deal with the developing situation in Vietnam."

At its meeting on October 4, the NSC group considered a draft of proposed action on the Taylor report prior to presenting the proposal to the President at a meeting the following day (October 5).[137] The draft report stated, "The recommended actions are designed to indicate to the Diem Government our displeasure at its political policies and activities and to create significant uncertainty in that government and in key Vietnamese groups as to the future intentions of the United States. At the same time, the actions are designed to have at most slight impact on the military or counterinsurgency effort against the Viet Cong, at least in the short term." "The test of the adequacy of these actions," the report added, "should be whether, in combination, they improve the effectiveness of the GVN effort to the point where we can carry on in confident expectation that the war effort will progress satisfactorily." There followed a list of specific action recommendations taken from the McNamara-Taylor report. These included the continued suspension of various aid programs, including the critically important commodity import program, as well as suspension of the extremely sensitive and important support for the Vietnamese Special Forces commanded by Colonel Le Quang Tung, and under the direct control of Nhu. These actions would not be announced, and any inquiries concerning them should be answered, the report said, "by the statement that affected programs have been suspended for technical review. . . ."

---

[136]Kennedy Library, NSF Presidential Meetings File, "Meeting in the Situation Room," Oct. 3, 1963.

[137]Kennedy Library, POF Country File, Vietnam Security, 1963. The file copy of the "Report to the Executive Committee," Oct. 4, 1963, does not indicate its source or drafters.

The second part of the report dealt with additional actions that Lodge could take at his discretion as part of his negotiations with Diem. "Lodge's policy toward the GVN and particularly Diem," the report said, "has been one of cool correctness, keeping his distance, in order to make Diem come to him. This policy is correct, and Lodge should continue it. However, it must be realized that it may not work and that at some later time Lodge may have to go to Diem to ensure the latter understands U.S. policy." There were two issues involved: "The first is a crisis of confidence in the American Government and public. The second is a crisis of confidence among the Vietnamese people, which is eroding the popular support for the GVN that is vital to victory. Both of these crises of confidence are caused by the form of government that has been evolving in Viet-Nam. His regime has the trappings of democracy but in reality it has been evolving into an authoritarian government maintained by police terrorist methods. What the GVN must do is to reverse this process of evolution." There followed a listing of the various actions, pursuant to the McNamara-Taylor report, which Lodge could take in seeking to accomplish this result.

On October 5, 1963, the President met with his NSC advisers to consider the action report, as revised by the group on October 4. The meeting was so sensitive and important that it included only Rusk, McNamara, Harriman, Taylor, McCone, Bell, McGeorge Bundy, Forrestal, and Vice President Johnson (who had not participated in previous meetings on the pressure plan).[138] The report was approved as submitted. The President said that there would be no public statement concerning this action, and that in testifying before executive sessions of congressional committees the following week, Rusk and McNamara "should confine themselves to saying that U.S. programs were under continuing review in light of the President's previously announced policy that we supported those things which furthered the war effort and would not support those things which do not."[139] He also said that no formal announcement should be made of implementation of the decision to withdraw 1,000 troops, nor should the matter be raised formally with Diem. "Instead the action should be carried out routinely as part of our general posture of withdrawing people when they are no longer needed."

On October 11, NSAM 263 promulgated the President's decisions.[140]

After the October 5 meeting, McGeorge Bundy sent the following cable to Lodge:[141]

. . . the President asked me to send you this personal message from him.

He thinks it of the greatest importance that, to the very limit of our abilities, we should not open this next stage in the press. The decisions and instructions in following telegram are being held most tightly here, and we are making every possible effort to limit public knowledge and to let the Vietnamese Gov-

[138]See Kennedy Library, NSF Presidential Meetings File, "Report of National Security Council," Oct. 5, 1963.
[139]"Presidential Conference on South Vietnam," Oct. 7, 1963, same location.
[140]PP, Gravel ed., vol. II, pp. 769-770.
[141]Kennedy Library, NSF Country File, Vietnam.

ernment itself learn from what we do and not what the papers say, so that your negotiations with Diem may run on your terms. Nothing could be more dangerous than an impression now that a set of major actions is being kicked off and a set of requirements imposed on GVN by U.S. This is of particular importance since some officals and reporters honorably believe in just such a public posture of disapproval and pressure. President therefore believes you should personally control knowledge of individual actions and tactics, and accept, as we will try to, necessary dissatisfaction of determined reporters with cryptic posture.

In a cable to the AID mission director in Saigon informing him of the new pressure plan, AID Director Bell said that Washington officials ". . . believe it of great importance that there should be no public impression of a package of sanctions and a package of demands. We are seeking necessary but limited improvements from a government very difficult to move, and we do not wish to encourage unjustified sense of optimism or of triumph from those who wish this situation was easier than it is. In particular, we would prefer press to consider us inactive than to trumpet a posture of 'major sanctions' and 'sweeping demands.' " He told the foreign aid mission that it should take this same line in briefing a delegation from the House Foreign Affairs Committee led by Representative Zablocki, which was on its way to Vietnam. He also told the mission not to reveal the contents of his cable to the Zablocki group.[142]

When Kennedy made the decision on October 5, 1963, to reject "reconciliation," and to apply most of the pressures under the category of phase 2 of the pressure track, he was fully aware not only that these actions were calculated to induce a coup, but that they were the precise signals of U.S. support for a coup that the opposition generals had said they needed to have before proceeding. Kennedy doubtless hoped that Diem and Nhu would respond to the pressures, and that a coup could be avoided, but he also knew that there was a very slim chance that this would happen. His advisers had told him that it appeared unlikely that Diem would banish Nhu, and there was little likelihood, therefore, that U.S. demands would be met.

Thus, October 5, 1963, was the day the President of the United States decided to move against President Ngo Dinh Diem, knowing that the result probably would be the overthrow of the Vietnamese President. He did so reluctantly, having in mind, no doubt, that his own support may have been instrumental in helping Diem to gain and hold office. By the same token, he probably felt betrayed by what he considered Diem's failure to continue to provide political leadership, as well as his failure to carry out the promises he had made to the United States.

Meanwhile, coup planning was underway again in Vietnam even before news of the new U.S. commitment to support a coup had been communicated to the Vietnamese generals. On October 2, Lucien Conein met accidently with General Don, who said that he

---

[142]Bell to Brent, Oct. 5, 1963, same location.

had been trying for some time to establish contact. At another meeting later that day, Don told Conein that the generals had a specific plan, and that General Minh wanted to meet with Conein on October 5. Conein did so with Lodge's (and presumably Washington's) approval, even before Lodge had been told about the President's final decision at the October 5 NSC meeting.[143]

At their October 5 meeting, Minh told Conein that the generals needed to know as soon as possible the position of the U.S. Government with respect to a coup. He said he did not need specific American assistance, but he did need assurances that the U.S. would not thwart the plan. He told Conein that there were three ways to accomplish the coup. The first and "easiest" was to assassinate Nhu and his brother Ngo Dinh Can, and to keep Diem in office as a figurehead. The other two involved military action by the Army against Special Forces stationed in Saigon which were loyal to Diem and Nhu. Conein, acting under specific orders, was noncommittal.

After Conein's conversation with Minh, the CIA team in Saigon recommended to Lodge that "we do not set ourselves irrevocably against the assassination plot, since the other two alternatives mean either a blood bath in Saigon or a protracted struggle."[144] This suggestion was rebuffed by CIA Director McCone, who cabled the CIA station in Saigon that it should withdraw the recommendation it had made to Lodge, "as we cannot be in position actively condoning such course of action and thereby engaging our responsibility therefore."[145] But McCone also told the station not to prevent the use of assassination:[146]

> [W]e certainly cannot be in the position of stimulating, approving, or supporting assassination, but on the other hand, we are in no way responsible for stopping every such threat of which we might receive even partial knowledge. We certainly would not favor assassination of Diem. We believe engaging ourselves by taking position on this matter opens door too easily for probes of our position re others, re support of regime, et cetera. Consequently believe best approach is hands off. However, we naturally interested in intelligence on any such plan.

Lodge immediately cabled Washington on October 5 to report Conein's conversation, and to ask for guidance.[147] He recommended that Conein tell Minh that the U.S. would not thwart the coup, and that Conein offer to review coup plans other than removal by assassination.

Meanwhile, before receiving Lodge's cable, Washington had sent Lodge a cable on this subject after the October 5 NSC meeting:[148] ". . . President today approved recommendation that no initiative should now be taken to give any covert encouragement to a coup. There should, however, be urgent covert effort with closest security

---

[143]"[first word or two deleted] Contacts with Vietnamese Generals, 23 August through 23 October 1963," cited above.
[144]Senate Report on Assassination Plots, p. 220.
[145]*Ibid.*, p. 221.
[146]*Ibid.*
[147]*PP*, Gravel ed., vol. II, pp. 767-768.
[148]*Ibid.*, p. 766.

under broad guidance of Ambassador to identify and build contacts with possible alternative leadership as and when it appears. Essential that this effort be totally secure and fully deniable. . . ."

On October 6, Washington replied to Lodge's cable of October 5:[149]

> While we do not wish to stimulate coup, we also do not wish to leave impression that U.S. would thwart a change of government or deny economic and military assistance to a new regime if it appeared capable of increasing effectiveness of military effort, ensuring popular support to win war and improving working relations with U.S. We would like to be informed on what is being contemplated but we should avoid being drawn into reviewing or advising on operational plans or any other act which might tend to identify U.S. too closely with change in government. We would, however, welcome information which would help us assess character of any alternative leadership.

On October 10, Conein accordingly assured Minh that the U.S. would not thwart the coup, would continue giving aid to Vietnam after the coup, and would be interested in further information on the plan. For the next three weeks, as plans for the coup progressed, the U.S. Government was kept fully informed through Conein's contact with the generals. There were literally hundreds of cables back and forth from Saigon to Washington on these developments, but this subject is so sensitive that almost all of these are still highly classified, and may remain classified indefinitely.

Congress Acquiesces in the Pressures on Diem

During October, as the pressures were being applied to Diem, Congress continued to approve of or acquiesce in the administration's handling of the situation. In part this can be attributed to a lack of information. Although a few Members may have been told privately what was happening, most Members were not informed. Testimony even in closed sessions of committees followed the President's instructions that Congress should be told only that the U.S. was supporting those things that would help the war, and was not supporting those things that would not.

One exception to this general pattern of approval or acquiescence was the position taken by freshman Senator George McGovern (D/S. Dak.), who on September 26, 1963, argued that the U.S. should withdraw both its forces and its aid from Vietnam. He, too, was highly critical of Diem.[150]

Morse also continued to criticize Diem and the role of the U.S. in keeping him in power, and to assert that ". . . South Vietnam is not worth the life of a single American boy."[151]

It is important to recognize that another reason for Congress' acquiescence, which may also help to account for the noticeable sparseness of congressional comment on Vietnam during the summer and fall of 1963, as well as after the coup, may have been that key Members of Congress, especially on the Foreign Relations

[149] *Ibid.*, p. 769.
[150] *CR*, vol. 109, p. 18205.
[151] *Ibid.*, pp. 15744-15745, 16488.

Committee, were either co-opted by the administration, or were privy to sensitive information that they refrained from discussing or acting upon. For example, in conjunction with executive sessions of the Foreign Relations Committee in early October at which U.S. activities and policy in Vietnam were discussed, President Kennedy held at least two private meetings with key members of the committee—Fulbright, Mansfield, Hickenlooper and Aiken on October 8, and Fulbright, Church, and Symington on October 10. There is apparently no record of these talks, but the composition of the group, especially for the October 10 meeting, suggests that Vietnam may have been discussed, in addition to discussion of the foreign aid bill itself. (The administration was concerned about House cuts in aid funds, which it was seeking to reverse in the Senate.)

There were probably other discussions during this pre-coup period between Rusk and McNamara and the leaders of the committees to which they reported.

The closest thing to a real examination of current U.S. plans and goals in Vietnam by Congress came in executive sessions of the Senate Foreign Relations Committee on October 8, 9, and 10.[152] On October 8, McNamara and Taylor reported to the committee on their trip.[153] Taylor said that the war was "going well," and that victory—which he defined as the point where the insurgency in South Vietnam was under such control that it could be handled by the "normal security forces"—could be attained by the end of 1965. Although Diem was unpopular, he said, this was not seriously affecting the war effort.

Senator Church asked about U.S. "leverage" on Diem, adding ". . . it seems to me that we are in a position to go further withholding certain kinds of aid, or taking action that can help to force changes in Government policy." "Yes," McNamara said, "it is within our capacity to exert pressures, but it's not within our capacity to assure action in accordance with our recommendations. This is an independent government and I think it is quite inappropriate for us to think of it as a colony or to expect it to act as a colony." The U.S., he said, was withholding support from Colonel Tung's special forces, and was reviewing other aid commitments in an effort to support those activities that furthered the war effort. Consistent with the President's orders, however, he did not comment further on the specific actions being undertaken, and at no point did he or Taylor indicate that the President had approved a general plan of action to bring pressure on Diem.

Taylor observed that no one had suggested an alternative to Diem. Moreover, he said, "We need a strong man running this country [South Vietnam], we need a dictator in time of war and we have got one." Referring to the U.S. Civil War, where "we also had dictatorial government," he added, "This country is in the heart of a civil war and I think to try to apply what we might call normal democratic standards to this government simply is not realistic."

[152]McNamara and Taylor also testified in an executive session of the House Foreign Affairs Committee on Oct. 8, 1963.
[153]U.S. Congress, Senate, Committee on Foreign Relations, unpublished executive session transcript, Oct. 8, 1963.

On October 9 the Foreign Relations Committee met again in executive session with Rusk as the witness.[154] The subject was the foreign aid bill, then in its final stages. Church again raised the question of using U.S. aid as leverage. Rusk replied that this was being done, and mentioned specifically the suspension of payment to Colonel Tung's Special Forces. He, too, did not reveal to the committee any additional details on the pressure plan, however, or even the existence of such a general plan of action.

On October 10, there was an executive session of the Senate Foreign Relations Committee with McCone and other CIA officials to discuss the role of the CIA in Vietnam.[155] This, as well as a discussion in the October 8 and 9 hearings, was touched off, at least in part, by a newspaper article asserting that "The story of the Central Intelligence Agency's role in South Viet Nam is a dismal chronicle of bureaucratic arrogance, obstinate disregard of orders, and unrestrained thirst for power."[156] A more proximate cause for the hearing with McCone, however, was the recall to Washington on October 5 of CIA Station Chief Richardson. One explanation was that he was being recalled because of "His identity having been compromised in recent press stories about internal policy struggles in the U.S. mission. . . ."[157] Another explanation, which is nearer the truth, is that he was close to Nhu and Diem, and was sent home by Lodge because he was not in favor of the pressure plan and the anticipated coup. The real explanation for Richardson's recall, however, was that it was undertaken as part of the plan to bring additional pressure to bear on Nhu and Diem by removing one of their allies and supporters from the U.S. mission.[158]

In the October 10 hearing, Senator Humphrey asked why Richardson had been recalled. McCone replied that this was done primarily to give the U.S. "more freedom for carrying forward on our current policy. . . ."

Humphrey also asked what would happen if Diem were overthrown. Both McCone and William Colby replied that there was no alternative in sight, and that there would be a political vacuum if Diem were removed.

The question of a coup against Diem was discussed. McCone said, ". . . we could only advise that we would have to move very slowly into this," in part because of the lack of an alternative.

There is no indication that any Member of Congress, save one, Representative Zablocki, indicated personally to the President or his advisers a serious concern about the possible effects of a coup, or about U.S. support for a coup. On the contrary, many leading Members of Congress, especially on the Senate Foreign Relations Committee, strongly supported the use of U.S. sanctions against Diem, and agreed with the position of the executive branch that Diem should be replaced if he did not make the reforms which the U.S. considered essential.

---

[154]*Ibid.*, Oct. 9, 1963.
[155]*Ibid.*, Oct. 10, 1963.
[156]This article, by Richard Starnes, appeared in the Scripps-Howard newspapers, including the *Washington Daily News*, on Oct. 1, 1963.
[157]*PP*, Gravel ed., vol. II, p. 217.
[158]See Hilsman, *To Move A Nation*, p. 515.

Following the trip he and seven other members of the House Foreign Affairs Committee made to Vietnam beginning October 6, Zablocki issued a report which concluded that U.S. assistance to Vietnam was essential, that the war was being won, and that the U.S. should be very cautious in supporting any change in the Vietnamese Government.[159] "Some have recommended as a solution," the group said, "the ouster of the Diem family. Those who advocate such a course offer no specific alternatives. The lesson of Cuba must not be forgotten—Batista was bad but Castro is worse." The Zablocki group summed up its general position as follows:

What kind of a victory do we seek in Vietnam? A decisive military victory is not to be expected in a guerrilla operation. Nor should we expect a resounding victory for democracy as we understand it. Our sights ought to be set at more modest goals for both—a high degree of internal security and a reasonably responsible and responsive government. The problem in Vietnam today is that the military effort of the Vietnamese and ourselves is not matched by a comparable political effort which must, of necessity, be that of the Government of Vietnam. There is no reason to expect quickly in Vietnam or in any other newly established state the full range of democratic processes we know. At best we can hope only for small increments of popular participation as the level of education rises and the people identify themselves more closely with the Government.

The war in Vietnam is far from its conclusion. We can be pleased with the progress made thus far, but all indications are that the conflict will be a long one. The United States presence will be required in Vietnam until there is a successful resolution of the military conflict.

When the Zablocki group returned to Washington, Zablocki met with Kennedy to report his finding. According to Zablocki, Kennedy said, "I hope you'll write an objective report and not put President Diem in a favorable light." Zablocki said he replied, "Mr. President, we intend to write that report as we've seen it, as we believe the situation to be, and I don't think we should be basing our policy on columnists who write their stories in the Caravelle bar after a few martinis." As he was leaving the White House, Zablocki said that the President's Press Secretary, Pierre Salinger, told him, "Well, you know what the boss wants." Zablocki said he replied, "The boss will get what we think is right. . . . Somebody's giving the boss some bad information."[160]

On October 22, 1963, the Senate Foreign Relations Committee reported as a part of the foreign aid bill the following substitute for the Church amendment:

It is the sense of the Congress that assistance authorized by this act should be extended to or withheld from the Government of South Vietnam, in the discretion of the President, to further the objectives of victory in the war against communism and the return to their homeland of Americans involved in that struggle.

---

[159]H. Rept. 88-893.
[160]CRS Interview with Clement J. Zablocki, Jan. 29, 1979.

This was subsequently approved by the Senate and the House after Diem's assassination, and became law.[161] In its report the Foreign Relations Committee said:[162]

> This new paragraph reflects the committee's conviction that stabilization of the political situation in Vietnam is of the utmost importance for winning the war against the Communist guerrillas. The committee takes note of the fact that there is still pending before it Senate Resolution 196 [the Church resolution] calling for discontinuance of aid to South Vietnam unless the Vietnamese Government puts needed reforms into effect. If the political situation in South Vietnam deteriorates further to the detriment of the war effort, the committee will be disposed to give further consideration to the more drastic steps called for by Senate Resolution 196.

Dénouement

Toward the end of October 1963, the U.S. was informed that the coup against Diem would occur before November 2. Coup leaders were reluctant to provide Conein with detailed plans, however, because they were concerned that U.S. military officials who continued to oppose a coup might reveal the plans to Diem or Nhu. Conein was told that he would be given the plans two days in advance.

In Washington, the White House was becoming very concerned about the situation. The President and his advisers were fearful that the coup would not be successful, as well as being worried that the U.S. would be held responsible if it did succeed. On October 24, the White House cabled Lodge expressing concern about the lack of "firm intelligence" on coup plans, as well as about the possible publicity that could arise from the role of Conein. Lodge replied on October 25 that he shared Kennedy's concern about the possible publicity arising from Conein's role, and was considering using two other persons as "cut-outs" (go-betweens) for communication between Conein and the generals. As for White House jitters about the coup, Lodge said that it was important for the U.S. to support the coup. To attempt to thwart it, he said, would be a mistake:[163]

> First, it seems at least an even bet that the next government would not bungle and stumble as much as the present one has. Secondly, it is extremely unwise in the long range for us to pour cold water on attempts at a coup, particularly when they are just in their beginning stages. We should remember that this is the only way in which the people in Vietnam can possibly get a change in government. Whenever we thwart attempts at a coup, as we have done in the past, we are incurring very long lasting resentments, we are assuming an undue responsibility for keeping incumbents in office, and in general are setting ourselves in judgment over the affairs of Vietnam.

The White House replied immediately:[164] "We are particularly concerned about hazard that an unsuccessful coup, however care-

---

[161]Public Law 88-205, Dec. 16, 1963.
[162]S. Rept. 88-588.
[163]PP, Gravel ed., vol. II, pp. 780-781. The White House cable is still classified.
[164]Ibid., p. 782.

fully we avoid direct engagement, will be laid at our door by public opinion almost everywhere. Therefore, while sharing your view that we should not be in position of thwarting coup, we would like to have option of judging and warning on any plan with poor prospects of success."

On Saturday, October 27, according to U. Alexis Johnson, then Deputy Under Secretary of State, the U.S. gave final approval to the coup, and a "green light" cable was sent to Lodge after approval by Ball. This is Johnson's account:[165]

> On Saturday, October 27, when I was playing golf with Undersecretary Ball at the Falls Road public course, Averell Harriman and Roger Hilsman interrupted our game, and they gave him a telegram to sign. George was Acting Secretary in Rusk's absence from Washington. I found it somewhat curious that they did not show it to me, but there was no special reason I had to see it, so I kept out of their discussion. Ball signed the telegram, the two departed, and we continued our game. It turned out that this was the "green light" telegram authorizing Ambassador Lodge to signal that we would not oppose a coup against Diem. Looking back on it, I am relatively sure that Ball, Hilsman, and Harriman knew that I would oppose it and excluded me from their discussion on purpose.

On October 29, Lodge cabled Kennedy a summary of developments, including the latest conversations of Conein with General Don, which concluded as follows:[166]

> In summary, it would appear that a coup attempt by the Generals' group is imminent; that whether this coup fails or succeeds, the USG must be prepared to accept the fact that we will be blamed, however unjustifiably; and finally, that no positive action by the USG can prevent a coup attempt short of informing Diem and Nhu with all the opprobrium that such an action would entail.

The NSC met twice that day (October 29) to review the Vietnam situation.[167] The summaries of these meetings are still classified. According to Arthur Schlesinger, (who has had exclusive access to Robert Kennedy's papers containing a summary of at least the first meeting on October 29), "Robert Kennedy thought the situation no different from August, when the generals talked big and did nothing. 'To support a coup,' he told the group, 'would be putting the future of Vietnam and in fact all of southeast Asia in the hands of one man not now known to us. A failure of a coup risks too much. The reports we have are very thin.' The President observed that,

---

[165] Johnson, *The Right Hand of Power*, p. 412. The Kennedy Library reports that no copy of such a cable on October 27 can be found in the library's records. Judging by the "withdrawal sheets" indicating which classified items have been removed from the files, it would also appear that there is no copy of the cable in the library's records in materials covering the day or two following that date. (Many important government cables, even some highly important ones, are not in Presidential libraries, however.) Queried about Johnson's reference to a "green light" cable on October 27, Ball and Hilsman contend that Johnson's account is misdated, and that the event as he described it occurred on Saturday, August 24. See Ball's account of the August 24 cable in *The Past Has Another Pattern*, pp. 371-372. Johnson, however, maintains that his account is correct.

[166] *PP*, Gravel ed., vol. II, p. 260. Lodge also cabled a report (Saigon to Washington 805, Oct. 29, 1963) on his day-long talk with Diem on Oct. 27. This is in the Kennedy Library, NSF Country File, Vietnam.

[167] For an outline of subjects to be discussed at the first meeting see Kennedy Library, NSF Country File, Vietnam, "Check List for 4 PM meeting."

since the pro-Diem and anti-Diem forces appeared about equal, any attempt to engineer a coup would be silly."[168]

Hilsman's account of Robert Kennedy's position in the October 29 meeting (he does not mention the President's position), makes it clear, however, that the Attorney General was not taking the position that the U.S. should back away from supporting a coup. According to Hilsman, Robert Kennedy concluded, "It was difficult to see where the United States' interest lay. It was important that the decisions in such matters be Vietnamese . . . but the United States would get the blame no matter what happened. It might be wise to try to find more about what was going on."[169]

Colby, who was also present at the October 29 White House meetings, says that in the meetings, ". . . the by-then much-hashed-over debate was repeated between the State Department view that the Diem regime had to go because it could not prosecute the war, and the Pentagon's (and McCone's and my) view that Diem was better than anyone on the horizon and that the real American interest was to avoid adversely affecting the war in the countryside by upsetting the political structure in Saigon. The President vacillated in the face of the intensity of argument among his closest advisers, and the only decision reached that day was the usual easy one to seek more information about what was really going on in Vietnam by sending out more cables."[170]

After the October 29 meetings, McGeorge Bundy sent Lodge a cable asking for additional information, and reemphasizing the importance of a quick, successful coup:[171] "We reiterate burden of proof must be on coup group to show a substantial possibility of quick success; otherwise, we should discourage them from proceeding since a miscalculation could result in jeopardizing U.S. position in Southeast Asia." Lodge was also told to share all of the cables on the coup with Harkins, partly because of Washington's concern about the exclusion of Harkins from the planning process. In addition, as a part of the plan, Lodge had been scheduled to return to Washington for consultation at the end of October, and in his absence Harkins' role would be even more important.

Harkins' reaction after he read the cables between Lodge and the White House was that he and Lodge had a different understanding of the guidance from Washington with respect to the U.S. role in a coup. In a cable to Taylor on October 30, Harkins said that, unlike Lodge, he assumed that the U.S. was not going to give any covert encouragement to a coup.[172] He added that he was not opposed to a "change in government," but he thought it should be in "methods of governing rather than a complete change of personnel."

---

[168]*Robert Kennedy and His Times*, p. 721. CRS requested mandatory review of the classification of the notes which were kept on the first of these meetings, and was informed by the Kennedy Library on Apr. 13, 1983, that the State Department and the NSC will not agree at this time to declassify the material, citing Executive Order 123561, Sec. 1.3 (a) (5)—"foreign relations or foreign activities"—and Sec. 1.3 (b) ". . . disclosure, either by itself or in the context of other information, reasonably could be expected to cause damage to the national security."

[169]*To Move A Nation*, p. 519.

[170]*Honorable Men*, p. 216.

[171]*PP*, Gravel ed., vol. II, p. 783.

[172]*Ibid.*, pp. 784-785.

"In my contacts here," Harkins said, "I have seen no one with the strength of character of Diem, at least in fighting communists. Clearly there are no Generals qualified to take over in my opinion."

Harkins said he did not agree with Lodge that the war was not being won. On the contrary, "Nothing has happened," he told Taylor, "in October to change the assessment you and Secretary McNamara made after your visit here."

Harkins concluded:

I would suggest we not try to change horses too quickly. That we continue to take persuasive actions that will make the horses change their course and methods of action. That we win the military effort as quickly as possible, then let them make any and all of the changes they want.

After all, rightly or wrongly, we have backed Diem for eight long hard years. To me it seems incongruous now to get him down, kick him around, and get rid of him. The U.S. has been his mother superior and father confessor since he's been in office and he had leaned on us heavily.

Leaders of other under-developed countries will take a dim view of our assistance if they too were led to believe the same fate lies in store for them.

That same day (October 30), Lodge replied to Bundy's cable of that date. He agreed that it was important to "get best possible estimate of chance of coup's success and this estimate must color our thinking," but he added that he did not think "we have the power to delay or discourage a coup." He added:

Heartily agree that a miscalculation could jeopardize position in Southeast Asia. We also run tremendous risks by doing nothing.

If we were convinced that the coup was going to fail, we would, of course, do everything we could to stop it.

"My general view," Lodge said, "is that the U.S. is trying to bring this medieval country into the 20th Century and that we have made considerable progress in military and economic ways but to gain victory we must also bring them into the 20th Century politically and that can only be done by either a thoroughgoing change in the behavior of the present government or by another government."

Lodge said he anticipated that after the coup there might be a need either to grant asylum in the U.S. Embassy to "key personalities" or to transport them out of Vietnam. "I believe," he said, "that there would be immediate political problems in attempting to take these personalities to another neighboring country and probably we would be best served in depositing them in Saipan where the absence of press, communication, etc., would allow us some leeway to make a further decision as to their ultimate disposition."

Lodge did not ask Washington for air transportation for this purpose. He did not need to. The Air Force had already sent a plane to Saigon for his use in returning to Washington, and commercial airlines also had planes available.

Lodge did ask Washington for money for the generals, who, he said, "may well have need of funds at the last moment with which to buy off potential opposition." (After the coup, Conein, who had received the money on October 24, gave $42,000 to the generals to pay troops that had participated and death benefits for those killed.)[173]

Lodge's cable ended with this statement: "Gen. Harkins has read this and does not concur."

Harkins then called Taylor. He said he had not concurred because he thought the U.S. needed more information, adding, "I feel we should go along with only a sure thing. This or continue with Diem until we have exhausted all pressures. The prestige of the U.S. is really involved one way or the other and it must be upheld at all costs."[174]

After receiving this cable from Lodge, the White House replied immediately (October 30).[175] In this, which may have been the final White House cable to Lodge before the coup on November 1, Bundy, speaking for Kennedy, told Lodge:

> We do not accept as a basis for U.S. policy that we have no power to delay or discourage a coup. . . . You say that if you were convinced that the coup was going to fail you would of course do everything you could to stop it. We believe that on this same basis you should take action to persuade coup leaders to stop or delay any operation which, in your best judgment, does not clearly give high prospect of success. . . . Therefore, if you should conclude that there is not clearly a high prospect of success, you should communicate this doubt to generals in a way calculated to persuade them to desist at least until chances are better.

Kennedy then gave Lodge these instructions:

> a. U.S. authorities will reject appeals for direct intervention from either side, and U.S.-controlled aircraft and other resources will not be committed between the battle lines or in support of either side, without authorization from Washington.
>
> b. In event of indecisive contest, U.S. authorities agree to perform any acts agreeable to both sides, such as removal of key personalities or relay of information. In such actions, however, U.S. authorities will strenuously avoid appearance of pressure on either side. It is not in the interest of USG to be or appear to be either instrument of existing government or instrument of coup.
>
> c. In the event of imminent or actual failure of coup, U.S. authorities may afford asylum in their discretion to those to whom there is any express or implied obligation of this sort. We believe however that in such a case it would be in our interest and probably in interest of those seeking asylum that they seek protection of other Embassies in addition to our own. This point should be made strongly if need arises.
>
> d. But once a coup under responsible leadership has begun, and within these restrictions, it is in the interest of the U.S. Government that it should succeed.

[173] Senate Report on Assasination Plots, p. 222.
[174] Kennedy Library, NSF Country File, Vietnam, MAC 2034, Oct. 30, 1963.
[175] PP, Gravel ed., vol. II, pp. 792-793.

The Coup

On November 1, at approximately 1:30 p.m. (Saigon time), the coup began, and U.S. officials in Saigon and Washington made every effort to carry out the President's directive that it should succeed. Conein joined the generals at their headquarters and kept Lodge informed by a direct telephone line. Lodge kept Washington fully informed.

At approximately 4 p.m., Diem called Lodge to ask about the attitude of the U.S. Government toward the coup. According to a CIA summary, "Lodge took refuge in the confusion of the situation and expressed concern for Diem's physical safety. Lodge told Diem that he had heard that the coup leaders had offered Diem and Nhu safe conduct out of the country and he asked Diem about this. Diem's only comment was that he was the Chief of State, that he had tried to do his duty, and that he was trying to reestablish law and order."[176]

This statement in the CIA summary is not entirely correct. According to the State Department's verbatim transcript of the conversation, Diem said he had not heard of the offer of safe conduct, and told Lodge, "You have my telephone number." Lodge's reply was, "Yes. If I can do anything for your physical safety, please call me."[177]

According to Conein, when he called the U.S. Embassy on the morning of November 2 to procure an airplane in which to take Diem and Nhu out of Vietnam, the answer was that there were none available:[178]

> . . . on October 30, 1963, Ambassador Lodge notified Washington that there might be a request by key leaders for evacuation and suggested Saigon as a point for evacuation. (Cable, Saigon to Washington, 10/30/63.) Conein was charged with obtaining the airplane. Between 6:00 and 7:00 on the morning of November 2, [General] Minh and [General] Don asked Conein to procure an aircraft. Conein relayed the request to a Station Officer at the Embassy who replied that it would not be possible to get an aircraft for the next twenty-four hours, since it would have to be flown from Guam. Conein testified that a Station representative told him that Diem could be flown only to a country that offered him asylum and that the plane could not land in any other country. There were no aircraft immediately available that had sufficient range to reach a potential country of asylum. (Conein, 6/20/75, p. 54.)[179]

Conein has also stated, "I asked the Embassy for an aircraft and I was told I had to wait 24 hours before I could get the aircraft that was necessary to transport Diem to a nation who would accept his exile, I spoke for the United States government and I was author-

[176] Kennedy Library, POF Country File, Vietnam Security, 1963, Central Intelligence Agency, OCI No. 3238/63, "Progress of the Coup d'Etat in Saigon (As of 0800 EST)."

[177] Kennedy Library, NSF Country File, Vietnam, Saigon to Washington 860, Nov. 1, 1963. See also *PP*, Gravel ed., vol. II, p. 268.

[178] Senate Report on Assassination Plots, p. 223, fn. 2.

[179] This citation to Conein is a reference to his testimony before an executive session of the Senate Select Committee to Study Governmental Operations with Respect to Intelligence Activities in connection with the committee's study of possible CIA involvement in assassination plots. All testimony on the subject of assassinations was in executive session, and remains unpublished and closed to public access.

ized and I informed the junta that I had an aircraft, but it would take me 24 hours to have that aircraft."[180]

As a staff study for the Senate Foreign Relations Committee put it, "One wonders what became of the U.S. military aircraft that had been dispatched to stand by for Lodge's departure, scheduled for the previous day."[181]

Later that day (November 2), Diem and Nhu escaped to a residence in the suburb of Cholon. The next morning, Diem called the generals and offered to surrender in return for safe conduct out of Vietnam. It is not clear from available evidence whether this offer was accepted. The whereabouts of the brothers was soon discovered, and they took sanctuary in a nearby Catholic church. Shortly afterwards they were taken captive, and on the way to the generals' headquarters they were assassinated.[182]

The NSC was meeting on November 2 when word of the assassinations was received. Taylor said that the President "leaped to his feet and rushed from the room with a look of shock and dismay on his face which I had never seen before." According to Taylor, Kennedy ". . . had always insisted that Diem must never suffer more than exile and had been led to believe or had persuaded himself that a change in government could be carried out without bloodshed."[183]

Some CIA officials were surprised to hear of Kennedy's reaction:[184]

> The following day, at McCone's regular morning meeting with the CIA's Deputy Director and the top officials, McCone described Kennedy's reaction to the news of Diem's murder. According to Lyman Kirkpatrick, who was present at the meeting, the reaction of those in the room was not entirely sympathetic. The coup was Kennedy's idea; his administration authorized it despite repeated CIA objections. What did he expect? When a coup takes place you can't control it. Helms, too, wondered at Kennedy's dismay, and concluded later that the President had not fully understood what he had ordered. He'd okayed the August cable which first put the U.S. Embassy on the side of the dissident generals, and when a coup appeared imminent at the end of October he authorized

---

[180]Quoted in U.S. Congress, Senate, Committee on Foreign Relations, *U.S. Involvement in the Overthrow of Diem, 1963,* Staff Study, 92d Cong., 2d sess. (Washington, D.C.: U.S. Govt. Print. Off., 1972), p. 23.

[181]*Ibid.,* p. 23, fn. 80. According to the study by *U.S. News and World Report,* cited above, ". . . the desire to conceal the U.S. role in the coup does not explain why, 17 hours after the coup began, there still had been no attempt to bring in a plane to fly Diem and Nhu out of the country."

[182]For additional details on these events see especially the excellent Foreign Relations Committee staff study by Ann L. Hollick, *U.S. Involvement in the Overthrow of Diem,* cited above. See also the Pentagon Papers; Shaplen, *The Lost Revolution;* Halberstam, *The Making of a Quagmire;* and Mecklin, *Mission in Torment.* In addition see L. Fletcher Prouty, "The Anatomy of Assassination," in Howard Frazier (ed.), *Uncloaking the CIA* (New York: Free Press, 1975), pp. 196-209. Prouty, for nine years the officer responsible for military liaison with the clandestine operations of the CIA, who was on the staff of the JCS at the time of the Diem coup, says (p. 205), "The actual killing was a simple thing, 'for the good of the cause.' The USA and CIA could wash their hands of it. They had had nothing to do with it. Like all assassinations, it had just happened. Nobody in Washington had said, 'Shoot Diem.' You don't do an assassination that way. The way people are assassinated is by taking away the power that has been created to keep them there. The deadly passive role of the CIA had permitted the termination of another ruler."

[183]*Swords and Plowshares,* p. 301.

[184]Powers, *The Man Who Kept the Secrets,* p. 165.

McGeorge Bundy to tell Lodge to use his own judgment—a roundabout way of saying, It's okay with me. But Kennedy's dismay at the result convinced Helms that Kennedy had never quite hoisted this operation aboard: he'd said yes, without fully realizing what he was saying yes to.

After the coup, a military junta (Military Revolutionary Council) of 12 generals, headed by General Duong Van "Big" Minh, assumed power. Vice President Tho became the civilian premier with an all-civilian Cabinet. The legislature was abolished, but a Council of Notables was appointed as an advisory body. Among the various actions taken by the new government was the release of political prisoners, including Dr. Phan Quang Dan, one of Diem's leading opponents, who had been imprisoned since 1960.

Diem's brother, Ngo Dinh Can, was later executed by the new government. His brother, Archbishop Thuc, was in Rome, and remained in Europe. His other brother, Ngo Dinh Luyen, then South Vietnam's Ambassador to London, also remained abroad. Madame Nhu was still abroad, but three of her four children were in Vietnam. She called journalist Marguerite Higgins, who called Hilsman to ask whether the U.S. Government could assist in getting the children out. Higgins told Hilsman, "Congratulations, Roger. How does it feel to have blood on your hands?" He replied, "Oh, come on now, Maggie. Revolutions are tough. People get hurt."[185] Hilsman said, however, that the U.S. would assist with the children. This was done, and they left Vietnam in a U.S. aircraft several days later.

Higgins' own reaction was that the U.S. ". . . allowed itself to forget that it was in Vietnam as an ally, not as a conqueror. In the fall of 1963 Washington went into the business of hiring and firing governments. We not only forgot the one overriding priority, the war effort, but also for the first time in history, conspired in the ouster of an ally in the middle of a common war against the Communist enemy, thus plunging the country and the war effort into a steep spiral of decline."[186]

Officials in Washington reacted as might have been expected, given their attitudes and their roles. Taylor, Colby, Richardson and others from the military and the CIA, as well as U. Alexis Johnson, Nolting and some other Foreign Service officers, took the position that the overthrow of Diem was a great mistake, perhaps even a fatal mistake, in terms of U.S. involvement. In his memoirs, Taylor said:[187]

[185]Marguerite Higgins, *Our Vietnam Nightmare,* (New York: Harper and Row, 1965), p. 225.
[186]*Ibid.,* p. 288.
[187]*Swords and Plowshares,* p. 302. A study prepared for the Strategic Studies Institute of the U.S. Army War College (BDM Corp.), *The Strategic Lessons Learned in Vietnam* [McLean Va.: 1980] (concluded in part) (vol. II, p. Ex-4):
"The overthrow of the Diem regime was one of the very few key watersheds of the Second Indochina War; although Diem might have lost the war eventually, his assassination resulted in:
"—political, military and economic chaos for almost three years
"—an irreversible loss of GVN legitimacy and popularity, particularly among the rural peoples
"—massive, prolonged and eventually self-defeating U.S. military intervention
"—erosion of the U.S. moral basis for the war, and conversely a deeper commitment to support the successive governments regardless of their worth. . . .'"

Diem's overthrow set in motion a sequence of crises, political and military, over the next two years which eventually forced President Johnson in 1965 to choose between accepting defeat or introducing American combat forces. The encouragement afforded the enemy of Diem's downfall found expression in a massive offensive, political and military, to exploit the removal of their mortal enemy. Taking into account all these effects, I would assess this whole episode as one of the great tragedies of the Vietnamese conflict and an important cause of the costly prolongation of the war into the next decade.

In his memoirs, Colby called the "American-sponsored overthrow of Diem," the "worst mistake of the Vietnam war. . . ."[188]

Lansdale had this reaction:[189]

> . . . I thought it was a terrible, stupid thing. First of all, Diem was a friend of mine, so it came as a personal shock when he was killed. Secondly, the action itself didn't make military sense to me. We divided our forces in the face of the enemy—a military "no-no." South Vietnam was up against a very aggressive, smart, and imaginative enemy who was fighting the war from a political basis. And on our side, we paid too little attention to the political basis which we needed to wage a war. By killing Diem we split our political side at least in two if not more parts, and doing that in the face of the enemy who would take advantage of it right away. I felt we were too weak to play around that way, and I thought it was the worst thing that we ever did. I still can't understand anybody's thinking on that. And the enemy did take advantage of it right away. I'm sure that someplace along the line we'll find all of the ways that they did. They became much stronger, and started going on towards winning the war from that moment. I think we should never have done it. We destroyed the Vietnamese Constitution, not we, but the people we were working with, threw it in the waste basket. The governmental structure was destroyed—the province chiefs and the district chiefs and so forth, the whole structure went down. And from then on, as they kept on having more and more coups and new generals would take over, they'd destroy the whole structure of government again, all of the province chiefs and so forth. There were always people who didn't quite know their jobs throughout the country, and we were thinking all of the time that they were all solid and held together, but they weren't people to do that. And we didn't realize it. Even today I don't think any of the historians have ever figured out that it happened that way, but we destroyed the whole government side of the social structure in one fell-blow.

Among those who had advocated the coup, the reaction was that it was necessary and that it had been successful. They argued that the mistake would have been to continue to depend on the Diem government. Lodge himself cabled Kennedy on November 6 that as a result of the coup "prospects for victory are much improved." ". . . this may be a useful lesson in the use of U.S. power," he

---

[188]*Honorable Men*, p. 203.
[189]CRS Interview with Edward Lansdale, Nov. 19, 1982.

added. "Perhaps the USG has here evolved a way of not being everywhere saddled with responsibility for autocratic governments simply because they are anti-Communist."[190]

On that same day, President Kennedy replied:[191]

Now that there is a new Government which we are about to recognize, we must all intensify our efforts to help it deal with its many hard problems. As you say, while this was a Vietnamese effort, our own actions made it clear that we wanted improvements, and when these were not forthcoming from the Diem Government, we necessarily faced and accepted the possibility that our position might encourage a change of government. We thus have a responsibility to help this new government to be effective in every way that we can, and in these first weeks we may have more influence and more chance to be helpful than at any time in recent years.

I am particularly concerned myself that our primary emphasis should be on effectiveness rather than upon external appearances. If the new Government can limit confusion and intrigue among its members, and concentrate its energies upon the real problems of winning the contest against the Communists and holding the confidence of its own people, it will have met and passed a severe test. This is what we must help in, just as it was ineffectiveness, loss of popular confidence, and the prospect of defeat that were decisive in shaping our relations to the Diem regime.

Lodge was also known to believe, as were others in the U.S. Government, that the coup averted an accommodation, led by Nhu, with North Vietnam, as the South Vietnamese generals themselves had feared when they began plotting. In an executive session of the Senate Foreign Relations Committee on June 30, 1964, Lodge declared: "Last fall, if the Diem Government hadn't come to an end and had gone on for another month, I think we might have had a Communist takeover. I think it had become that important."

George Ball has defended the decision, while criticizing the involvement of the United States in Vietnam:[192]

I think it would have been disastrous to have left Diem there with the Nhus using him as though he were a puppet. They were bringing disgrace on the United States. They were creating a situation which was quite intolerable, which I think had it continued would have led to a very great continued disorder in Saigon. I don't at all accept the thesis that this was a disaster which changed the course of the war. I think it was the kind of situation which illustrated the fact that we should never have been deeply engaged with these people under any circumstances.

---

[190]This cable, which is still classified, is quoted by Schlesinger, who had access to it in the Robert Kennedy papers. *Robert Kennedy and His Times*, pp. 721-722. In the same cable Lodge added that while the coup was a Vietnamese affair, "which we could neither manage nor stop after it got started and which we could only have influenced with great difficulty . . . it is equally certain that the ground in which the coup seed grew into a robust plant was prepared by us and that the coup would not have happened [as] it did without our preparation. . . ."

[191]Kennedy Library, NSF Country File, Vietnam, Washington to Saigon 746, Nov. 6, 1963.

[192]Charlton and Moncrieff, *Many Reasons Why*, p. 94. See also *The Past Has Another Pattern*, pp. 373-374.

William Bundy, who said he believed at the time that the change of government would be an improvement,[193] feels that the decision of the U.S. to pressure Diem and to precipitate a coup in Vietnam "came to rank almost along side those of 1961, barely below those of 1954-55 in importance and those of 1964-65 in both gravity and importance."[194] He defends these actions, however, ". . . because the chances of South Vietnam being preserved were rightly judged to be less under Diem even than under a disorganized succession." He also finds the decisions morally and ethically acceptable: ". . . it does seem to me clear that in the face of the kind of thing that was happening in South Vietnam from mid-August onward, a nation like the U.S. must subordinate its concern to let things alone to the concern for present deprivation of liberty and life."[195]

Bundy concludes, however, that the effect of the coup was to deepen U.S. involvement in Vietnam, and that this effect was given short shrift in the debate in the executive branch:[196]

The political fact was that through what it did in the fall of 1963 the U.S. deepened its commitment to the preservation of South Vietnamese national independence. This was not stated at the time by Vietnamese, nor was it any significant part of the argument within the U.S. Government. So far as either written record or oral recollection can establish, no participant in the debate rested any weight, or even dwelt, on the argument that to engage U.S. prestige and judgment in the internal politics of South Vietnam was inevitably to increase the investment of both in the wider contest for the country itself. . . . In an intangible way, Americans in both public and policy circles were bound henceforth to feel more responsible for what happened in South Vietnam.

Bundy has also commented on why the decision was made, and why an action with such serious consequences was debated without full consideration of those consequences:[197]

In part because the process was so confused, so laden with personality clashes, and so distorted and inflamed by publicity that it never got far away from the immediate issues of tactical judgment. The process of policy-making was almost at its worst from mid-August through the beginning of October, and thereafter events came so rapidly that time was not taken for reflection.

Yet this is only a part of the reason. The greater part is that all of the participants assumed that the stakes in South Vietnam were so serious as to warrant the deepened commitment, if that was what it came to.

. . . was any basic alternative considered? Might one have been? The answer to the first part of the question is, again, categorically negative. Up to the day of President Kennedy's death, no one in the policy circle suggested seriously that the U.S. start to think in terms of withdrawing with the task unfinished. . . . Out of government as within it, the general feel-

---

[193]*Many Reasons Why*, p. 87.
[194]Bundy MS., ch. 10, p. 1.
[195]*Ibid.*, pp. 4, 5.
[196]*Ibid.*, pp. 5-6.
[197]*Ibid.*, pp. 7-9.

ing that things would somehow be better if Diem left—strongest in liberal circles of course—tended to drown out any serious voices asking if the whole venture was worth it.[198]

In Congress, only a few Members commented publicly on the coup or the death of Diem. In the Senate, Mansfield said on November 1, before the news of Diem's assassination, that the reported "uprising" "appears to me to be a purely Vietnamese affair which the Vietnamese should settle among themselves." He added that the coup had come as a surprise to him and, he felt sure, to the Kennedy administration.[199] Zablocki made similar comments when queried by the press. "They told us [the Zablocki subcommittee]," he said, that "there was no advance information."[200]

Senator Hickenlooper, ranking Republican on the Foreign Relations Committee, said that it was a serious situation which should be watched closely. Senator Aiken said he did not know whether U.S. personnel had been involved, "But if we are at all involved we don't want another failure. I hope we don't have another Bay of Pigs on our hands."[201]

The *New York Times*, along with most of the major newspapers of the country, welcomed the coup. In an editorial on November 2 it said:

> The only surprising thing about the military revolt in Saigon is that it has not come sooner. The inefficiency, corruption, inflexibility and growing unpopularity of the Diem-Nhu regime has been increasingly evident for the last two years. The Buddhist revolt in May and subsequent non-Communist unrest in South Vietnam made the continuation of all-out American support impossible.

On November 5, Mansfield, referring to Diem's death, said that "recent events in Vietnam are tragic events." He went on to discuss U.S. policy in the aftermath of the coup:[202]

> We will not serve the interests of the Nation if:
>
> First. We regard the overthrow of the Diem government as a victory or defeat for this country. It is neither. It is more an inexorable development in the tragic postwar history of the Vietnamese people.
>
> Second. If we reassume that the successor military-dominated regime is an automatic guarantee of a permanent improvement in the situation in Vietnam. This successor authority in Vietnam is, at this point, at best a promise of something better. But if the Korean experience is at all relevant, it is apparent that such promises can be undone in short order.
>
> If these tragic events of the past few days are to have constructive significance for this Nation as well as for the Vietnamese people, we would be well advised to recognize that the effectiveness of our Asian policies cannot be measured by an

[198]The commitment of U.S. policymakers to the defense of Vietnam and of Southeast Asia continued to be shared during this period by at least some of America's foremost Asian scholars, as evidenced by the papers presented in May 1963 at a conference sponsored by the Asia Society and the Association for Asian Studies, and printed in William Henderson (ed.), *Southeast Asia: Problems of United States Policy* (Cambridge, Mass.: M.I.T. Press, 1963).

[199]*CR*, vol. 109, p. 20868.

[200]*New York Times*, Nov. 2, 1963.

[201]*Ibid.*

[202]*CR*, vol. 109, p. 21061.

overthrow of a government, by whether one government is "easier to work with" than another, by whether one government smiles at us and another frowns. In the last analysis, the effectiveness of our policies, and their administration with respect to the Vietnamese situation and, indeed, all of southeast Asia can only be weighed in the light of these basic questions:

First. Do these policies make possible a progressive reduction in the expenditures of American lives and aid in Vietnam?

Second. Do these policies hold a valid promise of encouraging in Vietnam the growth of popularly responsible and responsive government?

Third. Do these policies contribute not only to the development of internal stability in South Vietnam but to the growth of an environment of a decent peace and a popularly based stability throughout Asia—the kind of environment which will permit the replacement of the present heavy dependence upon U.S. arms and resources with an equitable and mutual relationship between the Asian peoples and our own?

This is, indeed, an appropriate time for the executive branch to reassess policies for Vietnam and southeast Asia in these terms.

In brief statements, two of the three Senators who had accompanied Mansfield on his 1962 trip to Vietnam—Pell and Boggs—concurred with his remarks.

Church, however, voiced his approval of the change of government:[203]

The U.S. Government—both the executive branch and the Congress—has, since the severe repression of the Vietnamese students and the Buddhists by the Diem government this summer, hoped for the creation of an atmosphere in South Vietnam which might regather popular support behind the war effort.

I think that the President has followed the correct course in relations to South Vietnam. Although we have favored reforms, we have left it entirely to the will of the Vietnamese to implement that reform. If they themselves had not so strongly desired the change, we would have seen no coup in South Vietnam. My one regret about the recent coup was the violent death of Diem and Nhu, and all others who fell in the fight.

Representative Zablocki said that curtailment of U.S. aid, especially to Colonel Tung's Special Forces, had been justified. "But there can be little doubt," he added, "that this curtailment of aid also heartened Diem's opponents and helped trigger the coup. It was a signal to the military leaders of Vietnam that the United States would support the overthrow of the Diem regime." Lamenting the death of Diem, Zablocki asked whether the U.S. had taken steps to warn Diem about the coup. "If officials of the U.S. Government knew of the coup, and failed to exert every possible pressure to gain assurances of safe conduct out of the country for President Diem, then the shadow of blame falls on our Nation."[204]

---

[203] *Ibid.*, p. 21056.
[204] *Ibid.*, p. 20940.

Three weeks after Diem's assassination, in one of the great tragedies and ironies of modern history, President Kennedy was assassinated.

CHAPTER 4

PREPARING FOR THE POSSIBILITY OF A WIDER WAR

On November 24, 1963, two days after becoming President, Lyndon Johnson met with Lodge, Rusk, McNamara, Ball, McCone, and McGeorge Bundy to discuss Vietnam. (This followed a meeting on Vietnam held in Honolulu on November 20, which was attended by all top-level U.S. officials from Washington and Saigon.) Lodge was optimistic. McCone reported that there had been a considerable increase in Communist activity, and that he "could see no basis for an optimistic forecast of the future." Johnson said he had "serious misgivings" about the situation, but that the U.S. had to persevere.[1] He said he was ". . . not going to lose Vietnam," and was "not going to be the President who saw Southeast Asia go the way China did."[2] William Bundy has cautioned, however, against exaggerating the implications of this last statement, noting that Kennedy "said almost the same thing in September. . . ."[3]

On November 26, Johnson approved NSAM 273, reaffirming the U.S. commitment to Vietnam and the continuation of Vietnam programs and policies of the Kennedy administration. These were its principal provisions:[4]

(1) That the withdrawal of forces announced on October 2 "remain as stated";

(2) that the U.S. should support the new government;

(3) that U.S. efforts be fully unified, and that inter-departmental criticism be avoided;

(4) that U.S. assistance programs be maintained at previous levels, and that special attention be given to the situation in the delta;

(5) that a plan be developed for incursions into Laos;

(6) that steps be taken to improve U.S. relations with Cambodia;[5]

---

[1] *The Vantage Point*, p. 43. McCone's notes of that meeting remain classified.

[2] Tom Wicker, *JFK and LBJ* (Baltimore, Md.: Penguin, 1972), p. 205. Bill Moyers recalls that Johnson said after the meeting, "They'll think with Kennedy dead we've lost heart. . . . The Chinese. The fellas in the Kremlin. They'll be taking the measure of us. . . . I told them to go back and tell those generals in Saigon that Lyndon Johnson intends to stand by our word." Quoted by Schlesinger, *Robert Kennedy and His Times*, p. 726. According to Jack Valenti, who was with Johnson on the night after Kennedy's assassination, "He talked little of Vietnam that first night. I suspect he felt that Vietnam would yield to reason and informed judgment. LBJ really believed that if he applied his total intellect and concentration to a problem and if there was any alternative possible, he would find a way to an agreement. In all his career this reliance on reason and face-to-face challenge had never failed. He had no doubts it would succeed in Vietnam." Valenti, *A Very Human President* (New York: W. W. Norton, 1975), p. 152.

[3] Bundy MS., ch. 12, p. 5.

[4] Summarized from the text of NSAM 273, which was provided by the Johnson Library.

[5] On Nov. 19, 1963, Prince Sihanouk, charging that U.S. military advisers and the CIA had been aiding opponents of his government, rejected further U.S. military and economic assistance to Cambodia. Subsequently President Johnson asked former Secretary of State Dean Acheson to talk to Sihanouk, but this offer was refused by the Prince on Dec. 17.

(7) that a strong case on the external control and provisioning of the insurgency in Vietnam be developed for public presentation.

In addition to these instructions, NSAM 273 directed that planning for "possible increased activity" should include an estimate of such factors as the damage to North Vietnam and possible retaliation from the North, other international reaction, and "the plausibility of denial." The "activity" in question was the proposed plan for covert military operations against North Vietnam, begun in May 1963 when the JCS directed CINCPAC to prepare a plan for "hit and run" operations against North Vietnam by the South Vietnamese with covert U.S military assistance. On September 9, 1963, this new plan—CINCPAC OPLAN [operations plan] 34-63—was approved by the Joint Chiefs of Staff. According to the *Pentagon Papers*,[6] the plan was not sent to the White House at that time, but it was discussed and approved at the November 20 Conference in Honolulu, and, based upon the guidance in NSAM 273, it was revised and sent to the President on December 19, 1963, as OPLAN 34A. In the form in which it was sent to the President it provided for "(1) harassment; (2) diversion; (3) political pressures; (4) capture of prisoners; (5) physical destruction; (6) acquisition of intelligence; (7) generation of intelligence; (8) diversion of DRV resources," in order to "convince the DRV leadership that they should cease to support insurgent activities in the RVN and Laos." Two thousand and sixty-two separate operations were listed. CINCPAC, however, took the position that of these 2,062 operations, only air attacks and a few other "punitive or attritional" operations would have any significant influence on the North Vietnamese.[7]

Within a few days after the issuance of NSAM 273, information coming in from the field began to create alarm in Washington. Communist pressure was rapidly increasing in Vietnam and in Laos, and this, together with the problems being experienced by the new Vietnamese Government, led to new proposals for action. Some of these contemplated greater U.S. involvement in administrative matters. According to the *Pentagon Papers,* "The tone of USG internal documents and of its dealings with GVN was that of a benevolent big brother anxious to see little brother make good on his own."[8]

Others recommended military action. According to Hilsman,[9] "General Curtis E. LeMay, Chief of Staff of the Air Force, was particularly vigorous in advocating the bombardment of North Vietnam. 'We are swatting flies,' LeMay said, 'when we should be going after the manure pile.'" Hilsman added that "General Thomas S. Powers said that with conventional bombs alone the Strategic Air Command, which he headed, and its B–52s could 'pulverize North Vietnam,' and he made a special trip to Washington to plead the case for bombing not only North Vietnam but the Viet Cong and their bases in South Vietnam."

[6]*PP,* Gravel ed., vol. III, p. 150.
[7]*ibid.,* pp. 150-151.
[8]*Ibid.,* vol. II, p. 303.
[9]*To Move A Nation,* pp. 526–527. See also Robert F. Futrell, *The Advisory Years to 1965* (Washington, D.C.: Office of Air Force History, United States Air Force, 1981), p. 201.

The CIA proposed low-level reconnaissance over Laos to gather information on infiltration down the Ho Chi Minh Trail, with the implication that this could lead to bombing the trail.[10]

In addition, there were proposals, probably from the military, for armed incursions from Vietnam into Laos to reduce infiltration from the Ho Chi Minh Trail. This was reflected in the provision in NSAM 273 for developing a plan for such operations.

Although the evidence is fragmentary, it would appear from Hilsman's account that the Harriman-Hilsman-Forrestal group resisted proposals for incursions into Laos or the use of U.S. airpower in either North or South Vietnam or in bombing the Ho Chi Minh Trail, and countered with a proposal that if Communist infiltration from the north increased, the U.S., in order to deter the North Vietnamese from escalating the war, should deploy a division of troops to Thailand, coupled with a warning to the North Vietnamese.[11] If necessary, the troops would then be moved up to the border of Laos and another division brought into Thailand. If these steps were not effective, another division could be brought into Vietnam, "and so on." This proposal, Hilsman said, was opposed by the "never again" school in the Pentagon that resisted any limitations on the use of force.[12]

It should be noted, however, that the Pentagon's Office of International Security Affairs (ISA), headed by William Bundy, also disagreed with proposed incursions into Laos, and ISA and State agreed that it would be preferable to continue CIA-sponsored covert activities in Laos in order not to threaten Laotian sovereignty or disturb the 1962 Geneva Accords.[13]

The December 1963 McNamara Report

Adding to the uncertainties of the situation were reports from Vietnam that the new junta was not performing as well as expected, and that the strategic hamlet plan was proving to be far less effective than originally anticipated. There was also evidence that the Communists had been able to take advantage of the conditions created by the coup, and were making new gains in some areas.

Although U.S. military leaders continued to express optimism, President Johnson, as he said in his memoirs, thought that the U.S. "had been misled into over-optimism," and sent McNamara (others on the trip included McCone and William Bundy) to Vietnam for a report on the situation.

After another of his whirlwind tours (he and McCone were in Vietnam for two days, December 19 and 20), McNamara returned on December 21 to give his report.

These were its major points:[14]

    1. *Summary.* The situation is very disturbing. Current trends, unless reversed in the next 2-3 months, will lead to

---

[10] *To Move a Nation*, p. 527.
[11] *Ibid.*, pp. 533-534.
[12] *Ibid.*, p. 534.
[13] *PP*, Gravel ed., vol. III, p. 117.
[14] Excerpted from the text in *ibid.*, pp. 494-496. On Dec. 23, 1963, McCone submitted a brief report of his own to the President, in which he said that he felt "a little less pessimistic" than McNamara. Johnson Library, NSF Country File, Vietnam.

neutralization at best and most likely to a Communist-controlled state.

2. *The new government* is the greatest source of concern. It is indecisive and drifting. . . .

3. *The Country Team* is the second major weakness. It lacks leadership, has been poorly informed, and is not working to a common plan. . . .

4. *Viet Cong progress* has been great during the period since the coup. . . . The Viet Cong now control very high proportions of the people in certain key provinces, particularly those directly south and west of Saigon. . . .

5. *Infiltration* of men and equipment from North Vietnam continues. . . . ["To counter this infiltration," McNamara added, "we reviewed in Saigon various plans providing for cross-border operations into Laos. On the scale proposed, I am quite clear that these would not be politically acceptable or even militarily effective. Our first need would be immediate U-2 mapping of the whole Laos and Cambodian border, and this we are preparing on an urgent basis. One other step we should take is to expand the existing limited but remarkably effective operations on the Laos side, the so-called Operation HARDNOSE. . . ."]

6. *Plans for Covert Actions into North Vietnam* were prepared as we had requested and . . . present a wide variety of sabotage and psychological operations against North Vietnam from which I believe we should aim to select those that provide maximum pressure with minimum risk. . . .

7. *Possible neutralization* of Vietnam is strongly opposed by Minh, and our attitude is somewhat suspect because of editorials by the *New York Times* and mention by Walter Lippmann and others. We reassured them as strongly as possible on this—and in somewhat more general terms on the neutralization of Cambodia. . . .

8. *U.S. resources and personnel* cannot usefully be substantially increased. . . .

Conclusion: My appraisal may be overly pessimistic. Lodge, Harkins, and Minh would probably agree with me on specific points, but feel that January should see significant improvement. We should watch the situation very carefully, running scared, hoping for the best, but preparing for more forceful moves if the situation does not show early signs of improvement.

McNamara recommended to Johnson that more U.S. advisers, military and economic/political, be sent to the provinces, and McCone proposed improving the U.S. intelligence system in Vietnam. Both recommendations were approved by the President.

President Johnson also approved on December 21 the establishment of an interdepartmental committee, chaired by Krulak, to study the proposed OPLAN 34-A, and to designate those operations with "least risk." The committee made its report on January 2, 1964, and on January 16 the President approved 34-A covert operations, beginning February 1. (Later in 1964, as will be seen, these operations appear to have played a key role in the incidents in the

Gulf of Tonkin which resulted in Congress' passage of the Gulf of Tonkin Resolution.)

A few days later, Johnson ordered the establishment of an inter-departmental Vietnam Coordinating Committee under the direction of William Sullivan to deal with Vietnam. This replaced the Vietnam Task Force, headed by Kattenburg, and, because it was deliberately created outside the confines of the State Department's Far East Bureau, it took all effective jurisdiction and control over Vietnam from Hilsman (who was relieved of his duties shortly thereafter), as well as removing Kattenburg from Vietnam responsibilities.

Before turning to the events of 1964, note should also be taken of another development in late 1963 that affected the role of the U.S. in Vietnam. This was the final implementation of Operation SWITCHBACK, under which all of the CIA's paramilitary activities in Vietnam were transferred to the military pursuant to the conclusions of General Taylor's study of the Bay of Pigs episode. This action, which was effective November 1, 1963, increased the control of the military in the war, and further weakened the CIA's efforts to wage an unconventional political war. As Colby said, "it soon became clear that the military wanted to do its own thing, and neither wanted nor listened to CIA's political ideas of how to fight the war."[15] At the November 20, 1963, Conference in Honolulu, Colby told McNamara that putting covert teams into North Vietnam would not work. "He listened to me with a cold look and then rejected my advice. The desire to put pressure onto North Vietnam prevailed, and there and then the United States military started the planning and activity that would escalate finally to full-scale air attacks."

As 1963 ended, the United States was, as Halberstam said, caught in a quagmire. There were almost 20,000 U.S. troops in Vietnam, more than twice the number Taylor had proposed two years earlier; strategic hamlets were failing; the overthrow of Diem had not produced the expected improvements in governmental efficiency and public support; and the Communists were stronger than ever. By the middle of December 1963, it was clear to Washington policymakers that the plan for withdrawing U.S. forces was no longer workable if the U.S. was going to continue to defend South Vietnam. Although no announcement was made of the fact, the scheduled withdrawal of 1,000 troops was achieved by juggling the figures to make it look as if there were 1,000 fewer men. This was done, as the Pentagon Papers stated, "by concentrating rotations home in December and letting strength rebound in the subsequent two months."[16] President Johnson later stated publicly, however, that 1,000 men had been withdrawn, and Secretary McNamara made similar statements to congressional committees.[17]

On January 2, 1964, General Krulak submitted the report of his covert operations committee.[18] The report recommended that the

[15] *Honorable Men*, pp. 219-220.
[16] *PP*, Gravel ed., vol. II, p. 303.
[17] *Public Papers of the Presidents*, Lyndon B. Johnson, 1963-1964, p. 345.
[18] See *PP*, Gravel ed., vol. III, pp. 150-153. The report itself, "Program of Operations Against North Vietnam," from Krulak to McNamara, Jan. 2, 1964, is still classified. Also classified are the covering memo, "North Vietnam Operations Paper," and the attachment, an undated memorandum for the President entitled "Operations Against North Vietnam."

U.S. initiate the 34-A plan, and by "progressively escalating pressure . . . to inflict increasing punishment upon North Vietnam, and to create pressures, which may convince the North Vietnamese leadership, in its own self-interest, to desist from its aggressive policies." The 34-A plan, which was to be directed by the military, was to consist of three phases over 12 months, each phase progressively more punitive. Phase 1 ". . . called for intelligence collection through U-2 and communications intelligence missions and psychological operations involving leaflet drops, propaganda kit deliveries, and radio broadcasts. It also provided for about '20 destructive undertakings . . . designed to result in substantial destruction, economic loss, and harassment.' The second and third phases involved the same categories of action, but of increased tempo and magnitude, and with the destructive operations extending to 'targets identified with North Vietnam's economic and industrial well-being.'"

Although the Krulak committee concluded that these operations might not cause the North Vietnamese to desist, there was some hope among members of the committee and others—although this apparently did not include any of the top policymakers, who tended to view 34-A operations as relatively insignificant—that, out of concern for their economy and fear of Chinese intervention, the North Vietnamese might be inclined as a result of 34-A to cease supporting the Communists in the South. According to W. W. Rostow, one of the administration's principal proponents of the use of such gradual pressure, "Ho has an industrial complex to protect: he is no longer a guerrilla fighter with nothing to lose."[19] But the Krulak committee also recognized that these operations had to be punitive enough to be effective: "Toughened, as they have been, by long years of hardship and struggle, they will not easily be persuaded by a punitive program to halt their support of the Viet Cong insurgency, unless the *damage* visited upon them is of great magnitude." (emphasis in original)

On January 16, 1964, the Krulak committee's recommendations were approved by the President.[20]

There is no indication that the decision to launch the new program of covert operations was revealed to Congress. A few Members dealing with military matters and the CIA were probably told. Fulbright also seems to have known. In a speech on March 25, 1964, he said that one of the options for the U.S. was to equip the South Vietnamese "to attack North Vietnamese territory, possibly by means of commando-type operations from the sea or the air," adding ". . . it seems to me that we have no choice but to support the South Vietnamese Government and Army by the most effective means available," pending other decisions.[21]

New Proposals for Neutralization of Vietnam, and a New Coup

As it became apparent that the new junta was not operating effectively, a number of U.S. and other public figures began to worry

---

[19]*PP*, Gravel ed., vol. III, p. 153 from a memorandum from Rostow to Rusk, "Southeast Asia," Feb. 13, 1964, still classified.
[20]No NSAM was issued.
[21]*CR*, vol. 110, p. 6232.

about the possibility of greater U.S. involvement in Vietnam and the escalation of the conflict into a full-scale war. Hilsman had predicted on September 10, in the course of planning the coup, that "if we start down this path we would have to be prepared to contemplate the use of U.S. forces on the ground in Vietnam." This is what Senator Russell probably had in mind when he is said to have told Johnson late in 1963, when the President asked him what he would do about Vietnam: "I'd spend whatever it takes to bring to power a government that would ask us to go home."[22]

Similar views about disengagement were being expressed privately to Johnson by Mansfield. On December 7, 1963, after talking with Johnson about the situation, Mansfield sent him a memorandum along with copies of the several memos he had sent to President Kennedy.[23] He told Johnson that it might not be possible to "win" the war in Vietnam, or to "win" it in South Vietnam. "There may be only a war which will, in time, involve U.S. forces throughout Southeast Asia, and finally throughout China itself in search of victory. What national interests in Asia would steel the American people for the massive costs of ever-deepening involvement of that kind? It may be that we are confronted with a dilemma not unlike that which faced us in Korea a decade ago."

Mansfield added that there might, however, be a "truce that could be won now in Viet Nam alone and eventually a peace which might be won throughout Southeast Asia at a price commensurate with American interests." This would involve three things: first, strengthening South Vietnam's control of its territory; second, a "diplomatic offensive," in which France would be the key participant, to bring an end to the "North-South Vietnamese conflict," which might be "on terms which reduced our influence (and costs) *provided* it also inhibited Chinese political domination"; and, third, U.S. "understanding, sympathy and sensible encouragement for the Cambodians desire to stand on its own feet without one-sided U.S. aid." "At this time," he added, "Cambodia would appear to be the principal prototype of any eventual peace for Southeast Asia. It would be an independent Southeast Asia, not dependent on a costly U.S. prop."

During Christmas week, Johnson telephoned Mansfield's assistant, Francis Valeo, and in response Mansfield sent him another memorandum on January 7, 1964.[24] He noted that Johnson had told Valeo, ". . . we do not want another China in Vietnam." Mansfield said:

> I would respectfully add to this observation: Neither do we want another Korea. It would seem that a key (but often overlooked) factor in both situations was a tendency to bite off more than we were prepared in the end to chew. We tended to talk ourselves out on a limb with overstatements of our purpose and commitment only to discover in the end that there were not sufficient American interests to support with blood and treasure a desperate final plunge. Then, the questions fol-

[22]Quoted by Tom Wicker, *New York Times,* May 1, 1966.
[23]A copy is in the Johnson Library, NSF Aides File, McGeorge Bundy Memos for the President.
[24]Same location.

lowed invariably: "Who got us into this mess?" "Who lost China?" etc.

We are close to the point of no return in Viet Nam. A way to avoid another Korea and, perhaps, another China may be found in the general policy approach suggested in the memo of December 7th. If so, there ought to be less official talk of our responsibility in Viet Nam and more emphasis on the responsibilities of the Vietnamese themselves and on a great deal of thought on the possibilities for a peaceful solution through the efforts of other nations as well as our own.

In early January 1964, at the President's request McGeorge Bundy sent him a memorandum, along with memos from Rusk and McNamara, in which all three advisers disagreed with Mansfield's position:[25]

1. To neutralize South Viet Nam today, or even for the United States Government to *seem to* move in that direction, would mean the following:

a. A rapid collapse of anti-Communist forces in South Vietnam, and a unification of the whole country on Communist terms.

b. Neutrality in Thailand, and increased influence for Hanoi and Peking.

c. Collapse of the anti-Communist position in Laos.

d. Heavy pressure on Malaya and Malaysia.

e. A shift toward neutrality in Japan and the Philippines.

f. Blows to U.S. prestige in South Korea and Taiwan which would require compensating increases in American commitment there—or else further retreat.

2. We may have to move in these painful directions, but we should do so only when there is a much stronger demonstration that our present course cannot work. If we neutralize, it should not be because *we* have quit but because *others* have. Today a move in this direction would be regarded as betrayal by the new regime in Saigon and by all anti-Communist Vietnamese. There are enough of them to lose us an election.

3. The right course is to continue to strengthen our stuggle against the Communist terror (which is exactly what it is). For this we need new and stronger leadership in the U.S. effort. In particular, we need a wholly rejuventated military command and a rapidly stepped-up political effort of the sort which Lodge has at last recommended in the attached cable.

On January 9, when he gave the three memos to the President, Bundy said in a cover memo:

The political damage to Truman and Acheson from the fall of China arose because most Americans came to believe that we could and should have done more than we did to prevent it. This is exactly what would happen now if we should seem to be the first to quit in Saigon.

---

[25] All of the memos are in the Johnson Library, NSF Country File, Vietnam.

It should also be noted that during the early months of 1964 the President was also being urged by Chester Bowles, U.S. Ambassador to India, to seek a neutralist solution, but he was ignored by Johnson as he had been by Kennedy. Kalb and Abel, *Roots of Involvement,* p. 167.

Mansfield's analogy with Korea neglects the fact that a very solid anti-Communist base existed in South Korea when the armistice was worked out in 1953. Moreover, the U.S. presence has continued. There is literally no comparison between this solution and proposals for "neutralization" and U.S. withdrawal in the present situation in South Vietnam. *When* we are stronger, *then* we can face negotiation.

Perhaps you can trade with Mike Mansfield: his support for the war effort against our support, which is real, for new and energetic political, social, and economic programs in South Vietnam.

McNamara's memorandum made these points.

1. *We should certainly stress that the war is essentially a Vietnamese responsibility,* and this we have repeatedly done, particularly in our announced policy on U.S. troop withdrawal. At the same time we cannot disengage U.S. prestige to any significant degree. . . .

2. *The security situation is serious, but we can still win,* even on present ground rules. . . .

3. . . . *any deal either to divide the present territory of South Vietnam or to "neutralize" South Vietnam would inevitably mean a new government in Saigon that would in short order become Communist-dominated.*

4. *The consequences of a Communist-dominated South Vietnam are extremely serious* both for the rest of Southeast Asia and for the U.S. position in the rest of Asia and indeed in other key areas of the world. . . .

5. Thus, the stakes in preserving an anti-Communist South Vietnam are so high that, in our judgment, we must go on bending every effort to win. In the final analysis, Senator Mansfield is challenging what he regards as the gross imbalance between the extent of our involvement in Southeast Asia and our narrow self-interests in the area. My assessment of our important security interests is that they unquestionably call for holding the line against further Communist gains. And, I am confident that the American people are by and large in favor of a policy of firmness and strength in such situations.

Rusk also disagreed with Mansfield's proposals. He called the proposal for neutralization "a phony," adding that "what the communists mean by 'neutralization' of South Viet-Nam is a regime which would not have support from the West and would be an easy prey to a communist takeover." In a statement submitted with his memo, Rusk said: "We do not believe that North Vietnam's terrorism can be called off by 'an astute diplomatic offensive' at this time. While diplomacy may eventually play a role, we believe this will happen only after the North Vietnamese become convinced that they cannot succeed in destroying the Republic of Vietnam by guerrilla warfare." The statement added: "We believe the fight against the Viet Cong can be won without major and direct United States involvement *provided* the new South Vietnamese Government takes the proper political, economic and social actions to win the support of the rural people *and* uses its armed forces effectively."

On January 13, Theodore Sorensen, Kennedy's assistant who was still on the White House staff, sent President Johnson a memorandum in which he said, ". . . I am certain that Messrs. McNamara, Rusk and Bundy are right in stating that the partition or neutralization of South Vietnam today, or even our proposing such partition or neutralization, would, *under present conditions*, lead to a Communist takeover in that country, a weakening of our prestige and security throughout Asia and an increase in the possibilities of a major military involvement in that area. This would have greater political liabilities than our present course. The commitment to preserve Vietnamese independence was not made by Democrats—but we are not free to abandon it."

Sorensen suggested, however, that if the U.S. proposed some form of neutralization of all of Vietnam, or a cease-fire, rejection of these by the Communists would make the burden for continued fighting fall on them, and thus improve the position of the U.S. at home and abroad.

He also suggested that the President should make it clear that it was up to the South Vietnamese to win the war, ". . . so that if during the next four months the new government fails to take the necessary political, economic, social and military actions, it will be their choice and not our betrayal or weakness that loses the area."[26]

On January 30, 1964, the government of General Minh was ousted by a coup led by General Nguyen Khanh, one of the Diem coup plotters. The U.S. Government was given several days notice of the Khanh coup, and Lodge was told not to become involved. The role, if any, of the U.S. Government in the coup is not known. Khanh told the U.S. in advance of the coup that some of the leading members of the junta were planning to negotiate the neutralization of Vietnam, but there is no evidence as to the possible effect of this on the attitudes and actions of U.S. officials in Saigon and Washington.[27]

Lodge attempted to justify the change of government in a cable to Washington saying, in part:[28]

> If Khanh is able, his advent to power may give this country one-man command in place of a junta. This may be good. We have everything we need in Viet Nam. The U.S. has provided military advice, training, equipment; economic and social help; and political advice. The Government of Viet Nam has put relatively large numbers of good men into important positions and has evolved civil and military procedures which appear to be workable. Therefore, our side knows how to do it; we have the means with which to do it; we simply need to do it. This requires a tough and ruthless commander. Perhaps Khanh is it.

---

[26]Johnson Library, NSF Country File, Vietnam. Available records do not indicate whether President Johnson replied in writing to Senator Mansfield, or talked personally with him.

[27]For a discussion of the factors involved in the coup see *PP*, Gravel ed., vol. II, pp. 306-309, and vol. III, pp. 37-39. Before and during the coup, the U.S. was kept fully informed by Col. Casper Wilson, the MAAG adviser for Khanh's I Corps, who was in Khanh's command post throughout the affair.

[28]*Ibid.*, vol. III, p. 39.

On January 31, 1964, French President Charles de Gaulle, an advocate for many years of a unified, independent Vietnam, repeated this recommendation.[29] In a news conference on February 1, President Johnson was asked about de Gaulle's proposal. He replied that neutralization of both South and North Vietnam "would be considered sympathetically," but that neutralization did not appear likely, and that the course the U.S. was following was "the only course for us to follow. . . . We plan to pursue it diligently and, we hope, successfully on a stepped-up basis." He was asked whether de Gaulle's proposal did not provide for neutralizing both North and South Vietnam, and how this differed from his statement that such a proposal would be considered sympathetically. He replied that the questioner would have to ask de Gaulle about his plan; as he understood it, proposals for neutralization applied only to South Vietnam.[30]

De Gaulle's proposal was praised, however, by Mansfield. In a speech in the Senate on February 19, 1964,[31] he said that while neutralization might be difficult to achieve, it should not be lightly dismissed. "Do we ourselves," he asked, "in terms of our national interests as seen in juxtaposition to the cost in American lives and resources, prefer what exists in South Vietnam to what exists in Laos or in Cambodia? Do we prefer another Vietnamese type of American involvement or perhaps a Korean-type involvement in these other countries and elsewhere in Southeast Asia?" "There has not been and there does not exist today," he declared, "a basis in our national interests which would justify the assumption of primary American responsibility in this situation which might well involve the sacrifice of a vast number of American lives not only in South Vietnam but, by extension, in North Vietnam, in Cambodia, in Laos, if not, indeed, in China itself."

In Saigon, according to one report, "Mansfield's statement strengthened a growing body of opinion among Vietnamese and Americans here that the United States is sick of this war and is looking for a way out. Officially there was no reaction. Privately and unofficially, reaction ran the gamut of clichés from shock to dismay to anger. 'Of course it wasn't the Senator's intention to give aid and comfort to the Communists and undermine Vietnamese and American morale,' said a top American official. 'But that's exactly what he did. And he couldn't have done a better job if his speech had been written in Hanoi.' "[32]

Walter Lippmann, the noted political columnist, also urged that de Gaulle's proposal be considered, but the New York Times' James Reston disagreed, saying:[33]

> The most dangerous and likely immediate prospect is not that the Communists will win the war in South Vietnam or that the United States will carry the war to North Vietnam

---

[29]De Gaulle was not suggesting neutralization per se, as Bernard Fall pointed out in an excellent analysis, "What De Gaulle Actually Said About Vietnam," *Reporter*, Oct. 24, 1963.

[30]*Public Papers of the Presidents,* Lyndon B. Johnson, 1963-1964, pp. 257, 259, 260.

[31]*CR,* vol. 110, p. 3114.

[32]Keyes Beech, Chicago Daily News Service, in the *Washington Post,* Feb. 22, 1964.

[33]*New York Times,* Mar. 1, 1964. A similar position against negotiations was taken by Zbigniew Brzezinski, subsequently a member of State's Policy Planning Staff under President Johnson, and national security adviser to President Carter. See *Washington Post,* Mar. 1, 1964.

but that in the atmosphere of rumor, confusion and intrigue in Saigon another coup d'etat, the third in 100 days, will bring in a neutralist South Vietnamese Government that will order us out and negotiate a settlement that will leave the Communists free to take over.

This would be almost as bad for the West as a military disaster. We could not impose our presence on a South Vietnamese Government that didn't want us, and with U.S. power out of Vietnam, the situation would really, in the President's phrase, "go to pot." The Communists would be free to expand in southeast Asia almost at will.

Senator Jacob K. Javits (R/N.Y.) took issue with Mansfield. While agreeing that it was important to consider alternatives, he said, ". . . the minute we begin to talk about neutralization and neutralism, the backbone and the spirit could go out of the action which is being taken in this stuggle."

There was a consensus among the American people, Javits said, that ". . . our presence there is important enough to warrant the risks we are running." Moreover, ". . . they will accept these risks—yes, even accept the casualties—if they believe there is the remotest chance in that way to keep the Communist grip from encompassing Vietnam."

There was also a consensus, he said, ". . . that if we adopted the attitude of General de Gaulle in that area, it would represent a diminution in the American effort, some lessening in our support, perhaps even a decision to pull out and let the Government of South Vietnam do whatever it pleases."

Javits added,

> . . . Let us remember that even a great nation must suffer casualties currently in order to avoid even greater casualties later. The present position in south and southeast Asia—representing still a rampart against the absolutely uncontrolled expansion of Communist China, which preaches to all its people that its ultimate aim is the destruction not only of the free world, but specifically the United States of America and its people—it seems to me is only insurance against a future which seems too foreboding in terms of the intentions at the moment which Communist China declared and reiterated for so very long.

Javits concluded by saying that what the U.S. was doing was ". . . worth doing. No one in the Pentagon or in the Senate need have the 'jitters' about it. It is high time that some people understand that the American people are adults. They understand that in order to make an omelet, some eggs must be broken."[34]

Representative Zablocki, chairman of the Far East Subcommittee of the House Foreign Affairs Committee, also took issue with proposals for neutralization. In a speech on February 20, which was intended to counter Mansfield's speech the previous day, Zablocki said:[35]

> Such expressions from Americans it seems to me, do a grave disservice to the brave Vietnamese people who have demon-

---

[34]*CR*, vol. 110, pp. 3277-3279.
[35]*Ibid.*, p. 3226.

strated, and are continuing to demonstrate their desire to win the present guerrilla conflict against the Communist Viet-cong. . . . The effect of statements, from American legislators, whether or not they have the sanction and approval of the administration, are bound to be construed by the Vietnamese as indications that the United States is growing weary of the grueling guerrilla war and want to pull out.

Nothing could be further from the truth. The people of the United States want Communist aggression defeated in Viet-nam.

. . . Besides worrying our Vietnamese allies, these statements give aid and comfort to the North Vietnamese and the Vietcong.

Zablocki added that neutralization would "result in complete Communist dominance in the whole of the Indochina Peninsula. . . . We cannot give way—or appear to give way before the expansionist policies of Communist China. Instead, we must make our stand in Vietnam as long as the freedom-loving people of that nation ask our assistance in this joint endeavor against communism."

Zablocki was not opposed to further U.S. military involvement. "While we do not wish additional commitments of men and equipment in South Vietnam, let us not hesitate to provide them should it become necessary. While we do not wish to involve U.S. troops in direct fighting in South Vietnam, let us not shrink from such involvement should it become necessary."

In conjunction with his speech, Zablocki had reprinted in the *Congressional Record* an article on February 16, 1964, by the esteemed military correspondent for the *New York Times,* Hanson W. Baldwin, in which Baldwin reported that "South Vietnam's moment of truth appears to be at hand. . . . The Communists hold the initiative in much of the country, and the ultimate outcome is in doubt."[36]

Baldwin concluded:

There is no doubt that the stakes are high in Vietnam. They are considerably more important than the economic, political, and strategic value of the country. For in Vietnam the United States has fielded, for the first time, its concept of counterinsurgency and has made its first all-out attempt to erect a defense against Communism's creeping aggressions and Premier Khrushchev's tactics of national wars of liberation. If the defense fails, if the dam breaks, there will be no clear-cut line drawn against Communist expansion in Southeast Asia or anywhere else in the world. A new victory for communism would have most serious international and domestic consequences.

Because the United States has been morally, militarily, and politically committed in South Vietnam, because its prestige is involved and because the consequences of failure would have worldwide repercussions, most, but not all, Washington officials believe the price of victory must be paid even if the price includes some limited commitment of U.S. combat forces.

---

36 *Ibid.,* pp. 3228-3229.

President Johnson's reaction to Mansfield, Lippmann and others was expressed in a cable he sent to Lodge on March 20, saying in part:[37]

I think that nothing is more important than to stop neutralist talk whenever we can by whatever means we can. I have made this point myself to Mansfield and Lippmann and I expect to use every public opportunity to restate our position firmly.

To buttress his argument, Johnson turned to his old Senate friend and ally, J. William Fulbright. On March 2, 1964, he telephoned Fulbright, and this is at least a partial transcript of their conversation:[38]

President. If we can just get our foreign policy straightened out.

Fulbright. Get that damn Vietnam straightened out. Any hope?

President. Well, we've got about four possibilities. The only thing I know to do is more of the same and do it more efficiently and effectively and we got a problem out there that I inherited with Lodge. I wire him every day and say what else do you recommend? Here is the best summary we have. [here the President apparently read from a document] (1) In Southeast Asia the free world is facing an attempt by the Communists of North Vietnam to subvert and overthrow the non-Communist government of South Vietnam. North Vietnam has been providing direction, control, and training for 25,000 Vietcong guerrillas. (2) Our objective, our purpose in South Vietnam, is to help the Vietnamese maintain their independence. We are providing the training and logistic support that they cannot provide themselves. We will continue to provide that support as long as it is required. As soon as the mission is complete our troops can be withdrawn. There's no reason to keep our military police there when the Vietnamese are trained for that purpose. (3) In the past four months there've been three governments in South Vietnam. The Vietcong have taken advantage of this confusion. Their increased activity has had success. At least four alternatives are open to us: (1) Withdraw from South Vietnam. Without our support the government will be unable to counter the aid from the North to the Vietcong. Vietnam will collapse and the ripple effect will be felt throughout Southeast Asia, endangering independent governments in Thailand, Malaysia and extending as far as India and Indonesia and the Philippines. (2) We can seek a formula that will neutralize South Vietnam à la Mansfield and De Gaulle but any such formula will only lead in the end to the same results as withdrawing support. We all know the Communist attitude that what's mine is mine, what's yours in negotiable. True neutralization would have to extend to North Vietnam and

[37] *PP*, Gravel ed., vol. III, p. 511.

[38] This is quoted from Doris Kearns, *Lyndon Johnson and the American Dream* (New York: Harper and Row, 1976), pp. 196-197. Kearns, who helped Johnson write his memoirs, said that Johnson gave her this and several other transcripts of telephone conversations to help her learn the realities of government. All other Johnson telephone transcripts are said to be closed to the public until 50 years after his death.

this has been specifically rejected by North Vietnam and the Communist China government, and we believe if we attempted to neutralize, the Commies would stay in North Vietnam. We would abandon South Vietnam. The Communists would take over South Vietnam. (3) We can send Marines à la Goldwater and other U.S. forces against the sources of these aggressions but our men may well be bogged down in a long war against numerically superior North Vietnamese and Chicom forces 100,000 miles from home. (4) We continue our present policy of providing training and logistical support of South Vietnamese forces. This policy has not failed. We propose to continue it. Secretary McNamara's trip to South Vietnam will provide us with an opportunity to again appraise the prospects of the policy and the future alternatives open to us.

Fulbright. I think that's right . . . that's exactly what I'd arrive at under these circumstances at least for the foreseeable future.

President. Now when he comes back though and if we're losing with what we're doing, we've got to decide whether to send them in or whether to come out and let the dominoes fall. That's where the tough one is going to be. And you do some heavy thinking and let's decide what we do.

Fulbright. Righto.

Fulbright reacted in part by giving a speech in the Senate on March 25 in which, among other things, he criticized the French:[39]

Recent initiatives by France, calling for the neutralization of Vietnam, have tended to confuse the situation, without altering it in any fundamental way. France could, perhaps, play a constructive mediating role if she were willing to consult and cooperate with the United States. For somewhat obscure reasons, however, France has chosen to take an independent initiative . . . the problem posed by French intervention in Southeast Asia is that while France may set off an unforeseeable chain of events, she is neither a major military force nor a major economic force in the Far East, and is therefore unlikely to be able to control or greatly influence the events which her initiative may precipitate . . . It is difficult to see how a negotiation, under present military circumstances, could lead to termination of the war under conditions that would preserve the freedom of South Vietnam. It is extremely difficult for a party to a negotiation to achieve by diplomacy objectives which it has conspicuously failed to win by warfare. The hard fact of the matter is that our bargaining position is at present a weak one; and until the equation of advantages between the two sides has been substantially altered in our favor, there can be little prospect of a negotiated settlement which could secure the independence of a non-communist South Vietnam.

Cacophony in Congress

Meanwhile, there were more discordant voices in the Senate. On March 4, Morse delivered a major speech on U.S. foreign policy in

---

[39] *CR*, vol. 110, p. 6232.

which he criticized the U.S. role in Vietnam: "We should never have gone in. We should never have stayed in. We should get out."[40] He continued:

American unilateral participation in the war of South Vietnam cannot be justified, and will not be justified in American history. As I have made clear to the State Department, this administration had better be warned now that when the casualty lists of American boys in South Vietnam increase until the mothers and fathers of those boys—and, yes, the American people generally—start crying "Murder," no administration will stand.

. . . let us not forget that the French people finally turned out a French government because they decided that French boys—the best of French blood—were being murdered in Indochina. . . .

The effort to continue dominating the western shores of the Pacific, not to mention any part of the Indian Ocean, will be increasingly costly to us in blood and money. I am flatly and completely opposed to any expansion of our commitments there, and to increasing the scale of our participation in the Vietnamese war.

I am opposed to it because American involvement in any Asian conflict is going to be a nuclear involvement. I am satisfied that there is no other way this country could meet the manpower and geographic advantages that a Chinese-backed force would have over us.

I am permitted to say, within the bounds of secrecy and in my capacity as a member of the Foreign Relations Committee who individually has passed a judgment upon American foreign policy in Asia, that we cannot win a land war in Asia with American conventional ground forces. That is fully recognized by outstanding military experts.

I cannot think of a greater mistake that this country could make than to seek to escalate the war in South Vietnam by using conventional American forces in North Vietnam or in any other areas to the north of South Vietnam.

Therefore I say to the American people, from the floor of the Senate this afternoon, "You have the right to ask your Government now, Do you have plans for sending American boys to their deaths by the tens of thousands in escalating the South Vietnam war above South Vietnam?"

Senator Allen J. Ellender (D/La.), a conservative Southern Democrat who was a top-ranking member of the Senate Appropriations Committee, and who had visited Vietnam several times during overseas study missions in the late 1950s-early 1960s, agreed with Morse that the U.S. should not be involved in Vietnam, and that U.S. forces should be withdrawn.

On March 10, Senator Ernest Gruening (D/Alaska) also made a major speech in which he advocated U.S. withdrawal from Vietnam.[41] "The war in South Vietnam," he said, "is not and never

---

[40] *Ibid.*, pp. 4357-4359.
[41] *Ibid.*, pp. 4831 ff. See also his remarks on Apr. 15, p. 8071.

has been a U.S. war. It is and must remain a fight to be fought and won by the people of South Vietnam themselves." "Let us get out of Vietnam," he concluded, "on as good terms as possible—but let us get out."

The next day (March 11), Senator Thomas Dodd (D/Conn.), answered Gruening, in a speech entitled "South Vietnam: Last Chance for Freedom in Asia," in which he said, "We must assume that at this moment, we are losing. Only a supreme effort by the South Vietnamese and an increased effort by the United States will turn back the Communist tide." If Vietnam fell, Dodd said, the Pacific would become a "Red ocean." Neutralization, he added, would be a "dishonest substitute for unconditional surrender." Dodd, speaking unofficially for the administration, recommended guerrilla operations against the coast of North Vietnam, and possible airstrikes against the north. The solution to the problem he said, would be to carry the war "to its source: North Vietnam."[42]

On March 11, Gruening wrote to President Johnson:[43]

> As the opposition is warming up and trying to blame you for some of the problems that you have inherited and in the creation of which you played no part, I thought it desirable to emphasize this in a speech on the Viet Nam situation, which I hope will be helpful.
>
> I was pleased that Dick Russell, Chairman of the Armed Services Committee, warmly congratulated me on this speech and said he agreed with me completely. He told me that at the time that the decision was made by the Eisenhower administration to go into Viet Nam, ten years ago, he strongly counselled against it, but his advice was not heeded.
>
> The reactions I have gotten so far lead me to the conclusion that our getting out and the putting of an end to the killing of American boys would be highly popular.

Gruening also wrote to Fulbright suggesting that the Foreign Relations Committee question McNamara about the extent to which, during his recent trip, he had committed the U.S. to provide assistance to Vietnam. (McNamara's trip, discussed below, occurred in early March 1964.) Gruening told Fulbright that he was apprehensive about the situation in Vietnam. "My study of the situation convinces me that this is largely a civil war inside of South Viet Nam and that we should try to disengage ourselves as rapidly as possible. I find no justification for continued intervention in view of all the past sacrificing of American lives there."

Fulbright replied that he shared Gruening's apprehension about the situation in South Vietnam. He said that the Foreign Relations Committee customarily asked McNamara for briefings on his trips, but that he had not had an opportunity to arrange a meeting on the Secretary's most recent trip.

Fulbright then sent Gruening's letter to the Foreign Relations Committee's acting chief of staff with a note suggesting that a meeting be arranged.[44] (The meeting was held on March 26.)

---

[42] *Ibid.*, pp. 4986-4992.
[43] Johnson Library, ND 19/C0312.
[44] This correspondence is in the University of Arkansas, Fulbright Papers, series 48, box 6.

Gruening's fellow Democratic Senator from Alaska, Senator E. L. "Bob" Bartlett, was also troubled by the increasing U.S. commitment in Vietnam. In a Senate speech on the same day as Mansfield's he said he did not think that the U.S. could or should withdraw at that time, but he noted, "We are attempting to find a military solution in Vietnam and if we are determined to win, the cost of this solution will have just begun." He welcomed, therefore, the diplomatic initiatives of the French, and urged that the U.S. take a more flexible, less rigid and dogmatic approach to the situation in the Far East, especially towards the Communist Chinese. French recognition of China (which had occurred in early 1964), he said, could help in bringing about a peaceful resolution of the conflict in Indochina. In the U.S., he added, China should be taken "out of domestic politics." Only by "defusing" the China issue could the U.S. begin reevaluating and reshaping its policy toward the Far East.

In another speech on March 7, Bartlett summed up his position:[45]

> We must at all costs avoid being cast in the role of an imperialistic, colonial power. If, through misadventure or folly, we should allow the struggle in Viet Nam to become one of Asian versus white intruders, we have lost a good deal more than South Viet Nam.
>
> The war in South Viet Nam is a South Vietnamese war. It will be won only by the South Vietnamese themselves. It will only be won when they have something worth winning it for.
>
> Our best hope appears, I believe, to hold and strengthen the military situation as best we can while at the same time to press hard for improvements in the central government. Unless the soldier and the peasant believe there is real hope for economic and social reform, we cannot win. If there is such hope, we shall not lose.

In the House, however, there was considerable support for a stronger U.S. role. Gerald R. Ford (R/Mich.) and Daniel J. Flood (D/Pa.), both of whom were on the House Appropriations Committee, took issue with McNamara and Taylor's reassurances about the situation in Vietnam in a closed hearing of that committee on February 17, 1964. Representative Flood said that there was division of command in Vietnam between the Vietnamese and the U.S., and that "We command and control nothing." Taylor agreed that the U.S. had no command responsibilities, but explained that the U.S. did have some control. Flood replied, "A division of command always results in the failure of national policy." He said he was not advocating the use of U.S. combat forces, but he told Taylor, "You have come to the Rubicon. Very, very soon in South Vietnam you are at the end of the line. You have to make up your mind very soon, General, that you are going to command, or you are not going to command. If you are not going to command, you are a dead duck, you cannot win." "Whether you are going to command or not," he added, "is a matter of politics vis-à-vis the people

---

[45]This speech by Senator Bartlett was given at a conference on Mar. 7, sponsored by The Johnson Foundation (Racine, Wisconsin), the proceeding of which were published by the foundation in 1964 under the title "Viet Nam." For a subsequent Senate speech by Bartlett on June 15, 1964, see *CR*, vol. 110, pp. 13842-13844.

and the Government of South Vietnam. But the question whether you are going to stay in there or not is—are you going to command?"[46]

Representative (later President) Ford also spoke up after one particular comment by McNamara in his testimony. McNamara said, "We hope that, with our full support, the new [Khanh] government can take hold and eventually suppress the Viet Cong insurrection. . . . However, the survival of an independent government in South Vietnam is so important to the security of all of southeast Asia and to the free world that I can conceive of no alternative other than to take all necessary measures within our capability to prevent a Communist victory. We must prove that Communist aggression cannot succeed through subversion, but will fail as surely as it has failed in direct confrontation."[47]

Responding to this, Ford—who, along with other Republicans on the committee, was to some extent baiting McNamara politically—said "I don't want you [McNamara] to hesitate to say, because of a fear you might be criticized, that we would use all necessary U.S. forces to achieve what you have indicated is so vitally important." McNamara replied off-the-record, and Ford added:[48]

. . . there somehow seems to be a reluctance on the part of Administration officials to commit U.S. forces to combat for a Vietnamese-United States victory, and I don't think this is a proper or prudent attitude. If we want victory or if we want to prevent a Communist victory I think we have to be prepared to make commitments. I don't like to see strong words used and then when we come to the point of implementing them, we back off. Now, I don't like the use of U.S. forces overseas any better than anybody else, but I think we have to make some hard choices every once in a while and if what you say here is what you believe, I don't see how you can back off from that viewpoint if the potential circumstances become realities.

McNamara replied, before again going off the record, "We will make whatever hard choices have to be made."

Anticipating a Crisis, the U.S. Increases Aid

The growing political and governmental problems of South Vietnam during the latter part of 1963 and early 1964 made it increasingly apparent that the "essential premise"—an effective system of self-government—was lacking, and that the U.S. would need to increase its commitment or find a way to withdraw. Harkins' quarterly MACV report from Saigon on February 2, 1964, concluded by

[46]U.S., Congress, House, Committee on Appropriations, *Department of Defense Appropriations for 1965*, Subcommittee Hearings, pt. 4, 88th Cong., 2d sess. (Washington, D.C.: U.S. Govt. Print. Off., 1964), p. 101. Also indicative of congressional skepticism about the progress of the war and the role of the U.S. were questions raised when McNamara testified in executive sessions of the House Armed Services Committee on Jan. 27 and 29, 1964, just before the Khanh coup. (These hearings are still closed, but there are excerpts in *PP*, Gravel ed., vol. III, pp. 35-36.) He was asked if he continued to be as optimistic about withdrawing U.S. forces as he had been in Oct. 1963, and whether the withdrawal plan was still in effect. He replied that it was a "South Vietnamese war," that the role of the U.S. was to help them, and that "by keeping the crutch there too long we would weaken the Vietnamese rather than strengthen them." He was asked whether the U.S. was planning "to do anything to bring this war to the VC . . . to change the modus operandi of this war, so far as the bleeding of this country is concerned?" Again, he replied that it was a Vietnamese war.
[47]*Department of Defense Appropriations for 1965*, p. 12.
[48]*Ibid.*, p. 117.

saying, ". . . no amount of military effort or capability can compensate for poor politics. Therefore, although the prospects for an improved military posture are good, the ultimate achievement of the established military goal depends primarily upon the quality of support achieved by the political leadership of the government of Vietnam at all levels." As the *Pentagon Papers* analysis notes, "Here again was an explicit judgment that the *sine qua non* of an effective counterinsurgency operation was a stable, broadly-based, popular and effective government. It was acknowledged at this time, as it had been acknowledged before concerning other governments, that a government of these qualities did not exist. But . . . there was apparently always the hope that fate would not close in before something happened to change the situation."[49]

During February 1964, the situation in Vietnam worsened rapidly as the Communists, who had accelerated their efforts in December 1963 after a decision by the North Vietnamese to provide greater assistance to the guerrillas in the south, increased their hold on the countryside. On February 12, supported by a survey in Vietnam by Lyman D. Kirkpatrick (then one of the highest ranking CIA officials), and Peer de Silva, the new station chief in Saigon (replacing Richardson), the CIA concluded in a Special National Intelligence Estimate that "the situation in South Vietnam is very serious and prospects uncertain. Even with U.S. assistance as it is now, we believe that, unless there is a marked improvement in the effectiveness of the South Vietnamese government and armed forces, South Vietnam has, at best, an even chance of withstanding the insurgency menace during the next few weeks or months." Kirkpatrick said he was "shocked by the number of our people and of the military, even those whose job is always to say we are winning, who feel that the tide is against us."[50]

From his post on the NSC staff, Forrestal felt the same way, and in a memorandum to McNamara on February 14, in which he made some suggestions for the trip McNamara was to make to Vietnam in the middle of March, Forrestal said, among other things, "I have the impression that since last November 1st [the date Diem was deposed] our own efforts in support of what we call the Strategic Hamlet Program have deteriorated badly . . . all of the mixed civil and military counterinsurgency programs which about a year ago seemed to be working well."[51]

Faced with this critical situation, the U.S. responded, first, politically, by efforts to achieve greater control over the machinery of government and the conduct of the war in South Vietnam, and, second, militarily, by stepping up pressures on the Communists, particularly by extending the war into North Vietnam.

The political response took the form primarily of increased pressure on the South Vietnamese to expand the role and influence of U.S. advisers, civilian as well as military. When this proposal (which was similar to General Lansdale's 1961 recommendation for *"encadrement"*) was first broached with the junta after the Novem-

---

[49] *PP*, Gravel ed., vol. III, p. 41.

[50] These and other excerpts from the Kirkpatrick report, and the excerpt from the SNIE, are in *ibid.*, pp. 41-42. Both reports are still classified.

[51] Johnson Library, NSF Aides File, McGeorge Bundy Memos to the President.

ber 1963 coup, General Minh argued that it would "play into the hands of the VC and make the Vietnamese officials look like lackeys. There would be a colonial flavor to the whole pacification effort. Minh added that even in the worst and clumsiest days of the French they never went into the villages or districts." He said that U.S. training of troops organized among political sects (he mentioned specifically the Cao Dai and the Hoa Hao) "was bad because they then became American type soldiers, not Vietnamese soldiers." "'We simply cannot govern this country if this kind of conduct continues.'"[52] Minh and his colleagues doubtless were concerned that they would suffer the same fate as Diem, and wanted to limit U.S. influence in the internal affairs of Vietnam. It is also arguable, however, that, like Diem and Nhu, they resented the growing dominance of the United States, and genuinely believed that Americanization of the war would play into the hands of the Communists.

Unable to persuade Minh, the U.S. attempted to get Khanh to accept the idea. On February 3, 1964, only a week after the coup, and the day before Khanh formally took office, the State Department urged the U.S. mission in Saigon to reopen the question of placing more U.S. advisers in sub-units of the Government of South Vietnam. State told Lodge, "It might be useful to point out to Khanh that . . . proposed extension U.S. advisory structure would represent expansion U.S. commitment to support GVN in war against VC." Moreover, if Khanh would not agree to a general plan, State told Lodge to suggest that U.S. advisers be used in several districts "to lay basis for determining whether there is any substantial ill effect in political sense from their presence." Khanh not only agreed to this latter suggestion (he accepted U.S. advisers in 13 districts in the delta), but went so far as to ask Lodge to recommend Vietnamese for the position of Prime Minister and for the Cabinet. Lodge suggested some names, but, according to the *Pentagon Papers,* he did not recommend individuals for specific posts.[53]

In addition to these political proposals, U.S. policymakers considered a range of new military programs. On January 22, 1964, General Taylor, Chairman of the JCS, sent a comprehensive JCS memorandum to McNamara recommending an expansion of military operations in Southeast Asia, especially Vietnam, which he said was needed to achieve the victory over Communist forces that President Johnson had reaffirmed as the U.S. goal in NSAM 273 (November 26, 1963). "In order to achieve that victory," Taylor said, "the Joint Chiefs of Staff are of the opinion that the United States must be prepared to put aside many of the self-imposed restrictions which now limit our efforts, and to undertake bolder actions which may embody greater risks."

These were the principal justifications and recommendations presented in that important memorandum:[54]

> Currently we and the South Vietnamese are fighting the war on the enemy's terms. He has determined the locale, the

[52]*PP,* Gravel ed., vol. II, pp. 307-308.
[53]*Ibid.,* p. 309, and Saigon to Washington 1451, Jan. 31, 1964, and 1483, Feb. 4, 1964, and Washington to Saigon 1192, Feb. 7, 1964. Johnson Library, NSF Country File, Vietnam.
[54]*PP,* Gravel ed., vol. III, pp. 496-499.

timing, and the tactics of the battle while our actions are essentially reactive. One reason for this is the fact that we have obliged ourselves to labor under self-imposed restrictions with respect to impeding external aid to the Viet Cong. These restrictions include keeping the war within the boundaries of South Vietnam, avoiding the direct use of US combat forces, and limiting US direction of the campaign to rendering advice to the Government of Vietnam. These restrictions, while they may make our international position more readily defensible, all tend to make the task in Vietnam more complex, time consuming, and in the end, more costly. In addition to complicating our own problem, these self-imposed restrictions may well now be conveying signals of irresolution to our enemies—encouraging them to higher levels of vigor and greater risks. A reversal of attitude and the adoption of a more aggressive program would enhance greatly our ability to control the degree to which escalation will occur. It appears probable that the economic and agricultural disappointments suffered by Communist China, plus the current rift with the Soviets, could cause the communists to think twice about undertaking a large-scale military adventure in Southeast Asia.

In adverting to actions outside of South Vietnam, the Joint Chiefs of Staff are aware that the focus of the counterinsurgency battle lies in South Vietnam itself, and that the war must certainly be fought and won primarily in the minds of the Vietnamese people. At the same time, the aid now coming to the Viet Cong from outside the country in men, resources, advice, and direction is sufficiently great in the aggregate to be significant—both as help and as encouragement to the Viet Cong. It is our conviction that if support of the insurgency from outside South Vietnam in terms of operational direction, personnel, and material were stopped completely, the character of the war in South Vietnam would be substantially and favorably altered. Because of this conviction, we are wholly in favor of executing the covert actions against North Vietnam which you have recently proposed to the President [34-A]. We believe, however, that it would be idle to conclude that these efforts will have a decisive effect on the communist determination to support the insurgency; and it is our view that we must therefore be prepared fully to undertake a much higher level of activity, not only for its beneficial tactical effect, but to make plain our resolution both to our friends and to our enemies.

Accordingly, the Joint Chiefs of Staff consider that the United States must make ready to conduct increasingly bolder actions in Southeast Asia; specifically as to Vietnam to:

    a. Assign to the US military commander responsibilities for the total US program in Vietnam.

    b. Induce the Government of Vietnam to turn over to the United States military commander, temporarily, the actual tactical direction of the war.

    c. Charge the United States military commander with complete responsibility for conduct of the program against North Vietnam.

d. Overfly Laos and Cambodia to whatever extent is necessary for acquisition of operational intelligence.

e. Induce the Government of Vietnam to conduct overt ground operations in Laos of sufficient scope to impede the flow of personnel and material southward.

f. Arm, equip, advise, and support the Government of Vietnam in its conduct of aerial bombing of critical targets in North Vietnam and in mining the sea approaches to that country.

g. Advise and support the Government of Vietnam in its conduct of large-scale commando raids against critical targets in North Vietnam.

h. Conduct aerial bombing of key North Vietnam targets, using US resources under Vietnamese cover, and with the Vietnamese openly assuming responsibility for the actions.

i. Commit additional US forces, as necessary, in support of the combat action within South Vietnam.

j. Commit US forces as necessary in direct actions against North Vietnam.

W. W. Rostow, Director of the State Department's Policy Planning Council, also called for bolder action against North Vietnam. In a memorandum to Rusk on February 13, 1964, he declared.[55]

South Vietnam is in danger. The internal position in South Vietnam created by the systematic operations conducted from North Vietnam is precarious. . . . although difficult tasks would still be faced in South Vietnam and Laos if North Vietnamese compliance with the 1962 agreement was enforced. We see no possibility of achieving short-run or long-run stability in the area until it is enforced.

In that same memorandum, according to the *Pentagon Papers*,[56] Rostow also said that there had been some State Department discussions "on the desirability of the President's requesting a congressional resolution, drawing a line at the borders of South Vietnam." "Even this early in the Johnson administration," Rostow said subsequently, "word had gotten back to the bureaucracy that Johnson disapproved of Truman's failure to seek a congressional resolution in the Korean War. We understood that, should the occasion arise, he intended to be governed by Eisenhower's precedent in the Formosa and Middle East resolutions, where broad congressional support was sought before policies that might lead to military confrontations were carried out."[57]

On February 18, the JCS followed up its memorandum of January 22 with recommendations to McNamara for specific immediate actions:[58]

a. Induce the GVN (General Khanh) military to accept U.S. advisors at all levels considered necessary by COMUSMACV [Commander, U.S. Military Assistance Command, Vietnam]. (This is particularly applicable in the critical provinces). . . .

---

[55] *Ibid.*, vol. II, p. 310. The memorandum—the *Pentagon Papers* refers to it as a letter—is still classified.
[56] *Ibid.*, vol. III, p. 153.
[57] *The Diffusion of Power*, p. 505.
[58] *PP*, Gravel ed., vol. III, pp. 44-45.

b. Intensify the use of herbicides for crop destruction against identified Viet Cong areas as recommended by the GVN.

c. Improve border control measures. . . .

d. Direct the U.S. civilian agencies involved in Vietnam to assist the GVN in producing a civilian counterpart package plan to the GVN National Pacification Plan . . . .

e. Provide U.S. civilian advisors to all necessary echelons and GVN agencies . . . .

f. Encourage early and effective action to implement a realistic land reform program.

g. Support the GVN in a policy of tax forgiveness for low income population in areas where the GVN determines that a critical state of insurgency exists . . . .

h. Assist the GVN in developing a National Psychological Operations Plan . . . to establish the GVN and Khanh's "images," create a "cause" which can serve as a rallying point for the youth/students of Vietnam, and develop the long term national objectives of a free Vietnam.

i. Intensify efforts to gain support of U.S. news media representatives in Washington . . . .

j. Arrange U.S. sponsored trips to Vietnam by groups of prominent journalists and editors.

k. Inform all GVN military and civilian officials . . . that the United States (a) considers it imperative that the present government be stabilized, (b) would oppose another coup, and (c) that the United States is prepared to offer all possible assistance in forming a stable government . . . all U.S. intelligence agencies and advisors must be alert to and report cases of dissension and plotting in order to prevent such actions.

According to the memorandum, these measures would not have a "decisive effect in the campaign against the Viet Cong," however, and the Joint Chiefs were continuing to study other, more drastic steps, including the following:

a. Intensified operations against North Vietnam to include air bombings of selected targets;

b. Removal of restrictions for air and ground cross-border operations;

c. Intelligence and reporting;

d. U.S. organizational changes;

e. Increased U.S. Navy participation in shore and river patrol activities;

f. Introduction of jet aircraft into the Vietnamese Air Force and the U.S. Air Commando unit. . . .

In mid-February, 1964 the JCS also recommended a concentrated counterinsurgency effort in the province of Long An (which had been the subject of discussion in December after reports that the situation in that key province was deteriorating, contrary to the optimistic reporting of Harkins and Krulak). Acting in Lodge's absence, Deputy Chief of Mission David G. Nes objected strongly to the proposal on the grounds that the U.S. did not have the influence to persuade the Government of Vietnam to take such action, nor was the GVN politically strong enough to launch an effective operation. Moreover, it was a mistake,. Nes said, to assume that such an "indigenous Communist insurgency with full external support could be defeated by an 'offensive' of finite duration."[59]

In a memorandum to Lodge on February 17, Nes explained his position, based on his observations during two months as Lodge's deputy. He said he had decided that de Gaulle was right in believing that the U.S. faced either the possible collapse of its counterinsurgency program in South Vietnam or an escalation which could lead to direct military conflict between the U.S. and North Vietnam and China. Nes did not think the U.S. counterinsurgency program could stem the tide:[60]

Nothing that I have seen or heard thus far in Saigon leads me to believe that against the background of recent Vietnamese history our counter-insurgency efforts can win through so long as the Viet Cong is backed politically and psychologically and to a lesser extent militarily by Hanoi and Peking.

The peasants who form the mass of the South Vietnamese population are exhausted and sick of 20 years of civil conflict. During this entire period they have never and are not now receiving either political leadership or orderly and just administration from the central authorities of the GVN. They have enjoyed little if any social or economic betterment.

On the other hand, the Viet Cong represents a grass roots movement which is disciplined, ideologically dedicated, easily identifiable with the desires of the peasantry and of course ruthless. The fact that the VC has the full backing of China is perhaps its most powerful asset in presenting itself as the inevitable winner.

I do not see in the present military regime or any conceivable successor much hope in providing the real political and social leadership or the just and effective country-wide administration so essential to the success of our counter-insurgency program.

I think we would be naive in the extreme to believe that any number or quality of American advisors can succeed in changing within a reasonable period of time the attitudes and patterns of thinking of senior Vietnamese military and political officialdom.

In developing a large conventional World War II Vietnamese military establishment organized into Four Corps and 9-10 divisions with other equally sizable supporting units, we may, in fact, have a Frankenstein on our hands which on the one hand serves little purpose in dealing effectively with the Viet Cong and on the other provides a perfect framework for spawning successive coups and so perpetuating the current political malaise.

On February 18, the President met with his top advisers (Rusk, McNamara, McCone and Taylor), and with the members of the newly-established interdepartmental Vietnam Coordinating Com-

---

[59] *Ibid.*, vol. II, p. 310. For confirmation of Nes' position, see the excellent study by Jeffrey Race, *War Comes to Long An* (Berkeley: University of California Press, 1972).
[60] "Where We Stand in Vietnam" Johnson Library, Nes Papers.

mittee.[61] At this meeting, the President directed that "Contingency planning for pressures against North Vietnam should be speeded up. Particular attention should be given to shaping such pressures so as to produce the maximum credible deterrent effect on Hanoi."[62]

On February 21, President Johnson used a speech in California as a vehicle for delivering a carefully prepared warning to the North Vietnamese to cease and desist or be prepared for the consequences:

> In South Viet-Nam, terror and violence, directed and supplied by outside enemies, press against the lives and liberties of a people who seek only to be left in peace. For 10 years our country has been committed to the support of their freedom, and that commitment we will continue to honor. The contest in which South Viet-Nam is now engaged is first and foremost a contest to be won by the government and the people of that country for themselves. But those engaged in external direction and supply would do well to be reminded and to remember that this type of aggression is a deeply dangerous game.[63]

There is no indication that Johnson's warning had any effect on the North Vietnamese.

On February 26, as pressure for attacking the North Vietnamese continued to grow, including actions against increased North Vietnamese activities in Laos, especially the infiltration of South Vietnam through Laos, the JCS recommended flights over Laos by Vietnamese and U.S. aircraft for both reconnaissance and the display of power. On February 25, the State Department, in a draft memorandum for the President, recommended, according to the *Pentagon Papers,* "deploying twelve F-100's to Thailand, with a view toward its potential deterrence and signalling impacts on communist activities in Laos."[64]

On March 2, 1964, the JCS sent two memoranda to McNamara recommending further action. The first, "Removal of Restrictions for Air and Ground Cross Border Operations," proposed that direct action be taken against the Communists in Laos to demonstrate that the U.S. was determined to eliminate their use of Laos as a "sanctuary" for conducting or supporting operations in South Vietnam. The second proposed direct airstrikes against North Vietnam to demonstrate U.S. determination to oppose Communist aggres-

---

[61]The interdepartmental committee on Vietnam, chaired by William H. Sullivan of the State Department, was established on Feb. 14, 1964, by NSAM 280. Its members were:
John T. McNaughton, DOD
Maj. Gen. Rollen H. Anthis, JCS
Maj. Gen. Lucius Clay, Jr., USAF
William Colby, CIA
Joseph Mendenhall, State
Walter Stoneman, AID
William Jorden, State

[62]*PP,* Gravel ed., vol. III, p. 154, from a White House memorandum for the record, "South Vietnam," Feb. 20, 1964, that is still classified. This decision was not promulgated by a NSAM.

[63]*Public Papers of the Presidents,* Lyndon B. Johnson, 1963-1964, p. 304.

[64]*PP,* Gravel ed., vol. III, pp. 156-157, from the unpublished classified paper, "Stabilizing the Situation in Southeast Asia." It is unclear as to where the State Department memorandum originated and who cleared it in the form cited by the *Pentagon Papers,* as well as whether it was ever sent to the President.

sion in Southeast Asia, and to convince the North to cease assisting the South.[65]

Report of the Vietnam Committee

After the February 18 White House meeting, the Vietnam Committee, as ordered by the President, quickly drew together plans for increasing the pressure on North Vietnam. Robert Johnson, Rostow's deputy on State's Policy Planning Council, was the coordinator of the planning process, and the proposals were in the form of a memorandum which he sent to William Sullivan (head of the Vietnam Coordinating Committee) in draft on March 1, with other versions on March 13 and 19, 1964. The subject of the memo was "Alternatives for Imposition of Measured Pressure Against North Vietnam," and, according to the *Pentagon Papers,* there were the following attachments: "a 'White Paper' detailing Hanoi's role; a Presidential statement of our rationale and limited intent; a Congressional resolution; and diplomatic consultations."[66]

Thus, by March 13, 1964, the draft text of a congressional resolution had been prepared by the Vietnam Committee as a key element in the series of steps leading to increased pressure on North Vietnam.

It is unfortunate that the Vietnam Committee memorandum—the first comprehensive plan for expanding the Vietnam war, and for using overt military force against North Vietnam—is still classified, but fortunately the *Pentagon Papers* contains a lengthy description of the plan and, based on that account, these appear to have been the principal points in the memorandum:[67]

(1) The strategic concept on which increased pressure on North Vietnam would be based was "North Vietnamese concern that their industrialization achievements might be wiped out or could be defended (if at all) only at the price of Chicom control," and "that their more powerful Communist allies would not risk their own interests for the sake of North Vietnam."

(2) There were five objectives of increased pressure against North Vietnam—

A. induce North Vietnam to cease support of the Communists in the South;

B. reduce the morale of the Communists in the South;

C. strengthen the Khanh government and discourage neutralization;

D. demonstrate to the world U.S. determination to combat Communist aggression;

E. strengthen morale in Asia.

In addition, it was argued that such pressure would improve the U.S. negotiating position. (Negotiation was considered "virtually inevitable.")

(3) Pressure against North Vietnam, however, was "no substitute for successful counterinsurgency in South Vietnam." "It

---

[65]This information, taken from a chronology in *ibid.,* p. 120, is the only information available on these two memoranda, both of which are still classified.
[66]*PP,* DOD ed., book 3, IV. C. 2. (a), fn. 27.
[67]*PP,* Gravel ed., vol. III, pp. 154-156. Portions in quotations are from the memorandum itself.

is not likely that North Vietnam would (if it could) call off the war in the South even though U.S. actions would in time have serious economic and political impact. Overt action against North Vietnam would be unlikely to produce reduction in Viet Cong activity sufficiently to make victory on the ground possible in South Vietnam unless accompanied by new U.S. bolstering actions in South Vietnam and considerable improvement in the government there. The most to be expected would be reduction of North Vietnamese support of the Viet Cong for a while and, thus, the gaining of some time and opportunity by the government of South Vietnam to improve itself."

(4) The U.S. should be prepared to "follow through against Communist China if necessary," but it was unlikely that the Chinese or the Russians would intervene militarily except for providing equipment and supplies.

After examining three alternative forms of pressure, (1) covert, non-attributable actions, (2) overt U.S. deployment and actions not directed toward North Vietnam, and, (3) overt U.S. actions against North Vietnam, the memorandum considered six military moves with the greatest potential, ranked, according to the *Pentagon Papers*, "in ascending order of the degree of national commitment":

(1) "deploy to Thailand, South Vietnam, Laos and elsewhere the forces, sea, air and land, required to counter a North Vietnamese or Chicom response of the largest likely order";

(2) "initiate overt air reconnaissance activities as a means of dramatizing North Vietnamese involvement," beginning with high-level flights and following with low-level missions;

(3) "take limited air or ground action in Cambodia and Laos, including hot pursuit across the Cambodian border and limited operations across the Laos border";

(4) "blockade Haiphong," which would "have dramatic political effect because it is a recognized military action that hits at the sovereignty of North Vietnam and suggests strongly that we may plan to go further";

(5) "establish a limited air defense capability around Saigon"; and

(6) conduct air strikes on key North Vietnamese LOC's, [lines of communication] infiltrator training camps, key industrial complexes, and POL [petroleum, oil, lubricants] storage.

Recognizing the desirability of rallying Congress and the public behind the position that U.S. actions against North Vietnam were in reaction to North Vietnamese aggression, as well as the importance of assuming such a position in U.S. relations with other countries, the memorandum also stated, "public justification of our action and its expressed rationale must be based primarily upon the fact of Northern support for and direction of the war in the South in violation of the independence of South Vietnam." It discussed a number of steps for accomplishing this, both in the United States and abroad.

The memorandum cautioned against undertaking any action without calculating what the U.S. could and might do depending upon the reaction from the north, including how far the U.S. would escalate militarily if the North Vietnamese did not respond to pressure or decided to escalate in response to pressure.

While new plans were being developed for responding to the situation in Vietnam, Roger Hilsman, who was preparing to leave the State Department on March 14, 1964, was summarizing his views in two final memoranda and a parting letter to Rusk. In the memoranda, he again urged that first priority should be given to establishing security in the villages, leading to the creation of a secure area which could then be extended—the "oil blot principle"— rather than having a scattering of fortified villages. He repeated his position that instead of conducting large military operations, "the way to fight a guerrilla is to adopt the tactics of a guerrilla. . . ." He favored covert operations against North Vietnam, but said that, with respect to overt operations, ". . . significant action against North Vietnam that is taken before we have demonstrated success in our counterinsurgency program will be interpreted by the Communists as an act of desperation, and will, therefore, not be effective in persuading the North Vietnamese to cease and desist. What is worse, I think that premature action will so alarm our friends and allies and a significant segment of domestic opinion that the pressures for neutralization will become formidable."[68]

In his letter to Rusk on March 17, 1964, however, Hilsman advocated strengthening "our overall military posture in southeast Asia in ways which will make it clear that we are single-mindedly improving our capability to take whatever military steps may be necessary to halt Communist aggression in the area."[69] He expressed concern that "since the fall of Dienbienphu, all Asians have wondered about our determination to fight in Southeast Asia, should fighting become necessary." In Vietnam itself, he said, "De Gaulle, Lippmann and Mansfield have set the neutralist hares running with self-fulfilling prophecies that dishearten those who wish to fight and encourage coup-plotting among both the true neutralists and the simple opportunists. But what gives these lofty, unrealistic thoughts of a peaceful neutralist Asia their credibility is, again, fundamental doubts about our ultimate intentions."

To impress upon the Communists that the U.S. "might escalate hostility to a level unacceptable to them," and "that we are prepared to go as far as necessary to defeat their plans and achieve our objectives," Hilsman recommended the deployment of "substantial" U.S. ground and air forces to Thailand, where they should be maintained "quite indefinitely," together with implications that

---

[68] *Ibid.*, pp. 40-44. See also *To Move A Nation*, pp. 535-536. The memoranda themselves are still classified. William Bundy (Bundy MS., ch. 12, p. 19) says that Hilsman's "'either/or' discussion of the 'military' and 'political' approaches simply does not square with the idiom of policy debate at any time in 1963-1964. . . . Nor, I might add, does it fit with the prescriptions in Mr. Hilsman's own farewell memoranda of Mar. 1964. In parts not quoted in his book, these included the greatest possible stress on demonstrative action, specifically a major deployment of ground forces to Thailand, to show Hanoi that the US would 'take whatever measures are necessary in Southeast Asia to protect those who oppose the Communists and to maintain our power and influence in the area.' As his book does show, Mr. Hilsman also stood quite ready to see bombing of infiltration bases and other targets in the north, but said this should come only after improvement in the south had been achieved—the very conclusion the Administration reached in March and June.

"Whether Mr. Hilsman's ideas on 'counter-guerrilla' warfare were ever practical for South Vietnam and for dealing such the infiltration routes is a question I must leave to others. For what it is worth, I (and I am sure many others at policy levels) always thought he was right in considerable degree, but asking more than a demoralized South Vietnamese force could deliver for years to come."

[69] Hilsman's letter is now available at the Johnson Library, NSF Aides File, McGeorge Bundy Memos for the President.

U.S. ground forces could also be sent to Laos if necessary. This should be accompanied, he said, "by a diplomatic offensive designed (1) to reassure our friends as to our determination, and (2) to warn the Communist side that they are indeed playing a 'deeply dangerous game.'"

Report of the McNamara-Taylor-McCone Mission, and the Approval of NSAM 288

By early March 1964, President Johnson was preoccupied with getting congressional approval of legislation for his proposed "war on poverty," as well as other domestic legislation which he considered important. He was also obviously concerned about and deeply involved in Presidential election politics in preparation for the November 1964 Presidential election. The situation in Vietnam had not improved, however, and with the draft report of the Vietnam Coordinating Committee in hand he was faced with making another round of decisions about U.S. policy. His reaction was to send McNamara on another mission to Vietnam on March 8, and then to use the report of that mission as the vehicle for making a decision which he hoped would meet the needs of the situation without adversely affecting either his domestic program or his political campaign. This limited action, however, resulted in the further involvement of the U.S. in Vietnam in 1964, and laid the groundwork for U.S. military intervention in 1965.

After spending five days in Vietnam, McNamara, accompanied by Taylor and McCone, reported back to the President on March 16, and filed his report on March 17. The report did not recommend bombing North Vietnam. It did recommend, however, that plans be made for bombing the North, both through "quick reaction strikes" and in more sustained actions, as a part of the application of greater pressure on North Vietnam.

On March 17, the NSC discussed the report.[70] According to the notes of the meeting, Johnson asked McNamara "if his program would reverse the current trend in South Vietnam. Secretary McNamara replied that if we carry out energetically the proposals he has made, Khanh can stem the tide in South Vietnam, and within four to six months, improve the situation there." General Taylor added that the Joint Chiefs believed the proposed program was acceptable, but thought that to make it effective the U.S. would have to take military action against North Vietnam.

"The President summarized the alternatives to the recommended course of action, i.e., putting in more U.S. forces, pulling out of the area, or neutralizing the area. He said the course we are following is the only realistic alternative. It will have the maximum effectiveness with the minimum loss," adding that this would not foreclose other action later if the situation did not improve. He asked the group whether there were any objections to the proposals. No one objected. That day the McNamara report was issued verbatim as NSAM 288.[71]

---

[70]Sanitized notes of the meeting are in the Johnson Library, NSF NSC Meetings File.
[71]The text of the report (and thus also the text of NSAM 288) is in *PP*, Gravel ed., vol. III, pp. 499-510.

These were the principal points made in the McNamara-Taylor-McCone report:

(A) The U.S. objective is to maintain an "independent, non-Communist South Vietnam." If this fails, all of Southeast Asia would be threatened. There would also be general ramifications for U.S. policy, because Vietnam was "regarded as a test case of U.S. capacity to help a nation meet a Communist 'war of liberation.'"

(B) Although the situation in South Vietnam has worsened, "it does not appear likely that major equipment replacement and additions in U.S. personnel are indicated under current policy." Replacement of Americans by Vietnamese was still sound, and would demonstrate that the war was a Vietnamese responsibility. Furthermore, "Substantial reductions in the numbers of U.S. military training personnel should be possible before the end of 1965."

(C) In terms of possible courses of action, a negotiated settlement leading to neutralization, as proposed by de Gaulle, "would simply mean a Communist take-over in South Vietnam." "Even talking about a U.S. withdrawal would undermine any chance of keeping a non-Communist government in South Vietnam, and the rug would probably be pulled before the negotiations had gone far."

(D) With respect to the other two alternatives—military action against North Vietnam, and steps to improve the situation in the South, the former would be "extremely delicate," and might not be effective. Moreover, until the Khanh government was more secure, "an overt extension of operations into the North carries the risk of being mounted from an extremely weak base which might at any moment collapse and leave the posture of political confrontation worsened rather than improved." There were, however, a number of steps that could and should be taken to help the South Vietnamese, and if the Khanh government "takes hold vigorously," the situation should improve "in the next four to six months."

(E) "If the Khanh government takes hold vigorously—inspiring confidence, whether or not noteworthy progress has been made—or if we get hard information of significantly stepped-up VC arms supply from the North, we may wish to mount new and significant pressures against North Vietnam. We should start preparations for such a capability now. . . . The reasoning behind this program of preparations for initiating action against North Vietnam is rooted in the fact that, even with progress in the pacification plan, the Vietnamese Government and the population in the South will still have to face the prospect of a very lengthy campaign based on a war-weary nation and operating against Viet Cong cadres who retained a measure of motivation and assurance."

(F) Accordingly, the President should instruct agencies of the U.S. Government:

1. To make it clear that we are prepared to furnish assistance and support to South Vietnam for as long as it takes to bring the insurgency under control.

2. To make it clear that we fully support the Khanh government and are opposed to any further coups.

3. To support a Program for National Mobilization (including a national service law) to put South Vietnam on a war footing.

4. To assist the Vietnamese to increase the armed forces (regular plus paramilitary) by at least 50,000 men.

5. To assist the Vietnamese to create a greatly enlarged Civil Administrative Corps for work at province, district and hamlet levels.

6. To assist the Vietnamese to improve and reorganize the paramilitary forces and to increase their compensation.

7. To assist the Vietnamese to create an offensive guerrilla force.

8. To provide the Vietnamese Air Force 25 A-1H aircraft in exchange for the present T-28s.

9. To provide the Vietnamese Army additional M-113 armored personnel carriers (withdrawing the M-114s there), additional river boats, and approximately $5-10 million of other additional material.

10. To announce publicly the Fertilizer Program and to expand it with a view within two years to trebling the amount of fertilizer made available.

11. To authorize continued high-level U.S. overflights of South Vietnam's borders and to authorize "hot pursuit" and South Vietnamese ground operations over the Laotian line for the purpose of border control. More ambitious operations into Laos involving units beyond battalion size should be authorized only with the approval of Souvanna Phouma. Operations across the Cambodian border should depend on the state of relations with Cambodia.

12. To prepare immediately to be in a position on 72 hours' notice to initiate the full range of Laotian and Cambodian "Border Control" actions (beyond those authorized in paragraph 11 above) and the "Retaliatory Actions" against North Vietnam, and to be in a position on 30 days' notice to initiate the program of "Graduated Overt Military Pressure" against North Vietnam.

According to the *Pentagon Papers*,[72] NSAM 288 ". . . outlined a program that called for considerable enlargement of U.S. effort. It involved an assumption by the United States of a greater part of the task, and an increased involvement by the United States in the internal affairs of South Vietnam, and for these reasons it carried with it an enlarged commitment of U.S. prestige to the success of our effort in that area. . . ."

The *Pentagon Papers* also makes the point[73] that "Although VC successes in rural areas had been the prime feature of the downswing over the past half year or more, pacification was to receive less comparative emphasis."

[72] *Ibid.*, p. 50.
[73] *Ibid.*, p. 54.

The Defense Department and the JCS immediately began planning for the implementation of items 11 and 12 on the above list of 12 actions, and on April 17 the JCS approved OPLAN 37-64, the proposed plan for exerting graduated military pressure on North Vietnam, which later served as the blueprint for the escalation of U.S. military action in 1965.

OPLAN 37 was "a three-phase plan covering operations against VC infiltration routes in Laos and Cambodia and against targets in North Vietnam. Phase I provided for air and ground strikes against targets in South Vietnam, and hot pursuit actions into Laotian and Cambodian border areas. Phase II provided for 'tit-for-tat' airstrikes, airborne/amphibious raids, and aerial mining operations against targets in North Vietnam. Phase III provided for increasingly severe airstrikes and other actions against North Vietnam, going beyond the 'tit-for-tat' concept."[74] As part of OPLAN 37, a list of North Vietnamese targets was drawn up, called the "94 Target List," which became the guide for target selection in bombing the North.

Although OPLAN 37 was developed in response to a current program of planning, Gen. William C. Westmoreland later said, "Those of us in Saigon who knew of OPLAN 37 saw little possibility that the President would implement it until after the November election. Indeed, we saw it strictly as a postelection plan."[75]

Even as the basis was being established for using overt military force against the North, Johnson continued to control the U.S. commitment to Vietnam, and, more importantly at that point, he attempted to control also the level of congressional and public concern about the situation. According to Doris Kearns, "He did know that there were difficult decisions to be made. But he needed time, and in any event an election year was no time to make them. The word went out that tough decisions on Vietnam should be deferred as long as possible. . . . Opinion surveys showed that more than two-thirds of the American public said they paid little or no attention to what was going on in Vietnam. Johnson wanted to keep it that way."[76]

On March 26, McNamara and Taylor met with the Foreign Relations Committee in an informal, unrecorded session.[77] McNamara reported that the situation in Vietnam had worsened. He was asked about Laos, and he replied that there, too, the situation was unstable and dangerous, and would be much worse if the U.S. withdrew from Vietnam. Cambodia would also fall quickly to the Communists, followed by Thailand.

Commenting on alternatives, McNamara said that withdrawal was not worth discussing, and that de Gaulle's proposal for a negotiated settlement and for neutrality could lead to a situation in

[74] *Ibid.*, p. 287. OPLAN 37-64 is still classified.

[75] William C. Westmoreland, *A Soldier Reports* (Garden City, N.Y.: Doubleday, 1976), p. 109.

[76] *Lyndon Johnson and the American Dream*, pp. 197-198. William Bundy says in response to Kearns: "If 'the word went out,' it never reached me. On the contrary I can recall at least one strong injunction from LBJ to call it as we saw it, regardless of politics or the election. Of course the election played a part, as did the fact that LBJ was in some sense a caretaker. But explicit mention of the sort described here was rare, and never came to me." William Bundy letter to CRS, Dec. 9, 1984.

[77] There is no transcript of this meeting. Comments here are based on notes in the committee files in the National Archives, RG 46.

which South Vietnam would be unable to ask for outside assistance, and would be taken over by the Communists. He added that, contrary to his public statements, de Gaulle privately did not think a negotiated settlement was possible.

General Taylor outlined for the committee the alternative of applying force against North Vietnam. Three kinds of military pressure were being considered, he said: first, border control operations; second, a selective program of retaliation; third, an escalation of military pressure against the north.

Senator Fulbright said that with regard to the third category (escalation), the French once had 200,000 men in Indochina, and he wondered whether, in the event of escalation, the U.S. would put in large numbers of forces. McNamara replied that the U.S. would not use large forces, and that the major pressures would be applied by airpower.

Senator Albert Gore asked how McNamara squared his comments about increasing pressures with his statements in the fall of 1963 regarding the reduction of U.S. forces. McNamara replied that a program of new military pressures should not require additional U.S. forces in Vietnam; that the U.S. would attack by air.

Meanwhile, after their telephone conversation of March 2, Fulbright, as was mentioned earlier, publicly supported the President's position on Vietnam in a speech in the Senate on March 25, 1964, entitled "Old Myths and New Realities."[78] U.S. foreign policy, said Fulbright, suffered from the divergence "between the realities of foreign policy and our ideas about it." ". . . we are handicapped . . . by policies based on old myths, rather than current realities." Americans needed, he said, "to start thinking some 'unthinkable' thoughts about the cold war and East-West relations, about the underdeveloped countries and particularly those in Latin America, about the changing nature of the Chinese Communist threat in Asia and about the festering war in Vietnam." After dealing with the other subjects, Fulbright concluded the speech with comments on Vietnam, noting that, as compared with reevaluation of basic U.S. foreign policy in the Far East generally, "The situation in Vietnam poses a far more pressing need for a reevaluation of American policy." Other than withdrawal, which he did not think "could be realistically considered under present circumstances," there were three options: first, to continue the war in the South, second, to end the war and negotiate neutralization of South Vietnam or all of Vietnam, and, third, to expand the war, "either by the direct commitment of large numbers of American troops or by equipping the South Vietnamese Army to attack North Vietnamese territory, possibly by means of commando-type operations from the sea or the air." He said that a negotiated settlement was not an alternative as long as South Vietnam was in such a weak bargaining position. He concluded, therefore, that there were only two options: expanding the war, or assisting the South Vietnamese "to prosecute the war successfully on its present scale."

---

[78] *CR*, vol. 110, pp. 6227-6232. This was subsequently printed as the lead chapter in Fulbright's book of the same title.

Morse responded to Fulbright[79] by repeating his proposal for taking the Vietnam problem to the U.N., after first attempting to solve it through the SEATO framework. Fulbright replied that he thought the U.N. approach was "futile," and that, "The Vietnamese situation is one in which I do not see any feasible way in which it will be possible to apply any rules of law." The U.S., he said, had "little choice but to try to stabilize conditions to see if we cannot help the present Government acquire, and I hope merit, the support of the people of that country who are free to exercise any choice." "Rightly or wrongly, we are deeply involved," he said; ". . . we are committed to the point where it would be quite disastrous for this country to withdraw." He added, however, that he was "extremely reluctant to expand the commitment."

During his speech Fulbright made the following cryptic statement, indicating that he had some knowledge of the fact that the executive branch was considering future options, and that he was not going to take a position that would foreclose his own consideration of such proposals as the President might subsequently make: "The matter [whether to expand the war] calls for thorough examination by responsible officials in the executive branch; and until they have had an opportunity to evaluate the contingencies and feasibilities of the options open to us, it seems to me that we have no choice but to support the South Vietnamese Government and Army by the most effective means available." "Whatever specific policy decisions are made," he added, "it should be clear to all concerned that the United States will continue to meet its obligations and fulfill its commitments with respect to Vietnam." What those "obligations" and "commitments" were, Fulbright did not say, but it was apparent that he was helping to lay the groundwork for the possible expansion of the war. It is also interesting to note his reference to the examination of options by officials in the executive branch, with no reference to the possible value of congressional participation in such a process.

At his news conference three days later (March 28), Johnson was asked about Fulbright's speech. He replied that he did not agree with some of Fulbright's comments, but he revealed that he had had dinner with Fulbright the Sunday before the March 25 speech, and that they had discussed Vietnam "in some detail."[80]

On March 26, the day he met with the Senate Foreign Relations Committee, McNamara, gave a major speech in which he used almost the same analytical framework as Fulbright had used. (The decision to make the speech had been made at a White House meeting on March 16, and the White House, as well as State, participated extensively in the writing of the speech.)[81] In the speech, McNamara discussed, and rejected, withdrawal or a negotiated settlement, and said that there remained only two options: expanding the war, and helping the South Vietnamese to win the war in the South. With respect to the former, McNamara said, "This course of action—its implications and ways of carrying it out—has been carefully studied." "Whatever ultimate course of action may be forced

[79] *Ibid.*, pp. 6238-6244. This was followed by a reply to Fulbright by Gruening.
[80] *Public Papers of the Presidents,* Lyndon B. Johnson, 1963-1964, p. 429.
[81] See Kennedy Library, Thomson Papers, folder entitled "1964 McNamara Vietnam Speech."

upon us by the other side," he added, "it is clear that actions under this option would be only a supplement to, not a substitute for, progress within South Vietnam's own borders." As for helping the Vietnamese, he said, this was essential, and the U.S. had pledged such assistance "for as long as it takes to bring the insurgency under control."[82]

The following day, March 27, 1964, McNamara formally (but without public notice) terminated the planning, begun in the summer of 1962, for withdrawing U.S. forces from Vietnam. The *Pentagon Papers* had this comment: "Although the Vietnamese knew that the 'withdrawal' of 1,000 men in December 1963 had been a pretense, his action now removed any remaining doubt about our intentions."[83]

Implementing NSAM 288 While Restraining Khanh

After the issuance of NSAM 288 on March 17, the development of plans for increasing pressure on North Vietnam intensified. The central point of coordination was the Office of International Security Affairs in the Defense Department, with assistance from Bundy's Far East bureau (William Bundy had replaced Hilsman) and the Vietnam Coordinating Committee in State, as well as from the JCS. During March and April several versions of these plans were produced, each consisting of "scenarios" of increasing pressures on the North, from covert U.S. support of South Vietnamese 34-A operations, to open U.S. and South Vietnamese attacks on the North. At each stage it was planned that there would be steps to secure congressional and public support, as well as support from other countries.[84]

On April 19-20, 1964, Rusk, William Bundy, General Wheeler and others met in Saigon with Lodge, Harkins and others to discuss the scenarios. "Much of the discussion," according to the *Pentagon Papers,*[85] "centered on the political context, objectives, and risks, of increasing military pressure on North Vietnam. It was understood that it would be first exerted solely by the Government of Vietnam, and would be clandestine. Gradually both wraps and restraints would be removed." There was considerable discussion as to how best to let the North Vietnamese know what the consequences would be if they did not cease supporting the Communists in the South.

During the meetings, Lodge suggested, as he had first proposed several months earlier, that a "carrot and stick approach" be tried before initiating any additional military pressures on the North. ". . . the carrot and stick concept envisioned a secret contact with Hanoi at which an ultimatum would be delivered demanding the DRV's cessation of support for the VC insurgency. Rewards for compliance would include our making available food imports to help alleviate the known food shortages affecting North Vietnam in late 1963 (and early '64). In the case of non-compliance, we

---

[82]*PP*, Gravel ed., vol. II, pp. 315-316. For the text, see *Department of State Bulletin*, Apr. 13, 1964. For Morse's reply to McNamara, see *CR*, vol. 110, pp. 6468-6470.

[83]*PP*, Gravel ed., vol. II, p. 316.

[84]None of these documents has been made public, and there is only a brief discussion of them in the *Pentagon Papers*. See *ibid.*, vol. III, pp. 121-123, and 157-162.

[85]*Ibid.*, p. 65.

would undertake previously threatened punitive strikes to which we would not admit publicly."[86] Lodge suggested that the secret contact be made by Canadian diplomat J. Blair Seaborn, whom he knew, who was about to be sent to Vietnam to serve on the International Control Commisssion. It was agreed that this would be done.[87]

Lodge did not object to the proposed program of increased pressure on North Vietnam, but he was unsure whether such a program would produce the desired result. He also took the position that massive intervention by the north in the south could not be met by conventional force.

During the meetings there was some discussion of the use of nuclear weapons against the north, and speculation as to whether this would cause the Russians to enter the war. Rusk apparently had reservations, both about the results of destroying North Vietnamese industrial installations, which he doubted would have much of an adverse effect on North Vietnam or on its support of the Communists in the south, and about the use of nuclear weapons. William Bundy, "for argument's sake," the *Pentagon Papers* said,[88] conjectured that the use of nuclear weapons in unpopulated areas for troop interdiction might have more of an impact on the Communists than if used otherwise.

Rusk made several suggestions for additional military pressure, including the stationing of a U.S. naval unit at Tourane or Cam Ranh Bay, to indicate to the North Vietnamese the determination of the United States to defend the south.

Although the meeting did not produce any significant new decisions or action (except for an agreement on the Seaborn mission), the "direction of thinking" in the group "was clearly away from measures internal to Vietnam, and clearly headed toward military action against the North." "In certain circles in Washington at least, there was what appears now to have been an amazing level of confidence that we could induce the North Vietnamese to abandon their support of the SVN insurgency if only we could convince them that we meant business, and that we would indeed bomb them if they did not stop their infiltration of men and supplies to the South."[89]

---

[86] *Ibid.*, p. 163.

[87] On Apr. 40, 1904, William Sullivan and Chester Cooper went to Ottawa and arranged with the Canadians to make such a diplomatic contact with North Vietnam, *Ibid*, pp. 65-66 and 163-164. On June 18 Seaborn met with North Vietnamese premier Pham Van Dong. He presented a statement of the U.S. position and offer of assistance, and warned of the consequences for North Vietnam of continued support of the Communists in the South. Then, and in another meeting on Aug. 15, Pham Van Dong is reported to have listened patiently, but indicated that the North Vietnamese, too, were confident of their cause. *Ibid.*, p. 292. In his memoirs, *(The Vantage Point,* p. 67), Johnson described the effort to communicate through Seaborn, and concluded, "Obviously, the Communist leaders believed they were winning in the South. . . . We could only conclude from his experience that the North Vietnamese had no desire to limit their actions or to negotiate. . . ." For the Seaborn mission, as well as subsequent U.S. efforts to negotiate with North Vietnam, see the four "negotiating volumes" of the *Pentagon Papers*, (book 12 of the DOD edition), which were declassified and made public after the release of the earlier volumes in that series. See also the excellent study by Wallace J. Thies, *When Governments Collide: Coercion and Diplomacy in the Vietnam Conflict, 1964-1968* (Berkeley: University of California Press, 1980).

[88] Gravel ed., vol. III, p. 65.

[89] *Ibid.*, pp. 64-65.

On April 22, members of the NSC met to hear a report on Rusk's trip. The President joined the group toward the end of the meeting. Among the more general points that Rusk made (some of the notes have been deleted) was the problem of the "Limitation of funds— we may not be doing some of the things that we ought to be doing in Vietnam because we still think that we must limit expenditures."[90] Yet, Rusk added, "As compared to the cost of a war or our withdrawal, the amount of money we are spending in Vietnam is small." McNamara agreed. The U.S., he said, was ". . . right on the margin in Vietnam and that he could not guarantee that we would still be there in six months or twelve months from now. Therefore, we should pour in resources now even if some of them were wasted because of the terrific cost that would be involved if we had to use U.S. forces."

Somewhat more optimistic statements were made by William Bundy and General Wheeler. Bundy said ". . . we are now getting good reporting in both the political and military fields. Newspaper reporters have been misleading us. Unrest within the South Vietnam government has been exaggerated. The security situation is much better than as reported in the press." Wheeler added, "We should be encouraged by the progress which was being made."

On April 23, W. W. Rostow sent Rusk another memo—"On How Much Flesh and Blood Can Stand: Laos and Vietnam"—in which he argued that if the U.S. did not act to prevent further deterioration in the situation in Vietnam and Laos it would become much more difficult to make a credible case for possible efforts to force the North Vietnamese to adhere to the 1954 and 1962 Geneva Accords.[91]

On May 4, 1964, Khanh told Lodge that he wanted to move against the North. He said he wanted to declare a state of war and put South Vietnam on a war basis, including ". . . getting rid of the so-called 'politicians' and having a government of . . . technicians." He wanted to threaten the North with reprisal if there was further interference in South Vietnam's affairs, and he asked Lodge if the U.S. would consider "tit-for-tat" reprisal bombing each time there was North Vietnamese interference in South Vietnam. He also urged that the U.S. deploy 10,000 Special Forces along the frontier with Cambodia and Laos. Lodge did not make any commitments on U.S. forces (although he told Khanh he was opposed to large U.S. ground force operations on the Asian mainland), but he did tell Khanh that the war came first, and that "democratic forms" could wait.[92] Washington's reaction was immediate and firm. After conferring with the President, the State Department sent a "flash" cable to Lodge stating that the meeting with Khanh posed extremely grave issues, and the U.S. response had to be developed with great care. On May 6, Johnson met with his advisers, and it was agreed that McNamara, who was preparing to go to Saigon, would tell Khanh that the U.S. did ". . . not intend to pro-

[90]Johnson Library, NSF NSC Meetings File.
[91]*PP*, Gravel ed., vol. III, p. 164; the memo is still classified.
[92]*Ibid.*, vol. II, p. 317. A copy of Lodge's cable, Saigon to Washington 2108, May 4, 1964, is in the Johnson Library, NSF Country File, Vietnam.

vide military support nor undertake the military objective of roll-
ing back Communist control in North Vietnam."[93]

On May 12-14, 1964, McNamara, General Taylor, John T.
McNaughton (who had replaced Bundy as Assistant Secretary of
Defense for International Security Affairs), General Wheeler, William Sullivan, and Michael Forrestal visited Vietnam to review implementation of the NSAM 288 decisions. Discussions were held
with Khanh, at which McNamara expressed concern about
Khanh's lack of progress, but also, as instructed by Johnson, told
Khanh that drastic measures against the north were not necessary
at that time.

Forrestal met with Vietnamese officials to review administrative
and financial matters, and it was agreed that the U.S. would increase its financial assistance. (Late in April Khanh had requested
that three U.S. experts in finance-economics, foreign affairs, and
press be assigned to him personally. "We Vietnamese want the
Americans to be responsible with us and not merely as advisors,"
he was reported to have said. This proposal, which was similar to
the one the U.S. had made to Minh, was agreed to, and the three
advisers were assigned to Khanh early in May 1964.)[94]

It is of interest to note that during the Saigon meetings McNamara stated that the use of U.S. personnel in combat had not been
authorized, and that efforts to use Vietnamese personnel should be
intensified. Exceptions to this policy, he said, obviously echoing
Johnson's concern, were to be considered undesirable and were not
to be viewed as precedents for the future. Operation FARM GATE,
in which, among other things, Vietnamese commando-reconnais-
sance teams were dropped in North Vietnam and Laos from U.S.-
manned aircraft, was, he said, a specific exception—a "supplementary effort transitory in nature," that he had approved reluctantly.
It should also be noted, however, that while in Saigon McNamara
authorized, doubtless after approval by the President, a doubling
each month of the number of such teams being dropped over North
Vietnam and Laos. McNamara, according to the record of the
meeting, was anxious to get more information about assistance
being given by North Vietnam to the Communists in the South.[95]

On May 15, McNamara reported to a meeting of the members of
the NSC to which the President had invited a group of Democratic
and Republican congressional leaders.[96] In his report, McNamara
said that the situation was worse than at the time of his last visit
in March. "The number of people under Viet Cong control and the
amount of Vietnamese territory they hold is increasing. The Viet
Cong holds the initiative in the military action. The Khanh government is fragmented and a religious crisis is brewing. . . . Khanh

---

[93]*PP*, Gravel ed., vol. III, p. 67. For a copy of the cable, Washington to Saigon 1838, May 5,
1964, see the Johnson Library, NSF Country File, Vietnam. Within the JCS, the Air Force and
Marine representatives favored low-level reconnaissance and airstrikes against North Vietnam.
See Futrell, *The Advisory Years to 1965,* p. 204.

[94]*PP*, Gravel ed., vol. II, p. 317. For the McNamara meetings in Saigon, May 12-14, see vol. III,
pp. 67-72, and 164-165, as well as vol. II, p. 318. According to Shaplen, *The Lost Revolution,* p.
250, ". . . the brain-trust plan was never accepted by the Vietnamese, in principle or in fact,
and the United States, as it had so often done before, simply backed down and didn't insist upon
its implementation."

[95]*PP*, Gravel ed., vol. III, p. 70.

[96]Johnson Library, NSF NSC Meetings File.

controls eight out of fourteen million South Vietnamese. His major problem is not military but civilian and religious."

McNamara added that Khanh ". . . does not feel that he should strike north before his security situation in the south is improved, possibly by this fall. No strike to the north is required now, but there may be a psychological requirement to hit North Vietnam at a later time."

"The President summarized the McNamara report by saying that the situation in South Vietnam was deteriorating and caused us to be extremely alarmed. The religious aspect is explosive. A great effort will be necessary to turn the tide back to our side." He said that he would soon be sending Congress a request for additional funds for Vietnam, but he added, ". . . even with increased U.S. aid the prospect in South Vietnam is not bright."

Criticism Rises

Meanwhile, congressional and public criticism of U.S. policy in Vietnam was increasing. On May 13, 1964, the *Wall Street Journal* printed an editorial entitled "Error Upon Error," commenting on McNamara's trip: ". . . no matter how many high officials visit Vietnam, or how frequently, nothing gets clarified. Except, that, is, the continuing failure of U.S. policy." The editorial continued:

. . . it is almost impossible to figure out what is the U.S. strategy, if any—that is, how it thinks it can in fact drive the Communists out and keep them out. Not that anyone expects the Pentagon to reveal its war plans in detail; it is rather that the evidence indicates the lack of any plan which promises to be workable against the varied and successful tactics of the Communists.

Not even the commitment of many more American soldiers or the bombing of Communist bases in the north, which has been talked of off and on, would be guaranteed to accomplish the objective. In other circumstances perhaps, but not necessarily against this particular enemy, in this particular terrain, with this particular ally.

At the same time the French solution of neutralizing all of Vietnam sounds like a proposal in a vacuum, at least for the present. Why should Ho Chi Minh, the dictator of the north, want to neutralize when he is doing so well as it is? Or if he did want to we may be sure he would see it as a means of continuing the conquest.

We do not rule out the possibility that the United States may somehow someday turn the tide, any more than we rule out the possibility that the realities of the situation may finally dictate withdrawal. But whatever happens, the U.S. involvement in Vietnam reveals a series of classic military and political errors from which it may be hoped the Government will eventually profit. . . .

No nation should count on military success, even limited, in the most unfavorable circumstances. No piece of territory is beyond all price, worth any cost, as the French finally discovered 10 years ago after such great cost. And the United States, for all its great power, cannot forever police the world alone and unaided.

Morse and Gruening, as well as Ellender, were also stepping up their attacks, with one or the other or both speaking at almost every meeting of the Senate on what Morse had begun calling "McNamara's War."[97]

McNamara's response was, "I must say, I don't object to its being called McNamara's war. I think it is a very important war and I am pleased to be identified with it and do whatever I can to win it."[98] "Well, at long last, we have smoked him out," Morse said, upon hearing of McNamara's comment. "We now have an admission from the Secretary of Defense that this Nation is engaged in war." He continued:[99]

> I ask the Secretary of Defense, I ask the Secretary of State, I ask the President: When are you going to ask for a declaration of war? I say from the floor of the Senate that the killing of American boys in South Vietnam cannot be justified, except on the basis of a declaration of war. I charge that McNamara's war stands today an unconstitutional war. It is now up to the President, the Secretary of State, and the Secretary of Defense to send to Congress a declaration of war proposal. They should ask for constitutional approval of the killing of American boys in McNamara's war.

On April 24, James Thomson, William Bundy's Special Assistant in the Far East Bureau (he was formerly with Under Secretary Bowles), sent Bundy a memorandum summarizing congressional comments on the far east, especially Vietnam, during Bundy's absence from Washington during the middle of April. "Although Morse and Gruening appear to have made no admitted converts in this period," Thomson said, "they have encountered little rebuttal from their colleagues. . . . At the same time, in addition to support previously expressed by Senator Ellender, friendly questioning has revealed backing for aspects of their view from Senators Symington, John L. McClellan (D/Ark.) and Long (of Louisiana). In addition, H [the Congressional Relations Office of the State Department] reports that a growing number of Senators are privately sympathetic with the Morse-Gruening position."[100]

On May 13, Bundy testified on Vietnam before a closed, un-recorded session of the Far East Subcommittee of the Senate Foreign Relations Committee chaired by Senator Lausche. In advance of the meeting, Bundy's staff prepared various documents for his use, including a memorandum rebutting Morse's doubts about the legal basis for U.S. involvement in Vietnam. In a cover memo to Bundy to which these documents were attached, his assistant, Jonathan Moore cautioned him with respect to certain weaknesses in the administration's legal case. ". . . we are on pretty thin ice in certain instances," Moore said, "and accordingly must be cautious when attempting to fight on his battleground." After citing these weaknesses he advised Bundy that although it was important to make the legal case for U.S. involvement, he should "shift gears rapidly

---

[97]Other Senate Democrats defended McNamara. See, for example, *CR*, vol. 110, p. 8411.
Of Morse's many speeches during April, the most important was one he delivered on Apr. 24, *ibid.*, pp. 8996-9013.
[98]*New York Times*, Apr. 25, 1964.
[99]*CR*, vol. 110, p. 9070.
[100]Kennedy Library, Thomson Papers. The "H" stands for (Capitol) Hill.

into a general (practical and political) rationale away from isolated technical details which the purely legal discussion tends to enhance." Morse was arguing that the Vietnam question should be taken to the U.N., Moore said, and "We have good answers to this question if we don't become exclusively embroiled in the legal discussion." He added, "I think that Senator Morse just might run out of gas on this one. At any rate, we should ignore him as much as possible rather than giving him more fuel for the fire."[101]

That same day (May 13), Morse returned to the attack in a speech in the Senate in which repeated many of the arguments he had been making.[102] "South Vietnam," he said, "is the Achilles' heel of this administration. South Vietnam is the Achilles' heel of our whole foreign policy. . . . It is a U.S. puppet, with its government controlled by the United States, taking U.S. orders. It is a U.S. protectorate." "We are trying," he added, "to pick up the failure of Great Britain, France, the Dutch, and every other colonial power in Asia of the last 50 years, and we will end with the same failure. Asia will not be run by white men. . . . In trying to fight on ground and terms alien to the United States, we are needlessly killing Americans for an objective we eventually will have to abandon."

Morse said that "the only answer is to withdraw American military forces from South Vietnam." The U.N., he said, should play a peace-keeping role in South Vietnam, "under some arrangement which for want of a better description I would label a form of United Nations trusteeship, [and] maintain peace in the area until the people there finally develop the ability and the incentive to govern themselves on the basis of exercising their own will as to what form of government they wish."

Morse was congratulated by Senator Olin Johnston, a Southern Democrat (South Carolina) who was a liberal on economic issues but conservative on defense and foreign policy. Johnston said he agreed with Morse's criticism of the U.S. role in Vietnam, and with the suggestion that the matter should be taken to the U.N.

During this time there were also the first signs of antiwar feeling among American college students. The earliest expression of this occured at Yale University on March 13-15, 1964, when participants in a student conference on socialism, including members of the new-left Students for a Democratic Society, *SDS*, (formerly the student department of the socialist League for Industrial Democracy), formed an ad hoc May Second Committee (subsequently known as the May 2nd Movement, or M2M) to organize a demonstration against the war in New York City on May 2, 1964. The march, which attracted about 1,000 people, was followed in the fall of 1964 by an M2M petition calling on draft-age college students to pledge that they would not fight in Vietnam. This also attracted only a small number of persons (about 1,000 signatures were collected), but it was, as one author has noted, "the first of the 'We Won't Go' statements and a precursor of the draft-refusal movement of later years."[103]

---

[101]Kennedy Library, same location.
[102]*CR*, vol. 110, pp. 10826 ff.
[103]Kirkpatrick Sale, *SDS* (New York: Random House, 1973), p. 161.

Students on other campuses were also beginning to express their opposition to the war. On May 20, 1964, a group of students at the University of California (Berkeley), which subsequently became known for extensive antiwar activities, sent a telegram to Senator Gruening asking for the withdrawal of U.S. military personnel from Vietnam.[104] Faculty were also becoming involved. On July 10, 1964, a petition on Vietnam which had been circulated by the National Committee for a Sane Nuclear Policy (SANE), and signed by more than 5,000 college and university professors (several thousand others were added afterwards), was presented to the Johnson administration. It called on the President not to enlarge the war, and to seek neutralization of the area. One of the signers and presenters was Hans Morgenthau who had been an active member of the American Friends of Vietnam in the 1950s.[105]

On the other hand, there continued to be considerable support for U.S. policy in Vietnam from Congress, the press and the public. On May 9, 1964, columnist C. L. Sulzberger of the *New York Times* (and a member of the family that owned the paper), who had numerous contacts among American and other government elites, argued that "a continued policy of neither war nor peace" would lead to the neutralization of Vietnam, which would be a "humiliating sham," a "political repetition of Dienbienphu." "The time for a showdown has come," he said. "We certainly don't want holocaust any more than we wanted holocaust in Cuba 18 months ago. But we cannot afford a self-defeating strategy. . . . So long as we permit the Communists to fight according to their own rules, to train and equip guerrillas in a northern safe-haven and then send them south, we cannot crush them. Our only hope of military triumph and positive political settlement would be to destroy their aggressive base. We should never contemplate invading North Vietnam. But it is time to announce that if aggression is not stopped, we will pulverize its bases and communications."[106]

Laos Flares Up Again, and Planning for U.S. Action in Vietnam Intensifies

In mid-May 1964, at about the time McNamara and his party returned from Vietnam, the Communists staged an offensive in Laos, (after a dispute within the coalition government and the arrest of Souvanna Phouma by the rightists), that produced great concern in Washington.[107] The JCS called for more intensive covert operations in the upcoming second quarter of 34-A, and urged that these plans be worked out as quickly as possible with South Vietnam. The Chiefs also advocated airstrikes against Laos and North Vietnam, and outlined the projected timetable and results of graduated operations, ranging from those conducted by the Vietnamese alone to those in which U.S. forces in the Pacific would play a major role.[108]

---

[104]*CR*, vol. 110, pp. 11754-11755.
[105]*New York Times*, July 11, 1964.
[106]*Ibid.*, May 9, 1964.
[107]For a description of these events see Dommen, *Conflict in Laos*, pp. 261 ff.
[108]For the JCS proposals, see *PP*, Gravel ed., vol. III, pp. 165-166.

On May 21, a little noted but important decision was made to begin the first direct, overt U.S. military action in Indochina. With the consent of Souvanna Phouma, the U.S. began reconnaissance flights over enemy-occupied territory in Laos.[109] In addition, a U.S. troop alert was ordered in Okinawa, and the Seventh Fleet was readied for action. U.S. planes began ferrying Laotian troops, and U.S. personnel flew combat missions in planes of the Laotian air force.[110]

That same day, Mansfield endorsed a proposal made the day before by President de Gaulle to reconvene the Geneva Conference on Laos. Not only was it in the interest of the United States to avoid military involvement in Laos, Mansfield said, but there was also "little likelihood that the situation in Vietnam can be improved without an understanding in Laos along the lines which General de Gaulle is apparently hopeful of achieving. . . . we must continue our economic and military assistance to Vietnam, but we should also consider most carefully the conference proposed by President de Gaulle. It may well be the last train out for peace in southeast Asia."[111]

On May 20, as a result of the events in Laos, and growing problems in Vietnam, the President directed his advisers to prepare two basic plans for action in Vietnam, one political and the other military, for his consideration. He may also have been prompted to do so by the advice of Dean Acheson, with whom he had maintained a close relationship for many years, which was reported to him on May 19 in a memorandum from one of his assistants, Douglass Cater. Cater said he had talked to Acheson the night before, and that "He is greatly concerned that situation in Viet Nam will soon enter phase when new initiatives become impossible because of convention and campaign period here at home. He urged that any assessment of stepping up involvement in Indo-China take into account that we must act quickly or be prepared to stall for a while."[112]

On May 21, Rusk sent Lodge an "eyes only" cable expressing his concern about the failure of the South Vietnamese to create a greater sense of solidarity against the Communists, all well as more effective actions by the government to increase public confidence and support. It is worth quoting in full:[113]

1. Situation in Southeast Asia is clearly moving toward basic decisions both in the Free World and in the communist world. The present activity with regard to Cambodia, Laos and Viet Nam illustrates that the central issue of pressures from the communist North will have to be faced not just by us but by other allies.

2. [words deleted] The Geneva Accords of 1962 are very specific and have been grossly violated by the continued presence of Viet Minh in Laos and the persistent use of Laos for infiltration of South Viet Nam. We intend to press very hard for the

---

[109]This may have been the subject of one of the two NSAMs issued on May 19, 1964, but even the titles of these are still classified.
[110]Stevenson, *The End of Nowhere*, pp. 201-202.
[111]*CR*, vol. 110, p. 11552.
[112]Johnson Library, NSF Name File, Cater Memos.
[113]Johnson Library, NSF Country File, Vietnam, Washington to Saigon 2027, May 21, 1964.

full and complete implementation of those Accords on the basis of an international and legal position which is very strong indeed.

3. At a time when we and other governments are facing decisions on further military action in Southeast Asia, including the possibility of actions against North Viet Nam, the fragility of the present sitution in South Viet Nam is very much on our minds. On the basis of my talks with Congressional leaders and committees and a sensing of public concern about Southeast Asia, I am convinced that the American people will do what has to be done if there is something to support. The prospect that we might strike the North, with all of the attendant risks, only to lose the south is most uninviting.

4. We need your judgment as to what more can be done to achieve both the reality and appearance of greater solidarity in South Viet Nam and to improve the actual administrative performance of the government itself in grappling with its awesome problems.

5. When I was in Saigon, we talked about whether the non-governmental community could be stimulated to demonstrate solidarity with the fight against the Viet Cong. Recent reports of new religious crises, grumblings among senior officials of government, delays in administration action to get on with the most elementary tasks of government are all disconcerting. From this end we are prepared to furnish men, material, funds on whatever scale is required to defeat the Viet Cong. But I feel the need to assure the President that everything humanly possible is being done both in Washington and by the Government of Viet Nam to provide a solid base of determination from which far-reaching decisions could proceed. I would greatly appreciate, therefore, your comments on such questions as the following, plus any others along the same lines which might occur to you.

(a) Is there any way in which we can shake the main body of leadership by the scruff of the neck and insist that they put aside all bickering and lesser differences in order to concentrate upon the defeat of the Viet Cong?

(b) Can we find some way to get the leaders of the religious communities to declare a moratorium on their differences until the anti-religious communist threat has been thrown back?

(c) How can we provide personnel experienced and trained in military government to work along side Viet Namese counterparts in order to galvanize the machinery of Government?

(d) Can we find some way by which General Khanh can convince larger segments of the people that they have a stake in the success of his leadership against the Viet Cong?

(e) Can we devise further incentives to enlist the full cooperations of ordinary people both in the cities and in the countryside to pursue the struggle as one in which they are personally involved?

6. Everyone here in Washington is deeply impressed by the magnitude and difficulty of the problems faced by General Khanh, yourself and General Harkins but, in the face of a prospect of a deepening crisis and the possible necessity for asking the American people to accept larger sacrifices and grave risks, we want to be sure that nothing is left undone which could be done to strengthen the position of South Viet Nam itself.

I find it hard to believe, for example, that General Khanh and General Minh cannot find a basis to work together as patriotic Viet Namese even though it may require General Khanh to take some chances on working with some of those he displaced when he assumed power. I do not understand why so much delay in strengthening the puny diplomatic effort of Viet Nam abroad. I can't see why we are just now able to approve a January budget. I can't see why materials in warehouses and pipelines cannot be moved promptly to the countryside to achieve the purpose from which such materials are being supplied. Surely administration can go on a war footing and French techniques of triple entry bureaucracy can be set aside in order to get prompt action. Having served in India, Burma and China during World War II I have had considerable personal experience with how deliberate all deliberate speed can be in that part of the world, but somehow we must change the pace at which these people move and I suspect that this can only be done with a pervasive intrusion of Americans into their affairs. I would deeply appreciate it if you would give me your best judgment as to how we on the American side can further stimulate Viet Namese solidarity and effort. In other words, what more can we do to make it quite clear to the American people that if a great deal more is required of them there is something solid to support and that what we may ask of them has point and the prospect of success.

On May 22, McGeorge Bundy reported to the President that four groups were working on the plans which were requested by the President on May 20.[114] One group under McNaughton was working on the military plan, the "theory" of which was "that we should strike to hurt but not to destroy, and strike for the purpose of changing the North Vietnamese decision on intervention in the south." The second group, under William Sullivan, was working on "marrying Americans to Vietnamese at every level, both civilian and military." "The object of this exercise is to provide what Khanh has repeatedly asked for: the tall American at every point of stress and strain." The third group, under Chester Cooper, was analyzing enemy reactions to possible U.S. moves. The fourth group, under George Ball, was "drafting alternative forms of a Congressional resolution so as to give you a full range of choice with respect to the way in which you would seek Congressional *validation* of wider action. (emphasis added) The preliminary consensus is that such a resolution is essential before we act against North Viet-

---

[114]Johnson Library, NSF Aides File, McGeorge Bundy Memos for the President.

nam, but that it should be sufficiently general in form not to commit you to any particular action ahead of time."

On May 23, the McNaughton group completed a new "scenario" for pressure against North Vietnam. Unlike previous scenarios, this one did not provide for intermediate "deniable" steps involving substantial attacks that would not be acknowledged. In a cable to Lodge on May 22, Rusk explained that it had been concluded that such operations could not be successfully concealed.[115] Lodge replied that firm action against the North by South Vietnam and the U.S. was the only way to achieve a significant improvement in South Vietnam's self-defense.[116]

The May 23 "Scenario for Strikes on North Vietnam" was based on the assumption that, as the memo stated, "additional efforts within South Vietnam by the U.S. will not prevent further deterioration there." This is the text of the proposed scenario for the 30-day period, D-30 to D-Day:[117]

1. Stall off any "conference on [Laos or] Vietnam until D-Day."

2. Intermediary (Canadian?) tell North Vietnam in general terms that U.S. does not want to destroy the North Vietnam regime (and indeed is willing "to provide a carrot"), but is determined to protect South Vietnam from North Vietnam.

3. (D-30) Presidential speech in general terms launching Joint Resolution.

4. (D-20) Obtain Joint Resolution approving past actions and authorizing whatever is necessary with respect to Vietnam.

Concurrently: An effort should be made to strengthen the posture in South Vietnam. Integrating (interlarding in a single chain of command) the South Vietnamese and U.S. military and civilian elements critical to pacification, down at least to the district level, might be undertaken.

5. (D-16) Direct CINCPAC to take all prepositioning and logistic actions that can be taken "quietly" for the D-Day forces and the forces described in Paragraph 17 below.

6. (D-15) Get Khanh's agreement to start overt South Vietnamese air attacks against targets in the North (see D-Day item 15 below), and inform him of U.S. guarantee to protect South Vietnam in the event of North Vietnamese and/or Chinese retaliation.

7. (D-14) Consult with Thailand and the Philippines to get permission for U.S. deployments; and consult with them plus U.K., Australia, New Zealand and Pakistan, asking for their open political support for the undertaking and for their participation in the re-enforcing action to be undertaken in anticipation of North Vietnamese and/or Chinese retaliation.

8. (D-13) Release an expanded "Jordan [sic] Report," including recent photography and evidence of the communications

<hr>

[115] *PP*, Gravel ed., vol. III, pp. 166-167. In another cable he asked Lodge to redouble his efforts to achieve greater solidarity in South Vietnam. "We need to assure the President that everything humanly possible is being done both in Washington and by the government of Vietnam to provide a solid base of determination from which far-reaching decisions could proceed."

[116] *Ibid.*, p. 166.

[117] *Ibid.*, pp. 167-168.

nets, giving full documentation of North Vietnamese supply and direction of the Viet Cong.

9. (D-12) Direct CINCPAC to begin moving forces and making specific plans on the assumption that strikes will be made on D-Day. . . .

10. (D-10) Khanh makes speech demanding that North Vietnam stop aggression, threatening unspecified military action if he does not. (He could refer to a "carrot.")

11. (D-3) Discussions with Allies not covered in Item 7 above.

12. (D-3) President informs U.S. public (and thereby North Vietnam) that action may come, referring to Khanh speech (Item 10 above) and declaring support for South Vietnam.

13. (D-1) Khanh announces that all efforts have failed and that attacks are imminent. (Again he refers to limited goal and possibly to "carrot.")

14. (D-Day) Remove U.S. dependents.

15. (D-Day) Launch first strikes. . . . Initially, mine their ports and strike North Vietnam's transport and related ability (bridges, trains) to move South; and then against targets which have maximum psychological effect on the North's willingness to stop insurgency—POL storage, selected airfields, barracks/training areas, bridges, railroad yards, port facilities, communications, and industries. Initially, these strikes would be by South Vietnamese aircraft; they could then be expanded by adding FARMGATE, or U.S. aircraft, or any combination of them.

16. (D-Day) Call for conference on Vietnam (and go to UN). State the limited objective: Not to overthrow the North Vietnam regime nor to destroy the country, but to stop DRV-directed Viet Cong terrorism and resistance to pacification efforts in the South. Essential that it be made clear that attacks on the North will continue (*i.e.*, no cease-fire) until (a) terrorism, armed attacks, and armed resistance to pacification efforts in the South stop, and (b) communications on the networks out of the North are conducted entirely in uncoded form."

On May 24 and 25 the principal members (called the Executive Committee, or ExCom) of the NSC considered the scenario, and on May 25 a memorandum from them, "Basic Recommendations and Projected Course of Action on Southeast Asia," was signed and sent to the President by McGeorge Bundy.

These were its recommendations:[118]

1. It is recommended that you make a Presidential decision that the U.S. will use selected and carefully graduated military force against North Vietnam, under the following conditions: (after appropriate diplomatic and political warning and preparation, (2) and unless such warning and preparations—in combination with other efforts—should produce a sufficient improvement of non-Communist prospects in South Vietnam and in Laos to make military actions against North Vietnam unnecessary.

---

[118]Johnson Library, NSF Country File, Vietnam.

2. This basic Presidential decision is recommended on these premises:

(1) that the U.S. cannot tolerate the loss of Southeast Asia to Communism;

(2) that without a decision to resort to military action if necessary, the present prospect is not hopeful, in South Vietnam or in Laos.

(3) that a decision to use force if necessary, backed by resolute and extensive deployment, and conveyed by every possible means to our adversaries, gives the best present chance of avoiding the actual use of such force.

The memorandum added, however, "It is further recommended that our clear purpose in this decision should be to use all our influence to bring about a major reduction or elimination of North Vietnamese interference in Laos and in South Vietnam, and *not* to unroll a scenario aimed at the use of force as an end in itself."

In making these recommendations, the memorandum stated:

It is the hope and best estimate of most of your advisers that a decision of this kind can be executed without bringing a major military reply from Red China, and still less from the Soviet Union. It is also the prevailing estimate that selective and carefully prepared military action against North Vietnam will not trigger acts of terror and military operations by the Viet Cong which would engulf the Khanh regime. *Nevertheless, it is recognized that in making this decision we must accept two risks:* (1) the risk of escalation toward major land war or the use of nuclear weapons; (2) the risk of a reply in South Vietnam itself which would lose that country to neutralism and so eventually to Communism." (emphasis in original)

The memorandum recommended the following course of action, to be taken in the sequence given:

(1) A Presidential decision. . . .

(2) *The establishment of communication with Hanoi (through the Canadians) and with other adversaries of major importance (USSR, France, [sic] Red China).*

The purpose of these communications would be to make very clear both the seriousness of U.S. will and the limited character of U.S. objectives. We intend that Communism shall not take over Southeast Asia, but we do not intend or desire the destruction of the Hanoi regime. If terror and subversion end, major improvement in relations is possible. It is only if they do not end that trouble is coming.

(3) *A Honolulu conference and discussion with Thailand.*

This meeting, which might occur early next week, would be directed to the establishment of full understanding with Ambassador Lodge and MACV, and to possible intense consultations with Ambassador Unger and Ambassador Martin from Thailand. At the same time, or just after, we would communicate our basic determination and our opening strategy to the governments of Thailand, Laos and South Vietnam. This Honolulu meeting would imply major decisions also to intensify our efforts in South Vietnam (along lines to be presented in a separate paper).

(4) *Action at the UN.*
This would probably take a double form:
(a) *in the broadest terms,* we would present the problem of Communist aggression in Southeast Asia, together with much hitherto secret evidence proving Hanoi's responsibility;
(b) *in parliamentary terms,* we would probably ask a resolution confined to the Pathet Lao aggression in Laos. It is the current estimate of our UN experts that on a wider resolution involving South Vietnam we might not have the necessary seven votes for affirmative action. The one thing we do not want is to take our basic political case to the UN and fail to muster a majority.
The basic object of this exercise would be a double one:
(a) to give worldwide publicity to the basic problem through the voice of Stevenson, and
(b) to make it perfectly plain if we move to further action that we had done our best at the UN.

(5) *A formal announcement by us and by our friends that the requirements of the UN resolution (whether or not it was vetoed) are not being met.*
The purpose of this step is to clarify again that we have tried the UN and that it is not our fault that there has been an inadequate response.

(6) *Consultation of SEATO allies.*
We believe this should take place both by a meeting of the SEATO Council in Bangkok and by more intense consultations in the capitals of the more energetic members of SEATO, notably Australia, New Zealand, Great Britain, The Philippines, and Thailand. We do not expect Pak or French support. The object would be to obtain basic agreement on the next steps toward action and commitment of forces at as high a level as possible.

(7) *The first deployments toward Southeast Asia of U.S. and, hopefully, allied forces.*
It is our recommendation that these deployments be on a very large scale, from the beginning, so as to maximize their deterrent impact and their menace. We repeat our view that a pound of threat is worth an ounce of action—as long as we are not bluffing.

(8) *A Congressional Resolution.*[119]
We agree that no such resolution should be sought until Civil Rights is off the Senate calendar, and we believe that the preceding stages can be conducted in such a way as to leave a free choice on the timing of such a resolution. Some of us recommend that we aim at presenting and passing the resolution between the passage of Civil Rights and the convening of the Republican Convention. Others believe that delay may be to our advantage and that we could as well handle the matter later in the summer, in spite of domestic politics.

---

[119]For the text of the draft congressional resolution proposed on May 25, see *PP,* DOD ed., book 4, IV. C. 2., following p. 42.

(9) *A further and expanded deployment of military force toward the theater.*

The object of this continuing deployment, after the passage of the resolution, is to give still more time for threat to do the work of action.

(10) *Initial strike against the north.*

This would be very carefully designed to have more deterrent than destructive impact, as far as possible. This action would be accompanied by the simultaneous withdrawal of U.S. dependents from south Vietnam and by active diplomatic offensives in the Security Council, or in a Geneva Conference, or both, aimed at restoring the peace throughout the area. This peace-keeping theme will have been at the center of the whole enterprise from the beginning.

There is no declassified record of the actions President Johnson took on these proposals, but he did approve the recommendation for a meeting of high-level U.S. officials to give further consideration to the situation, and this was hastily convened in Honolulu on June 1-3, 1964.

Meanwhile, Sullivan's Vietnam Coordinating Committee had completed its report on having "Americans assume de facto command of GVN's machinery." Americans, Sullivan said, should be "integrated into the Vietnamese chain of command, both military and civil," at all levels of government. "For cosmetic purposes," however, he said, "American personnel would not assume titles which would show command functions, but would rather be listed as 'assistants' to the Vietnamese principals. . . ."[120]

It is not clear in what form the Sullivan proposals were presented to the President, but they were discussed—and dismissed—at the Honolulu Conference. (When the cable describing the agenda for that meeting was sent to Lodge, it stated that although U.S. personnel would be listed as "assistants" to the Vietnamese, "In practice . . . we would expect them to carry a major share of the burden of decision and action. . . .")[121]

On May 30, Rusk, who had attended the funeral of Prime Minister Jawaharlal Nehru of India, and was en route to the Honolulu Conference, stopped by Saigon to see Khanh. He pointed out to Khanh, as stated in the cable to Washington summarizing the meeting,[122] that, ". . . one of main problems President faces is justifying to American people whatever course of action may be necessary or indicated as matter of internal solidarity of SVN. Secretary noted that if struggle escalates, only U.S. will have the forces to cope with it. This basic reality means President has heavy responsibility of making vital decisions and leading American public opinion to accept them. Difficult to do this if SVN appears hopelessly divided and rent by internal quarrels." Khanh, in turn, stressed the need for acting against the Communists in eastern Laos and

---

[120]On May 27, a meeting of McGeorge Bundy, McNaughton, and General Goodpaster was held to discuss Sullivan's proposals, as slightly revised by Mendenhall in the interim. At this meeting the proposals presumably were endorsed, but there is no declassified record of that discussion. See *PP*, Gravel ed., vol. II, pp. 319-320. For a summary of the Mendenhall paper see *ibid.*, vol. III, p. 74.

[121]*Ibid.*, vol. III, p. 73.

[122]*Ibid.*, pp. 320-322.

North Vietnam, and wanted to know what U.S. intentions were with respect to widening the war. Rusk replied that he did not know, but that the matter would be considered in Honolulu, and that the President would have to decide.

In his discussion with Khanh, Rusk emphasized the following points:

A. Since 1945 U.S. had taken 165,000 casualties in defense of free world against Communist encroachments, and most of these casualties were in Asia.

B. U.S. would never again get involved in a land war in Asia limited to conventional forces. Our population was 190,000,000. Mainland China had at least 700,000,000. We would not allow ourselves to be bled white fighting them with conventional weapons.

C. This meant that if escalation brought about major Chinese attack, it would also involve use of nuclear arms. Many free world leaders would oppose this. Chiang Kai-Shek had told him fervently he did, and so did U Thant. Many Asians seemed to see an element of racial discrimination in use of nuclear arms; something we would do to Asians but not to Westerners. Khanh replied he certainly had no quarrel with American use of nuclear arms, noted that decisive use of Atomic bombs on Japan had in ending war saved not only American but also Japanese lives. One must use the force one had; if Chinese used masses of Humanity, we would use superior fire power.

D. Regardless what decisions were reached at Honolulu, their implementation would require positioning of our forces. This would take time. Khanh must remember we had other responsibilities in Asia and must be able react anywhere we had forces or commitments. Not by chance was this Conference being held at Honolulu; the combined headquarters of all American forces in Pacific was there.

On May 28, General LeMay, Air Force Chief of Staff, and its representative on the JCS, who, in Taylor's absence, was acting chairman of the JCS at the time, advised the other chiefs that the U.S. was "losing Asia fast." At the Honolulu meeting, he said, the JCS should present a plan by which the U.S. and the South Vietnamese could "start winning." The only way to prevent North Vietnam's support of Communist activity in Laos and South Vietnam, he said, was to destroy their ability to do so. He proposed air attacks on infiltration points at Dien Bien Phu and Vinh. The other Chiefs agreed, and the JCS notified McNamara of this position. When Taylor returned to Washington, he told McNamara that he agreed with the need to put additional pressure on the north, but preferred more limited action against targets that were less risky than Dien Bien Phu and Vinh.[123] Taylor said that there were three main alternatives:[124]

a. A massive air attack on all significant military targets in North Vietnam for the purpose of destroying them and thereby making the enemy incapable of continuing to assist the Viet Cong and the Pathet Lao.

---

[123]Futrell, *The Advisory Years to 1965*, p. 205.
[124]*PP*, Gravel ed., vol. III, p. 179.

b. A lesser attack on some significant part of the military target system in North Vietnam for the dual purpose of convincing the enemy that it is to his interest to desist from aiding the Viet Cong and the Pathet Lao, and, if possible, of obtaining his cooperation in calling off the insurgents in South Vietnam and Laos.

c. Demonstrative strikes against limited military targets to show U.S. readiness and intent to pass to alternative *b* or *a* above. These demonstrative strikes would have the same dual purpose as in alternative *b*.

Taylor said he preferred the second alternative, but that "political considerations will incline our responsible civilian officials" to opt for the third. In a memo to Taylor on June 10, McNamara agreed.

The Honolulu Conference, June 1-3, 1964

At the Honolulu Conference, attended by all top U.S. officials from Washington and Saigon, the principal subjects of discussion were how best to apply pressure to North Vietnam, what to do in Laos if diplomatic efforts failed and the military situation worsened, how South Vietnam could be strengthened, and how to prepare the U.S. public for an expanded war. "Our point of departure," according to the State Department guidance cable, "is and must be that we cannot accept overrunning of Southeast Asia by Hanoi and Peiping."[125] In the same cable the State Department said that the President was consulting closely with congressional leaders, and that he "will wish Congress associated with him on any steps which carry with them substantial acts and risks of escalation."

At the Conference, Lodge argued for attacking the north in order to help the south. ". . . if we bombed Tchepone [on the Ho Chi Minh Trail in eastern Laos] *or attacked the [North Vietnamese torpedo] boats,*" he said (emphasis added), this would produce greater unity in the South.[126] The general consensus of those at the Conference, however, was that attacks on the north or on Laos were not required at that time (the JCS disagreed), and that plans for such action needed to be prepared more carefully. U.S. public opinion would also have to be prepared for expansion of the war. (McNamara said it would take at least 30 days to prepare the public.) Moreover, it was felt that the Khanh government would not be strong enough to participate in such a war until the end of the year. These factors suggested that major military action against the north should be delayed until the necessary preparations could be made. Rusk took the position that the U.S. "should not be considering quick action unless the Pathet Lao lunged toward the Mekong."

The question of possible Chinese intervention was considered, and General Taylor said the assumption in Washington was that it was unlikely the Chinese would intervene in force. If they did, it would take five to seven divisions, mostly U.S., to stop them.

---

[125]*Ibid.,* p. 73.
[126]This and other references to the Conference are from *ibid.,* vol. II, pp. 323-325, and vol. III, pp. 171-176.

The use of nuclear weapons was raised by McNamara. "Admiral [Harry D.] Felt [CINCPAC] responded emphatically that there was no possible way to hold off the communists on the ground without the use of tactical nuclear weapons, and that it was essential that the commanders be given the freedom to use these as had been assumed under the various plans. He said that without nuclear weapons the ground force requirement was and had always been completely out of reach." General Taylor, however, was more doubtful about the need for nuclear weapons. Rusk "said that another possibility we must consider would be the Soviets stirring up trouble elsewhere. We should do everything we could to minimize this risk, but it too must be considered. He went on to stress the nuclear question, noting that in the last ten years this had come to include the possibility of a nuclear exchange, with all that this involved." General Taylor's response was, "there was a danger of reasoning ourselves into inaction. From a military point of view . . . the U.S. could function in Southeast Asia about as well as anywhere in the world except Cuba."[127]

Concerning the strengthening of South Vietnam, both Lodge and Gen. William Westmoreland (who had replaced Harkins) objected to Sullivan's plan, which Taylor said was favored by the President,[128] for *encadrement* of American personnel. They thought it would create an anticolonialist reaction, and could lead to even greater dependence on the United States.

Westmoreland proposed increasing U.S. civilian and military personnel in eight critical provinces, and this was accepted by the conferees in lieu of the Sullivan proposal. (Westmoreland also agreed with Lodge about the need for military action, such as airstrikes in eastern Laos, to galvanize the South Vietnamese.)

About 3 weeks later, on June 25, 1964, Westmoreland asked for 900 additional U.S. military advisers. By mid-July he asked for another 4,200 U.S. military personnel. McNamara's only objection was to Westmoreland's schedule; he thought that all of the additional advisers should be sent to Vietnam by the end of September. (None was sent until after the Presidential election.)[129]

Considerable attention was given at the Honolulu Conference to the question of influencing U.S. public opinion, and to the desirability of a congressional resolution. According to the *Pentagon Papers*,[130] "The conference concluded that the crucial actions for the immediate future were (1) to prosecute an urgent information effort in the United States toward dispelling the basic doubts of the value of Southeast Asia which were besetting key members of Congress and the public in the budding 'great debate,' and (2) to start diplomatic efforts with the Thais, Australians, New Zealanders, Philippines, and the French on matters within their cognizance which impinged on our effort in South Vietnam."

Concerning the congressional resolution, the text of which was read to the group by Sullivan, Lodge said he did not think it would be required if the U.S. were to engage only in tit-for-tat reprisal

[127] *Ibid.*, vol. III, p. 175.
[128] *Swords and Plowshares*, p. 313.
[129] *PP*, Gravel ed., vol. II, pp. 468-470.
[130] *Ibid.*, p. 325.

bombing. Rusk, McNamara and McCone, however, argued for a resolution. Rusk said that some of the military requirements might require calling up the reserves, which was a sensitive political issue. "He also stated," according to the *Pentagon Papers,*[131] "that public opinion on our Southeast Asia policy was badly divided in the United States at the moment and that, therefore, the President needed an affirmation of support." McNamara pointed out that such action by Congress would be desirable in view of the possibility that as many as seven divisions might have to be deployed to protect South Vietnam against possible action by China. McCone said that passage of a resolution should act as a deterrent to North Vietnam and China.

The Honolulu Conference ended on June 3, 1964 with agreement on three points: first, that the U.S. advisory effort would be expanded in key provinces; second, that plans for pressures on North Vietnam would be refined, and, meanwhile, that stronger military action would be delayed; third, that a campaign would be launched to influence U.S. public opinion and to secure the support of allied countries. Rusk subsequently cabled Saigon this list of expanded actions in the provinces that had been agreed upon at the Conference:[132]

(1) Move in additional VN troops to assure numerical superiority over VC.

(2) Assign control of all troops in province to province chief.

(3) Develop and execute detailed hamlet by hamlet "oil spot" and "clear and hold" operations plans for each of the approximate 40 districts.

(4) Introduce a system of population control (curfews, ID papers, intelligence network).

(5) Increase the province police force.

(6) Expand the information program.

(7) Develop a special economic aid program for each province.

(8) Add additional U.S. personnel

   320 military province and district advisors
    40 USOF province and district advisors
    74 battalion advisors (2 from each of 37 battalions)

   434

(9) Transfer military personnel to fill existing and future USOM shortages.

(10) Establish joint US/GVN teams to monitor the program at both national and provincial level.

On June 3, Rusk, McNamara, McCone and others met with the President to report on the Conference. There is no declassified document on this meeting, but the *Pentagon Papers* states[133] that a memo from William Bundy to Rusk may indicate what the President was told:

Citing a "somewhat less pessimistic estimate" of conditions in South Vietnam, the "somewhat shaky" but hopeful situa-

---

[131]*Ibid.,* vol. III, p. 174.
[132]*Ibid.,* vol. II, p. 325.
[133]*Ibid.,* vol. III, p. 176.

tion in Laos, and the military timing factors reported above, Bundy counseled taking more time "to refine our plans and estimates." Criticizing CINCPAC's presentation on military planning, he stated that it "served largely to highlight some of the difficult issues we still have." These he identified as: "(1) the likely effects of force requirements for any significant operations against the [Laotian] Panhandle"; (2) the trade-off between the precautionary advantages of a major build-up of forces prior to wider action and the possible disadvantages of distorting the signal of our limited objectives; (3) the sensitivity of estimates of communist reactions to different levels and tempos of a military build-up; and (4) the need for "more refined targeting and a clearer definition of just what should be hit and how thoroughly, and above all, for what objective."

In particular, Bundy emphasized to Secretary Rusk the need for immediate efforts in the information and intelligence areas. These were needed, he said, "both for the sake of refining our plans and for preparing materials to use for eventual support of wider action if decided upon"—particularly to support the diplomtic track in Laos. He called for "an urgent U.S. information effort" to "get at the basic doubts of the value of Southeast Asia and the importance of our stake there . . ." However, noting the problem of "handling the high degree of expectations flowing from the conference itself," Bundy recommended "careful guidance and consideration of high-level statements and speeches in the next two weeks" to assure that our posture appeared firm.

According to William Bundy, the President accepted the Honolulu recommendations "without hesitation."[134]

On June 4, Lodge met with Khanh to tell him about the Conference, and "the main thrust of his talk with Khanh was to hint that the USG would in the immediate future be preparing U.S. public opinion for actions against North Vietnam."[135]

A few weeks later, President Johnson approved some increases in the U.S. advisory effort, and apparently gave McNamara and the military clearance to study further the question of applying pressure on North Vietnam, as well as permission to prepare logistically for the introduction of U.S. ground forces into Indochina.

During this period (the end of May and the first part of June 1964) congressional Republicans, especially in the House, prompted in part by a request on May 18 for $125 million in additional funds for the U.S. program, became more vocal in their criticism of the administration's management of the war in Vietnam. They said it was a "no-win" policy, and that the U.S. should decide to win, or get out.[136] William S. Broomfield (R/Mich.), a member of the House Foreign Affairs Committee, introduced a resolution[137] on May 21 calling on the President to use every means to support South Vietnam and to prevent infiltration from outside its borders, and to reassert U.S. determination to defend South Vietnam and

[134]Bundy MS., ch. 13, p. 21.
[135]*PP,* Gravel ed., vol. II, p. 325.
[136]See *CR,* vol. 110, pp. 11116, 11397-98, 11402-03, 11451.
[137]H.J. Res. 1034, 88th Cong.

Southeast Asia. "There should remain," the resolution concluded, "not the slightest doubt as to the determination of the United States Government to pursue this course of action, and to fully inform the American people of what will be necessary to defend freedom in South Vietnam and in southeast Asia."[138]

Republican Senator Aiken of Vermont, a member of the Foreign Relations Committee, was opposed, however, both to military escalation and to precipitate withdrawal, and said that the U.S. should maintain a "stalemate with the rebels for the time being if that is the best we can do." He favored efforts to achieve a political settlement, but also said he would support the stationing of some U.S. forces in Thailand "for defensive purposes if the government of that country requests it and if the government and the people of Thailand are willing to defend their own country with full force, and if such action is not a prelude to a wide expansion of the war."[139]

On May 26, Senate Republican leader Dirksen declared that the administration's "indecision" on Vietnam was "dribbling away both American lives and American prestige in Southeast Asia." President Johnson responded that same day by asking Dirksen and eight other Republican Senators to a meeting at the White House to discuss the situation in Southeast Asia.[140]

On June 2, partisan feuding became a bit more intense when Melvin R. Laird (R/Wis.) complained in a speech in the House that the President was not being "completely forthright" in a statement in his press conference that morning about U.S. contingency plans for attacking North Vietnam.[141] Laird said that in his work as chairman of the Republican platform committee for the 1964 Republican national convention he had been informed by Secretary of State Rusk that the U.S. was preparing contingency plans for Vietnam, including "the preparation of plans to go north into North Vietnam. . . ." He added that he had used this information, which was not classified, in a radio interview the previous Sunday. Yet, Laird said, the President had stated in his press conference, "I know of no plans being made to that effect."[142] "I regret that the President of the United States used his news conference in this way," Laird continued, "because the American people deserve to be informed and have the right to know." This comment was immediately reported by one of the wire services, as follows: "Representative Melvin R. Laird, Republican, of Wisconsin, today charged that President Johnson 'deliberately misled the American people in stating that there were not plans to take the war in Vietnam to the Communist north.'"[143] This wire service story appeared on the

---

[138]For Broomfield's discussion of the need for Congress to express its commitment to defending Vietnam and Southeast Asia see *CR*, vol. 110, pp. 13249-13251. Broomfield and many other congressional Republicans also took the position that the U.S. program in Vietnam should be better funded, and they succeeded in amending the 1964 foreign aid authorization bill to earmark $200 million in military support (supporting assistance) funds for use only in Vietnam unless the President decided otherwise and reported his decision to Congress. See Public Law 88-633, sec. 107. The President's request for an additional $125 million for Vietnam was passed by Congress without significant opposition or debate.
[139]*CR*, vol. 110, p. 12373.
[140]*New York Times*, May 27, 1964.
[141]*CR*, vol. 110, p. 12460.
[142]See *Public Papers of the Presidents*, Lyndon B. Johnson, 1964, p. 739.
[143]*CR*, vol. 110, p. 12476.

press ticker in the House lobby (adjacent to the Chamber), and a few minutes later senior Democrats on the Defense Appropriation Subcommittee of the House Appropriations Committee, on which Laird served, accused Laird of misleading the public, and implied that he had used secret information on such contingency plans given to the subcommittee by McNamara a short time earlier. Laird stood his ground, repeating his statements he had been given the information from the Department of State, and that the President was not being forthright.[144]

Republican Representative Eugene Siler, from a rural district in Kentucky, marched to a different drummer. On June 8, 1964, he said in a speech in the House:[145]

> . . . I rise to announce my candidacy for President of the United States.
>
> I am running with the understanding that I will resign after 24 hours in the White House and let my Vice President take over the duties thereafter. Accordingly, I want an able and sufficient Vice President to run with me and then succeed me after that first day.
>
> What I propose to do in my 1 day as President is to call home our 15,000 troops in South Vietnam and cancel our part of that ill fated, unnecessary, and un-American campaign in southeast Asia. . . .

Despite these few protests from Congress, general congressional opinion, as summarized on June 2, 1964, by Frederick Dutton, the head of the State Department's office of congressional relations, was "cautious or noncommittal." "Even most of those supporting the Administration's present course are often wary about it," he said, adding, "Actually the level of interest in Southeast Asia is not at all high, which suggests to me not merely political caution in an election year but low understanding or care about the problem. I suspect the overwhelming majority of Congress would support a Presidential initiative—but would also still try to keep sufficiently remote to be able to second-guess it if things went bad or were prolonged."[146]

Preparing a Congressional Resolution

After the Honolulu Conference, planning continued for a congressional resolution, and between June 8 and 15, 1964, several interdepartmental meetings were held on the subject. For the meeting on June 10, William Bundy prepared a discussion paper, "Alternative Public.Positions for U.S. on Southeast Asia for the Period July 1-November 15."[147] (Note the post-Presidential election date of November 15.) "It is agreed," the paper said, "that the U.S. will wish to make its position on Southeast Asia as clear and strong as possible in the next five months. The immediate watershed decision is whether or not the Administration should seek a Congressional resolution giving general authority for action which

---

[144]*Ibid.*, pp. 12475-12477.
[145]*Ibid.*, pp. 12889-12890.
[146]"Loose Congressional Breakdown on Southeast Asia Situation," June 2, 1964, sent by Dutton to McGeorge Bundy on that date. Johnson Library, NSF Country File, Vietnam.
[147]Johnson Library, NSC History File, Gulf of Tonkin Attacks.

the President may judge necessary to defend the peace and security of the area."

According to Bundy's paper, the "scenario" for a congressional resolution would entail, first, "to prepare the case in favor." There would then have to be a ". . . major public campaign by the Administration. A very important element in such a campaign would be early and outspoken support by leading members of Congress." The resolution would be preceded by a Presidential message. The resolution would not be sent to Congress, however, ". . . unless careful Congressional soundings indicate rapid passage by a very substantial majority."

In preparing the case for the resolution certain questions would arise, one of which would be, "Does this resolution imply a blank check for the President to go to war over Southeast Asia?" The proposed answer was as follows:

> The resolution will indeed permit selective use of force, but hostilities on a larger scale are not envisaged, and in any case any large escalation would require a call-up of Reserves and thus a further appeal to the Congress. More broadly, there is no intent to usurp the powers of the Congress, but rather a need for confirmation of the powers of the President as Commander in Chief in an election year. The basic precedents are the Formosa Resolution, the Middle East Resolution, and, in a sense, the [Arthur H.] Vandenberg Resolution.

A decision to seek a congressional resolution, the paper stated, would not be "a small undertaking," and such a move would have "heavy implications." "A strong campaign in defense of this resolution will require a substantial increase in the commitment of U.S. prestige and power to success in Southeast Asia."

The advantages and disadvantages of seeking a resolution at that time were summarized as follows:

> The great advantages of an early Congressional resolution are international. It would give additional freedom to the Administration in choosing courses of action; still more important, it would give a signal of this new freedom of action and firmness of purpose in a number of important capitals, the most important of which are in Southeast Asia, on both sides of the line.
>
> If we do not seek a Congressional Resolution, the international disadvantages are obvious, in that we may seem to have a relative lack of freedom of action and will not have built the major new base of commitment and of authority which in the best of cases such a resolution, with its attendant debate, might provide. On the other hand, if we do not have a resolution, we do not have the risks of a contest at home, nor do we pin ourselves to a level of concern and public notice which might be embarrassing if in fact we do not find it wise to take drastic action in the months immediately ahead. Thus we need to consider how much our course of action may be limited if we *do not* seek a Congressional Resolution.
>
> First, it should be recognized that there are alternative forms of bipartisan support for action: consultation with Eisenhower and the Republican candidate; discussion with bipartisan leadership of Congress; direct Presidential appeal to the

people; ample, if not always encouraging, precedent for Presidential action, as in Korea.

Second, there is a wide range of actions which are plainly permissible without a resolution. These include direct military action by South Vietnamese forces, and very substantial deployments of U. S. air, sea and ground forces. Within the framework of SEATO, and in defense of the agreements of 1962, we can plausibly move troops even into Vietnam, Thailand and Laos itself if the appropriate governments request it. Short of direct U. S. military action against North Vietnam, we could almost surely maintain adequate freedom of action even without a Congressional Resolution.

Third, the only time we can get a resolution, in the absence of acute emergency, is within the next three weeks. A strong case can be made that we do not now need to commit ourselves so heavily, and that if the situation changes drastically, we could readily respond by emergency session, certainly in November, and conceivably in September too. (emphasis in original)

Bundy's paper came down on the side of waiting: "On balance, it appears that we need a Congressional Resolution if and only if we decide that a substantial increase of national attention and international tension is a necessary part of the defense of Southeast Asia in the coming summer."

At the interdepartmental meeting on June 10 where this paper was discussed it was agreed, according to a memorandum later that day from McGeorge Bundy to the President, that, ". . . we do not now recommend an attempt to get an early resolution. We think the risks outweigh the advantages, unless and until we have a firm decision to take more drastic action than we currently plan."[148]

On June 11, the State Department prepared a draft of a congressional resolution, with alternative language for two of the resolution's three sections.[149] After the "Whereas" or policy statement, the proposed resolution was as follows:

Sec. 1. That the maintenance of international peace and security in Southeast Asia and the preservation of the political independence and territorial integrity of the non- Communist nations of the area, including the Republic of Viet-Nam and Laos, is required by the national interest of the United States:

*   *   *   *   *   *   *

Alternative Drafts of Section 2

Alternative Based on the Middle East Resolution of 1957:

Sec. 2. To this end, if the President determines the necessity thereof, the United States is prepared, upon request from any nation in Southeast Asia, to take, consistently with the Charter of the United Nations, all measures including the use of armed forces to assist that nation in the defense of its political

---

[148]Johnson Library, NSF Aides File, McGeorge Bundy Memos for President.

[149]The text is in the Johnson Library, NSC History File, Gulf of Tonkin Attacks. An earlier and similar version dated June 5 is located in NSF Aides Files, McGeorge Bundy, Meetings on SE Asia.

independence and territorial integrity against aggression or subversion supported, controlled or directed from any Communist country. Any such measures shall be reported to the Security Council of the United Nations.

* * * * * * *

Alternative Based on the Cuba Resolution of 1962:
Sec. 2. That the United States is determined to prevent by whatever means may be necessary, including the use of arms, the Communist regime in North Viet-Nam, with the aid and support of the Communist regime in China, from extending, by force of threat of force, its aggressive or subversive activities against any non- Communist nation in Southeast Asia.

* * * * * * *

Alternative Drafts of Section 3

First Alternative:
Sec. 3. This Resolution shall expire when the President shall determine that the peace and security of Southeast Asia is reasonably assured by international conditions created by action of the United Nations or otherwise, and shall so report to the Congress.

* * * * * * *

Second Alternative:
Sec. 3. This Resolution shall expire on January 8 (?), [sic] 1965 [date of convening of the next Congress.]
As will be seen in the following chapter, the Gulf of Tonkin Resolution, while containing provisions similar to section 1 and to the first alternative for both sections 2 and 3 of this draft of June 11, was an even stronger grant of power to the President than the language in the June 11 draft.
According to William Bundy,[150] the June 11 resolution was prepared by the staffs of State, Defense and the White House, and was reviewed "with care" by a group consisting of McGeorge Bundy, William Bundy, Douglass Cater (a White House assistant) and James Thomson (who had moved from the State Department to the NSC staff).
On June 12, there was further discussion of a congressional resolution, based on William Bundy's June 12 "Memorandum on the Southeast Asia Situation: Probable Developments and the Case for a Congressional Resolution." The *Pentagon Papers* summarized the memorandum as follows:[151]

Even though the Administration did not expect "to move in the near future to military action against North Vietnam," it recognized that significant changes in the local situations in both Laos and South Vietnam were "beyond our control and could compel us to reconsider this position." Although our diplomatic track in Laos appeared hopeful, and our now firm escorted reconnaissance operations provided an image of U.S. re-

---

[150]Bundy MS., ch. 13, p. 24.
[151]*PP*, Gravel ed., vol. III, p. 180. (emphasis in original) The full text of the memorandum is now available at the Johnson Library, NSC History File, Gulf of Tonkin Attacks, vol. III.

solve to complement the Polish negotiating scheme, we needed to be able to augment this posture in the event negotiations stalemated. If Souvanna were to become discouraged, or if Khanh were to view our efforts to obtain a Laotian settlement as a sign of willingness to alter our objectives, we would need additional demonstrations of our firmness to keep these leaders from being demoralized. Since additional military actions in Laos and South Vietnam did not hold much promise, actions or the strong threat of actions against the North might need to be considered. For these reasons, an immediate Congressional resolution was believed required as "a continuing demonstration of U.S *firmness* and for complete *flexibility in the hands of the Executive in the coming political months.*"

A congressional resolution, Bundy's memorandum stated, should be drafted in consultation with congressional leaders in such a way as to ensure its immediate and strong support and passage without extended and divisive debate. It should "support any action required but must at the same time place maximum stress on our peaceful objectives and our willingness to accept eventual negotiated solutions so that we might hope to have the full support of the school of thought headed by Senator Mansfield and Senator Aiken and leave ourselves with die-hard opposition only from Senator Morse and his very few cohorts."

With respect to timing, the memorandum stated that July would be difficult because of the Republican convention, as would August because of the possible last-minute rush of Congress to adjourn before the Democratic convention. The memorandum concluded, therefore, that the resolution should be sent to Congress during the week of June 22. It added this very interesting point: "It may be argued that a Congressional Resolution under present circumstances faces the serious difficulty that there is no drastic change in the situation to point to. The opposing argument is that we might well not have such a *drastic* change even later in the summer and yet conclude—either because of the Polish consultations [meetings then being planned for negotiating a new settlement in Laos] or because of the South Viet-Nam situation—that we had to act." (emphasis in original)

Some years later, William Bundy had this comment:[152]

The case for a Resolution seemed to many, including myself, strong. The country was heading into an election campaign, in which the Congress would be away much of the time till early January of 1965. Yet there might at any time be some development in Southeast Asia that would call for quick action of a directly military character. Moreover, the strongest possible deterrent to Hanoi's pressing its local advantages in Laos and South Vietnam would surely be a Congressional expression of US steadiness and willingness to go further if need be. No longer, of course, was a Congressional Resolution being put forward in the context of a sequential plan to get Hanoi to pull back, but even without such a plan there seemed much that it could accomplish. Many of us harked back to the Middle East

---

[152]Bundy MS., ch. 13, pp. 23-24.

Resolution the Congress had adopted in March of 1957, at a time when there was no drastic or immediate threat in the area, but when the US posture was felt to need definition.

Suspending Action on a Congressional Resolution

While his advisers were completing plans for a congressional resolution, President Johnson was trying to devise a way by which to increase pressures on the Communists while avoiding a substantial escalation of the war. He knew at least by June 1964 that the Republican Presidential nominee would be Senator Barry Goldwater, (R/Ariz.), who was critical of Johnson and the Democrats for their failure to apply sufficient force in Vietnam. Johnson also knew that there was considerable support in Congress and the public, as well as from many of his military and some of his civilian advisers, for Goldwater's point of view. Moreover, there was strong public and congressional support, shared by Johnson and most of his top advisers, for taking steps to prevent Communist domination of Vietnam and of Southeast Asia. Personally he was—and politically he needed to be—committed to helping the South Vietnamese.

On the other hand, Johnson was keenly aware of the opposition in Congress and the public to U.S. military involvement in Vietnam, and he recognized the political advantage of portraying Goldwater as a saber rattler.

These factors led the President to conclude by late June 1964 that during the next six months he should demonstrate strength and firmness of purpose, while avoiding escalating U.S. involvement or substantially widening the war. He also concluded (see discussion below of June 15 memo, "Elements of a Southeast Asia Policy that does not include a Congressional Resolution") that, prior to the election, and in the absence of a congressional resolution, the U.S. could defend its interest, and could shift to a higher level of military activity if the Communists escalated the conflict.

The decision to postpone major military moves and generally to avoid any significant new actions in Vietnam, combined with the effects of the President's campaign activities, resulted, as Michael Forrestal (former NSC staff member who succeeded Sullivan as head of the Vietnam Coordinating Committee in July 1964) has described it, in a confused situation in the government, especially from the middle of August through October:[153]

> The President was out of Washington a great deal. He was difficult to see, and it was very hard to learn from him what he wanted to do. If I had been an older and wiser person, I would have perfectly well understood why. He didn't want to take a position during a campaign. But for somebody who was working for him, having to handle the problem from day to day, it was very frustrating. The result was that the division in the government between those who felt you've got to stay in and put in more, and those who were beginning to feel we have to somehow calm this thing down, was getting very strong, and particularly the philosophical division between those who felt that force was the only answer and those who

---

[153]CRS Interview with Michael Forrestal, Oct. 16, 1978.

felt that the political problem was more important than the military one. It got to the point where people weren't talking to each other.

While work continued during the second week in June on the congressional resolution, Johnson received advice from others. W. W. Rostow recommended "a more aggressive approach" and a speech on Vietnam by the President.[154] Johnson did not make the suggested statement, however, and generally avoided the subject of Southeast Asia in public appearances during this period.

On June 9, the Board of National Estimates of the CIA submitted its conclusions, as of that time, on the question of the effect of a Communist takeover of Laos and South Vietnam:[155]

> With the possible exception of Cambodia, it is likely that no nation in the area would quickly succumb to communism as a result of the fall of Laos and South Vietnam. Furthermore, a continuation of the spread of communism in the area would not be inexorable, and any spread which did occur would take time—time in which the total situation might change in any of a number of ways unfavorable to the communist cause.

The statement went on to argue that the loss of South Vietnam and Laos "would be profoundly damaging to the U.S. position in the Far East," because of its impact on U.S. prestige and on the credibility of our other commitments to contain the spread of communism. It did not suggest that such a loss would affect the wider U.S. interest in containing overt military attacks. Our island base, it argued, would probably still enable us to employ enough military power in the area to deter Hanoi and Peking from this kind of aggression. It cautioned, however, that the leadership in Peking (as well as Hanoi) would profit directly by being able to justify its militant policies with demonstrated success and by having raised "its prestige as a leader of World Communism" at the expense of the more moderate USSR.

On June 6-7 an incident occurred that tended to highlight both the advantages and the disadvantages of the Johnson administration's approach to the situation in Southeast Asia. Two U.S. reconnaissance planes were shot down over Laos, and the U.S. announced that future flights would be escorted by U.S. fighters. Supporters of U.S. involvement applauded Johnson's firmness. Opponents of U.S. involvement, however, were displeased, and Mansfield sent a memorandum to the President warning that such flights were provocative and could lead to escalation.[156]

For Johnson, the Laos incident had an effect similar to Kennedy's experience with Laos in the spring of 1961. Faced with a situation in which some of his advisers, notably Air Force Chief of Staff Gen. Curtis LeMay, called for strong action, Johnson's instinct, according to one account of the NSC meeting on June 7, was to probe for a better explanation and justification: "At this meeting, the decision was made to continue reconnaissance but the President pressed for more specific recommendations and plans. 'Where are

[154]*PP*, Gravel ed., vol. III, p. 178.
[155]Summarized in *ibid.*
[156]Johnson Library, NSF Country File, Vietnam.

we going?' he asked with some vehemence." After the meeting, the President was reported to have said "that he was worried about LeMay and his truculent visions. 'I get anxious and look for the fire exits when a general wants to get tough. LeMay scares the hell out of me.'"[157]

Consideration of a congressional resolution climaxed at a meeting of top NSC officials on June 15, 1964. Six papers were prepared for this meeting: first, a memo of June 15, "Elements of a Southeast Asian Policy that does not include a Congressional Resolution," second, a Sullivan memo on the general political situation in Vietnam, third, William Bundy's memo of June 12 on "Probable Developments and the Case for a Congressional Resolution," fourth, a draft congressional resolution, fifth, a paper by William Bundy on "Themes in Presenting the Resolution," and, sixth, questions and answers for an accompanying public relations campaign.[158]

The memo on actions that could be taken in the absence of a congressional resolution was prepared by the White House staff and obviously reflected the President's views, including his assumption that, as the memorandum stated, "This outline does not preclude a shift to a higher level of action if actions of the other side should justify or require it. It does assume that in the absence of such drastic action, defense of U.S. interests is possible, within these limits, over the next six months." The outline of possible actions was as follows:

    1. *Possible military actions*

        a. Reconnaissance, reconnaissance-strike, and T-28 operations in all parts of Laos.

        b. Small-scale reconnaissance strike operations, after appropriate provocation, in North Vietnam (initially VNAF?).

        c. VNAF strike operations in Laotian corridors.

        d. Limited air and sea deployments toward Southeast Asia, and still more limited ground troop movements. (Major ground force deployments seem more questionable, without a decision "to go north" in some form.)

    2. *Political actions*

        a. Internationally—a continued and increased effort to maximize support for our diplomatic track in Laos and our political effort in South Vietnam. Higher authority particularly desires a maximum effort with our allies to increase their real and visible presence in support of Saigon.

        b. Laos—an intensive effort to sustain Souvanna and to restrain the right wing from any rash act against the French. Possible increase of direct support and assistance to Kong Le in appropriate ways.

[157]Valenti, *A Very Human President,* p. 138.

[158]The Sullivan memorandum remains classified, but the others are in the Johnson Library in NSC History File, Gulf of Tonkin Attacks, except for the June 15 memorandum on "Elements . . .," which is in NSF Country File, Vietnam.

The Bundy draft of "Basic Themes in Presenting the Resolution," was similar to his earlier paper on June 10 cited above. The files do not contain the draft of a congressional resolution prepared and submitted for the June 15 meeting.

c. South Vietnam—rapid development of the critical province program and the information program, strengthening of country team, and shift of U.S. role from advice toward direction; emphatic and continued discouragement of all coup plots; energetic public support for Khanh Government.

d. In the U.S.—continued reaffirmation and expanded explanation of the above lines of action, with opposition to both aggressive adventure and withdrawal, and a clear open door to selected action of the sort included in paragraph 1.

Although the White House memo was the central point of discussion at the June 15 meeting, the *Pentagon Papers* says that the Sullivan memo "warrants special attention" because of its significance in relation to the policymaking process.[159] This memo described the stalemate in South Vietnam, and the feeling of Lodge and Westmoreland that a way had to be found to cause the South Vietnamese to become committed to the war. This, the memo stated, ". . . could come from the external actions of the U.S. internal leadership in Vietnam, or from an act of the [*sic*] irreversible commitment by the United States." Such a commitment by the U.S., the memo said, could also lead to "executive involvement into the Vietnamese structure," i.e., the *encadrement* of U.S. personnel that the Vietnam Coordinating Committee, as well as Lansdale, had been recommending.

At its June 15 meeting, the NSC officials agreed with the position taken in the White House memo that a resolution was not necessary at that time, and that there were steps that could and should be taken in the absence of such action.

This is William Bundy's comment:[160]

. . . in the end the case against the resolution seemed overwhelming . . . the general consensus was that in the absence of a considered decision for a sustained course of action, the need for a resolution was impossible to explain adequately to the Congress and the public. It was also argued that the existence of a resolution would tend to determine the decision in the direction of military force.

Although the President suspended actions on a congressional resolution, he permitted the launching of the public information campaign that had been agreed upon in Honolulu, and was reaffirmed by ExCom agreement on the June 15 memo. (See "Political Actions—d." in the outline reproduced above.) This decision was promulgated by NSAM 308, June 22, 1964.

The President also sought to clarify his own authority to use the armed forces, and on June 22 he asked the State Department for advice on that subject. The reply on June 29 from the Legal Adviser at State (Leonard C. Meeker), cleared by William Bundy and by the Justice Department, was that Johnson did not need action by Congress in order to deploy troops in Southeast Asia or anywhere

---

[159] *PP*, Gravel ed., vol. III, p. 78.
[160] Bundy MS., ch. 13, p. 22.

else in the world. This was the central point in Meeker's memorandum:[161]

The assignment of United States military personnel to duty in Viet-Nam involving participation in combat rests on the constitutional powers of the President as Commander-in-Chief of the armed forces, as Chief Executive, and in the field of foreign affairs. There have been numerous precedents in history for the use of these powers to send American forces abroad, including various situations involving their participation in hostilities. In the case of Viet-Nam, the President's action is additionally supported by the fact that South Viet-Nam has been designated to receive protection under Article IV of the Southeast Asia Collective Defense Treaty; both the Treaty and the Protocol covering Viet-Nam received the advice and consent of the Senate.

Persuading Congress and the Public to Support Executive Policy

The information campaign to be conducted under NSAM 308 was to be aimed at both Congress and the public. "Of special concern was a recent Gallup poll showing only 37 percent of the public to have some interest in our Southeast Asia policies. Administration officials viewed this group as consisting primarily of either those desiring our withdrawal or those urging our striking at North Vietnam. A general program was proposed with the avowed aim of eroding public support for these polar positions and solidifying a large 'center' behind the thrust of current Administration policies. These aims were to be accomplished by directing public comment into discussions of the precise alternatives available to the United States, greater exposure to which it was believed would alienate both 'hawk' and 'dove' supporters." Robert Manning (Assistant Secretary of State for Public Affairs) was named by the President to direct the campaign.[162]

As part of its public information campaign the administration held two executive session briefings for the Senate Foreign Relations Committee, one on June 15 with Rusk and William Sullivan as the witnesses, and the other on June 30 with Lodge as the witness.[163] In the June 15 session, Senator Church again argued that only the South Vietnamese could win the war, and that U.S. military intervention would not be a decisive factor in that struggle and might involve the United States in a war with North Vietnam or China. Fulbright expressed an interest in Church's views, but did not express his own opinion.

In the June 30 meeting, Lodge, who had resigned as U.S. Ambassador to Vietnam in order to participate in the Presidential campaign, and had been replaced by General Taylor, said that the situation was improving, but it would take time for the necessary political strength to be developed in South Vietnam.[164] His point of

---

[161]Johnson Library, NSF Country File, Vietnam 7B Legality.
[162]*PP,* DOD ed., book 4, IV. C. 2. (b), p. 2
[163]The unpublished transcript of the June 15 hearing has been declassified and opened, and is in the papers of the Foreign Relations Committee in the National Archives, RG 46.
[164]U.S. Congress, Senate, Committee on Foreign Relations, unpublished executive session transcript, June 30, 1964. During the process of choosing Lodge's successor, several of the Presi-

Continued

view seemed to have the support of the committee, except for Morse, who again urged a negotiated settlement.

Several days after the meeting with Rusk, Church, who was chairman of the U.N. Subcommittee of the Foreign Relations Committee, made a major Senate speech on June 26 on the accomplishments and changing role of the United Nations, in which he suggested that the U.N. might help to bring peace to Indochina:[165]

> If experience proves anything at all it is that upheaval among the black, brown, and yellow peoples, now emerging in their own right throughout Africa and Asia, is not likely to be assuaged for long through the unilateral intervention of any white nation. The empires which Western power could not hold, that power cannot now pacify. But because the United Nations has proved itself to be theirs, as well as ours, it can often play the role of "honest broker," and even that of the welcome policeman on the beat, when violence breaks out within, or between, the newly independent countries which were so recently the restive possessions of the Western World.
>
> For this reason, it seems to me that we would be well advised to probe all the possibilities for using the peacekeeping machinery of the United Nations, not only in the matter of the smoldering border dispute between Cambodia and South Vietnam, but also in the broader effort to end the fighting in Laos and South Vietnam itself, under some form of negotiated settlement. Administered by the U.N. such an accord might succeed in preserving the independence of these countries, guaranteeing their neutrality, and permitting them to peaceably proceed to fashion their own destinies through self-determination.

Fulbright welcomed Church's suggestion, but said he doubted whether the U.N. could play such a role until there was greater stability in South Vietnam. ". . . under the circumstances that now exist," he said, "if it became current, if the people, particularly the people of South Vietnam, thought we were about to withdraw and turn the matter over to the U.N., it could well cause a crisis in the affairs of the Government of South Vietnam. In other words, I think our determined support at this time is indispensable to the survival of that regime. . . . If we could establish a firm position in which things were going better for the South Vietnamese and they had greater confidence in their capacity to survive, a consideration of some substitute, by way of the U.N., not only would be tenable, but I would be favorable toward it." Church agreed that

---

dent's prominent advisers had volunteered to take the assignment, including Rusk, McNamara, Taylor, McGeorge Bundy, and Attorney General Robert Kennedy, who sent Johnson this handwritten note on June 11, (from Schlesinger, *Robert Kennedy and His Times*, p. 728):

"Dear Mr. President:

"I just wanted to make sure you understood that if you wished me to go to Viet Nam in any capacity I would be glad to go. It is obviously the most important problem facing the United States and if you felt I could help I am at your service.

"I have talked to both Bob and Mac about this and I believe they know my feelings. I realize some of the other complications but I am sure that if you reached the conclusion that this was the right thing to do then between us both or us all we could work it out satisfactorily.

"In any case I wished you to know my feeling on this matter."

Johnson declined Kennedy's offer: "I feared, as did Secretaries Rusk and McNamara, that the potential danger to the late President's brother was too great." *The Vantage Point*, p. 99. See also Jack Valenti, *A Very Human President*, pp. 138-143.

[165] *CR*, vol. 110, pp. 14790-14796.

the U.S. had to continue its efforts in South Vietnam, but he was "concerned lest we eliminate other alternatives to military action alone":

> Now it is said that perhaps we must go further and extend the war to North Vietnam, Laos, or northward. What troubles me is that if this war—which is essentially a political war, that can be won only by the people of South Vietnam—is being waged on terms so advantageous, with the enemy restricted to 25,000 hard core Vietcong, how on earth will the situation be improved by extending the war to the north? Will it help to take on the army of North Vietnam? Do we think that the bombing of North Vietnam will break the spirit of the Government, and cause it to discontinue to aid and abet the insurrection in the south? Why should we? The bombing of North Korea never broke the spirit there. And we bombed every house, bridge, and road until there was nothing left but rubble. Expanding the war is not getting out, Mr. President. It is getting further in.

"If we become involved in that region," Church added, ". . . we could waste our troops endlessly in the interminable jungle." What for? he asked:

> Do we think it will be a war in which world opinion will be on our side? Do we think that the history of the last 20 years means that a white nation is going to be upheld in fashioning the destiny of Asia? Do we think that if we occupy this region with our naked power, we would then have solved the problem? Do we think that the Asians concerned would then say, "We are saved. We are liberated by the Western power, the United States, and her occupation will be our shield"? Why, the tides of history will wash over us in time. For Asia does belong to the Asians now, and will forevermore.

These comments were indicative of a position which Church had been developing for several months, and according to Bryce Nelson, who was assisting him, Church's speech was an important one:[166]

> In my mind, it was one of the first forceful expressions of some senatorial discontent on Vietnam. During this period, Morse and Gruening had been the most outspoken senators against American involvement in Vietnam. And I think that one of the feelings of the younger and more cautious senators was that they did not want to identify too much with opposition to involvement in Vietnam because they thought that the comments of people like Morse and Gruening were so strident. They did not want to be lumped in with people like Morse and Gruening, at least initially.

Hubert Humphrey, who was about to be chosen by President Johnson as his Vice Presidential running mate also commented on Church's speech. He agreed that the U.N. could play a role, and he said he was opposed to escalating the war. "What is needed in Vietnam," he added, "is a cause for which to fight, some sort of inspiration for the people of South Vietnam to live for and die for."

---

[166]CRS Interview with Bryce Nelson, Dec. 12, 1978.

Humphrey obviously was being very cautious. The President had asked him for his views on Vietnam, and Humphrey had been advised by John Rielly, his foreign policy assistant, to avoid discussing Vietnam with the President or becoming one of the his spokesmen on Vietnam. Rielly told Humphrey: "'(1) Do not make any speech on the subject of Vietnam. (2) Do not present to the President any memoranda on Vietnam. (3) Do not permit yourself, if at all possible, to be maneuvered into the position by the President where you become the principal defender of the Administration's policy in the Senate against critics like Mansfield, Church, Morse, Gruening and others.'"[167]

Humphrey replied to Johnson's request in a memorandum prepared by General Lansdale and Rufus Phillips, in which he argued for U.S. restraint. "The Vietnamese," he said, must be skillfully and firmly guided, but it is they (not we) who must win their war. . . . A political base is needed to support all other actions. . . . No amount of additional military involvement can be successful without accomplishing this task. . . . Direct U.S. military action against North Vietnam, U.S. assumption of command roles, or the participation in combat of U.S. troop units is unnecessary and undesirable."[168]

The memorandum also criticized the over-reliance on a conventional military response, and the excessive use of heavy artillery, napalm, and airstrikes. The war was primarily a guerrilla war, it said, and should be fought as such.

In conclusion, Humphrey suggested to the President that a new team of U.S. experts, headed or selected by Lansdale and Phillips, should be sent to Vietnam to take charge of implementing the counterinsurgency program. Maj. Gen. Chester V. Clifton, Jr., President Johnson's military aide, in a memorandum to the President on June 25, 1964 commenting on Humphrey's memorandum, said, ". . . fine as these men are, they have a reputation for using the 'lone wolf' approach rather than being men who can participate as part of a team effort." "I do not recommend that you inject Lansdale-Phillips into the action at this time."[169]

Toward the end of June 1964, while the administration's public information campaign was getting underway, congressional Republicans continued pressing Johnson and the Democrats to take a stronger stand on Vietnam. In a public hearing of the Foreign Relations Committee on June 23, on the 1964 foreign aid authorization bill, Senator Hickenlooper, the ranking Republican on the committee, told McNamara, the witness at that point, that he was concerned about what U.S. objectives were in Vietnam, and about how serious the situation was and how committed the United States was in its policies and programs. He thought the time had come for a congressional resolution: "We have had lots of speeches on the vital necessity of some of these things. But in the past we have had resolutions concurred in by Congress establishing policy. It seems to me the time had come when we had better have the

---

[167]CRS Interview with John Rielly, Mar. 29, 1979.
[168]Hubert H. Humphrey, Norman Sherman (ed.) *The Education of a Public Man, My Life and Politics* (New York: Doubleday, 1976) pp. 482-483.
[169]Johnson Library, NSF Country File, Vietnam.

administration and the Congress get together on some understood policy and some definite directional trends here so that we know what potentials we may have to face."

Hickenlooper added that, in the absence of such a consensus, it was becoming more difficult to explain U.S. policy on Vietnam to the public, as well as more difficult for Congress to approve funds. "I can vote lots of money when I think I understand the objectives and I am willing to support the objectives when they are reliable. But to vote money on a rather indefinite and still undefined purpose is a rather difficult thing." McNamara replied that the President and his advisers had defined U.S. objectives. Hickenlooper said that he still did not know whether it was U.S. policy "to win." "Is victory in South Vietnam the essential objective? I think we had better get down to the point where we determine whether we do that. Then if the American people or the Congress want to say, 'All right, we will accept the thesis and the objective that victory in South Vietnam is absolutely essential to the well-being of the country and to the free world; therefore, if it is, we will support all necessary action from here on out to guarantee that victory.'"[170]

A few days later (June 29), the House Republican Conference issued a statement generally criticizing Johnson and the Democrats for "letting down our guard" against the Communists, and specifically criticized the administration for not taking steps to win the war in Vietnam. It said the administration was following a "why win?" policy in Vietnam, and that "A victory in South Vietnam over the military and subversive threats of communism is urgently required. We must repeal today's complacent commitment to prevent a Communist victory and substitute a commitment to insure a victory for freedom." In making public the report of the group, Representative Gerald Ford said that the U.S. should immediately ". . . take command of the forces in Vietnam and not simply remain advisers," and that more U.S. Special Forces should be sent to Vietnam in order to seal the borders against infiltration from the north.[171]

Senator Mansfield was very critical of the statement, calling it a "tirade." "I am not surprised that the partisan political knives should be drawn on this issue," he said. "What amazes me is that they have come out of the sheaths so early. I can only conclude that they are intended to be used in a preliminary rumble in San Francisco [site of the July 1964 Republican National Convention] as a warmup for the political war later on."[172] Senator John Sherman Cooper (R/Ky.) however, defended the action of the House Republicans, as did Senator Javits, who said he believed "regardless of party, that we must stick it out in Vietnam. I do not believe that we ought to pull out. I believe there is too much at stake for us to pull out. Also, I do not believe we should overtly extend the war to North Vietnam which has been recommended by some."[173]

[170] U.S. Congress, Senate, Committee on Foreign Relations, *Foreign Assistance 1964*, Hearings, 88th Cong., 2d sess. (Washington, D.C.: U.S. Govt. Print. Off., 1964), pp. 542-552.
[171] *New York Times*, June 30, 1964.
[172] *CR*, vol. 110, p. 15666.
[173] *Ibid.*, pp. 15672-15673.

CHAPTER 5

STRIKING BACK: THE GULF OF TONKIN INCIDENTS

During the latter part of June and continuing through July 1964, the U.S. proceeded to carry out various of the military measures outlined in the June 15 White House memo which had been approved by the top members of the NSC and by the President. The *Pentagon Papers* provides a good summary of these actions:[1]

Among the more important *military-political* actions, carried out with considerable publicity, were the accelerated military construction effort in Thailand and South Vietnam, the prepositioning of contingency stockpiles in Thailand and the Philippines, the forward deployment of a carrier task force and land-based tactical aircraft within close striking distance of relevant enemy targets, and the assignment of an unprecedentedly high-level "first team" to man the U.S. Diplomatic Mission in Saigon. These measures were intended both to convince Hanoi and to reassure the GVN of the seriousness and durability of the U.S. commitment.

In addition, the U.S. undertook a number of unpublicized and more provocative actions, primarily as low-key indications to the enemy of the U.S. willingness and capability to employ increased force if necessary. Chief among these were the occasional DE SOTO Patrols (U.S. destroyer patrols conducted deep into the Gulf of Tonkin along the cost [*sic*] of North Vietnam), both as a "show of strength" and as an intelligence gathering device; Laotian air strikes and limited GVN cross-border operations against VC infiltration routes in Laos; GVN maritime raids and other harassing actions against North Vietnam; YANKEE TEAM, low-level photo reconnaissance missions over Laos, conducted by U.S. jet aircraft with fighter escorts for suppressive or retaliatory action against enemy ground fire. . . .

Many U.S. officials, however, continued to feel that a stronger, more dramatic commitment by the United States was required in order to rally the South Vietnamese. On July 13, William Sullivan, head of the Vietnam Coordinating Committee, who was about to leave for Vietnam as Taylor's deputy, drafted a memorandum on the situation in Vietnam again calling for such a commitment.[2] Sullivan referred to the "great doubt and confusion in Vietnam about U.S. determination." He added, "The daily speeches of Senator Morse, the columns of Walter Lippmann, the *New York Times*

---

[1] *PP*, Gravel ed., vol. III, p. 291.

[2] Sullivan's July 13 memorandum, Johnson Library, NSF Country File, Vietnam, would appear to be quite similar to his memo of about June 13, cited above, which is apparently still classified. Either he used much of the same material, or the July 13 memorandum is misdated, or the *Pentagon Papers* incorrectly attributed it to a date in June.

editorials, AFP [Agence France-Presse] distortions of George Ball's meeting with General de Gaulle [early June], the diplomatic negotiations with respect to Laos, and the absence of any clear signal concerning US intentions in Southeast Asia have worried the Vietnamese."

Given this sort of atmosphere in South Viet Nam, it is very difficult to persuade the Vietnamese to commit themselves to sharp military confrontations with the communists if they suspect that something in the way of a negotiated deal is being concocted behind their backs.

Both Ambassador Lodge and General Westmoreland, at the Honolulu Conference, expressed the opinion that the situation in South Viet Nam would "jog along" at the current stalemated pace unless some dramatic "victory" could be introduced to put new steel and confidence into Vietnamese leadership. General Westmoreland defined "victory" as a determination to take some new vigorous military commitment, such as air strikes against Viet Cong installations in the Laos corridor. Ambassador Lodge defined "victory" as a willingness to make punitive air strikes against North Viet Nam. The significant fact about both the Ambassador's and the General's suggestions was that they looked toward some American decision to undertake a commitment which the Vietnamese would interpret as a willingness to raise the military ante and eschew negotiations begun from a position of weakness. . . .

The general conclusion from this analysis is that we can anticipate no sharp upturns in the Vietnamese willingness or ability to press for the extermination of the insurgency if the current situation continues. Indeed, if they continue to worry about American will and determination, we could expect further political fragmentation and increasing disabilities. On the other hand, we cannot guarantee that a dramatic "victory" or active commitment by the U.S. would produce the sharp infusion of spirit which both the Ambassador and General Westmoreland predict.

It is clear, however, that unless some improvement in spirit and leadership can be introduced, we will have great difficulty in introducing more effective American assistance or in obtaining more effective Vietnamese utilization of that assistance. . . .

During July 19-23, there was new agitation by South Vietnamese leaders for "marching North," and Ambassador Taylor, fearing that Khanh might resign, and that the Vietnamese might even move toward negotiating with the Communists if they were unable to get more action out of the U.S., recommended to Washington on July 25 that the U.S. propose joint contingency planning for bombing North Vietnam.[3] Such planning, he said, would have several advantages, including forcing the Vietnamese "to look at the hard facts of life which lie behind the neon lights of the 'March North' slogans."

---

[3] Johnson Library, NSF NSC History File, Saigon to Washington 214, July 25, 1964.

A CIA cable on July 22 reported that Khanh told one of his associates, "my plan now is to get the Americans involved in North Vietnam." In a discussion with Taylor and U. Alexis Johnson on July 27, however, Khanh, according to Taylor's cable to Washington, "again spoke strongly about a natural war-weariness and the need to bring hostilities to a prompt end. Once more it came out clearly that he is thinking about reprisal tit-for-tat bombing rather than a movement north withdrawal forces or massive bombing. . . . He wants to do this reprisal bombing to encourage his people and to hasten Ho Chi Minh to conclude that the support of the VC should end."[4]

A meeting of the NSC was held on July 25, presumably to discuss the situation in Vietnam, and it would appear that several proposals for further military actions were considered during and immediately after the meeting. The *New York Times,* citing a summary of a Department of Defense command and control study of Tonkin Gulf decisionmaking prepared by the Institute for Defense Analyses for the Defense Department, which it said it obtained at the same time it obtained the *Pentagon Papers,* reported that after the meeting the JCS proposed "air strikes by unmarked planes flown by non-American crews against several targets in North Vietnam, including the coastal bases for Hanoi's flotilla of torpedo boats." McNaughton reportedly sent the plan to Rusk on July 30.[5]

On July 27, it was decided that 5,000 more U.S. military advisers would be sent to Vietnam in response to Westmoreland's June 25 request for 4,200 additional men, and the Vietnamese were so informed. This, too, may have been timed to placate Khanh, and as a further demonstration of the commitment of the United States to the defense of South Vietnam.

Provocation: 34-A Raids and DE SOTO Patrols

Of the various actions being undertaken to bring greater pressure on the North, the most provocative were the 34-A raids and the DE SOTO patrols. The 34-A raids on coastal areas of North Vietnam were being carried out by high-speed boats manned by commandos from South Vietnam and other countries who had been recruited and were supported and led by the CIA. DE SOTO patrols, which had been approved by President Kennedy in 1962, were highly-classified missions off the coast of North Vietnam by destroyers of the U.S. Navy equipped with specialized electronic gear which was manned by personnel from the National Security Agency (NSA, the U.S. Government's communications intelligence agency). The purpose of the patrols was to gather information on North Vietnam's radar systems, as well as various other kinds of military intelligence, and to conduct a "show of force." They had been conducted intermittently, and reportedly without incident. None of them, however, had been conducted concurrently with 34-A raids against the North Vietnamese coast.

---

[4] Johnson Library, NSF Country File, Vietnam.
[5] *The Pentagon Papers as published by the New York Times* (New York: Bantam Books, 1971), p. 258. The command and control study, which was subsequently denied to the Foreign Relations Committee, remains classified.

According to studies of the period, the most recent DE SOTO patrol of North Vietnam prior to the patrol conducted on July 31, 1964 occurred on March 10, 1964. This is not correct. There was another patrol in July 1964 immediately preceding the July 31 mission, and along almost the same course. In fact, the destroyer which made the July 31 patrol picked up the "black box" containing NSA's electronic gear from the destroyer which had just returned from patrol.[6] There had been no incidents during the patrol which had just ended, but neither had there been any 34-A operations against the North Vietnamese coast in the vicinity of the patrol.

In addition to the 34-A operations and the DE SOTO patrols, other military activities were being directed at North Vietnam during the summer of 1964, and may have contributed to a perception of threat by the north. In addition to those noted above, U-2 aircraft were making high-altitude reconnaissance flights over North Vietnam, and on July 25, U.S. reconnaissance planes based in Thailand also began flying communications intercept missions off the North Vietnamese coast.[7]

On July 15, 1964, the decision was made to send another DE SOTO patrol into the Gulf of Tonkin on July 31, using the destroyer U.S.S. *Maddox*. It is not entirely clear how the decision to undertake the patrol was made, who was involved in making it, or what debate there was, if any. Responsibility for all major U.S. covert operations worldwide, including both DE SOTO patrols and 34-A operations, had been vested in the so- called "303 Committee" of the NSC (this name was bestowed by NSAM 303 of June 2, 1964, the sole purpose of which was to change the name of the group after public disclosure of the term "special group") the successor to the NSC's Special Group under President Kennedy, composed of the Deputy Secretary of Defense, the Deputy Under Secretary of State for Political Affairs, the Deputy Director (Plans) of the CIA, and the Special Assistant to the President for National Security Affairs. As of July 1964 these were: Cyrus Vance (DOD), U. Alexis Johnson (State), Richard Helms (CIA), and McGeorge Bundy (White House). Bundy was Chairman of the group.[8]

The 303 Committee had delegated operational responsibility for both the DE SOTO patrols and 34-A operations to the JCS. The JCS assigned responsibility for the DE SOTO patrols to the Joint Reconnaisance Center, Operations Directorate (Ops Center), in the Defense Intelligence Agency (DIA), which drew up tentative schedules for patrols, based in part on intelligence requests from the CIA and NSA and sent them to CINCPAC (Commander in Chief, Pacific, then Adm. Ulysses S. Grant Sharp, Jr.), presumably after approval by the 303 Committee. CINCPAC selected the dates for pa-

---

[6]CRS Interview with Comdr. John J. Herrick (USN, Ret.), Nov. 27, 1984. See also McNamara's testimony in U.S. Congress, Senate, Committee on Foreign Relations, *The Gulf of Tonkin, The 1964 Incidents,* Hearing on February 20, 1968, 90th Cong., 2d sess. (Washington, D.C.: U.S. Govt. Print Off., 1968), p. 27.

[7]Futrell, *The Advisory Years to 1965,* p. 228.

[8]Within State, responsibility, at least for 34-A operations, apparently had been delegated to William Bundy, Llewellyn Thompson, and Michael Forrestal. William C. Trueheart, formerly with the U.S. mission in Saigon, was also involved. In Defense, responsibility for 34-A apparently had been delegated to John McNaughton, Assistant Secretary for International Security Affairs.

trols and issued orders to the Commander, Seventh Fleet, and gave copies of the orders to MACV in Saigon.[9]

The 34-A operations were planned initially by MACV in Saigon, and were sent through CINCPAC to Washington for approval by the JCS Special Assistant for Counterinsurgency and Special Activities (then Maj. Gen. Rollen Anthis), who sent a copy of the proposed schedule for the next month to the 303 Committee for its approval.

Thus, there were four points in the decisionmaking system where information about both the proposed DE SOTO patrols and the proposed 34-A operations was available: MACV (Westmoreland's headquarter in Saigon), CINCPAC, the JCS, and the 303 Committee. The division of responsibility for the two programs could have resulted, however, in a compartmentalization of knowledge that may have contributed to one hand not being fully informed as to what the other was doing. MACV was responsible for operating the 34-A program, but it was not in charge of the DE SOTO patrols even though it was informed about the schedule for those patrols. CINCPAC, which was responsible for the DE SOTO patrols, was informed about the 34-A operations, but was not directly involved in their conduct. The JCS was involved in scheduling both 34-A operations and DE SOTO patrols, but the two programs were handled by separate entities within the JCS staff system. The 303 Committee had responsibility for approving and overseeing both 34-A operations and DE SOTO patrols, but apparently left many of the details to the JCS, CINCPAC and MACV. In a real sense, therefore, coordination between the two programs may have occurred primarily at the operational level in CINCPAC and MACV, where the functional relationships between the two programs could be expected to come into sharpest focus.

According to a document prepared at the time, the July 15 decision to send the *Maddox* on a patrol on July 31 was made by the 303 Committee, as requested by CINCPAC.[10] Evidence is not available, however, as to whether at this or any of the other three points in the system there was any consideration of the fact that a 34-A raid on the coast of North Vietnam near the route to be taken by the *Maddox* had already been ordered for the night of July 30. Nor is there any evidence that at one or more of these points any consideration was given as to whether the North Vietnamese might assume that there was a connection between the July 30 34-A raid and the July 31 DE SOTO patrol.

On the night of July 30, 1964, 34-A South Vietnamese and other commandos, led by American advisers, raided the North Vietnamese islands of Hon Me and Hon Niem in the Gulf of Tonkin, while

---

[9]According to Joseph C. Goulden, *Truth is the First Casualty* (Chicago: Rand McNally, 1969), p. 123, the intelligence gathering part of the plan for the July 31 DE SOTO patrol was reviewed and approved by McCone for the CIA, by the Deputy Director of Defense Research and Engineering for the DIA, by Eugene G. Fubini for NSA, and "routinely" by the Bureau of Intelligence and Research (INR) of the State Department and the NSC.

[10]Johnson Library, NSC History File, Gulf of Tonkin Attacks, "Chronology of Events Relating to DESOTO Patrol Incidents in the Gulf of Tonkin on 2 and 4 August 1964," p. 1. This 3-page summary; and an attached 11-page chronology, were prepared by the Department of Defense, Joint Reconnaisance Center, Operations Directorate, and sent to the White House on Aug. 10, 1964, by Col. Ralph Steakley, Chief. The 11-page chronology consists mainly of technical details on the location of the *Maddox*, and brief reports from the ship during the Aug. 2 attack.

about 120 miles away the U.S.S. *Maddox* was headed toward the same area to conduct its DE SOTO patrol the following day. It is not known whether either group was aware of the other's existence and mission. How much more awareness there may have been in Saigon, Honolulu, and Washington is also unknown, and may even be unknowable. What is clear is that the U.S. and South Vietnam were provoking North Vietnam, and it may be reasonable to assume that at some point in the decisionmaking system these various operations were being orchestrated toward that end. George Ball said as much in discussing the Tonkin Gulf incidents of August 2 and 4, 1964, in an interview with Michael Charlton of the British Broadcasting Company:[11]

Ball. At that time there's no question that many of the people who were associated with the war saw the necessity of bombing as the only instrument that might really be persuasive on the North Vietnamese, and therefore were looking for any excuse to initiate bombing.

Charlton. And this may have been the incident that those people were waiting for.

Ball. That's right. Well, it was: the "de Soto" patrols, the sending of a destroyer up the Tonkin Gulf was primarily for provocation.

Charlton. To provoke such a response in order to pave the way for a bombing campaign?

Ball. I think so. I mean it had an intelligence objective. But let me say, I don't want to overstate this, the reason the destroyer was sent up was to show the flag, to indicate that we didn't recognize any other force in the Gulf; and there was *some* intelligence objective. But on the other hand I think there was a feeling that if the destroyer got into some trouble, that would provide the provocation we needed.

Early on the morning of Sunday, August 2, 1964, the *Maddox* was attacked in the Gulf of Tonkin by three North Vietnamese torpedo boats, and the *Maddox,* as well as planes from the carrier U.S.S. *Ticonderoga,* returned their fire, reportedly sinking one and damaging if not sinking the other two.[12]

---

[11]Charlton and Moncrieff, *Many Reasons Why,* p. 108.

[12]See the excellent article in *U.S. News and World Report,* "The 'Phantom Battle' That Led to War," July 23, 1984.

For primary materials on the Gulf of Tonkin incidents, two files in the Johnson Library are most useful: the "Gulf of Tonkin Attacks" in the NSF NSC History File, and "Gulf of Tonkin Miscellaneous," as well as the chronological material for Aug. 1964 in the NSF Country File, Vietnam. For original congressional materials, see especially the printed hearings of the joint executive session on Aug. 6, 1964, of the Senate Foreign Relations and Armed Services Committees, published in sanitized form in 1966: *Southeast Asia Resolution* (Washington, D.C.: U.S. Govt. Print. Off., 1966), and the subsequent hearings in Feb. 1968, in which the Foreign Relations Committee reexamined the 1964 incidents: *The Gulf of Tonkin: The 1964 Incidents,* cited above. Another important source is the series of three Senate speeches by Senator Morse on Feb. 21, 28, and 29, 1968, which consisted primarily of the draft report prepared by the staff of the Foreign Relations Committee. *CR,* vol. 114, pp. 3813-3817, 4578-4581, 4691-4697. See also *PP,* Gravel ed., vol. V., pp. 320 ff, which contains a complete text of this part of the report, some sections of which were missing from Vol. III; Goulden, *Truth is the First Casualty;* Anthony Austin, *The President's War* (Philadelphia: J. B. Lippincott, 1971), in the writing of which Austin had access to files of the Foreign Relations Committee; Eugene C. Windchy, *Tonkin Gulf* (New York: Doubleday, 1971). John Galloway did a brief study of the passage (and subsequent reexamination by the Senate) of the resolution, *The Gulf of Tonkin Resolution* (Rutherford, N.J.: Fairleigh Dickinson University Press, 1970), which also contains all of the pertinent documents, hearings, and debates on the resolution, as well as the key statements from the North Vietnamese on the Gulf of Tonkin incidents. Also useful is David Wise, "Remember the Maddox!" *Esquire,* (April 1968).

Several hours earlier, Comdr. John J. Herrick, the commander of Destroyer Division 192, who was then on the *Maddox* as commander of Task Group 72.1, had become concerned about the possibility of an attack, and had ordered the captain of the *Maddox*, Comdr. Herbert L. Ogier, to change course, while sending a message to their superior that "continuance of patrol presents an unacceptable risk. . . ."[13] Herrick was told that the *Maddox* should return to the assigned course when it was prudent to do so, but that it could change course again if need be. (The *Maddox* resumed course soon thereafter, but shortly before the attack began Herrick received information from electronic monitors aboard the *Maddox* that the torpedo boats were being ordered to attack, and he again ordered the ship toward the open sea.)

After receiving word of the attack on the morning of August 2, President Johnson met with Rusk, Ball, Vance, Wheeler for a briefing on the situation. According to one account, "He did not seem overly upset. He was more interested in the postal bill and, for more than an hour, treated his advisers to a lecture on the problems of moving such a bill through Congress."[14]

On August 2, the President ordered an augmented patrol to continue, and on August 3 the U.S.S. *Turner Joy* joined the *Maddox*. Johnson said in his memoirs: "We were determined not to be provocative, nor were we going to run away. We would give Hanoi the benefit of the doubt—this time—and assume the unprovoked attack had been a mistake."[15]

According to George Ball,[16]

> Though some of the President's advisers urged an immediate retaliatory move, the President wished for an even stronger record. So, rather than keeping our ships out of this now established danger zone, the President approved sending both the *Maddox* and the destroyer *C. Turner Joy* back into the Gulf. I was upset by this decision; the argument that we had to "show the flag" and demonstrate that we did not "intend to back down" seemed to me a hollow bravado.

Later that day, several congressional leaders were briefed on the attack (including Minority Leader Dirksen, Russell, Humphrey), and they were said to have voiced strong support for the President's actions.[17]

On the afternoon of August 3, the President met with Rusk, McNamara and Wheeler, and it was agreed that, for the moment, no additional action was required.[18] There are as yet no available notes of that meeting, but apparently one of the subjects discussed was the 34-A operations scheduled for the night of August 3, and the addition of more targets for those raids. After the meeting, Rusk sent Taylor a cable informing him that more targets were

[13]*CR*, vol. 114, p. 4693. This and several other important messages could not be found in the files of the Johnson Library. They were obtained by the Senate Foreign Relations Committee in 1967-68 in conjunction with the committee's reconsideration of the Gulf of Tonkin incidents, and were quoted in the committee's hearing or by Morse in his three speeches.

[14]Kalb and Abel, *Roots of Involvement*, p. 171.

[15]*The Vantage Point*, p. 113.

[16]*The Past Has Another Pattern*, p. 379.

[17]Austin, *The President's War*, p. 25, and Goulden, pp. 24-25.

[18]Johnson Library, NSC History File, Gulf of Tonkin Attacks, McGeorge Bundy Chronology of Events August 3-7, a memorandum to George Reedy dated Aug. 7, 1964.

going to be added. He also told Taylor, contrary to the denials of the executive branch is its discussions with Congress and in its public statements, that there was, indeed, a direct connection between the 34-A operations and the North Vietnamese attack on the *Maddox,* and that the attack on the *Maddox,* rather than being unprovoked, was directly related to the 34-A raids. This is what Rusk's cable said: "We believe that present OPLAN 34A activities are beginning to rattle Hanoi, and MADDOX incident is directly related to their efforts to resist these activities. . . . We have no intention yielding to pressure."[19] In a meeting of the NSC on August 4, after a second attack on the *Maddox* was thought to have occurred, CIA Director McCone took the same position, as will be seen, arguing that in attacking U.S. ships the North Vietnamese were reacting defensively to 34-A raids, and were not trying to provoke the United States.

A secret meeting was then held later on the afternoon of August 3 at the Capitol, attended by members of the Senate Foreign Relations and Armed Services Committees, and the majority and minority leaders, at which 25 Senators, including Fulbright, Mansfield and Morse, were briefed on the situation by Rusk, McNamara, and General Wheeler. According to one account, it was revealed at the meeting that the *Maddox* had deliberately gone inside the 12-mile coastal limit claimed by North Vietnam (the U.S. recognized only a three-mile limit), that South Vietnamese 34-A vessels had bombarded the coast of North Vietnam on July 31, and that, according to McNamara, the North Vietnamese may have mistaken the *Maddox* for a South Vietnamese boat. Both Rusk and McNamara called the attack "entirely unprovoked."[20] After the meeting, Senator Russell, chairman of the Armed Services Committee, told the press that there had been some South Vietnamese naval operations in the Gulf of Tonkin, and these could have "confused" the North Vietnamese. The State Department denied Russell's statement, saying that such a mistake was highly unlikely.[21]

Judging by an exchange in Senate debate on the Gulf of Tonkin Resolution several days later, it would appear that those who attended this highly secret meeting on August 3 were also told by administration officials that the *Maddox* had the capability of intercepting North Vietnamese radio messages—the so-called "radio intercepts" that were to play such an important role in the subsequent debate about the occurrence of a second attack on August 4. Those Senators present at the meeting were apparently cautioned, however, about the sensitivity of this information. When Senator Morse mentioned during the debate on the resolution that the *Maddox* moved out to sea "because there was some concern about some intelligence that we are getting," Senator Lausche began to ask him about it and Morse cut him off, saying "I am not going to comment on that. I think I have said all that I have a right to say within the proprieties. . . . I do not think I should say it. I do not believe the Senator from Ohio should say it, either."[22]

[19]Johnson Library, NSF Country File, Vietnam, Washington to Saigon 336, Aug. 3, 1964.
[20]Austin, p. 28. There are apparently no notes or summary of that meeting.
[21]*New York Times,* Aug. 4, 1964, and Austin, p. 28.
[22]*CR,* vol. 110, p. 18424.

As the DE SOTO patrol resumed on August 2-3, Rear Adm. Robert B. Moore, the Commander of carrier Task Group 77.5 (which included the flagship *Ticonderoga*) sent Herrick this message:[23]

> It is apparent that DRV has thrown down the gauntlet and now considers itself at war with the United States. It is felt that they will attack U.S. forces on sight with no regard for cost. U.S. ships in Gulf of Tonkin can no longer assume that they will be considered neutrals exercising the right of free transit. They will be treated as belligerents from first detection and must consider themselves as such.

Faced with the fact that, as Moore so flatly stated, U.S. vessels in the Gulf of Tonkin would be treated by North Vietnam as belligerents, even in international waters, Herrick requested on August 3 that the patrol be terminated. This was rejected by Adm. Thomas H. Moorer, Commander in Chief of the Pacific Fleet, who said:[24] "Termination of DE SOTO patrol after two days of patrol ops subsequent to *Maddox* incident does not in my view adequately demonstrate United States resolve to assert our legitimate rights in these international waters." The only course modification by CINCPAC was to direct the *Maddox* and the *Turner Joy,* at the request of U.S. officials at the U.S. military command (MACV) in Saigon to remain somewhat north of their scheduled location "to avoid interference with 34-A Ops." In a message to Admiral Sharp (CINCPAC), Admiral Moorer also stated that this change in location would "possibly draw NVN [North Vietnamese Navy] PGMs [patrol boats] to northward away from area of 34-A Ops . . . ," thus suggesting that U.S. officials, at this point at least, despite denials by the executive branch, were using the DE SOTO patrol in conjunction with 34-A operations.

On the night of August 3, another 34-A raid was made on the coast of North Vietnam, and on the morning of August 4 Herrick sent a message that, based on electronic monitoring of North Vietnamese communications, North Vietnam ". . . considers patrol directly involved with 34-A ops. DRV considers U.S. ships present as enemies because of these ops and have already indicated their readiness to treat us in that category."[25] When he was asked on August 6 during testimony before the Foreign Relations Committee on the Gulf of Tonkin Resolution about the 34-A operations, McNamara did not mention the raids on August 3.[26] Later he stated that he learned of those raids only after he had testified on August 6.[27] The record shows, however, that McNamara met with the President on the afternoon of August 3 to discuss, among other things, the 34-A operations scheduled for that night. In addition, there was at least one message sent to his office prior to his testimony on August 6 providing information on the August 3 raids.[28]

[23] *CR*, vol. 114, p. 4580.
[24] *Ibid.*, p. 4694.
[25] *The Gulf of Tonkin, The 1964 Incidents,* p. 40.
[26] See *Southeast Asia Resolution passim.*
[27] *The Gulf of Tonkin, The 1964 Incidents,* p. 15.
[28] On the morning of Aug. 4, a cable from Westmoreland's headquarters in Saigon, a copy of which went to "OSD [Office Secretary of Defense] McNamara," reported on the details of the raids. The cable, 040955Z, is in the Johnson Library, NSF Country File, Vietnam.

August 4, 1964: The U.S. Retaliates Against North Vietnam

At 7:40 p.m. Saigon time on the evening of August 4, (7:40 a.m. in Washington), Herrick sent a message to Admiral Moorer that, based on radio monitoring, the North Vietnamese appeared to be preparing to attack the *Maddox* and the *Turner Joy.*[29]

At 9:12 a.m., McNamara called the President to tell him about the information. Although there still had not been an attack, the President told Democratic congressional leaders, who were at the White House for their weekly legislative breakfast meeting, about the situation, and said that if there were to be an attack he thought the U.S. would have to retaliate.[30] The leaders agreed, and there was also agreement on the desirability of a congressional resolution. White House assistant Kenneth O'Donnell, a former Kennedy aide, said that after the meeting Johnson wondered about the political effects of military retaliation, and O'Donnell said that he and Johnson "agreed as politicians that the President's leadership was being tested under these circumstances and that he must respond decisively. His opponent was Senator Goldwater [who had been nominated for the Presidency by the Republican Party at its convention in late July] and the attack on Lyndon Johnson was going to come from the right and the hawks, and he must not allow them to accuse him of vacillating or being an indecisive leader."[31]

After his breakfast meeting with the leadership, Johnson told Majority Leader Carl Albert (D/Okla.) that he wanted to discuss another subject. The conversation that followed was interrupted by a phone call, probably the second (at 9:43 a.m.) of four that McNamara made to the President during the morning, in which McNamara reported that the two ships were under attack. According to Albert, Johnson said to the person who was calling, "They have? Now, I'll tell you what I want. I not only want those patrol boats that attacked the *Maddox* destroyed, I want everything at that harbor destroyed; I want the whole works destroyed. I want to give them a real dose."[32]

Meanwhile, McNamara met at the Pentagon, beginning at about 9:25 a.m., with representatives of the JCS. At 9:30 a.m. Herrick reported that vessels which were evaluated as hostile were closing rapidly.[33] At 9:52 a.m., Herrick radioed that the *Maddox* and the

---

[29]Saigon time was 12 hours ahead of Washington during daylight savings time. The *Maddox* was in the next time zone, with a 13-hour difference, but was operating on Saigon time.

[30]Present were from the House, Speaker McCormack, Albert, and Boggs, and from the Senate, Humphrey, Carl Hayden (D/Ariz.) and George Smathers. Mansfield was absent.

[31]Austin, pp. 29-30.

[32]CRS Interview with Carl Albert, Oct. 31, 1978.

[33]These and other facts about the events of Aug. 4 are derived from the 48-page "Chronology of Events Tuesday, August 4 and Wednesday, August 5, 1964 Tonkin Gulf Strike," Third Draft, Aug. 25, 1964, located in the Johnson Library, NSF Country File, Vietnam. This, as well as other materials cited below, including a 74-page transcript of selected telephone conversations on Aug. 4 between the Pentagon, CINCPAC and the White House, was prepared in conjunction with compilation by the White House staff of information on the Gulf of Tonkin incidents. There is no information on who prepared the chronology or the telephone transcript, or on the criteria for selection of material. For whatever reason, the chronology does not contain, nor does the telephone transcript, any material relating to the messages to and from the *Maddox* and the *Turner Joy* seeking to confirm that an attack had occurred, except for the initial message from Herrick at 1:27 p.m. on Aug. 4 (see below) suggesting further evaluation.

This chronology should not be confused with the chronology cited earlier which was prepared by the office of Col. Steakley.

Turner Joy were under "continuous torpedo attack." At approximately 11:30 a.m., Rusk, McGeorge Bundy and McCone joined the group. It was agreed to recommend to the President a limited airstrike on the torpedo boat bases.

At about 1 p.m., Rusk, McNamara, Vance, McCone and McGeorge Bundy met with the President for lunch. Johnson's first reaction was that the North Vietnamese must be punished. He agreed that the response should be an airstrike, and he ordered preparations to be made.

George Ball, General Wheeler and CIA Deputy Director (for Plans) Helms joined the group after lunch for a discussion of the details of the airstrike.

At 1:27 p.m. Herrick sent this "flash"message: "Review of action makes many reported contacts and torpedoes fired appear doubtful. Freak weather effects on radar and overeager sonarmen may have accounted for many reports. No actual visual sightings by Maddox. Suggest complete evaluation before any further action taken."[34]

At 1:59 p.m., before the full printed text of Herrick's 1:27 p.m. message was available in Washington, Gen. David A. Burchinal, Director of the Joint Staff (JCS), who was serving as McNamara's contact with Admiral Sharp (CINCPAC), was talking by telephone to Sharp in Honolulu. Sharp had received Herrick's new message, and told Burchinal what it said. Burchinal asked him to secure more information. At 2:08 p.m., Sharp told Burchinal that despite Herrick's message, there was no doubt that a torpedo attack had occurred. He said, however, that many of the reported attacks may have been due to inaccurate sonar reports, ". . . because whenever they get keyed up on a thing like this everything they hear on the sonar is a torpedo."[35]

McNamara was at the White House at this point, but was receiving reports from Burchinal, including the information about Herrick's 1:27 p.m. message suggesting further evaluation, which he, in

---

[34]Johnson Library, NSF Country File, Vietnam. In the 1968 hearings of the Senate Foreign Relations Committee reexamining the 1964 Gulf of Tonkin incidents, (*The Gulf of Tonkin, The 1964 Incidents*, p. 80), Senator Fulbright, referring to the 1:27 p.m. message from Herrick, said this to McNamara:

"But that alone almost, if I had known of that one telegram, if that had been put before me on the 6th of August, I certainly don't believe I would have rushed into action."

[35]Johnson Library, NSF Country File, Vietnam, "Transcript of Telephone Conversations, 4-5 August," p. 31.

There is no available information concerning the coverage of the 74-page transcript, and thus no way, at present at least, of knowing how to evaluate the document as a source. There is no information on what phone calls pertaining to the Gulf of Tonkin were recorded in the Pentagon during Aug. 4, and which calls may have been excluded from the transcript. Nor is there any indication as to who compiled the transcript, or whether any changes were made in it, and, if so, what changes were made and by whom. Judging from the transcript, most if not all of the important calls between the Pentagon and Admiral Sharp and within the Pentagon, as well as between the White House and the Pentagon, were recorded on Aug. 4. Yet there are no phone calls in the transcript dealing with efforts, discussed below, after Herrick's 1:27 p.m. message, to get him to confirm that an attack occurred. In this respect, the transcript bears a strong resemblance to the Chronology of Events, Aug. 25 Draft, which, as was noted above, also does not refer to any of those messages after Herrick's 1:27 p.m. message.

The only available evidence that the White House staff attempted to collect all of the "pertinent" (the word used in the memo) recorded telephone calls made on Aug. 4 is a one-page document in the Johnson Library, NSF Country File, Vietnam, entitled "Steps in Remaking Gulf of Tonkin Tape," dated Aug. 24, 1964. It is apparently an internal Pentagon document, which is unattributed, directing those concerned to search the "master tape" for recorded conversations that were not included on an "original small tape" (which may have been sent earlier to the White House), and to send the new tape to the White House by the next day. In the memo, there is reference to the "goal of getting EVERYTHING recorded."

There is also no evidence as to whether any of the tapes themselves are still in existence.

turn, gave to the President. At 4:08 p.m., after he returned to the Pentagon, McNamara called Admiral Sharp to ask about the latest information on the attack. Sharp described what had happened, and McNamara said, "There isn't any possibility there was no attack, is there?" Sharp replied, "Yes, I would say there is a slight possibility." He added that he was trying to get further information. McNamara said, "We obviously don't want to do it [carry out the retaliatory strike] until we are damned sure what happened." He asked Sharp, "how do we reconcile all this?" Sharp said that the order to retaliate should be held "until we have a definite indication that this happened." McNamara told him to leave the "execute" order in effect (it was sent to Sharp a few minutes later) and to call him by 6 p.m.[36]

Meanwhile, in the Gulf of Tonkin, where it was about 2 a.m. on August 5, the battle finally seemed to have ended, but verification of the attack on the two ships was extremely difficult. Besides the darkness, bad weather had added to the problem of visibility. Because of the cloud cover, most of the star shells (flares) fired by the ships to illumine the area burned out before they came out of the clouds. Planes from the *Ticonderoga*, which were supporting the destroyers, also reported restricted visibility (3 miles) and deteriorating weather conditions (3,000 feet broken), but also said they could see clearly enough to see the two American ships, and, because of the dark, could have seen gunfire from any attacking ship. "Returning pilots," according to a message from the *Ticonderoga* (at 3:28 p.m. Washington time), "report no visual sightings of any vessels or wakes other than Turner Joy and Maddox. Wakes from Turner Joy and Maddox visible for 2-3000 yards."

At 1:54 p.m. Washington time, Herrick sent this message:[37]

> Maddox and Joy now apparently in clear further recap reveals Turner Joy fired upon by small calibre guns and illuminated by search light. Joy tracked 2 sets of contacts. Fired on 13 contacts. Claims positive hits 3, 1 junk, probable hits 3.
>
> Joy also reports no actual visual sightings or wake. Have no recap of aircraft sightings but seemed to be few. Entire action leaves many doubts except for apparent attempted ambush at beginning. Suggest thorough reconnaisance in daylight by aircraft.

This message, as well as Herrick's message at 1:27 p.m., were sent after Herrick and Commander Ogier of the *Maddox* had conducted an experiment once the engagement appeared to be over. After 26 sonar reports (all from the *Maddox*, and none from the *Turner Joy*) which had been identified as torpedoes, they suspected that the sonar operator on the *Maddox* was hearing reflections from the *Maddox* as it made its evasive weaving turns. So they experimented with a few high speed turns, and, as they suspected, each one was reported by the sonar operator in the same manner as the previous reports. Herrick said later, "It was the echo of our outgoing sonar beam hitting the rudders, which were then full

[36] Johnson Library, NSF Country File, Vietnam. "Telephone Conversation between Secretary McNamara and Admiral Sharp." This conversation was not included in the compilation of telephone transcripts cited above.
[37] Johnson Library, NSF Country File, Vietnam, 041754Z.

over, and reflected back into the receiver. Most of the *Maddox's* reports were probably false."[38]

At 2:48 p.m., in response to continuing efforts of his superiors to get further confirmation of the attack, Herrick sent this message:[39]

Certain that original ambush was bonafide. Details of action following present a confusing picture. Have interviewed witnesses who made positive visual sightings of cockpit lights or similar passing near Maddox. Several reported torpedoes were probably boats themselves which were observed to make several close passes on Maddox. Own ship screw noises on rudders may have accounted for some. At present cannot even estimate number of boats involved. Turner Joy reports 2 torpedoes passed near her.

At 4:47 p.m., McNamara and Vance met with the JCS "to marshal the evidence to overcome lack of a clear and convincing showing that an attack on the destroyer had in fact occurred."[40] Five factors were considered to be especially important:

1. The TURNER JOY was illuminated when fired on by automatic weapons.

2. One of the destroyers observed cockpit lights.

3. A PGM 142 shot at two U.S. aircraft (From COMINT).[41]

4. A North Vietnamese announcement that two of its boats were "sacrificed." (From COMINT)

5. Sharp's determination that there was indeed an attack.[42]

McNamara and the JCS concluded, based on these five points that there had been an attack, and at 4:49 p.m., the National Military Command Center (NMCC) in the Pentagon transmitted the "strike execute" message to CINCPAC.

Throughout the afternoon of August 4, the White House was relying on McNamara for confirmation of the August 4 attack. It was August 7 before McGeorge Bundy asked for copies of the NSA intercepts. According to a memorandum for the record on August 8 from the White House Situation Room, which handled the request, he asked for "all intercepts which preceded and related" to the second attack. He received some but apparently not all of the intercepts. The memorandum stated that "the attached messages" were "selected by CIA and NSA."[43]

While McNamara and the military were examining the evidence of the attack and preparing plans for retaliating, a congressional resolution was quickly prepared on August 4 by Abram Chayes

---

[38]*U.S. News and World Report,* July 23, 1984, and CRS Interview with Commander John J. Herrick (USN, Ret.), Nov. 27, 1984.

[39]Johnson Library, NSF Country File, Vietnam, 041848Z.

[40]"Chronology of Events, Tuesday, August 4 and Wednesday, August 5, 1964 Tonkin Gulf Strike," cited above.

[41]COMINT, communications intelligence, refers here to National Security Agency communications intercepts.

[42]Sharp had called the Pentagon at 5:23 p.m., during McNamara's meeting with the JCS, to report that the COMINT intercept about the sacrifice of the two boats was convincing evidence for him that the attack had occurred. It is interesting, however, that when Sharp asked Gen. David A. Burchinal, who was Director of the Joint Staff, whether he had seen that message, Burchinal said he had not. Later in the conversation, however, Burchinal said that McNamara was "satisfied with the evidence," even though at that point McNamara also apparently had not seen the COMINT intercept in question. Transcript of Telephone Conversations, p. 37.

[43]Johnson Library, NSF Country File, Vietnam. The "attached messages" are not attached to the copy of this memorandum contained in this particular file, however.

working with George Ball[44] According to Chayes, who had been the State Department's Legal Adviser from 1961 until June of 1964, "The main thing . . . that Ball wanted me to deal with, . . . was this question of Executive-Congressional relationships. . . . the whole problem . . . was how do you get a resolution without acknowledging that Congress had any authority in this? . . . I didn't look at whatever the evidence was. . . . It was simply that he [Ball] wanted me to look at the resolution and make sure that we're not giving away any part of the President's power in this resolution. And so I spent . . . a couple of hours, talking about the resolution, going over it and making sure that it didn't go beyond the earlier resolutions in the acknowledgment of a requirement of congressional participation."[45]

When George Ball was asked later about his role, he replied:[46]

> . . . I don't think I ever saw the resolution until it was in final form. . . . the President asked me to help get it through and I went up and talked to Bill Fulbright and some of the others, and did what I was supposed to do. . . . I don't think I thought about it very much. I was just doing a chore. I don't think I fully realized the total implications. The President wanted to get some legitimizing action for what he was doing. The war distressed me, to be quite frank about it.

Ball added, "I don't think that Congress ought to give that kind of open-ended authority to any President."

At 6:15 p.m., the President met with the NSC. McNamara outlined the plan to strike the North Vietnamese torpedo boat bases and to conduct armed reconnaissance along the North Vietnamese coast, as well as to send reinforcements to the area to demonstrate the U.S. "will to escalate." The attack would be accompanied by a Presidential announcement and a congressional resolution. Rusk stated, "An immediate and direct reaction by us is necessary. The unprovoked attack on the high seas is an act of war for all practical purposes."[47] The President asked, "Do they want a war by attacking our ships in the middle of the Gulf of Tonkin?" CIA Director McCone replied, "No. The North Vietnamese are reacting defensively to our attacks on the off-shore islands. They are responding out of pride and on the basis of defense considerations. The attack is a signal to us that the North Vietnamese have the will and determination to continue the war. They are raising the ante." (Following this, a comment by the President as to how the U.S. should respond has been deleted from the notes of the meeting.) Carl Rowan, Director of the U.S. Information Agency, asked, "Do we know for a fact that the North Vietnamese provocation took place? Can we nail down exactly what happened? We must be prepared to be accused of fabricating the incident." McNamara replied, "We will know definitely in the morning." (The remainder of his reply has been deleted from the notes.) After this discussion,

---

[44]"Draft Joint Resolution on Southeast Asia," undated, but filed under 8/4/64, is in the Johnson Library, NSF NSC Meetings File. This is probably the Chayes-Ball version, which, after changes in wording but not in substance, became the Gulf of Tonkin Resolution.

[45]CRS Interview with Abram Chayes, Oct. 13, 1978.

[46]CRS Interview with George Ball, Sept. 30, 1980.

[47]Johnson Library, NSF NSC Meetings File. The notes of this meeting have been sanitized in several places.

which lasted about 20 minutes, the President asked the members of the NSC whether they had any objections to the plan. "All NSC members approved the plan."[48] The President ordered the attacks to take place, thus putting into effect the "strike execute" message which had been sent at 4:49.

At 5 p.m., the White House started asking 16 congressional leaders and committee chairmen and ranking members to attend a meeting with the President. At 6:45 p.m., the President opened the meeting with a report on the attack.[49] He then explained that he had already ordered retaliation, and would make a public announcement later in the evening after U.S. planes were over their targets. Rusk, McNamara, McCone and General Wheeler also spoke. Rusk emphasized the importance of demonstrating U.S. resolve in defending Southeast Asia, as well as affirming the right of U.S. ships to use the international waters of the Gulf of Tonkin. The President added: "We want them to know we are not going to take it lying down, but we are not going to destroy their cities. We hope we can prepare them for the course we will follow."

Speaker McCormack said that the attacks were an act of war, and that the U.S. had to respond. Senator Russell urged the President to "get the last one of them [torpedo boats]."

Mansfield was the only congressional leader to express opposition to Johnson's decision. He read a prepared statement which is summarized in the notes of the meeting: "I don't know how much good it will do," he said. "May be getting all involved with a minor third rate state. Then what is to come in response, if not Korea for China? The Communists won't be forced down. A lot of lives to mow them down." The President asked Mansfield if he had an alternative. Mansfield replied that the U.S. should consider the attacks as "isolated acts of terror," and should take the matter to the U.N. Rusk said that one problem with that suggestion was that China had not committed itself, and that a limited attack would impress the Chinese with the seriousness of the United States' purpose, while also demonstrating that the U.S. would keep the conflict limited.

Senator Hickenlooper, while feeling that the U.S. should not be seeking a "confrontation," also supported retaliation, and added, "There should be no doubt as to whether the President should have the right to order the Armed Forces into action. Should not have to quarrel for weeks as to whether he had the authority or not. It is my own personal feeling that it is up to the President to prepare the kind and type of resolution he believes would be proper. It is up to Congress to say whether they will pass it or not." President

[48] Chronology of Events, Aug. 25 draft, p. 30.

[49] The following discussion is based on notes on the Aug. 4 meeting with congressional leaders which have been declassified and are in the Johnson Library, NSF Meetings Notes File. See also Austin, p. 42; *Washington Post*, Aug. 5, 1964; and the *New York Times*, Aug. 5 and 8, 1964. These Members of Congress were present at the meeting: from the House, Speaker McCormack, Albert, Vinson, and Morgan, and Republicans Halleck, Leslie C. Arends (Ill.) and Frances P. Bolton (Ohio); from the Senate, Democrats Mansfield, Russell, Fulbright, and Humphrey, and Republicans Dirksen, Saltonstall, Kuchel, Hickenlooper, and Aiken. There are several versions of the notes of this meeting. For an explanation and a discussion of the meeting see Mark A. Stoler, "Aiken, Mansfield and the Tonkin Gulf Crisis: Notes from the Congressional Leadership Meeting at the White House, August 4, 1964," *Vermont History* 50 (Spring 1982), pp. 80–94. The author is grateful to Dr. David Humphrey, Archivist at the Johnson Library, for calling this article to his attention.

Johnson replied, "I had that feeling but felt I wanted the advice of each of you and wanted to consult with you. We felt we should move with the action recommended by the Joint Chiefs, but I wanted to get the Congressional concurrence. I think it would be very damaging to ask for it and not get it." "I don't think any resolution is necessary," he added, "but I think it is a lot better to have it in the light of what we did in Korea." McCormack responded, "I think the Congress has a responsibility and should show a united front to the world."

House Republican Leader Charles A. Halleck (R/Ind.) said, "The President knows there is no partisanship among us," and he noted that in the case of the Cuban missile crisis he had been the first to speak up in support of President Kennedy. But he wondered, "Are we getting fouled up here on something we could put off?"

As the meeting ended, Halleck said, "If we are going to have it [the resolution], it has to be overwhelming. . . . I think it will pass overwhelmingly as far as I am concerned."

The President said, "I have told you what I want from you," and he proceeded to go around the table and ask each Member of Congress to state his position. Every Member, including Mansfield and Fulbright, said he would support the resolution. Aiken indicated his reluctance, as well as his acceptance of the reality of the situation in which Congress was being placed, when he commented, "By the time you send it up here there won't be anything for us to do but support you."

Later in the evening Johnson talked by telephone with Senator Goldwater, who said he supported the decision. Goldwater told the press, "I believe it is the only thing he can do under the circumstances. We cannot allow the American flag to be shot at anywhere on earth if we are to retain our respect and prestige."

In an interview some years later, Senator Goldwater commented:[50]

> I'll be perfectly honest with you. I have very grave doubts that there was ever any incident in the Gulf of Tonkin that would have required congressional action. I think it was a complete phony, and I've yet to run into a Navy man that will tell me there was. . . . I think Johnson plain lied to the Congress and got the resolution. . . . About the only way he could have gotten congressional support was to insinuate that there had been an attack on an American ship. . . .

Goldwater added, however, that the U.S. could have retaliated without action by Congress, based on the power of the Commander in Chief to use the armed forces.

Goldwater was also asked if, even before the 1964 Presidential campaign began, President Johnson was planning on going to war after the election. He replied: "Oh, I don't think there's any question. You might say the troops had gotten their orders but nobody knew about it."

Efforts to confirm the second attack continued throughout the late afternoon and evening of August 4. At about 5:30 p.m., Admiral Sharp, possibly in the call at 5:23 p.m. cited above, is said to

---

[50]*New York Times*, Aug. 5, 1964, and CRS Interview with Barry Goldwater, Aug. 20, 1980.

have reconfirmed his belief that an attack took place, and after the call McNamara is said to have told a top aide to make doubly sure that Sharp was willing to state that the attack had occurred.[51] Sharp then sent an urgent message to Herrick at 5:34 p.m. asking for further confirmation:[52]

1. Can you confirm absolutely that you were attacked?
2. Can you confirm sinking of PT boats?
3. Desire reply directly supporting evidence.

At 5:58 p.m. (5:58 a.m. on the *Maddox*), Herrick sent his final situation report, in which he said:[53]

. . . Turner Joy claims sinking one craft and damage to another with gunfire. Damaged boat returned confire-no hits. Turner Joy and other personnel observed bursts and black smoke from hits on this boat. This boat illuminated Turner Joy and his return fire was observed and heard by T J personnel. Maddox scored no known hits and never positively identified a boat as such.

4. The first boat to close Maddox probably fired torpedo at Maddox which was heard but not seen. All subsequent Maddox torpedo reports are doubtful in that it is suspected the sonarman was hearing the ships own propeller beat reflected off rudders during course changes (weaving). Turner Joy detected 2 torpedo runs on her one of which was sighted visually passed down port side 3 to 5 hundred yards.

5. Weather was overcast with limited visibility. There were no stars or moon resulting in almost total darkness throughout action.

Finally a message was sent to both the *Maddox* and the *Turner Joy* asking in part: "Can you confirm you were attacked by PT or Swatow (patrol boat)?" The *Maddox* did not reply, but at 7:10 p.m., Cdr. Robert C. Barnhart, the commanding officer of the *Turner Joy*, sent this message:[54]

1. Confirm being attacked by 2 pt craft. Evidence as Fol:
   A. Target fired torpedo sighted by director off and dir crew plus port lookout.
   B. Target burned when hit. Black smoke seen by co [commanding officer] and many other personnel.
   C. Target silhouette sighted by some topside personnel.
   D. Target tracked on surface search and fire control radar at high speeds erratic maneuvers.
2. Sinking only highly probably and as fols:
   A. Target tracked on search and fire control radars.
   B. Shell bursts observed on radar all over contact.
   C. Hits reported visually.
   D. Target disappeared from radar scope while within radar range.
   E. No further burning or smoke seen.

At about 9 p.m., Admiral Moorer sent this message to the *Turner Joy*: "Who were witnesses? what is witness reliability? most impor-

[51]Goulden, p. 155.
[52]*CR*, vol. 114, p. 4695.
[53]Johnson Library, NSF Country File, Vietnam, 042158Z.
[54]Johnson Library, NSF Country File, Vietnam, 042310Z.

tant that present evidence substantiating type and number of attacking forces be gathered and disseminated."[55] The reply, the text of which is not available, was reported to have been received in Washington at 1:15 a.m. on August 5.[56]

In Washington at 11:37 p.m. on the night of August 4, while Admiral Sharp and others were still collecting evidence that the attack on the *Maddox* and the *Turner Joy* had occurred, President Johnson went on nationwide television to announce that the U.S. was retaliating with airstrikes (Operation PIERCE ARROW) on North Vietnamese torpedo boat bases and POL (petroleum, oil, lubricants) supplies.[57] ". . . renewed hostile actions against United States ships on the high seas in the Gulf of Tonkin," he said, "have today required me to order the military forces of the United States to take action in reply. The initial attack on the destroyer *Maddox* on August 2 was repeated today by a number of hostile vessels attacking two U.S. destroyers with torpedoes. . . . repeated acts of violence against the armed forces of the United States must be met not only with alert defense but with positive reply. . . ." "firmness in the right is indispensable today for peace. That firmness will always be measured. Its mission is peace."[58]

Aftermath

On August 7, Herrick submitted eyewitness statements from himself, Commander Ogier, and other officers and members of the crew of the *Maddox*, on the events of August 4. In his statement, Herrick concluded:[59] "I had no opportunity to visually sight by unaided human eye any of the action. However, it is my opinion that certainly a PT boat action did take place. The number of boats involved and the number of torpedoes fired I cannot accurately determine." Commander Ogier said, "I believed [at] the time that the Maddox was under attack by PT boats. Later I doubted that so many torpedoes could have been fired and have missed. I am now convinced that the torpedo attacks did take place."

Ogier also said that he was forwarding to the fleet commander a recorded tape of the sonar effects which had occurred during the August 4 incident, and that "an evaluation . . . of the dydrophone effects may disclose proof of the presence of the torpedoes." Whether this evaluation was ever made, and what disposition was made of the tape, is not known.

On August 9, 1964, a team of two Department of Defense civilians and two military men was sent from Washington to investigate the August 4 incident. They interviewed personnel from the *Maddox* and the *Turner Joy*, as well as pilots on the *Ticonderoga*.

[55]*CR*, vol. 114, p. 4695.

[56]*Ibid.*, p. 4695.

[57]*Public Papers of the Presidents*, Lyndon B. Johnson, 1963-1964, pp. 927-928.

[58]On Aug. 5, in a speech at Syracuse University, the President said, among other things, "The attacks were deliberate. The attacks were unprovoked." The Government of North Vietnam, he said, had committed an act of aggression against the United States, "Aggression—deliberate, willful and systematic aggression—has unmasked its face to the entire world. The world remembers—the world must never forget—that aggression unchallenged is aggression unleashed." *Ibid.*, pp. 928-930.

[59]0710512, from CINCPCFLT (Commander in Chief, Pacific Fleet), Johnson Library, NSF Country File, Vietnam. McNamara used some of the eyewitness accounts when he tesified in 1968, but apparently did not use others in which doubts about the attack may have been expressed. See *The Gulf of Tonkin, The 1964 Incidents*, pp. 16-17.

In a copy of their draft report—the final report is still classified—they reported eyewitness accounts of a torpedo wake, hits on enemy craft that were verified by radar and black smoke, sightings of the PT boats themselves, and a search light. They concluded: "Although details engagement will require considerable data refinement, believe attack clearly occurred essentially as described in [this] cable."[60]

Although two U.S. pilots aboard the *Ticonderoga* were later quoted by McNamara as supporting eyewitnesses for the August 4 attack on the two U.S. destroyers,[61] one other Navy pilot on the *Ticonderoga*, Commander James B. Stockdale, leader of another attack squadron and later a prisoner of war of the North Vietnamese for eight years, thought that there had been no attack, and that the U.S. was ". . . about to launch a war under false pretenses, in the face of the on-scene military commander's advice to the contrary." Stockdale also had been flying over the two destroyers that day, as he had when he and others from the *Ticonderoga* attacked the North Vietnamese PT boats on August 2. On August 4, despite limited visibility, he said he could see the destroyers clearly, but never saw any other boats: "Not a one. No boats, no boat wakes, no ricochets off boats, no boat impacts, no torpedo wakes—nothing but black sea and American firepower."[62]

When Stockdale was then ordered to lead the reprisal strike against North Vietnam on the morning of August 5, his reaction was "'Reprisal for what?' . . . I felt like I had been doused with ice water. How do I get in touch with the President? He's going off half-cocked."[63]

In the several days after the August 4 incident, questions were also being raised by at least one high-ranking offical of the CIA, and then or later by a high ranking official of the NSA as well. Ray S. Cline, Deputy Director of the CIA, began looking at the evidence, and within about three days after the incident he decided that there probably had not been an attack. He based his conclusion on the fact that the intercepts being used as evidence were too close in time to the events to have been "real time" intercepts.[64] As he commented some years later, "I began to see that the [intercepts] which were being received at the time of the second attack almost certainly could not have referred to the second attack because of the time difference involved. Things were being referred to which, although they might have been taking place at that time, could not have been reported back so quickly."[65]

Cline thinks that the intercepts which were purported to be from the incident on August 4 were after-action reports on the attack of

[60] Johnson Library, NSF Country File, Vietnam, 101155Z.

[61] McNamara stated in his 1968 testimony: "The commanding officer of Attack Squadron 52 from the *Ticonderoga* (Comdr. G. H. Edmonson, USN) and his wingman (Lt. J. A. Burton), while flying at altitudes of between 700 and 1,500 feet in the vicinity of the two destroyers at the time of the torpedo attack both sighted gun flashes on the surface of the water as well as light anti-aircraft bursts at their approximate altitude. On one pass over the two destroyers, both pilots positively sighted a 'snakey' high speed wake 1½ miles ahead of the lead destroyer, U.S.S. *Maddox*." *The Gulf of Tonkin, The 1964 Incidents*, p. 16.

[62] For similar reports by two other pilots see *U.S. News and World Report*, July 23, 1984, p. 62.

[63] James Bond Stockdale and Sybil B. Stockdale, *In Love and War* (New York: Harper and Row, 1984), pp. 21, 23.

[64] CRS Interview with Ray S. Cline, Dec. 14, 1984.

[65] Quoted by *U.S. News and World Report*, July 23, 1984, p. 63.

August 2. Those involved in reacting to the incident were probably too keyed-up, he says, to evaluate the evidence dispassionately. They also wanted to get on with tit-for-tat military action against North Vietnam, and this, too, created a psychological climate which did not encourage a calm study of the facts.

Several days after the August 4 incident, Cline testified before the President's Foreign Intelligence Advisory Board, which was inquiring, as it usually does in cases involving substantial U.S. intelligence activity, into the Gulf of Tonkin attacks. He discussed the attack on August 2, but told the group he did not have the evidence to confirm that there had been an attack on August 4.

When he became Director of Intelligence and Research in the Department of State in 1967, Cline had occasion to study Gulf of Tonkin files in that office, and found that the August 4 incident had also been examined afterwards by analysts in State. He says he came across memoranda which raised questions about the incident, and that the file convinced him that there had not been a second attack.

In 1972, Louis Tordella, then Deputy Director of NSA, is also reported to have told staff members of the Senate Foreign Relations Committee that intercepts purportedly pertaining to the August 4 incident pertained instead to the August 2 attack.[66]

In addition to the inquiry made by the President's Foreign Intelligence Advisory Board, a study of the August 4 Gulf of Tonkin incident was also made soon afterwards for the Weapons Systems Evaluation Group in the Pentagon by the Institute for Defense Analyses, a private arm of the Pentagon. It's title was *Command and Control of the Tonkin Gulf Incident, 4-5 August 1964*. It is not known what kind of a report, if any, was made by the Intelligence Advisory Board, but whatever report there might have been is still classified. The command and control study is also still classified, despite efforts of the Foreign Relations Committee, beginning in 1968, to obtain a copy on a classified basis.[67] Based on a description by the committee's staff, the document ". . . will show that the Administration was becoming more and more uncertain about the nature of the incident in the Gulf of Tonkin but decided to go ahead with the attack on North Vietnam in spite of this increasing uncertainty."[68]

Some of those who were involved at the time have taken the position that the DE SOTO patrols and the 34-A operations were intended to provoke the North Vietnamese into responding, thereby creating a "crisis" that could be used to galvanize congressional and public support for U.S. action against the North Vietnamese. George Ball is one of these:[69]

> . . . I think that there was a feeling on the part of the President that he had to get a new grant of power from the Congress, that some overt act of aggression might justify it, and if such an act of aggression occurred then he wanted to be ready

[66]*U.S. News and World Report*, July 23, 1984, p. 64.
[67]See *The Gulf of Tonkin, The 1964 Incidents*, p. 2.
[68]A note at the conclusion of a staff memorandum, Jan. 30, 1968, on "Examples of Misinformation Given to SFRC and Armed Services at time of Incident," in the papers of the Committee on Foreign Relations, National Archives, RG 46.
[69]Charlton and Moncrieff, *Many Reasons Why*, p. 109.

so he could use that opportunity to get the kind of support from the Congress so that he wouldn't be acting alone . . . it was a tactical opportunity that they were looking for . . . he had a feeling that if he were going to take the measures which the military were telling him were going to have to be taken if we were going to win the war, that he had to be sure of his ground and get a much firmer support. The Tonkin Gulf Resolution was that kind of expression of support from the Congress which he felt he needed.

Another is James Thomson, a member of the NSC staff at the time, although he was not directly involved in the events of August 4:[70]

Mr. Thomson. I was in the White House, the NSC staff at the time, and some of my colleagues indicated very clearly that there was no credible evidence that the second incident had, in fact, ever taken place. It was judged, however, to be useful nonetheless, to show, as the papers regularly put it, our will or our resolve, regardless of the absence of a clear *causus belli.*

The Chairman [Senator Fulbright]. And this was interpreted to mean if we showed the will then the North Vietnamese would surrender. I mean, being faced with such overwhelming power, they would stop. Is that really the way they were thinking?

Mr. Thomson. "Would be brought to their knees" was the phrase that was used.

The Chairman. And, in effect, be willing to settle it on our terms; is that correct? Is that a fair summary?

Mr. Thomson. That was the hope, yes.

The Chairman. So, again, that was rather a serious mistake in judgment, too; wasn't it?

Mr. Thomson. It was, sir.

Thomson explained that beginning in late May or early June 1964 the administration wanted to obtain broad discretionary authority from Congress which it could use if the situation in Vietnam required it, especially if the Executive needed to act when Congress was not in session. When the first attack occurred on August 2, the administration began to think that this could provide such an opportunity. The second attack, although "more dubious," gave "imprudent, harassed people" the chance they needed to get congressional approval. The evidence to support the attack was inconclusive, Thomson added, but by then the decision was so far along that it could not be reversed; "the operational procedures had gone so far that the Administration had to fish or cut bait."[71]

Other key participants have argued, however, that the U.S. did not intend to create a crisis, and that the Gulf of Tonkin incidents were not "engineered" as an excuse for U.S. military action. In fact, William Bundy says, ". . . it didn't fit in with our plans at all, to be perfectly blunt about it. We didn't think the situation had deteriorated to the point where we had to consider stronger action

---

[70]U.S. Congress, Senate, Committee on Foreign Relations, *Causes, Origins, and Lessons of the Vietnam War,* Hearings, 92d Cong., 2d sess. (Washington, D.C.: U.S. Govt. Print. Off., 1972), p. 54.

[71]Memorandum of conversation between Thomson and Carl Marcy, chief of staff of the Senate Foreign Relations Committee, Jan. 3, 1968, SFRC Papers, National Archives, RG 46.

on the way things lay in South Vietnam . . . nobody would have planned this, nobody did plan it. It was totally unexpected and the response was entirely on the level."[72]

". . . the case on any Administration intent to provoke the incidents [on August 2 and 4]," Bundy says, "is not simply weak, it is non-existent. Not at any level of command is there a scintilla of evidence, after exhaustive internal and external searches, that points to any anticipation by the Administration of the incidents, much less any intent to provoke them."[73] This is his analysis of what happened:

> Miscalculation by both the US and the NVN is, in the end, at the root of the best hindsight hypothesis of Hanoi's behavior. In simple terms, it was a mistake, for an Administration sincerely resolved to keep its risks low, to have the 34A operations and the destroyer patrol take place even in the same time period. Rational minds could not readily have foreseen that Hanoi might confuse them . . . but rational calculations should have taken account of the irrational . . . in the form of a few days' postponement of the patrol. . . .

Bundy adds, ". . . there is a major element of straight misunderstanding in what took place. Washington did not want an incident, and it seems doubtful that Hanoi did either. Yet each misread the other, and the incidents happened."

The Gulf of Tonkin Resolution

On August 5, Johnson sent the proposed Gulf of Tonkin resolution to Congress.[74] Before the resolution was officially transmitted it had been reviewed by congressional leaders at the meeting on August 4, and ". . . in light of their comments redrafts continued in the evening, and at a breakfast meeting in the Department of State [on August 5] the Secretary and his associates hammered out a short, basic, agreed version with the bipartisan leaders."[75]

In a conversation with the President on August 4, McGeorge Bundy questioned whether the events in the Gulf of Tonkin should be used to obtain a resolution.

"My first reaction," he said in an interview some years later, "was that this was not the right way to get the kind of resolution that would really ensure that the Congress meant what it said." It was just a little episode. . . . I would have just ridden out that particular episode." "That was just one conversation between me and the President," Bundy added. "His reaction was that he had already decided the other way, and to climb on board."[76] "It is perfectly plain," Bundy said, "that when you get to the Gulf of Tonkin that he [Johnson] knew in his own mind that he had a problem of a resolution, and he seized that episode to get the resolution."

---

[72]Charlton and Moncrieff, *Many Reasons Why,* p. 117. Bundy, who was on vacation the first week of August 1964, had written a memorandum on July 31 stating his understanding that the U.S. would continue on its existing course in Vietnam until at least the end of the U.S. Presidential campaign, and that although further actions might be required in Vietnam, they would not be undertaken during the campaign.
[73]Bundy MS., appendix to ch. 14, p. 14A-36.
[74]For his statement see *Public Papers of the President,* Lyndon B. Johnson, 1963-1964, pp. 930-931.
[75]McGeorge Bundy chronology, cited above.
[76]CRS Interview with McGeorge Bundy, Jan. 8, 1979.

Bundy is reported to have held a White House staff meeting on the morning of August 5 at which he stated that the President was requesting a congressional resolution. "After Bundy finished, Douglass Cater, a White House adviser on domestic issues, was one of the first to speak up. 'Isn't this a little precipitous?' he asked. 'Do we have all the information?'

"Bundy looked quickly at him and said 'The President has decided and that's what we're doing.'

"Cater, new in the White House, persisted: 'Gee, Mac, I haven't really thought it through.'

"Bundy, with a very small smile: 'Don't.'"[77]

This was the text of the Gulf of Tonkin Resolution as it was submitted to and approved (with one minor change) by Congress:

Joint Resolution[*]

To promote the maintenance of international peace and security in southeast Asia.

Whereas naval units of the Communist regime in Vietnam, in violation of the principles of the Charter of the United Nations and of international law, have deliberately and repeatedly attacked United States naval vessels lawfully present in international waters, and have thereby created a serious threat to international peace; and   Whereas these attacks are part of a deliberate and systematic campaign of aggression that the Communist regime in North Vietnam has been waging against its neighbors and the nations joined with them in the collective defense of their freedom; and

Whereas the United States is assisting the peoples of southeast Asia to protect their freedom and has no territorial, military or political ambitions in that area, but desires only that these people should be left in peace to work out their own destinies in their own way: Now, therefore, be it

Resolved by the Senate and House of Representatives of the United States of America in Congress assembled, That the Congress approves and supports the determination of the President, as Commander in Chief, to take all necessary measures to repel any armed attack against the forces of the United States and to prevent further aggression.

Sec. 2. The United States regards as vital to its national interest and to world peace the maintenance of international peace and security in southeast Asia. Consonant with the Constitution of the United States and the Charter of the United Nations and in accordance with its obligations under the Southeast Asia Collective Defense Treaty, the United States is, therefore, prepared, as the President determines, to take all necessary steps, including the use of armed force, to assist any member or protocol state of the Southeast Asia Collective Defense Treaty requesting assistance in defense of its freedom.

Sec. 3. This resolution shall expire when the President shall determine that the peace and security of the area is reasonably

---

[77]Halberstam, *The Best and the Brightest,* p. 44.
[*]Public Law 88–408

assured by international conditions created by action of the United Nations or otherwise, except that it may be terminated earlier by concurrent resolution of the Congress.

The language of the Gulf of Tonkin Resolution was a hybrid of language from previous resolutions, but it was closer to that of the Middle East Resolution of 1957 than to any of the others.[78] Like that resolution, the Gulf of Tonkin Resolution provided that the security of the area concerned was vital to U.S. interests and to world peace. It also provided, as did the Middle East Resolution, that the U.S. was prepared to use its armed forces to assist affected nations, and that it would do so "as the President determines." This contrasts with the statement in the Middle East Resolution: "if the President determines the necessity thereof." Although the Middle East Resolution required the President to determine the need for such action, the Gulf of Tonkin Resolution went beyond that to give full advance approval to the President to decide whether, how, when and where to use force, and how much force to use. In this respect, the Gulf of Tonkin Resolution was stronger than the Middle East Resolution, and more comparable to the 1955 Formosa Resolution's provision that the President could use force "as he deems necessary." The Formosa Resolution, however, specifically authorized the President to do so, whereas the Gulf of Tonkin stated it as a given. Thus, the Gulf of Tonkin Resolution appears to have been the strongest and most complete, in terms of its approval of Presidential power, of any of the five foreign policy resolutions passed by Congress between 1955 and 1965. (See below for the Executive Branch's interpretation of the Gulf of Tonkin Resolution.)

On the day (August 5) the Gulf of Tonkin Resolution was introduced, Morse made a major speech in the Senate in which he called the resolution a "predated declaration of war."[79] ". . . our actions in Asia today are the actions of warmaking," he said. The Gulf of Tonkin incident was ". . . as much the doing of the United States as it is the doing of North Vietnam. For 10 years, the United States, in South Vietnam, has been a provocateur, every bit as much as North Vietnam has been a provocateur. For 10 years, the United States, in South Vietnam, has violated the Geneva agreement of 1954. For 10 years, our military policies in South Vietnam have sought to impose a military solution upon a political and economic problem." "We have been making covert war in southeast Asia for some time," he added, "instead of seeking to keep the peace. It was inevitable and inexorable that sooner or later we would have to engage in overt acts of war in pursuance of that policy. . . ."

---

[78]The Middle East Resolution provided: ". . . the United States regards as vital to the national interest and world peace the preservation of the independence and integrity of the nations of the Middle East. To this end, if the President determines the necessity thereof, the United States is prepared to use armed forces to assist any nation or group of such nations requesting assistance against armed aggression from any country controlled by international communism: *Provided,* That such employment shall be consonant with the treaty obligations of the United States and with the Constitution of the United States." For more information on the Middle East Resolution, as well on the 1955 Formosa Resolution, see pt. I of this study. For a discussion of the 1962 Cuba and Berlin Resolutions, see pp. 129-130 above. For a discussion of the June 1964 draft of a congressional resolution on Vietnam, see pp. 266-270 above.

[79]*CR,* vol. 110, pp. 18133-18139.

Morse then referred to the bombardment of islands off the coast of North Vietnam by the South Vietnamese, an action, he said, that the U.S. Government knew was occurring at a time when U.S. ships were on patrol in the vicinity. "Was the U.S. Navy standing guard," he asked, "while vessels of South Vietnam shelled North Vietnam? That is the clear implication of the incident."

Unknown, reportedly, to anyone in the Senate or the press, Morse had received a phone call that morning from a source in the Pentagon, who has never been named, who told him that the *Maddox* was not on a "routine patrol," as the administration had claimed, but was an intelligence ship, and that its mission was associated with the 34-A raids. The U.S., the source said, was engaging in provocation in the Tonkin Gulf.[80]

Morse confided some of his doubts to fellow Senators, but found them unwilling to oppose the President. One said to him,[81] "Hell, Wayne, you can't get in a fight with the President at a time when the flags are waving and we're about to go to a national convention. All Lyndon wants is a piece of paper telling him we did right out there, and we support him, and he's the kind of president who follows the rules and won't get the country into war without coming back to Congress."

That afternoon (August 5), a meeting of leaders from the Senate Foreign Relations and Armed Services and the House Foreign Affairs Committees was held in Mansfield's office to decide how the resolution would be handled. Present were Mansfield, Fulbright, Hickenlooper, Aiken, Russell, and Leverett Saltonstall (R/Mass.), and from the House, Dr. Thomas E. Morgan (D/Pa.), chairman of the Foreign Affairs Committee, and Mrs. Frances Bolton (R/Ohio), the ranking Republican on the committee. There were also several staff members present, including Pat Holt, a senior member of the Foreign Relations Committee staff, and then acting chief of staff in the absence of Carl Marcy. Holt later recalled his reaction to the group's plan to act quickly on the resolution:[82]

> We'd have a joint hearing of Foreign Relations and Armed Services the next morning, report it, call it up, have a quick debate and pass it. I listened to all of this with growing disbelief, and I remember Bill Darden [William H. Darden, chief of staff of the Senate Armed Services Committee] and I talked to each other about it. We thought it was wildly unrealistic for senators to expect action to be taken on it that quickly, because Bill and I had been through the debate on the Middle East Resolution in '57 which tied up the two committees for weeks. The Formosa Resolution in '55 didn't take very long, but it took some days anyhow. Both of these had caused a good deal of unhappiness on the part of some senators who eventually voted for them, and we didn't see that there was any way under heaven that either the joint committee or the Senate could act on the Gulf of Tonkin thing as fast as it did, particularly in view of the way the thing was worded, which looked to us like pretty much a blank check and a pre-dated declaration

[80]Goulden, p. 48 and Austin, pp. 67-68.
[81]Goulden, p. 49.
[82]CRS Interview with Pat Holt, Dec. 13, 1978.

of war. Well, that just shows how much more senators know about the Senate than the staff does.

At the meeting, there was a brief discussion of the language of the resolution, and according to Chairman Morgan, Mansfield argued that it should be left unchanged, and that it should be passed in the same form that had been sent to Congress by the President.[83]

On August 6, executive session hearings were held on the resolution in both the House and the Senate. The hearing of the House Foreign Affairs Committee lasted 40 minutes. The combined hearing of the Senate Foreign Relations and Armed Services Committees lasted 1 hour and 40 minutes.

Prior to the meeting of the House committee, Chairman Morgan held a caucus of the Democratic members of the committee at which he urged them to approve the resolution without change. At the conclusion of the hearing he made the same plea to the full committee. "I had to practically get down on my hands and knees to plead with my committee, please don't change a single word in this resolution."[84]

At the hearing of the House Foreign Affairs Committee, Secretary Rusk said that the administration was asking for the resolution because ". . . it has seemed clearly wise to seek in the most emphatic form a declaration of congressional support both for the defense of our Armed Forces against similar attacks and for the carrying forward of whatever steps may become necessary to assist the free nations covered by the Southeast Asia Treaty." "We cannot tell what steps may in the future be required to meet Communist aggression in southeast Asia," he added.

Secretary of Defense McNamara described the events preceding the request for the resolution, and characterized the attacks as "deliberate and unprovoked." The *Maddox,* he said (without mentioning that it was an intelligence ship), was on a "routine patrol in international waters."

Rusk commented on the specific provisions of the resolution. He pointed out that the wording of section 1 of the resolution ("That the Congress approves and supports the determination of the President, as Commander in Chief, to take all necessary measures to repel any armed attack against the forces of the United States and to prevent further aggression") was a recognition of the President's "authority and obligation" to defend U.S. forces against attacks. With respect to the language in section 2 stating that the U.S. was "prepared, as the President determines, to take all necessary steps, including the use of armed force" to defend Vietnam, Rusk said that this was "similar to the authority embraced in the Formosa resolution of 1955, the Middle East resolution of 1957, and the Cuba resolution of 1962." He gave copies of each of these to members of the committee so that they could compare the language. "There can be no doubt," he added ". . . that these previous resolutions form a solid legal precedent for the action now proposed. Such action is required to make the purposes of the United States clear and to protect our national interest."

---

[83]CRS Interview with Thomas E. Morgan, Apr. 3, 1979.
[84]*Ibid.*

Rusk said that although he would not take the committee's time to discuss the constitutional aspects of the resolution, "I believe it to be the generally accepted constitutional view that the President has the constitutional authority to take at least limited armed action in defense of American national interest. . . ."[85]

In his "briefing book," a large black looseleaf notebook with materials covering all of the possible points on which he might have to testify, Rusk had a memorandum prepared by State's legal adviser, "Legal Questions and Answers on the Gulf of Tonkin," August 5, 1964, which he could use if necessary to answer questions about constitutional aspects of the resolution. That memorandum made it clear that in the view of the executive branch, as was subsequently maintained, the President did not need congressional approval or authorization to use U.S. forces in Vietnam, even against North Vietnam, and that the resolution, therefore, was a political rather than a legal or constitutional instrument. These were some of the key points made in the memorandum:[86]

Question. *What is the authority for using U.S. combat forces in the Tonkin Gulf action?*

Answer. The constitutional authority of the President as Commander-in-Chief.

Question. *Does the President have authority to use the forces of the U.S. now in Viet-Nam for combat action?*

Answer. (1) Yes. The use of U.S. forces for combat duty in Viet-Nam rests on the Constitutional powers of the President as Commander-in-Chief and as Chief Executive, and on his power to conduct foreign affairs.

(2) Presidents have ordered the armed forces to take combatant action abroad, without Congressional authorization and in the absence of a Declaration of War, on a large number of occasions.

Question. *How does the Joint Resolution affect the authority of the President to use force in Viet-Nam?*

Answer. The Resolution does not detract from or enlarge the constitutional authority of the President as Commander-in-Chief and Chief Executive.

Question. *Then why seek a Congressional Resolution?*

Answer. The Resolution would constitute a declaration of the common purpose of the U.S. in this situation. It would record the approval and support of the Congress for the actions of the President.

Question. *Does the Joint Resolution constitute an anticipatory declaration of war; that is, does it constitute a delegation of Congress' constitutional authority to declare war?*

Answer. (1) No. The Joint Resolution in no way affects the constitutional prerogative of the Congress to declare war.

(2) A declaration of war, however, has always been thought of as implying a massive commitment of U.S. forces. That is not the case here.

---

[85]Rusk's and McNamara's statements were printed as an appendix to the report of the House Foreign Affairs Committee, H. Rept. 88-1708. The transcript of the hearing has not been made public.

[86]Johnson Library, NSC History File, Gulf of Tonkin Attacks.

Questions. *Does this Resolution cover the use of U.S. forces for combat in North Viet-Nam?*

Answer. (1) Sec. 2 declares that the U.S. is prepared "to take all necessary steps, including the use of armed force, to assist any Protocol or Member State of the Southeast Asia Collective Defense Treaty requesting assistance in defense of its freedom."

(2) Under Sec. 2, such steps would have to be "consonant with the Constitution and Charter of the United Nations and in acccordance with [the] obligations [of the U.S.] under the Southeast Asia Collective Defense Treaty."

(3) If, in a particular situation, the use of U.S. combat troops in North Viet-Nam would meet all of the required conditions, and if the President determined that it was necessary, such use would be within the Resolution.

Immediately after its hearing, the House Foreign Affairs Committee voted 29-0 to approve the resolution. Two members voted "present." They were H. R. Gross (R/Iowa), who said that he wanted the words "United States of America" added after the word "Constitution" in the resolution (this was done by the Senate), and Edward J. Derwinski (R/Ill.), who said that he voted present to protest the fact that Congress was never informed by the President and his advisers "until they get in a jam."[87]

In its report,[88] the Foreign Affairs Committee stated:

As it had during earlier action on resolutions relating to Formosa and to the Middle East, the committee considered the relation of the authority contained in the resolution and the powers assigned to the President by the Constitution. While the resolution makes it clear that the people of the United States stand behind the President, it was concluded that the resolution does not enter the field of controversy as to the respective limitations of power in the executive and the legislative branches. As stated in the committee report on the Formosa resolution:

Acting together, there can be no doubt that all the constitutional powers necessary to meet the situation are present.

According to the report, the committee also considered the question of the duration of the resolution, but decided not to make any changes. "Given the persistent Communist pressures in southeast Asia, the committee did not consider it advisable to insert a specific time limitation on the resolution. . . . In any case the resolution specifically reserves to Congress the right to terminate the force of the resolution by concurrent resolution."

The mood in the Foreign Affairs Committee and in the House as a whole was one of action, in which the "facts" may not have been that important, according to Dante B. Fascell (D/Fla.), a member (and later chairman) of the committee:[89]

My own impression of what happened at that time was that most everybody said, well, the President wants this power and

[87]Galloway, *The Gulf of Tonkin Resolution,* p. 78.
[88]H. Rept. 88- 1708.
[89]CRS Interview with Dante Fascell, Feb. 23, 1979.

he needs to have it. It had relatively little to do with the so-called incident. I don't know why so much stress has been made on whether or not there was an incident or whether or not the President was deceitful or whatever. . . . The President needed the authority. Who cared about the facts of the so-called incident that would trigger this authority? So the resolution was just hammered right on through by everybody.

Nicholas deB. Katzenbach (then Deputy Attorney General, and later Under Secretary of State), has taken a similar position with respect to the reaction of both Congress and the Executive:[90]

. . . the Tonkin Gulf incident itself was an absolute nothing. Sure, the facts of that were exploited by President Johnson and by the executive branch, but I don't think it made any difference what the facts were. All they were looking for was a vehicle for the resolution. Then they chose this incident in the Tonkin Gulf to do it. If that hadn't come around, they would have found something else. I don't think it made one iota of difference in any congressman's or senator's vote as to what happened or didn't happen in the Tonkin Gulf.

Katzenbach said that the 1964 Presidential election was a key factor in congressional action on the resolution, adding, "And there is no question in my mind that that is what motivated Bill Fulbright and other good Democrats to go along with it and vote for it." He also explains how this affected the role of Congress thereafter: "They created a situation there that Congress was tied up in its underwear the whole rest of the time. You couldn't have gotten anything through that was like the Tonkin Gulf Resolution; you couldn't have gotten anything through that was going to take it away. Having done it, they were just absolutely tied."

On Friday, August 7, acting under a suspension of the rules (a parliamentary devise for limiting debate and amendments), the House of Representatives passed the Gulf of Tonkin Resolution 416-0, after considering it for only 40 minutes. No Member spoke against the resolution.[91] On the vote to pass the resolution, Representative Adam Clayton Powell (D/N.Y.), saying that he was a "pacifist," voted "present." Representative Eugene Siler of Kentucky (who had voted against SEATO, and had made the statement in June 1964 about running for President in order to serve one day) refrained from voting, saying that such resolutions were "unnecessary," and were used "to seal the lips of Congress against future criticism."[92]

During the brief discussion of the resolution, House Democratic and Republican leaders gave it their strong endorsement. Democratic Majority Leader Carl Albert (D/Okla.) referring to previous actions by Congress supporting the President, said:

The United States is presently facing in southeast Asia a challenge similar to the ones we have faced in the past in Turkey, Berlin, Lebanon, the Straits of Taiwan, and Cuba. The President has asked us as representatives of the American

---

[90]CRS Interview with Nicholas deB. Katzenbach, Nov. 7, 1978.
[91]The proceedings are in *CR*, vol. 110, pp. 18539-18555.
[92]*Washington Post*, Aug. 8, 1964. In the *Congressional Record*, Representative Siler was listed as being paired against the resolution, making him the only Member of the House to have been recorded in the negative.

people for our support. It is now time for all of us to join together as a nation firmly united behind our Commander in
Chief and to express our complete confidence in him and in his
leadership.

House Republican Leader Charles Halleck said he supported the
resolution "as a clear indication on the part of the Congress of our
determination to be a united people in the face of any threats to
our liberty." He pointed out, however, that "orders for retaliatory
action against the forces of North Vietnam had been issued prior
to the meeting [of congressional leaders with the President on
August 4] and that the apparent purpose of the meeting was to
inform us that such decisions had been made."

Other leading Republicans questioned the Johnson administration's policy on the war. Representative Melvin Laird said he
agreed with the President's action and with the resolution, but that
". . . the land war remains. And we still have a policy to develop.
We still must decide whether to follow the Gaullist proposal of
withdrawal by neutralization or whether to stiffen our commitment by resolving to take whatever steps are necessary to win the
war in that beleaguered area within a reasonable period of time."

Representative Gerald Ford said that he supported the resolution, but that "The military results raise the legitimate question—
similar U.S. military action affecting our own ground forces on
prior occasions in Vietnam might have turned the tide our way
much sooner. The United States in Vietnam is not winning now
and has not been in the past months. I hope and trust what appears to be a new administration policy will bring victory for the
people of Vietnam and the United States."

Representative Paul Findley (R/Ill.), was concerned about the
broad language of the resolution, and asked Ford whether he could
be allocated some time to speak during the debate. According to
Findley, Ford said there was no time available, and that ". . . I
shouldn't be concerned. This was a symbolic gesture of support to
the President at a critical time, when our ships were under attack.
We wanted to show solidarity behind the President, but it didn't
have any far-reaching implications. And, on that assurance, I voted
for it and, of course, regretted it thereafter."[93]

Chairman Morgan of the Foreign Affairs Committee told the
House that the resolution would not adversely affect Congress' constitutional role: "This is definitely not an advance declaration of
war. The committee has been assured by the Secretary of State
that the constitutional prerogative of the Congress in the respect
will continue to be scrupulously observed." These assurances were
echoed by Representative E. Ross Adair of Indiana, the second-
ranking Republican on the committee, who said:

> Secondly, the question has been raised as to whether by
> voting for this resolution we say in effect that we are approv-
> ing all of the U.S. policies in southeast Asia in the past and
> are giving approval, in advance, for such actions as the Presi-
> dent may see fit to take in the future. Here again the answer
> is in the negative. By voting for this resolution it is my under-

---

[93]CRS Interview with Paul Findley, Feb. 2, 1979.

standing that we are meeting a specific situation. The American flag has been fired on. We are saying we will not and cannot tolerate such things. We will stand in defense of our flag and our freedoms solidly behind the President. This we are saying by this resolution.

Representative John B. Anderson (R/Ill.) who became a national figure during his campaign for President in 1980, took a similar position when he noted statements to the effect that the resolution did not give the President "carte blanche authority to launch an all-out war or even limited war in any part of the southeast Asia theater of operations. We are merely expressing our determination to stand firm and resolute as a nation in the face of enemy attack, and to repel any aggressions." But Anderson called on the administration to make clear that any attack on North Vietnam or elsewhere in Southeast Asia would be based on the principle of "joint action" with U.S. allies.

Representative Bruce Alger (R/Tex.) was the only Member of the House to express doubts about the resolution during the debate, but even he voted for it "for reasons of unity." ". . . I have grave reservations," he said, "involving congressional abdication of responsibility in declaring war. . . . This resolution does not assure us that the President will come back to Congress, as the gentleman from Indiana [Mr. Adair] assured us, before involving this Nation further. I agree to the resolution, therefore, only assuming that Congress will not be bypassed later."

Senate Hearings on the Resolution

The joint hearing of the Senate Foreign Relations and Armed Services Committees were also held on the morning of August 6, with McNamara and Rusk as the witnesses. Before the hearing began, according to Pat Holt, McNamara, who had arrived early, talked informally in the back room of the committee's suite in the Capitol with several Senators who were already on hand, including Fulbright and Russell. He told them that if the question came up as to why the administration was so sure of what had happened to U.S. ships in the Gulf of Tonkin, and Morse was in the room, he (McNamara) would not answer.[94] McNamara was apparently concerned about protecting the fact that radio intercepts had been used, even though this information appears to have been imparted, at least to some extent, in the informal meeting on August 3 which Morse attended. (Morse, as it turned out, hinted during Senate debate on the resolution that there was secret intelligence data, but he refused to be drawn into a discussion on that point.)[95]

At the joint executive session of the two Senate committees Rusk and McNamara again testified that the *Maddox* was on a "routine patrol in international waters." Rusk also made this important statement with respect to future consultation:[96]

. . . this resolution, and this consultation which the executive and legislative branches are now having in the course of

[94]CRS Interview with Pat Holt, Dec. 13, 1978.
[95]See p. 287.
[96]See *Southeast Asia Resolution* (cited above), from which the quotations that follow have been taken.

today, will in no sense be the last contact between the executive and the legislative branches on these problems in southeast Asia. There will continue to be regular consultations not
only with committees but between the President and the congressional leaders, and on a bipartisan basis. That has been the
practice of Presidents in this postwar period. Therefore, as the
southeast Asia situation develops, and if it develops, in ways
which we cannot now anticipate, of course there will be close
and continuous consultation between the President and the
leaders of the Congress.

All of the senior Democrats and Republicans on the two committees supported the resolution. Senator Russell Long, then a
member of the Foreign Relations Committee, commented, "As
much as I would like to be consulted with on this kind of thing the
less time you spend on consulting and the quicker you shoot back
the better off you are."

Senator Strom Thurmond (R/S.C.), a member of the Armed Services Committee, was in favor of the resolution and of the retaliatory action, but felt that ". . . we ought to make up our minds that
we are going to have a victory in the war in Vietnam or get out."
He was concerned about having another "stalemate"—"another
Korea."

Senator Clifford P. Case, a liberal Republican from New Jersey,
who had just joined the Foreign Relations Committee, approved the
President's actions saying, "I think it would be unfortunate if we
did not support immediate action in response to aggression and on
the spot because this is where the decisions are made and anything
we do afterward will be affected favorably or adversely by our failure to take action on whatever action we take." (Case's support of
the President and of the war made his later opposition to the war,
which he announced in mid-1967, all the more galling to the administration.)

The only member of either Senate committee who attempted to
raise any serious objections to the administration's case in the
August 6 hearing was Senator Morse. He said he was ". . . unal-
terably opposed to this course of action which, in my judgment, is
an aggressive course of action on the part of the United States [de-
leted].[97] I think what happened is that Khanh got us to backstop
him in open aggression against the territorial integrity of North
Vietnam. I have listened to briefing after briefing and there isn't a
scintilla of evidence in any briefing yet that North Vietnam engaged in any military aggression against South Vietnam either
with its ground troops or its navy."

Rusk and McNamara took issue with Morse's statement, and
argued at some length that there was no basis for his allegations.

In questions that were deleted from the printed hearing by the
executive branch, Morse asked, as he had asked in his speech in
the Senate on August 5, about the relationship between the DE
SOTO patrols and the 34-A operations. McNamara's response was
also deleted in part.[98] Some of the deleted portions were subse-

---

[97]This deletion in the transcript of the hearing was made by the executive branch.
[98]Morse denounced the deletions. See the *Washington Post,* Nov. 24, 1966.

quently provided, however, by Goulden.[99] This was that section of McNamara's response, with the deleted material in brackets:

Secretary McNamara. First [our Navy played absolutely no part in, was not associated with, was not aware of any South Vietnamese actions, if there were any. I want to make that very clear to you.] The *Maddox* was operating in international waters, was carrying out a routine patrol of the type we carry out all over the world at all times. [It was not informed of, was not aware of, had no evidence of, and so far as I know today had no knowledge of, any South Vietnamese actions in connection with the two islands, as Senator Morse referred to.]

I think it is extremely important that you understand this. If there is any misunderstanding on that we should discuss the point at some length.

Senator Morse. I think we should.

Secretary McNamara. I say this flatly. This is the fact.

About a month later (September 10), the Foreign Relations Committee met in executive session with Maxwell Taylor, U.S. Ambassador to South Vietnam. Morse returned to the Gulf of Tonkin incidents, and asked Taylor about his knowledge of 34-A operations, especially the attacks on North Vietnamese islands at the end of July. As frequently happens in situations of this kind, the Member of Congress asking the question did not know enough about the subject to word the question precisely, and the executive branch witness, wanting to avoid discussing the subject, answered in such a way as to take advantage of the questioner's lack of knowledge. Thus, Morse, apparently accepting the administration's cover story that the 34-A operations were conducted by the Vietnamese, asked Taylor whether he had been consulted by General Khanh, Prime Minister of South Vietnam, prior to the July 30 raids on the islands, and Taylor's reply was that these operations were going on constantly, and that "Any specific action of that sort I would not be counselled about." He did not answer the question directly. To do so would have required that he admit that Khanh did not consult him, and this might have given Morse an opening to explore further the question of consultation, and how such decisions were made. The fact was that 34-A operations were planned and controlled by the U.S., even though South Vietnamese military personnel were involved, and there would have been no reason for General Khanh to consult Taylor.

Morse tried again. He said that in conjunction with the Gulf of Tonkin testimony it had been mentioned that South Vietnamese boats attacked the islands. He had asked McNamara whether U.S. officials knew of these attacks, and McNamara had replied that U.S. officials in Saigon may have known, but the commander of the *Maddox* did not. The possibility that U.S. officials in Saigon knew about the raids, Morse added, raised the question as to whether the raids might involve the U.S., in terms of creating the impression in the minds of the North Vietnamese that the U.S. was involved. Again Taylor replied that he knew of these naval activities, but that what happened day to day were not his business.

---

[99]See *The Gulf of Tonkin, The 1964 Incidents*, p. 29, and *Truth is the First Casualty*, p. 59.

Morse then asked how long the 34-A naval raids had been going on. Taylor, who knew that they had been started the previous February, again evaded by saying that he imagined they had been going on for some months, but he "really couldn't tell." Morse asked whether the raids have resulted in escalating the war into North Vietnam. Taylor, who was fully informed of the provocation involved, said he did not think so; that the raids were merely counteraction against North Vietnamese infiltration. Taylor said he did not know where the ships were that were engaged in countering this infiltration, and that although he thought it was a very sound program, he was not in charge of it.

The August 6 joint hearing of the two committees on the Gulf of Tonkin Resolution lasted 1 hour and 40 minutes. Fulbright asked no questions, nor did Russell or Mansfield. "Imagine," Fulbright was reported to have said later, "we spent all of an hour and 40 minutes on that resolution. A disaster; a tragic mistake. We should have held hearings. [sic] The resolution would have passed anyway, but not in its present form. At the time, I was not in a suspicious frame of mind. I was afraid of Goldwater."[100]

Besides being "afraid of Goldwater," Fulbright was still very close to Johnson. Several days earlier he and Mrs. Fulbright had given a dinner party at their home for President and Mrs. Johnson, which was also attended by Secretary of the Treasury Douglas Dillon and Mrs. Dillon, Senator Russell, and Mr. and Mrs. James Reston (noted columnist of the *New York Times)*. A few weeks later (September 3), the Fulbrights and Russell were guests of the Johnsons at a private dinner at the White House.[101]

After concluding the August 6 hearing, the Foreign Relations and Armed Services Committees voted 31-1, with Morse in the minority, to report the, Gulf of Tonkin resolution favorably to the Senate. In its report, the joint committee, calling the attacks "unprovoked," stated:[102]

> The basic purpose of this resolution is to make it clear that the Congress approves the actions taken by the President to meet the attack on U.S. forces in southeast Asia by the Communist regime in North Vietnam. Full support by the Congress also is declared for the resolute policy enunciated by the President in order to prevent further aggression, or to retaliate with suitable measures should such aggression take place.

Without even mentioning the possible constitutional questions posed by the resolution, or its impact on the role of Congress in decisions involving the use of the armed forces, the joint committee concluded:

> On the basis of testimony submitted by the Secretaries of State and Defense and the Chairman of the Joint Chiefs of Staff, the committee was satisfied that the decision of the President to retaliate against the North Vietnamese gunboat attacks was both soundly conceived and skillfully executed. In

the circumstances, the United States could not have done less and should not have done more.

Several years later, in a memorandum to Chairman Fulbright to help him prepare for a CBS television interview, Carl Marcy, chief of staff of the Foreign Relations Committee, discussed the question of the committee's quick approval of the resolution:[103]

You will probably be asked why the joint Committees on Armed Services and Foreign Relations approved the Tonkin Resolution so quickly.

A possible answer is to recall that the Administration did not tell all at that time. For example, it was only after the Committee investigated the incident in late 1967 and at the hearing with McNamara on February 20, 1968, that members learned that Commander Herrick, about four hours after the August 4 attack allegedly occurred, sent a message to Washington reading as follows:

"Review of action makes many recorded contacts and torpedoes fired appear doubtful. Freak weather effects and over-eager sonarman may have accounted for many reports. No actual visual sightings by Maddox. Suggest complete evaluation before any further action." That message was sent on August 4 at 1:30 p.m. Eastern Daylight Time. That was ten hours before President Johnson went on the air (11:38 p.m.) to announce our military response.

The Committee was not informed in 1964 that the Maddox was on an intelligence mission. Secretary McNamara had described the attack as being on the "high seas" while the Maddox was on a "routine patrol."

The Committee didn't know that after the first attack, the commander of the Carrier Task Force in the Pacific had told the Maddox and the Turner Joy that North Vietnam had "thrown down the gauntlet and now considers itself at war with the United States . . . and . . . they will be treated as belligerents from the first detection. . . ."

In short, this was a case in which if the facts *as they were then known to the Administration* had been given to the Committee, there might have been more deliberation than was the case when the Administration snowed the Congress and the American people.

Pat Holt has suggested that the political situation was also determinative:[104]

This was early August. Goldwater had been nominated as the Republican candidate for President in July. Goldwater was taking a very hard line about Vietnam, in comparison to which Johnson looked like a model of restraint and moderation. The Democrats on the two committees felt much constrained to support a moderate Democratic President, or what looked like a moderate Democratic President, against the onslaughts of this bomb-them-out, shoot-them-up Republican. The Republicans on the committees could scarcely refuse to support even

---

[103]Memorandum, Jan. 27, 1971, University of Arkansas, Fulbright Papers, series 48, box 46. (emphasis in original)
[104]CRS Interview with Pat Holt, Dec. 13, 1978.

this much, and there it was. And the politics of it also were such that the Democrats almost had to support the thing, not only for the reason that I mentioned, but because if they didn't, then they would be in the position of opening themselves to the charge of knuckling under to this little two-bit communist power in Southeast Asia and that sort of thing.

Holt's explanation may shed some light on the puzzling question of why Wayne Morse did not make more of an issue of the information he had received, and why he refrained from asking for further hearings. According to Fulbright, ". . . I didn't at the time have any suspicion that it hadn't happened like we were told it had happened, and Morse didn't undertake a very determined effort to reveal it or to say that he had information. . . . he didn't ask the committee to hear his informant or do anything like that, that I know of. . . . If he had any information he was relying on, why he didn't prolong it [the debate] and demand that we have hearings and require these people to come forward and examine the reasons for the thing. Why didn't he? Because he certainly wasn't a very timid man. . . . My guess is that he had a kind of feeling about it but he wasn't certain about it."[105]

Asked for his explanation, Joseph Goulden, who interviewed Morse while writing his book, replied that Morse could have done more, but that for some reason he did not. Goulden was asked why. "Well, you also have a juxtaposition of events . . . where the Democratic Convention is opening in the next week, and maybe Lyndon made a phone call to him."[106]

Whether or not it is coincidence, or their conversation involved some other subject, the President's appointment calendar shows that there was, indeed, a phone call to Morse from the President on August 3, and it is quite possible that in that conversation Johnson asked for Morse's help in protecting him, the Democratic Party, and the country, from the possibility of Goldwater's election by not pushing the Gulf of Tonkin matter too hard. (Although this phone call was made before the second attack was said to have taken place on August 4, the secret meeting on August 3 between Rusk and McNamara and members of the Foreign Relations and Armed Services Committees, in which the possibility of another attack was apparently considered, was about to occur, and Johnson may have wanted to make his case with Morse beforehand.)

A similar instance of this kind of politician-to-politician collaboration between Morse and the President may well have occurred a few weeks earlier in conjunction with Senate confirmation of Johnson's appointment of Maxwell Taylor as U.S. Ambassador to Vietnam. Morse opposed the appointment, but he was not on the Senate floor on July 1 when the nomination was considered and approved by voice vote with no debate or opposition. Later that afternoon, Morse made a statement in the Senate giving his reasons for opposing the appointment, and explaining that when the nomination had been brought up for approval he was "downstairs in the Committee on Foreign Relations presenting an argument against a shocking waste of taxpayer funds in a foreign aid pro-

---

[105]CRS Interview with J. William Fulbright, Feb. 18, 1983.
[106]CRS Interview with Joseph Goulden, Dec. 10, 1978.

gram that is in need of drastic revision. I was not aware that the Taylor nomination was to be brought up at that time."[107] Given the way the Senate operates, including the standard practice of notifying a Senator when a matter in which he or she has expressed strong interest is about to be called up for action on the floor, Morse's explanation suggests that he had decided not to debate or delay the nomination, and thus made his appearance after it was approved.

The Senate Debates the Resolution

On August 6-7, 1964, the Senate acted on the Gulf of Tonkin Resolution.[108] Majority Leader Mansfield began by praising Johnson: "The President . . . has acted with a cool head and a steady hand in a most critical situation. He has acted as the leader of a great free nation, fully aware of a great nation's responsibilities to itself, to freedom, and to the peace of the world."

Chairman Fulbright then discussed the resolution. He said that North Vietnam had acted "without provocation," and that the second attack "was without any doubt a calculated act of military aggression." He, too, praised Johnson's "limited and measured" reaction, saying that "The single, most notable fact about the American action was its great restraint as an act of retaliation taken by a great power in response to the provocation of a small power." Had the attacks not been part of a pattern of North Vietnamese aggression, he added, "it might have been appropriate to respond by a lesser act of force than that employed, or even by measures short of force." But the North Vietnamese regime "has made an international career of aggression almost since its inception in 1954." Therefore, ". . . it was incumbent upon the United States to act, as it did, in a manner proportionate to the provocation. Viewed in the context of the immediate provocation, the retaliatory measures taken by the United States were necessary and justified. Viewed in the context of a decade of reckless and irresponsible behavior on the part of the North Vietnamese regime, the action taken by the United States was the minimum consistent with its own vital interests and with its obligations to its allies and partners in Southeast Asia." It should be made clear to the Communists, Fulbright said, ". . . that their aggressive and expansionist ambitions, wherever advanced will meet precisely that degree of American opposition which is necessary to frustrate them. The resolution now before the Senate is designed to shatter whatever illusions our adversaries may harbor about the determination of the United States to act promptly and vigorously against aggression."

Fulbright inserted in the *Congressional Record* editorials from the August 6 issues of several leading newspapers. One of them was from the *Washington Post,* which said, "President Johnson has earned the gratitude of the free world as well as of the Nation for his careful and effective handling of the Vietnam crisis." The *Post* went on to suggest that as a result of the attacks, the U.S. was now in a position to become more involved in the war:

---

[107]*CR,* vol. 110, p. 15765.
[108]The debate is in *ibid.,* pp. 18399-18471.

Whatever restraint had previously been exercised through lack of precedent or provocation has been removed by the events in the Tonkin Gulf. No one can tell at this point the precise form which the Vietnam war will take, but it is bound to be a new form, and the newness would seem inevitably to be on the side of more direct American participation and more direct action against the North.

The *New York Times* also praised the President, but warned that the situation was now more uncertain and dangerous. The U.S. had become a direct combatant in the war, and "The sword, once drawn in anger, will tend to be unsheathed more easily in the future."

Commenting on the resolution, the *Times* approved of its open-ended wording, saying that the President "has rightly asked" Congress to approve language providing that "all necessary measures" shall be taken.

Other Senators from both parties joined Mansfield and Fulbright in commending the President and in endorsing the resolution. Minority Leader Dirksen praised the President for consulting Members of Congress. "The President," he said, "could have taken this action [retaliatory strikes] in his own right as the Commander in Chief. . . . What is involved is a demonstration that the executive and legislative branches of the Government stand together in an hour of need and threat. . . ."

Senator Javits, a liberal Republican from New York (who, it will be recalled, was an active participant in discussions of Indochina policy in the early 1950s while serving on the House Foreign Affairs Committee), said, "I shall support the resolution, because I think we must defend freedom in that area, or else see the balance of a large segment of the population of the world tipped against freedom. The degree of our resistance under the action that may be taken in southeast Asia, under the resolution, will determine not only future events in Vietnam, but also the freedom of Malaya, India, Pakistan, and Indonesia, and perhaps even Australia and New Zealand." Javits added, "we who support the joint resolution do so with full knowledge of its seriousness and with the understanding that we are voting a resolution which means life or the loss of it for who knows how many hundreds or thousands? Who knows what destruction and despair this action may bring in the name of freedom?"

Asked later whether he thought Congress had been misled on the facts of the Gulf of Tonkin attacks, Javits said:[109]

There is a doctrine in the law which says that on some occasions there is a duty to tell, and I believe that this was such an occasion. Congress, in my judgment, was not misled by anything that was actually said or represented. But I believe there was a duty on the part of the administration, which alone had this information—after all, we don't man naval ships at sea. The administration made certain representations as to what had occurred. The representations were clearly an armed attack on the American naval vessels, without any question of identification as to the sources of that attack. That was clearly

---

[109]CRS Interview with Jacob Javits, Apr. 25, 1979. See also Javits' comments in his book, *Who Makes War* (New York: William Morrow, 1973), pp. 258-261.

delineated. Under those circumstances, I believe there was a duty on the part of the administration to state the facts, which, when they later came out, cast very considerable doubt on whether this was clearly attributable to the North Vietnamese.

Senator Hugh Scott (R/Pa.), an influential Republican, said that one of the reasons he supported the resolution was that it did not limit the President's right to repel attacks or prevent further aggression in Southeast Asia.

Armed Services Committee Chairman Russell said that while he had had "grave doubts" about U.S. involvement in Indochina in 1954, that was not the issue before the Senate. He referred to previous resolutions (Formosa, Middle East, Cuba), which he said had helped to prevent more serious military action, and said he hoped this would be the case in this instance. ". . . there is much more danger in ignoring aggressive acts," he concluded, "than there is in pursuing a course of calculated retaliation that shows we are prepared to defend our rights."

Senator Leverett Saltonstall of Massachusetts, the ranking Republican on the Armed Services Committee, and Senator Bourke Hickenlooper of Iowa, the ranking Republican on the Foreign Relations Committee (who had suggested during a hearing in June 1964 that a resolution would be advisable), also expressed their strong support for the resolution.

Senator John Stennis, of Mississippi, second-ranking Democrat on the Armed Services Committee, who had been very active in 1954 in trying to prevent U.S. involvement in Indochina, said, "None of us are happy about the situation in Vietnam and about our position there. But that bridge has long since been crossed. We are already there. We dare not run away, certainly not while we are under attack."

Senator John Sherman Cooper a highly respected moderate Republican from Kentucky, said he would vote for it "because it expresses the unity of one purpose to defend our country."

Senator Humphrey, liberal Democrat from Minnesota, Senate Democratic whip and a member of the Foreign Relations Committee, who was about to be named by Johnson as his running mate in the 1964 election, said that the resolution was patterned after previous resolutions, and that, in his opinion, ". . . the President has the authority under the Constitution to order the Armed Forces of the United States to protect the vital interests of this country whenever those interests are threatened."

Senator Church of Idaho, a Democratic member of the Foreign Relations Committee, (who, it will be recalled, had offered the amendment in September 1963 to condition aid to Vietnam on reforms), said that the situation called for action rather than debate: "There is a time to question the route of the flag, and there is a time to rally around it, lest it be routed. This is the time for the latter course, and in our pursuit of it, a time for all of us to unify."

Humphrey agreed. The function of the Senate was to debate policy, he said, "But there comes a time when the aggressor may feel that because of our discussions, we are disunited, and he then could launch an attack."

Church said that while he still had doubts about U.S. policy in Southeast Asia and in Vietnam, the U.S. Government, including Congress, was responsible for the consequences of that policy:

. . . who can say that these events are not the natural consequence of the hazards we have assumed by the policy we have adopted in this part of the world?

We had every reason to expect that some such incident might occur. It is a risk we assumed, necessarily, when we chose to intervene, following the defeat of the French, in that great peninsula which was once French Indochina—when we assumed an American responsibility for the future of this remote region of the world.

I have entertained and continue to entertain, serious misgivings about the correctness of American policy in southeast Asia. It seems to me that this policy is more the product of our own addiction to an ideological view of world affairs—an affliction which affects us as well as the Communists—rather than a policy based upon a detached and pragmatic view of our real national interests.

However, my dissent, to the extent that I hold it, and to the degree that I have been able to define it, is not appropriate for this occasion. This is not a time to decry the policy. A country must live with the policy it adopts, whether it be wise or foolish.

We have adopted the policy. It was initiated under the Eisenhower administration, when the original decision was made for the United States to intervene actively in South Vietnam. It has been inherited and upheld by the Kennedy administration, and by the Johnson administration, in the years which have followed.

Congress shares its responsibility for that policy. If we have not formulated it, we have funded it, from year to year, with our votes. Who is there to say that we have not acquiesced in it down through the years? . . .

So, we must accept the consequences of our own actions. We must now face the fact that the difficulties in which we find ourselves are our responsiblity, in having chosen to pursue a course of action which exposed us to such hazards.

It is in this spirit that I approach the pending joint resolution. Under the circumstances, we must unite behind the President.

Senator Bartlett, Democrat of Alaska, who had previously urged that serious attention be given to negotiations, said that negotiations required a position of strength, and that while he regretted U.S. involvement in Vietnam, "Our honor, our integrity, our vital interests are assuredly now at issue. We can do but one thing as I see it—unite behind the President."

Senator Aiken of Vermont, a Republican member of the Foreign Relations Committee, said that he continued to be opposed to expanding the war, and was still "apprehensive" about the outcome of Johnson's decision to retaliate, but that after the decision had been made ". . . I feel that I, as an American citizen, can do no less than support the President in his capacity as leader of our Nation."

Senator Albert Gore of Tennessee, a Democratic member of the Foreign Relations Committee, who had opposed U.S. involvement in Vietnam in 1954, and had frequently questioned U.S. policy toward Vietnam since that time, said, "Now, however, when U.S. forces have been attacked repeatedly upon the high seas, . . . whatever doubts one may have entertained are water over the dam. Freedom of the seas must be preserved. Aggression against our forces must be repulsed."

Senator Frank Carlson of Kansas, a Republican member of the Foreign Relations Committee, who had co-sponsored Church's reform amendment in 1963, said he had been concerned about the increasing involvement of the United States in Vietnam, and wanted to prevent further escalation of the war. But the time for questioning U.S. policy in Vietnam, he said, had passed. "We have reached a place where we have not only to support the President, because he has the responsibility, but we have a duty and a privilege today [to vote on the resolution], and we should exercise it."

During debate on the resolution, Senator Morse continued to hammer away at what he called the provocative acts of the United States. The attacks on U.S. ships was not justified, he said, but "As in criminal law, crimes are committed, but they are sometimes committed under provocation." He added:

My point is, if we are to talk about provocation, that the United States was a provocateur by having any ships anywhere within striking distance or bombing distance; and the South Vietnamese boats did bomb those islands. We should have been completely out of the scene.

If Senators want my opinion, a "snow-job" is being done on us by the Pentagon and the State Department in regard to that bombardment. Not only had we full knowledge of it, but it was being done with our tacit approval. If we did not want to escalate the war into North Vietnam, that was the time for the United States to stop escalating.

. . . when the United States became aware of the fact that South Vietnamese planned to bomb the two islands, the United States should have moved in and done everything it could to prevent an escalation of the war.

In my judgment, that act constituted a major escalation of this war.

After the second attack, Morse said, the U.S. should have taken the matter to the U.N., rather than striking back at North Vietnam. U.S. air raids against the north, he said, were "not necessary for self-defense," and "At that point the United States was guilty of an act of aggression."

Morse also discussed at some length the constitutionality of the resolution, and how Congress could check the President ". . . if the President should commit an unconstitutional act under the joint resolution, or if the joint resolution in effect . . . is an attempt to give to the President an unconstitutional power. . . ." Under the Constitution, Morse argued, the President had the inherent power to respond to an attack on U.S. forces and then to come to Congress for a declaration of war. "We should require those steps," he said, "rather than give the President blanket authority under the joint resolution to proceed to wage war without a declaration of war." After the resolution was passed, what action could Congress take to check the President if he proceeded to make war? It would be difficult, although not impossible, he said, to bring the President before the Supreme Court, and impeachment would be "unthinkable" in view of the fact that the President would be exercising his powers to protect the interests of the U.S. If neither of these checks was usable, Congress would be forced to rely on its power over appropriations. Repeal of the resolution by concurrent resolution of Congress, Morse added, was not an adequate remedy. It would create a "havoc of disunity" in the country.

Morse also criticized the use of U.S. forces to defend countries like Vietnam:

> Have we reached the point in American foreign policy where we are going to permit the President to send American boys to their death in the defense of military dictatorships, monarchies, and fascist regimes around the world with which we have entered into treaty obligations involving mutual security, no matter what the provocation and no matter what wrongs they may have committed that cause an attack upon them? Are we going to do that without a check of Congress by way of a declaration of war? What are we thinking of? What time factor would justify such precipitate action?

The Gulf of Tonkin Resolution, Morse said, "would put the United States in the middle of the Vietnam civil war," and he added:

> We could never win such a war. We might win military victory after military victory. If we did not stop the escalation, we would kill millions of people, because the escalation, step by step, would lead to all-out bombing of North Vietnam and Red Chinese cities. When we were through, we should have killed millions, and won military victory after military victory, but we should still have lost the war.
>
> The United States can never dominate and control Asia, with 800 million people in China alone. That kind of war would create a hatred for the United States and for the white man generally that would persist for centuries. Dominating Asia, after destroying her cities and killing her millions by bombings—that is the danger that we are walking into—would not make the white man supreme in Asia, but only hated.
>
> We know what the floods of human history do. Eventually the white man will be engulfed in that Asiatic flood and drowned. . . .
>
> I say most respectfully and sadly that in my judgment, in this resolution, we are planting seeds not of peace, but of war. Those who will follow us in the years to come will cry out in anguish and despair in criticism over the mistake that was made in 1964 when the joint resolution was passed.

During the two days in which the resolution was considered by the Senate there was very little discussion of its substance. Democratic and Republican leaders in the Senate and on the Foreign Relations and Armed Services Committees, acting at the request of the President, as well as in response to what they, too, viewed as a situation requiring prompt action, were determined to pass the resolution quickly and without change. As Fulbright later said,

". . . there was a great sense of urgency and we were asked to pass it immediately. . . . I was told that it would be most unfortunate if there were any amendments allowed or any delay, because this would evidence a lack of confidence and unity within the Congress with our President. So we were requested not to accept amendments."[110]

One explanation of the lack of discussion and of the Senate's ready acceptance of the resolution was given later by Senator Charles Mathias of Maryland, a thoughtful, moderate Republican:[111]

> What we were familiar with was a pattern or practice that had existed since the end of World War II, whereby the United States, by merely passing a resolution of the Congress, could bring about certain dramatic events in the world. . . . So I think we were, to some extent, the victims of success, in dealing with the Tonkin Gulf Resolution. It had worked so well in those previous situations that, speaking for myself, I think I was over-confident that it would work again, and that merely by enacting a resolution which seemed, at least, to show a high degree of national unity, that we could in some way dissipate the forces which we at that moment, saw as a threat. And as a result of that, I feel personally culpable that I didn't pursue questions. I didn't raise issues which, in a different climate and a different atmosphere, I certainly would have.
> . . . in the context of what had gone before, we were saying, "Well, we'll sign this blank check, but we don't have any expectation that it will ever have to be used. All you'll have to do is wave it in front of your creditors and they'll all go away."

In response to the few substantive questions that were raised during debate in the Senate, Fulbright took the position that the facts about the Tonkin Gulf incidents were as they had been presented by the administration, that the resolution was needed for national unity, and that the President, who had acted so wisely and prudently, could be trusted to continue doing so. Senator Ellender asked whether U.S. naval forces "could have done anything which might have provoked these attacks." Fulbright replied, "Nothing that they were not entitled to. . . . whatever provocation there may have been arose, if it did arise, from the activity of the North Vietnamese ships."

Senator Daniel B. Brewster (D/Md.) asked if the resolution contained any language "which would authorize or recommend or approve the landing of large American armies in Vietnam or in China." Fulbright replied:

> There is nothing in the resolution, as I read it, that contemplates it. I agree with the Senator that that is the last thing we would want to do. However, the language of the resolution would not prevent it. It would authorize whatever the Commander in Chief feels is necessary. It does not restrain the Executive from doing it. Whether or not that should ever be done

---

[110]U.S. Congress, Senate, Committee on Foreign Relations, *U.S. Commitments to Foreign Powers*, Hearings, 90th Cong., 1st sess. (Washington, D.C.: U.S. Govt. Print. Off., 1967), p. 139.
[111]CRS Interview with Charles Mathias, Jan. 25, 1979. In 1970, Mathias introduced a resolution to repeal four of the foreign policy area resolutions which had been passed by Congress, beginning with the Formosa Resolution, and including the Gulf of Tonkin Resolution.

is a matter of wisdom under the circumstances that exist at the particular time it is contemplated. This kind of question should more properly be addressed to the chairman of the Armed Services Committee. Speaking for my own committee, everyone I have heard has said that the last thing we want to do is to become involved in a land war in Asia; that our power is sea and air, and that this is what we hope will deter the Chinese Communists and the North Vietnamese from spreading the war. That is what is contemplated. The resolution does not prohibit that, or any other kind of activity.

Senator Thruston B. Morton, an influential Republican moderate from Kentucky, who was involved in Vietnam policymaking in the 1950s as Assistant Secretary of State for Congressional Relations under Dulles (and who became an opponent of the war in 1967), made a similar point.

Mr. Morton. I believe the action taken by the President helps to avoid any miscalculation on the part of either the North Vietnamese or the Chinese Communists. I believe the joint resolution gives that policy further strength. In my opinion, the three major wars in which we have been involved in this century have come about by miscalculation on the part of the aggressor.

I believe Congress should speak loud and clear and make it plain to any would-be aggressor that we intend to stand here. If we make that clear, we will avoid war, and not have to land vast land armies on the shores of Asia. In that connection I share the apprehension of my friend the Senator from Maryland [Mr. Brewster].

Mr. Fulbright. The Senator has put it very clearly. I interpret the joint resolution in the same way. This action is limited, but very sharp. It is the best action that I can think of to deter an escalation or enlargement of the war. If we did not take such action, it might spread further. If we went further, and ruthlessly bombed Hanoi and other places, we would be guilty of bad judgment, both on humanitarian grounds and on policy grounds, because then we would certainly inspire further retaliation.

This situation has been handled in the best way possible under the circumstances, so as to calm the situation, and not escalate it into a major war.

Senator Gaylord Nelson (D/Wis.) was troubled, however, by the broad language of the resolution, and he asked Fulbright:

Am I to understand that it is the sense of Congress that we are saying to the executive branch: "If it becomes necessary to prevent further aggression, we agree now, in advance, that you may land as many divisions as deemed necessary, and engage in a direct military assault on North Vietnam if it becomes the judgment of the Executive, the Commander in Chief, that this is the only way to prevent further aggression"?

Fulbright replied:

If the situation should deteriorate to such an extent that the only way to save it from going completely under to the Communists would be action such as the Senator suggests, then that would be a grave decision on the part of our country as to whether we should confine our activities to very limited personnel on land and the extensive use of naval and air power, or whether we should go further and use more manpower.

I personally feel it would be very unwise under any circumstances to put a large land army on the Asian Continent.

It has been a sort of article of faith ever since I have been in the Senate, that we should never be bogged down. We particularly stated that after Korea. We are mobile, we are powerful on the land and on the sea. But when we try to confine ourselves and say that this resolution either prohibits or authorizes such action by the Commander in Chief in defense of this country, I believe that is carrying it a little further than I would care to go.

I do not know what the limits are. I do not think this resolution can be determinative of that fact. I think it would indicate that he would take reasonable means first to prevent any further aggression, or repel further aggression against our own forces, and that he will live up to our obligations under the SEATO treaty and with regard to the protocol states.

I do not know how to answer the Senator's question and give him an absolute assurance that large numbers of troops would not be put ashore. I would deplore it. And I hope the conditions do not justify it now.

Mr. Nelson. We may very well not be able to nor attempt to control the discretion that is vested in the Commander in Chief. But the joint resolution is before the Senate, sent to us, I assume, at the request of the executive branch.

Mr. Fulbright. The Senator is correct.

Mr. Nelson. It was sent to the Congress in order to ascertain the sense of the Congress on the question. I intend to support the joint resolution. I do not think, however, that Congress should leave the impression that it consents to a radical change in our mission or objective in South Vietnam. That mission there for 10 years, as I have understood it, has been to aid in the establishment of a viable, independent regime which can manage its own affairs, so that ultimately we can withdraw from South Vietnam. . . .

Mr. Fulbright. . . . it seems to me that the joint resolution would be consistent with what we have been doing. We have been assisting the countries in southeast Asia in pursuance of the [SEATO] treaty. But in all frankness I cannot say to the Senator that I think the joint resolution would in any way be a deterrent, a prohibition, a limitation, or an expansion on the President's power to use the Armed Forces in a different way or more extensively than he is now using them. In a broad sense, the joint resolution states that we approve of the action taken with regard to the attack on our own ships, and that we also approve of our country's effort to maintain the independence of South Vietnam.

The Senator from Wisconsin prompts me to make a remark which perhaps I should not make. He has said that we might be mistaken in our action. If any mistake has been made—and I do not assert that it has been—the only questionable area is whether or not we should ever have become involved. That question goes back to the beginning of action in this area, and I do not believe it is particularly pertinent or proper to the debate, because in fact we have become involved. However, the Senator has mentioned it. As an academic matter, the question might be raised. But having gone as far as we have in 10 years, it seems to me that the question now is, How are we to control the situation in the best interest of our own security and that of our allies? I believe that what we did was appropriate. The joint resolution is appropriate, because it would fortify the strength of the Executive and the Government. It would put the Congress on record—and we are the most representative body that we have under our system—as supporting the action. If anything will deter aggression on the part of the North Vietnamese and the Chinese, I believe it would be the action taken together with the joint resolution supporting the action. That is the best I can do about justification of the resolution. In frankness, I do not believe the joint resolution would substantially alter the President's power to use whatever means seemed appropriate under the circumstances. Our recourse in Congress would be that if the action were too inappropriate, we could terminate the joint resolution, by a concurrent resolution, and that would precipitate a great controversy between the Executive and the Congress. As a practical question, that could be done.

Senator Cooper raised similar points:

Mr. Cooper. . . . are we now giving the President advance authority to take whatever action he may deem necessary respecting South Vietnam and its defense, or with respect to the defense of any other country included in the [SEATO] treaty?

Mr. Fulbright. I think that is correct.

Mr. Cooper. Then, looking ahead, if the President decided that it was necessary to use such force as could lead into war, we will give that authority by this resolution?

Mr. Fulbright. That is the way I would interpret it. If a situation later developed in which we thought the approval should be withdrawn, it could be withdrawn by concurrent resolution. That is the reason for the third section. . . .

One of the reasons for the procedure provided in this joint resolution, and also in the Formosa and Middle East instances, is in response, let us say, to the new developments in the field of warfare. In the old days, when war usually resulted from a formal declaration of war—and that is what the Founding Fathers contemplated when they included that provision in the Constitution—there was time in which to act. Things moved slowly, and things could be seen developing. Congress could participate in that way.

Under modern conditions of warfare—and I have tried to describe them, including the way the Second World War developed—it is necessary to anticipate what may occur. Things move so rapidly that this is the way in which we must respond to the new developments. That is why this provision is necessary or important. Does the Senator agree with me that this is so?

Mr. Cooper. Yes, warfare today is different. Time is of the essence. But the power provided the President in section 2 is great.

Mr. Fulbright. This provision is intended to give clearance to the President to use his discretion. We all hope and believe that the President will not use this discretion arbitrarily or irresponsibly. We know that he is accustomed to consulting with the Joint Chiefs of Staff and with congressional leaders. But he does not have to do that.

Mr. Cooper. I understand, and believe that the President will use this vast power with judgment.

Mr. Fulbright. He intends to do it, and he has done it. . . . I have no doubt that the President will consult with Congress in case a major change in present policy becomes necessary.

Mr. Cooper. . . . I know it is understood and agreed that in the defense of our own ships and forces any action we might take to repel attacks could lead to war, if the Vietnamese or the Chinese Communists continued to engage in attacks against our forces. I hope they will be deterred by the prompt action of the President.

We accept this first duty of security and honor. But I would feel untrue to my own convictions if I did not say that a different situation obtains with respect to South Vietnam. I know that a progression of events for 10 years has carried us to this crisis. Ten years have passed and perhaps the events are inevitable now, no one can tell. But as long as there is hope and the possibility of avoiding with honor a war in southeast Asia—a conflagration which, I must say, could lead into war with Communist China, and perhaps to a third world war with consequences one can scarcely contemplate today—I hope the President will use this power wisely with respect to our commitments in South Vietnam, and that he will use all other honorable means which may be available, such as consultations in the United Nations, and even with the Geneva powers.

We have confidence in the President and in his good judgment. But I believe we have the obligation of understanding fully that there is a distinction between defending our own forces, and taking offensive measures in South Vietnam which could lead progressively to a third world war.

Senator Cooper said later that he considered offering an amendment to split the resolution into two parts, the first part to consist of section 1, which he said was "perfectly constitutional, that is, we have the right to protect the troops. . . ." The second part would consist of section 2, which dealt with the question of authorizing or approving the use of force prospectively. He said he did not offer the amendment in part because he believed there had been an attack, and retaliation therefore was permitted by the "rules of war."[112]

Senator McGovern was also concerned about the resolution, "despite private assurances," he said later in his autobiography, "that it was primarily a ploy to defuse the Vietnam issue during the

[112]CRS Interview with John Sherman Cooper, Jan. 12, 1979.

presidential campaign."[113] He, too, asked Fulbright about the relationship between the U.S. ships and the 34-A operations, and was assured by Fulbright that the U.S. patrols were "entirely unconnected or unassociated with any coastal forays the South Vietnamese themselves may have conducted."

On August 7, the second and final day of Senate debate on the resolution, Senator Nelson decided to offer an amendment stating the concern of Congress about escalating the war. After section 1 of the resolution (which read, "That the Congress approves and supports the determination of the President, as Commander in Chief, to take all necessary measures to repel any armed attack against the forces of the United States and to prevent further aggression") he wanted to add this provision:

> (b) The Congress also approves and supports the efforts of the President to bring the problem of peace in southeast Asia to the Security Council of the United Nations, and the President's declaration that the United States, seeking no extension of the present military conflict, will respond to provocation in a manner that is "limited and fitting." Our continuing policy is to limit our role to the provision of aid, training assistance, and military advice, and it is the sense of Congress that, except when provoked to a greater response, we should continue to attempt to avoid a direct military involvement in the southeast Asian conflict.

According to Senator McGovern, Nelson showed him the amendment, and the two of them went to see Fulbright. This is McGovern's later account of that meeting:[114]

> Fulbright reiterated the plea that we had to help Johnson against Goldwater. We were just backing the President on his Tonkin response, not giving him a blank check for war. The resolution was "harmless," Fulbright insisted. It would have to go to [a Senate-House] conference if there was an amendment and that would frustrate Johnson's purpose—"to pull the rug out from under Goldwater." Nelson agreed to withdraw his amendment in return for a colloquy on the floor in which Fulbright emphasized the resolution's limiting effect.

---

[113]George S. McGovern, *Grassroots* (New York: Random House, 1977), p. 103. In a Senate speech on Aug. 8, the day after passage of the Gulf of Tonkin Resolution, McGovern said he voted for the resolution "because our leaders assured us that the military evidence was such that it constituted a military challenge which had to be met with a military response." He said he continued to be opposed, however, to further U.S. military involvement, and he proposed that there be an international conference, as suggested by de Gaulle, to negotiate a political settlement in southeast Asia. "In my judgment," he added, "an indefinite continuance of the military conflict in South Vietnam is a hopeless course that will lead in the end either to defeat or entanglement in the kind of major war which we are ill-prepared to fight in Asia." Morse said he found McGovern's speech "very interesting, and very belated. . . . Although conversion is always welcome, in my judgment, if Senators who have held the views of the Senator from South Dakota—and many of them have held them privately for these many months—had joined the Senator from Alaska [Gruening] and the Senator from Oregon 5 or 6 months ago in urging an economic, political, and diplomatic settlement of the Asiatic strife under the rules of international law, we might have been able to change the war making course of our Government in Asia. . . . one of the saddest things is that during all those months the talk of many Senators in the cloakroom has been noticeably different from their silence on the floor of the Senate." *CR*, vol. 110, pp. 18668-18669. Nelson made a brief statement in which he supported McGovern's call for a conference. *Ibid.*, p. 18672.

[114]McGovern, *Grassroots*, p. 103.

In keeping with this agreement, Nelson asked Fulbright during the debate whether he would accept the amendment (which Nelson had not formally offered). Fulbright replied:

The Senator has put into his amendment a statement of policy that is unobjectionable. However, I cannot accept the amendment under the circumstances. I do not believe it is contrary to the joint resolution, but it is an enlargement. I am informed that the House is now voting on this resolution. The House joint resolution is about to be presented to us. I cannot accept the amendment and go to conference with it, and thus take responsibility for delaying matters.

I do not object to it as a statement of policy. I believe it is an accurate reflection of what I believe is the President's policy, judging from his own statements. That does not mean that as a practical matter I can accept the amendment. It would delay matters to do so. It would cause confusion and require a conference, and present us with all the other difficulties that are involved in this kind of legislative action. I regret that I cannot do it, even though I do not at all disagree with the amendment as a general statement of policy.[115]

Nelson's proposal was the only amendment to the Gulf of Tonkin Resolution to be suggested in either the Senate or the House.

Shortly after Fulbright declined Nelson's amendment, debate on the resolution ended. Fulbright told the Senate that he was very pleased with the action of the House in passing the resolution unanimously, and that he hoped the Senate "will approach that unanimity, if possible." He added:

I realize that we all have our apprehensions about what may happen in South Vietnam or elsewhere. But fundamentally, under our system, it is the President, as our representative in these activities, who must necessarily have the dominant role, however jealous we may be of our own privileges—and we rightly should be in many areas. But in dealing with the Nation's security or with threatened warfare, we must rely to a great extent on the decisions of the Executive. We always have a reserve power, when we see that the President has made a mistake. We can always later impeach him, if we like, if we believe that he has so far departed from the sense of duty that he has betrayed the interests of our country.

But essentially the joint resolution is an exhibition of solidarity in regard to the will and determination of this country as a whole, as represented in Congress, to support the broad

---

[115]On Oct. 2, 1964, Senator Nelson wrote to the *New York Times* in response to a couple of news articles to the effect that officials in the Johnson administration were urging broader U.S. military action in Vietnam, including possible provocation of an incident which could be used to justify such an expanded program. "It appears," Nelson said, "that those within the Administration who urge a change in our policy and a larger involvement in Vietnam have mistaken the intent of Congress in approving a resolution supporting the President's response to provocation in the Gulf of Tonkin in early August. The Congressional resolution endorsed the President's specific action, but, it in no way approved in advance or gave Congressional endorsement to an expansion of the war." Nelson added that in his opinion, ". . . as I believe most Senators feel, our basic mission in Vietnam is one of providing material support and advice. It is not to substitute our armed forces for those of the South Vietnamese government, nor to join with them in a land war, nor to fight the war for them."

Nelson sent Fulbright a copy of the letter. Fulbright replied, "I think it is an excellent presentation of the matter, and I agree with your point of view." University of Arkansas Library, Fulbright Papers, series 48, box 35.

policies that have been well announced and well described in the words of the President, both recently and in past months. We are exhibiting a desire to support those policies. That will have a strong psychological effect upon our adversaries wherever they may be.

I believe the joint resolution is calculated to prevent the spread of the war, rather than to spread it, as has been alleged by some critics of the resolution. I have considered every possible alternative, both those that have been suggested on the floor of the Senate and elsewhere, and I still have come back to my own conclusion that the action that was taken; the resistance that was made in the Gulf of Tonkin; the joint resolution adopted in committee; and all our actions in this connection, are best designed to contribute to the deterrence of the spread of war.

No one knows, in this uncertain world, whether the war will spread. It could easily spread because of the determination of our adversaries, in spite of anything we might do. But I sincerely believe that this action, taken with such general support by both Houses of Congress, will result in deterring any ambitions or reckless adventuresome spirit on the part of the North Vietnamese or the Communist Chinese. So I ask and hope that Members of this body will support the joint resolution.

Morse was the last to speak. He said that passage of the Gulf of Tonkin Resolution would be a "historic mistake":

I believe that history will record that we have made a great mistake in subverting and circumventing the Constitution of the United States, article I, section 8, [declaration of war by Congress] thereof by means of this resolution.

As I argued earlier today at some length, we are in effect giving the President of the United States warmaking powers in the absence of a declaration of war.

I believe that to be a historic mistake, I believe that within the next century, future generations will look with dismay and great disappointment upon a Congress which is now about to make such a historic mistake.[116]

Ninety Senators out of one hundred were present and voting on the passage of the resolution. Eighty-eight voted aye. Morse and Gruening voted nay. The ten absentees were all recorded in the affirmative. Among those voting for the resolution were southern conservatives who had opposed U.S. involvement in the war, including Russell, Stennis, Harry F. Byrd, Jr., (D) of Virginia, Ellender, Sam J. Ervin, Jr. (D/N.C.), Robertson. Also voting for the resolution were all of the moderate and liberal Democrats and Republicans from all sections of the country. These included, besides Fulbright, all of the leaders of the antiwar movement of later years: Mansfield, Cooper, Church, Case, McGovern, Edward M. Kennedy (D/Mass.), Gore, Pell, Nelson, Eugene J. McCarthy (D/Minn.) Javits, Edmund S. Muskie (D/Maine), Aiken, Morton, Vance Hartke (D/Ind.), Clark. Others voted for it because they favored strong U.S. military action in Vietnam, including Goldwater, Dirk-

---

[116]Morse continued to make frequent Senate speeches on Vietnam during the following weeks. See, for example, *CR*, vol. 110, pp. 22037-22040.

sen, Thurmond, John G. Tower (R/Tex.), McGee, Paul H. Douglas (D/Ill.) Hickenlooper, Gordon Allott (R/Colo.), Dodd, and Lausche.

Executive Branch Interpretation of the Gulf of Tonkin Resolution

Unlike the Formosa Resolution (but like the Middle East and Cuba Resolutions), the Gulf of Tonkin Resolution did not specifically *authorize* the President to use the armed forces, but such authorization was claimed to have been given, based on the language of section 1 that Congress "approves and supports the determination of the President, as Commander in Chief, to take all necessary measures to repel any armed attack against the forces of the United States and to prevent further aggression," and especially the language of section 2, that "the United States is, therefore, prepared, as the President determines, to take all necessary steps, including the use of armed force. . . ." to defend Vietnam. Thus, the executive branch argued in a 1966 State Department legal memorandum: "Section 2 thus constitutes an authorization to the President in his discretion, to act—using armed force if he determines that is required—to assist South Viet-Nam at its request in defense of its freedom. . . . the grant of authority 'as the President determines' is unequivocal." The memorandum further asserted, however, that a resolution or even a declaration of war by Congress was not required in order for the President to wage war in Vietnam: "No declaration of war is needed to authorize American actions in Vietnam. . . . the President has ample authority to order the participation of United States armed forces in the defense of South Viet-Nam. . . . In the Korean conflict, where large-scale hostilities were conducted with an American troop participation of a quarter of a million men, no declaration of war was made by the Congress. The President acted on the basis of his constitutional responsibilities. . . . If the President can act in Korea without a declaration of war, *a fortiori,* he is empowered to do so now in Viet-Nam."[117]

This interpretation, which is probably the most extreme assertion of its type ever to have been made by the executive branch, was considered to be too extreme by some legal and constitutional authorities, however. One of the most respected of these, John Norton Moore, who was known as a principal exponent of the government's position, made this comment in an interview:[118]

> Well, to be candid, that [the 1966 State Department legal memorandum] was not the finest legal document that has ever been produced. In fairness, it was, I'm sure, done under the usual time pressure of the Legal Adviser's office. . . . at the time it was written there was, indeed, congressional participation and Congress had, in fact, authorized the hostilities. I would have preferred not to place the principal authorization on the exclusive power of the Commander in Chief.

---

[117]"The Legality of United States Participation in the Defense of Viet-Nam," *Department of State Bulletin,* Mar. 28, 1966. This is sometimes referred to as the Meeker memorandum, after Leonard C. Meeker, the State Department's Legal Adviser at the time. A number of lawyers and legal scholars challenged the State Department's position as stated in this as well as an earlier memorandum in March of 1965, "Legal Basis for U.S. Actions Against North Vietnam." For an answer to the latter paper, see, for example, the memorandum of law prepared in Sept. 1965 by the Lawyers Committee on American Policy Toward Vietnam, which was reprinted in *CR,* vol. 112, p. 2666 ff.
[118]CRS Interview with John Norton Moore, Dec. 7, 1978.

Despite the claim of the Legal Adviser of the State Department that the "grant of authority" of the Gulf of Tonkin Resolution was "unequivocal," and similar claims by the Justice Department in the many lawsuits in which the legality of the war was an issue, some key officials in the executive branch believed that in passing the resolution Congress was not approving a large-scale war. They also believed that Congress expected to be consulted prior to any substantial changes in the U.S. military posture in Vietnam subsequent to the passage of the resolution.[119]

One of the most persuasive witnesses on this point is McGeorge Bundy, who said later: "They [Congress] didn't decide to put 150,000 people in Vietnam. They didn't decide to bomb the north. They decided to fire a warning shot and they passed a resolution that endorsed firing a warning shot as they saw it. But, of course, in formal language it endorsed a lot more."[120]

Bundy also testified on this point when Congress was holding hearings on the War Powers Resolution:[121]

> . . . the exact trouble with the Tonkin Gulf Resolution was that it was misperceived, both by the Congress and by the executive branch. . . . The Congress surely did not believe, in 1964, that it was voting for the war that happened. And the executive branch, while I believe it was mistaken in describing the resolution as the functional equivalent of a declaration of war,[122] was thinking and acting in a framework of legal and traditional experience in which there was no clear middle-ground between unauthorized hostilities and . . . a formal declaration [of war].

With respect to consultation with Congress prior to engaging in a large-scale war, which Rusk, on behalf of the President, promised the Foreign Relations Committee when he testified on the Gulf of Tonkin Resolution, McGeorge Bundy, together with James Thomson of the NSC staff, confirmed Congress' expectation of consultation in a memorandum they sent to the President on June 11, 1965, in conjunction with preparations to send U.S. ground forces to Vietnam in July. This is the text of that memo:[123]

> The following points emerge from a review of last August's Congressional debate on the Southeast Asia Resolution:
>
> 1. Neither the Resolution itself nor the Floor discussion specifically *authorizes* or *prohibits* unlimited expansion of our force levels in Vietnam or Southeast Asia.
>
> 2. Senators who spoke in support of the Resolution were generally apprehensive of direct U.S. involvement in ground warfare anywhere in Asia; the Korean War analogy was frequently cited.

---

[119]For a discussion of legal commentary and judicial opinions on the Gulf of Tonkin Resolution see the appendix to this volume.

[120]CRS Interview with McGeorge Bundy, Jan. 8, 1979.

[121]Testimony by McGeorge Bundy, U.S. Congress, Senate, Committee on Foreign Relations, *War Powers Legislation*, Hearings, 92d Cong., 1st sess. (Washington, D.C.: U.S. Govt. Print. Off., 1972), p. 421.

[122]This was stated in 1967 by Under Secretary of State Nicholas deB. Katzenbach in testimony before the Senate Foreign Relations Committee on *U.S. Commitments to Foreign Powers*, cited above.

[123]Johnson Library, James Thomson, National Security Staff, Presidential Chron File, 6/65.

3. The Resolution's Floor manager, Senator Fulbright, indicated in his replies to questioners that the Resolution should be interpreted as permitting the President "to use such force as could lead to war," if necessary.

4. Senator Fulbright noted that the Congress had the ultimate option of withdrawing its approval at a later date by a concurrent resolution that would rescind the Southeast Asia Resolution.

5. The Resolution was passed on the understanding that there would be consultation with the Congress "in case a major change in present policy becomes necessary."

In advance of the July 1965 decision, the President asked his legal advisers for opinions on whether he needed additional authority to commit large-scale forces to Vietnam, or whether the Gulf of Tonkin Resolution was sufficient. All of them replied that the President had full constitutional authority to deploy and use the armed forces, short of what Attorney General Nicholas deB. Katzenbach called an "all-out war" which might call for Congress to declare war, and therefore that the President did not even need the Gulf of Tonkin Resolution.[124] Katzenbach said that there was "some legislative history to indicate that Congress . . . did not intend to approve a large scale land war in Asia" when it passed the resolution, but that the number of troops to be sent (he had been given the figure of 95,000) did not represent a commitment to fight such a war. For this reason, as well as to avoid having Congress place any conditions on deployment of U.S. forces to Vietnam, Katzenbach recommended against requesting a new resolution or any other form of approval.

Leonard C. Meeker, the State Department's legal adviser, concluded that although there was no requirement to consult Congress, ". . . the record shows that the Resolution was passed on the understanding that there would be consultation with the Congress 'in case a major change in policy becomes necessary.'" Committing new forces to combat in Vietnam, Meeker said, could represent such a major change, and therefore constitute a reason for consulting Congress. "Consultation would not require new affirmative action by Congress," Meeker added, "but would afford the Congress an opportunity for review."[125]

In August 1967, testifying before the Senate Foreign Relations Committee on a resolution to provide that Congress should approve major U.S. national commitments—the so-called National Commitments Resolution, which passed the Senate in 1969—former Attorney General Katzenbach, then Under Secretary of State, declared that the combination of the SEATO Treaty and the Gulf of Tonkin Resolution ". . . fully fulfill the obligation of the Executive in a situation of this kind to participate with the Congress to give the Con-

---

[124]In 1970, Katzenbach, testifying before the House Foreign Affairs Committee on the war powers bill then being considered, took a somewhat different tack. He stated: "In my opinion, the constitutional authority to use our Armed Forces in Vietnam rests squarely on Tonkin and cannot otherwise be constitutionally justified." U.S. Congress, House, Subcommittee on National Security Policy and Scientific Developments of the Committee on Foreign Affairs, *Congress, The President, and the War Powers,* Hearings, 91st Cong., 2d sess. (Washington, D.C.: U.S. Govt. Print Off., 1970), p. 302.

[125]For a further discussion of these legal opinions see pt. III of this study, forthcoming.

gress a full and effective voice, the functional equivalent of the constitutional obligation expressed in the provision of the Constitution with respect to declaring war."[126] Senator Fulbright replied that the Executive had not asked for a declaration of war, and Katzenbach countered with ". . . but didn't that resolution authorize the President to use the armed forces of the United States in whatever way was necessary? Didn't it? What could a declaration of war have done that would have given the President more authority and a clearer voice of the Congress of the United States than that did?" Fulbright: "It was presented as an emergency situation; the repelling of an attack which was alleged to have been unprovoked upon our forces on the high seas. . . . It wasn't a deliberate decision by the Congress to wage war in that full-fledged sense against a foreign power." Katzenbach: "Mr. Chairman, how much debate was there on that resolution as compared with a declaration of war when President Roosevelt sent that up? How quickly did the Congress respond? If you say there was pressure, there was the urgency. Maybe people regret afterward a declaration of war or a vote for it, but that situation inherently is one of urgency, it is one of commitment." The Gulf of Tonkin Resolution, Katzenbach added, ". . . is as broad an authorization for the use of armed forces for a purpose as any declaration of war so-called could be in terms of our internal constitutional process. . . ."

When Senator Eugene J. McCarthy (D/Minn.), heard Katzenbach's remark that the Gulf of Tonkin Resolution was the functional equivalent of a declaration of war, he left the hearing room, and said in the presence of a nearby reporter that someone would have to take the issue of the war to the country, which he soon proceeded to do.[127]

At several other points in the 1967 hearing on the making of national commitments there were extended discussions of the Gulf of Tonkin Resolution.[128] It was apparent that some Members of Congress, especially in the Senate Foreign Relations Committee, were becoming increasingly convinced that "institutional problems" had developed with respect to Congress' exercise of its war power that needed to be redressed.

Congressional Reconsideration of the Gulf of Tonkin Resolution

In 1970, Congress repealed the Gulf of Tonkin Resolution. The Executive first opposed but then acquiesced in that action, saying that the resolution had not been necessary in the first place, and had not been relied upon for the actions taken by the President in fighting the war.[129]

Congressional dissatisfaction and regret with respect to the Gulf of Tonkin Resolution had been building for several years prior to repeal.[130] Many Members of Congress had felt the sting of President Johnson's frequent reminders of their vote in favor of the resolution. According to one report in early 1966, "'He [Johnson] has

---

[126] *U.S. Commitments to Foreign Powers*, p. 82. Following quotes are from pp. 82-89.
[127] See pt. III of this study, forthcoming, for more details.
[128] See especially pp. 190-224 of *U.S. Commitments to Foreign Powers*.
[129] For details, see pt. III of this study, forthcoming.
[130] Events discussed here are discussed more fully in pt. III, where full citations of sources also are given.

used it [the Gulf of Tonkin Resolution] all year,' one Republican Senator said today. 'He pulls it out of his pocket and shakes it at you.' 'It was so damned frayed and dog-eared the last time I talked to him,' a Democratic Senator said, 'that I wanted to give him a fresh copy.'"[131]

Johnson was particularly critical of Fulbright after Fulbright began to oppose the war. "It was a shame somebody didn't think of calling it the Fulbright Resolution, like the Fulbright Scholars thing," Johnson said in an interview shortly after leaving office, "because Senator Fulbright introduced it with his approval, his consent. . . . Don't tell me a Rhodes scholar didn't understand everything in that resolution, because we said to him at the White House that the President . . . is not about to commit forces . . . unless and until the American people through their Congress sign on to go in."

In the same interview, Johnson said he did not want to ask for a declaration of war because of the administration's concern that the North Vietnamese had secret mutual defense treaties with China and Russia which might be activated by such a formal action by the U.S. But he added that the resolution provided all the support he needed. Referring to Morse's position that the resolution was a pre-dated declaration of war, Johnson said Morse ". . . could read the language and understand it. . . . Congress gave us this authority to do 'whatever may be necessary'—that's pretty far-reaching; that's 'the sky's the limit'. . . ."[132]

For his part, Fulbright has continued to take the position that Congress not only was misled, but that in passing the resolution Congress was not intending to approve a large-scale war:[133]

> In Vietnam we fought a long, costly and ultimately futile war with no more cover of constitutional sanction than the dubious and later discredited Gulf of Tonkin Resolution. To my lasting regret I played a major role in securing the enactment of that Resolution, which I surely did not anticipate would be invoked as legal sanction for a full-scale war. If the Gulf of Tonkin Resolution was, as claimed, the "functional equivalent" of a declaration of war, it must stand as the only instance in the nation's history in which Congress authorized war *without knowing* that it was doing so—indeed, in the belief, as the legislative history shows, that it was acting to prevent war.

According to George E. Reedy, Jr., one of Johnson's top aides for many years, who was White House Press Secretary at the time of the Gulf of Tonkin incidents, Fulbright "got a terribly raw deal" as a result of Johnson's action in interpreting the Gulf of Tonkin Resolution as approval by Congress of the large-scale war that ensued:[134]

> He [Fulbright] had very definite assurances from Johnson that the Tonkin Gulf Resolution was not going to be used for anything other than the Tonkin Gulf incident itself. And, as you know, Johnson later turned the Gulf Resolution virtually

---

[131]*New York Times*, Jan. 30, 1966.
[132]From CBS-TV interview with Walter Cronkite, Feb. 6, 1970.
[133]J. William Fulbright, "The Legislator as Educator," cited above, p. 725. (emphasis in original)
[134]CRS Interview with George Reedy, Mar. 29, 1979.

into a declaration of war. I myself think that, psychologically, Johnson was quite capable of telling himself that he had never given Fulbright any such assurances, that conditions had developed to a point where logically going into Vietnam was an extension of the Tonkin Gulf Resolution. . . . I think Johnson could convince himself of that, and he did convince himself of that. But I'll be damned if he could convince Fulbright. And I don't blame Fulbright. I wouldn't be convinced either, because Fulbright had really laid himself on the line for it.

Asked later what the Foreign Relations Committee should have done when presented with the Gulf of Tonkin Resolution, Fulbright said, "Well, immediately, of course, what should have been done is to have long hearings and to stall it and demand they bring in the commander of the *Maddox,* and so on, to get it right then. But we were overwhelmed by this argument that we should show a united front and get this passed quickly and show support of the President's action. . . ." "What should have been done is that the resolution should have been denied and the President told to go chase himself; we're not interested in going forward. . . . But, obviously, under those circumstances, that's just a fantasy in the light of hindsight."[135]

Although the Gulf of Tonkin Resolution was not repealed until 1970, pressure for its reconsideration, which had been growing during 1965, after the President had cited the resolution as adequate authority for expanding the war, increased during 1966. On February 1966, Morse offered an amendment to repeal the resolution. This was tabled by a vote of 92-5, with Gruening, Eugene McCarthy, and Stephen Young voting with Morse.

In August 1967, as the increasingly costly war continued without apparent progress, there was renewed consideration of the Gulf of Tonkin Resolution. For example, a group of about 25 Republicans in the House of Representatives, led by Paul Findley, then a member of the Foreign Affairs Committee, introduced a resolution calling for the committee to hold hearings on whether the Gulf of Tonkin Resolution should be modified or replaced.

At about the same time, the Senate Foreign Relations Committee held its national commitment hearings, following which it made this statement in its report:[136]

> The Gulf of Tonkin resolution represents the extreme point in the process of constitutional erosion that began in the first years of this century. Couched in broad terms, the resolution constitutes an acknowledgment of virtually unlimited Presidential control of the Armed Forces. It is of more than historical importance that the Congress now ask itself why it was prepared to acquiesce in the transfer to the executive of a power which, beyond any doubt, was intended by the Constitution to be exercised by Congress.
> Several answers suggest themselves:
> First, in the case of each of the resolutions discussed, Congress was confronted with a situation that seemed to be urgent

---

[135]CRS Interview with J. William Fulbright, Feb. 18, 1983.
[136]S. Rept. 90-797, pp. 21-22. The National Commitments Resolution was passed by the Senate in 1969.

and, lacking firm historical guidelines for the discharge of its foreign policy responsibilities in a real or seeming emergency, it acquiesced in an expedient which seemed to meet the needs of the moment, the foremost of which at the time of each of the resolutions seemed to be an expression of national unity. In the case of the Gulf of Tonkin resolution, the Senate responded to the administration's contention that the effect of the resolution would be lost if it were not enacted quickly. The desired effect was a resounding expression of national unity and support for the President at a moment when it was felt that the country had been attacked. In order, therefore, to avoid the delay that would arise from a careful analysis of the language of the resolution and the further delay that would arise if the resolution had to go to a Senate-House conference to reconcile differing versions, the Foreign Relations Committee and the entire Senate speedily approved the resolution in the language in which it had already been adopted by the House of Representatives. The prevailing attitude was not so much that Congress was granting or acknowledging the executive's authority to take certain actions but that it was expressing unity and support for the President in a moment of national crisis and, therefore, that the exact words in which it expressed those sentiments were not of primary importance.

Second, in the course of two decades of cold war the country and its leaders became so preoccupied with questions of national security as to have relatively little time or thought for constitutional matters. Insofar as the question of authority to commit the country to war was thought of at all, the general attitude was one of acceptance of the power of the President, in his capacity as Commander in Chief, to commit the Armed Forces to at least limited war. At the same time Congress showed a marked reluctance to attempt to define the constitutional division of authority between the President and Congress in matters of war and peace. More important, however, than what was thought about the war power was the paucity of thought about it.

Third, in the case of the Gulf of Tonkin resolution, there was a discrepancy between the language of the resolution and the intent of Congress. Although the language of the resolution lends itself to the interpretation that Congress was consenting in advance to a full-scale war in Asia should the President think it necessary, that was not the expectation of Congress at the time. In adopting the resolution Congress was closer to believing that it was helping to *prevent* a large-scale war by taking a firm stand than that it was laying the legal basis for the conduct of such a war.

The committee concluded that in adopting a resolution with such ". . . sweeping language . . . Congress committed the error of making a *personal* judgment as to how President Johnson would implement the resolution when it had a responsibility to make an *institutional* judgment, first, as to what *any* President would do with so great an acknowledgment of power, and, second, as to whether, under the Constitution, Congress had the right to grant or concede the authority in question." (emphasis in original)

Finally, on February 20, 1968, the Foreign Relations Committee, after receiving confidential information from at least one authoritative source, held a one-day hearing on the 1964 Gulf of Tonkin incidents.[137] In preparation for the hearing, a new committee staff member, William Bader, who had been an officer in the Navy and knew how to interpret ships' logs and communications, reexamined the evidence for the 1964 incidents and concluded that the administration had not proven that the second attack had taken place. In one of a series of memoranda, Bader stated:[138]

> In staff judgment, a wide variety of circumstances made it seem to Administration officials at high levels, and to operating officers in Vietnam, that some firm act was required by the U.S. The Vietnamese Government was falling, Senator Goldwater was demanding escalation, Congress was about to adjourn, and there was a feeling attributed to Mr. [Bill] Moyers that we might "bluff" the other side into desisting.
>
> It must be recalled that the first incident had occurred and the U.S. had decided not to retaliate but to warn. There was, therefore, a need to show the flag, a need to show the U.S. Navy could not be shoved around—a need to put the chip on the shoulder and to bloody someone's nose. Communications traffic reflects this air of tension and preconception.
>
> In our judgment circumstances were ripe—so ripe indeed that a flight of birds, a fish stake (both mentioned by naval officers), a balky sonar, or a falling star, would trigger a response out of proportion to the stimulus.
>
> So the U.S. reacted—from the lookout to the Commander-in-Chief and, once embarked in this framework, the movement toward retaliation became almost irresistable. Frantic communications asking for confirmation encountered delayed replies. Communications suggesting the early reports of 30 or more torpedo firings were erroneous, were brushed aside. By then aircraft on the *Ticonderoga* were fueled and armed for retaliation; the President was scheduled to go on television; Congressional leaders had been alerted. Retaliation was on the road.

In another memorandum Bader commented on the administration's handling of the questions raised by Commander Herrick as to whether there had been an attack:[139]

> Secretary McNamara misled the Committee by not telling the Committee how increasingly ambiguous the reports on the second incident became as the hours move on. What he described in such positive terms was actually a highly confused event. On the basis of the evidence from the communications

---

[137]*The Gulf of Tonkin, The 1964 Incidents*, cited above. The principal informant was Navy Commander Jack Cowles, who had been in the Flag Plot, the Navy's war room in the Pentagon, on Aug. 4, 1964, and, based on the messages he saw, had decided that evidence of the attack was very dubious if not nonexistent. In Sept. 1967, after he had read a press report of Fulbright's regrets about his role in the passage of the Gulf of Tonkin Resolution, Cowles approached Fulbright's staff with information on the subject. See Austin, pp. 165-168. Correspondence from Commander Cowles, as well as several other informants, is in the papers of the Senate Foreign Relations Committee at the National Archives, RG 46, and one of his letters is reprinted in *The Gulf of Tonkin, The 1964 Incidents*, pp. 84-85.

[138]"Tentative Staff Conclusions," Jan. 18, 1968, Records of the Senate Foreign Relations Committee, National Archives, RG 46.

[139]"Examples of Misinformation Given to SFRC and Armed Services at Time of Incident," Jan. 30, 1968, same location.

traffic it would seem that the facts increasingly demanded caution—but the operational requirements of the retaliatory raid and the bureaucratic and press momentum that developed after the first reports came in were just too strong.

Prior to the February 1968 hearing, the committee staff gathered detailed information on the August 4 incident, including a number of cables as well as information from the ships' logs. The staff also attempted to get access to the NSA intercepts, and finally the executive branch decided that it would be desirable to let the chairman see them. A meeting was arranged in the office of Senator Russell, in order for the matter to be handled under the auspices of the Armed Services Committee to which the Pentagon was responsible, where Deputy Secretary of Defense Paul H. Nitze showed the intercepts to Fulbright and Russell. Nitze and the administration hoped that Fulbright could be persuaded not to hold new hearings on the Gulf of Tonkin incidents. After looking at the intercepts and expressing some doubt that they were conclusive evidence, Fulbright asked Nitze for additional messages and logs. Russell told Nitze that the Foreign Relations Committee was entitled to have the information.[140]

The February 20, 1968 hearing of the committee, held in executive session, opened with a statement by McNamara in which he reviewed the events of August 2 and 4, 1964. He examined four questions: "Was the patrol in fact for legitimate purposes. Were the attacks unprovoked? Was there indeed a second attack? If there was a second attack, was there sufficient evidence available at the time on our response to support this conclusion?" His answers were that the patrol was legitimate, that the attacks were not provoked, and that there was a second attack supported by adequate evidence to justify the U.S. response. He said that in addition to all of the other forms of confirming evidence, ". . . intelligence reports received from a highly classified and unimpeachable source [radio intercepts] reported that North Vietnam was making preparations to attack our destroyers with two Swatow boats and one PT boat if the PT could be made ready in time." "No one within the Department of Defense has reviewed all of this information," he added, "without arriving at the unqualified conclusion that a determined attack was made on the *Maddox* and *Turner Joy* in the Tonkin Gulf on the night of August 4, 1964." Moreover, at the time the order was given for the airstrikes, "Sufficient information was in the hands of the President . . . to establish beyond any doubt then or now that an attack had taken place."

McNamara also took strenuous exception to allegations that the U.S. ". . . induced the incident on August 4 with the intent of providing an excuse to take the retaliatory action which we in fact took. I can only characterize such insinuations as monstrous." U.S. warnings after the first attack, and assertions of the right of free passage, as well as the order for the ships to remain 11 rather than 8 miles off the coast after resuming the patrol were, he said, "hardly indicative of an intent to induce another attack." "But beyond that," McNamara said, "I find it inconceivable that anyone

---

[140]See the account in Austin, pp. 168-172.

even remotely familiar with our society and system of Government could suspect the existence of a conspiracy which would include almost, if not all, the entire chain of military command in the Pacific, the Chairman of the Joint Chiefs of Staff, the Joint Chiefs, the Secretary of Defense, and his chief civilian assistants, the Secretary of State, and the President of the United States."[141]

Fulbright denied that there was any thought of a conspiracy, and explained his own views for holding the inquiry:

. . . I don't think anyone, I don't believe anyone, certainly myself, entertained the idea this was a plot or a conspiracy.

The point really is, and I think there is evidence sufficiently to justify an inquiry as to whether or not the decisionmaking process, with all these conflicting reports coming in, is sufficiently accurate and reliable to justify taking such a decision to declare war on another country, which was the immediate outgrowth of this particular series of events. . . .

I think this committee, and certainly as chairman of the committee I think it was very unfair to ask us to vote upon a resolution when the state of the evidence was as uncertain as I think it now is, even if your intercepts are correct. Of course, none of those intercepts were mentioned to us, I don't believe in the testimony on August 6. Your statement and General Wheeler's was without any doubt, any equivocation that there was an all-out attack.

I submit that even if you give the most favorable interpretations to these reports that it was far less than positive and unequivocal as your statement before the committee indicates.

This has been very serious to me and all members of this committee and the Senate.

We have taken what is called the functional equivalent of a declaration of war upon evidence of this kind, and action as precipitate as this was. Even the commander, that is one of the crucial cablegrams from the commander of the task force, recommended that nothing be done until the evidence was further evaluated. I read it this morning, I won't read it again.

But that alone almost, if I had known of that one telegram, [Herrick's 1:27 p.m. message suggesting further evaluation] if that had been put before me on the 6th of August, I certainly don't believe I would have rushed into action.

We met, if you will recall for 1 hour and 40 minutes, in a joint meeting of the Armed Services and this committee and we accepted your statement completely without doubt. I went on the floor to urge passage of the resolution. You quoted me, as saying these things on the floor. Of course all my statements were based upon your testimony. I had no independent evidence, and now I think I did a great disservice to the Senate. I feel very guilty for not having enough sense at that time to have raised these questions and asked for evidence. I regret it.

I have publicly apologized to my constituents and the country for the unwise action I took, without at least inquiring into

---

[141]These quotations are from *The Gulf of Tonkin, The 1964 Incidents,* cited above, pp. 17-19. *Ibid.,* pp. 79-81.

the basis. It never occurred to me that there was the slightest doubt, certainly on the part of Commander Herrick who was in charge of the task force that this attack took place. He obviously had doubts, his own cablegram so states. That is the reason for it. I feel a very deep responsibility, and I regret it more than anything I have ever done in my life, that I was the vehicle which took that resolution to the floor and defended it in complete reliance upon information which, to say the very least, is somewhat dubious at this time. . . .

If I had had enough sense to require complete evaluation I never would have made the mistake I did. If I had had notice of that particular cable in 1964 I think I would have had enough sense at least to raise a warning sign, and normally this committee does have hearings and questions. I don't know why, what possessed me, the background was such that I went along, of course I wasn't the only one. Both committees, except for the Senator from Oregon, unanimously accepted your testimony then as the whole story, and I must say this raises very serious questions about how you make decisions to go to war.

I mean, this is not a small matter that we are in, in Vietnam, and I think for the future, the least I can do and the committee can do, is to alert future committees and future Senates that these matters are not to be dealt with in this casual manner.

I felt very badly about it, about the matter. I must say that I don't blame you personally for this. These communications were very conflicting, and I don't think—I never meant to leave the impression that I thought you were deliberately trying to deceive us, but I must confess I think the evidence is very conflicting and warrants what Mr. Herrick suggested— time to evaluate what the evidence was—which we didn't do.

The hearing consisted largely of a recapitulation of the events of August 4, with frequent reference to the various messages sent that day, especially that suggesting further evaluation, and those which followed. A number of questions were asked about the relationship betweeen the DE SOTO patrol and the 34-A operations, why the patrol was not suspended after the first attack, and, of course, whether there had been a second attack. McNamara reminded the members of the committee that he had told them about the July 31 34-A operations, as well as the intercepts, at the meeting on August 3. As a part of his response to the question of evidence of the second attack, McNamara, after the hearing room was cleared of all but McNamara and his aides and the Senators themselves, showed the Senators the intercepts. (How many and which ones is not known, except for McNamara's comment that he was going to show them the intercept ordering the PT boats to attack. All of the intercepts are still classified as of this writing, 20 years later.)

The committee was obviously divided, and reluctant to express its judgment on the 1964 incidents. Except for Cooper, none of the Republican members questioned McNamara at any length. Among the Democrats, most of the questions were from Fulbright, and to a lesser extent Morse and Gore, and Lausche, who defended the administration.

Morse said that the hearing had not changed anything he had said in the Senate in August 1964, and had verified all of the information he had received at that time from his secret informant in the Pentagon. He said that the United States had engaged in "constructive aggression" in the Tonkin Gulf, and that the North Vietnamese were justified in thinking that the presence of the destroyers was related to the 34-A operations, and in striking back as they did.[142]

Gore said that in 1964 he had been misled into believing that the U.S. ships were on a routine patrol, while in fact they were on provocative intelligence missions. His tentative conclusion, he said, was "that the administration was hasty, acted precipitately, inadvisedly, unwisely, out of proportion to the provocation in launching 64 bombing attacks on North Vietnam out of a confused, uncertain situation on a murky night, which one of the sailors described as one dark as the knob of hell; and, particularly, 5 hours after the task force commander had cabled that he doubted that there were any attacks, and recommended that no further action be taken until it was thoroughly canvassed and reviewed."[143]

Pell said he did not question McNamara's integrity, but he thought that the reaction of the U.S. was "excessive to the offense." Aiken expressed more of an interest in the years ahead than in looking back three years. Mansfield and Symington said that they thought McNamara had been candid and honest in 1964, and again in the 1968 hearing. As Symington stated: ". . . if there was a mistake, and you [McNamara] do not believe there was a mistake, it was an unintentional mistake; and there was no conspiracy, no effort to formulate something to mislead the American people so as to justify going into a more active state of belligerency with North Vietnam. Does that sum it up?" McNamara replied that it did.[144]

Mansfield said, ". . . three and a half years ago is a long time, and you [McNamara] were under pressure, we were under pressure. Maybe we did some things we wouldn't do if we would be more careful. . . ."[145]

The Foreign Relations Committee did not issue a report on its 1968 hearing on the Gulf of Tonkin incidents of 1964—Fulbright said he could not get a consensus—but the case against the administration, which was based on the committee's staff reports, was made by Morse in three speeches in the Senate following the hearings.[146]

In 1970, as was mentioned above, the Gulf of Tonkin Resolution was repealed. There the matter rests, except that it does not rest. Those who were involved in the debate over the Gulf of Tonkin incidents have continued to argue their respective points of view. And although some additional evidence has become available, the radio intercepts are still classified, as are many of the cables between Washington and the field during the period in question, the

[142]*Ibid.*, pp. 82-87.
[143]*Ibid.*, p. 102.
[144]*Ibid.*, p. 106.
[145]*Ibid.*, p. 82.
[146]CRS Interview with J. William Fulbright, Feb. 18, 1983, and *CR*, vol. 114, pp. 3813-3817, 4578-4581, 4691-4697.

report of the President's Intelligence Advisory Board, and the command and control study.

There is, however, no gainsaying the fact that the 1964 Gulf of Tonkin incidents achieved the purposes for which they were used. They were used as the occasion on which to secure congressional approval of an open-ended resolution sanctioning if not authorizing Presidential use of force in the Vietnam war. They also served a political purpose in the 1964 U.S. Presidential election campaign. President Johnson, as well as Democrats running for Congress, could answer Republican claims of weakness and inaction by this demonstration that the U.S. was determined to prevent aggression, while using its strength sparingly and for purposes of deterrence.

In addition, the U.S. response to the incidents in the Gulf served an important political purpose in South Vietnam, where the Khanh government was at least temporarily boosted, and the pressure to "go north" was assuaged.

Most importantly, the incidents provided an opportunity to demonstrate to the North Vietnamese, as well as to the Chinese and the Russians, that the U.S. would defend its forces. In addition, the limited and selective nature of the "crime" permitted a limited and selective "punishment," whereby the U.S. could seek to convey to North Vietnam and its allies that American interests and goals were limited and specific, and that force would be used sparingly. Thus, in his public statement announcing that the U.S. was retaliating against North Vietnam, President Johnson said, ". . . our response, for the present, will be limited and fitting. . . . We still seek no wider war."[147]

---

[147]These few words expressed what the airstrikes were supposed to demonstrate: that the U.S. was acting in accordance with the policy or doctrine of "coercive diplomacy," an essential ingredient of which is "reprisal"—using force to compel an opposing nation to change its behavior, rather than achieving a military victory in the traditional sense. See William R. Simons, "The Vietnam Intervention, 1964-65," in Alexander L. George, David K. Hall, and William E. Simons, *The Limits of Coercive Diplomacy: Laos, Cuba, and Vietnam* (Boston: Little, Brown, 1971); Theis, *When Governments Collide;* Gordon A. Craig and Alexander L. George, *Diplomatic Problems of Our Time* (New York: Oxford University Press, 1983).

One of the leading proponents of this approach to the study and use of the "diplomacy of violence" has been Thomas C. Schelling of Harvard University. Thomas C. Schelling, *Arms and Influence* (New Haven: Yale University Press, 1966). The references here are to p. vii and ch. 4. Schelling said he approved of U.S. reprisal after the Gulf of Tonkin incidents. It was, he said, "fitting" and "appropriate." "What made it seem fitting was not its success as a military threat. It was as an act of reprisal—as a riposte, a warning, a demonstration—that the enterprise appealed so widely as appropriate." Airstrikes against the torpedo boat bases and supporting facilities made it an act directly connected with the act committed against the U.S.. "Equivalent damage on other military sources might have made as much sense militarily, but the symbolism would have been different." Moreover, "Had the United States returned to the attack day after day, shooting at naval installations, port facilities, and warehouses, the entire operation would have lost neatness; the sensation of 'justice' would have been diluted; and the 'incident' would have been less well-defined; and it would have been harder to tell what was reprisal for the destroyer attack and what was opportunistic military action."

The Gulf of Tonkin reprisal, Schelling added, was, as a reprisal should be, "a reciprocal action, some punishment for a break in the rules." "Nominally, at least," he said, "the reprisal is related to the isolated breach of conduct, not the underlying continuing dispute. The motivation and intent can of course be more ambitious than that; the object can be a display of determination or impetuosity, not just to dissuade repetition but to communicate a much broader threat. One can even hope for an excuse to conduct the reprisal, as a means of communicating a more persuasive threat."

CHAPTER 6

TALKING PEACE AND PLANNING WAR

Immediately after the U.S. reprisal against North Vietnam on August 5, 1964, the U.S. resumed the DE SOTO patrols in the Gulf of Tonkin. At about 1:30 a.m. on August 5 (Vietnam time), prior to the retaliatory raids later that night, the order was given by CINC-PAC for the patrol to resume at daylight. The *Maddox* and the *Turner Joy* did so, but later that day they were ordered to stop for rest and replenishment.[1] It is not clear when or whether they resumed their patrol, but a short time later CINCPAC requested authority to conduct still another patrol on August 12-17. This was deferred. The next patrol was made in mid-September.[2]

Ambassador Taylor favored resumption of the DE SOTO patrols, together with continuing U.S. air sweeps over the Gulf of Tonkin "with authority to engage DRV boats and aircraft. . . ." In a cable to Washington on August 9, in which he said that 34-A operations would be suspended while Washington reviewed the situation, Taylor also advocated U.S. armed reconnaissance mission over the Ho Chi Minh Trail area of Laos, with authority to conduct air-strikes. "Any public statement regarding flights," he said, "would stress the need to protect our reconnaissance operations in Laos and avoid any other comment on operations."[3]

Taylor also proposed that on about January 1, 1965, the U.S. should begin implementing OPLAN 37-64 (the graduated pressure plan) by launching airstrikes against North Vietnam.

At an NSC meeting on August 10, Rusk recommended that further DE SOTO patrols, as well as any additional military activities, should be held up "at least until we see what the other side does." As McGeorge Bundy's notes of the meeting state, "He [Rusk] emphasized, as he has repeatedly before and since, the importance from his point of view of keeping the responsibility for escalation on the other side."[4]

The notes further state:

> The President expressed his basic satisfaction with what had been accomplished in the last week. He said the reaction from Congress was good, and also from the people, judging by the polls. He said this response was quite a tribute to the Secretaries of State and Defense. He warned, however, that if we

---

[1]"Chronology of Events, Tuesday August 4 and Wednesday August 5, 1964, Tonkin Gulf Strike," cited above, pp. 20, 47-48.

[2]Information about these subsequent patrols is contained in "Chronology of Events Relating to DE SOTO Patrol Incidents in the Gulf of Tonkin on 2 and 4 August 1964," cited above. Information concerning the response of Washington to the CINCPAC request for a patrol on Aug. 12-17 has been deleted, however.

[3]Johnson Library, NSC History File, Gulf of Tonkin Attacks, Saigon to Washington 364, Aug. 9, 1964.

[4]Johnson Library, NSF Aides File, McGeorge Bundy Memos to the President.

should fail in the second challenge, or if we should do nothing further, we could find ourselves even worse off than before this last set of events. The President did not wish to escalate just because the public liked what happened last week. We would have to pick our own ground, nonetheless, instead of letting the other side have the ball, we should be prepared to take it. He asked for prompt study and recommendations as to ways this might be done with maximum results and minimum danger. He did not believe that the existing situation would last very long.

Plans for Increasing the Pressure on North Vietnam

In the aftermath of the U.S. airstrikes and passage of the Gulf of Tonkin Resolution, U.S. policymakers, as the President had directed, continued planning for further action against the Communists. This included steps to increase U.S. readiness, one of which was to leave, rather than to withdraw, most of the military reinforcements, primarily air, that had been moved to the Pacific and to Vietnam and Thailand during the Gulf of Tonkin episode.[5]

The *Pentagon Papers* suggests that the use of airstrikes in the reprisal raids had the effect, however, of "denying options which had been considered useful alternatives to strikes against the North."[6] One of these was negotiation. In June, de Gaulle had again called for neutralization of Indochina and the withdrawal of all foreign forces. In July, he had advocated reconvening the 1954 Geneva Conference to deal with Vietnam. Then, on August 5, U.N. Secretary-General U Thant called for a Geneva Conference on the Gulf of Tonkin incidents, and on August 6 he told Rusk and Adlai Stevenson, U.S. Ambassador to the U.N., that the U.S. and North Vietnam should meet to discuss ending the war.[7] The French, the Chinese, and the North Vietnamese supported such a move, but wanted the Conference to address the entire problem of Vietnam, as it had in 1954.

There was strong opposition to these suggestions among U.S. policymakers, partly because of distrust of Communist diplomacy, and partly because such moves would undercut the gains made in response to the Gulf of Tonkin incidents. There seems to have been a new resolve that the U.S. should not allow itself to be "negotiated out" of the war, and should not negotiate until it could negotiate from strength.[8]

---

[5] *PP*, DOD ed., IV, C. 2. (b), p. 13.

[6] *Ibid.*, p. 15.

[7] For the outcome of this see Walter Johnson, "The U Thant-Stevenson Peace Initiatives in Vietnam, 1964-1965," *Diplomatic History*, 1 (Summer 1977), pp. 285-290, and Thies, *When Governments Collide*, pp. 48-49. In addition, as well as for Stevenson's own position on Vietnam during this time, see John Bartlow Martin, *Adlai Stevenson and the World* (Garden City, N.Y.: Doubleday, 1977), pp. 793 ff.

[8] Saigon to Washington 363, Aug. 9, 1964, the full text of which is in *PP*, Gravel ed., vol. III, pp. 522-524. In response to demands for negotiation on Laos, the State Department suggested a countermove, namely, dropping the previous demand that Communist forces withdraw from the Plaine des Jarres. Lao Government gains in Western Laos, it was argued, permitted this concession to be made safely. The suggestion produced a sharp reaction from various officials, however, including Ambassador Taylor, who argued that it would have a "potentially disastrous effect." Morale and will to fight particularly willingness to push ahead with arduous pacification task . . . would be undermined by what would look like evidence that U.S. seeking to take advantage of any slight improvement in non-communist position as excuse for extricating itself from Indo-

Continued

To reemphasize U.S. determination, and to warn of possible additional actions, as well as to continue to hold out the carrot of "economic and other benefits," Canadian diplomat Seaborn again conferred with the North Vietnamese on August 10, 1964, at the request of the U.S. The U.S. position reportedly angered North Vietnamese Premier Pham Van Dong, but there was also said to be some indication that the North Vietnamese might be receptive to negotiations.[9]

By mid-August, policymakers in Washington were beginning to discuss the next phase in U.S. policy, while the President turned his attention to the Democratic National Convention and the nomination of Hubert Humphrey for the Vice Presidency. W. W. Rostow circulated a memorandum proposing a program of "limited, graduated military actions," which the *Pentagon Papers* summarized as follows:[10]

> By applying limited, graduated military actions reinforced by political and economic pressures on a nation providing external support for insurgency, we should be able to cause that nation to decide to reduce greatly or eliminate altogether support for the insurgency. The objective of these pressures is not necessarily to attack his ability to provide support, although economic and certain military actions would in fact do just that. Rather, the objective is to affect his calculation of interests. Therefore, the threat that is implicit in initial U.S. actions would be more important than the military effect of the actions themselves.

Rostow's proposal was sent to all of the relevant offices of the government, and a critique was prepared for the JCS by Henry Rowen in the Office of International Security Affairs in the Department of Defense, with contributions from Rostow's own Policy Planning Staff in State.[11] The effectiveness of Rostow's proposal in influencing the North Vietnamese, the Rowen paper said, would depend upon three factors:[12]

> The opponents would have to be persuaded that: (1) the United States was "taking limited actions to achieve limited objectives"; (2) "the commitment of the military power of the United States to the limited objective is a total commitment—as total as our commitment to get the missiles out of Cuba in October 1962"; (3) the United States has "established a sufficient consensus to see through this course of action both at home and on the world scene." Further, unless such an opponent were so persuaded, "the approach might well fail to be effective short of a larger U.S. military involvement."

China via conf route." He said that a "rush to conference table would serve to confirm to CHICOMS that US retaliation for destroyer attacks was transient phenomenon and that firm CHICOM response in form of commitment to defend NVN has given the US 'Paper Tiger' second thoughts." "Under circumstances," he concluded, "we see very little hope that results of such a conference would be advantageous to us. Moreover, prospects of limiting it to consideration of any Laotian problem appear at this time juncture to be dimmer than ever. . . ."

[9]See Thies, *When Governments Collide*, pp. 47-48, and Allan E. Goodman, *The Lost Peace: America's Search for a Negotiated Settlement of the Vietnam War* (Stanford: Hoover Institution Press, 1978), pp. 19-20.

[10]*PP*, Gravel ed., vol. V, p. 336.

[11]See *ibid.*, vol. III, pp. 201-202.

[12]*Ibid.*, with passages in quotes from the Aug. 21 Rowen memorandum.

The critique pointed out, further, that there might not be the necessary domestic consensus. "Given present attitudes, application of the Rostow approach risks domestic and international opposition ranging from anxiety and protest to condemnation, efforts to dissociate from U.S. policies or alliances, or even strong countermeasures. . . ." This problem, Rowen said, would be compounded by the fact that in order to make the Rostow proposal an explicit, declared policy of the United States, the U.S. would be required to make it public before applying it, and that in turn would necessitate a public commitment. Debate on such a commitment might produce the kind of negative reaction which would prevent a firm, positive consensus from being formed, and thus prevent the plan from being carried out.

Almost obscured by the esoteric language of this critique is the very plain suggestion that for these reasons such a U.S. plan of military action against the north should begin when there was an "occasion"—an "emergency situation"—for doing so:

> . . . the controlled, limited military actions implied in the Rostow approach would be far more acceptable to the extent that they were seen to follow from Presidential conviction of vital national *necessity* in a specific context, and even more to the extent that this conviction were shared by Congress and the U.S. public. An attempt to legitimize such actions in general terms, and in advance of an emergency situation, would not only be likely to fail, but might well evoke public expression of domestic and allied opposition and denunciation . . . from opponents that would make it much *more* difficult for the President to contemplate this approach when an occasion actually arose. . . .

On August 11 the State Department circulated a memorandum drafted by William Bundy, "Next Course of Action in Southeast Asia," a slightly different version of which was sent on August 14 to Saigon, Vientiane and CINCPAC for comment.[13] Bundy said that as a result of the Gulf of Tonkin reprisal the North Vietnamese and the Chinese were convinced only "that we will act strongly where U.S. force units are directly involved." The ". . . solution in both South Viet-Nam and Laos will require a combination of military pressure and some form of communication under which Hanoi (and Peiping) eventually accept the idea of getting out. . . . After, *but only after,* we have established a clear pattern of pressure, we could accept a conference broadened to include the Viet-Nam issue." (emphasis in original) Bundy proposed a three-phase series of action:

> Phase One—Military Silence (through August)
>
> Phase Two—Limited Pressure (September through December)
>
> Phase Three—More Serious Pressures (January 1965 and following)

Phase One he described as a "short holding phase, in which we would avoid actions that would in any way take the onus off the

---

[13] For the complete text of the memo of Aug. 11, see *ibid.*, pp. 524-529. The Aug. 14 cable is on pp. 533-537.

Communist side for escalation." The DE SOTO patrols and most 34-A operations would be suspended.

In Phase Two, most 34-A operations would be resumed, as would joint U.S.-Vietnamese military planning. Training of Vietnamese pilots would expand, and cross-border operations would be conducted against the corridor in Laos. Specific "tit-for-tat" actions, or "actions of opportunity," would be conducted in response to Communist attacks.

Phase Two also would include the resumption of DE SOTO patrols, but "Both for present purposes and to maintain the credibility of our account of the events of last week, they *must* be clearly dissociated from 34A operations both in fact and in physical appearance."

Phase Three, for which Bundy suggested adopting Taylor's planning date of January 1, 1965, would include "action against infiltration routes and facilities," and "action in the DRV against selected military-related targets," including the bombing of bridges, railroads, and petroleum facilities, as well as the mining of Haiphong harbor. *"Beyond these points,"* Bundy added, "it is probably not useful to think at the present time."[14] (emphasis in original)

There was general agreement from the field with the plan proposed by Bundy.[15] CINCPAC said that it was important not to lose the "momentum" from the U.S. reaction to the Gulf of Tonkin attacks, and that ". . . pressures against the other side once instituted should not be relaxed. . . ." He urged that, in addition to the steps recommended in the Bundy memo, the U.S. consider establishing a base in South Vietnam, preferably at Danang, that would facilitate U.S. operations and symbolize America's determination to stay the course.

The U.S. mission in Saigon emphasized in its reply the need to strengthen Khanh's government. Until the viability of that government could be demonstrated, Taylor said, the U.S. should proceed with caution: "Since any of the courses of action considered in this cable carry a considerable measure of risk to the US, we should be slow to get too deeply involved in them until we have a better feel of the quality of our ally." In addition, Taylor said that it was important for the Khanh government and the South Vietnamese military to be strong enough to defend the country against possible Communist ground attacks which might result from U.S. air attacks on the north, thereby relieving the U.S. of the need to make a major ground force commitment.

The Joint Chiefs of Staff also approved generally of the Bundy plan, but said, ". . . accelerated and forceful action with respect to North Vietnam is essential to prevent a complete collapse of the

---

[14]The memorandum concluded with comments on the handling of Laos negotiations. "We would wish to slow down any progress toward a conference," Bundy wrote, "and to hold Souvanna to the firmest possible position." The conference should be put off until at least January 1965. "If, despite our best efforts, Souvanna on his own, or in response to third country pressures, started to move rapidly toward a conference, we would have a very difficult problem. If the timing of the Laos conference, in relation to the degree of pressures we had then set in motion against the DRV, was such that our attending or accepting the conference would have major morale drawbacks in South Viet-Nam, we might well have to refuse to attend ourselves and to accept the disadvantages of having no direct participation. In the last analysis, GVN morale would have to be the deciding factor."

[15]See the texts of the cables from Vientiane, Saigon, and CINCPAC in *PP*, Gravel ed., vol. III, pp. 541-548.

US position in Southeast Asia."[16] They also took issue with Taylor's "go-slow" approach, saying that they did not agree ". . . that we should be slow to get deeply involved until we have a better feel for the quality of our ally. The United States is already deeply involved . . . only significantly stronger military pressures on the DRV are likely to provide the relief and psychological boost necessary for attainment of the requisite governmental stability and viability." The JCS reiterated their previous position that "The military course of action which offers the best chance of success remains the destruction of the DRV will and capabilities as necessary to compel the DRV to cease providing support to the insurgencies in South Vietnam and Laos." There were at least two mid-August meetings of the President and his advisers to discuss these ideas, but notes of those sessions are not yet available.

By early September 1964, after considerable political turmoil in South Vietnam during the latter part of August, "a general consensus had developed among high-level Administration officials," according to the *Pentagon Papers,* "that some form of additional and continuous pressure should be exerted against North Vietnam."[17] In addition to the State (Bundy) proposal, McNaughton prepared for McNamara a "Plan of Action for South Vietnam," that presaged the decisions ultimately made by the administration in 1965. (Ironically, the memorandum reportedly was drafted by Daniel Ellsburg, one of McNaughton's assistants, who later released the *Pentagon Papers* to the press, and was very active in the antiwar movement.)[18] "U.S. policy," said McNaughton, "has been to pacify South Vietnam by aid and advice and actions within the borders of South Vietnam. This policy will not work without a strong government in Saigon. It has become apparent that there is no likelihood that a government sufficiently strong to administer a successful pacification program will develop. It follows that our current U.S. policy . . . will not succeed." In order to "reverse the present downward trend," and to prevent "a succession of government changes ending in a demand for a negotiated settlement," the memo said, the U.S. had to "inject some major new elements" into the situation, both inside and outside South Vietnam. Inside—and here the memo anticipated the major decisions of 1965—it was proposed that the U.S. establish a naval base, perhaps at Danang, and (then under study, the memo said) enlarge the U.S. role "e.g., large numbers of US special forces, divisions of regular combat troops, US air, etc., to 'interlard' with or to take over functions or geographical areas from the South Vietnamese armed forces."

Outside the borders of South Vietnam, the McNaughton memo proposed a program beginning around October 1, but postponing to November or December any major escalation, designed to "put increasing pressure on North Vietnam," but also to "create as little risk as possible of the kind of military action which would be difficult to justify to the American public and to preserve where possible the option to have no US military action at all." Three specific

---

[16] *Ibid.,* pp. 550-552.
[17] *Ibid.,* p. 192. For political developments in South Vietnam, see Shaplen, *The Lost Revolution.*
[18] See the text in *PP,* Gravel ed., vol. III, pp. 556-559.

actions, similar to those suggested by William Bundy, were recommended by McNaughton: "(1) *South Vietnamese air attacks on the Laotian infiltration routes.*" These, the memo said, could provoke reactions from the Communists that would justify U.S. bombing of targets in North Vietnam as well as air combat with North Vietnamese MIG fighter planes. "(2) *South Vietnamese sea attacks on North Vietnamese junks and shore facilities by bombardment and landings.*" North Vietnamese reaction could justify U.S. sea or air protection, as well as mining of North Vietnamese harbors. "(3) *DE SOTO patrols.*" North Vietnamese reaction could justify U.S. "limited retaliation" airstrikes against the North, or, "especially if a US ship were sunk, to commence a full-fledged squeeze on North Vietnam." The memo said that the patrols should be dissociated from 34-A operations, and operated "far out in international waters of the Gulf of Tonkin," but it also noted, "It is unlikely that the DRV will attack our ships if they are outside the "12-mile limit."" (emphases in original)

In addition to these actions, the memo stated that there would be other "actions of opportunity" that might justify U.S. retaliation.

The concept underlying these proposals, the memorandum stated, ". . . in essence is: by doing legitimate things to provoke a DRV response and to be in a good position to seize on that response, or upon an unprovoked DRV action, to commence a crescendo of GVN-US military actions against the DRV." But care would have to be exercised during the election: "During the next two months, because of the lack of 'rebuttal time' before election to justify particular actions which may be distorted to the US public, we must act with special care—signaling to the DRV that initiatives are being taken, to the GVN that we are behaving energetically despite the restraints of our political season, and to the US public that we are behaving with good purpose and restraint."

"In hindsight," William Bundy commented later,[19] "the McNaughton paper reads like a *reductio ad absurdum* of the planner's art, combining *realpolitik* with the hyper-rationalist belief in control of the most refined American 'think-tank.' The Tonkin Gulf events had been unplanned but had turned out favorably; this paper can be read as an attempt to devise more Tonkin Gulfs to order. In the whole experience of the Vietnam War, the proposal was perhaps the most extreme attempt to plan systematically."

McGeorge Bundy also favored consideration of stronger military actions, including ground troops. In a memorandum to the President on August 31, in which he said that there was some question as to Khanh's ability to control the situation, he said:[20]

> The larger question is whether there is any course of action that can improve the chances in this weakening situation. A number of contingency plans for limited escalation are in preparation. They involve three kinds of activities—naval harassments, air interdiction in the Laos panhandle, and possible U.S. fleet movements resuming a presence on the high seas in the Gulf of Tonkin. The object of any of these would be more to heighten morale and to show our strength of purpose than to

---

[19]Bundy MS., ch. 15, pp. 8-9.
[20]Johnson Library, NSF Aides File, McGeorge Bundy Memos to the President.

accomplish anything very specific in a military sense—unless and until we move toward a naval quarantine.

One other possibility which we are discussing is the increase of a U.S. military presence in South Vietnam, perhaps by a naval base, or perhaps by landing a limited number of Marines to guard specific installations. Bob McNamara is very strongly against the latter course, for reasons that are not clear to me, and you may wish to question him on it if we have a luncheon meeting tomorrow.

A still more drastic possibility which no one is discussing is the use of substantial U.S. armed forces in operations against the Viet Cong. I myself believe that before we let this country go we should have a hard look at this grim alternative, and I do not at all think that it is a repetition of Korea. It seems to me at least possible that a couple of brigade-size units put in to do specific jobs about six weeks from now might be good medicine everywhere.

Johnson Approves Some Additional Pressure

On September 9, 1964, the President held a meeting to discuss U.S. policy toward Vietnam, especially the question of additional military pressures on North Vietnam. It was attended by all of the top policymakers, including Taylor, Rusk, McNamara, General Wheeler, McCone, William Bundy, McNaughton, and McGeorge Bundy. On September 6, before leaving for Washington, Taylor had cabled Rusk concerning the situation in South Vietnam.[21] Recent events, he said, had caused him to conclude, contrary to his earlier position on the Bundy memorandum of August 11, that the U.S. had no choice but to resort to increased pressure on North Vietnam, which he again suggested should begin around December 1, 1964. ". . . after this recent experience . . . we must accept the fact that an effective government, much beyond the capacity of that which has existed over the past several months, is unlikely to survive. We now have a better feel for the quality of our ally. . . . Only the emergence of an exceptional leader could improve the situation and no George Washington is in sight." Taylor stressed the importance of Vietnam in relation to "total world responsibilities" of the United States, and said, "If we leave Vietnam with our tail between our legs, the consequences of this defeat in the rest of Asia, Africa, and Latin America would be disastrous."

Prior to the September 9 meeting, William Bundy and Michael Forrestal drafted a paper, "Courses of Action for South Vietnam," (September 8, 1964), in which they summarized the consensus reached by Rusk, McNamara, Taylor, and General Wheeler. This was its text:[22]

COURSES OF ACTION FOR SOUTH VIETNAM

This memorandum records the consensus reached in discussions between Ambassador Taylor and Secretary Rusk, Secretary McNamara, and General Wheeler, for review and decision by the President.

---

[21]*PP*, Gravel ed., vol. II, pp. 336-337, from Saigon to Washington 768, Sept. 6, 1964.
[22]Johnson Library, NSF Meetings File. An earlier and slightly different draft of this paper was printed in *PP*, Gravel ed., vol. III, pp. 561-562. (emphases in original)

The Situation

1. Khanh will probably stay in control and may make some headway in the next 2-3 months in strengthening the government (GVN). The best we can expect is that he and the GVN will be able to maintain order, keep the pacification program ticking over (but not progressing markedly), and give the appearance of a valid government.

2. Khanh and the GVN leaders are temporarily too exhausted to be thinking much about moves against the North. However, they do need to be reassured that the US continues to mean business, and as Khanh goes along in his government efforts, he will probably want more US effort visible, and some GVN role in external actions.

3. The GVN over the next 2-3 months will be too weak for us to take any major deliberate risks of escalation that would involve a major role for, or threat to, South Vietnam. However, escalation arising from and directed against US action would tend to lift GVN morale at least temporarily.

4. The Communist side will probably avoid provocative action against the US, and it is uncertain how much they will step up VC activity. They do need to be shown that we and the GVN are not simply sitting back after the Gulf of Tonkin.

Courses of Action

We recommend in any event:

1. US naval patrols in the Gulf of Tonkin should be resumed immediately (about September 12). They should operate initially beyond the 12-mile limit and be clearly dissociated from 34A maritime operations. The patrols would comprise 2-3 destroyers and would have air cover from carriers; the destroyers would have their own ASW [Anti-Submarine Warfare] capability.

2. 34A operations by the GVN should be resumed immediately thereafter (next week). The maritime operations are by far the most important. North Vietnam is likely to publicize them, and at this point we should have the GVN ready to admit that they are taking place and to justify and legitimize them on the basis of the facts on VC infiltration by sea. 34A air drop and leaflet operations should also be resumed but are secondary in importance. We should not consider air strikes under 34A for the present.

3. Limited GVN air and ground operations into the corridor areas of Laos should be undertaken in the near future, together with Lao air strikes as soon as we can get Souvanna's permission. These operations will have only limited effect, however.

4. We should be *prepared* to respond on a tit-for-tat basis against the DRV in the event of any attack on US units or any *special* DRV/VC action against SVN. The response for an attack on US units should be along the lines of the Gulf of Tonkin attacks, against specific and related targets. The response to special action against SVN should likewise be aimed at specific and comparable targets.

The main further question is the extent to which we should add elements to the above actions that would tend deliberately to provoke a DRV reaction, and consequent retaliation by us. Examples of actions to be considered would be running US naval patrols increasingly close to the North Vietnamese coast and/or associating them with 34A operations. We believe such deliberately provocative elements should not be added in the immediate future while the GVN is still struggling to its feet. By early October, however, we may recommend such actions depending on GVN progress and Communist reaction in the meantime, especially to US naval patrols.

The JCS agreed with the four recommendations in Bundy's draft, but the Chiefs were split on the question of provocation.[23] The Chairman of the JCS, General Wheeler, the Chief of Staff of the Army, Gen. Harold K. Johnson, and the Chief of Naval Operations, Adm. David L. McDonald, "consider that, based upon Ambassador Taylor's recommendations, we should not purposely embark upon a program to create an incident immediately but that . . . we must respond appropriately against the DRV in the event of an attack on U.S. units." The Chief of Staff of the Air Force, Gen. John P. McConnell, and the Commandant of the Marine Corps, Gen. Wallace M. Greene, Jr., however, "believe that time is against us and military action against the DRV should be taken now."

The Chiefs also agreed that the war was not being won, and that U.S. forces would have to be used in order to win.

At the meeting on September 9, the President asked if anyone disagreed with the four recommendations in Bundy's Paper. "No differing view was expressed," according to McGeorge Bundy's notes of the meeting.[24] "Secretary McNamara said we could try other things later on. Secretary Rusk concurred. General Wheeler said that of course a clear-cut incident might require appropriate action at any time, and there was general agreement with this thought."

The President asked each of the principal officials who were present to comment on the four proposals. Taylor said that the Khanh government "was in a more uncertain condition than before," and that for this reason the U.S. should postpone major military actions against North Vietnam. But he also emphasized that in the long run such moves would be necessary.

McCone agreed that a sustained air attack on the north would be dangerous in view of the political fragility of the south.

When asked for his opinion, "Mr. Rusk said that a major decision to go North could be taken at any time—'at 5-minutes' notice.' He did not recommend such decision now. He thought we should take the four recommended actions and play for the breaks."

Rusk added that a split might be developing in the "Communist Bloc," and if this happened the Chinese and the North Vietnamese might become more inhibited in Southeast Asia.

Johnson asked Taylor what would happen if the Khanh government grew weaker, despite U.S. help. "Ambassador Taylor replied that as long as the armed forces are solid, the real power is

---

[23]Johnson Library, NSF Country File, Vietnam, JCS Memorandum CM-124-64, Sept. 9, 1964.
[24]Johnson Library, NSF Meeting Notes File.

secure." There was some discussion of who would assume power if Khanh "went out." Johnson also asked Taylor ". . . to compare Khanh and Diem in the people's affections. The Ambassador replied the people did not care for either one."

"The President asked if anyone doubted whether it was worth all this effort. Ambassador Taylor replied that we could not afford to let Hanoi win, in terms of our overall position in the area and in the world. General Wheeler supported him most forcefully, reporting the unanimous view of the Joint Chiefs that if we should lose in South Vietnam, we would lose Southeast Asia. Country after country on the periphery would give way and look toward Communist China as the rising power of the area. Mr. McCone expressed his concurrence and so did the Secretary of State, with considerable force."

For his part, the President, who concluded the meeting by approving the four recommended actions, said, ". . . the reason for waiting, then, must be simply that with a weak and wobbly situation it would be unwise to attack until we could stabilize our base." He told General Wheeler to explain to his military colleagues in the JCS that ". . . we would be ready to do more, when we had a base. . . . [He] did not wish to enter the patient in a 10-round bout, when he was in no shape to hold out for one round. We should get him ready to face 3 or 4 rounds at least."

The President's decisions were promulgated by NSAM 314, September 10, 1964,[25] which directed that additional pressures be exerted on North Vietnam in the four categories agreed upon, but that "the first order of business at present is to take actions which will help to strengthen the fabric of the Government of South Vietnam," and that "to the extent that the situation permits, such action should precede larger decisions." However, "If such larger decisions are required at any time by a change in the situation, they will be made."

In passing, it is of interest to note that on September 10-15, 1964, a "war game" was run on the effects of bombing North Vietnam. Called Sigma II, the game was conducted by the Joint War Games Agency, Cold War Division, Joint Chiefs of Staff, and had as participants some of the government's top Vietnam policymakers, including General LeMay, General Wheeler, McGeorge Bundy, William Bundy, and John McNaughton. The results were startling, to say the least. What the game revealed, according to George Ball, was that "exhausting the 1964 target list presently proposed for airstrikes would not cripple Hanoi's capability for increasing its support of the Viet Cong, much less force suspension of present support levels on purely logistical grounds."[26] David Halberstam, who provides some of the details of the game, said that it demonstrated "not how vulnerable the North was to U.S. bombing, but rather how invulnerable it was. . . ."[27]

---

[25]For the text, see *PP*, Gravel ed., vol. III, pp. 565-566. For a detailed discussion of the position of the various parties and interests involved with respect to the actions discussed at the Sept. 9 meeting see pp. 202-206.

[26]George Ball, "Top Secret: The Prophecy the President Rejected," *Atlantic* (July 1972), p. 39.

[27]*The Best and the Brightest*, p. 462.

Continued

William Bundy has said that Sigma II had very little effect on those who participated in the game. This is his explanation:[28]

> Essentially we must have thought that the men who ran the game (civilians from outside government . . .) were too harsh in their judgments of how the two Vietnams would respond. . . . I suppose the effect may have been greatest among those who had the time to immerse themselves in it; yet I cannot recall that any of the relevant staff members ever invoked the outcome in later discussions. Perhaps this reflects one of the most basic elements in this whole story—how much of planning and policy review came in the middle of days already full, and without the chance to stop and reflect.

Some problems developed in implementing NSAM 314. In order for the U.S. to carry out military operations in Laos, it was necessary to avoid a cease-fire and to continue to delay the holding of another international conference on Laos. Working closely with Souvanna Phouma, the U.S. was able to prevent both the cease-fire and the conference, while laying plans for conducting cross-border operations in Laos in October 1964. The President refused to allow either U.S. airstrikes or any cross-border ground actions in Laos during September-October, probably because of the pending U.S. election, but in a cable to Vientiane on October 2[29] Rusk told the U.S. Ambassador to urge the Laotians to begin airstrikes on the corridor areas. These, he said, would be supported at a later time by U.S. airstrikes, which were "part of the over-all concept," but were not authorized at that time. On October 14, T-28s of the Royal Laotian Air Force (some with Thai pilots), under the direction of U.S. advisers, conducted bombing raids on the corridor areas, with the combat air patrol support of U.S. planes. The U.S. air support role, however, was not acknowledged, partly to avoid publicly embarrassing Souvanna Phouma, who had accepted the plan. It was also not acknowledged that the T-28 program was directed by the United States.

There were also delays in implementing other aspects of NSAM 314. The DE SOTO patrols were resumed on September 12, but were suspended by the President on September 18, (and not resumed until February 1965), after an incident on September 17 in which U.S. destroyers fired at and reportedly hit several boats, presumed to be North Vietnamese torpedo boats, despite the lack of torpedo sightings or gunfire from the other vessels. (As a result, 34-A maritime operations were not resumed until October 4, and then only with very explicit advance approval each month by the 303 Committee of the NSC.)[30]

The conclusions of Sigma I, conducted in the spring of 1964, were also contrary to many of the assumptions being made by U.S. policymakers. Rather than being deterred by U.S. (Blue Team) bombing, the North Vietnamese (Red Team) took steps to defend themselves, while continuing their support of Communists in the south. For each U.S. move, the North Vietnamese made an apparently effective countermove. General LeMay finally told McGeorge Bundy at one of the intermissions that the U.S. should make full use of its air power, and, if necessary, should "bomb them into the Stone Age." Halberstam, p. 462. According to William Sullivan (CRS Interview with William Sullivan, July 31, 1980), by the end of Sigma I, (1970 in the time frame of the game), the U.S. had 500,000 troops in Vietnam but was still faced with a stalemate and with draft riots at home. For more details see Sullivan, *Obbligato, 1939–1979: Notes on a Foreign Service Career* (New York: W. W. Norton, 1984), pp. 178–181.

[28]Bundy MS., ch. 15, appendix 1, p. 3.
[29]The text is in *PP*, Gravel ed., vol. III, pp. 576–577.
[30]See the directive for these procedures, *ibid.*, p. 571.

In contrast to the August 4 incident, the President questioned whether there had been an attack, and seemed reluctant to act without better evidence. Conceivably, he may have wanted to avoid a further display of U.S. military power at that point in his campaign, particularly since he had already done so in August, and, having the Gulf of Tonkin Resolution, did not feel the same need for congressional approval. He may also have doubted the value, either in the war or in the campaign, of another retaliatory strike at that time against North Vietnam, especially when the South Vietnamese Government was so unstable. In a meeting on September 18 to discuss the report of an attack he said he was "not interested in rapid escalation on so frail evidence and with a very fragile government in South Vietnam," and at a meeting on September 19 he "pointed out that nothing would be more useful in the next six weeks than a real success on the ground [by South Vietnamese forces], for both domestic and international reasons."[31]

Moreover, even though the reports of the August 4 and September 18 incidents were similar, there were basic differences in the circumstances surrounding the two events. For one thing, there was only one ship involved in the September 18 incident, and although McNamara said that there were eyewitness reports of an attack, and one intercept that "appeared to indicate," that North Vietnamese ships were under attack, the reporting was said to be much "thinner," and the evidence of actual hostile attack "thin to non-existent." The August 4 incident had also been preceded by a confirmed attack on August 2, thus creating the expectation that another attack might occur at any time, and a receptivity to believing that a second attack had occurred when it was so reported. There was also the need, strongly felt on August 4, to respond to a second attack after not responding to the first.

It is also likely that the President was more cautious after the August 4 incident. He was reported, in fact, to have commented several days later, "Hell, those dumb stupid sailors were just shooting at flying fish."

Thus, in the meeting at 2:30 p.m. on September 18, after the report of an air attack was received at 9:15 a.m., President Johnson "proved very skeptical about the evidence to date, and he was deeply annoyed that leaks apparently from the Pentagon were producing pressure for a public statement before we knew what we wanted to say." Although he authorized preparations for retaliation against targets in the southern part of North Vietnam (the JCS proposed attacking oil supplies in the Hanoi/Haiphong area, preceded by attacks on North Vietnamese MIG fighter planes, but Rusk preferred a smaller scale strike, and the Chiefs were told by McNamara to plan for attacks on targets in the southern part of North Vietnam which were not defended by MIGs), additional reports during the afternoon raised further doubts that an attack had occurred, and the preparatory order was cancelled. A daylight

---

[31] These and other quotes are from McGeorge Bundy's Memorandum for the Record of Sept. 20, 1964, Johnson Library, NSF Aides File, McGeorge Bundy Memos to the President, "The Gulf of Tonkin Incident, September 18." The President's remark about "flying fish" is from Karnow, *Vietnam*, p. 374, and Ball's comment is from *The Past Has Another Pattern*, pp. 379–380.

search was ordered of the area in which the attack was said to have occurred.

By the next morning (September 19), "it was clear that the search had proven negative. Summary reports from CINCPAC and others had somewhat hardened the evidence that [North Vietnamese] vessels had been in the area, but the general conclusion was that these vessels had not attempted an aggressive attack." In a meeting at 11 a.m. with top officials, the President "continued to make clear his very grave doubt that there had been any hostile vessels, let alone an intent to attack." The President "found only the intercept persuasive." (Even the intercept was subsequently discounted.) He asked Gen. Marshall S. Carter of the CIA for his opinion, and Carter replied that there probably had been North Vietnamese vessels in the area. Rusk said this was 99 percent probable, and stressed the importance of "not seeming to doubt our naval officers on the spot. The President replied somewhat sharply that he was not planning to make a radio broadcast on the matter but that he did think it important to find out exactly what happened. He also repeated his irritation at having his hand forced by an AP [Associated Press] report obtained from some junior military officer."

McNamara suggested that the DE SOTO patrols be renewed, but George Ball questioned whether this would be wise, and the President is said to have found "considerable force" in Ball's argument. This is Ball's rendition:

. . . Secretary McNamara proposed a further DE SOTO Patrol to show the flag and prove to Hanoi and the world that we were not intimidated. The project was briefly discussed; there was general agreement around the table; the President indicated his approval to go forward. I had said little during the discussion, but I now spoke up, "Mr. President, I urge you not to make that decision. Suppose one of those destroyers is sunk with several hundred men aboard. Inevitably, there'll be a Congressional investigation. What would your defense be? Everyone knows that the DE SOTO Patrols have no intelligence mission that couldn't be accomplished just as well by planes or small boats at far less risk. The evidence will strongly suggest that you sent those ships up the Gulf only to provoke attack so we could retaliate. Just think what Congress and the press would do with that! They'd say you deliberately used American boys as decoy ducks and that you threw away lives just so you'd have an excuse to bomb. Mr. President, you couldn't live with that.

No one spoke for a long moment. The President seemed disconcerted and confused. Then he turned to McNamara: "We won't go ahead with it, Bob. Let's put it on the shelf."

According to the notes of the meeting, after Ball's comment the President asked General Wheeler to explain the military value of the patrols. Wheeler did so, adding that more important than the intelligence-gathering functions of the patrols was the "general proposition that we should not allow ourselves to be denied free movement on the high seas." Rusk "supported this argument strongly by saying that the 'bandits' in North Vietnam finally needed to know that we were in the area and had no intention of being driven out." The President said he accepted these arguments, and was prepared to continue the patrols if there was adequate justification. He asked McNamara and Wheeler to prepare such a justification, and for Ball to "serve as critic" of their argument.

The Vietnam Issue in the Presidential Campaign

During the Presidential election campaign then in progress, President Johnson stressed his combination of firmness and restraint in dealing with matters of war and peace, as exemplified by his response to the Gulf of Tonkin attacks. This is one reporter's description of the way in which Johnson used the peace-war issue:[32]

> . . . having shown his strength, [Gulf of Tonkin] having diminished Goldwater's ability to charge him with a "no-win" policy and with soft-headedness toward Communism, having established his own "restraint," Johnson seemed free to do what came so naturally to so political a creature. With every rattle of the Goldwater sword, every reference to the use of nuclear weapons by the Air Force general [Goldwater, who was a general in the Air Force Reserve] on the Republican ticket, every provocative remark about bombing the North from the avid jet pilot [Goldwater] who was his opponent, Johnson was lured by politics into the profitably contrasting position of deploring—even forbidding—war, escalation, and nuclear brinkmanship.

As one part of his strategy of contrasting his restraint with the alleged lack of restraint of his opponent, Johnson made a very pointed issue of his policy toward Vietnam, especially with respect to the possible use of U.S. combat forces. The most frequently quoted of his statements was the one in Akron, Ohio, on October 21, 1964, where he said, "Sometimes our folks get a little impatient. Sometimes they rattle their rockets some, and they bluff about their bombs. But we are not about to send American boys 9 or 10,000 miles away from home to do what Asian boys ought to be doing for themselves."[33] This theme was repeated in many other speeches given by Johnson during the campaign.

Johnson said in his memoirs[34] that those who decided that he was the "'peace candidate' . . . were not willing to hear anything they did not want to hear." He said he wanted peace, but not at "any price." "They knew Lyndon Johnson was not going to pull up stakes and run. . . . They know too that I was not going to wipe out Hanoi or use atom bombs to defoliate the Vietnamese jungles." A review of the themes of his campaign speeches in the *Public Papers of the Presidents* confirms that he made the keeping of peace the central issue in the campaign. In a speech in Atlanta, Georgia, on October 26, 1964, he said as much: "There is only one real issue in this campaign, and it is a very important issue, and it is probably the most important issue that you will ever decide in your lifetime. That issue is peace or war." He went on to contrast

---

[32]Tom Wicker, "The Wrong Rubicon," *Atlantic Monthly* (May 1968), p. 75. See also Kearns, *Lyndon Johnson and the American Dream*, pp. 198-199.
[33]*Public Papers of the Presidents*, Lyndon B. Johnson, 1963-1964, pp. 1390-1391.
[34]*The Vantage Point*, p. 68.

his qualifications for keeping the peace with those of Goldwater, without mentioning names, and added, "There are parents in this crowd that took their son down to the depot to say goodby to him in World War I and World War II, and I pray they will never have to do that again."[35]

One of Johnson's strongest supporters during the 1964 campaign was Senator Fulbright. He was convinced that Goldwater was dangerous, and that Johnson, as Fulbright said of him in a seconding speech at the Democratic National Convention, was "a man of understanding with the wisdom to use the great power of our nation in the cause of peace."[36] In another speech Fulbright said:[37]

> The foreign policy issue in this campaign is as profound as any that has ever arisen between the two great American political parties. The Goldwater Republicans propose a radical new policy of relentless ideological conflict aimed at the elimination of Communism and the imposition of American concepts of freedom on the entire world. The Democrats under President Johnson propose a conservative policy of opposing and preventing Communist expansion while working for limited agreements that will reduce the danger of nuclear war.

Fulbright's fear of Goldwater and his confidence in Johnson were also, as was indicated earlier, a key factor in his strong support of the Gulf of Tonkin Resolution. As he said later:[38] "I did so because I was confident that President Johnson would use our endorsement with wisdom and restraint. I was also influenced by partisanship: an election campaign was in progress and I had no wish to make any difficulties for the President in his race against a Republican candidate whose election I thought would be a disaster for the country."

"A part of Fulbright's future anguish over his role in the resolution," according to two of his biographers,[39] "concerned what he felt was his own blindness at the time. Fulbright was so deeply involved in the Goldwater-Johnson campaign that he lost his critical detachment. He was so opposed to Goldwater, so certain Goldwater was rash and improvident, that he could not believe Johnson capable of aggressive military actions. As he would say in private later, . . . 'It just seemed sort of really treasonable to question that damn Tonkin Gulf resolution at that time. But looking back on it now, there's just no excuse for it. I mean, in the first place, it's obviously questionable on its face as to whether it was provoked or not. I mean, from what I know now and what I knew then—it would look to me that the whole damn thing was provoked, that it was planned that way.' He would add: 'This sort of leaves you very, very doubtful.'"

Many other prominent Americans appear to have been persuaded to support Johnson, in part, at least, because of the restraint he seemed to be demonstrating in Vietnam, as well as in the use of force as an instrument of national policy. This seems to have been

---

[35]*Public Papers of the Presidents,* Lyndon B. Johnson, 1963-1964, pp. 1452-1453.
[36]From the text of the speech, University of Arkansas Library, Fulbright Papers, series 72, box 24.
[37]*CR,* vol. 110, p. 21677.
[38]J. William Fulbright, *The Arrogance of Power* (New York: Random House, 1966), pp. 51-52.
[39]Johnson and Gwertzman, *Fulbright the Dissenter,* p. 198.

an important factor, for example, in the decision of some leading businessmen, primarily Republicans, to endorse and work for Johnson through an "independent" committee set up in late August 1964 by Henry H. Fowler, then Deputy Secretary of the Treasury, and chaired by John T. Connor, a Democrat and President of Merck & Company, and John I. Loeb, a registered Republican and senior partner in a Wall Street brokerage firm. One member of this group was Marriner Eccles, a financier and former chairman of the Federal Reserve System, who had strong connections with Democratic politicans. Eccles said that Johnson's announced opposition to sending American boys to fight in Asia was the principal reason for his decision to join the group.

Sixteen other prominent figures became members of a bipartisan group which became known as the "Wise Men," officially called the Advisory Panel on Foreign Affairs. It was announced on September 9, 1984 in connection with the Presidential campaign, and an internal White House memorandum on September 17, reporting on the assistance being given by the NSC staff to the campaign, stated: "We have had our little triumphs. The timely announcement of the Presidential Peace Consultants was one." On September 22, McGeorge Bundy recommended to the President that he meet with the group and release the text of his statement to them. "The object would be to get a headline on Johnson, bipartisanship, and peace, together with a picture of you meeting with these men. It is not a big story, but it is a good one."[40] It should be noted, however, that although the group was organized in connection with the campaign, it subsequently played a role of some importance in supporting Johnson's decision to go to war in July 1965, and in persuading him in March 1968 that the U.S. should seek a negotiated settlement.

Ball's Dissent

While Lyndon Johnson was campaigning on keeping American boys out of Vietnam, his advisers were worrying about what they considered to be the increasing fragility of South Vietnam. A special intelligence estimate on October 1, 1964 concluded that the political situation was continuing to deteriorate, and that there were no prospects that the Khanh government would be able to reverse the trend.[41]

In a memorandum to Johnson on October 1, giving him some pointers for a press interview, McGeorge Bundy suggested he "give a hint of firmness." Bundy added:[42]

It is a better than even chance that we will be undertaking some air and land action in the Laotian corridor and even in

---

[40]For the announcement of the group, see the *New York Times*, Sept. 10, 1964. The memo of Sept. 17, from Chester Cooper to McGeorge Bundy, is in the Johnson Library, NSF Name File, Cooper Memos, and the Sept. 22 Bundy memo is in NSF Aides File, McGeorge Bundy Memos to the President, where there is additional material in a folder labelled "President's Consultants on Foreign Affairs (Peace Plan)." Members of the group were: Dean Acheson, Eugene R. Black, Gen. Omar N. Bradley, John Cowles, Arthur H. Dean, Allen W. Dulles, Roswell L. Gilpatric, Paul G. Hoffman, George B. Kistiakowsky, Arthur Larson, Morris I. Liebman, Robert A. Lovett, John J. McCloy, Teodoro Moscoso, James Perkins, and James J. Wadsworth.

[41]SNIE 53-2-64, summarized in *PP*, Gravel ed., vol. III, p. 133. For the South Vietnamese political situation see Shaplen, *The Lost Revolution*.

[42]NSF Aides Files, McGeorge Bundy Memos to the President.

North Vietnam within the next two months, and we do not want the record to suggest even remotely that we campaigned on peace in order to start a war in November. The middle course we are on could well require pressure against those who are making war against South Vietnam, but the timing and techniques of such pressure are a very delicate business, as you have said several times before.

On October 2, James Reston of the *New York Times* reported that some of Johnson's advisers were talking openly about expanding the war, ". . . and not only advocating but almost lobbying for such a course of action. It is even possible now to hear officials of this Government talking casually about how easy it would be to 'provoke an incident' in the Gulf of Tonkin that would justify an attack on North Vietnam. . . ."[43]

On October 3, the President returned to Washington for a meeting with his advisers. They discussed the situation and U.S. options, especially the systematic bombing of North Vietnam, which McNamara said was the only alternative being considered by those making contingency plans. Under Secretary of State George Ball attended the meeting, and expressed his opposition to increased U.S. military involvement, and to the bombing of North Vietnam.

On October 5, Ball completed a long (67 pages, single-spaced) memorandum for Rusk, McNamara and McGeorge Bundy in which he articulated these views.[44] Because of the deteriorating political situation in South Vietnam, Ball said, the U.S. faced a "major decision of national policy." There were four options:[45]

(1) We could continue along current lines, recognizing that at some point we should either be thrown out by a neutralist coup in Saigon or be forced to a deeper involvement "by the manifest hopelessness of the present course of action."

(2) We could take over the war by injecting substantial United States ground forces, but in that event "our situation would, in the world's eyes, approach that of France in the 1950s."

(3) We could mount an offensive against the North to improve our bargaining position for negotiation. But though preferable to a ground force commitment, that would lead to the same result by provoking the North Vietnamese to send ground forces to the South that could be effectively countered only by United States ground forces.

(4) Finally, we might try to bring back a political settlement without direct US military involvement that would check, or at least delay, the extension of Communist power into South Vietnam.

In his discussion of these options Ball said, "The maintenance of a non-Communist South Vietnam is of considerable strategic value to the United States . . . [but] our primary motive . . . is unquestionably political. It is to make clear to the whole Free World that we will assist any nation that asks for our help in defending itself

---

[43]*New York Times,* Oct. 2, 1964.
[44]For the text see the *Atlantic* (July 1972), cited above. See also Ball's, *The Past Has Another Pattern,* and Halberstam, *The Best and the Brightest,* pp. 491-499.
[45]The summary of these options is from Ball, *The Past Has Another Pattern,* pp. 380-381.

against Communist aggression." U.S. policy, he said, was "defended on the proposition that America cannot afford to promote a settlement in South Viet-Nam without first demonstrating the superiority of its own military power—or, in other words, giving the North Vietnamese a bloody nose. To do otherwise would enormously diminish American prestige around the world and cause others to lose faith in the tenacity of our purpose and the integrity of our promises." This policy, he said, needed to be reexamined "before we commit military forces to a line of action that could put events in the saddle and destroy our freedom to choose the policies that are at once the most effective and the most prudent."

Ball questioned the efficacy of military action against North Vietnam, particularly in view of the instability of the Government of South Vietnam. "If the political situation in Saigon should continue to crumble," he said, "air action against North Viet-Nam could at best bring a Pyrrhic victory. Even with diminished North Vietnamese support for the Viet Cong, a disorganized South Vietnamese Government would be unable to eliminate the insurgency." Moreover, North Vietnam believed victory was near, and as long as it did it would "probably be willing to accept very substantial costs from United States air action."

If there were a large increase in infiltration from the north, or the direct use of North Vietnamese forces, U.S. ground troops would be required, Ball said, and this would have a number of adverse consequences. The U.S. would have to take charge of the war, and thus would tend to be put in the earlier position of the French. It would also create problems at home, and "The frustrations and anxieties that marked the latter phases of the Korean struggle would be recalled and revived—and multiplied in intensity."

Once military action was undertaken against the north, it would be difficult to prevent or control escalation: "Once on the tiger's back we cannot be sure of picking the place to dismount." If ground fighting were prolonged, and especially if the Chinese entered the war, there would be pressure to use nuclear weapons. This, in turn, could affect the "fragile balance of terror on which much of the world has come to depend for the maintenance of peace," as well as creating "discouragement and a profound sense of disquiet" in the U.S.

Ball summed up his analysis as follows:

1. Unless the political base in Saigon can be made secure, the mounting of military pressure against the North would involve unacceptable risks.

2. To persuade the North Vietnamese Government to leave South Viet-Nam alone, military pressure against Hanoi would have to be substantial and sustained.

3. Even with substantial and sustained military pressure it is improbable that Hanoi would permanently abandon its aggressive tendencies against South Viet-Nam so long as the governmental structure in South Viet-Nam remained weak and incapable of rallying the full support of the South Vietnamese people.

4. The United States cannot substitute its own presence for an effective South Vietnamese Government and maintain a free South Viet-Nam over a sustained period of time.

5. We must be clear as to the profound consequences of a United States move to apply sustained and substantial military pressure against North Viet-Nam. The response to that move—or even the deployments required by prudence in anticipation of a response—would radically change the character of the war and the United States's relation to the war. The war would become a direct conflict between the United States and the Asian Communists (North Viet-Nam cum Red China).

6. Once the United States had actively committed itself to direct conflict with the North Vietnamese and Hanoi had responded, we could not be certain of controlling the scope and extent of escalation. We cannot ignore the danger—slight though some believe it to be—that we might set in train a series of events leading, at the end of the road, to the direct intervention of China and nuclear war.

7. Finally, it remains to be proved that in terms of U.S. prestige and our world position, we would risk less or gain more through enlarging the war than through searching for an immediate political solution that would avoid deeper U.S. involvement.

With respect to a political settlement, Ball concluded that better results could be obtained if negotiations were conducted before rather than after an air offensive. After weighing the various factors and alternatives he said he thought a large-scale conference along the lines of the 1962 Conference on Laos would be the most propitious, but he also saw some hope in working through the U.N.

This is Ball's description of the response to his memorandum:[46]

When I completed the memorandum, I sent it to Secretary McNamara, Mac Bundy, and Secretary Rusk. Bob McNamara in particular seemed shocked that anyone would challenge the verities in such an abrupt and unvarnished manner and implied that I had been imprudent in putting such doubts on paper. My colleagues seemed somewhat more concerned with a possible leak than with the cogency of what I had written. We agreed, however, to meet and discuss the specific points in the memorandum, reserving two Saturdays for that purpose. But it required only one meeting, which took place on Saturday, November 7, 1964, to convince me that there was no point in carrying the argument further. My colleagues were dead set against the views I presented and uninterested in the point-by-point discussion I had hoped to provoke. They regarded me with benign tolerance; to them, my memorandum seemed merely an idiosyncratic diversion from the only relevant problem: how to win the war.

For his part, McGeorge Bundy said, "My principal difficulty with George's arguments through that winter and the spring of '65 was not with his worries that things might not work, because it was perfectly clear that they might not work. . . . I never found his picture of the alternative very persuasive, or, indeed, persuasive at all."[47]

[46] *Ibid.*, pp. 383-384.
[47] CRS Interview, McGeorge Bundy, Jan. 8, 1979.

In mid-October 1964, Ambassador Taylor stepped up his campaign for stronger U.S. military action, warning that the political situation in South Vietnam was becoming more serious, and that with higher infiltration from the north and the end of the rainy season the Communists were more of a threat than ever. "I feel sure," he cabled Washington on October 14, "that we must soon adopt new and drastic methods to reduce and eventually end such infiltration if we are ever to succeed in South Vietnam."[48]

The JCS agreed. To defeat the guerrillas in South Vietnam, they said on October 21, the U.S. should attack the problem at its source—North Vietnam—by "control of the boundaries or by eliminating or cutting off the source of supply and direction."[49]

On October 27, the Chiefs again proposed a major military program for "applying military pressures on the . . . DRV to the extent necessary to cause the DRV to cease support and direction of the insurgency," and for accelerating the counterinsurgency program in South Vietnam. Among the actions recommended were a resumption of the DE SOTO patrols and airstrikes by Vietnamese and unidentified U.S. planes (with U.S. pilots) against targets in Laos and North Vietnam.[50]

Agreement on a General Plan of Action

While the JCS proposal of October 29 was being considered, the Communists staged a raid on the air base at Bien Hoa on November 1, killing five Americans, wounding 76, and destroying or damaging 27 of the 30 B-57s that, according to the *Pentagon Papers* ". . . had been deployed to South Vietnam to serve notice upon Hanoi that the United States had readily at hand the capacity to deliver a crushing air attack on the North."[51] Townsend Hoopes gave this description of how the decision was made to move the planes to Bien Hoa:[52]

> Shortly after the Tonkin episode, there occurred another of those consequential inadvertencies that seem an unavoidable element of the U.S. governmental process—in which so much is asked of a few overworked men. It came to the attention of the White House staff that the Air Force was planning, within a few days, to move a squadron of B-57 bombers from the Philippines to Bien Hoa in South Vietnam. These were obsolescent aircraft being used to provide jet training for the South Vietnamese. The training was being conducted at Clark Field in the Philippines, but no decision had been taken to turn the aircraft over to South Vietnam (among other difficulties, the introduction of jet equipment would involve a violation of the 1954 Geneva Accords). The Air Force now wished however to shift the training to Vietnam.
>
> Both Michael Forrestal . . . and William Bundy . . . thought the proposed move was a bad idea, for they feared that U.S. aircraft sitting in Vietnam would become an irresistible target for Viet Cong attack. Hastily they took the issue to Rusk in an

[48]*PP,* Gravel ed., vol. III, p. 207.
[49]*Ibid.,* p. 208.
[50]*Ibid.*
[51]*Ibid.,* p. 288.
[52]Townsend Hoopes, *The Limits of Intervention* (New York: David McKay, 1970), p. 27.

effort to head off the move, getting an appointment with him late on a September afternoon. Rusk was not particularly impressed by their argument, but agreed to pick up the phone and call McNamara. While Forrestal and Bundy stood by the edge of his desk, he talked to McNamara for perhaps five minutes. Then, putting down the phone, he said "Bob has so many issues with the JCS that he would rather finesse this one unless we are prepared to take a very strong position. I don't think we are. It seems to me a rather small matter."

The B-57s were duly moved to Bien Hoa. After sitting on that air base for about two months, six of the aircraft were demolished by Viet Cong mortars on November 1, just two days before the U.S. election; five Americans were killed and seventy-six wounded.

Taylor and the Joint Chiefs urged the President to retaliate for Bien Hoa by airstrikes on the north.[53] The Joint Chiefs argued that failure to retaliate would encourage the Communists to undertake additional attacks. Taylor said that if airstrikes were rejected there should be increased pressure through selective bombing and 34-A operations. The President, supported by Rusk and McNamara, decided against such a move. In his memoirs Johnson said: "Most of us were very much aware of the continuing unsteadiness of the South Vietnamese government and its military weakness. We judged the concerns of September still valid. I was worried too about possible Viet Cong retaliation against U.S. dependents in Saigon. With all of these considerations in mind, I decided against a retaliatory strike."[54]

The possible adverse effects on the Presidential election, then only two days away, was another unspoken reason for the decision not to retaliate at that point. Louis Harris of the Harris Poll reported receiving a telephone call on November 1 from Bill Moyers, one of Johnson's top assistants, who said that the President, Rusk and McNamara were meeting at the White House to discuss the U.S. response to the Bien Hoa raid, and that "The president would like to know if a failure to respond to this attack immediately will be taken by the voters as a sign of weakness by the Administration." Harris' advice to the President via Moyers was, "That is the sort of thing people would expect from Barry Goldwater and probably the main reason they are voting for him."[55]

Although he did not agree to immediate airstrikes, the President, after meeting with his advisers on November 1, asked Taylor for his opinion on moving U.S. air and ground units into Vietnam to protect U.S. dependents and military units and bases against attack, as well as the possible withdrawal of U.S. dependents from Vietnam before beginning airstrikes. Taylor "replied quickly that, at least for the time being, we did not want U.S. ground forces for the close defense of bases unless needed as an accompaniment of a

---

[53] *PP,* Gravel ed., vol. III, pp. 209-210. According to Halberstam (*The Best and the Brightest,* p. 485), the attack "infuriated" Taylor, and was a decisive factor in his becoming more of an advocate of bombing the North. By contrast, Halberstam says, the CIA station chief in Saigon at the time, Peer de Silva, thought bombing would not work, and would result in increased North Vietnamese infiltration of the South.

[54] *The Vantage Point,* p. 121. See also *PP,* Gravel ed., vol. III, p. 209.

[55] Louis Harris, *The Anguish of Change* (New York: W. W. Norton, 1973), p. 23.

program of air pressure against North Vietnam." Taylor said later, "I was greatly surprised that the offer of ground troops was made so casually, as it seemed to me a much more difficult decision than the use of our air forces against military targets north of the seventeenth parallel."[56] He also noted that when Vietnam was hit by a major flood a short time later, Washington ". . . inquired if we needed American logistical troops to help in flood relief, supported by U.S. combat troops to give them local protection. This was essentially the proposal which I had made to President Kennedy in the wake of the Mekong Delta flood in 1961, and which he had not approved. This time I declined the proposal on about the same grounds as Kennedy had—the lack of clear need justifying a course of action difficult to control or to reverse."[57]

Another important factor in the decision not to retaliate for the Bien Hoa attack was the effect on North Vietnam. "'The other side would not have believed in any response we made during the election campaign,' said one man in close touch with the President's thinking at the time. 'He felt he had to get Goldwaterism defeated soundly in order to make it an American response, instead of a political response.'"[58]

On November 3, 1964, the day he was elected President by an overwhelming vote, Johnson began immediately to lay plans for a broader plan of retaliation through the establishment of the so-called "NSC Working Group on SVN/SEA," an interagency group chaired by William Bundy. Other members included Marshall Green, Michael Forrestal, and Robert Johnson from the State Department; John McNaughton and Vice Adm. Lloyd Mustin from Defense; Harold Ford and George Carver from the CIA. The group was directed to study "immediately and intensively" alternative courses of action in Southeast Asia, and to report to the NSC principals group, (Rusk, McNamara, McCone, General Wheeler, Ball, McGeorge Bundy), which would then make recommendations to the President.[59]

According to a memorandum by Chairman William Bundy on November 5, the President was ". . . clearly thinking in terms of maximum use of a Gulf of Tonkin rationale, either for an action that would show toughness and hold the line till we can decide the big issue, or as a basis for starting a clear course of action under the broad options."[60] Bundy went on to suggest how relations with Congress should be handled in conjunction with such moves:

> Congress must be consulted before any major action, perhaps only by notification if we do a reprisal against another Bien Hoa, but preferably by careful talks with such key leaders as Mansfield, Dirksen, the Speaker, Albert, Halleck, Fulbright, Hickenlooper, Morgan, Mrs. [Frances P.] Bolton [R/Ohio], Rus-

---

[56] *Swords and Plowshares,* pp. 324-325.
[57] *Ibid.*
[58] Philip Geyelin, *Lyndon B. Johnson and the World* (New York: Praeger, 1966), p. 200. Geyelin asserts, however, (p. 202), ". . . a strong case can be made, retrospectively, that American inaction at Bien Hoa encouraged Communist miscalculation of U.S. interests, and indeed, convinced the Communists that they could step up infiltration and engage in acts of terrorism aimed deliberately at Americans in South Vietnam with impunity."
[59] *PP,* Gravel ed., vol. III, p. 210.
[60] "Conditions for Action and Key Actions Surrounding Any Decision," Nov. 5, 1964, *ibid.,* pp. 593-594.

sell, Saltonstall, [L. Mendel] Rivers [D/S.C.], (Vinson?) [*sic*], [Leslie C.] Arends [R/Ill.], Ford, etc. He probably should wait till his mind is moving clearly in one direction before such a consultation, which would point to some time next week. Query if it should be combined with other topics (budget?) [*sic*] to lessen the heat.

Bundy added:

We probably do not need additional Congressional authority, even if we decide on very strong action. A session of this rump Congress might well be the scene of a messy Republican effort.

During the remainder of November there occurred one of the most intensive and important periods of planning of the entire Vietnam war. In a very real sense it was the month that the United States Government made final plans to enter the war. Although the order to begin executing the decisive second phase of these plans was not issued until February 1965, agreement was reached in November 1964 on the course of action that should be taken, and the first phase of that plan was authorized to begin. Phase two of the plan was then put into effect when the President finally decided that he had no better alternative, and thus no choice.

This is the matter-of-fact description in the *Pentagon Papers*:[61]

In their Southeast Asia policy discussions of August-October 1964, Administration officials had accepted the view that overt military pressures against North Vietnam probably would be required. Barring some critical developments, however, it was generally conceded that these should not begin until after the new year. Preparations for applying such pressures were made in earnest during November.

The planning process in November was action-oriented—not whether to act, but what to do. There was almost no debate over U.S. diplomatic or strategic interests in Vietnam, or whether the U.S. could succeed where the French had failed. It was generally assumed that the U.S. was already committed to stopping the Communists, and that this required the use of U.S. forces. It was also agreed that to win in the south, it would be necessary to take the war to the north.

Two points are especially worth noting. First, it was generally agreed that U.S. objectives should be limited, and that force should be used as a political/diplomatic instrument, with a negotiated settlement rather than military "victory" as the goal. Second, it was generally thought that force would prevail, and that at some point the North Vietnamese would respond affirmatively to graduated pressure from the United States—the so-called "breaking point."[62]

There was also a shift of emphasis on the one "essential condition" policymakers previously had said was necessary for "winning" in Vietnam, namely, a viable government in South Vietnam. During the November debate the consensus was that the Government of South Vietnam was critically weak, and that if it "collapsed" the United States would have to withdraw or fight the war

---

[61]*Ibid.*, pp. 206-207.
[62]See the seminal analysis by John E. Mueller, "The Search for the 'Breaking Point' in Vietnam," *International Studies Quarterly* 24 (December 1980), pp. 497-518.

unilaterally. To forestall that eventuality, it was agreed that the U.S. should, in effect, assume primary responsibility for both the pacification program in the south and the war against the north. One result of this was the virtually complete assumption by the U.S. of direct responsibility for the new pacification program in seven provinces around Saigon (the Hop Tac program) that had been proposed by Lodge, approved at the Honolulu meeting in July, and implemented by Taylor and Westmoreland. As the *Pentagon Papers* notes:[63] "Ironically, Hop Tac is the Vietnamese word for 'cooperation,' which turned out to be just what Hop Tac lacked."

There were some uncertainties and differences of opinion among policymakers, as William Bundy has explained:[64]

> In case of failure in Vietnam would the US appear as a more reliable guarantor elsewhere for having tried? McNamara, McNaughton and I thought so, at least to the point where the effort in Vietnam appeared plainly hopeless. Rusk and Ball thought that if we failed, we would be worse off for having tried—and in the end drew diametrically opposite conclusions. Rusk came to be convinced that if we did do more, we simply could not afford to fail; Ball never wavered that we should not try to do more, beyond the most temporary effort to get a balance.

The central point of debate was how fast and how far to use force, and in keeping with good bureaucratic procedure this was reduced to a choice among three "Broad Options." This, says George Ball, ". . . was what we referred to as 'the Goldilocks principle.'" "Working groups of seasoned bureaucrats deliberately control the outcome of a study assignment by recommending three choices. . . . By including with their favored choice one 'too soft' and one 'too hard,' they assure that the powers deciding the issue will almost invariably opt for the one 'just right.'"[65]

These options were framed initially by Bundy in an outline for the Working Group issued on November 3,[66] and after lengthy debate but few basic changes they were presented to the principals.[67] The first option, Option A, was to be a continuation of programs and policies then in effect. Option B would be fast, heavy military pressure against the North, called "fast/full Squeeze" by McNaughton. Option C would be a continuation of existing policies but with additional military pressure, called "Progressive squeeze-and-talk" by McNaughton.[68] Option B was also referred to as "in cold blood," and Option C as "hot blood."

In their final or nearly final form the options were stated by Bundy and McNaughton as follows:[69]

> A. Option A would be to continue present policies indefinitely: Maximum assistance within South Vietnam, limited external actions in Laos and by the GVN covertly against North

[63]*PP,* Gravel ed, vol. II, p. 521.
[64]Bundy MS., ch. 18, p. 13.
[65]*The Past Has Another Pattern,* p. 388.
[66]*PP,* Gravel ed., vol. III, pp. 588-590.
[67]For a good analysis of the changes that were made, and the arguments pro and con, see *ibid.,* pp. 220-222.
[68]For McNaughton's phraseology, see his memo of Nov. 6, *ibid.,* p. 598-601.
[69]"Summary—Courses of Action in Southeast Asia," as revised on Nov. 21 and 26, 1964, *ibid.,* pp. 659-660.

Vietnam, specific individual reprisal actions not only against such incidents as the Gulf of Tonkin attack but also against any recurrence of VC "spectaculars" such as Bien Hoa. Basic to this option is the continued rejection of negotiations.

B. Option B would add to present actions a systematic program of military pressures against the north, with increasing pressure actions to be continued at a fairly rapid pace and without interruption until we achieve our present stated objectives. The actions would mesh at some point with negotiation, but we would approach any discussions or negotiations with absolutely inflexible insistence on our present objectives.

C. Option C would add to present actions an orchestration of (1) communications with Hanoi and/or Peiping, and (2) additional graduated military moves against infiltration targets, first in Laos and then in the DRV, and then against other targets in North Vietnam. The military scenario should give the impression of a steady deliberate approach, and should be designed to give the US the option at any time to proceed or not, to escalate or not, and to quicken the pace or not. These decisions would be made from time to time in view of all relevant factors. The negotiating part of this course of action would have to be played largely by ear, but in essence we would be indicating from the outset a willingness to negotiate in an affirmative sense, accepting the possibility that we might not achieve our full objective.

Among those involved in the policy debate there was no apparent support for Option A alone. A combination of Option B and C was strongly supported by most of the military. A combination of Option A and C was favored by most civilian policymakers. The final consensus of both the Working Group and the principals, however, was for a combination of Option A and C, with agreement also that certain actions should be taken immediately prior to deciding the future course of action.

There were some significant differences in the positions taken by participants in the planning process. The intelligence panel of the Working Group, with some dissent from the Defense Intelligence Agency (DIA), took the position that "The basic elements of Communist strength in South Vietnam remain indigenous," but because the "VC insurrection" was managed from the north, the Communists in the south could be controlled by the North Vietnamese if the latter were to be so persuaded. In the opinion of the panel, "US ability to compel the DRV to end or reduce the VC insurrection rests essentially upon the effect of US sanctions on the will of the DRV leadership, and to a lesser extent upon the effect of sanctions on DRV capabilities." But the intelligence assessment report added that even though U.S. military actions against North Vietnam and Laos might buy time for strengthening South Vietnam, ". . . it would almost certainly not destroy DRV capabilities to continue, although at a lessened level."[70]

---

[70]These quotes are from the Bundy-McNaughton "Summary" memo, *ibid* pp. 656-657, based on a paper prepared by the intelligence panel, Nov. 24, 1964, "Section 1: Intelligence Assessment: The Situation in Vietnam," which is contained in *ibid.*, pp. 651-66.

The intelligence panel of the Working Group also pointed out that one of the basic problems confronting the U.S. was the assumption of the Communists that "the difficulties facing the US are so great that US will and ability to maintain resistance in that area [South Vietnam] can be gradually eroded—without running high risks that the US would wreak heavy destruction on the DRV or Communist China." Although the North Vietnamese were concerned about possible destruction, "they would probably be willing to suffer some damage in the country in the course of a test of wills with the US over the course of events in South Vietnam."[71]

Vice Adm. Lloyd Mustin, the JCS representative on the Working Group, thought that the intelligence assessment was too negative, although he admitted that it was difficult to estimate the level of force that might be required to persuade the North to cease and desist. "This is the reason," he said, "for designing a program of progressively increasing squeeze," but he added that "obviously that program may have to continue through substantial levels of military, industrial, and governmental destruction in the DRV."[72]

Mustin also disagreed strongly with an early State Department draft of the section of the report dealing with U.S. objectives. He said that the risks of war with China were overstated, as were the difficulties of prevailing over the North Vietnamese. There was no alternative, he said, to "our holding South Vietnam," and "a resolute course of action in lieu of half measures, resolutely carried out instead of dallying and delaying, offers the best hope of minimizing *risks, costs,* and *losses* in achieving our objectives." (emphasis in original) With respect to the effect of the "loss of South Vietnam" on other countries that look to the U.S. for help, he said:[73] "In JCS view, near-disastrously, or worse."

In general, the Joint Chiefs of Staff took the position that force had to be used, and used decisively, against North Vietnam and in Laos. They were leery of a land war, however, and advocated primary use of the Air Force and the Navy.[74]

Ambassador Taylor's own view was that "'too much' in this matter of coercing Hanoi may be as bad as 'too little.' At some point, we will need a relatively cooperative leadership in Hanoi willing to wind up the VC insurgency on terms satisfactory to us and our SVN allies. What we don't want is an expanded war in SEA and an unresolved guerrilla problem in SVN."[75]

At the meeting of the principals on November 27, Taylor, who had come to Washington to participate in the discussions of U.S. policy, gave an extensive report on the current situation in Viet-

---

[71] *Ibid.,* pp. 654-655.

[72] "Comments on CIA-DIA-INR Panel Draft Section I—The Situation," Enclosure to Joint Staff Memo, Nov. 10, 1964, from the text in *ibid.,* pp. 619-621.

[73] "Comments on Draft Section II—US Objectives and Stakes in South Vietnam and Southeast Asia," no date, the text of which is in *ibid.,* pp. 622-628.

[74] For an analysis of the JCS position see *ibid.,* pp. 231-234. On Nov. 14 the JCS again recommended additional covert activities by the South Vietnamese (CJCS Memorandum to McNamara, "Operation Plan 34A—Additional Actions," CM 258-64, Nov. 14, 1964), as well as airstrikes against North Vietnam and Laos in retaliation for Bien Hoa and to divert the Communists from U.S. preparations for widening the war. CJCS Memorandum to McNamara, "Courses of Action in Southeast Asia," Nov. 14, 1964, JCSM 955-64, the partial text of which is in *ibid.,* pp. 628-630. See also the CJCS memo to McNamara on Nov. 18, JCSM 267-64, with the same title as JCSM 955-64, which is in *ibid.,* pp. 639-640.

[75] Cable, Nov. 3, 1964, the text of which is in *ibid.,* pp. 590-591.

nam.[76] He said that it was ". . . impossible to foresee a stable and effective government under any name in anything like the near future," and that "Without an effective central government with which to mesh the US effort, the latter is a spinning wheel unable to transmit impulsion to the machinery of the GVN."[77] The U.S., he said, needed to "establish an adequate government" in South Vietnam, adding:

> . . . it is hard to visualize our being willing to make added outlays of resources and to run increasing political risks without an allied government which, at least, can speak for and to its people, can maintain law and order in the principal cities, can provide local protection for the vital military bases and installation, can raise and support Armed Forces, and can gear its efforts to those of the United States. Anything less than this would hardly be a government at all, and under such circumstances, the United States Government might do better to carry forward the war on a purely unilateral basis.

Taylor favored immediate action to increase covert operations against North Vietnam, as well as counterinfiltration attacks in Laos and reprisal bombing for incidents such as Bien Hoa, all of which he said would improve morale in South Vietnam. He also favored the Working Group's proposed plan of graduated pressure on the north. He said that before making any final decisions on expanding the war, however, the U.S. would need to have a "heart-to-heart talk" with Vietnamese leaders. "We should make every effort to get them to ask our help in expanding the war. If they decline, we shall have to rethink the whole situation. If, as is likely, they urge us with enthusiasm, we should take advantage of the opportunity to nail down certain important points such as:[78]

> a. The GVN undertakes (1) to maintain the strength of its military and police forces; (2) to replace imcompetent military commanders and province chiefs and to leave the competent ones in place for an indefinite period; (3) to suppress disorders and demonstrations; (4) to establish effective resources control; and (5) to obtain US concurrence for all military operations outside of South Vietnam.

> b. The US undertakes responsibility for the air and maritime defense of South Vietnam.

> c. The GVN takes responsibility for the land defense of South Vietnam to include the protection of all US nationals and installations.

> d. The GVN accepts the US statement (to be prepared) of war aims and circumstances for negotiations.

In conclusion, Taylor stated, the U.S. should adhere to three principles:[79]

> a. Do not enter into negotiations until the DRV is hurting.

> b. Never let the DRV gain a victory in South Vietnam without having paid a disproportionate price.

---

[76]See the text in *ibid.*, pp. 666-673.
[77]Note Taylor's assumption that the "impulsion" of the Vietnamese depended upon the U.S.
[78]*Ibid.*, p. 670.
[79]*Ibid.*, p. 672.

c. Keep the GVN in the forefront of the combat and the negotiations.

Taylor's preference for air power and his desire to avoid having the U.S. in the forefront of the combat were not shared by W. W. Rostow, who took the position that the U.S. needed to deploy ground forces to Vietnam, and possibly to Laos, in order to send the North Vietnamese a sufficiently strong "signal" of U.S. intentions, as well as to have ground forces in position to strengthen the American hand in any diplomatic negotiations that might subsequently occur. He also called for the "introduction into the Pacific Theater of massive forces to deal with any escalatory response, including forces evidently aimed at China as well as North Viet Nam, should the Chinese Communists enter the game." Rather than using as a basis for reprisal the narrow concept of attacks on U.S. units or bases or single incidents in South Vietnam, he also urged that North Vietnam be told that it would be "vulnerable to retaliatory attack for continued violation of the 1952-1962 Accords." The U.S., Rostow said, would have to demonstrate that it was committed to restoring those accords. Otherwise the Communists would not be convinced, and would not back down.[80]

As November drew to a close, William Bundy sent the principals a memorandum on "Issues Raised by Papers on Southeast Asia" in which he listed a number of points that they might want to discuss.[81] With respect to immediate courses of action, he raised a question about the existing CINCPAC order for reprisal bombing. None of the options provided by the order called for less than 175 airstrikes, he pointed out, and questioned whether this large scale of operations "could throw off all calculations based on the theory of 'squeeze' under Option C and even under Option B."

In choosing among the options, Bundy said, "All concede there is *some* chance that the GVN would come apart under any Option." With respect to Option A, he asked whether ground forces could or should be deployed to Vietnam (all three options provided for U.S. ground forces), a move that he said the advocates of A had recommended as a "bargaining counter."[82] His comment was that "most of us think that, apart from lacking any military necessity in the absence of attacks on the DRV, it would appear as a bluff and not help any negotiations."

With respect to Option B, Bundy asked whether ground invasion of North Vietnam was a "military necessity or advantage that outweighs the increased risks the Chicoms would then come in force?" (He said the same question applied to Option C.) Also, there was the question with respect to B: "At what stage, if ever, might nuclear weapons be required, and on what scale? What would be the implications of such use?"

With respect to Option C, one very basic question, he said, was whether it could be "carried out in practice under the klieg lights of democracy, in view of its requirement that we maintain a credi-

[80]See *ibid.,* pp. 632-633. and 645-647 for the two Rostow memos, "Military Dispositions and Political Signals," Nov. 16, 1964, to McNamara; and "Some Observations As We Come to the Crunch in Southeast Asia," Nov. 23, 1964, to Rusk. For an analysis of Rostow's position see pp. 234-236.

[81]For the text, see *ibid.,* pp. 648-650; the papers of the Working Group are still classified.

[82]On this point, see *ibid.,* p. 226.

ble threat of major action while at the same time seeking to negotiate, even if quietly?" Bundy's comment was: "The parallel to Korea
in 1951-53 is forbidding. Even advocates of C concede the difficulties."

In his memo Bundy listed "Congressional consultation" among
"active issues applicable to any decision," but he did not elaborate.
In his earlier memo on November 5 he had said that the Executive
probably did not need any additional authority from Congress, even
for "very strong action," and in a memo of November 8 analyzing
Option C he said that "the present Congressional Resolution provides an adequate legal basis for initiating this course of action."[83]
One of the papers prepared by the Working Group[84] had taken the
position, however, that Option B might pose some problems with
respect to Congress. It noted that U.S. military moves against
North Vietnam should be consistent with the provisions of the Gulf
of Tonkin Resolution, and that, in the case of Option B, "Charac-
terizing the use of force in the context of this alternative as a legitimate exercise of the right of individual or collective self-defense
in response to an "armed attack' from the North would be a major
public relations effort." Furthermore, in view of the military measures contemplated under Option B, "the constitutional prerogatives
of the Congress, for example, to declare war [would] become pertinent."[85]

On November 24 the NSC principals met to review the material
from the Working Group and to prepare recommendations for the
President. According to the *Pentagon Papers* it was the consensus
of the group that "South Vietnam could be made secure, provided
the Saigon government could maintain itself." There was also a
"clear consensus" (defined by the *Pentagon Papers* as "no more
than a single dissenting opinion") on the following points:[86]

(2) That the situation in South Vietnam would deteriorate
further under Option A even with reprisals, but that there was
a "significant chance" that the actions proposed under B or C
would result in an improved GVN performance and "make
possible" an improved security situation (George Ball indicated
doubt).

(3) That any negotiating outcome under Option A (with or
without U.S. negotiating participation) probably would be
clearly worse than under Option B or C.

(4) That it was doubtful (contrary to the view expressed in
the Working Group papers) that Option B would have the best
chance of achieving the full U.S. objectives (General Wheeler
expressed agreement with the Working Group statement).

(5) That the requirement of Option C, "that we maintain a
credible threat of major action while at the same time seeking
to negotiate," could be carried out despite acknowledged public
pressures.

[83] *Ibid.*, p. 611.
[84] "Alternate Forms of Negotiation—Alternative B," Nov. 6, 1964.
[85] *Ibid.*, p. 229.
[86] *Ibid.*, p. 237. Item (1) is not in the *Pentagon Papers* text.

(6) That the Administration could safely assume that South Vietnam could "only come apart for morale reasons, and not in a military sense," as a result of intensified VC effort.

(7) That early military actions against North Vietnam under Option C should be determined, but low in scale (General Wheeler disagreed, stating that our losses might be higher in the long run with such an approach).

(8) That the loss of South Vietnam would be more serious than stated in Section II of the Working Group's draft papers and that the Administration's assessment should be revised at least in the direction of the JCS viewpoint (George Ball argued against this judgment).

According to the *Pentagon Papers*,[87] ". . . there was no clear decision as to which option was favored by the principals. It seems likely that A was favored by Ball. Wheeler clearly favored B, and he may have had support from McCone, although this was far from clear . . . it is clear that C was favored by McNamara, McNaughton, Rusk, and the Bundy brothers. However, McGeorge Bundy and McNamara apparently favored a 'firm C,' whereas the other three wanted a more restrained, incremental approach."

Several other important issues were discussed at the November 24 meeting. At the beginning of the meeting, Rusk said that the public might be concerned about making a greater commitment to Vietnam in view of that country's internal instability. The feeling of the group appeared to be that even if the North Vietnamese were to withdraw their support for the Communists fighting in the south, the struggle in the south would be protracted. Ball asked if bombing the North would benefit the south, and McNamara replied that it would not unless it reduced infiltration. McNamara and Wheeler "conceded the propriety of this concern but warned that the situation in the GVN would only get worse if additional steps were not taken to reverse present trends," and McNamara posed a question that, according to the *Pentagon Papers*, "addressed the whole rationale for contemplated U.S. courses of action." He asked whether South Vietnam could be strengthened "in time to save it" if the North Vietnamese continued to provide support.

On the question of deploying U.S. ground forces, McNamara took the position that there was no military requirement for them, and that he would prefer massive use of airpower. McCone suggested that U.S. ground forces could help to stabilize South Vietnam, but McNamara disagreed. Rusk and McGeorge Bundy said such forces might have a useful "preemptive effect" as a signal of our determination. The use of U.S. troops as a "bargaining counter" for negotiations was not discussed, however.[88]

With respect to the possible use of nuclear weapons, McNamara said he could not imagine a case where they would be considered, but McGeorge Bundy said that there might be considerable pressure for their use in certain situations, both from military and political circles.

---

[87] *Ibid.*, p. 239.
[88] This, says the *Pentagon Papers, ibid.*, p. 239, was "one more indication of the Principals' reluctance to deal with the issue of negotiation."

On November 27, the principals met again, and heard the above-mentioned briefing from Taylor on the situation in Vietnam. Taylor offered a "Suggested Scenario for Controlled Escalation," the actions in which, the *Pentagon Papers* states, "were quite similar to an extended Option A or a low-order Option C without declared negotiating willingness."[89] In a discussion of Taylor's report, the question of "neutralism" was raised, and Taylor "noted that 'neutralism' as it existed in Saigon appeared to mean throwing the internal political situation open and thus inviting Communist participation." Ball commented that "neutralism in the sense of withdrawal of external assistance" was not possible until the Communists were defeated and neutralism could be maintained.

In response to a remark by Taylor that the U.S. might have to wage war unilaterally if the Government of South Vietnam collapsed, Rusk said he "couldn't see a unilateral war," and Taylor replied that he meant only "punitive actions." McNamara agreed with Rusk, but said the U.S. would need to try Option C or A if South Vietnam continued to weaken. "The consensus was that it was hard to visualize continuing in these circumstances [if the GVN collapsed or told the U.S. to get out], but that the choice must certainly be avoided if at all possible."

The options were discussed, and McNamara said that the U.S. would be justified in taking Option C even if the political situation did not improve. Taylor and others felt that stronger actions would have a beneficial effect in South Vietnam, but might not be sufficient to improve the situation. McNamara agreed, but argued that Option C might buy time, even years. Taylor recommended that over the next two months the U.S. adopt a combination of Option A and the first stages of Option C, but added that the situation in Vietnam was so serious, and the likelihood of improvement in the government so doubtful, that the U.S. should "move into C right away."

The group asked William Bundy to draft a more precise plan for immediate actions that could be taken during a 30-day period in advance of a decision to move into the full Option C.[90]

On November 29, the principals met again. As requested, William Bundy suggested steps that should be taken whether or not Option C was approved. In the cover memo for this proposal, however, he said "Frankly, the Working Group inclines more and more to the view that at least a contingent decision to go on [with C] is now required."[91]

The principals discussed specific steps that should be recommended to the President. These included a Presidential statement supported by evidence on infiltration that would also be presented to Congress and leaders of other countries. The question of resuming DE SOTO patrols was discussed. Taylor, McNamara and McGeorge Bundy were opposed, and General Wheeler was in favor. It was agreed that they would not be resumed during the initial 30-

[89]*Ibid.*, p. 241. For the text of the scenario, see pp. 672-673.
[90]"Memorandum of Meeting on Southeast Asia," William P. Bundy, Nov. 27, 1964, the text of which is in *ibid.*, pp. 674-676.
[91]For the text of both the memo and the proposed plan, see *ibid.*, pp. 676-677.

day period. William Bundy was then asked to draft a NSAM outlining the plan to be recommended to the President.

On November 30 the principals met to discuss Bundy's new draft NSAM.[92] The draft stipulated that the U.S. would join with South Vietnam and Laos in a program "to help GVN morale and to increase the costs and strain on Hanoi, foreshadowing still greater pressures to come." During the first 30 days, there would be intensified military activity, as well as covert action. After that time, the paper called for two phases of graduated military pressure on North Vietnam, the first of which would be specific, tit-for-tat reprisal, and the second would be systematic air attacks, combined with other forms of generalized pressure.

William Bundy had also drafted the text of a note for Taylor to give to the Government of South Vietnam explaining the U.S. position. Among other things, the statement emphasized the necessity of having at least minimal political stability in South Vietnam before the U.S. and South Vietnam could begin the second phase of military pressure on North Vietnam.

The note expressed the hope, however, that the necessary political stability could be achieved, and toward this end "It is hoped that this phase [I] will prove to be merely preliminary to direct military pressure on the DRV after the GVN has shown itself firmly in control."[93]

At the meeting of principals to discuss the draft NSAM, it was apparent that McGeorge Bundy, for one, had conferred with the President, and on his advice the group dropped the idea of a Presidential speech. The principals also decided to recommend to the President a combination of Option A and the lowest order of C, which, as the *Pentagon Papers* notes,[94] was a "substantial deviation" from the position of the Working Group that Option A would not be effective. All of these changes appear to have been made, as the *Pentagon Papers* suggests, to avoid public commitments by the President. The group approved, however, the two-phase program of military pressure on North Vietnam.

On December 1, the principals met with the President to present their recommendations. Ambassador Taylor and Vice-President-Elect Humphrey also attended the meeting. The Bundy draft NSAM was discussed, and the two-phase program of military pressure, which was, in effect the first two phases of OPLAN 37 prepared in May 1964 in response to NSAM 288, was approved by the President.[95] He authorized the beginning of the first phase,[96] to consist primarily of additional 34-A raids, and armed reconnaissance operations in Laos (BARREL ROLL) by which U.S. planes would conduct bombing raids in the corridor areas.[97]

---

[92]For the text see *ibid.*, pp. 678-683. Note that there were tabs, which are still classified.
[93]*Ibid.*, p. 680.
[94]*Ibid.*, p. 246.
[95]*Ibid.*, pp. 248-251, and Westmoreland, *A Soldier Reports,* p. 113.
[96]No NSAM was issued, however.
[97]At a meeting of the principals on Dec. 12 to discuss BARREL ROLL it was agreed "that there would be no public statements about armed reconnaissance operations in Laos unless a plane were lost. In such an event, . . . the Government should continue to insist that we were merely escorting reconnaissance flights as requested by the Laotian government." This was done at the insistence of Souvanna Phouma, who agreed to the new plan but did not want it publicized. *PP*, Gravel ed., vol. III, pp. 253, 254.

According to notes of the meeting kept by John McNaughton, the only record which is currently available.[98] Taylor told the group that pacification was bogging down, the government was more unstable, and there was greater infiltration from the north. The President then remarked that a stable government in South Vietnam was "most essential." "They do it *or else,*" he said. "No point hitting North if South not together. . . . Why not say 'This is it!'? Not send Johnson City boy out to die if they [are] acting as they are."

The President added, "Day of reckoning coming. Want to be sure we've done everything we can. . . . Before Wheeler saddles up [and U.S. Army goes in] try everything. . . . If need be, create a new Diem, so when tell Wheeler to slap we can take slap back." But he did not appear to be optimistic. He asked McNamara if he agreed "that it's downhill in SVN no matter what we do *in* country." McNamara agreed. Before taking military action, however, the President said he wanted to give Taylor "one last chance," but that if the response was "more of the same, then I'll be talking to you General [Wheeler]."

As the meeting ended, the President told his advisers that they should inform a few Members of Congress. "Give good and bad; ask for suggestions." Rusk, and presumably also McNamara, was to meet with Fulbright, Hickenlooper, Russell and Saltonstall.[99] It should be a small meeting, the President said, to avoid any publicity. McNamara and Rusk should decide which members of the House to see. "[George] Mahon [D/Tex.] if here. [Gerald] Ford maybe." (Congress was not in session at the time.) Taylor should "touch base with the Hill" before returning to Saigon.

After the President's approval of the new plan by which to bring additional pressure on North Vietnam, culminating, if necessary, in a large-scale air war, and even an eventual ground war, the public itself was told only that according to the Gulf of Tonkin Resolution the U.S. was reaffirming its "policy of providing all possible and useful assistance," and that the President had told Taylor to "consult urgently with the South Vietnamese Government as to measures that should be taken to improve the situation in all its aspects."[100]

As a result of the President's suggestion that Taylor touch base with Congress, there was an executive session of the Senate Foreign Relations Committee on December 3, 1964, at which Taylor testified, which gave members of the committee the opportunity of telling him (and through him, the President and his other advisers) what they felt.[101] It is important to understand, however, that al-

---

[98] McNaughton's notes are in the Johnson Library, NSF Meeting Notes File. The account in the *Pentagon Papers,* Gravel ed., vol. III, pp. 248–251, appears to be based on McNaughton's notes.

[99] On Nov. 26, 1964, Russell commented on his return to Washington from visiting the President in Texas, "I would want to explore every avenue before extending the war. We either have to get out or take some action to help the Vietnamese. They won't help themselves. We made a big mistake in going there, but I can't figure out any way to get out without scaring the rest of the world." *New York Times,* Nov. 27, 1964. (Congress, it should be noted, had adjourned for the year in early October.)

[100] *New York Times,* Dec. 2, 1964.

[101] U.S. Congress, Senate, Committee on Foreign Relations, unpublished executive session transcript, Dec. 3, 1964.

though attentive Members of Congress knew that plans for further U.S. action were being made, except for those few, like Russell, who may have been told by the President, or contacted by Rusk or McNamara, they did not know what had been decided. Nor did members of the Foreign Relations Committee learn about these plans and decisions from Taylor, although from several of his comments they could have deduced that a plan for U.S. military pressure against North Vietnam had been developed and would be put into effect at the propitious time.

Taylor told the committee that most U.S. policymakers felt that such action against the north would have to be taken at some point. When asked whether there was any disagreement with this position, he said "I know of none in the councils I have attended." His own opinion continued to be that the U.S. had to stay and to win.

According to Taylor, such action should not be taken, however, when the South Vietnamese Government was as weak as it was at that time. Fulbright said he was willing to try working with the present government, but if it fell he would not support an attack on North Vietnam by the United States just because the South Vietnamese Government had fallen. Taylor, who was critical of "these vacillating, unpatriotic, unreliable politicians in Saigon," replied that the United States could accept a "military dictatorship" at that point, which would provide the political stability in Vietnam that the U.S. needed as a precondition for attacking the north.

Fulbright agreed that the problem was the lack of a workable, reliable government in the south which was supported by the people, and said that unless such a government existed, "What are you fighting for? We don't want the country." He, as well as Church, expressed concern over reports that the U.S. would attack the North. ". . . if you want to go to war, I don't approve of it. I don't give a damn what the provocation is. I am not going to vote to send a hundred thousand men, or it would probably be 300,000 or 400,000. The French had 500,000." Taylor replied that the U.S. could attack by air, and punish the North Vietnamese, and "let it go at that." Fulbright was skeptical. "Well, if it doesn't succeed—America never fails—once it engages in that they will just go all out."

Neither Fulbright nor the Foreign Relations Committee, however, took any further action at that point. Only Mansfield appears to have followed-up. In a memorandum to the President on December 9, 1964, he said, among other things:[102]

> We remain on a course in Viet Nam which takes us further and further out on the sagging limb. . . .
> At this point, . . . the Communists are not likely to be in the mood for a bonafide peaceful settlement, even if the wherewithal for such a settlement were to exist on our side. It would appear that the government in Saigon, at this point, is not adequate even for negotiating a bonafide settlement, let alone for going ahead into North Viet Nam. . . . we are now in the

---

[102]Johnson Library, NSF Name File, Mansfield, reprinted in Gareth Porter (ed.), *Vietnam: A History in Documents*, 2 vols. (New York: New American Library, 1981), vol. II, pp. 333-335.

process of putting together makeshift regimes in much the same way that the French were compelled to operate in 1952-1954.

If developments continue in the present pattern we are sooner or later going to have to face up to the fact that the preponderant responsibility for what transpires in South Viet Nam really rests with us even as it once had with the French. We will find ourselves saddled in South Viet Nam, no matter what we will, with a situation that is a cross between the present South Korean quasi-dependency and the pre-independence Philippine colony and at the 1964 level of cost in lives and resources.

This grim prospect, moreover, presupposes no major extension of the war beyond South Viet Nam. But it would still be the best that we would have to look forward to for the next decade or more unless there is a significant improvement in the situation, an improvement which is not and has not even been in sight for a year or more.

If a significant extension of the conflict beyond South Viet Nam should occur then the prospects are appalling. Even short of nuclear war, an extension of the war may well saddle us with enormous burdens and costs in Cambodia, Laos and elsewhere in Asia, along with those in Viet Nam.

Mansfield made several suggestions for avoiding such an outcome. First, the U.S. should not undertake military action beyond the borders of South Vietnam. U.S. forces should also remain clear of the Cambodian border, and support should be given to nationalist forces in Cambodia (Sihanouk) and in Laos (Souvanna Phouma) in the effort being made to maintain the independence and stability of those countries.

He made this recommendation for dealing with the Government of Vietnam:

Begin to think and act in a political sense in South Viet Nam in terms of assisting in evolving a government which can speak with some native validity and authority for that section should the time come with negotiation of a bonafide peaceful settlement, perhaps on the basis of confederation, is possible. To be effective this late in the game, such a government, it would seem would have to begin now to speak in terms of eventual *peaceful* [emphasis in original] unification of all Viet Nam rather than in terms of either liberation of the north or establishing an isolated independence in South Viet Nam. The first is illusory without total United States involvement. The second, an independent and isolated South Viet Nam is also illusory in present circumstances since it would require such a vast United States involvement as to negate the meaning of independence.

The very stress on peaceful unification of all Viet Nam by a South Vietnamese government in Saigon may be helpful in bringing about an increase in that government's acceptance in South Viet Nam. And such an increase would have to develop before it could speak with the authority which bonafide negotiations would require.

Mansfield concluded by saying, "If some such course as the above is not practical we had better begin now to face up to the likelihood of years and years of involvement and a vast increase in the commitment, and this should be spelled out in no uncertain terms to the people of the nation."

On December 17, the President replied to Mansfield in a letter drafted by McGeorge Bundy: "I think we have the same basic view of this problem, and the same sense of its difficulties. The one suggestion in your memorandum which I myself would take direct issue with is that we are 'overcommitted' there. Given the size of the stake, it seems to me that we are doing only what we have to do."[103] In transmitting to Johnson the draft reply to Mansfield, McGeorge Bundy said that the letter was "designed to treat him gently. We could get into a stronger debate, but I doubt if it is worth it."[104]

Implementing the December 1 Decision

On December 3, Taylor met with the President, joined only by McGeorge Bundy, to go over final plans for presenting the U.S. position to the South Vietnamese, and based on the President's instructions Taylor told the Vietnamese upon his return to Saigon that the ". . . unsatisfactory progress being made in the Pacification Program was the result of two primary causes from which many secondary causes stem. The primary cause has been the governmental instability in Saigon, and the second the continued reinforcement and direction of the Viet Cong by the Government of North Vietnam."[105] Although both factors had to be dealt with, "First and above all, there must be a stable, effective Vietnamese Government able to conduct a successful campaign against the Viet Cong even if the aid from North Vietnam for the Viet Cong should end." This point was restated in order to emphasize the fact that an effective South Vietnamese Government was a prerequisite for U.S. help in widening the war:

> Thus, since action against North Vietnam would only be contributory and not central to winning the war against the Viet Cong, it would not be prudent to incur the risks which are inherent in an expansion of hostilities until there were a government in Saigon capable of handling the serious problems inevitably involved in such an expansion, and capable of promptly and fully exploiting the favorable effects which may be anticipated if we are successful in terminating the support and direction of the Viet Cong by North Vietnam.

The Vietnamese were also told by Taylor, in a statement which again reflected the tendency to apply American values and ideas, what the U.S. expected of them:

> . . . In the view of the United States, there is a certain minimum condition to be brought about in South Vietnam before new measures against North Vietnam would be either justified or practicable. At the minimum, the Government in Saigon

---

[103]Johnson Library, NSF Name File, Mansfield.
[104]Johnson Library, NSF Aides File, McGeorge Bundy Memos to the President.
[105]These quotes are from the paper, "Actions Designed to Strengthen the Government of Vietnam," which Taylor presented to the Vietnamese, *PP*, Gravel ed., vol. II, pp. 343-345.

should be able to speak for and to its people who will need special guidance and leadership throughout the coming critical period. The Government should be capable of maintaining law and order in the principal centers of population, assuring their effective execution by military and police forces completely responsive to its authority. The Government must have at its disposal means to cope promptly and effectively with enemy reactions which must be expected to result from any change in the pattern of our operations.

To bring about this condition will require a demonstration of far greater national unity against the Communist enemy at this critical time than exists at present. It is a matter of greatest difficulty for the United States Government to require great sacrifices by American citizens on behalf of South Vietnam when reports from Saigon repeatedly give evidence of heedless self-interest and shortsightedness among so many major political groups.

Better performance in the prosecution of the war against the Viet Cong needs to be accompanied by actions to convince the people of the interest of their government in their well-being. Better performance in itself is perhaps the most convincing evidence but can be supplemented by such actions as frequent visits by officials and ranking military officers to the provinces for personal orientation and "trouble shooting." The available information media offer a channel of communication with the people which could be strengthened and more efficiently employed. The physical appearance of the cities, particularly of Saigon, shows a let-down in civic pride which, if corrected, would convey a message of governmental effectiveness to their inhabitants. Similarly, in the country an expanded rural development program could carry the government's presence into every reasonably secure village and hamlet.

If governmental performance and popular appeal are significantly improved, there will be little difficulty in establishing confidence in the government. However, this confidence should be expressed, not merely implied. It is particularly important that the military leaders continue to express public confidence in the government and the firm intention to uphold it. While giving an impression of submitting to pressure, the government might explore honorable ways of conciliating its most important opponents among the minority groups. The United States Government is prepared to help by oral statements of support and by further assistance to show our faith in the future of South Vietnam.

The U.S., said Taylor, wanted improvement in eight specific areas:

1. and 2. Increasing RVNAF, paramilitary, and police to and above existing authorized strengths.

3. Better performance by civilian and military officials.

4. Speeding up budgetary procedures and spending in the provinces.

5. Strengthening the province chiefs.

6. Strengthening police powers.

7. More vigor in Hop Tac.

8. After a delay, "review cases of political prisoners from previous regimes."

For its part, the U.S., Taylor said, was willing to launch a two-phase military program against North Vietnam:

. . . While the Government of Vietnam is making progress toward achieving the goals set forth above, the United States Government would be willing to strike harder at infiltration routes in Laos and at sea. With respect to Laos, the United States Government is prepared, in conjunction with the Royal Laos Government, to add United States air power as needed to restrict the use of Laotian territory as a route of infiltration into South Vietnam. With respect to the sea, the United States Government would favor an intensification of those covert maritime operations which have proved their usefulness in harassing the enemy. The United States would regard the combination of these operations in Laos and at sea as constituting Phase I of a measured increase of military pressures directed toward reducing infiltration and warning the Government of North Vietnam of the risks it is running.

. . . If the Government of Vietnam is able to demonstrate its effectiveness and capability for achieving the minimum conditions set forth above, the United States Government is prepared to consider a program of direct military pressure on North Vietnam as Phase II. . . .

As contemplated by the United States Government, Phase II would, in general terms, constitute a series of air attacks on North Vietnam progressively mounting in scope and intensity for the purpose of convincing the leaders of North Vietnam that it is to their interest to cease aid to the Viet Cong and respect the independence and security of South Vietnam . . .

Beginning in late December 1964 and continuing until the end of February 1965, there was a period of intense political turmoil in South Vietnam. On December 20, following several days of political unrest among Buddhists and students, General Khanh, under pressure from a group of young Vietnamese generals, including Nguyen Cao Ky and Nguyen Van Thieu, each of whom was later premier, announced the formation of an Armed Forces Council as the new governing body for South Vietnam. Taylor objected strenuously to the action of the generals, and with the support of Deputy Ambassador U. Alexis Johnson he called the "Young Turks" together for a meeting. As reported to Washington by the U.S. mission, this is how the meeting opened:[106]

. . . Ambassador Taylor. Do all of you understand English? (Vietnamese officers indicated they did, although the understanding of General [Nguyen Chanh] Thi was known to be weak.) I told you all clearly at General Westmoreland's dinner we Americans were tired of coups. Apparently I wasted my words. Maybe this is because something is wrong with my French because you evidently didn't understand. I made it

[106] Ibid., p. 346. For Taylor's version see Swords and Plowshares, pp. 330-331. For a detailed description of these and other political developments in South Vietnam, which have been greatly oversimplified here, see Shaplen, The Lost Revolution, and the extensive reporting of the New York Times.

clear that all the military plans which I know you would like to carry out are dependent on governmental stability. Now you have made a real mess. We cannot carry you forever if you do things like this.

On December 21, Taylor asked Khanh to resign and leave the country. On December 23, the Young Turks criticized Taylor, and asked for his recall as Ambassador. Finally, in early January the U.S. accepted some rearrangements in the Vietnamese Government, including the membership of Young Turks in the Cabinet, and the Vietnamese made their peace with the U.S. Political turmoil continued, however, and it was June of 1965 before some apparent stability was reached when Thieu and Ky assumed leadership of the government.

During December 1964, Phase I of the U.S. plan of graduated pressure on North Vietnam got underway with the opening on December 14 of U.S. armed reconnaissance bombing along infiltration routes in Laos (BARREL ROLL).[107] According to the *Pentagon Papers*, however,[108] "This and other signs of increased American commitment against North Vietnam's involvement in the South showed no results in terms of increasing GVN stability."

On December 24, 1964, a U.S. officers' billet in Saigon was bombed by the Communists. Two Americans were killed and 38 Americans and 13 Vietnamese injured. There were strong recommendations for U.S. reprisal airstrikes on North Vietnam from Taylor and Westmoreland, CINCPAC, and the JCS, but the President, joined by Rusk and McNamara, rejected the idea.[109] In a personal NODIS cable to Taylor on December 30, 1964, Johnson explained why:[110] First, he said, there was the problem of the "political turmoil" and "general confusion" in South Vietnam, which made it difficult for the U.S. to know what was happening, including who was responsible for such an attack on a U.S. position. (He also criticized the lack of adequate security at U.S. installations.) In this regard, Johnson told Taylor that he continued to be worried by the lack of progress ". . . in communicating sensitively and per-

---

[107] For a description of this and other activities in Phase I, see *PP*, Gravel ed., vol. III, pp. 251 ff. There were NSC meetings on Dec. 12 and 19, but there is almost no information or documentation on these in the *Pentagon Papers*, and the notes or summaries of the meetings are still classified.

[108] *Ibid.*, p. 92.

[109] *Ibid.* Rusk appears to have been particularly skeptical about bombing the north or widening the war, even though he was a strong supporter of the U.S. role in South Vietnam. This is one description of his position:

In those days, Rusk was arguing with what appeared to be great personal conviction that it would serve no useful purpose to bomb North Vietnam or to send in American fighting men. In his "bottle club" sessions, with newsmen on the eighth floor of the State Department, Rusk would say that white men should not fight an Asian nation's war; that large numbers of U.S. troops would only lead to future and serious hostility with Vietnamese. On the question of bombing, Rusk always would say "the war must be won in the South." When pressed to be more specific, he would beg the question, for, as he would remark, the President had said he was not "going North" but was undecided about what action he might take to counter specific situations.

His public appearances backed up his private remarks. On Jan. 3, 1965, for instance, when interviewed on a television program, he said that an expansion of the Vietnam war would lead to a multiplication of casualties and subject the people to devastation.

Such remarks contributed to what came to be known in Washington as a "credibility gap" between the Government and its citizens. No one spelled out the frustrating prospects of Vietnam better than Rusk himself at that time. To expand the war, he said in the same January television show, would lead down the trail "the end of which no one in any country could possibly see with assurance." Johnson and Gwertzman, *Fulbright, the Dissenter*, p. 201.

[110] These excerpts are from the President's cable, which is in the Johnson Library, NSC History File, Deployment of Forces.

suasively with the various groups in South Vietnam. . . . In particular, I wonder whether we are making full use of the kind of Americans who have shown a knack for this kind of communication in the past . . . even if they are not always the easiest men to handle in a country team. To put it another way, I continue to believe that we should have the most sensitive, the most persistent, and attentive Americans that we can find in touch with Vietnamese of every kind and quality, and reinforced by Englishmen, and Buddhists, and labor leaders, and agricultural experts, and other free men of every kind and type, who may have skills to contribute in a contest on all fronts." Johnson was apparently referring to Lansdale, and to Taylor's long-standing disinclination to include Lansdale on the U.S. team in Saigon.

Johnson also questioned the validity of large-scale bombing of the north, preferring instead the use of more U.S. forces in an anti-guerrilla capacity:

> Everytime I get a military recommendation it seems to me that it calls for large-scale bombing: I have never felt that this war will be won from the air, and it seems to me that what is much more needed and would be more effective is a larger and stronger use of Rangers and Special Forces and Marines, or other appropriate military strength on the ground and on the scene. I am ready to look with great favor on that kind of increased American effort, directed at the guerrillas and aimed to stiffen the aggressiveness of Vietnamese military units up and down the line. Any recommendation that you or General Westmoreland make in this sense will have immediate attention from me, although I know that it may involve the acceptance of larger American sacrifices. We have been building our strength to fight this kind of war ever since 1961, and I myself am ready to substantially increase the number of Americans in Vietnam if it is necessary to provide this kind of fighting force against the Viet Cong.

"I recognized this suggestion," Taylor said in his memoirs, "as a reflection of the President's conviction, which I shared, of the importance of the ground operations in South Vietnam over anything which could be accomplished by air power in North Vietnam. However, I felt that there was an important secondary role for the air campaign in supplementing and advancing our efforts in the South."[111]

According to Westmoreland, Taylor was "stung by the President's implied criticism and disturbed that he saw introducing ground troops as a less serious step then bombing the North. . . ."[112]

What is the Alternative?

By the end of 1964, the Vietnam war was on the verge of being "Americanized." What was the alternative? Some supported neutralization, although there were few U.S. policymakers who thought it was a realistic possibility. Withdrawal was even less ac-

---

[111] *Swords and Plowshares*, p. 333.
[112] *A Soldier Reports*, p. 114.

ceptable. Taylor said,[113] ". . . it never occurred to me to recommend withdrawal." "First, there were many untried military and other possibilities for improving the situation." In addition, ". . . we had every reason to keep up the American will to persist in Saigon following the expression of national determination after the Tonkin Gulf affair. . . . Had not the Congress declared with only two dissenting votes that 'The U.S. regards as vital to its national interest and to world peace the maintenance of international peace and security in Southeast Asia'? With this authoritative confirmation of the essentiality of our mission, no senior official could in conscience harbor thoughts of retreat." The complicity of the U.S. in Diem's demise also increased U.S. responsibility for the Vietnamese, he said.[114]

On the other hand, there was considerable doubt among U.S. officials about the outcome of the struggle in Vietnam, and a feeling on the part of many that it would, as Paul Kattenburg had predicted, poison anyone who touched it. No one was more aware of this than Lyndon Johnson. In December 1964, Johnson met privately for three hours with a group of three reporters, one of whom gave this account of the President's perception of his own dilemma:[115]

> . . . he appeared to know that Vietnam was a trap, and that he was probably doomed to failure no matter what policy he adopted. He likened his situation to standing on a copy of a newspaper in the middle of the Atlantic Ocean. "If I go this way," he said, tilting his hand to the right, "I'll topple over, and if I go this way"—he tilted his hand to the left—"I'll topple over, and if I stay where I am, the paper will be soaked up and I'll sink slowly to the bottom of the sea." As he said this, he lowered his hand slowly toward the floor.

Amid the increasing pressure for U.S. military action, those in the executive branch, primarily in the CIA, who continued to advocate a "political" solution rather than military escalation, found little support. One of them was William Colby:[116]

> After one of the many meetings I attended at the White House, I stopped McGeorge Bundy outside the Situation Room and told him plaintively that we must get our attention and our programs back to the real contest at the village level, and build up from there instead of endlessly debating where to bomb North Vietnam and what new projects to impose on the overloaded Saigon government. He replied that I might be right in my approach, but that he thought the structure of the American government would never permit it to be applied. And his appreciation of the role of the Pentagon's and the rest

---

[113]*Swords and Plowshares*, pp. 327-328.
[114]Another opponent of both neutralization and withdrawal was David Halberstam, who wrote in late 1964 that "Neutralization would only delay the inevitable momentarily," and that "we would dishonor ourselves and our allies by pulling out. . . ." He was skeptical about the use of U.S. troops, but at the same time he considered Vietnam to be "perhaps one of only five or six nations in the world that is truly vital to U.S. interests," and "may be worth a larger commitment on our part. . . ." "The basic alternatives for Vietnam," he said, "are the same now as they were in 1961; they are not different, no more palatable, no less of a nightmare." Halberstam, *The Making of a Quagmire*, pp. 315 ff.
[115]Wise, *The Politics of Lying*, p. 295.
[116]*Honorable Men*, p. 225.

of Washington's juggernaut staff machinery was correct at the time.

In an article on "Viet Nam: Do We Understand Revolution?" which appeared in *Foreign Affairs* for October 1964, General Lansdale discussed publicly the position he and others had been advocating.[117] Vietnam, he said, was a "people's war," the fighting of which would affect future "people's wars" in other parts of the world. The "harsh fact," he continued, was that "despite the use of overwhelming amounts" of U.S. aid and assistance, the Communists were stronger than ever. This had happened because ". . . the Communists have let loose a revolutionary idea in Viet Nam . . . [which] will not die by being ignored, bombed or smothered by us. Ideas do not die in such ways." The answer, he said, was "to oppose the Communist idea with a better idea and to do so on the battleground itself, in a way that would permit the people, who are the main feature of that battleground, to make their own choice."

This was Lansdale's description of that "better idea":

A political base would be established. The first step would be to state political goals, founded on principles cherished by free men, which the Vietnamese share; the second would be an aggressive commitment of organizations and resources to start the Vietnamese moving realistically toward those political goals. In essence, this is revolutionary warfare, the spirit of the British Magna Carta, the French "Liberté, Egalité, Fraternité" and our own Declaration of Independence. . . .

Lansdale referred to the counterguerrilla wars in the Philippines and Malaya, and suggested this formula for success in "people's wars":

When the right cause is identified and used correctly, anti-Communist fight becomes a *pro*-people fight, with the overwhelming majority of the people then starting to help what they recognize to be their own side, and the struggle is brought to a climax. When the *pro*-people fight is continued sincerely by its leaders, the Communist insurgency is destroyed.

Lansdale recognized that assisting with the internal political problems of another country required "great wisdom and sensitivity," but his position was the U.S. had done it before and could do it again.

He then turned to the question of developing political goals with public appeal. "The great cause in Viet Nam which last united the overwhelming majority of Vietnamese, both North and South was "independence."'" But Ho Chi Minh, Vietnam's "Benedict Arnold," had substituted Communism for nationalism. "At this point in time and experience," he said, "perhaps the most valuable and realistic gift that Americans can give Viet Nam is to concentrate above everything else on helping the Vietnamese leadership create the conditions which will encourage the discovery and most rapid possible development of a patriotic cause so genuine that the Vietnamese willingly will pledge to it "their lives, their fortunes, their sacred honor.'"

---

[117] Maj. Gen. Edward G. Lansdale, "Viet Nam: Do We Understand Revolution," *Foreign Affairs* (October 1964), pp. 75-86.

Lansdale concluded his article with several proposals, primarily having to do with the election of a government to replace the military junta ruling the country, the reestablishment of a national legislative assembly (which the junta had abolished), and the use of U.S. economic aid to support political development at the local level, as well as to increase agricultural production (which he stressed would be very beneficial politically). He stressed that military activities should be directed at protecting and helping the people, and supporting the recommended political activities.

On November 25, Rufus Phillips, one of Lansdale's 1954 team, who had returned to Vietnam in 1962 as Assistant Director of the Rural Development Office, restated his and Lansdale's position in a paper that was circulated among some of the policymakers involved in the November discussions of U.S. policy. This was his summary:[118]

The United States must soon adopt one, or a combination, of four approaches to the problem in Vietnam:

1. Punitive/Interdictory bombardment of installations and activities in North Vietnam/Laos. This would not seriously adversely affect the Viet Cong/DRV effort; it would solidify opinion against us; its failure would seriously lower morale in Vietnam and the U.S., and lead either to the commitment of ground forces or negotiated withdrawal.

2. Ground force intervention to:

a. Establish a cordon sanitaire; using U.S., and SEATO conventional forces;

b. Harass and throw off-balance the Viet Cong, by the employment of a limited number of international volunteers—footborne Flying Tigers; or

c. Assault the North by surprise, employing airborne forces, principally U.S., and a major psychological—"liberation"—effort; and follow this up with sound political-economic counter-insurgency efforts. The first of these would be as futile as bombardment, and would entail an U.S. assumption of command in Vietnam, a sure way to lose that war. The second would be dramatic and useful, but would be endangered by tacit and explicit internal opposition. The third would be effective, given greater ability, understanding and determination than we have yet exhibited in our efforts in Vietnam.

3. Negotiated withdrawal: This would be recognized by our enemies and friends alike as total, ignominious, political and military defeat; a cowardly betrayal of our allies; and an abandonment of any American claim to honor or morality.

4. A positive, politically-oriented, integrated program. Essentially an expression of belief that the traditional "American way" can triumph, this would be a rejuvenat-

---

[118]Kennedy Library, Thomson Papers, from Phillips' one-page summary which accompanied his 11-page paper, "United States Policy Options in Vietnam," Nov. 25, 1964. In the same location is a similar 22-page paper by Lansdale, "Concept for Victory in Vietnam," June 8, 1964.

ed, redirected effort to establish stable, popular, effective government on a sound political and economic base. Success is assured, *if* the effort is guided by advisors with successful experience in such wars who are backed by the very top; failure, no worse and less costly than the other positive courses would entail, is probable if the effort does not have such guidance and backing.

5. Only the last course of action offers real hope of an outcome consonant with United State national objectives, principles, and honor.

Recommendations for Stronger Action

On January 6, 1965, Ambassador Taylor cabled a long reply (in which his deputy, U. Alexis Johnson, and Westmoreland concurred, to the President's cable of December 30.[119] ". . . we are presently on a losing track," Taylor said, "and must risk a change. . . . To take no positive action now is to accept defeat in the fairly near future." This was his description of the situation:

> We are faced here with a seriously deteriorating situation characterized by contrived political turmoil, irresponsibility and division within the armed forces, lethargy in the pacification program, some anti-US feeling which could grow, signs of mounting terrorism by VC directly at US personnel and deepening discouragement and loss of morale throughout SVN. Unless these conditions are somehow changed and trends reversed, we are likely soon to face a number of unpleasant developments ranging from anti-American demonstrations, further civil disorders, and even political assassinations to the ultimate installation of a hostile govt which will ask us to leave while it seeks accommodations with the National Liberation Front and Hanoi.

Taylor said that there were three general causes for "this unhappy state of affairs": "lack of a stable government, inadequate security against the VC and nation-wide war-weariness." He continued:

> Until the fall of Diem and the experience gained from the events of the following months, I doubt that anyone appreciated the magnitude of the centrifugal political forces which had been kept under control by his iron rule. The successive political upheavals and the accompanying turmoil which have followed Diem's demise upset all prior US calculations as to the duration and outcome of the counterinsurgency in SVN and the future remains uncertain today. There is no adequate replacement for Diem in sight.
>
> At least we know now what are the basic factors responsible for this turmoil—chronic factionalism, civilian-military suspicions and distrust, absence of national spirit and motivation, lack of cohesion in the social structure, lack of experience in the conduct of govt. These are historical factors growing out of national characteristics and traditions, susceptible to change only over the long run. Perhaps other Americans might marginally influence them more effectively but generally speaking

---

[119]Taylor's five-part report was contained in Saigon to Washington 2052-2058, Jan. 6, 1965, Johnson Library, NSC History File, Deployment of Forces.

we Americans are not going to change them in any fundamental way in any measurable time. We can only recognize their existence and adjust our plans and expectations accordingly.

Based on this analysis, Taylor said that there were "some things we clearly cannot do—change national characteristics, create leadership where it does not exist, raise large additional GVN forces or seal porous frontiers to infiltration . . . in the time available we cannot expect anything better than marginal govt and marginal pacification progress with continued decline of national morale—unless something new is added to make up for those things we cannot control." The "something new" was "graduated air attacks directed against the will of the DRV"—Phase II. "I know that this is an old recipe with little attractiveness," Taylor said, "but no matter how we reexamine the facts, or what appear to be the facts, we can find no other answer which offers any chance of success." Air attacks, he added, would be "the most flexible weapon in our arsenal of military superiority to bring pressure on the will of the chiefs of the DRV. As practical men, they cannot wish to see the fruits of ten years of labor destroyed by slowly escalating air attacks (which they cannot prevent) without trying to find some accommodations which will excise the threat."

Taylor again objected to the use of U.S. ground forces whose, ". . . military value would be more than offset by their political liability. The Vietnamese have the manpower and the basic skills to win this war. What they lack is motivation. The entire advisory effort has been devoted to giving them both skill and motivation. If that effort has not succeeded there is less reason to think that U.S. combat forces would have the desired effect. In fact, there is good reason to believe that they would have the opposite effect by causing some Vietnamese to let the U.S. carry the burden while others, probably the majority, would actively turn against us. Thus intervention with ground combat forces would at best buy time and would lead to ever increasing commitments until, like the French, we would be occupying an essentially hostile foreign country."

Included in the report was an analysis by Westmoreland of several alternative methods for using U.S. forces, which concluded that the only acceptable alternative was to use such forces in a supporting role for Vietnamese forces. Taylor and Westmoreland did not recommend that alternative, however, nor did they favor an expansion of the advisory effort. (At that time there were approximately 23,000 U.S. military personnel in Vietnam, 5,000 of whom were serving as advisers, and 18,000 in operational support.)

Taylor's recommendation was that the U.S. give the Vietnamese a "conditional commitment that if, in the U.S. judgment, the GVN reaches a certain level of performance, the USG will join in an escalating campaign against the DRV. Hopefully, by such action, we could improve the government, unify the armed forces to some degree, and thereupon move into the Phase II program without which we see little chance of breaking out of the present downward spiral." ". . . we should look for an occasion," he added, "to begin air operations just as soon as we have satisfactorily compromised the current political situation in Saigon and set up a minimal govt. . . . At the proper time, we can set the stage for action by exposing to the public our case against infiltration, and by initiating aggressive DE SOTO patrols . . . when decided to act, we can justify that decision on the basis of infiltration, of VC terrorism, of attacks on DE SOTO patrols or any combination of the three." Meanwhile, Taylor said he hoped that, regardless of the political situation in Saigon, the U.S. would conduct appropriate reprisal strikes in the event of major acts of terrorism by the Communists.

Taylor did not agree with the President's suggestion for using more Americans with skill and experience in communicating with the Vietnamese, saying that the U.S. already had extensive political contacts in Vietnam, and that, "On the whole, the quality of our personnel in Vietnam is high and I believe they meet pretty well your description of 'sensitive, persistent and attentive Americans.' We could perhaps improve on our use of them but we definitely do not need more. The Vietnamese may even be somewhat smothered now by the quantity of US contacts." But Taylor said that it would be well for Johnson to assure himself on this point, and suggested that the President send McGeorge Bundy, or someone like him, to review that particular aspect of the U.S. program.

On January 6, 1965, William Bundy sent a memorandum to Rusk in preparation for a meeting that afternoon with the President to discuss the Vietnamese situation, especially Taylor's cable. The subject of the Bundy memo was "Notes on the South Vietnamese Situation and Alternatives."[120] The memorandum represented, Bundy said, the consensus of his ideas and those of the State Department's other top advisers on Vietnam—Michael Forrestal (head of the Vietnam Coordinating Committee) and Leonard Unger (one of Bundy's deputies).

According to Bundy's memo, "the situation is now likely to come apart more rapidly than we had anticipated in November." This was his prognosis:[121]

> We would still stick to the estimate that the most likely form of coming apart would be a government of key groups starting to negotiate covertly with the Liberation Front or Hanoi, perhaps not asking in the first instance that we get out, but with that necessarily following at a fairly early stage. In one sense, this would be a "Vietnam solution," with some hope that it would produce a Communist Vietnam that would assert its own degree of independence from Peiping and that would produce a pause in Communist pressure in Southeast Asia. On the other hand, it would still be virtually certain that Laos would then become untenable and that Cambodia would accommodate in some way. Most seriously, there is grave question whether the Thai in these circumstances would retain any confidence at all in our continued support. In short, the outcome would be regarded in Asia, and particularly among our friends, as just as humiliating a defeat as any other form. As events have developed, the American public would probably not be too sharply critical, but the real question would be whether Thailand and other nations were weakened and taken over thereafter.

---

[120]For the text see *PP*, Gravel ed., vol. III, pp. 684-686.
[121] *Ibid.*, p. 685.

Bundy recommended that the U.S. take stronger action against North Vietnam to prevent the defeat of the U.S. in Southeast Asia, but cautioned that "its stiffening effect on the Saigon political situation would not be at all sure to bring about a more effective government, nor would limited actions against the southern DRV in fact sharply reduce infiltration or, in present circumstances, be at all likely to induce Hanoi to call it off."[122] This was his reasoning:[123]

Nonetheless, on balance we believe that such action would have some faint hope of really improving the Vietnamese situation, and, above all, would put us in a much stronger position to hold the next line of defense, namely Thailand. Accepting the present situation—or any negotiation on the basis of it—would be far weaker from this latter key standpoint. If we moved into stronger actions, we should have in mind that negotiations would be likely to emerge from some quarter in any event, and that under existing circumstances, even with the additional element of pressure, we could not expect to get an outcome that would really secure an independent South Vietnam. Yet even on an outcome that produced a progressive deterioration in South Vietnam and an eventual Communist takeover, we would still have appeared to Asians to have done a lot more about it.

Bundy's memo cited three specific kinds of action that could be taken:

a. An early occasion for reprisal action against the DRV.

b. Possibly beginning low-level reconnaissance of the DRV at once.

c. Concurrently with a or b, an early orderly withdrawal of our dependents.

The memo added, however, that such actions ". . . would be a grave mistake in the absence of stronger action, and if taken in isolation would tremendously increase the pace of deterioration in Saigon. If we are to clear our decks in this way—and we are more and more inclined to think we should—it simply *must* be, for this reason alone, in the context of *some* stronger action." (emphasis in original) By "stronger action" Bundy was referring to U.S. ground forces. "Introduction of limited US ground forces into the northern area of South Vietnam," he said, "still has great appeal to many of us, concurrently with the first air attack into the DRV. It would have a real stiffening effect in Saigon, and a strong signal effect to Hanoi." The memo added, "On the disadvantage side, such forces would be possible attrition targets for the Viet Cong."

McNaughton took a similar position. In a memo on January 4, 1965,[124] he stated, "Our stakes in South Vietnam are: (a) Buffer real estate near Thailand and Malaysia and (b) Our reputation. The latter is more important than the former. . . ." McNaughton also felt that "The best present estimate is that South Vietnam is being 'lost.'" Unlike Bundy, Forrestal, and Unger, however, he did

---

[122]Others also doubted the efficacy of bombing North Vietnam, and urged that the U.S. concentrate on improving South Vietnamese forces rather than increasing the use of U.S. forces. See, for example, Cooper, *The Lost Crusade,* pp. 258-259.

[123]*PP,* Gravel ed., vol. III, p. 685.

[124]For the text see *ibid.,* pp. 683-684.

not favor U.S. ground forces: "Additional U.S. soldiers are as likely to be counterproductive as productive." He did advocate a reprisal raid on North Vietnam and the removal of U.S. dependents. We should "keep slugging away," and "if we leave be sure it is a departure of the kind that would put everyone on our side, wondering how we stuck it and took it so long."[125]

At the January 6 meeting with Rusk, McNamara, and McGeorge Bundy, however, the President reportedly "was clearly in no mood to make new decisions," and made none.[126] In a cable back to Taylor on January 7, the President said that he and others in Washington generally agreed with Taylor's analysis, but he did not want to make a commitment on the "timing and scale of Phase II."[127] He agreed that the U.S. should begin contingency planning with the Vietnamese in anticipation of Phase II, but said that further decisions would depend on "experience in reprisal actions, on joint efforts to achieve victories within South Vietnam, and on joint efforts to achieve political stability."

Johnson also agreed with Taylor that the U.S. should have a firm policy, established jointly with the Vietnamese, of reprisal in the case of "Viet Cong atrocities," but he repeated his opinion that before such reprisals were carried out the U.S. should evacuate its dependents from Vietnam.

Taylor replied on January 11, expressing satisfaction with the President's cable of January 7.[128] He said he hoped he could assume from that cable that the U.S. was planning "prompt passage into Phase II operations against the DRV as soon as possible," in addition to conducting reprisals in return for specific Communist attacks. In this connection, Taylor said that "in applying the criteria for governmental performance, I am sure we will have to use much common sense and great leniency if we are ever going to take action . . . we may have to be satisfied with little more than the continued existence of a government in whose name we can act and to whose request for assistance we can respond." He recommended, therefore, that the President approve a policy statement that would include the following point: "It is the intention of the USG to initiate Phase II operations as soon as the GVN meets or shows reasonable promise of meeting the criteria being able to

---

[125]During 1964, McNaughton began discussing with Forrestal his doubts about U.S. policy toward Vietnam. According to Halberstam, *The Best and the Brightest*, p. 368, "Having finished with Forrestal, McNaughton would go back and pour out his doubts to one man, Robert S. McNamara, a man he was still in awe of. McNamara would override them, he would dampen them, it would be business as usual, and McNaughton, the secret dove, would emerge from the Secretary's office and hide his doubts, because he still wanted to be a player, and he knew there was no power at the Pentagon if he differed from McNamara at all."

Halberstam also reports the following (p. 366):

"In late 1964, he [McNaughton] assigned Daniel Ellsberg to the job of looking for ways of rationalizing the American way out of Vietnam—if everything collapsed. It was in effect to be a covering White Paper along the lines of the China White Paper. The secrecy involved in Ellsberg's assignment was paramount: Ellsberg, McNaughton made clear, was to talk to no one else about his assignment, not even his colleagues in the McNaughton shop. He was not to use a secretary on his reports but to type them himself. In addition McNaughton wanted to make clear that this very assignment might damage Ellsberg's career, that a repeat of the McCarthy period was possible. 'You should be clear,' he repeatedly warned Ellsberg, 'that you could be signing the death warrant to your career by having anything to do with calculations and decisions like these. A lot of people were ruined for less.'"

[126]Bundy MS., ch. 20, p. 19.

[127]Johnson Library, NSC History File, Deployment of Forces, Washington to Saigon 1419, Jan. 7, 1965.

[128]Saigon to Washington 2116, Jan. 11, 1965, same location.

speak for and to its people; to maintain law and order in principal cities; and to make plans for the conduct of operations and to assure effective execution of such plans by military and police forces of SVN."

Taylor proposed that "If, after giving about another month's run to our effort in Laos, the Huong government [on November 1, 1964, Tran Van Huong, a civilian, had been named Premier under Khanh and the military junta] is still in business, my feeling is that we should be ready to embark on Phase II operations, if only for the pulmotor effect upon the internal situation in SVN." Almost one month after this recommendation was made, it is of interest to note, Phase II began.

On January 14, the President replied. He directed Taylor to begin the evacuation of U.S. dependents, and to recommend reprisal action in the event of a "spectacular enemy action." He still declined, however, to make a commitment with respect to when Phase II would begin.[129]

In later conversations with Doris Kearns, Johnson described his perception of the situation in early 1965:[130]

> I knew from the start that I was bound to be crucified either way I moved. If I left the woman I really loved—the Great Society—in order to get involved with that bitch of a war on the other side of the world, then I would lose everything at home . . . But if I left that war and let the Communists take over South Vietnam, then I would be seen as a coward and my nation would be seen as an appeaser and we would both find it impossible to accomplish anything for anybody anywhere on the entire globe.
>
> Oh, I could see it coming all right. History provided too many cases where the sound of the bugle put an immediate end to the hopes and dreams of the best reformers: the Spanish-American War drowned the populist spirit; World War I ended Woodrow Wilson's New Freedom; World War II brought the New Deal to a close. Once the war began, then all those conservatives in the Congress would use it as a weapon against the Great Society. You see, they'd never wanted to help the poor or the Negroes in the first place. But they were having a hard time figuring out how to make their opposition sound noble in a time of great prosperity. But the war. Oh, they'd use it to say they were against my programs, not because they were against the poor—why, they were as generous and as charitable as the best of Americans—but because the war had to come first. First, we had to beat those Godless Communists and then we could worry about the homeless Americans. And the generals. Oh, they'd love the war, too. It's hard to be a military hero without a war. Heroes need battles and bombs and bullets in order to be heroic. That's why I am suspicious of the military. They're always so narrow in their appraisal of everything. They see everything in military terms. Oh, I could see it coming. And I didn't like the smell of it. I didn't like

---

[129]Washington to Saigon 1477, Jan. 14, 1965, same location.
[130]Kearns, *Lyndon Johnson and the American Dream*, pp. 251-252. See also *The Best and the Brightest*, p. 507.

anything about it, but I think the situation in South Vietnam bothered me most. They never seemed able to get themselves together down there. Always fighting with one another. Bad. Bad.

Yet everything I knew about history told me that if I got out of Vietnam and let Ho Chi Minh run through the streets of Saigon, then I'd be doing exactly what Chamberlain did in World War II. I'd be giving a big fat reward to aggression. And I knew that if we let Communist aggression succeed in taking over South Vietnam, there would follow in this country an endless national debate—a mean and destructive debate—that would shatter my Presidency, kill my administration and damage our democracy. I knew that Harry Truman and Dean Acheson had lost their effectiveness from the day that the Communists took over in China. I believed that the loss of China had played a large role in the rise of Joe McCarthy. And I knew that all these problems, taken together, were chicken-shit compared with what might happen if we lost Vietnam.

For this time there would be Robert Kennedy out in front leading the fight against me, telling everyone that I had betrayed John Kennedy's commitment to South Vietnam. That I had let a democracy fall into the hands of the Communists. That I was a coward. An unmanly man. A man without a spine. Oh, I could see it coming all right. Every night when I fell asleep I would see myself tied to the ground in the middle of a long, open space. In the distance, I could hear the voices of thousands of people. They were all shouting at me and running toward me: "Coward! Traitor! Weakling!" They kept coming closer. They began throwing stones. At exactly that moment I would generally wake up . . . terribly shaken. But there was more. You see, I was as sure as any man could be that once we showed how weak we were, Moscow and Peking would move in a flash to exploit our weakness. They might move independently or they might move together. But move they would—whether through nuclear blackmail, through subversion, with regular armed forces or in some other manner. As nearly as anyone can be certain of anything, I knew they couldn't resist the opportunity to expand their control over the vacuum of power we would leave behind us. And so would begin World War III. So you see, I was bound to be crucified either way I moved.

Doubtless some of this was LBJ hyperbole and hindsight, but there can be no question that in January 1965, as he was about to be inaugurated after campaigning on a peace platform, Lyndon Johnson was loath to lead the country into war.[131]

---

[131]His inaugural address on Jan. 20 was general in nature, and Vietnam was not mentioned. The only related remarks were, "The American covenant called on us to help show the way for the liberation of man. And that is still our goal. . . . If American lives must end, and American treasure be spilled, in countries that we barely know, then that is the price that change has demanded of conviction and of our enduring covenant." *Public Papers of the Presidents,* Lyndon B. Johnson, 1965, p. 72.

Growing Opposition in Congress

Johnson also had good reason, as he learned later, to be concerned about the growing opposition in Congress to an expanded U.S. military role in Vietnam. An Associated Press poll of the Senate on January 6, 1965, showed strong support for a negotiated settlement. Of 63 Senators responding, 31 were for a negotiated settlement after improving the U.S.-South Vietnamese bargaining position, and 10 favored negotiating immediately. Three were for an immediate withdrawal. Eight favored using U.S. forces in Vietnam, while another eleven favored continuing the program of strengthening the South Vietnamese.[132]

Although there was considerable congressional opposition to further U.S. involvement in Vietnam, Congress, according to a report in the *New York Times* on January 11, 1965, ". . . is just as baffled and frustrated over what the U.S. should do in Vietnam as the Administration is."

Senate Republican Leader Dirksen was not among the skeptics. On January 3, 1965, he said that if the U.S. pulled out of Vietnam "the rank of the United States in the Orient would plummet. And from the standpoint of the Philippines and Guam, we would have no anchor point left." He suggested, however, that the President might want to meet with congressional leaders and arrive at a decision to fight or to withdraw. Although he believed that the President could act without congressional approval if there was a "danger to national security," he thought Johnson would want to have the support of congressional leaders, if not Congress as a whole, as was the case in earlier crises in Lebanon, Berlin, and the Formosa Straits.[133]

Among those Senators who questioned U.S. policy toward Vietnam, Church and McGovern, both of whom had voted reluctantly for the Gulf of Tonkin Resolution, but had supported Johnson in the 1964 Presidential election, were becoming increasingly concerned about the trend toward greater U.S. involvement and the possible extension of the war into North Vietnam. Although they were young, junior Members of the Senate, they were considered intelligent moderate-liberal Democrats, whose internationalist viewpoints contrasted rather sharply with those of their constituencies in Idaho (Church) and South Dakota (McGovern). (Church, a member of the Foreign Relations Committee, represented the same state that had been represented by Senator William Borah, chairman of the Foreign Relations Committee in the 1920s, who was thought of by those of internationalist persuasion as being an "isolationist"—a fact that Lyndon Johnson did not let Church forget as the two began to part company on the issue of Vietnam.) As a result of these factors, both Church and McGovern were viewed as being part of the moderate, centrist sector of senatorial and public opinion on Vietnam, and as representative of the kind of electoral support Johnson had received from traditionally isolationist areas in the Midwest and West.

---

[132]*New York Times*, Jan. 7, 1965.
[133]*Ibid.*, Jan. 3, 1965.

In the post-Gulf of Tonkin and post-1964 election period, when Johnson's political strength was so formidable, the views of Church and McGovern may not have seemed very important to the President. He doubtless knew, however, that if the war became unpopular, it would be the Churches and McGoverns in Congress who, as spokesmen for those who opposed the war, especially those from the moderate-liberal Democratic center, would help to bring him down and to repudiate his policies.

For their part, Church and McGovern and others like them in Congress were well aware of Johnson's political power and prowess, and of the political and personal risk they would run if they opposed him on an important issue. By the end of 1964, however, they felt compelled to speak out. Church was the first to do so. In an interview for the *New York Times,* on December 26, 1964, he advocated the neutralization of Southeast Asia, with the U.N. as the guarantor of the settlement. Neutralization, however, should not be "camouflage for a Communist takeover." Church was also opposed to extending the war to the north. He said that the U.S. must honor its commitments, but that the war could be won only by the South Vietnamese themselves. He hoped that the U.S. would not be forced to withdraw, but said, "we must be prepared for that possibility." He added: "Unless we come to accept the fact that it is neither within the power nor the interest of the United States to preserve the status quo everywhere, our policy is doomed to failure."[134]

On January 15, 1965, McGovern made a major speech in the Senate in which he took a somewhat comparable position. The U.S. was not winning in Vietnam, he said, and expansion of the war would be "an act of folly designed in the end to create simply a larger, more inglorious debacle." The problem, he said, was political rather than military. "The United States can accomplish much through foreign aid and military support, but we cannot create strong, effective, and popular national leadership where that leadership either does not exist or does not exert itself." "The United States," he added, "can at most only hold a finger in the dike until the South Vietnamese find themselves." He, too, was opposed to increasing U.S. involvement or extending the war, but he said, "we cannot simply walk out and permit the Vietcong to march into Saigon." He preferred a prolonged conflict if necessary, and said he hoped "we would be prepared to wage such a conflict rather than to surrender the area to communism."

According to McGovern, "the most practical way, if we are to take further action in Vietnam, is to put pressure on North Vietnam quietly through infiltration and subversion by South Vietnamese units." The purpose of such action, he added, would be to force the North Vietnamese to negotiate, and "The most viable and practical policy for the United States in Vietnam is negotiation and a political settlement." Alluding to his speech on August 8, 1964, immediately after passage of the Gulf of Tonkin Resolution, in which he suggested that the U.S. might accept the French proposal for an international conference, he concluded by discussing possible mini-

---

[134]*Ibid.,* Dec. 27, 1964.

mal terms by which a settlement acceptable to both sides might be reached.[135]

The administration's own survey of the Senate and the House, which was conducted by State Department staff during January, concluded that both Congress and the public generally supported the President, and would especially do so in a "crunch," but were frustrated and confused, and needed further persuasion as to the justice and necessity of the U.S. position:[136]

We find largely that there is a generalized frustration with the situation in Vietnam and our involvement there. The great majority of Congressmen are neither satisfied nor dissatisfied; their thoughts are fragmented and they are genuinely perplexed. In this state, they are willing to go along with the people who have the direct responsibility, the experts, in the Executive Branch. Of the remainder, there are substantially more people who are definitely with us or think we might do slightly more in the way of demonstrating our resolve in a military sense than there are who are definitely against us and think we should really pour our efforts into withdrawing, call it what they will.

There are some differences between the House and the Senate. There are fewer individuals in the House who are willing to take any precise stand; the general instinct is to keep with the herd, watch the situation, stick it out, pester the Administration to solve the problem but go along with it in its efforts. . . . On the Senate side there are more who will take individual stands and . among those more who are moving gradually, although cautiously, in the direction of negotiation-neutralization-U.N. responsibility-political settlement.

The report gave this rundown on individuals in the Senate:

. . . You now know how McGovern stands; Morse is somewhat inclined to institute a tough but limited reprisal policy as our next move.

There is a fairly definable Senate group who should be watched closely in this regard. They are the Church-McGovern-Pell-Gore-Nelson bunch, which is partially dormant, and could expand. What might be characterized as the [A. S. Mike] Monroney [D/Okla.]-Saltonstall-Scott group, much larger in size, is right with us, and feeling we conceivably might do more in the way of selective pressures on the North. Lausche is right with us; . . . Russell is obviously unhappy but staying on the reservation. Young [Milton R. Young, R/N. Dak.] has stated that he doesn't feel Vietnam is a hopeless cause and [Karl E.] Mundt [R/S. Dak.] says that neutralization has never worked before. We know about Fulbright and Mansfield; most Senators reject Morse and Gruening, as well as Thurmond and Tower; Dirksen is looking, so far unsuccessfully, for a handle; Jackson and Cooper should be watched as indicators.

---

[135]*CR*, vol. 110, pp. 784-786.
[136]Memorandum for William Bundy from his assistant, Jonathan Moore, "Congressional Attitudes on SVN," no date, but written in Jan. 1965, and located in the Kennedy Library, Thomson Papers, in a folder covering the period 1-65 to 2-65.

Thus, the report stated, referring to the overall situation in Congress:

1. We've got adequate support for the moment, largely passive but strong enough in a crunch to more than offset the opposition, and left largely alone it will stay this way.

2. There is in the Senate a group of fairly junior liberals growing in size and boldness who advocate finding a way to withdraw honorably and under the protection of international safeguards as the first order of business.

3. Without more active efforts to present and persuade on the Hill in order actually to develop and solidify support, the passage of time and unhappy developments in SEA could erode our position and enhance the persuasiveness and numbers of the opposition.

In conclusion, the report stated:

The Congressional opinion—as it should—largely mirrors what is going on throughout the country. The public opinion trend there is toward the middle even more notably. That is, there are less people who are really behind us and more whose opinions about U.S. policy in Vietnam are frustrated and fragmented. This body of citizens is not against us and will not be for the time being; in a crunch they would back us up rather strongly. But left alone they can become increasingly discontent and impatient, and gradually—particularly if helped by continuingly dismal reports from the area—shift to a more negative position which could become very influential. If that trend ever did really set in, it might grow tenaciously.

Johnson had his own thoughts on some of the "problem" Senators. He told Adlai Stevenson (U.S. Ambassador to the U.N.) in a private conversation at the White House on January 4, 1965, that Stevenson should talk to Morse, and that he should remind Morse that as majority leader he (Johnson) had put him on the Foreign Relations Committee on the day Morse switched from the Republican to the Democratic Party. "Stevenson replied that Morse had said so many nasty things about him that he doubted he would have much influence. Johnson observed that Morse had said nasty things about everyone except his wife." Johnson also said ". . . he was having trouble with Senator Mansfield, whom he considered 'mean and small,' who would not give Humphrey's wife a ticket to the State of the Union ceremonies, who refused to give Vice President Humphrey a suitable office in the Capitol, and who had once told Johnson that he, Mansfield, would run the Senate and that if Johnson sent Humphrey to run it Mansfield would oppose him."[137]

With respect to Russell's position, it is likely that during the period around Christmas 1964, Johnson, who was at his ranch in Texas, discussed the Vietnam situation with Russell, as well as others, by telephone. Although the necessary documentation as to what Russell recommended is not available (if, in fact, it exists), according to William Bundy, ". . . at least one Senior Senator who

---

[137]Martin, *Adlai Stevenson and the World,* pp. 823-824. Morse resumed his Senate speeches on Jan. 6, 1965. See *CR,* vol. 111, pp. 331-341. For a good statement of his position see his article in the *New York Times* Magazine, Jan. 17, 1965, "We Must Leave Vietnam." In the same issue is a contrary view by Henry Cabot Lodge, "We Can Win in Vietnam."

enjoyed the President's total confidence and high respect had advised him bluntly that now was the time to find a way out."[138] Russell's only public comment was a remark made to reporters on January 11, 1965, after a briefing of the Senate Armed Services Committee by CIA Director McCone. Russell said there could be no victory in Vietnam unless "a more stable government" was established. "The situation is at best a stalemate that promises to be prolonged endlessly," he added.[139]

In early January, Johnson also had a report from Rusk on the state of opinion in the Foreign Relations Committee, where Rusk and William Bundy had testified on Vietnam in an executive session on January 8, following another executive session on January 7 at which the concern of some members of the committee about the situation in Vietnam had been sharpened by secret testimony from a group of witnesses assembled by Vice-President-Elect Humphrey.[140] (Johnson had been told of the January 7 hearing by Humphrey, and his reaction, according to Humphrey, was ". . . 'if you feel that some of these things should be done get ahold of Rusk and talk to these people and bring these boys in.'")

The witnesses on January 7 were General Lansdale, Rufus Phillips, and two officials from the U.S. foreign aid mission in Vietnam, Bertram Fraleigh and George H. Melvin.[141] They told an informal meeting of the committee attended by Fulbright, Sparkman and Humphrey, that the situation in Vietnam was deteriorating, and that a military response was not the answer. As Fraleigh said, "This is not a war of more dollars, more guns or more people. . . ." Melvin added, "I know it would be unpolitic to reduce the budget for Vietnam, but we need only a fraction of the money that you are spending in Vietnam, and only a fraction of the people you have out there."

The war, they said, was a "political war," and could only be won politically. But it had to be won. ". . . if we don't win it there," Fraleigh said, "we are going to have to fight it everywhere, Central America, Africa, the whole works."

In a memorandum (included in the transcript of the hearing) summing up his own position, which appears to have been generally shared by the other witnesses, Lansdale said, "The United States needs a win in Vietnam. . . ," and ". . . a win is possible." The key, he said, reiterating some of the ideas he had expressed in his October 1964 article in *Foreign Affairs,* was to recognize, first, that the Vietnamese could win the struggle against the Communists, and, secondly, that the U.S. had to give Vietnam the kind of assistance, from the kinds of people, that would enable the Vietnamese to win. "Thus," he concluded, "the United States must place Americans into Vietnam, in positions where their influence can be decisive, whom the Vietnamese trust to share the Vietnamese desire to

---

[138]Bundy MS., ch. 20, p. 14.

[139]*New York Times,* Jan. 12, 1965.

[140]U.S. Congress, Senate, Committee on Foreign Relations, unpublished transcripts of the informal hearing on Jan. 7 and of the executive session on Jan. 8, 1965.

[141]At this time Lansdale had technically retired from the Air Force, and was a Consultant to the White House on Food for Peace. Phillips, who had been replaced in 1964 as head of the office of rural affairs in the U.S. mission by George Tanham, was president of Intercontinental Consultants, Inc.

be free in a way understood by Vietnamese, and whom the Vietnamese realists believe can give practical advice worthy of their heeding on how to defeat Communist subversive insurgency as it is waged in Asia. . . ."

As the meeting with the Lansdale group concluded, Sparkman, who tended to be a staunch supporter of the executive branch in the conduct of foreign policy, said he was deeply troubled by the testimony. Humphrey said that he was too. Sparkman asked what could be done. Fulbright said, "There is only one man that can do anything . . . and that would actually be the President." Sparkman asked, "How are you going to get that word to the President?" Fulbright replied, ". . . we have got the Vice President here. I will go with him . . . the only thing I can think of is that you and I and the Vice President talk to the President about it." It was at this point that Humphrey said he had talked to the President, who had told him to go ahead. "The President hasn't a closed mind on this," Humphrey added, and he suggested that the material from the hearing be summarized and that he, Fulbright, Sparkman and Hickenlooper, the ranking Republican on the committee, ask to see the President to talk about it. Referring to the witnesses, Humphrey added, ". . . I feel like these men do. It is just a tragedy to think we are losing when we don't need to. I know some of the decisions . . . that are being made as we sit here and talk right now. I feel that maybe we are going to make some decisions that will be disastrous."

Fulbright also suggested that at the hearing the next day (January 8) with Rusk, some questions be asked based on the hearing with the Lansdale group. Humphrey disagreed. His explanation was off the record, but it presumably had to do with the fact that the hearing with the Lansdale group had been set up for the benefit of the committee, and the witnesses were speaking informally, off-the-record, and out of official channels.

Several months later, in an executive session of the Foreign Relations Committee on May 19, 1965, Fulbright referred to the hearing in January with the Lansdale group, and said that he had "mentioned" to the President the need for more attention to the political side of the war, and "got a very cool reception." He added that Fraleigh had been "fired" by the administration for testifying on this subject, an act which Fulbright said was considered by the AID mission chief in Vietnam to be "disloyal."[142]

In the executive session on Vietnam with Rusk and William Bundy on January 8, various members of the Foreign Relations Committee expressed concern about the situation in Vietnam and the ineffectiveness of U.S. policy.[143] "The only reason I and others," Fulbright said, "have entertained the possibility . . . that maybe we might have to negotiate is simply it looks hopeless. It isn't because we want to but . . . we are faced with the fact [that] it just isn't working. . . ." Without revealing that he and others on the committee had discussed the "political war" with the Lansdale group the previous day, Fulbright said, ". . . maybe we have

[142]U.S. Congress, Senate, Committee on Foreign Relations, unpublished executive session transcript, May 19, 1965.
[143]Ibid., Jan. 8, 1965.

thought of this entirely as a military operation or practically so, and that we have not been . . . willing and able . . . to help them generate a stable political organization which could then be the basis with which we work. . . ." Gore took a similar position.

Church and Morse advocated using the U.N. Rusk, saying that he did not think that the U.N. would fight in Vietnam, commented that it would be tempting to take the issue to the U.N. to prove to Morse, in particular, that this was not a feasible solution.

Fulbright referred to Taylor's testimony before the committee in December 1964 that the war would not be escalated unless and until a stable government was established in South Vietnam. He wanted to know whether this was still the policy of the administration. Rusk replied, "Mr. Chairman that is present policy. I think I should say if the President should come to any other conclusions he would do so in consultation with the leadership of the Congress." What about the argument that an attack on the north was necessary in order to bring about a stable government in the south? Fulbright asked, adding, "I don't think anything can justify the escalation of the war. . . ." Rusk replied, "Well, Mr. Chairman, I think that is something that the President and the leadership will talk to each other about." The exchange continued:

The Chairman. Will we be told after the decision is made or before. Will we be invited to a meeting at the White House and told we have made up our mind tomorrow morning or in 30 minutes launch an attack.

Secretary Rusk. We have never ourselves guaranteed North Vietnam as a safe haven for all those depradations which have been coming out of North Vietnam. There have been incidents down the coast and other things which have happened.

The Chairman. I understand covert attacks have been made and we know about it. But I am talking about a rather major attack on North Vietnam by forces which are not just a hit and run.

Secretary Rusk. I take it you are going beyond the possibility of retaliation at this point.

The Chairman. Yes.

Secretary Rusk. There was the Gulf of Tonkin.

The Chairman. Yes.

Secretary Rusk. That was retaliation.

The Chairman. I just want to know what the idea is. I would hate for this decision to be made before the committee had the opportunity to consider it. . . . [Fulbright then mentioned the restraining role of Congress when the U.S. was considering military action at Dien Bien Phu and in Laos.] In this case it is so important that I hope the administration won't make a decision of that nature. Before they make the decision, at least feeling the pulse of this committee. Do you think that would be a reasonable thing to expect?

Secretary Rusk. I think Mr. Chairman, perhaps the reasonable thing on a matter of such importance is to report your remarks to the President.

The Chairman. That is right.

On January 15, Rusk testified again before the Foreign Relations Committee in an executive session on the committee's annual review of the "state of the world."[144] There was a brief discussion of Vietnam, including a question by Sparkman about news stories that the U.S. was planning airstrikes on North Vietnam. Rusk replied: "I myself feel that strikes against the North are a part of the problem on which the leadership and President would be in consultation, because this would be a significant development of the situation. I have reported the views expressed by members of the committee on that point at our last meeting."

During the last two weeks of January and the first week of February, as various other Members of Congress were expressing concern about the situation in Vietnam, and the possibility of military escalation, Fulbright replied to a friend who was an overseas employee of the U.S. foreign aid program, and who had written to him about U.S. policy in Vietnam:[145]

> . . . it is not exactly within my power to influence the course of events in South Viet Nam, other than to express a personal opinion, as the matter is run by the Executive Branch, as you well know. We are only told whatever is thought suitable for our sensitive ears. All I can say is that there is a great deal of discussion under the surface. I feel sure the majority of my colleagues do not wish to see it expanded, but would like very much to see it administered more effectively. I hope some way can be found to persuade the Vietnamese to work together. While I have a very high opinion of Ambassador Taylor as a military leader, he has not demonstrated a very effective political talent when it comes to inspiring the Vietnamese to pull together, but perhaps no one can do it.

Conclusion

These last weeks of January 1965 proved to be the end of another phase of U.S. involvement in Vietnam. Within a few weeks, the United States began systematic bombing of North Vietnam, followed by the deployment of U.S. ground forces to fight in South Vietnam. At the end of 1964, there were about 23,000 U.S. military personnel in Vietnam, only about 3,000 more than a year before, and most of them were still serving in an advisory capacity. By the end of 1965, there were 183,000 U.S. troops in Vietnam, and the United States had assumed major responsibility for the war.

Neither the President nor most Members of Congress wanted to become more involved militarily in South Vietnam. There was a general reluctance to commit U.S. forces to a land war on the mainland of Asia; memories of the Korean war were still fresh, and the "never again club" still active. A major war could also seriously interfere with Johnson's Great Society. Yet a year's experience with the situation since the death of Diem also had convinced many policymakers that the U.S. had no choice; either it had to withdraw from Vietnam, a position with little support, or it had to become more involved alongside the South Vietnamese. Seemingly, only American power could prevent a Communist victory. As the President had told Taylor and his other associates at the meeting

---

[144]U.S. Congress, Senate, Committee on Foreign Relations, unpublished executive session transcript, Jan. 15, 1965.
[145]University of Arkansas, Fulbright Papers, series 48, box 35.

in December 1, 1964, the Vietnamese would be given one last chance to pull themselves together, but if that failed, he would have to send in the troops.

APPENDIX

Legal Commentary and Judicial Opinions on the Gulf of Tonkin Resolution

In the legal and political controversy that developed subsequent to the passage of the Gulf of Tonkin Resolution, especially after opposition to the war intensified, numerous questions were raised by legal scholars about the legality and constitutionality, as well as the appropriateness, of the Gulf of Tonkin Resolution. Among other things, it was argued that the resolution was an impermissible delegation of power, that it was not sufficiently specific, that it authorized military action but not a large-scale war, and that it was obtained from Congress by misinformation if not deception. Professor Richard Falk, a legal scholar and political activist who was a most vigorous critic of the U.S. role in the Vietnam war, declared, "The Gulf of Tonkin Resolution was obtained from Congress in August 1964 by fraud, the Executive branch distorting the circumstances of alleged attack by North Vietnamese torpedo boats on U.S. warships and masking from Congress the Executive's plans to extend the war to North Vietnam in subsequent months."[1]

Alexander Bickel, a noted professor of constitutional law, contended that the U.S. entered the Vietnam war in 1965 "unconstitutionally" because of Congress' impermissible delegation of power to the Executive. ". . . the real answer to the Gulf of Tonkin resolution," he said, "is that if it authorized anything, beyond an immediate reaction, beyond its own factual context, it was an unconstitutionally broad delegation." ". . . standard delegation doctrine," he added, "requires that whenever Congress authorizes anybody to do something prospectively . . . that it be done under standards, and that the delegation be relatively narrow and specific . . . as opposed to, as compared with, a broad prospective delegation of power to act in circumstances not now foreseeable."[2]

Lawrence R. Velvel, another professor of constitutional law, and a very active participant in efforts to challenge the constitutionality of the war (he was founder of the Constitutional Lawyers Committee on Undeclared War which opposed the war, and he also initiated two court cases in his own name), contended that the war "represents a flagrant executive usurpation of Congress' power to declare war." In explaining his position, Velvel said, among other things, that Congress may have been "deceived" by the Executive with respect to the Gulf of Tonkin incidents. ". . . while it is unnecessary to rely on the possibility of such deception, it must be ad-

---

[1]Richard Falk, Foreword to Lawrence R. Velvel, *Undeclared War and Civil Disobedience: The American System in Crisis* (New York: Dunellen, 1970), p. ix.
[2]Senate hearings on *War Powers Legislation,* cited above, pp. 563, 575-576.

mitted," he added, "that the alleged deception does not aid the executive's case that the Tonkin Resolution authorizes it to conduct the current war. For it can be argued that, somewhat like the restitution doctrine of mistake of fact, even if Congress had intended to authorize the current war, its authorization would be void if based on an improper understanding of the facts of the Tonkin Gulf attack, let alone a deliberate deception as to the facts of the attack."[3]

Velvel took the position that the Gulf of Tonkin Resolution did not and was not intended to authorize a "sustained and large-scale offensive and defensive war in Viet Nam":[4]

As the text of the Resolution illustrates, any reasonable man must concede that, if one considers only the language of the Resolution and totally ignores the congressional intent expressed in its ample legislative history, its language is broad enough to authorize the President, in his sole discretion, to fight a large-scale land, sea, and air war on the continent of Asia. Indeed, if one considers only the language of the Resolution and ignores the intent expressed in its legislative history, its language is broad enough to authorize the President, in his sole discretion, to initiate the atomic holocaust of World War III should he alone believe that World War III must be commenced in order to stop Communist aggression in Southeast Asia. This fact graphically demonstrates that, as is true with any legislation, the language of the Resolution cannot be considered in isolation from the congressional intent displayed in the legislative history. That history shows that Congress did not intend to authorize the executive, in its sole discretion, to fight the present long-sustained and large-scale land, sea, and air war on the continent of Asia.

In one of the most definitive statements on the subject, an unnamed student at the Harvard Law School prepared a paper, published by the *Harvard Law Review* in 1968, examining the powers of the President and Congress to commit U.S. forces to combat. This paper concluded, ". . . instead of assuming that the President may deploy American forces as he sees fit and only in the exceptional case need he seek congressional approval, the presumption should be that congressional collaboration is the general rule whenever the use of the military is involved, with presidential initiative being reserved for the exceptional case."[5]

The Gulf of Tonkin Resolution, the paper said, was broad enough to enable the President to ". . . conduct the war as he sees fit. He has the power to bomb North Vietnam and presumably even China if that is deemed necessary to defend South Vietnam's freedom." The author concluded, however, that the resolution was imperfect,

[3]Lawrence R. Velvel, "The War in Viet Nam: Unconstitutional, Justiciable, and Jurisdictionally Attackable," *Kansas Law Review*, 16 (1968), pp. 449-503, reprinted in Richard A. Falk, ed., *The Vietnam War and International Law*, Volume II (Princeton: Princeton University Press, 1969), pp. 650-710. (See also Velvel's book cited above.) The four-volume work edited by Falk for the American Society of International Law, and published by Princeton, 1967-76, is an excellent collection of readings on the legal aspects of the war.
[4]Falk, vol. II, p. 675.
[5]"Congress, the President, and the Power to Commit Forces to Combat," Note from *Harvard Law Review*, 81 (1968), pp. 1771-1805, reprinted in Falk, vol. II, pp. 616-650.

and that Congress should have been asked to approve the large commitments of forces made in 1965:[6]

Despite apparent statements to the contrary when the bill was being debated, Senator Fulbright claims, however, that there was no understanding that the resolution extended to the authorization of war. In his defense it must be admitted that the circumstances surrounding the passage of the resolution hardly lent themselves to minimizing misunderstandings. The resolution was presented in an atmosphere of great urgency immediately after the attack. This factor, coupled with the allusions to that attack and the request for approval of a response to it, created a strong impression that the implications of the second section [of the resolution] were overlooked. Although such a result is surely as much the fault of Congress as of the administration, under the circumstances, compliance with the principle that Congress should be given the closest possible participation in such decisions would have demanded at the least that prior to the decision the following year vastly to increase the commitment of troops to the area, congressional reassertion of its approval be sought.

The *Harvard Law Review* paper reached this conclusion:[7]

At best, the Gulf of Tonkin Resolution, even coupled with subsequent appropriations, leaves unclear the extent to which congressional authorization of the war has been expressed.

With respect to the future, the problem can be avoided by placing a strict time limit on the resolution, giving Congress adequate time to deliberate and review the resolution and encouraging the Executive to seek further specific support later. With respect to the present, although the *fait accompli* problem can no longer be avoided, the ambiguity is best resolved, not by relying on Congress' failure to repeal the resolution as provided for in the third clause, but by resubmitting for congressional approval a resolution specifically phrased to give consent to the war.

Louis Henkin, one of the foremost authorities on constitutional aspects of the U.S. Government's foreign affairs powers, has argued, however, that for "constitutional purposes" Congress approved the war by passing the Gulf of Tonkin Resolution and appropriations for the war. Henkin also has dismissed suggestions that Congress did not know what it was doing, that the President exceeded or misused the resolution, or that Congress was barred from taking corrective action:[8]

That, as some later claimed, Congress did not appreciate what it was doing, or that its hand was forced to do it, is constitutionally immaterial. . . . It would be constitutionally material if, as some claimed, the resolutions [Gulf of Tonkin and a statement of purpose contained in a subsequent appropriations act in 1965] did not authorize full-scale war, that the President misinterpreted them and exceeded the authority they granted;

---

[6]*Ibid.*, pp. 649-650. (footnotes in original have been omitted)
[7]*Ibid.*, p. 650.
[8]Louis Henkin, *Foreign Affairs and the Constitution* (Mineola, N.Y.: Foundation Press, 1972), pp. 101-102.

there is no evidence, however, that Congress (as distinguished from some Congressmen) thought so, and Congress had the power and many opportunities to tell the President so, and did not seize them. (The Tonkin Resolution itself expressly reserved the power to withdraw the authorization it granted by concurrent resolution.) Congress also had the power to withhold appropriations, at least to make them with disclaimer and protest, and to check the President in other ways; and surely it could have readily and justifiably done so if it believed he had exceeded the authority granted him. Similarly, that Congress could not muster a majority to terminate or redefine the President's authority; that it could not openly break with the President without jeopardizing major national interests; that it could not discontinue support for the war because it "could not let the troops down"—these do not indicate that Congress did not authorize or continue to support the war; rather, they show that, and why, Congress did. . . .

For the constitutional lawyer, as well as for the citizen, then, it is important to distinguish in these controversies between appeals to the Constitution and complaints against it. The claim on Vietnam, properly, was less that the President usurped power than that the Constitution gave him "excessive" power; or, since Congress has the authority to check the President, that the constitutional distribution does not work because, in the end, the restraints on the President are not effective. Many were really asking whether, in essential respects, we have a desirable system for conducting foreign relations.

John Norton Moore, another noted authority, takes the position that the Gulf of Tonkin Resolution "completely—and in my opinion unquestionably—satisfied the constitutional requirement of congressional authorization of hostilities in the Indo-China War," and that Congress was aware that the resolution "gave the President the authority, within his discretion, to take whatever action he deemed necessary with respect to the defense of South Vietnam." Moreover, he says, the language of the resolution was sufficiently broad to embrace the large-scale war that followed. Nor has Moore found merit in the invalid delegation argument: ". . . even if there is a constitutional requirement as to the breadth of congressional delegation of the war power to the President, a proposition open to considerable doubt, the Congress which passed the Tonkin Gulf Resolution was, I believe, reasonably informed of the circumstances giving rise to the need for the use of U.S. forces."[9]

Moore has contended, however, that the Executive should have attempted to avoid the "authority deflation" that resulted from the controversy over the Gulf of Tonkin Resolution:[10]

---

[9] Letter to CRS from John Norton Moore, Nov. 20, 1968, and John Norton Moore, "The National Executive and the Use of the Armed Forces Abroad," *Naval War College Review* (January 1969), pp. 28-38, reprinted in Falk, vol. II, pp. 808-821. "If there is to be a delegation test," Moore said, "I would suggest that it be one asking whether there has been meaningful participation by a congress reasonably informed of the circumstances giving rise to the need for the use of U.S. forces." Falk, vol. II, p. 818. For a more extensive statement of Moore's views see his *Law and the Indo-China War* (Princeton: Princeton University Press, 1972).
[10] CRS Interview with John Norton Moore, Dec. 7, 1978.

I think the emphasis, in all of this, on the question of precisely where is the constitutional line between congressional and executive branch power, which is the usual focus, is not as interesting in terms of future policy for the United States as an effort to try to develop some meaningful procedures, in which Congress and the President could attempt to work together in ways that would both insure meaningful congressional involvement and protect the President from the severe kind of authority deflation that occurs when there is a controversy as to whether he has the authority to do it. Because even if he's going constitutionally to the limit of his authority, and he has the authority to do it, it may be very poor policy to press that if, in fact, there is going to be such a substantial controversy about the issue that we will suffer a severe authority deflation, with associated criticism and law suits and all of the rest, at a time when we need particularly to pull together.

Moore would have preferred congressional action at a different time, even prior to August 1964, and under circumstances that would not have involved the factual and other ambiguities of the Gulf of Tonkin incidents. He has suggested that one test of the time for obtaining congressional authorization, would be when "regular combat units are committed to sustained hostilities." Based on this test, he has argued that congressional authorization for the Vietnam war should have been required in February 1965, when the U.S. began bombing the North on a continuing basis, and in the summer and fall of 1965 when U.S. ground forces began sustained combat.[11]

Moore has made the additional point that if congressional authorization needed to be requested at the time of the Gulf of Tonkin incidents, the executive branch should have been clearer in its reporting of the facts and in its request for authorization, in order to "make it clear to adversaries abroad and to those who have to participate domestically that, in fact, there is complete authorization and national congruence between Congress and the Executive in that kind of serious undertaking." It was the failure to do so, he feels, that helped to precipitate the domestic political controversy which followed, and which became the "cost"—the avoidable cost, in his opinion—of obtaining the Gulf of Tonkin Resolution in the manner in which it had been obtained.[12] ". . . if, in fact, the debate is filled with discrepancies and arguments back and forth, and it accompanies a *Maddox* type incident, and there is not very substantial clarity in the record at the time, then it seems to me that it leads to the kind of authority deflation that undercuts the effort abroad and hurts us at home." Moore added:[13]

Government really is, I'm convinced, and presidential power really is, the ability to build a consensus. And you're successful if you can do it. And if you can't, your policy won't work. You may push it through, but the chances are that you won't. They'll get you in the courts or they'll get you somewhere else, at some point.

---

[11]Falk, vol. II, pp. 814, 819.
[12]CRS Interview with John Norton Moore, Dec. 7, 1978.
[13]*Ibid.*

Abram Chayes, who helped draft the resolution, said that Congress was not fully informed about the incidents in the Gulf of Tonkin, "And, in a legal-political sense that means that you didn't have them on the hook the same way you would have had them if you had exposed the situation more fully. That is, the criticism by congressmen who had voted for the resolution—the subsequent criticism—you couldn't foreclose by simply saying, well you voted, you're in this with me."[14]

The Reactions of the Judiciary

During the latter 1960s and early 1970s, numerous efforts were made to get the courts to rule on the legality of the war.[15] They refused to do so primarily because of the political question doctrine, the traditional judicial position with respect to controversies between the political branches of the Government, Congress and the Executive, by which the courts refrain from adjudicating political disputes between the two branches.[16]

In most of the court cases on the war the plaintiffs challenged the legality and constitutionality of the war based on the argument that the Gulf of Tonkin Resolution was not constitutional authorization for the war, particularly for the large-scale war waged after 1965. In 1967, the Supreme Court was asked to hear *Mora* v. *McNamara* involving servicemen who were being sent to Vietnam, and who wanted the war declared illegal.[17] The Court declined to consider the case, but Justices William Douglas and Potter Stewart dissented on the grounds that the questions being raised were serious and deserved a hearing.[18] Some of these questions Justice Stewart said, were:

---

[14]CRS Interview with Abram Chayes, Oct. 13, 1978.

[15]Unfortunately there is no single comprehensive analysis of the role of the judiciary in the war. In addition, much of the literature was produced by those opposed to the war, and tends to reflect that position. The only general, nontechnical study is of that genre: Anthony A. D'Amato and Robert M. O'Neil, *The Judiciary and Vietnam* (New York: St. Martin's Press, 1972).

For a discussion of court cases resulting from efforts by activists who deliberately broke the law in order to challenge the legality and morality of the war, see John F. and Rosemary S. Bannan, *Law, Morality and Vietnam: The Peace Militants and the Courts* (Bloomington: University of Indiana Press, 1974). The best analysis of the role of the U.S. Supreme Court, also written by a lawyer opposed to the war, is Philippa Strum, "The Supreme Court and the Vietnamese War," in Falk, vol. IV, pp. 535-572. For the numerous additional sources see the footnotes contained in the selections reprinted in Falk.

[16]Perhaps the best definition of "political question" is contained in Justice Brennan's opinion in *Baker* v. *Carr*, 369 U.S. 186 (1962): "Prominent on the surface of any case held to involve a political question is found a textually demonstrable constitutional commitment of the issue to a coordinate political department; or a lack of judicially discoverable and manageable standards for resolving it; or the impossibility of deciding without an initial policy determination of a kind clearly for nonjudicial discretion; or the impossibility of a court's undertaking independent resolution without expressing lack of the respect due coordinate branches of government; or an unusual need for unquestioning adherence to a political decision already made; or the potentiality of embarrassment from multifarious pronouncements by various departments on one question."

[17]389 U.S. 934 (1967).

[18]Justice Brennan joined Justice Douglas in voting to grant certiorari in the case of *Orlando* v. *Laird*, 404 U.S. 869 (1971). Justice Douglas dissented for similar reasons in several other cases on the war, one of the most prominent of which was *Massachusetts* v. *Laird*, 400 U.S. 886 (1970), in which Justices Stewart and Harlan joined Douglas in voting to hear arguments on the case. For comments on dissents on the justiciability of Vietnam war cases by justices of the Supreme Court, see Strum in Falk, vol. IV, p. 542. For a brief discussion of the position taken by the justices on the Massachusetts case see Bob Woodward and Scott Armstrong, *The Brethren* (New York: Simon and Schuster, 1979), pp. 125-127. For a good discussion of the justiciability of Vietnam war cases see John Norton Moore, "The Justiciability of Challenges to the use of Military Forces Abroad," *Virginia Journal of International Law*, 10 (December 1969), pp. 85-107. For the importance of adjudicating such cases, see Warren F. Schwartz, "The Justiciability of Legal Objectives to the American Military Effort in Vietnam," *Texas Law Review*, 46 (1968), pp. 1033 ff.

I. Is the present United States military activity in Vietnam a "war" within the meaning of Article I, Section 8, Clause 11, of the Constitution?

II. If so, may the Executive constitutionally order the petitioners to participate in that military activity, when no war has been declared by the Congress?

III. Of what relevance to Question II are the present treaty obligations of the United States?

IV. Of what relevance to Question II is the Joint Congressional ("Tonkin Gulf") Resolution of August 10, 1964?

Justice Douglas, who had first argued in *Mitchell* v. *United States*[19] the need for the Supreme Court to consider these kinds of questions, added these questions to those posed by Stewart:

(a) Do present United States military operations fall within the terms of the Joint Resolution?

(b) If the Joint Resolution purports to give the Chief Executive authority to commit United States forces to armed conflict limited in scope only by his own absolute discretion, is the Resolution an impermissible delegation of all or part of Congress' power to declare war?

"We do not, of course, sit as a committee of oversight or supervision," Douglas said. "What resolutions the President asks, and what the Congress provides are not our concern. With respect to the Federal Government, we sit only to decide actual cases or controversies within judicial cognizance. . . ." But Douglas said that the court should "squarely face" these "large and deeply troubling questions." "We cannot make these problems go away simply by refusing to hear the case of three obscure Army privates."[20]

The U.S. Supreme Court refused, however, all appeals to hear Vietnam war cases, provoking this comment by a lawyer who opposed the war and thought that the Court should have been more active:[21]

United States involvement in Southeast Asia has been a key—if not *the* key—issue of American national politics in the 1960's and 1970's. Nevertheless, superficial examination of the role played by the Court in cases involving the constitutionality of American involvement would seem to indicate that the Court refused to play any role whatsoever. The Court denied certiorari not only to cases challenging the constitutionality of the war itself, but to related cases involving the issues of the right of the military to order servicemen to Vietnam and the right of the executive to draft civilians for service in Vietnam. Obviously, this raises the question of the Court's policy-making role in war-time. It is tempting but insufficient to postulate that the Court has no alternative other than to maintain a "hands-off" approach during war. Closer examination reveals that the Court's refusal to grant certiorari can be interpreted as an attempt to preserve lower court decisions that held the alleged unconstitutionality of a President-initiated war to be

---

[19]386 U.S. 972 (1967).
[20]See also William O. Douglas' comments in his autobiography, *The Court Years 1939-1955* (New York: Random House, 1980), pp. 55-56, 151-152.
[21]Strum in Falk, vol. IV, pp. 535-536.

justiciable. A total of four justices voted to grant certiorari in the war cases, although at no time did all four vote to do so in the same case. The Court also played an extremely active role in considering the collateral questions of conscientious objector exemptions, the permissible limits of anti-war speech, and the right of the press to print information which the government deemed inimical to national security. Even in the latter areas, however, the Court's record is erratic. While it perverted the language of a statute in order to extend draft exemptions as far as possible, the Court stopped short of adopting the selective conscientious objector standard. It upheld the right of school children to protest the war symbolically but declined to recognize draft card burning as symbolic speech. While rejecting one instance of prior restraint, it accepted the theory of restraint before publication.

Despite the Supreme Court's refusal to hear Vietnam war cases, the decisions of district and appeals courts produced some interesting case law, which, while it had little if any practical effect during the Vietnam war, may suggest the direction of judicial action should similar questions be posed in the future. (The existence of the War Powers Resolution, of course, created a new legal framework within which such disputes could be adjudicated in the future.) In 1970, in *Berk* v. *Laird*,[22] a lower court found that because Congress and the Executive must both authorize, under certain circumstances, the use of the armed forces, the question of whether the Vietnam war involved "mutual legislative-executive action" was justiciable in view of the existence of a "discoverable and manageable standard," namely, whether the executive branch had complied with the duty of acting with congressional authority. *Berk* left open, however, the question of what action by Congress would be sufficient to constitute authorization by the legislature. This was taken up in *Orlando* v. *Laird*[23] in 1971, in which the court found that judicial review of the adequacy of congressional authorization of a war was not barred by the political question doctrine, and, further, that several actions by Congress satisfied the standard for "mutual participation in the prosecution of war." Not only had Congress passed the Gulf of Tonkin Resolution; it had passed appropriations bills to fund the war, and an extension of the draft in order to provide the necessary manpower. Thus, the court concluded:

> . . . the constitutional propriety of the means by which Congress has chosen to ratify and approve the protracted military operations in Southeast Asia is a political question. The form which Congressional authorization should take is one of policy, committed to the discretion of the Congress and outside the power and competency of the judiciary because there are no intelligible and objectively manageable standards by which to judge such actions.

Berk and *Orlando* were also significant because of the courts' firm rejection of the government's claim that the President's power

---

[22]429 F. 2d 302 (2d Cir. 1970).
[23]404 U.S. 869 (1971).

to commit U.S. forces to combat is as broad as his foreign affairs power.[24]

The *Berk* and *Orlando* cases were carried one step further in 1973, by one of the last of the Vietnam court cases, *Mitchell* v. *Laird*,[25] in which a number of liberal Democrats in the House of Representatives[26] sought an injunction to prohibit further prosecution of the war "unless, within 60 days from the date of the order, the Congress of the United States shall have explicitly, intentionally and discretely authorized a continuation of the war, with whatever limitations Congress may place upon such continuation."[27] The *Mitchell* case went to the U.S. Court of Appeals for the District of Columbia, which made a significant determination with respect to the form of congressional authorization of the Vietnam War. Reversing earlier decisions, it found that congressional approval of appropriations acts and of the draft was not a "constitutionally permissible form of assent."[28]

---

[24]For a full-length record of the *Orlando* case, see the book edited by two of the counsels for the plaintiffs: Leon Friedman and Burt Neuborne (eds.), *Unquestioning Obedience to the President: The ACLU Case Against the Legality of the War in Vietnam* (New York: W. W. Norton, 1972).

[25]476 F. 2d 533 (2d Cir. 1973). There were several other important cases, as described succinctly in the "Plaintiff's Memorandum of Law" in the case of *Holtzman* v. *Richardson*, D.C.E.D., N.Y., 73 C 537, mimeo, pp. 11-13 (footnotes in the original have been omitted):

"In *DaCosta* v. *Laird*, 448 F. 2d 1368 (2nd Cir. 1971) *cert den* 31 L. Ed. 2d 255 (1972), this Circuit reaffirmed its decision in *Orlando* and ruled that military appropriations, standing alone, (in the absence of the Tonkin Gulf resolution) constituted sufficient authorization of the Vietnam war.

"However, the *DaCosta* court, as did each court accepting the analysis of the *Orlando* court, explicitly noted that should the Executive attempt to escalate the war or to continue the war without Congressional authorization, its actions would violate Article I, Section 8 of the Constitution.

"The passage of the Mansfield Amendment (PL 92-156, 85 Stat. 430) and its immediate public repudiation by the President on Nov. 17, 1971, ushered in the fourth phase of this Circuit's consideration of the legality of military operations in Vietnam.

"In *DaCosta* v. *Laird*, 72 Civ. 207 (Feb. 16, 1971) this Court ruled that the national policy of military withdrawal from Indochina enunciated in the Mansfield Amendment was binding upon the President, but that the Executive's actions through February 16, 1972 had not been inconsistent with such a binding national policy. This Court's opinion was summarily affirmed without opinion, on February 25, 1972.

"The Executive's unilateral decision to mine North Vietnam's coastal waterways led to the fifth phase of judicial inquiry into the legality of Executive warmaking in Indochina. . . . Judge Kaufman, writing for the Circuit, ruled that once initial Congressional authorization for the commitment of American forces to combat in Vietnam was found in the passage of military appropriations bills, the question of whether subsequent military tactics designed to protect the lives of American troops in the field fell within the original Congressional grant of authority constituted a non-justiciable political question. He noted, however, that the judiciary continued to recognize a threshold obligation to determine whether, within the meaning of Berk and Orlando, sufficient Congressional authorization existed for the commitment of American forces to combat."

[26]These included Representatives Parren J. Mitchell (D/Md.), Michael J. Harrington (D/Mass.), Benjamin S. Rosenthal (D/N.Y.), Bella S. Abzug (D/N.Y.), Phillip Burton (D/Calif.), Herman Badillo (D/N.Y.), William Clay (D/Mo.), Shirley Chisholm (D/N.Y.), John Conyers, Jr. (D/Mich.), Charles C. Diggs, Jr. (D/Mich.), Charles B. Rangel (D/N.Y.), Thomas M. Rees (D/Calif.), Louis Stokes (D/Ohio), Robert L. Leggett (D/Calif.), Donald M. Fraser (D/Minn.), Edward R. Roybal (D/Calif.), Don Edwards (D/Calif.), and William R. Anderson (D/Tenn.). For a copy of their brief see *CR*, Vol. 119, pp. 16846-16880.

[27]In their brief, the plaintiffs explained these criteria, all three of which they said must be met in order for a war-authorizing resolution "to be sufficient under the declaration of war clause without being a formal declaration."

[28]"This court cannot be unmindful of what every schoolboy knows: that in voting to appropriate money or to draft men a Congressman is not necessarily approving of the continuation of a war no matter how specifically the appropriation or draft act refers to that war. A Congressman wholly opposed to the war's commencement and continuation might vote for the military appropriations and for the draft measures because he was unwilling to abandon without support men already fighting."

The court also found in the *Mitchell* case that the Gulf of Tonkin Resolution, which had been repealed by Congress in 1970, could not be used as justification for the *"indefinite* continuation of the war." (emphasis in original) The court held, however, that despite the apparent lack of authorization from Congress for continuing the war, President Nixon was trying to bring the war to an end, and because the court could not presume to judge whether he was doing so, the case was dismissed on the political question doctrine.

Following the *Mitchell* case, another member of Congress, Representative Elizabeth Holtzman (D/N.Y.), and four members of the U.S. Air Force, filed suit in 1973 to enjoin U.S. bombing of Cambodia on the grounds that it had not been authorized by Congress and was unconstitutional. The district court held for the plaintiffs,[29] but the appeals court eventually found for the government on the political question doctrine, and the Supreme Court rejected review.[30] One leading antiwar legal analyst charged:[31]

Thus the [Supreme] Court, having steered its way dextrously through the dangerous waters churned up by most of the war cases, foundered on *Holtzman.* Its previous non-decisions had had the happy effect of leaving full responsibility for American actions in Southeast Asia with what the Court delights in calling the "political" branches of the federal government and with the American people. When the Congress and the people had finally spoken, however, the Court paid no heed. Thus there is still no definitive ruling that a Presidential war is unconstitutional or that as Judge Judd[32] indicated, it "cannot be the rule that the President needs a vote of only one-third plus one of either House in order to conduct a war." As the law now stands, it is possible to argue that, in clear contradiction of Article I, Section 8, "Congress must override a Presidential veto in order to terminate hostilities which it has not authorized," and that the Court has tacitly concurred in Congress' loss of its monopoly over the power to declare war.

---

[29] *Holtzman* v. *Schlesinger,* 361 F. Supp. 553 (1973).
[30] See Strum's excellent account in Falk, vol. IV, pp. 664-569.
[31] *Ibid.,* pp. 570-571 (footnotes in original are omitted).
[32] This refers to action by Congress banning U.S. military action in Cambodia. Judge Orin Judd of the U.S. District Court in New York enjoined the government in the *Holtzman* case.

INDEX

413

Library of Congress Cataloging-in-Publication Data

Gibbons, William Conrad.
   The U.S. government and the Vietnam war.

   "Prepared for the Committee on Foreign Relations,
United States Senate, by the Congressional Research
Service, Library of Congress."
   "Originally published by the U.S. Government
Printing Office in April 1984"—T.p. verso.
   Includes bibliographical references and indexes.
   Contents: pt. 1. 1945-1960—pt. 2. 1961-1964
   1. Vietnamese Conflict, 1961-1975—United States.
2. Indochinese War, 1946-1954—United States.
3. United States—Politics and government—1945-.
I. United States.   Congress.   Senate.   Committee on
Foreign Relations.   II. Library of Congress.
Congressional Research Service.   III. Title.
IV. Title: US government and the Vietnam war.

DS558.G52   1986   959.704'33'73   86-3270
ISBN 0-691-07715-0 (v. 2 : alk. paper)
ISBN 0-691-02255-0 (pbk. : v. 2)